W9-BGC-003

MANAGING SOFTWARE REUSE

A Comprehensive Guide to Strategically Reengineering
the Organization for Reusable Components

ISBN 0-13-552373-7

THE REVIEWS ARE IN

"A very important book on how to improve software development productivity through reuse of software development products. Wayne Lim has done it and is sharing his insights. Exhaustive and meticulous in its coverage, this is the definitive book on how to implement this approach. His book is to the Information Age what process automation was to the Industrial Age."

—Dr. F. Warren McFarlan
Albert H. Gordon Professor of Business Administration and Senior Associate Dean
External Relations, Harvard University Graduate School of Business Administration

"In this book, Wayne Lim addresses the key problems of reuse economics and reuse technology transfer in the best way: with data, case studies, and empirically based guidance. Wayne draws on a Harvard M.B.A., industrial experience at Hewlett-Packard, and consulting experience to create a valuable reference for managers trying to make reuse pay off."

—Dr. William Frakes, Associate Professor and Director,
Computer Science Department
Virginia Tech and Chair, IEEE TCSE Reuse Committee

"Software reuse researchers and practitioners have learned that success with software reuse requires careful attention to many issues, both non-technical and technical. Foremost, success requires a commitment by upper management, followed by careful planning and execution by middle management. Reuse *is* a business and management issue—reusable software becomes a corporate asset, to be invested in, improved, and used consistently. Wayne has always been tremendously concerned about how reuse would be managed as a business strategy. This excellent book reflects his care and attention to detail, focusing squarely on the key management, measurement, and economic issues. It is a superb handbook, providing a comprehensive set of tools, models, and metrics needed to assess the current state of reuse, develop economic models, and plan a reuse program. But the book offers far more. It provides a coherent and illuminating study of how various trends in business, manufacturing, economics, and organization design have influenced the understanding of how to effect a successful reuse program."

—Dr. Martin L. Griss, Senior Laboratory Scientist, Hewlett-Packard Laboratories
Co-author, *Software Reuse: Architecture, Process and Organization
for Business Success*
Addison-Wesley-Longman, 1997

MANAGING SOFTWARE REUSE

A Comprehensive Guide to Strategically Reengineering
the Organization for Reusable Components

Wayne C. Lim

Prentice Hall PTR
Upper Saddle River, NJ 07458
http://www.phptr.com

Library of Congress Cataloging-in-Publication Data

Lim, Wayne C.
      Managing software reuse / Wayne C. Lim.
         p.   cm.
      Includes index.
      ISBN 0-13-552373-7
      1. Computer software--Reusability.   I. Title.
QA76.76.R47L56   1998
005.1--dc21   97-36429
                                    CIP

Editorial/production supervision: *Patti Guerrieri*
Cover design director: *Jerry Votta*
Cover designer: *Scott Weiss, Design Source*
Manufacturing manager: *Alexis R. Heydt*
Marketing manager: *Kaylie Smith*
Acquisitions editor: *Greg Doench*
Editorial assistant: *Mary Treacy*

 ©1998 by Prentice Hall PTR
Prentice-Hall, Inc.
A Simon & Schuster Company
Upper Saddle River, NJ 07458

Prentice Hall books are widely used by corporations and government agencies for training, marketing, and resale.

The publisher offers discounts on this book when ordered in bulk quantities. For more information, contact: Corporate Sales Department, Phone: 800-382-3419; Fax: 201-236-7141; E-mail: corpsales@prenhall.com; or write: Prentice Hall PTR, Corp. Sales Dept., One Lake Street, Upper Saddle River, NJ 07458.

Lotus 123 is a registered trademark of Lotus Development Corporation. All other products or services mentioned in this book arc thc trademarks or service marks of their respective companies or organizations.

Printed in the United States of America
10 9 8 7 6 5 4 3 2 1

ISBN   0-13-552373-7

Prentice-Hall International (UK) Limited, *London*
Prentice-Hall of Australia Pty. Limited, *Sydney*
Prentice-Hall Canada Inc., *Toronto*
Prentice-Hall Hispanoamericana, S.A., *Mexico*
Prentice-Hall of India Private Limited, *New Delhi*
Prentice-Hall of Japan, Inc., *Tokyo*
Simon & Schuster Asia Pte. Ltd., *Singapore*
Editora Prentice-Hall do Brasil, Ltda., *Rio de Janeiro*

Dedication

This book is dedicated to:

My immediate family,
my friends,
Bryant Elliot,
Dr. Ralph Bolton,
Dr. Robert Mifflin,
Dr. James Likens,
and
Dr. Sylvia Kwan

Contents

Chapter 25

Chapter 26

Chapter 27

INTRODUCTION

The importance and prevalence of software has increased significantly in nearly every aspect of everyday life, from automation of offices to control of electronics at home. Both consumer and industrial products increasingly depend upon software for controlling and monitoring functions. This importance has naturally driven demand—and expenditures—for complex, quality software. Its demand continues to grow at rates which outpace current software production capacity. Software expenditures in 1985 were estimated to be about $70 billion in the U.S. and $125 billion worldwide. Such expenditures in 1990 were estimated to be $125 billion in the U.S. and $250 billion globally [1]. As a result of such a crisis, engineers have been challenged to develop ways of increasing productivity without compromising quality. One very promising solution is the reuse of previously developed software.

The explosive growth in demand for software dictates that it can no longer be developed as a throwaway product. Quality software reflects many person-hours of development, testing, and debugging and, as such, should no longer be viewed as an expense but rather treated as an investment. Active use of reusable software is recognized as one of the most promising avenues for preserving and utilizing the value inherent in software.

The goal of this book is to provide the practitioner with a handbook for implementing software reuse within an organization or across multiple organizations. The book offers an integrated, yet flexible, reuse adoption and institutionalization model which encompasses the managerial, organizational, and economic aspects of software reuse, and describes the various tools and techniques used in its implementation. It is not meant as a technical manual but rather, a managerial handbook for both managers and engineering professionals who wish to gain an understanding of the nontechnical areas in reuse. Its purpose is not only to provide its readers with an overview of reuse issues, but also to help them identify important factors to consider in deciding and embarking on reuse, and to discuss ways of managing, organizing, and marketing a reuse program. Whenever possible, real-life examples are used to illustrate the concepts.

This book is organized into nine major sections. The first section discusses the supply and demand predicament in software development; describes the sources from which productivity and quality may come; defines the terms which will be used in this book; examines how the concept of reuse has evolved; surveys how reuse has been utilized in various industries; and finally, describes a reuse adoption and institutionalization model. The second section covers issues in initiating reuse. Topics discussed include establishing the role of a corporate reuse program; identifying reuse potential at the organizational level; and selecting a reuse pilot project among candidates. The third section focuses on investigating whether reuse is appropriate for the targeted organization. It describes how to conduct a cost–benefit analysis; how to decide on whether to pursue reuse as a strategy; and a description of various reuse assessments used to determine the suitability of an organization for reuse. The fourth section spotlights planning for software reuse. This entails creating a reuse vision; determining the necessary staff members, training, and incentives; designing the appropriate organizational structure; handling funding and accounting issues as they relate to reuse; marketing reusable software internally in the organization; managing the legal and contractual issues in reuse; and understanding manufacturing concepts as they relate to reuse. The fifth section discusses the processes and tools used in implementing reuse. This includes processes for producing, brokering, and consuming assets and tools such as reuse repositories. The sixth section discusses implementation strategies for reuse. Areas explored include change management and technology transfer. The seventh section describes the phase after implementation: monitoring and improving the reuse program. The eighth section covers future trends in software reuse. This includes discussions on the rate of technology adoption and the factors necessary for accelerating the assimilation of reuse.

In order to provide readers with a comprehensive exposure to the full body of reuse research, we include surveys of other practitioners' and researchers' works in appendices at the end of each chapter when appropriate. Specifically, the areas surveyed include: 1) adoption models; 2) success factors; 3) economic models; 4) maturity models; 5) assessments; 6) organizational structures; 7) metrics; 8) processes; 9) domain analyses; 10) guidelines; 11) prologues; and 12) certification levels. Readers may wish to skim or skip these sections at first and return to them later for further study.

We continue this section with a discussion of systemic industry problems and challenges confronting software developers, followed by a brief examination of the possible solutions for meeting those challenges. This is followed by the definition and discussion of the reuse terms used throughout the book and an investigation into the evolution of the software reuse concept. The section closes with an overview of current applications of reuse in industry.

Reference

1. B. W. Boehm and P. N. Papaccio, "Understanding and controlling software costs.," *IEEE Transactions on Software Engineering,* vol. 14, no. 10, pp. 1462(16), Oct.1988.

ACKNOWLEDGMENTS

My acknowledgments are not only for those who supported me during the creation of this book, but also for those who encouraged or aided me in the path that I have chosen.

In the course of writing *Managing Software Reuse,* I have become indebted to many individuals who were involved in or influenced the creation of this manuscript. Although impractical to name all such individuals, I wish to offer special mention to some.

My editor, Greg Doench, is undoubtedly the most patient editor in this millennium. Fortunately, he saw the timeless value of and acknowledged the effort required to write such a detailed and comprehensive manuscript. I am truly indebted to him for sharing his knowledge of book publishing and helping me overcome obstacles in publishing this book.

My production editor, Patti Guerrieri, meticulously examined the manuscript and significantly improved it with her suggestions. She deftly coordinated the individuals involved in this endeavor and never failed to maintain high spirits. It has been my privilege and pleasure to have worked with her.

Joyce Rosinger, Bill Camarda, and Kevin Lisankie who are affiliated with Prentice Hall also helped improve this book.

Others played a significant role in my education and experience in reuse. Dorothy McKinney and Sylvan Rubin introduced me to the topic of reuse. Brad Lew and Vincent Young were instrumental in formulating and brainstorming on the topic during the early stages of the book. Guy Cox and the Software Quality and Productivity Analysis team at Hewlett-Packard offered their insights on analysis of reuse data. Martin Griss and I shared many hours working together in the early days to establish the HP Corporate Reuse Program. Known as the "reuse rabbi," Martin was visionary and instrumental in transforming HP divisions to reuse-based software engineering. The experiences in implementing reuse with the Hewlett-Packard Corporate Reuse Team led to insights revealed in this book. I am tremendously indebted to Alvina Nishimoto both as a colleague and a friend. She was responsible for allowing me to collect much of the reuse data shown in this book. Masahiro Yokokawa also generously provided information used in the manuscript.

Several individuals offered their time in discussing reuse issues with me or inspired my writings. They include Ted Biggerstaff, Ruben Prieto-Diaz, John Favaro, Bill Frakes, Chris Kemerer, Charles Lillie, Shari Lawrence Pfleeger, and Jeff Poulin. Please forgive me if I have overlooked anyone.

I would also like to acknowledge my colleagues, Terry Startsman, Eric Aranow, John Brackett, Greg Burdick, and Bob Howell. Steve Lee has always supported me in my endeavor. Karen Choy provided me encouragement and Angela Ren helped untangle the mystery of cash flow statements in the finance chapter.

Dr. Evelyn Oka has always believed in me and I thank her for the vote of confidence. Others who provided their vote of confidence in me include Ralph Bolton, Oliver de La Grandville, Bryant Elliott, James Likens, F. Warren McFarland, Robert Mifflin, Leslie Porter, and Gio Wiederhold. Louis Sivo, Brian Chan, Katie Chong, Brett Stutz, Ginny Fong, Randy Cox, Angela Cheung, Don Huey, Erin Nishimura, Tom Griggs, Michelle Lee, Carolyn Choi, Greg Wong, Michael Eckhardt, Steve Lew, Hiroshi Tominaga, Linda Takagaki, and George Yeo encouraged me and understood the schedule by which I was living. Frederick Chew has been an enduring friend, unselfishly helping me with my computer problems. Thanks also to D.H., E.C., N.S., and T.Y.

Dr. Sylvia Kwan has been a tremendous source of support and encouragement. Her insights and contribution are shown in chapter 16. Without her encouragement, this book probably would not have been written and for that I am especially grateful.

I have always had encouragement from my immediate family with whom I share a common experience. Thank you always for your support, Sue, Nancy, Mae, Fay, and Robert.

Forgive me if I have omitted anyone. All figures and quotations have been reprinted by the kind permission of various associations and organizations that are too numerous to mention here. A reasonable effort was made to locate copyright owners and any errors or omissions called to the publisher's attention will be rectified in future editions.

Wayne C. Lim
Wayne_Lim@post.harvard.edu
http://www.lombardhill.com
Silicon Valley, California U.S.A.
May 8, 1998

CHAPTER
1

THE SOFTWARE DEVELOPMENT CRUNCH

Simple economics dictates that a growing imbalance of supply and demand leads to instability. Within the software industry, this phenomenon, termed the "software crunch or crisis" [1], [2] (Fig. 1–1) has been the result of an explosive growth in software demand accompanied by lagging productivity in software development and a shortage in the supply of software professionals [3] (Fig. 1–2). Boehm [4] observes that the supply of software engineers is increasing at about 4% per year whereas the demand for software is rising by at least 12% per year. Engineer productivity is increasing at only 4% a year, resulting in a cumulative deficit of roughly 4% per year. The processing capacity of hardware, however, has increased at a rate of 40% or better per year [5], [6]. Increased power, along with declining hardware costs, have made computers affordable to many users who in turn demand more sophisticated software for their needs. As expected, complex software takes more time to develop, debug, and maintain.

As if productivity were not enough of a challenge, the lack of software quality has plagued the industry as well. A 1995 study by the Standish Group [7] based on 365 interviews with Information Systems executives revealed that only 16% of software projects were completed within budget, on time, and with all features (Fig. 1–3). In addition, a U.S. Government study of nine software projects revealed that less than 5% of the total dollar amount invested in the nine projects resulted in software that was usable as delivered [8]. Unless development processes become more productive and deliver higher quality output, the shortfall of software will severely limit future innovations and developments within the computer industry. This challenge, well-recognized in the industry, has served as the impetus to the search for new methods to create software that is of higher quality and requires less resources.

1

The Software Crunch

As companies spend more on software...

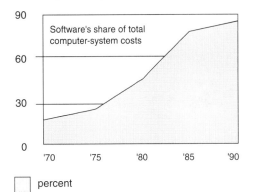

☐ percent

...programs are getting more complex...

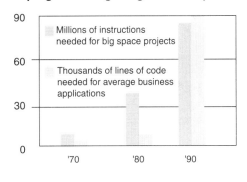

...stretching out software development times...

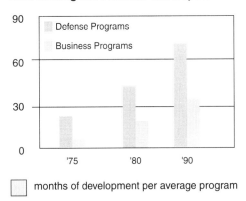

☐ months of development per average program

...and spurring the push to automate programming

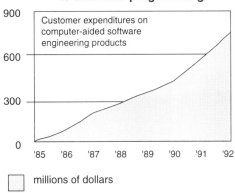

☐ millions of dollars

FIGURE 1–1   The software development crunch. *Source:* O. Port, "The software trap: automate or else," in *Business Week,* May 1988, p. 142.

1.1   Improving Software Productivity and Quality

Different techniques, including reuse, contribute to software productivity and quality improvement in different ways and at varying levels. As shown in Fig. 1–4, Jones [9] categorizes these methods into four different levels of improvement.

The lowest level includes the use of structured, modular high level languages, design reviews, and code inspections. Combining techniques used at the lowest level results in even higher productivity and quality gains—up to 50%. Further enhancements can also be achieved through careful selection of software engineers and a reduction of human labor through the use of program generators and shared

While software jobs are still growing...

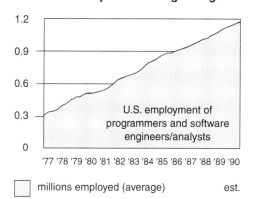

U.S. employment of programmers and software engineers/analysts

'77 '78 '79 '80 '81 '82 '83 '84 '85 '86 '87 '88 '89 '90

☐ millions employed (average)   est.

...fewer students are taking up programming

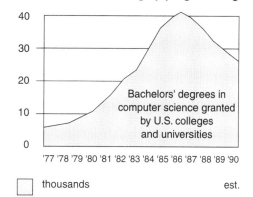

Bachelors' degrees in computer science granted by U.S. colleges and universities

'77 '78 '79 '80 '81 '82 '83 '84 '85 '86 '87 '88 '89 '90

☐ thousands   est.

FIGURE 1–2   Supply and demand of software engineers. *Source:* R. Brandt, "Can the U.S. stay ahead in software?," in *Business Week*, Mar. 1991, p. 105.

programs. The recognized sources of improvement in the highest ranges include reusable and shared modules, programs generators, standard functional modules, and the employment of superb software engineers. As is indicated by Fig. 1–4, one of the few techniques remaining at the top of the pyramid is software reuse. The ability to reach these levels of improvement using reuse depends upon several critical success factors, including the creation of a catalog of standard software, a com-

Outcome of Software Development Projects

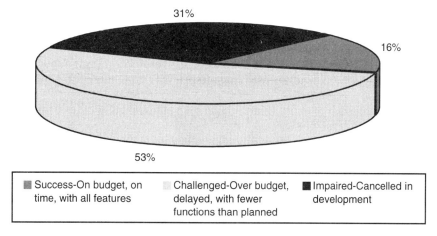

31%

16%

53%

☐ Success-On budget, on time, with all features   ☐ Challenged-Over budget, delayed, with fewer functions than planned   ☐ Impaired-Cancelled in development

FIGURE 1–3   Survey of software projects. *Source:* "Failed technology projects in *Investor's Business Daily*. Los Angeles, Jan. 25, 1995, p. A8.

Plateaus of Improvement

Percent Productivity and Quality Improvement	Technique
> 75%	generators, reusable modules
50–75%	superstars, generators, reusable modules
25–50%	combination of:
	design and control review, code inspections, structured code, high-level languages, direct aids, personnel selection and training
5–25%	structured code, high-level languages, review and inspections, interactive tools and equipment

FIGURE 1–4   Four levels of software development techniques and corresponding improvements. Reprinted by permission from IBM Guide/Share Application Development Symposium Proceedings, copyright 1979 by International Business Machines Corporation.

mon language for describing domains, and the identification of an optimal set of reusable modules.

In addition to high levels of improvement in productivity and quality, reuse can significantly contribute to cost reduction. As shown in Fig. 1–5, Maranzano [10] of AT&T systematically examined potential sources of cost reduction from various methods and found that among the methods investigated, reuse showed the highest level of cost reduction throughout the development life cycle.

Boehm [11], in his study of U.S. Department of Defense (DoD) software costs, reports similar results. Fig. 1–6 shows the impact of sources of savings with reuse constituting savings of nearly 50% from the baseline totals by the year 2008.

Because of its potential impact on improving software productivity and quality, reuse has quickly become a popular method of choice in some organizations. In Fig. 1–7 Matsumoto [12] reports the 1985 results of a semi-annual questionnaire of Fuchu Software Factory members. Reuse was cited more often than all of the other methods combined.

Sources of Cost Reduction

Reuse	12%
Process improvement	8%
Architecture	7%
Planning and administration	5%
C++ and OOP	2%

FIGURE 1–5   Sources of cost reduction. *Source:* J. Maranzano, AT&T, 1990.

Estimated Results by Source of Savings

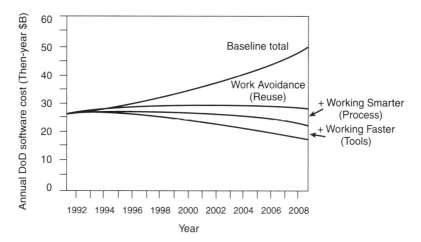

FIGURE 1–6   Estimated results by sources of savings. *Source:* B. W. Boehm, "DoD software technology strategy: forum overview," presented at Department of Defense Software Technology Strategy Public Program, Falls Church, VA, Mar. 1992, p. 47.

Toshiba Software Factory
Most Popular Methods of Achieving Target Productivity and Quality

Method	*Percent Using Method*
Reusing	52.1%
Improvement of functional decomposition	6.7%
Use of higher level language	6.3%
Application of new software engineering	7.2%
Application of new software tools	9.7%
Improvement of work steps, procedures, and environments	18.0%

FIGURE 1–7   Methods of improving productivity and quality at Toshiba. *Source:* Y. Matsumoto, "Experiences from software reuse in industrial process control applications," presented at Advances in Software Reuse. Selected papers from the Second International Workshop on Software Reusability, Lucca, Italy, Mar. 1993, p. 193.

References

1. W. W. Gibbs, "Software's chronic crisis," in *Scientific American (International Edition)*, vol. 271, Sept. 1994, pp. 72–81.
2. O. Port, "The Software Trap: Automate : Or Else," in *Business Week*, May 1988, pp. 142–154.
3. R. Brandt, "Can the U.S. Stay Ahead in Software?," in *Business Week*, Mar. 1991, pp. 98–105.
4. B. W. Boehm and T. A. Standish, "Software technology in the 1990s: using an evolutionary paradigm," *Computer*, vol. 16, pp. 30–7, 1983.
5. J. H. Morrissey and L. S. Y. Wu, "Software engineering . . . an economic perspective," presented at The 4th International Conference on Software Engineering, 1979.
6. E. J. Joyce, "Reusable Software : Passage to Productivity?," in *Datamation*, vol. 34, Sept. 1988, pp. 97–102.
7. "Failed technology projects (The Standish Group Report)," in *Investor's Business Daily*. Los Angeles, Jan. 1995, pp. A8.
8. B. Cox, *Object Oriented programming: An Evolutionary Approach*. Reading: Addison-Wesley, 1986.
9. T. C. Jones, "The limits of programming productivity," presented at IBM Guide/Share Application Development Symposium, Oct. 1979.
10. J. Maranzano, "private communication," 1990.
11. B. W. Boehm, "DoD Software Technology Strategy: Forum Overview," presented at Department of Defense Software Technology Strategy Public Program, Falls Church, VA, Mar. 1992.
12. Y. Matsumoto, "Experiences from software reuse in industrial process control applications," presented at Advances in Software Reuse. Selected Papers from the Second International Workshop on Software Reusability (Cat. No. 93TH0495-2), Mar. 1993.

CHAPTER

2

SOFTWARE REUSE—DEFINITION, SCOPE, AND FRAMEWORK

Precise definitions of reuse and its related terms have evolved throughout the years in response to changes in the software development field. In the 1960's and 1970's, reuse meant the use of already developed code in new situations. Since then, the term "reuse" has broadened to include not only the use of code but algorithms, designs, ideas, and components. In 1980, Freeman [1] expanded the concept to be "any information which a developer may need in the process of creating software." The focus then is not simply the reuse of programs by multiple end-users upon multiple occasions, but rather, all relevant information required by the developer or maintainer of a system.

2.1 Basic Definitions

For this book, the following definitions will be used:

Asset (or "workproduct" or "component"). Assets are the products or byproducts of the software development process. They include both tangible (e.g., code, design, algorithms, test plans, and documentation) and intangible (e.g., knowledge and methodologies) elements.

Reuse. Reuse is the use of existing assets in the development of other software with the goal of improving productivity, quality, and other factors (e.g., usability).

Leverage (or "leveraged reuse" or "white box reuse"). Leverage, a form of reuse, is the use of existing assets *with modification* to develop other software with the goal of improving productivity, quality, and other factors.

7

Systematic Reuse.   Systematic reuse is the reuse of assets within a structured plan with well-defined processes and life cycles and commitments for funding, staffing, and incentives for production and use of the reusable assets [2].

Proper scoping and defining reuse for an organization that is embarking on such a program is a critical task because it often dictates the specific forms of reuse an organization will utilize in the future. Thus, if the scope is too narrowly defined (e.g., reuse of code only), other potentially viable types of reuse such as design and test suites might be excluded. For example, an organization may unwittingly discourage reuse of previous versions of a software product if it defines, measures, and rewards reuse only on the basis of using components from a library. Thus, reuse should not be defined so narrowly as to exclude other viable forms and methods of reuse, but not so broadly that no distinctions are made.

2.2   Reusable Assets

As we discussed earlier, software reuse consists of more than just code and includes any information that may be needed in the course of developing or monitoring a system. Jones [3] describes ten types of assets which may be reused:

1. architectures	**6.** estimates
2. source code	**7.** human interfaces
3. data	**8.** plans
4. designs	**9.** requirements
5. documentation	**10.** test cases

In addition to the above, intellectual capital, such as knowledge and expertise of personnel, may also be reused. In Fig. 2–1, Cusumano [4] lists potential reusable assets by development phase.

Phase	Reusable Asset
Requirements	requirements/specifications, trade studies, cost models
Analysis	project models, histories, system simulations
Design	designs, standards, frameworks, consumer reports, historical reengineering costs, design simulations
Develop	code modules, programmer's manuals, operating manuals, unit test cases, codes simulations, operator training programs
Integrate and Test	system and subsystem test plans, procedures and cases, detailed interface simulations
Maintain	problem/trouble report tracking systems, regression test plans, procedures, cases

FIGURE 2–1   Potential reusable assets. Adapted from M. Cusumano, Ed., J. Morrison, project director, *Software Reuse in Japan*, Colorado Springs, CO: Technology Transfer International, Inc., 1992, p. 360.

Percentage of Life Cycle Assets Consisting of Reusable Parts

Asset	Mean
Requirements	20.8%
Design	26.1%
Code	33.0%
Test plans	26.1%
Test cases	24.8%
User documentation	30.4%

FIGURE 2–2   Results of Frakes' and Fox's reuse survey. *Source:* W. B. Frakes and C. J. Fox, "Software reuse survey report," Software Engineering Guild, Sterling, VA, 1993, pp. 38–50.

From a software reuse survey of 29 organizations, Frakes and Fox [5] determined the percentage of life cycle assets created by the organization and consisting of reusable parts. As shown in Fig. 2–2, the data indicated that code and user documentation were the assets that, on average, had the highest percentage of reusable parts.

2.3   A Framework for Reuse

Successful adoption and institutionalization of software reuse can be best achieved through a holistic and multidisciplinary approach (Fig. 2–3). Although software reuse originated from the fields of computer science and software engineering, re-

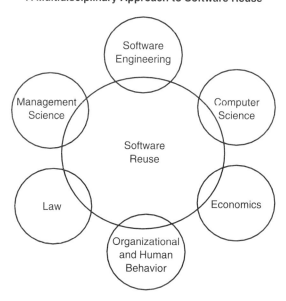

A Multidisciplinary Approach to Software Reuse

FIGURE 2–3   Example of fields affecting reuse.

searchers and practitioners have drawn from a host of disciplines to address the wide range of technical and nontechnical issues that have surfaced in practice [6] (Fig. 2–4).

Current thinking is that reuse is most effective when practiced systematically. The first step toward this goal is to develop a framework for identifying and discussing the key aspects of reuse. Nontechnical areas of reuse comprise the issues of adoption, economics, strategy, personnel, organization, finance, metrics, marketing, legal, and manufacturing as they relate to reuse. Technical areas include processes and tools. Because this book emphasizes the managerial aspects of reuse, the nontechnical aspects of reuse are highlighted in our framework.

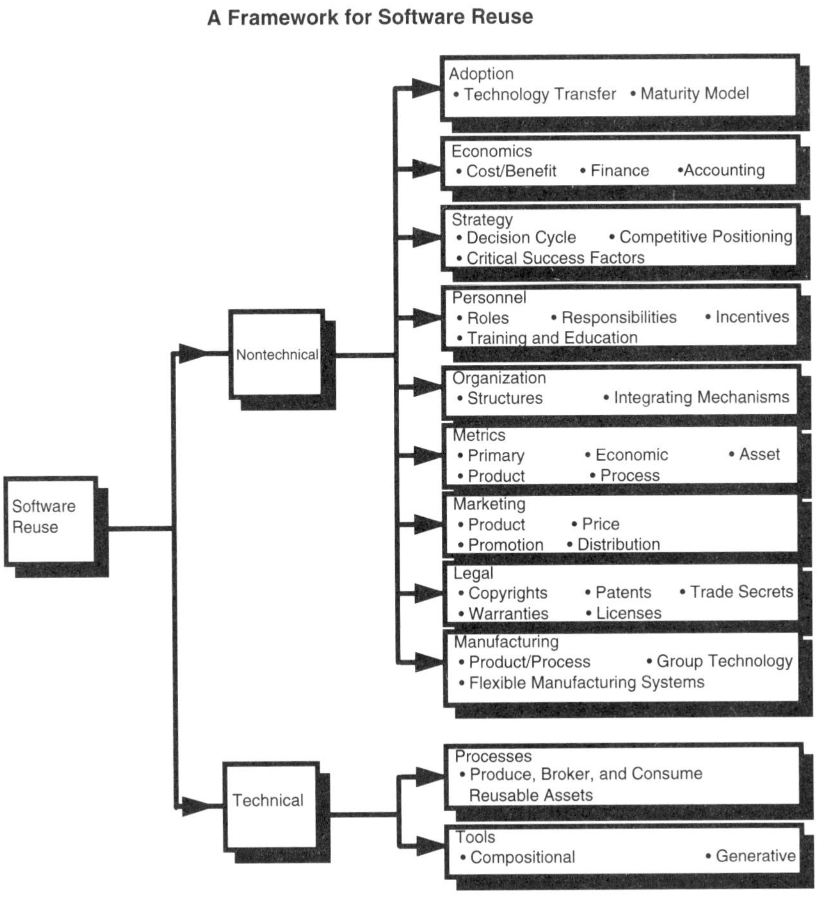

A Framework for Software Reuse

FIGURE 2–4   Fields contributing to reuse.

Adoption is the process of formally accepting and institutionalizing reuse. Topics which directly relate to reuse adoption include technology transfer techniques and maturity models, which are patterns showing the emergence of characteristics through growth.

Economics concerns the production, brokering, and consumption of reuse goods and services. Within this category are topics such as cost/benefit analysis, finance, and accounting. Cost/benefit analyses determine the economic worthiness of pursuing a reuse program or creating a reusable asset; finance relates to the funding of a reuse program; and accounting deals with tracking and controlling a reuse program.

Strategy refers to how reuse will be employed to meet the organization's goals. In certain situations, reuse will help formulate the organization's strategies. Related to strategy are the decision cycle the organization uses to determine the role of reuse; competitive positioning, or how the organization may capitalize on reuse to obtain a defensible position in the marketplace; and critical success factors, a technique used to identify the organization's priorities.

Personnel concerns the definition of the roles and responsibilities of the people involved with reuse. This includes the establishment of incentives necessary to motivate engineers to produce, broker, and consume reusable assets as well as the training and education necessary for them to reuse effectively.

The reuse *organizational structure* refers to the formal system of working relationships that permit both the division of labor and coordination of tasks for individuals and groups to achieve the common goal of reusing software. Related to the organizational structure is the concept of "integrating mechanisms," rules, and procedures that may be used to facilitate coordination between different parties.

A reuse *metric* defines a way of measuring some attribute of developing software with reusable assets. Not limited to code, these metrics also measure the reuse infrastructure, the underlying foundation or basic framework that supports reuse. Several categories of reuse metrics exist: primary, economic, library, asset, product, and process.

Effective *marketing* helps the reuse organization achieve its goals by accurately determining the needs and wants of the target organizations and delivering the desired value. Associated with reuse marketing is the need to identify the appropriate product/services, price, promotion, and distribution channels.

The key to successful reuse within the *legal* context is to strike the appropriate balance in allocating known risks among all parties so that reuse can be encouraged and not encumbered by unnecessary and undesirable legal problems. Topics within the legal and contractual arena include the use of copyrights, patents, trade secrets, warranties, and licenses.

Manufacturing for reuse involves the manner in which the process is linked to the product. Popular strategies for reuse include the application of group technology, a manufacturing technique used to identify and group similar parts so that their manufacture is streamlined, and flexible manufacturing systems which capitalize on economies of scale and reduce labor costs.

Reuse *processes* are systematic procedures to be employed in producing, brokering, and consuming reusable software. Reuse *tools* are broadly defined as those instruments which facilitate the reuse of products or byproducts of the software development life cycle. These would include, for example, reuse libraries, application templates, and generators. These tools, in turn, may be categorized into compositional or generative reuse techniques. Compositional reuse involves constructing new software products by assembling existing reusable assets, while generative reuse involves the use of application generators to build new applications from high-level descriptions.

To complete the reuse framework, we integrate and link together the key elements identified into a *"reuse diamond"* (Fig. 2–5).

Each of the six facets in this structure depicts an important reuse area that not only impacts the success of an entire reuse program but that of each of the other

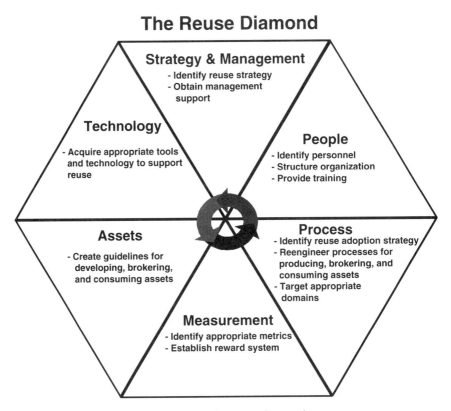

FIGURE 2–5   The reuse diamond.

areas as well. For example, the choice of a reuse strategy will impact the identification of appropriate metrics, and the selection of appropriate tools will affect the type of training personnel should receive. Depending upon its current state, different organizations should emphasize different areas when implementing reuse.

Within strategy and management, an appropriate reuse strategy needs to be charted within the context of the organization's existing plan. In some cases, reuse will play a pivotal role in the formulation of the organization's overall strategy. Procuring management support is extremely important before and during a reuse program. Within the people facet, the appropriate personnel and organizational structure needs to be identified as well as a training process for transitioning to a reuse paradigm. In the process area, an outline for a reuse adoption strategy tailored for the organization should be developed. Existing processes should be reeengineered for producing, brokering, and consuming assets. Appropriate domains for reuse and the organizations in which they reside need to be identified. In the measurement area, appropriate metrics and their integration into the reward system need to be established. In the assets area, guidelines for producing, brokering, and consuming should be made available and incentives for adhering to them instituted. Finally, in technology, the selective implementation of appropriate tools and technology can contribute substantially to successful reuse.

References

1. P. Freeman, "Reusable software engineering: a statement of long-range research objectives," Department of Information and Computer Science, University of California at Irvine, Irvine, CA, Technical Report 159, Nov 10, 1980.
2. M. Ogush, "Terms in transition: a software reuse lexicon," *Crosstalk: The Journal of Defense Software Engineering*, pp. 41–45, Dec. 1992.
3. T. C. Jones, "Software Return on Investment Preliminary Analysis," Software Productivity Research, Inc., Burlington, MA, 1993.
4. "Software Reuse in Japan," M. Cusumano, Ed., Colorado Springs, CO: Technology Transfer International, Inc., 1992, pp. 360.
5. W. B. Frakes and C. J. Fox, "Software reuse survey report," Software Engineering Guild, Sterling, VA, 1993.
6. M. L. Griss and M. Wosser, "Making reuse work at Hewlett-Packard," *IEEE Software*, vol. 12, pp. 105–7, Jan. 1995.

EVOLUTION OF THE SOFTWARE REUSE CONCEPT

In this chapter, we investigate historically the concept of reuse—the motivation for its inception, the initial spread of interest, and its continuing development into a systematic process. An examination of the industrial revolution and its impact on manufacturing processes will assist us in understanding the implications of industrialization on software development.

Numerous analogies have been made linking software development to the evolution of manufacturing processes. For example, gunsmithing in the 1800's was largely a specialized trade, with each gunsmith crafting his (or her) product in a unique style. Similarly, software development has been described as a cottage industry where "companies specializing in software reveal their deeply ingrained cottage mentality when they refer to themselves as software houses"[1]. Just as the production of firearms eventually moved to an interchangeable parts paradigm [2], the software industry's use of the terms "software factory" and "software tools" suggest that manufacturing models are being adapted for software production [3]. Although there are significant differences between manufacturing and software development, we can nonetheless learn some valuable lessons by looking at the implications of such industrialization on software production. Since the Industrial Revolution has had such a profound impact on manufacturing, we begin with an examination of this era.

3.1   The Industrial Revolution and the Software Development Process—
An Analogy

"Before the (assembly) line was introduced (in August 1913), each auto chassis was as-
sembled by one man in about 12 1/2 hours. Eight months later, when the line was in its
final form, with each worker performing a small unit of work and the chassis being
moved mechanically, the average labor time per unit was 93 minutes."
– Chase and Aquilano, Production and Operations Management,
Richard D. Irwin, Inc., 1973, p. 8

"What is unique in unique-product production is the product. In fact, unique-product
production is always organized around standard tools, and it typically works with standardized materials . . .
    In unique-product production, the basic unit is by homogeneous stages . . . every
man engaged in the work of a particular stage must be able to do everything needed in
that stage . . . no skill is needed by individual or team that goes beyond the requirements of that particular stage . . .
    It was not mass-production that resulted in the unprecedented output of ships
(during World War II). It was the division of the work into homogeneous stages; the
systematic organization of the work group for the specific requirements of each stage;
and the systematic training of a large number of people to do all the work required
within one stage . . ."
Drucker, P., Management, *Harper & Row, New York, 1974, pp. 205-206*

The industrial revolution is generally acknowledged to have begun in England
during the 1760's and refers to the process of change from a handicraft, agrarian society to an industrialized economy. The most salient characteristic of the industrial
revolution was the unprecedented and sustained increase in the rate of growth of
both total and per capita output [4]. Accompanying such change was the increase
in the number of goods due in part to the introduction of power-driven machinery
and the factory-organization. Prior to the revolution, products were the handiwork
of craftspeople. Each product was created as though it were unique, either by hand
or simple machinery [5]. The revolution popularized the practice of mass production which depended upon the standardization of parts and division of labor. As a
consequence, it became evident that products could be produced using a wide
range of available manufacturing processes.
    Production processes differ in many aspects. One important difference is "the
degree of variability (or customization) in the products or services that the system is
required to produce at any one time"[6]. At one extreme are the project processes
which allow for high tailorization and at the other extreme are the continuous
processes which capitalize on economies of scale or scope. *Economies of scale* is
defined as the long-term reduction in average costs that occurs when the scale of the
output is increased [7]. Related to this concept is *economies of scope* which refers to
the achievement of lower unit costs by manufacturing similar products in quantity.

Some processes are better suited for production of certain products than others. For example, as shown in Fig. 3–1, in the production of automobiles, a high-performance racing car may be best produced using a project process because of its unique requirements and its one-of-a-kind nature. An automobile with relatively unique requirements and limited demand (e.g., Mercedes) may be best suited for batch processes. A general transportation automobile, on the other hand, may be best manufactured with more assembly line processes. These processes exploit the economies of scale, scope, or both, through standardization when these cars are produced in high volume. Other analogies are presented in Fig. 3–2.

While a given product may be produced using any number of these processes, the choice of an appropriate process depends upon the demands of the market, the strategy of the company and the nature of the product. The manufacturing of automobiles discussed here is a clear example. This spectrum of processes, however, has not been aggressively pursued by software developers until recently.

In fact, most software has been viewed as though it were unique and developed with a project process. However, much software actually is potentially common and generic and can be developed through other processes which utilize more standard, interchangeable software parts and specialization of labor. Results from several studies show that software redundancy is as high as 85%. A California study found that 75% of application code, 50% of systems programs, and 70% of telecommunications programs shared identical code or functions [8]. Another sur-

The Choice of a Production Process Depends on Your Market

Projects ←——————→ Batch ←——————→ Assembly Line

Product:

| Highly-Customized, Unique, One-of-a-Kind Item | Small Production Volumes | Standardized, High Volume |

Examples:

| Racing Cars, Space Shuttles, Ocean-Going Vessels | Rolls Royce, Musical Instruments | World Cars, Lightbulbs |

FIGURE 3–1   Production processes. *Source:* W. E. Sasser, R. P. Olsen, and D. D. Wyckoff, *Management of Service Operations: Text, Cases and Readings.* Boston, MA: Allyn and Bacon, 1978, pp. xiv–xvii.

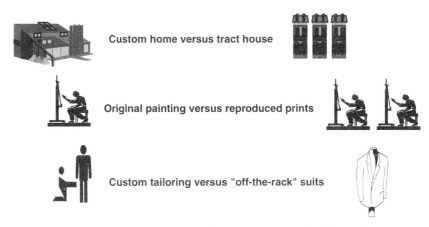

Production Processes Exploiting Economies of Scale and Scope

Custom home versus tract house

Original painting versus reproduced prints

Custom tailoring versus "off-the-rack" suits

FIGURE 3–2   Processes which exploit economies of scale and scope. *Source:* J. Poldolsky, Hewlett-Packard.

vey showed that only 15% of all programming code written in 1983 was unique, novel, and specific to individual applications [9].

Economist Paul Samuelson [10] describes a number of advances affiliated with mass production:

1. the use of nonhuman and nonanimal power sources (water and wind power, steam, electricity, turbines and internal-combustion engines, internal nuclear energy);
2. the use of automatic self-adjusting mechanisms (lathes, jigs, servomechanisms);
3. the use of standardized, interchangeable parts;
4. the breakdown of complex processes into simple repetitive operations;
5. the specialization of function and division of labor.

Some of these advances have already been attained in software development. For example, since the 1970's, we have seen a division of labor between applications engineers and systems software developers [11]. Accelerated progress towards industrialization can be further achieved through CASE tools, automated program generators, reusable assets, analysis and design, and producer and consumer paradigms. Such advances are often motivated by consumer demand and not from within the industry. For example, in the case of firearm industrialization, Cox [2] notes that the gunsmiths had played no role in influencing the way the arms would be manufactured, but rather, *consumers* "created an economic incentive for those vendors who would serve their interest (i.e., the ability to reuse, interchange, and repair parts)." Cox further predicts that "the software industrial revolution will occur, sometime, somewhere, whether programmers want it to or not, because the consumers determine the outcome."

Software reuse is not a new concept. It is an outcome of the engineer's motivation to avoid developing redundant code. In fact, one could argue that it is an inevitable consequence of evolution and a sign of a maturing discipline and industry.

3.2 The Evolution of Reuse

We continue this section by summarizing key developments in the industrialization of software reuse. Some reuse milestones are illustrated in Fig. 3–3.

1940s. The engineer's desire to avoid repetitive tasks has been evident since the early days of programming. Use of the subroutine and subroutine library was pioneered on the EDSAC at Cambridge University in 1949.

1950s. By the late 1950's, more than 200 subroutines resided in the EDSAC library [12]. In addition, various computer manufacturers began using the basic

Timeline for Software Reuse

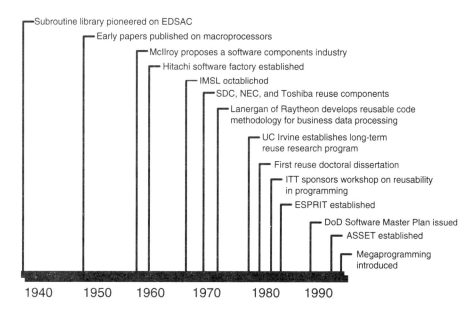

FIGURE 3–3   Software reuse timeline.

concepts of a system to replace text which would save countless hours of repetitive coding. These text replacement systems became known as macroprocessors.

1960s.   One of these macroprocessor pioneers, Douglas McIlroy [13], made a presentation one decade later at a 1968 NATO conference which has been largely credited with presenting the vision of a software components industry:

> "My thesis is that the software industry is weakly founded, and that one aspect of this weakness is the absence of a software components subindustry. . . . What I have just asked for is simply industrialism, with programming terms substituted for some of the more mechanically oriented terms appropriate to mass production. I think there are considerable areas of software ready, if not overdue, for this approach.
>
> Software production . . . would be enormously helped by the availability of spectra of high quality routines, quite as mechanical design is abetted by the existence of families of structural shapes, screws, or resistors."

In 1969, Hitachi started its software factory, a process which attempts to integrate and automate software development activities, usually with the sharing of standard parts and processes.

1970s.   International Mathematical and Subroutine Libraries (IMSL) was founded in 1970 by Charles W. Johnson to produce FORTRAN subroutine libraries for constructing mathematical and statistical analysis applications [14].

By 1974, the System Development Corporation had registered the term "software factory" as a trademark [15], [16]. In the same year, NEC Fuchu began pushing software development toward a level of productivity comparable to modern engineering and factory operations. They emphasized concepts such as process standardization, quality control, reusability, and automated tools [17].

In 1976, NEC formed a distributed software factory network to more effectively meet the varying demands of consumers. Not all consumers required state-of-the-art products. Consequently, products were made for such consumers using standardardized methods and tools.

In the mid-1970's, Lanergan, Poynton, Grasso, and Dugan reported on the Raytheon Company's success in implementing reuse for business applications with COBOL [18], [19]. By reusing software, eight Raytheon programmers managed to rewrite the entire company's large manufacturing system software in a period of only four months [20].

By 1977, Toshiba had established a software factory for creating real-time control software for industrial applications which emphasized the reuse of components [21].

1980s. Reusability became more practical in this decade, due to increased adoption and integration of specific tools and techniques designed to support reuse of designs and coded subroutines, mainly in applications programs.

In the early 1980s, work in reusable software was reported by Boeing, on reusable avionics software [22]; IBM, in the form of a reuse survey and compilation of definitions [23], [24]; and Softech, where the effects of software structure on reusability were examined [25]. The University of California at Irvine established a long-term reusable software research program in 1981 [26]. In addition, the first dissertation on software reuse was written by James Neighbors, who coined the term "domain analyst" [27]. In 1981, the U.S. Department of Defense established the Software Technology for Adaptable Reliable Systems (STARS) program for the purpose of improving productivity while achieving greater system reliability and adaptability [28], [29]. Over subsequent years, the program evolved to emphasize greater reuse [28].

Also in 1981, the Hartford Insurance Group formed a task force to investigate the potential of reusable code and subsequently implemented a program to support reusable code [30]. By 1982–83, Ford Aerospace developed guidelines for implementing reuse for Air Force-related software development efforts, including those for designing for reuse and for cataloging reusable software [31], [32].

In September 1983, the ITT Workshop on Reusability in Programming was one of the first organized workshop efforts in reuse and provided a collection of seminal works in reuse [33]. In 1984, the European Programme for Research in Information Technology (ESPRIT) was established, which eventually resulted in two projects heavily focused on reuse, Portable Common Tools and Environment (PCTE) and REuse Based on Object-Oriented Techniques (REBOOT). The PCTE project researched the reuse of tools [28] and REBOOT was formed to "provide methods and tools to support creation and use of domain-oriented components" [34].

In 1986, the Eureka Software Factory (ESF) was established to investigate the software factory concept and "establish the technical and economic foundations for software factory engineering in Europe" [35]. ESF is comprised of 13 European software organizations whose common goal is to create a tailorable software environment supported by standard "plug-compatible" tools [28].

1990s. The 1990's began with the issuance of the U.S. Department of Defense (DoD) Software Master Plan which focused on software repositories and domain engineering [28], [36]. The Asset Source for Software Engineering Technology (ASSET) was also established with the mission "to provide a distributed support system as a focus for software reuse within the DoD and eventually help foster a software reuse industry in the United States" [37]. In 1992, Megaprogramming (MP), the "practice of building software by components in a context of architecture conventionalization and reuse," was introduced as the main emphasis of the STARS Program [38].

References

1. P. Bassett and J. Giblon, "Computer aided programming. I," presented at SOFTFAIR. A Conference on Software Development Tools, Techniques, and Alternatives. Proceedings, 1983.
2. B. J. Cox, "There is a silver bullet (reusable software components)," in *Byte*, vol. 15, Oct. 1990, pp. 209–10, 212, 214, 216, 218.
3. P. Wegner, "Capital-intensive software technology," *IEEE Software*, vol. 1, pp. 7–45, July 1984.
4. R. M. Hartwell, *The Causes of the Industrial Revolution: An Essay in Methodology in the Causes of the Industrial Revolution*. London, U.K.: Methuen & Co. Ltd., 1967.
5. E. Lampard, "Industrial Revolution," in *World Book Encyclopedia*. Chicago, IL: World Book, Inc., 1994.
6. W. E. Sasser, R. P. Olsen, and D. D. Wyckoff, *Management of Service Operations: Text, Cases and Readings*. Boston, MA: Allyn and Bacon, 1978.
7. C. Pass, B. Lowes, L. Davis, and S. J. Kronish, *The Harper Collins Dictionary of Economics*. New York, N.Y.: Harper Collins, 1991.
8. N. Maginnis, "Specialist: reusable code helps increase productivity," in *Computerworld*, Nov. 1986.
9. E. J. Joyce, "Reusable Software : Passage to Productivity?," in *Datamation*, vol. 34, Sept. 1988, pp. 97–102.
10. P. Samuelson, *Economics*, 10th ed. New York, N.Y.: McGraw Hill, 1976.
11. J. Moad, "Cultural barriers slow reusability (programming)," *Datamation*, vol. 35, pp. 87–92, Nov. 1989.
12. M. Campbell-Kelly, *Introduction to macros*. New York, N.Y.: American Elsevier, 1973.
13. M. D. McIlroy, "Mass produced software components," in *Software Engineering Concepts and Techniques*, J. M. Buxton, P. Naur, and B. Randall, Eds. New York, N.Y.: Petrocelli/Charter, 1976, pp. 306.
14. J. Metzer, "Anatomy of a Merger," in *Software Publisher*. Aurora, CO: Webcom Communications Corp, Mar./Apr. 1994.
15. R. Prieto-Diaz, "Status report: software reusability," *IEEE Software*, vol. 10, pp. 61–6, May 1993.
16. H. Bratman and T. Court, "The software factory," *Computer*, vol. 8, pp. 28-37, May 1975.
17. M. Cusumano, *Japan's Software Factories*. New York, N.Y.: Oxford University Press, 1991.
18. R. Lanergan and B. Poynton, "Reusable Code-the Application Development Technique of the Future," presented at IBM Guide/Share Application Symposium, Oct. 1979.
19. R. Lanergan and B. Poynton, "Software Engineering with Standard Assemblies," presented at Association of Computing Machinery Proceedings, Washington D.C., Dec. 1978.

20. W. Rausch-Hindin, "Reusable Software: special series on system integration," in *Systems & Software*, Feb. 1983, pp. 78–92.

21. T. Matsubara, O. Sasaki, K. Nakajim, K. Takezawa, S. Yamamoto, and T. Tanaka, "SWB System: A Software Factory," in *Software Engineering Environments*. Amsterdam, The Netherlands: North-Holland Publishing Company, 1981, pp. 305–318.

22. R. F. Bousley, "Reusable avionics executive software," presented at NAECON 1981. *Proceedings of the IEEE 1981 National Aerospace and Electronics Conference*, May 1981.

23. C. S. Chandersekaran, "Survey of Reusable Software," IBM Unpublished Technical Report, 1982.

24. S. J. Schappelle, "Reusable Software Definitions," IBM Technical Reports Center, Owego, N.Y., Technical Report, 82-550-006, June 11, 1982.

25. J. B. Goodenough and R. V. Zara, "The effect of software structure on software reliability modifiability, and reusability: a case study and analysis," SofTech, Inc., Waltham, MA, Technical Report DAAA 25-72C 0667, 1974.

26. P. Freeman, "Reusable software engineering: a statement of long-range research objectives," Department of Information and Computer Science, University of California at Irvine, Irvine, CA, Technical Report 159, Nov. 10, 1980.

27. J. Neighbors, "Software Construction Using Components," Department of Information and Computer Science, University of California, Irvine, Irvine, CA, Technical Report 160, 1980.

28. R. Prieto-Diaz, "Historical Overview in Software Reusability," in *Software Reusability*, W. Schafer, R. Prieto-Diaz, and M. Matsumoto, Eds., West Sussex, England: Ellis Horwood, 1994, pp. 160.

29. L. E. Druffel, S. T. Redwine, Jr., and W. E. Riddle, "The STARS program: overview and rationale," *Computer*, vol. 16, pp. 21 9, Nov. 1983.

30. M. Cavaliere and P. Archambeault, "Reusable code at the Hartford Insurance Group," presented at ITT Workshop on Reusability in Programming, Newport, R.I., Sept. 1983.

31. S. Rubin and W. C. Lim, "Guidelines for Modularization and Reusability," presented at Hewlett-Packard Software Engineering Productivity Conference, Palo Alto, CA, 1987.

32. W. C. Lim and S. Rubin, "Guidelines for Cataloging Reusable Software," presented at Hewlett-Packard Software Engineering Productivity Conference, Palo Alto, CA, Aug. 1987.

33. A. Perlis, T. Biggerstaff, and T. Cheatham, "ITT Workshop on Reusability in Programming," Newport, R.I.: ITT, Sept. 1983.

34. J.-M. Morel and J. Faget, "The REBOOT Approach," *Reuse Improvement*, 1992.

35. R. Rockwell and M. H. Gera, "The Eureka Software Factory CoRe: A Conceptual Reference model for software factories," *Proceedings 1993 Software Engineering Environments*, pp. 80–93, 1993.

36. G. Millburn, "Department of Defense Software Master Plan, Volume1: Plan of Action," Department of Defense, Washington, D.C. Feb. 1990.

37. J. Moore and C. Lillie, "Asset Source for Software Engineering Technology (ASSET)," presented at National Symposium: Improving the Software Process and Competitive Position via Software Reuse and Re-engineering, Apr. 1991.

38. B. W. Boehm and W. L. Scherlis, "Megaprogramming," presented at DARPA Software Technology Conference, Los Angeles, CA, Apr. 1992.

MAJOR TRENDS IN REUSE

Over the last quarter of a century, a number of trends in reuse have and continue to influence software development practice. Fig. 4–1 illustrates one of the dimensions of this progress, from code-focused reuse to strategy-driven reuse. In the early 1970's, reuse meant reuse of code only. Experiences at Raytheon and Boeing typified this mindset. By the 1980's, work had begun on creating libraries to centrally store this code. Work in classification schemes and search mechanisms marked this period. By the 1990's, reuse had moved towards a more holistic view. Some organizations emphasized domain-specific, architecture-centric reuse. In addition, research in reuse expanded to include areas of management, metrics, culture, and economics. With the 21st century on the horizon, we hope to see reuse emerge from a technique utilized only in research and development departments for automation of software engineering to a foundation upon which corporations will base their business strategies. In this realm, reuse becomes not only a tool used to reduce costs, increase productivity, and shorten time to market, but one that will be considered for creating new products and entering new markets. Examples of organizations implementing strategy-driven reuse are available today and are described later in the book.

4.1 The Upstream Value of Reuse

The upstream value of reuse traces the impact and importance of reuse within an organization and is closely tied to trends in reuse. As shown in Fig. 4–2, the value of reuse increases over time as organizations begin to incorporate reuse into earlier stages of the product or system development phases. During the 1970's, reuse pri-

Phases in Reuse Evolution

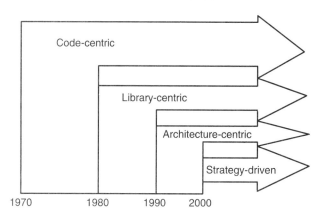

FIGURE 4–1   Phases in reuse evolution.

marily impacted the coding phase of the software development cycle, playing a relatively small role in the total development process [1], [2]. In the 1980's, several researchers advocated the reuse of designs because of the potential order of magnitude increase in quality and productivity [3], [4]. Part of the motivation for considering reuse further upstream in the development cycle was because coding constitutes only a small portion of the total cost of creating a system, and errors introduced in the early phases of the life cycle become much more expensive to fix downstream [5]. Furthermore, some felt that reuse of high-level assets should be easier since they were less dependent on hardware and operating system characteristics [4]. As a result, the practice of reuse began to include reuse of designs, specifications, and requirements.

Strategy-driven reuse, which is discussed in chapter 13, is a logical progression of the trend in which reuse has an impact further upstream in the development phases of a product or system. Potential added value from reuse in the product strategy and corporate strategy phases can be realized if organizations take reuse

The Upstream Value of Reuse

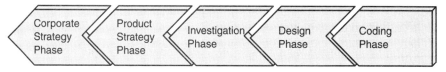

FIGURE 4–2   Upstream value of reuse.

into consideration while formulating product positioning and corporate strategies for competing in the marketplace.

4.2   Trends Which Enable Software Reuse

A number of trends in multiple areas have encouraged and enabled reuse. These areas include both non-technological and technological areas such as: management, law, processes, organizations, methods, environment, standards, application services, tools, and languages (Fig. 4–3). We will briefly describe the trends in each area and their impact on reuse.

Management.   In the 1970's, management focused on corporate growth in three ways: 1) intensive (achieving further growth within the company's current business scope); 2) integrative (building or acquiring businesses that are related to the company's current businesses); and 3) diversification (adding attractive businesses that are unrelated to the company's current businesses) [6]. The 1980's stressed the creation of sustainable competitive strategy [7]. Spurred by the thinking of Juran, Deming, and others, companies seeking to maintain competitive advantages went through total quality management (TQM) programs. TQM principles emphasize the prevention of problems rather than problem resolution, involvement of all levels of the organization in quality, and a commitment of continuous improvement. The recession of the economy in the late 1980's and early 1990's resulted in a need for rationalization and downsizing. This contraction in part popularized the concept of core competency, or, identifying the set of core skills that makes a company competitive [8]. It also fueled business process reengineering (BPR), defined as "the fundamental rethinking and radical redesign of business processes to achieve dramatic improvement in critical measures of performance" [9]. Reengineering can result in a leaner organization that is aligned to the processes of the business.

Intellectual capital or the reuse of intellectual assets is defined by Larry Prusak as "intellectual material that has been formalized, captured, and leveraged to produce a higher value asset" [10]. These include, for example, "knowledge in the form of: patents, processes, management skills, technologies, information about customers and suppliers and old fashioned experience" [11]. Hugh MacDonald of International Computers Limited (ICL), a large British computer maker, defines intellectual capital as existing knowledge within an organization which can be used to create special advantages. In other words, intellectual capital is "the sum of everything everybody in your company knows that gives you a competitive edge in the market place" [11].

The trend in downsizing has fueled the need for reusability because reuse allows an organization to accomplish more using less resources. Business process reengineering has identified a set of techniques that may be applied to achieve

Management and Technology Trends That Encourage and Enable Reuse

Area	1970's	1980's	1990's
Management	Intensive, integrative, and diversified growth	Competitive strategy; core competence; total quality management (TQM)	Business process reengineering (BPR); downsizing; intellectual capital reuse
Economics, finance, and accounting	Capital budgeting	Allocation; transfer pricing	Activity-based cost accounting
People	Theory Z	Informate	Empowerment; self-directed teams; learning organizations
Organizations	Functional; project	Matrix	Flat
Metrics	Code analytic	Design analytic	Function analytic
Marketing	Sales-oriented	Customer-focused	Constituent-oriented
Legal	Copyright Act of 1976	Computer Software Act of 1980	17 United States Code 202
Manufacturing	Mass production	Flexible manufacturing; Lean production	Mass customization; agile production
Process	Traditional waterfall	Incremental spiral	Produce; broker; consume
Methods	*ad hoc*	Structured analysis; Structured design	Object-oriented analysis (OOD); domain analysis; domain engineering
Environment	Mainframe and terminals	Personal workstations	Distributed computing
Standards	Portability	Interoperability	Reusability
Application services	Programming by questionnaire; decision tables	Spreadsheets	Problem-oriented languages
Tools	Construction tools	Design tools	Generation tools
Languages	Procedural (e.g., FORTRAN)	Modular (e.g., Ada)	Megaprogramming (e.g., MILs); object-oriented (e.g., C++)

FIGURE 4–3   Trends which enable reuse. *Note:* Parts of this table were adapted from M. Griss and J. Gustafson, Hewlett-Packard and H. Rubin, "Measuring 'rigor' and putting measurement into action," *American Programmer*, vol. 4, no. 9, Sept. 1991, pp. 9–20.

reuse [12]. Similar to software reuse, the leveraging of intellectual capital enables the capture, preservation and reuse of corporate assets.

Economics.   In the area of economics, finance, and accounting/control, several trends have enabled the implementation of reuse. Although work in cost–

benefit analyses and capital budgeting (a selection technique for evaluating and prioritizing long-term investments) had already begun in the early 1930's [13], it wasn't until the 1960's that the net present value method was established as an effective tool for project evaluation [14]. The 1970's saw increased usage as well as further refinements and applications to information economics [15]. Significant work on transfer prices and allocation also occurred during this time. Transfer pricing involves the method or mechanism by which one part of an organization is charged for using another part's services. Allocation is the distribution of costs of services according to some prearranged scheme. Other techniques developed include activity-based cost (ABC) accounting, which is the allocation of fixed costs according to specific activities. Under ABC, expenses are not allocated to the production of individual units, but rather, they are separated and matched to the type of activity that consumes the resource [16]. ABC reveals the relationships between activities and resource consumption and leads to better decision-making.

These developments in economics aid in determining the costs and benefits of reuse, more equitable cost allocation schemes for reuse, and a better understanding of the costs associated with reuse activities. A number of reuse economic models have been developed for inter- and intra-project assessments and for comparing and evaluating reuse and reuse-related programs. Presently, close to 20 different economic models have been developed for reuse [17].

People.   In the 1970's, Ouichi introduced Theory Z, a participatory management style reinforced with shared socioeconomic values and cultural traditions and characterized by collective decision making and responsibility [18]. The results of using such an approach are high levels of trust, holistic career planning, delayed promotion, and lifetime employment.

In the late 1980's, the concept of "informating" was introduced. Informating refers to "provid(ing) people with access to a rich variety of information that would otherwise not be available" [19]. For example, technology is not used to automate but to inform, and personnel are encouraged to utilize on-line databases and real-time measurements of critical variables to get immediate answers to questions [19], [20].

The trend from the organization to the individual continued into the 1990's with the concepts of empowerment, learning organizations, and self-directed teams. Empowerment refers to the decentralization of authority and delegation of decision making to lower levels of an organization. This empowers people to care for themselves more effectively and results in a "self-organizing system for managing a complex world"[21].

The learning organization is an entity "where people continually expand their capacity to create the results they truly desire, where new and expansive patterns of thinking are nurtured, where collective aspiration is set free, and where people are continually learning how to learn together" [22]. Senge describes five tools for creating learning organizations:

1. the capability to see the relationships and patterns within an organization;
2. continuous improvement of the individual;
3. understanding the traditions that direct an organization;
4. creation of a shared vision;
5. emphasis on the importance of teams.

Self-directed teams are based upon the idea that people who perform the work are the most knowledgeable in those areas and, thus, should be empowered to make the appropriate decisions within those areas.

These trends toward decentralization of responsibility and empowerment of individuals parallels similar trends in reuse such as leverage of specialized personnel knowledge and increasing the amount of engineers' time for productive and effective creation, as opposed to resource wasteful re-creation.

Organizations.   In the 1970's, most organizations could be characterized by either functional or project structures. The *functional* form is organized around the inputs to the tasks. An organization with a pure functional form would have a separate department for each task (e.g., marketing, finance). The *project* form is structure around the outputs of the task such as the organization's product. These project teams consists of members, each of whom focuses on a particular market or product and has responsibility for providing various resources for accomplishing specific tasks. Halfway between each extreme lies the *matrix* structure. The matrix structure is a combination of the functional and project structure. It is characterized by having functional departments; however, personnel from these departments reside or have indirect reporting obligations to project managers. Although the matrix structure had its beginnings in the late 1950's, primarily in the aerospace industry, it was not until the 1980's that it gained a strong following in industries such as electronics, financial services, and healthcare.

In the 1990's, interest in flat organizations began to take hold. An outcome of business process reengineering, a flat organization is organized around the processes, not the tasks, of a business. A hierarchical organization, for example, would be "flattened" by rearranging the organization into teams performing many steps within a process rather than many teams performing fewer steps [23]. These trends have implications when designing an organization for software reuse, which will be discussed later in this book.

Metrics.   Rubin [24] describes the 1970's as being a generation of code-analytic measures. Examples of this include measures of complexity, structuredness, and coupling. In the 1980's, design analytic measures emerged. Such metrics included graph theoretic and DeMarco's bang metric. Function analytic metrics were introduced in the mid-1980's and maintains its popularity in the 1990's. Such metrics include function points, feature points, and process maturity measures.

The development of processes for identifying metrics, and the increase in metrics focused on measuring business objectives, has helped further work in reuse metrics and improved our understanding of their application.

Marketing. Over the past several decades, marketing strategies have evolved from being (adapted from [25]):

> product-oriented—where the assumption is that a marketing effort is not required for a product that is well-made and reasonably priced;
> to
> sales-oriented—where the problem was not to make enough products but to sell the output, which required a great amount of promotional effort;
> to
> customer-oriented—where the focus was on the needs of the customer;
> to
> constituent-oriented—where the view is that of community and a focus on the many constituents that the organization has relationships with in the community, e.g., customers, shareholders, workers, local community, international community—essentially a focus on a higher quality of life.

These trends have facilitated the marketing of reuse in organizations, encouraging them to attend to the needs of internal as well as external constituents.

Law. In the legal area, several developments have occurred that affect software reuse. Among them are the 1980 amendments to the Copyright Act of 1976 (P.L. 94-553) where "Congress confirmed its intention that copyright protection applies to computer programs" [26]. With the support of the National Commission on New Technological Uses of Copyrighted Works (CONTU), Congress moved toward placing software within the protection of copyright by providing a definition of computer programs [26]. In addition, the signing of the Berne Convention agreement extended national treatment to works produced by authors from member nations. Consequently, software authors from nondomestic member nations have the same exclusive rights of ownership as those within the U.S. who market their programs domestically. Conversely, U.S. software exported to other members' countries have full copyright protection under that nation's laws [26].

The 1980 Computer Software Act allows for the copying of software if it is an essential step in the usage of the program. Regulation 17 United States Code 202 stipulates that works after March 1, 1989, no longer need a copyright notice for the work to be copyright protected. While legal issues are currently not a major inhibitor to reuse [27], they may potentially become a greater concern in the future as reuse expands both nationally and internationally.

Manufacturing.   Mass production techniques introduced by Ford in the early 1900's dominated manufacturing practices for nearly half a century. Mass production "uses narrowly skilled professionals to design products made by unskilled or semiskilled workers tending expensive, single-purpose machines" [28]. These techniques were internationally diffused through the 1970's. However, by the 1980's, the concept and practice of lean production had gained momentum. This strategy employs "teams of multiskilled workers at all levels of the organization and uses highly flexible, increasingly automated machines to produce volumes of products in enormous variety" [28].

Although the concept of flexible manufacturing systems (FMS) was introduced back in 1965, installation of FMS in companies such as Caterpillar, Chrysler, and Volkswagen did not take place until the early 1980's. An FMS is "a self-contained grouping of machinery—machine tools, robots, and so on—that can perform all the operations required in the manufacture of a number of parts with *similar* processing requirements" [29]. Such systems can process a wide variety of parts without significant delay in changing between parts by using very flexible machines which have high-level controls and automated materials handling. The goal of FMS is to reduce work in process and direct labor costs, gain economies of scale, and optimize productivity, product quality, consistency, and the use of capital equipment.

In the 1990's, mass customization began gaining popularity. Mass customization provides a product or service that is "constantly changing in response to what each customer wants and needs" through the interaction of autonomous processes or tasks [30]. These processes, called *modules*, are placed together in the right combination and sequence to "tailor-make" a product or service to the unique tastes of the consumer. Software reuse can be an important element in mass customized applications [31]. The concept of agile manufacturing—the production of highly customized products when and where the customer desires—also encourages the use of reusable assets [32].

Process.   In the area of process, the 1970's were characterized by the use of the traditional waterfall life cycle, a process which consists of a single pass through a series of phases (e.g., investigation, design, code, test, maintenance, etc.). In the 1980's, Boehm [33] introduced the notion of an incremental, spiral life cycle that revolved around risk reduction. A spiral life cycle advocates multiple passes through a series of phases (similar to the phases of the traditional waterfall life cycle), creating the system in an incremental fashion with an emphasis on prototyping. The 1990's has seen the introduction of a producer/broker/consumer process, where assets are created, maintained, and integrated into subsequent products or other assets. Such a process is meant to support the implementation of systematic reuse within an organization.

Methods.   Ad hoc methods were largely used in the 1970's until the advent of structured analysis and design methodologies in the 1980's. In the 1990's, object-oriented analysis and design methodologies such as Booch, Fusion, Coad and Yourdan, Rumbaugh, Jacobson, Mellor-Schlaer, etc., have gained momentum. Domain analysis and domain engineering have increased in popularity and have been important in identifying and creating reusable assets.

Environment.   The 1970's were characterized by centralized computing—the use of a mainframe computer and terminals. Tremendous growth in the use of personal computers and workstations occurred in the 1980's. Distributed and client–server computing is the trend in the 1990's. This trend has influenced the development of distributed programming that utilizes portable, reusable assets.

Standards.   Portability, the ability to move and operate applications on different platforms, sparked interest in the 1970's, and is even more popular today. In the 1980's, with the emphasis on open systems, interoperability standards received widespread attention. The 1990's have been focused on standards that reinforce reusability (as well as reusability reinforcing standards).

Application Services.   One of the first application developments was "automatic programming by questionnaire" in the 1970's. Users who were not programmers would complete a questionnaire on the features and characteristics of the application they wanted, using simple "yes," "no," or "don't care" responses. The program was then produced accordingly [34]. This application was the pre-cursor of spreadsheets which appeared in the 1980's. VisiCalc and Lotus 123® were notable examples.

   In the 1990's, we should continue to see domain-specific problem-oriented languages that enable end-user programming. Problem-oriented languages are dedicated-purpose languages and have narrow applicability but are powerful within the domain for which they are created. Since their semantics contain extensive problem-specific information, they are domain-specific. The current trend is toward *end-user programming*, where the level of skill and understanding required on the part of the end-users is minimal, enabling them to perform their own programming. In fact, an increasing number of end-users unskilled in programming, such as accountants and bankers, are building their own applications using tools such as macro languages [35]. Code libraries and prepackaged debuggers facilitate the customization of software without the need to write code. Software reuse is an important technique in furthering this trend in end-user programming [36]. Likewise, this trend encourages reuse because strong end-user programming techniques require and utilize preexisting software.

Tools.   During the 1970's, the coding and development of software were primarily aided by construction tools. As the value of focusing on the front-end of the software development process became more apparent, researchers turned their attention to the creation of design tools. The increase of reuse activities has helped intensify the investigation and creation of generation tools to aid development. In the 1990's, interest and work in generation tools have aided reuse. Such tools build new applications from high-level descriptions by automating many of the tasks of finding, modifying, and integrating reusable assets.

Languages. The 1970's were characterized by procedural languages such as FORTRAN. By the early 1980's, modular languages such as Ada were introduced. Later in the decade, object-oriented (OO) languages were introduced and have grown in popularity well into the 1990's. OO languages, which possess specific properties, have played a major role in enabling reuse. In 1992, megaprogramming (MP), the "practice of building software by components in a context of architecture conventionalization and reuse" was introduced [37], [38]. The purpose of MP, the main thrust of the U.S. Government's STARS program, is to "integrate current reuse technology such as reuse library tools, repositories, and reuse techniques into a systematic framework of industrialized reuse" [39]. Related to MP is the module interconnection language (MIL), a notation or language for describing the interfaces for large components.

References

1. R. Lanergan and B. Poynton, "Reusable Code-the Application Development Technique of the Future," presented at IBM Guide/Share Application Symposium, 1979.
2. M. D. McIlroy, "Mass produced software components," in *Software Engineering Concepts and Techniques*, J. M. Buxton, P. Naur, and B. Randall, Eds. New York, N.Y.: Petrocelli/Charter, 1976, pp. 306.
3. T. Biggerstaff and C. Richter, "Reusability Framework, Assessment and Directions," in *Software Reusability*, vol. 1. Reading, MA: Addison-Wesley, 1989.
4. W. Wong, "Management Guide to Software Reuse," National Bureau of Standards, Gaithersburg, MD, NBS Special Publication 500-155, Apr., 1988.
5. P. Freeman, *Tutorial: Software Reusability*. Los Alamitos, CA: IEEE Computer Society Press, 1987.
6. P. Kotler, *Marketing Management*, 7th ed. Englewood Cliffs, NJ: Prentice-Hall, 1991.
7. M. E. Porter, *Competitive Strategy*. New York, N.Y.: The Free Press, 1980.
8. C. K. Prahalad and G. Hamel, "The Core Competence of the Corporation," *Harvard Business Review*, vol. 68, no. 3, pp. 79–91 : Charts, May-June, 1990.
9. M. Hammer and J. Champy, *Reengineering the Corporation: A Manifesto for Business Revolution*. New York, NY: Harper Business, 1993.
10. T. A. Stewart, "Your company's most valuable asset : Intellectual capital," *Fortune*, pp. 68–74; European 28–33, Oct., 1994.

11. T. A. Stewart, "Brain power : Who owns it . . . How they profit from it," *Fortune*, pp. 104–110, June, 1997.
12. G. H. Anthes, "Software reuse plans bring paybacks," *Computerworld*, pp. 73, 76, Dec. 6, 1993.
13. I. Fisher, *The Theory of Interest as Determined by Impatience to Spend Income and Opportunity to Invest.* New York, N.Y.: A. M. Kelley, 1965.
14. J. Hirschleifer, "On the Theory of Optimal Investment Decision," *Journal of Political Economy*, vol. 66, Aug., 1958.
15. R. T. Due, "Determining economic feasibility: four cost/benefit analysis methods," *Journal of Information Systems Management*, vol. 6, no. 4, pp. 14–19, Fall, 1989.
16. R. Cooper and R. S. Kaplan, "Profit Priorities from Activity-Based Costing," *Harvard Business Review*, pp. 130–135 : Charts, June, 1991.
17. W. C. Lim, "Reuse economics: a comparison of seventeen models and directions for future research," *Proceedings Fourth International Conference on Software Reuse (Cat. No.96TB100015)*, pp. 41–50, Apr. 23–26, 1996.
18. W. Ouichi, "Type Z Organizations," *Academic Management Review*, Apr., 1978.
19. D. A. Norman, "Toward Human-Centered Design," *Technology Review*, July, 1993.
20. S. Zuboff, *In the Age of the Smart Machine: The Future of Work and Power.* New York, NY: Basic Books, 1988.
21. W. E. Halal, "Global strategic management in a new world order," *Business Horizons*, pp. 5–10, Nov./Dec., 1993.
22. P. Senge, T*he Fifth Discipline: The Art and Practice of the Learning Organization.* New York, NY: Doubleday, 1990.
23. F. Ostroff and D. Smith, "The horizontal organization," *McKinsey Quarterly*, pp. 148–168 : Charts, 1992.
24. H. Rubin, "Measuring 'Rigor' and Putting Measurement into Action," *American Programmer*, vol. 4, no. 9, pp. 9–20, Sept., 1991.
25. W. J. Stanton, *Fundamentals of Marketing.* New York, NY: McGraw-Hill, 1981.
26. "Intellectual property issues in software," National Academy Press, National Research Council (U.S.). Steering Committee for Intellectual Property Issues in Software, Washington, D.C, 1991.
27. W. B. Frakes and C. J. Fox, "Sixteen questions about software reuse," *Communications of the ACM*, vol. 38, no. 6, pp. 75–87, 112, June, 1995.
28. J. P. Womack, D. T. Jones, and D. Roos, *The Machine that Changed the World.* New York, NY: Rawson Associates, 1990.
29. C. Young and A. Greene, "Flexible Manufacturing System," American Management Association, New York, NY, 1986.
30. B. J. Pine, B. Victor, and A. C. Boynton, "Making mass customization work," *Harvard Business Review*, vol. 71, no. 5, pp. 108–111, Sept.–Oct., 1993.

31. S. Whitmore, "Objects of Desire," *PC Week*, vol. 10, no. 27, July 12, 1993.

32. J. H. Sheridan, "Agile manufacturing : Stepping beyond lean production," *Industry Week*, pp. 30–46, Apr. 19, 1993.

33. B. W. Boehm, "A spiral model of software development and enhancement," *Computer*, vol. 21, no. 5, pp. 61–72, May, 1988.

34. A. F. Cardenas, "Technology Generation for Automatic Generation of Application Programs," *MIS Quarterly*, pp. 49–72, Sept., 1977.

35. J. McMullen, "End users create PC applications," *Datamation*, vol. 35, no. 23, pp. 41–3, Dec. 1, 1989.

36. D. Marques, G. Dallemagne, G. Klinker, J. McDermott, and D. Tung, "Easy programming: empowering people to build their own applications," *IEEE Expert*, vol. 7, no. 3, pp. 16–29, June, 1992.

37. B. W. Boehm and W. L. Scherlis, "Megaprogramming," presented at DARPA Software Technology Conference, Los Angeles, CA, 1992.

38. G. Wiederhold, P. Wegner, and S. Ceri, "Toward mega programming," *Communications of the ACM*, vol. 35, no. 11, pp. 89-99, Nov., 1992.

39. R. Prieto-Diaz, "Historical Overview in Software Reusability," in *Software Reusability*, W. Schafer, R. Prieto-Diaz, and M. Matsumoto, Eds. West Sussex, England: Ellis Horwood, 1994, pp. 160.

REUSE IN INDUSTRY

5.1 Overview

A survey of executives conducted by CSC Index from 1992 to 1994 [1], [2], [3] shows that reuse is increasing among both North American and European companies. Fig. 5–1 and Fig. 5–2 illustrate the percent of respondents with reuse programs in various stages of deployment. During this period, implementation of reuse grew from 32% of responding companies to 44% in North America, and 45% to 48% in Europe. The decrease in the number of companies reporting no reuse at all is also encouraging: this figure dropped from 23% to 17% in North America and from 21% to 12% in Europe. In its report, CSC Index stated that "reuse is (a) broader phenomenon than object-oriented development environments, as more companies report implementation of software reuse than object-oriented tools" [3]. In addition, executives polled in the 1994 survey "agreed that reuse . . . is a critical development strategy for the future" [3].

As shown in Fig. 5–3, 89% of respondents in North America and 88% in Europe concurred that reuse of assets (e.g., designs, code modules, and documentation) will be a key development approach.

In 1991 and 1992, Frakes and Fox surveyed 113 individuals from 29 organizations, 28 of which are U.S. companies [4]. Nearly half of the respondents indicated that their organizations maintained reuse repositories. Eight percent of the respondents did not know whether or not their organization had a repository. Twenty-five percent of the respondents worked for companies with reuse organizations, and 17% reported planning one. Although general reuse activity appears to be occurring, formal and systematic reuse still seems to be lacking.

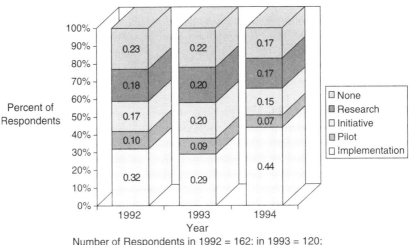

FIGURE 5–1 Reuse by stage of deployment—North America. *Sources:* Vitalari, Nicholas and Elizabeth Braun, 1992 Index Summit: Survey of Systems Development Directors, CSC Index, Cambridge, MA, 1992; Vitalari, Nicholas and Elizabeth Braun, 1993 Index Summit: Survey of Systems Development Directors, CSC Index, Cambridge, MA, 1993; Vitalari, Nicholas and William Matorelli, Index Summit: Survey of Systems Development Directors, CSC Index, Cambridge, MA, 1994.

Software reuse has been effectively applied in many fields, from pharmaceuticals to finance. A small sample of firms practicing reuse in such fields is shown in Fig. 5–4.

5.2 Industry Reuse Programs

Aerospace. The aerospace industry's strict specifications and need to continually upgrade its systems in a timely and cost-effective manner have motivated the industry to seek out new development technologies, such as reuse. This industry was among the first to research reuse. In the early 1980's, Ford Aerospace undertook an internal research and development effort to incorporate reuse into development projects for the U.S. Air Force. Early work included the creation of guidelines for cataloging, classifying, and retrieving from a reusable software library, and design and coding guidelines for modularity and reusability [5], [6]. The Boeing Company has also been involved with software reuse since the early 1980's when it examined the concept of developing real-time avionics software from a common set of functional modules [7]. More recently, Boeing is "explor(ing) the application of

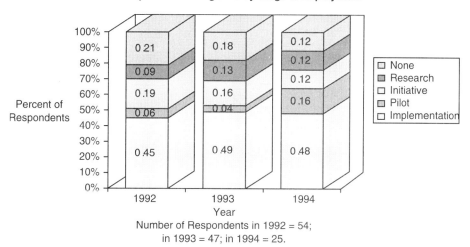

Europe: Reuse Programs by Stage of Deployment

FIGURE 5–2   Reuse by stage of deployment—Europe. *Sources:* Vitalari, Nicholas and Elizabeth Braun, 1992 Index Summit: Survey of Systems Development Directors, CSC Index, Cambridge, MA, 1992; Vitalari, Nicholas and Elizabeth Braun, 1993 Index Summit: Survey of Systems Development Directors, CSC Index, Cambridge, MA, 1993; Vitalari, Nicholas and William Matorelli, Index Summit: Survey of Systems Development Directors, CSC Index, Cambridge, MA, 1994.

the latest technology in automatic code generation and software reuse" with the goal of transferring this technology to software production within the company [8]. The Lockheed Software Technology Center is "providing facilities for reusing large scale software systems" [9]. Frontier Technologies designed a real-time remotely piloted vehicle (RPV) control workstation in Ada using common, reusable software components. Out of the 20,000 lines of code required, approximately 13% was from reusable components [10].

In addition, several development efforts in air traffic control (ATC) systems have employed software reuse. Thomson-CSF has been using the Ada language to develop systems for in-flight detection and guidance of aircraft in ATC centers throughout Europe. Reuse of software from one development site to another has enabled Thomson-CSF to offer a lower cost in developing such systems within the international marketplace [11]. Another large-scale Ada project, the United States Federal Aviation Administration's Advanced Automation System, has also measured and accrued significant economic benefits from reuse [12].

Reuse is also being applied in nonflight operational software. For example, by reusing an application template from Trans World Airlines, Inc., Canadian Airlines International Ltd. reduced the time required to develop their frequent flier application by one-half [13].

Reuse, in any dimension of designs, code modules, documentation, etc., is a critical development strategy for the future.

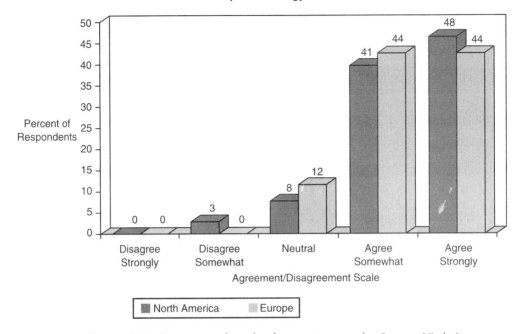

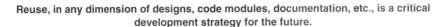

FIGURE 5–3   Reuse as a key development approach. *Source:* Vitalari, Nicholas and William Matorelli, Index Summit: Survey of Systems Development Directors, CSC Index, Cambridge, MA, 1994.

**Examples of Reuse Programs
in Industry**

 Aerospace: Boeing, Lockheed, Thomson-CSF

 Banking: Citicorp, Chemical Bank, First Boston,
                        Mellon Bank, Montreal Trust

 Government: Army, Air Force, NASA, Navy

 Insurance: Hartford, Northwest Mutual Life, USAA

 Manufacturing: HP, Foxboro, NEC

 Telecommunications: AT&T, BNR, Ellemtel-Ericsson,
                        GTE, Motorola, NEC, NTT,
                        PacBel, Sprint, MCI

Utilities: NEC, Sema-Metra   FIGURE 5–4   Firms practicing reuse.

Software systems developed for airborne applications will continue to require very strict specifications [8]. This requirement, along with the need for upgrades to ATC systems in a timely and cost-conscious manner, will provide motivation for the aerospace industry to continue using and researching reusability.

Banking.   The market for banking, investment advice, and money management services has become extremely competitive as both domestic and foreign investment banks and brokerage firms expand their operations. Increased global competition, rapidly changing markets, and the continued growth of complex financial instruments are challenging the information technology resources of many banks. As a result of such challenges, many noted firms such as the Bank of Montreal [14], [15]; Chemical Bank (later acquired by Chase Manhattan Bank) [16]; Citicorp [17]; First Boston [18]; Irving Trust (merged with The Bank of New York Group in 1988) [19]; Mellon Bank [20]; Montreal Trust [21]; and Westpac [22], have turned to reusability as a strategy to help relieve their software development backlog. In addition, a Finnish electronic systems conglomerate, Nokia, has developed an automatic teller machine network using Ada and reuse [23].

Shortening the time required to deliver an application or a financial instrument is essential because of the opportunity cost in forgone market share and profits, as well as the additional revenue and recognition of being first in the market. The field of financial engineering—the creation and valuation of financial contracts with nonstandard packages of cash flows has relied upon a reusability strategy and has shown every indication of continuing this strategy [24], [25]. Improvement in software quality is necessary because of the potential cost incurred due to defects. Examples include downtime due to a defect in a trading system and calculation errors in creating and pricing financial instruments. For these reasons, we expect to continue seeing greater reusability in the information systems [26] and financial engineering activities of bank operations.

Computer and Electronic Equipment.   Two of the largest firms in the computer and electronics industry, Hewlett-Packard [27] and IBM [28], have expended and continue to expend resources for reuse research and practice. The IBM Myers Corners Laboratory has implemented a support infrastructure for reusing software on operating systems. GenRad Fareham, Ltd., a maker of electronic computer-aided engineering (CAE) products, was led into reuse by marketing requirements [29].

Information Systems (IS) and Business Applications.   One the earliest examples of a formal reuse program was implemented at Raytheon in a COBOL data processing environment [30]. A formal internal study of more than 5000 COBOL production programs showed that the programs could all be classified into a few functional categories, and that 40–60% of the code in these programs was repetitive. A reuse program was successfully implemented which included training, standards, a centralized library, and certification procedures.

American Management Systems (AMS) has successfully created a reuse infrastructure for developing several classes of business applications [31]. These generic application architectures are accompanied by a "standard set of components" which may be tailored to create customer-specific solutions. Reuse has impacted AMS' business prospect review process to the extent that incoming requests for proposals to develop information systems are explicitly reviewed to see how AMS' existing generic architecture and standard components may be utilized as well as for the degree of customization required to develop the customer-specific system. A proposal is declined if its domain is unfamiliar to AMS. We expect to continue seeing reusability in information systems development [32].

Analytical Instruments. The benefits of reusable software in developing analytical instruments were noted as early as the 1980's [33]. The Analytical Products Group (APG) of Hewlett-Packard, which creates instruments for gas chromatography, liquid chromatography, mass spectrometry, spectrophotometry, and automated sample preparation, turned to reuse in order to "enhance value to customers through consistency and compatibility across products," and "improve productivity by reducing redundant development efforts" [34], [27]. APG currently practices reuse at three sites in the U.S. and Europe.

Insurance. In one of the earliest cases of reuse, in 1981 the Hartford Insurance Group established a project team to address reusable code, tools, and techniques [35], [36]. Hartford pursued reusable software to reduce program creation time and resource consumption. Northwestern Mutual Life began its investigation of reuse in the early 1980's, as a solution to its need to build systems that could be changed, extended, or reused more quickly. After analyzing their two major lines of business, data administrators uncovered about 100 common data entities with eight physical implementations for each data entity. Reuse was employed in an effort to reduce this redundancy [19], [37]. The United States Automobile Insurance Association (USAA) utilizes a "plug-compatible architecture" in its reusability approach and reports achieving levels of 55–80% reuse in its development portfolio [38]. Other insurance firms such as The Zurich Insurance Group [39] and the UNUM Life Insurance Company [40] are also turning to reusability as a strategy. In addition, Andersen Consulting offers an industry template—high-level designs tied in with computer-aided software engineering tools—for vertical reuse in the life insurance industry [13]. In collaboration with some of the largest insurance companies in the U.S., IBM is developing a set of reusable software components specific to the insurance industry [41]. Reuse in the insurance industry is expected to continue, driven by the need to reduce redundancy and shorten the time-to-market in offering new insurance products.

Manufacturing. Among manufacturers, software reuse has been utilized mainly in the creation of systems for materials management and process control in manufacturing. The Manufacturing Productivity Section of the Software Technology Division of Hewlett-Packard specializes in the development of manufacturing productivity software in the areas of materials management [42]. For more than 10 years, the section has extensively reused software in the form of components and generated code. Reuse of component software alone has resulted in a 51% defect reduction and a 57% increase in productivity relative to new code development only [43].

The Foxboro Company, which specializes in developing and delivering real-time process control system solutions, created a generic architecture and a set of standard objects for developing and solving common process control problems [31]. In addition, NEC Corporation utilized reuse to create industrial process control systems for steel industries and factory automation [44].

Pharmaceuticals. NEC Corporation established a three-year, three-stage process for creating "program parts" in the development of pharmaceuticals [45]. The first stage resulted in the creation of program parts and a registration system. In the second stage, the program parts collected in phase one were integrated and standardized. The third phase consisted of standardizing the accompanying documents to these parts. Similarly, Oracle Corporation offers an industry template for vertical reuse for the pharmaceutical industry [13].

Telecommunications. The potential for reuse in telecommunications is particularly noteworthy. A California study showed that 70% of telecommunications programs shared identical code or functions [46]. AT&T Information Systems reported working on reusing C source code as early as 1985. A study was conducted to create a source reuse system for development environments. "The system consist(ed) of a specification language for specifying general purpose components, its compiler, and an instantiator that transforms a general purpose component into a family of concrete program segments" [47]. AT&T Bell Laboratories has developed the Reusable Architectures for Productivity Improvement in Development/Network Management (RAPID/NM) platform, an architectural framework for large-scale reuse. In addition, special development tools, called software information systems, help programmers working in large software projects with "discovery," the problem of getting information they need to do their tasks [48]. One of these systems, called LaSSIE, is a classification-based software information system which consists of "a large knowledge base, a reasoning mechanism for query processing" coupled with a user interface. AT&T applied these reuse tools to applications in the telecommunications, manufacturing, medical information system, and business office system domains [49].

Bellcore has researched creating a reusable library of generic object classes [50]. Bell-Northern Research (now Nortel) has pursued a reusability strategy for its Digital Multiplex System (DMS), a central office switch system consisting of 15 million lines of code. This strategy encompasses a single development process and a proprietary software library system in which requirements, designs, and software are maintained [51].

Contel (now part of GTE) conducted reuse research and technology transfer on its business units. As part of this effort, a generic network management architecture was created for reuse [52]. Ellemtel-Ericsson, a telecommunications leader, applies total quality management principles in the application of reuse. It has also recognized the importance of identifying motivators for reuse at all levels and designing the organization for reuse [53].

Because of the redundancy of large-scale telecommunications software systems, the Fujitsu Telecommunications Software Division has been pursuing software reusability by standardizing its development methodology and establishing a development support system. This support system includes a knowledge and software asset database and automated creation of code and document workproducts from design information [54].

GTE Data Services, Inc., Tampa, FL, responsible for creating business applications for GTE telephone companies, has enjoyed a 20–30% software productivity increase by using its repository of 960000 lines of PC spreadsheet code and COBOL, C, and assembler languages [55]. GTE Data raises the target percentage for reused software each year [13].

Motorola has formed a reuse task force with representatives from a number of sectors including automotive, cellular, corporate research, government systems, and semiconductor [56]. The goal of the task force is to investigate organizational, educational, motivational, technological, methodology, and implementation reuse issues.

The Advanced Switching Laboratory of NEC America has developed a software reuse repository system which "will store . . . organization(al) software knowledge in one centralized system" [57]. The Nippon Telegraph and Telephone (NTT) Corporation pursued an experimental reuse project for four years. Reuse was supported via "program code modules stored in a common library" [58]. Support for reuse included the creation of a reusability committee, a support group, and a tool development group. Reuse levels of up to 15% were achieved. In addition, the Electrical Communications Laboratory of NTT developed software design automation (SoftDA) which includes features for supporting software reuse. The goals of the system were to acquire related information that previously would have been lost in the course of conventional software development, "to store documents and program codes with their elements interrelated in a network form," and "to utilize total software information in the network to facilitate software reuse" [59].

Sprint Telecommunications established a reuse support group to plan efforts for the company's 3000 software developers. Assets which will be reused include system architectures to object classes [60]. MCI Telecommunications reused designs and functions which enabled the company to increase market share by two to four percentage points [61].

Finally, in 1986, Pacific Bell established a Unix/C reusability library, "an on-line archive of catalogued, reusable code and support information" [62]. The library, comprised of employee contributed C language components that run on multiple computers made by different manufacturers, is accessible to about 250 software engineers. Its user interface is based on a hierarchical tree of function categories and subcategories.

Transportation. Reusability has been utilized very successfully in the transportation industry. In the railway sector, Canadian National Railway developed a complex freight-car optimization system using just eight person months of effort by reusing 137,600 lines from its application software library and writing 10,600 lines of new code [13]. In addition, reuse has been utilized in the development of traffic control systems [44]. With the increasing content of information and process control in such transportation systems, we expect to continue to see increasing levels of interest in reuse.

Utilities. Oracle Corporation offers a set of industry templates for vertical reuse in the oil, gas, and utility industries [13]. NEC has implemented reuse in the creation of "industrial process control systems for electric power network, nuclear/thermal power generation, city water/gas supply as well as the equipment used to control these systems" [44]. In addition, Sema-Metra, a large French conglomerate, is standardizing control software for the French nuclear power industry using Ada and reuse [23].

5.3 Government Reuse Programs

The government sector has been one of the most active participants in the research and application of software reuse. In 1992, the Department of Defense (DoD) Software Reuse Vision and Strategy Document articulated a vision "to drive the DoD software community from its current 'reinvent the software' cycle to a process-driven, domain-specific, architecture-centric, library-based way of constructing software" [63]. Numerous organizations, working groups, projects, and programs have been established in carrying out this vision. These efforts include:

- ASSET, an organization which provides an interoperating network of reuse libraries [64];
- ADA Software Repository which contains more than 43 million bytes of components and information [65],[66];
- Army Reuse Center (ARC), established to "support the development and fielding of reliable, high quality systems while reducing the time and resources required to develop and maintain those systems" [67];

- United States Air Force Central Archive for Reusable Defense Software (CARDS), the focus of which is on domain-specific reuse applicable to command and control software [64];
- Joint Avionics Integrated Working Group (JIAWG), the goal of which is to increase the effectiveness and supportability of aircraft systems while minimizing development costs, shortening schedules, and reducing risk via reuse;
- NASA's Goddard Space Flight Center, which reported that 12 of the 16 software programs used for satellite control operations control centers are 68–95% based on existing software [68];
- Software Technology for Adaptable, Reliable Systems (STARS) program the mission of which is to accelerate the shift to a new software development paradigm, one which is process-driven, domain-specific, reuse-based, and technology-supported. STARS focuses mainly on software-intensive DoD Systems. Three STARS contractors, Boeing, IBM, and Unisys, are "jointly developing a description of the reuse aspects of such a software development paradigm" [69].

5.4   Other Reuse Efforts

The purpose of the Software Engineering Institute (SEI) is "to provide leadership in software engineering and to transition new software engineering technology into practice" [70]. The reusability program at SEI links reusability and automation in projects in direct reuse, leveraging, and transforming high-level specification(s) into a lower level form. SEI research has included work in processes, feature-oriented domain analysis, and creation of a generic application and development model for unifying various types of reuse [71], [72], [73], [74].

The Software Productivity Consortium was founded in 1985 by a group of aerospace, defense, electronics, and systems integration companies [75]. Members include, for example, Boeing, General Dynamics, and Rockwell. The Consortium's goal is to "advanc(e) the fundamental processes and methods required to build large, complex, software intensive systems" [76]. Research areas include reuse libraries, domain analysis (in the form of a project called "Synthesis"), methodology, and measurement. In conjunction with the Virginia Center for Innovative Technology, SPC established the Virginia Center of Excellence (VCOE) in 1992 which "seeks to improve the nation's software engineering practices through the development of reuse technologies and effective technology transfer mechanisms" [77]. Work at VCOE has included, for example, research into reuse economic models, adoption strategies, and domain engineering.

The European Programme for Research in Information Technology (ESPRIT) was established in 1984. Two projects sponsored by ESPRIT which emphasize reuse include the Portable Common Tools and Environment (PCTE) and the REuse Based on Object-Oriented Techniques (REBOOT) projects. The PCTE project researched the reuse of tools [78]. REBOOT provides methods and tools to support creation and use of domain-oriented components [79].

The Eureka Software Factory consists of 13 European software organizations and was established in 1986 to examine and transfer the software factory concept to industry. Its emphasis has been on developing software production processes based on effective management control evolution control. Effective management control refers to predictable as well as correctable production schedules, costs, and results. Evolution control occurs when "development tools and methods exist and are put to use in such a way that they evolve in verifiable steps, supported by an active market of 'plug-compatible' products and factory engineering services" [80].

References

1. N. Vitalari and E. B. Braun, "1992 Index Summit: Survey of Systems Development Directors," CSC Index, Cambridge, MA, 1992.
2. N. Vitalari and E. B. Braun, "1993 Index Summit: Survey of Systems Development Directors," CSC Index, Cambridge, MA, 1993.
3. N. Vitalari and W. Matorelli, "1994 Index Summit: Survey of Systems Development Directors," CSC Index, Cambridge, MA, 1994.
4. W. B. Frakes and C. J. Fox, "Software reuse survey report," Software Engineering Guild, Sterling, VA, 1993.
5. S. Rubin and W. C. Lim, "Guidelines for Modularization and Reusability," *Hewlett-Packard Software Engineering Productivity Conference*, Aug., 1987.
6. W. C. Lim and S. Rubin, "Guidelines for Cataloging Reusable Software," *Hewlett-Packard Software Engineering Productivity Conference*, Aug., 1987.
7. R. F. Bousley, "Reusable avionics executive software," *NAECON 1981. Proceedings of the IEEE 1981 National Aerospace and Electronics Conference*, pp. 31–6 vol.1, 1981.
8. S. Moody, "Exploring Frameworks," *The 4th Annual Workshop on Institutionalizing Software Reuse*, Nov. 18–21, 1991.
9. S. Patel, W. Chu, R. Baxter, B. Sayrs, and S. Sherman, "A Top-Down Software Reuse Support Environment," *The 4th Annual Workshop on Institutionalizing Software Reuse*, Nov. 18–22, 1991.
10. A. Wildblood, "Ada Reuse: The Promises Ring True," *Defense Science*, vol. 9, no. 4, pp. 38–39, Apr., 1990.
11. P. Andribet, "Cost effectiveness of using ADA in air traffic control systems," *Ada: Experiences and Prospects. Proceedings of the Ada-Europe International Conference*, pp. 11–23, June 12–14, 1990.
12. J. Margono and T. E. Rhoads, "Software reuse economics: cost-benefit analysis on a large-scale Ada project," *International Conference on Software Engineering*, pp. 338–48, May, 1992.
13. G. H. Anthes, "Software reuse plans bring paybacks," *Computerworld*, pp. 73, 76, Dec. 6, 1993.

14. "Managing Workflow and Paper : Reusability Speeds Development," *Banking Software Review*, vol. 16, no. 3, pp. 10–12, Autumn, 1991.
15. S. Sivaraman, "Reusability as a By-Product of Systems Strategic Planning," *The 5th Annual Workshop on Institutionalizing Software Reuse*, Oct. 26–29, 1992.
16. K. Spinner, "Chemical Banks on object middleware for global trading," *Wall Street & Technology*, vol. 13, pp. 28–30, 32, 34, Aug., 1995.
17. B. Crockett, "Citicorp in Ambitious Project to Modernize Software Systems," *American Banker*, vol. 159, no. 47, pp. 16, Mar. 10, 1994.
18. R. D. Banker and R. J. Kauffman, "Reuse and productivity in integrated computer-aided software engineering: an empirical study," *Management Information Systems Quarterly*, vol. 15, no. 3, pp. 375–401, Sept., 1991.
19. "Improving Large Application Development," *I/S Analyzer*, vol. 26, no. 3, pp. 1–12, 1988.
20. U. M. Apte, C. S. Sankar, M. Thakur, and J. E. Turner, "Reusability-Based Strategy for Development of Information Systems : Implementation Experience of a Bank," *MIS Quarterly*, vol. 14, no. 4, pp. 421–433, 1990.
21. A. Abran, "Drowning in Costly Maintenance or Leveraging Costs?," *The 5th Annual Workshop on Institutionalizing Software Reuse*, Oct. 26–29, 1992.
22. E. J. Joyce, "Reusable Software : Passage to Productivity?," *Datamation*, vol. 34, no. 18, pp. 97–102, 1988.
23. J. S. Morrison, "The Emerging Market in Adaptable Reusable Software Components," *The 4th Annual Workshop on Institutionalizing Software Reuse*, Nov. 18–22, 1991.
24. T. Eggenschwiler and E. Gamma, "ET++ SwapsManager Using Object Technology in the Financial Engineering Domain," presented at 1992 OOPSLA, Vancouver, B.C., Canada, 1992.
25. C. W. Smith and C. W. Smithson, *The Handbook of Financial Engineering*. New York, NY: Harper Business, 1990.
26. J. Karimi, "An asset-based systems development approach to software reusability," *Management Information Systems Quarterly*, vol. 14, no. 2, pp. 179–98, June, 1990.
27. P. Collins, "Toward a Reusable Domain Analysis," *The 4th Annual Workshop on Institutionalizing Software Reuse*, Nov. 18–22, 1991.
28. J. R. Tirso, "Establishing a software reuse support structure," ICC 91. *International Conference on Communications Conference Record (Cat. No. 91CH2984-3)*, pp. 1500–4 vol.3, 1991.
29. P. A. V. Hall, "Software components and reuse-getting more out of your code," *Information and Software Technology*, vol. 29, no. 1, pp. 38–43, Jan.–Feb., 1987.
30. R. Lanergan and B. Poynton, "Reusable Code-the Application Development Technique of the Future," presented at IBM Guide/Share Application Symposium, 1979.

31. R. Drake and W. Ett, "Reuse: Two Concurrent Life Cycles Paradigm," presented at Tri-Ada 90, 1990.

32. F. Capozza, "Experiences of Reuse in EDP Software Development," presented at 2nd International Conference on Software Reuse, Lucca, Italy, 1993.

33. Y. C. Ling, "Background correction by digital data processing," Ph.D. dissertation, *Dep., Chemistry*: Florida State University, Tallahassee, FL, 1983.

34. R. Martin, G. Jackoway, and C. Ranganathan, "Software Reuse Across Continents," presented at The Fourth Annual Workshop on Institutionalizing Software Reuse, Reston, VA, 1991.

35. M. Cavaliere and P. Archambeault, "Reusable code at the Hartford Insurance Group," presented at ITT Workshop on Reusability in Programming, Newport, R.I., 1983.

36. J. Crawford, "Automating the automators (programmer productivity)," *Best's Review—Property/Casualty Insurance Edition*, vol. 87, no. 1, pp. 76–8, May, 1986.

37. A. Bernstein and J. Vitiello, "Financial Services—Tight Fists, Warm Handshakes at Northwestern Mutual," *Computerworld*, Sept. 10, 1991.

38. E. Yourdan, "U.S.A.A.: An Exemplary Data Processing Organization," *American Programmer*, vol. 2, no. 2, pp. 21–28, Feb., 1989.

39. R. Adhikari, "Code recycling saves resources," *Software Magazine*, vol. 15, no. 7, July, 1995.

40. J. Moad, "Where to Turn for Client/Server Skills," *Datamation*, vol. 37, no. 18, pp. 79–80, 1991.

41. E. Heichler, "Insurance firms speed development with shared objects," *Computerworld*, vol. 29, no. 37, pp. 28, 1995.

42. A. Nishimoto, "Evolution of a Reuse Program in a Maintenance Environment," presented at 2nd Irvine Software Symposium, Irvine, CA, 1992.

43. W. C. Lim, "Effects of reuse on quality, productivity, and economics," *IEEE Software*, vol. 11, no. 5, pp. 23–30, Sept.1994.

44. Y. Matsumoto, "A Software Factory: An Overall Approach to Software Production," in *IEEE Tutorial: Software Reusability*, P. Freeman, Ed. Los Alamitos, CA: IEEE Computer Society Press, 1987, pp. 155–178.

45. K. Kouno, "Enhancement of Productivity and Quality of Software by Standardization and Software Part Development," presented at 1st International Conference on Software Reuse, Dortmund, Germany, 1991.

46. N. Maginnis, "Specialist: reusable code helps increase productivity," *Computerworld*, Nov. 24, 1986.

47. S. K. Afshar, "Software reuse via source transformation," *Proceedings of COMPSAC 85. The IEEE Computer Society's Ninth International Computer Software and Applications Conference (Cat. No. 85CH2221-0)*, pp. 54–61, 1985.

48. P. Devanbu, "Acquiring Knowledge for Software Information Systems," presented at 1st International Workshop on Software Reusability, Dortmund, Germany, 1991.

49. R. P. Beck, S. R. Desai, R. P. Radigan, and D. Q. Vroom, "Software reuse: a competitive advantage," *ICC 91. International Conference on Communications Conference Record (Cat. No. 91CH2984-3)*, pp. 1505-9 vol.3, June, 1991.

50. H. Kilov, "Reuse of generic concepts in information modelling," *The 4th Annual Workshop on Institutionalizing Software Reuse*, Nov. 18–22, 1991.

51. S. Fraser, "Pragmatic Approaches to Software Reuse at BNR, Ltd," *The 4th Annual Workshop on Institutionalizing Software Reuse*, Nov. 18–22, 1991.

52. C. Braun, "Reuse at Contel," presented at National Conference on Software Reusability, Arlington, VA, 1989.

53. P. Jauhiainen, "Software Reuse at Ellemtel-Ericsson," *The 4th Annual Workshop on Institutionalizing Software Reuse*, Nov. 18–22, 1991.

54. S. Machida, "Approaches to software reusability in telecommunications software system," *Proceedings of COMPSAC 85. The IEEE Computer Society's Ninth International Computer Software and Applications Conference (Cat. No. 85CH2221-0)*, pp. 206, 1985.

55. C. McClure, *The Three Rs of Software Automation.* Englewood Cliffs, N.J.: Prentice-Hall, 1992.

56. R. Joos, "Software Reuse in an Industrial Setting," *The 4th Annual Workshop on Institutionalizing Software Reuse*, Nov. 18–22, 1991.

57. M. Diab, "Software Reuse Repository," *The 4th Annual Workshop on Institutionalizing Software Reuse*, Nov. 18–22, 1991.

58. S. Isoda, "An experience of software reuse activities," *Proceedings of the Fifteenth Annual International Computer Software and Applications Conference (Cat. No. 91CH3023-9)*, pp. 8–9, 1991.

59. S. Yamamoto and S. Isoda, "SoftDA-a reuse-oriented software design system," *Proceedings 10th Anniversary COMSAC '86. The IEEE Computer Society's Tenth Annual International Computer Software and Applications Conference (Cat. No. 86CH2356-4)*, pp. 284–90, 1986.

60. J. I. Cash, Jr., "Spend now, save tomorrow," *Informationweek*, no. 545, pp. 222, 1995.

61. M. Crego, "The Story of MCI Friends and Family: A Case Study in Very Large-Scale Reuse for Strategic Advantage," *American Programmer*, vol. 6, no. 8, pp. 28, Aug., 1993.

62. R. Anderson, "Unix/C reusability library," *IEEE Software*, vol. 4, no. 4, July, 1987.

63. J. Piper, "DoD Software Reuse Vision and Strategy," *Crosstalk: The Journal of Defense Software Engineering*, no. 37, pp. 2, Oct., 1992.

64. J. W. Moore, "A National Infrastructure for Defense Reuse," presented at The Fourth Annual Workshop on Institutionalizing Software Reuse, Reston, VA, 1991.

65. R. Conn, "ADA Software Repository in Software Libraries: Real-world reuse," *IEEE Software*, vol. 4, no. 4, July, 1987.

66. R. Conn, "The ADA Software Repository and Software Reusability," in *Software Reusability*, W. Tracz, Ed. Los Alamitos, CA: IEEE Computer Society, 1988.

67. "Army Reuse Center literature," Army Reuse Center, Fort Belvoir, VA, 1993.

68. B. G. Silverman, "Software Cost and Productivity Improvements: an Analogical View," *Computer*, vol. 18, no. 5, pp. 86–96, 1985.

69. M. Davis, "STARS Framework for Reuse Processes," *The 4th Annual Workshop on Institutionalizing Software Reuse*, Nov. 18–22, 1991.

70. M. R. Barbacci, A. N. Habermann, and M. Shaw, "The Software Engineering Institute: bridging practice and potential," *IEEE Software*, vol. 2, no. 6, pp. 4–21, Nov., 1985.

71. S. Cohen, "Software Reuse Technology," presented at Software Reuse: Principles and Practice, Irvine, CA, 1990.

72. K. Kang, S. Cohen, J. Hess, W. Novak, and A. S. Peterson, "Feature-Oriented Domain Analysis (FODA) Feasibility Study," Software Engineering Institute, Pittsburgh, PA, Technical Report CMU/SEI-90-TR-21, Nov., 1990.

73. J. M. Perry, "Perspective on Software Reuse," Software Engineering Institute, Pittsburgh, PA, Technical Report CMU/SEI-88-TR-22, Sept., 1988.

74. A. S. Peterson, "Coming to terms with software reuse terminology: a model-based approach," *SIGSOFT Software Engineering Notes*, vol. 16, no. 2, pp. 45–51, Apr., 1991.

75. A. Pyster and B. Barnes, "The Software Productivity Consortium Reuse Program," The Software Productivity Consortium, Herndon, VA, SPC-TN-87-016, Dec., 1987.

76. "Software Productivity Consortium literature," Software Productivity Consortium, Herndon, VA, 1993.

77. "Virginia Center of Excellence for Software Reuse and Technology Transfer literature," Virginia Center of Excellence for Software Reuse and Technology Transfer, Herndon, VA, 1992.

78. R. Prieto-Diaz, "Historical Overview in Software Reusability," in *Software Reusability*, W. Schafer, R. Prieto-Diaz, and M. Matsumoto, Eds. West Sussex, England: Ellis Horwood, 1994, pp. 160.

79. J. M. Morel and J. Faget, "The REBOOT Approach," *Reuse Improvement*, 1992.

80. R. Rockwell and M. H. Gera, "The Eureka Software Factory CoRe: A Conceptual Reference model for software factories," *Proceedings 1993 Software Engineering Environments*, pp. 80–93, 1993.

6

ORGANIZATIONAL REENGINEERING FOR REUSE: A REUSE ADOPTION AND INSTITUTIONALIZATION MODEL

Developing a reuse adoption strategy is the art and science of generating and employing resources for the formal acceptance and institutionalization of software reuse within an organization. Formal acceptance is achieved when the organization approves of and integrates the strategy into its business in accordance with established custom or procedures. Institutionalization of reuse is realized when its establishment becomes an ongoing concern. An adoption strategy is useful because it systematically outlines the resources, personnel, activities, and desired outcomes that need to be considered and employed in order to maximize the benefits of software reuse. It serves as a blueprint for deciding on, designing for, implementing, and managing reuse. In this chapter, we will describe *"organizational reengineering for reuse"* (ORR), a reuse adoption and institutionalization strategy that synthesizes concepts from business process reengineering (BPR) and diffusion of innovation (DOI).

Previous work involving reuse adoption strategies are summarized in Appendix 6–A. Some of these strategies were designed for specific types of organizations, and may not be effective for all situations. However, familiarity with the range and coverage of different adoption strategies will facilitate a discussion of this important process, as well as the design of an effective strategy customized for your organization.

6.1 A Reuse Adoption Strategy

The reuse adoption strategy we describe in this section encompasses a comprehensive outline for investigating, planning, implementing, and monitoring reuse. It focuses attention on the evaluation of reuse as a feasible and suitable software technology and makes no assumptions about whether or not an organization has decided on reuse. Rather, it begins with guidelines on investigating whether or not reuse is appropriate for an organization. The reuse adoption strategy described in this book distinguishes itself from previous reuse adoption strategies through its organizational and managerial perspective; by recognizing the varying needs, goals, and characteristics of organizations of different types and sizes; and by outlining an approach to adopting reuse which offers a range of alternatives within each step of the adoption process.

While some previous models describe a single approach to adopting reuse, we present a systematic, yet flexible approach that attempts to treat previously reported adoption approaches for a specific organization as a *special case* within our adoption framework. For example, in our adoption approach, instead of advocating a single, specific organizational structure for reuse, the advantages and disadvantages of several archetypes are examined and prescribed within the context of the target organization.

The organizational reengineering for reuse (ORR) methodology synthesizes concepts from business process reengineering and diffusion of innovation. For readers unfamiliar with these concepts, we briefly describe them below.

Business Process Reengineering.   As defined by Hammer [1], business process reengineering (BPR) is the "fundamental rethinking and radical redesign of an entire 'business system'—the business processes, jobs, organizational structures, management systems, and values and beliefs of an organization to achieve dramatic improvements in critical measures of performance." The term "reengineering" may be somewhat of a misnomer because many organizations have never really been "engineered" in the first place [2]. At best, many of them are the result of patchwork over time, or at worst, an antiquated organization that has drifted or degraded to its current state. ORR emphasizes the processes which enable reuse to occur. A process is "a set of linked activities that produce a specific product or service for a customer or for some other individual in the surroundings of the business" [3].

ORR applies a set of reengineering principles that can help an organization achieve greater efficiency and effectiveness through reuse. For example, it identifies the core processes for successfully achieving reuse (see chapter 23) and describes how to organize around those processes (see chapter 17). Reengineering an organization for reuse has enabled significant increases in performance (see chapter 11). We believe that a holistic (e.g., organizational structure, management systems) redesign of the way we capture, preserve, and utilize information is necessary to institutionalize reuse.

Diffusion of Innovation.   Diffusion of innovation (DOI) is "a process by which an innovation is communicated through certain channels, over time, among members of a social system" [4]. Essentially, it is the study of how invention is adopted by users and involves, for example, change agents and opinion leaders, social structure, culture and norms, and the propensity of the individual to adopt the innovation [4]. Recent work has provided insight into DOI as it applies to software engineering [5], [6], [7]. Refer to chapter 25 for more discussion on the diffusion of innovation for reuse.

Both activities and mindsets differ after an organization has been reengineered for reuse:

Software development under traditional organization	After organization has been reengineered for reuse
Develop from scratch	Develop with reusable assets
Each product or system viewed individually	Products or systems viewed as a portfolio
Engineers rewarded for number of lines of code written	Engineers rewarded for how few lines of code need to be written
Single life cycle for creating system or product	Multiple processes for producing, brokering, and consuming assets
Tools for traditional software development	Tools for supporting and linking producers, brokers, and consumers
Each engineer does his/her own work	Culture of reusing assets throughout consumer life cycle

Our philosophy is that there is no one correct way to successfully achieve software reuse. Just as no company or organization is identical, nor should the strategy to implement reuse be identical. Aside from the conspicuous differences among companies (e.g., different industry, geography, etc.), there are differences that in fact serve as "differentiators" of that company within its business area (e.g., low-cost producer, unique feature producer, etc.). It is these differences which enable a company to successfully differentiate itself and compete in the marketplace, and which must be carefully considered while deriving a reuse adoption strategy that is aligned with the company's business goals.

Because of these differences, the strategy described below should be modified as appropriate for your organization.

This reuse adoption strategy consists of five steps (Fig. 6–1)[1]:

- initiating;
- investigating;
- planning;
- implementing;
- continuous improvement.

---

[1]Each of the five steps is used to illustrate how to implement a pilot project. To implement reuse through the rest of the organization after a successful pilot, one can cycle back and start at step 2. Some organizations prefer to explicitly include the pilot in their reuse adoption strategy. Such a reuse adoption strategy may consist of the following steps: 1) initiate reuse program, 2) investigate reuse program, 3) plan pilot, 4) implement pilot, 5) institutionalize reuse, 6) continuously improve reuse program.

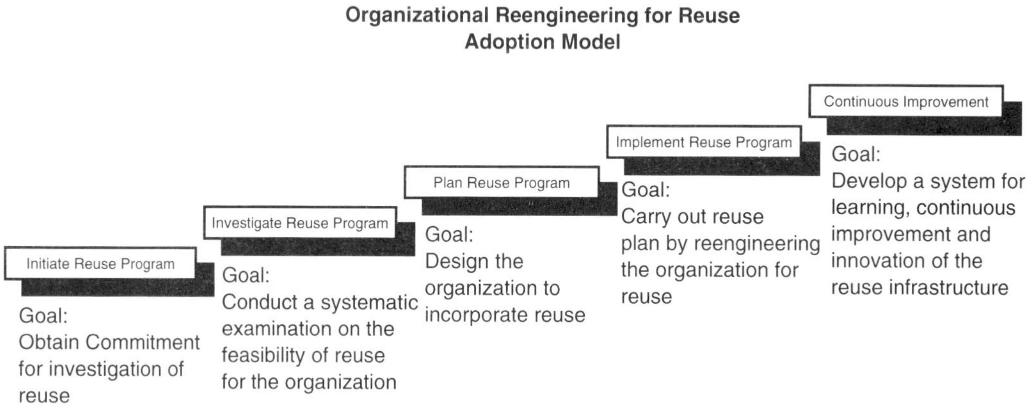

Organizational Reengineering for Reuse
Adoption Model

FIGURE 6–1   Organizational reengineering for reuse adoption model.

We will describe each stage by outlining its goals, the personnel responsible for seeing that its goals are met, the activities that must occur to meet the goals, and lastly, the criteria that determines when the goals are achieved.

Stage 1: Initiate reuse program

Goal: Obtain commitment for an investigation of reuse.

Personnel involved: Reuse champion, sponsor.

Activity: In some organizations, interest in software reuse may originate from an engineer who has read about or attended a conference on software reuse. This engineer takes upon the task of championing software reuse. In other organizations, a manager has heard about software reuse and may either champion reuse him/herself or relegate this task to one of his/her engineers. The reuse champion is responsible for educating others on the concept of reuse, its long-term benefits, its inhibitors, and the motivation behind its implementation. The reuse champion gathers basic information on software reuse. This includes understanding what reuse is; what reuse benefits have been reported; who is reusing software both in and out of the organization; and why it is worthwhile to pursue an investigation on the appropriateness of reuse for his/her organization. At the very least, he/she becomes an expert on the general issues of software reuse and raises awareness of reuse in his/her organization. He/she also identifies a sponsor who will provide and/or generate commitment from management to proceed to the next phase—an investigation into the feasibility of reuse for the organization.

Performance measures:

- commitment from management to proceed with investigation;
- allocation of time, personnel, and resources.

Stage 2: Investigate reuse program

Goal: Conduct a systematic examination of the feasibility of software reuse for the organization, or some portion of the organization.

Personnel involved: Reuse champion, managers and engineers, marketing personnel, reuse economist/metrician, and domain experts.

Activity: All reuse personnel, especially engineers and domain experts, need to identify and determine reuse potential throughout the organization. First and foremost, this requires a clear understanding of the business goals and objectives of the organization, as well as what its problems are. Within this context, the team needs to determine the applicability and project the economic feasibility and value of reuse.

This can be accomplished first by obtaining baseline measurements, if available, on existing software processes, and by examining the current infrastructure available to support a reuse effort via a reuse assessment. All aspects of reuse should be considered, including managerial, economic, metric, process, technology, asset, and personnel issues.

Performance measure: A decision whether or not to pursue reuse.

Stage 3: Plan reuse program

Goal: Design or reengineer the organization to incorporate software reuse.

Personnel involved: Reuse champion; producer and consumer managers and engineers; marketing personnel; domain experts; domain analyst; domain asset manager; reuse analyst; librarian; reuse economist/metrician.

Activity: Planning a reuse program first requires a specific vision statement for software reuse. This statement should describe the goals of reuse within the context of an organization's business. Second, a strategy detailing how the vision will be implemented should be created. Such a plan outlines an appropriate organizational structure; the creation and modification of new and existing roles and responsibilities in the new organization; the development of appropriate metrics to track reuse progress; and the strategy for marketing the reuse vision and for educating and training personnel.

These steps are the crux of BPR. Careful thought must be given to how the existing organizational and personnel structure and development and marketing processes should be changed to support reuse.

Reuse managers need to investigate and understand the economic, financial, legal, and contractual issues of reuse so that projects can be prioritized. Reuse engineers should investigate and develop the appropriate tools and techniques for implementing reuse.

Performance measure: Creation of vision statement and design of the organization for reuse.

Stage 4: Implement reuse program

Goal: Carry out the reuse program plan by reengineering the organization for reuse.

Personnel involved: Reuse champion; producer and consumer managers and engineers; marketing personnel; domain experts; domain analyst; domain asset manager; reuse analyst; librarian; reuse economist/metrician.

Activity: This stage involves the transfer of reuse technology, processes, and knowledge into the pilot program. The implementation of reuse for the pilot project should take into consideration issues such as technology transfer, change management, as well as implementation by speed (evolutionary, revolutionary) and driver (top-down, bottom-up, or both). Although the reuse program reaches a steady-state after implementation, changes within the organization through the diffusion of reuse and changes to the available resources will dictate when or whether the organization wishes to revisit previous stages in order to bring the organization to a new steady-state level.

Performance measure: Adoption of reuse infrastructure.

Stage 5: Continuous improvement

Goal: Develop a system for learning, continuous improvement, and innovation of the reuse infrastructure.

Personnel involved: Reuse champion; producer and consumer managers and engineers; marketing personnel; domain experts; domain asset manager; librarian.

Activity: Particularly critical at this stage is the systematic tracking of reuse performance through appropriate metrics. Based upon such "progress reports," managers will be able to identify mechanisms for continuous improvement of the reuse infrastructure and process. Changes within the organization or a slowdown in progress may signal the need to revisit Stage 1 in order to bring the organization to a new level of reuse.

Performance measure:

- ability to identify problem areas and opportunities for the reuse infrastructure;
- ability to identify when to begin cycle for changing the reuse infrastructure as business and technical conditions change.

The organizational reengineering for reuse strategy described in this chapter is intended as a flexible framework for implementing reuse. Depending upon the situation in your organization, steps in this process may be revisited, skipped, or done in parallel. If you already have effective organizational mechanisms established, these mechanisms may be substituted for activities in the ORR process. For example, if your organization already has an effective strategic planning mechanism, the technique described in chapter 13 may simply be used to augment the existing method. The intent of ORR is to bring awareness of the issues, viewpoints, and alternatives in implementing a reuse program, and serve as a decision support, not substitute, for managerial judgment.

Summary

A reuse adoption and institutionalization strategy allows an organization to systematically consider the resources, personnel, activities, and desired outcomes in order to establish software reuse. This chapter outlines a five-step adoption strategy from an organizational and managerial perspective. These steps are: initiate, investigate, plan, implement, and continuously improve.

References

1. M. Hammer and J. Champy, "The promise of reengineering," *Fortune*, vol. 127, no. 9, May 3, 1993.
2. M. Lenzi, "Editor's column," *Object Magazine*, pp. 4, Feb., 1994.
3. I. Jacobson, "Business process reengineering with object technology," *Object Magazine*, May, 1994.
4. E. M. Rogers, *Diffusion of Innovations*. New York, N.Y.: Free Press, 1983.
5. R. G. Fichman and C. F. Kemerer, "Adoption of software engineering process innovations: the case of object orientation," *Sloan Management Review*, vol. 34, no. 2, pp. 7–22, Winter, 1993.
6. S. M. Przybylinski, P. J. Fowler, and J. H. Maher, "Software Technology Transition Tutorial," *13th International Conference on Software Engineering*, May 12, 1991.
7. S. A. Raghavan and D. R. Chand, "Diffusion of Software Engineering Methods," Wang Institute, Boston, MA, Technical Report TR-86-10, Nov., 1986.

6–A

A Survey of Reuse Adoption Strategies

In the following appendix, we review several reuse adoption strategies: Bongard; Buxton and Malcolm; Caldiera; Durek; Holibaugh; Joos; Parkhill; Prieto-Diaz; Software Productivity Consortium; U.S. Army Information Systems Engineering Command (USAISEC); and Whittle, Lam, and Kelly. Some of these strategies were designed for specific types of organizations and may not be effective in all situations. However, familiarity with the range and coverage of different adoption strategies will facilitate a discussion of this important process as well as the design of an effective strategy customized for your organization.

Bongard. Bongard et al. [1], describe a four-step strategy for introducing software reuse.

1. Feasibility study for reuse introduction:
   - study current software practice;
   - identify and estimate the reuse potential;
   - evaluate return on investment;
   - propose an implementation plan.
2. Preparation for reuse introduction:
   - select or adapt methods and tools;
   - modify organizational structures for reuse;
   - get personnel involved.

3. Introduction of reuse to the organization:
   - define generic architectures;
   - select and build reusable components;
   - instruct and motivate personnel;
   - assist developers.
4. Tracking of the reuse introduction process:
   - measure benefits;
   - evaluate reuse behavior;
   - correct and improve reuse behavior.

Buxton and Malcolm.   Buxton and Malcolm [2] provide a generic high-level model not specifically for reuse but relating primarily to the transfer of software process technology. They note that in developing software, an organization faces "two innovation issues at the same time: the introduction of software technology into well established products, and the potential introduction of new software engineering techniques." This observation clearly applies to software reuse.

Buxton and Malcolm's view of the phases that take place within an organization involved in the transfer of technology include:

1. awareness;
2. assessment and choice;
3. adoption for real use;
4. assimilation into a new organizational orthodoxy.

In the awareness phase, they point out that awareness of a new technology may begin with management or a technologist who assumes the role of a "gatekeeper," a person who stays in touch with new developments and plays a key part in the identification of promising technologies. In the assessment and choice phase, the gatekeeper chooses the plausible new technology and advances with a "demonstrator" (pilot) project. If the pilot project is successful, the adoption for real use phase is pursued. This phase, which is the "first real application of the new technology" will meet the greatest resistance from personnel. Top management must take a proactive role and provide the necessary resources. Training for all personnel is crucial at this phase. The final phase occurs only after the technology has been used successfully. Education gradually takes place as an apprenticeship within the normal working environment. The authors believe that in order for a technology to be transferred successfully, it must be visible and its value to the organization must be quantified.

Caldiera.   Caldiera [3] describes a four-step process for use in a domain factory for establishing reuse: plan, execute, analyze, and formalize. These steps and their substeps follow.

1. Plan
   1. Characterize the domain and the environment.
   2. Set the goals and refine them into a measurable form.
   3. Choose the execution process model, the product models, the application engineering environment, and the associated control measurement.
2. Execute
   1. Supply the domain-specific units to the project organization and perform or support their adaptation.
   2. Control the process while executing, using the chosen measurement (the process during its execution is controlled by both the project organization and the domain factory).
   3. Provide immediate feedback on the process to the project organization.
3. Analyze the results and compare them to the goals defined in the planning phase.
4. Formalize
   1. Synthesize the results into new process and product models, quality models, measures, etc., or updates of the existing ones.
   2. Package processes products and experience into domain-specific units.

Durek.   Durek [4] describes a three-step strategy for implementing reuse:

1. define and qualify the domain;
2. define canonical requirements;
3. derive canonical architecture.

The first step, define and qualify the domain, consists of two activities: describing the domain and analyzing the feasibility of reuse. In describing the domain, the boundaries of the domain are defined and a taxonomy relating the domain concepts is established. Analyzing the feasibility of reuse is done by examining the business environment, the volatility of the requirements, organizational readiness, and availability of domain knowledge. The second step consists of defining canonical requirements. This is achieved by determining end-user requirements, studying existing systems, and obtaining feedback on a prototype. The third step is deriving a canonical architecture. The outputs of this step are the definition of a reusable architecture and components for implementation.

Holibaugh.   Holibaugh [5] outlines a life cycle for the adoption of reuse. The life cycle consists of seven steps, beginning with business planning. At this level, an organization's goals and current business processes are examined and evaluated within the context of reuse. These include opportunities and plans for the business in the domain; stability of the domain-specific technology; availability of domain expertise within the organization; depth of experience in the domain; availability of resources to commit to reuse; and the expected benefit of reuse. The second step is called life cycle and methodology. Its goal is to develop a reuse methodology to identify, develop, and apply reusable resources. Activities in this step include using a domain model and software architecture as a road map through the life cycle; identifying reusable resources early; including reuse in each phase of the life cycle; looking ahead for reusable components in later phases to ensure they are used; including reuse in planned reviews to ensure reusable assets are used; and monitoring through code reviews. The third stage is domain analysis. In this step, activities include defining the domain; identifying and collecting information and resources; selecting a representation mechanism; organizing, representing, and analyzing the information; and reviewing and validating the results. The fourth step, domain engineering, is concerned with producing the reusable assets which include designs, components, and tools. In the fifth step, library construction, the library is constructed with the goal of making the assets easily accessible to the consumers. This includes selecting the classification scheme and representation structure. The sixth step, systems construction, involves identifying the goals of reuse for any system to be created with reusable assets. Metrics are also collected to measure the achievement of these goals as well as to compare the use of reusable assets against development without reusable assets. The seventh and final step involves feeding back results to the previous steps. This is done through the collection and analysis of data from each life cycle phase. Such analysis identifies the impact of reuse on factors such as quality, personnel, and schedules.

Joos. Rebecca Joos [6] describes a proposal by members of a reuse working group at Motorola to implement reuse. The plan consists of eleven points.

1. Find a reuse champion for each role in the reuse organization (i.e., manager, reuse engineer, reuse architect, and librarian). The individuals should possess strong software engineering backgrounds.
2. Provide the above personnel with reuse training (i.e., object-oriented analysis/design, software reuse, and domain analysis).
3. Analyze the target domain.
4. Establish standards (templates, documentation, classification).
5. Select and obtain state-of-the-art tools for the department.
6. Gain expertise in the use of these tools.
7. Populate a reuse repository.
8. Collect and record baseline metrics data.
9. Begin training other software engineers on how to utilize the tools.
10. Begin designing all software *with* reuse and *for* reuse from day one.
11. Provide incentives for reuse.

Parkhill. Parkhill [7] describes seven guidelines that his organization, US West, has learned in their implementation of object-oriented technology.

1. Use only those portions of the technology that are ready.
2. Use the technology in both design and implementation phases of the project.
3. Target projects that can absorb additional risk.
4. Transfer technology through people and mentors.
5. Start small; don't be too ambitious.
6. Utilize "just-in-time" training.
7. Measure key process indicators.

Parkhill also advocates the creation of a technology receptor organization which would consist of three to four key people who serve as experts in the technology, and whose expertise can "facilitate the migration process."

Prieto-Diaz. Prieto-Diaz [8] proposes a strategy for the implementation of software reuse which implicitly assumes a minimal level of commitment to reuse and existing managerial and organizational support within the organization. The model describes implementation in four stages.

1. initiation;
2. expansion;
3. contraction;
4. steady state.

In the initiation stage, existing software is analyzed for potentially reusable assets and an early version of a catalog is created with the intent of raising the level of awareness on software reuse and stimulating others to seek and identify other potential assets. In the second stage, expansion, the size of the catalog increases and, as a consequence, a faceted classification scheme is created to manage it and, at the same time, facilitate the domain analysis process. If feasible, an automated library system is implemented as well. Domain analysis is the primary focus in the contraction stage where standard architectures and functional models are created, and assets with limited reuse potential are pruned from the library. In the final stage, existing assets are replaced by assets that address domain-specific functions. The Prieto-Diaz model emphasizes a learning environment and an incremental approach to establishing a reuse program.

Software Productivity Consortium. *The Software Productivity Consortium Reuse Adoption Guidebook* [9] provides a thorough examination of the process of "institutionalizing and improving an organization's software reuse practice." Its reuse adoption strategy consists of the following six steps.

1. initiate reuse program development;
2. define reuse program;

3. establish reuse adoption goals;

4. analyze reuse adoption strategies;

5. develop reuse action plan; and

6. implement and monitor reuse program.

This book shares the SPC philosophy in not specifying a single reuse adoption process for all organizations, but rather describing a flexible process where activities may be performed in parallel, skipped, or repeated as necessary. The *Reuse Adoption Guidebook* also includes tools for assessing the effectiveness of the current reuse process, identifying and evaluating potential candidates for reuse, and determining risky reuse-related situations that an organization should monitor and manage. The guidebook includes three major components: the reuse adoption process, domain assessment guidelines, and the reuse capability model. The reuse adoption process is an outline of steps that may be used to initiate, plan, implement, and institutionalize reuse. The domain assessment guideline is used to estimate the potential for reuse within a business area. The reuse capability model is a self-assessment aid which is used to understand an organization's process [10].

U.S. Army Information Systems Engineering Command (USAISEC). The USAISEC [11] provides the following guidelines for implementing reuse:

1. Establish an organizational entity whose charter is to promote reuse.

2. Assess suitability of establishing a reuse matrix structure.

3. Structure software development by domains amenable to reuse considerations.

4. Establish connections between reuse and maintenance.

5. Provide reuse education and training at all levels of the organization.

6. Hold people accountable for reuse.

7. Allow 2 to 3 years before expecting any economic payback.

8. Provide a corporate "safety net" for projects practicing reuse (provide extra resources).

Whittle, Lam, and Kelly. Whittle *et al.* [12] of the University of York describe their reuse introduction process to the Control Systems Engineering Department of Rolls-Royce Aerospace in Derby, England. Most of the steps are intended to be sequentially implemented. However, some phases, such as "define program" and "develop reuse strategies," may be done in parallel.

1. *Initiate program.* Decide that reuse is a likely option to help in achieving one or more organizational goals and obtain resources to proceed.

2. *Define program.* Define the scope of the reuse introduction, particularly the domain you wish to improve and the improvements you would like reuse to contribute toward.

3. *Develop reuse strategies.* Select and develop appropriate strategies, and show how the strategies can be linked together, i.e., an incremental approach.

4. *Analyze strategies and select.* Enable the selection of the most appropriate strategy.

5. *Develop action plan.* Develop an implementation plan for the chosen strategy.

6. *Implement.* Put the plan into action.

7. *Monitor and improve.* Measure the plan against the action plan and the organizational goals to which it intends to contribute.

References

1. B. Bongard, B. Gronquist, and D. Ribot, "Impact of Reuse on Organizations," Cap Gemini Innovation, Esprit project REBOOT, Grenoble, France, Sept. 4, 1992.
2. J. N. Buxton and R. Malcolm, "Software technology transfer," *Software Engineering Journal*, vol. 6, no. 1, pp. 17–23, Jan., 1991.
3. G. Caldiera, "Domain Factory and Software Reusability," *Software Engineering Symposium: New Frontiers for Software Maintenance*, May, 1991.
4. T. Durek, "Strategies and Tactics for Software Reuse Tutorial," presented at Improving the Software Process and Competitive Postion via Software Reuse and Reengineering, Alexandria, VA, 1991.
5. R. Holibaugh, S. Cohen, K. Kang, and S. Peterson, "Reuse: where to begin and why," *Proceedings. TRI-Ada '89*, pp. 266–77, Oct. 23-26, 1989.
6. R. Joos, "Software Reuse in an Industrial Setting," *4th Annual Workshop on Software Reuse*, Nov. 18–22, 1991.
7. D. Parkhill, "Object-oriented technology transfer: techniques and guidelines for a smooth transition," *Object Magazine*, pp. 57–59, May/June, 1992.
8. R. Prieto-Diaz, "Making software reuse work: an implementation model," *SIGSOFT Software Engineering Notes*, vol. 16, no. 3, pp. 61–8, July, 1991.
9. "Reuse adoption guidebook," Software Productivity Consortium, Herndon, VA, SPC-92051-CMC, Version 01.00.03, Nov., 1992.
10. T. Davis, "Reuse Capability Assessment: Case Study Results," *6th Annual Workshop for Institutionalizing Software Reuse*, Nov. 2–4, 1993.
11. "Software Reuse Guidelines," U.S. Army Information Systems Engineering Command (USAISE), ASQB-GI-90-015, Apr., 1990.
12. B. Whittle, W. Lam, and T. Kelly, "A pragmatic approach to reuse introduction in an industrial setting," *Systematic Reuse: Issues in Initiating and Improving a Reuse Program. Proceedings of the International Workshop on Systematic Reuse*, pp. 104–15, 1996.

THE ROLE OF A CORPORATE REUSE PROGRAM

In this chapter, we discuss the role, goals, and responsibilities of a corporate reuse program. Such a program often serves as the hub for reuse activities and services which are common to multiple projects or divisions. It provides a level of consistency and economies of scale across an organization, minimizes occurrences of duplicated tasks, and facilitates the measurement of the impact of reuse on the organization. For our discussion, we use the term "corporate" but it may easily be substituted with "enterprise" or any other appropriate term that denotes the high level organization which oversees or supports multiple suborganizations.

The choice of the role will determine the level of corporate involvement in projects, the types and scope of activities performed, and the level of interaction with constituents. Likewise, deciding on an effective role will depend on the reuse needs of the program's constituents, as well as the reuse goals of the entire organization. Thus, defining the responsibilities and roles of the corporate reuse program is best determined after having assessed constituents' needs. However, we address this issue early in the book to provide readers a more complete context as we progress through the adoption model.

We discuss a range of possible roles and levels of responsibility for a corporate program in reuse and present their advantages, disadvantages, types of deliverables, and measures of success. We will illustrate these roles with examples of corporate reuse programs from various companies.

7.1   Responsibilities of a Corporate Reuse Program

As shown in Fig. 7–1, the role and scope of the corporate reuse program ranges from consultancy to a fully integrated business center with profit accountability.

A consultancy may consist of a team or a single individual who provides information and advice and acts as a central source of reuse expertise. A consultancy does not create and maintain assets, libraries, or tools. Its role is to support and spur the development of local reuse programs. Hewlett-Packard [1] is an example of an organization which has implemented the consultant role.

The librarian/broker role requires a further commitment of resources as it not only provides information and expertise. It does not actually create reusable assets but catalogs them and facilitates their access. This role has also been implemented in some organizations including Hewlett-Packard.

In addition to the roles assumed by a consultancy and library, a producer/ business program creates, maintains, and procures assets. In some cases, the program is operated as a profit center. Although not a profit center, IBM's Reuse Technology Support Center acts in this fashion by "sponsor(ing) work that benefits more than one site, such as the creation of standards, parts, and tools."

Each of these roles has advantages and disadvantages, and the choice of an appropriate role along the continuum is dependent on a number of factors.

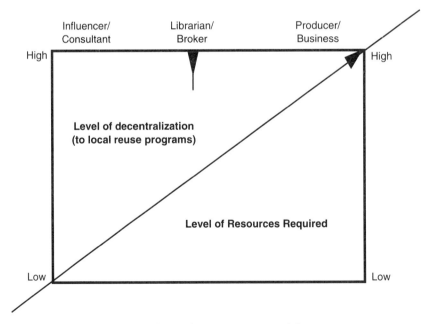

FIGURE 7–1   Range of roles and resources required for a corporate reuse program.

Influencer/Consultancy. Role: The consultancy program acts as a central source of reuse information, advice, and expertise. It acts as a catalyst for the development of local reuse programs within the organization and keeps abreast of reuse developments within industry, academia, and consortiums.

Advantages:
- less resources required from corporation;
- provides more control to local or divisional reuse programs;
- local reuse organizations may be more aware and responsive to needs of consumers.

Disadvantages:
- potential for projects to deviate from standards;
- future libraries may not be integrable;
- value of consulting services to projects difficult to measure.

Deliverables and typical activities:
- organize corporate reuse steering committee;
- capture and transfer technology and knowledge through classes, tutorials, handbooks, and consulting.

Measures of success:
- demand for materials and services.

When role is appropriate:
- highly decentralized corporation;
- more common needs within projects than across projects;
- localized expertise in creating specific assets;
- demand for specific assets localized;
- bulk of responsibility for reuse assumed by projects.

Example: The Corporate Reuse Program at Hewlett-Packard is a consultancy which consists of a core team of reuse experts. This core team is involved in developing and conducting reuse assessments to diagnose the various people, management, process, and technology issues; collecting metrics; developing and testing processes for domain analysis, architectures, and the production and reuse of software; and collecting reuse best practices in a reuse handbook [1].

Librarian/Broker. Role: The librarian program provides information, advice, and a reuse library tool, in addition to maintaining a centralized collection of reusable assets.

Advantages:
- standardized, corporate-wide repository;
- certification process is standardized;
- potential economies of scale.

Disadvantages:
- accessibility to divisions may be limited;
- responsiveness to divisions may be limited;
- requires more resources from corporation.

Deliverables and typical activities:
- deliverables and activities of influencer/consultancy role;
- standardized library service.

Measures of success:
- success measures for influencer/consultancy role;
- demand for library services.

When role is appropriate:
- highly centralized corporation;
- more common needs across projects than within projects;
- expertise for creating specific assets spread throughout the corporation;
- demand for assets spread throughout corporation;
- a centralized reuse library is worthwhile because of economies of scale.

Example: Another organization within Hewlett-Packard has served as a repository for reusable assets collected and reused by development projects. In addition, reuse information and expertise were provided by this entity to the projects.

Producer/Business. Role: In addition to providing the services of a library program, the business program creates, procures, and maintains assets. It may also operate as a profit center.

Advantages:
- advantages of library role;
- profit center status requires assets to be of value to divisions;
- corporate control results in the creation of assets that are consistent in terms of quality and standards.

Disadvantages:
- disadvantages of library role;
- more resources required (but if profit center, paid for via revenues);
- may only create and maintain profitable assets; assets which are applicable only to a specific division may be overlooked.

Deliverables and typical activities:
- deliverables and activities of library role;
- reusable assets;
- more emphasis on delivering courses on "designing with reuse."

Measures of success:
- success measures for library role;
- demand for assets;
- profit (if program is a profit center).

When role is appropriate:
- highly centralized corporation;
- more common needs across projects than within projects;
- expertise for creating specific assets can be centralized at the corporate level;
- demand for assets spread throughout corporation.
- a centralized reuse library is worthwhile because of economies of scale.

Activities Associated with the Different Roles of a Corporate Reuse Program

Influencer/Consultant

Education
- Newsletters
- Seminars and classes
- Book and magazine resources

Mentoring
- Assist divisions in starting reuse programs
- Pilot reuse projects
- Change management

Coordination and Communication
- Reuse intranet or bulletin board
- Organize corporate reuse steering committee
- Reuse workshops
- Contacts with academia, consortia, and industry

Marketing
- Promoting awareness of reuse
- Understanding constituents' needs and wants

Standards and Guidelines
- Interoperating libraries
- Compatible assets
- Core set of metrics
- Handbook of standards and guidelines

Vendor Relationships
- Evaluation of external reuse products and services
- Single point of contact for vendors

Librarian/Broker

In addition to Influencer/Consultant role:

Broker Reusable Assets
- Asset evaluation
- Assess external asset catalogs
- Procure assets
- Understand legal and contractual issues
- Certify assets
- Operate reuse library
- Delete obsolete assets

Producer/Business

In addition to Librarian/Broker role (with more emphasis on helping divisions consume and less emphasis on helping them produce):

Produce Reusable Assets
- Domain analysis
- Architecture reviews
- Create guidelines for desigining, coding, testing, and validating assets
- Maintain and enhance assets

FIGURE 7–2 Activities associated with the different roles of a corporate reuse program.

Example: IBM's Corporate Reuse Council is an example of a nonprofit center, business corporate reuse program [2]. "The mission of this group is to increase the amount of reuse within IBM." This work is handled by the Reuse Technology Support Center which deals with management and coordination issues, and provides support and tools. The Reusable Parts Technology Centers provides parts to meet each site's requirements.

In Fig. 7–2, we outline specific tasks and activities of corporate reuse programs and suggest a mapping between these activities and the types of reuse programs discussed in this chapter.

7.2   Other Issues

A process or method needs to be implemented to measure the return or benefit of investing resources in a corporate reuse program. This is important not only to justify its existence and measure its success, but to gain further support and funds from upper management. Quantitative metrics include dollars saved, increased profit, and the number of reuse projects benefitted. Examples of qualitative measures are satisfaction survey ratings by projects and internal customers.

A corporate reuse program may also evolve and adapt in conjunction with the stages of its constituents' reuse practices. For example, constituents usually go through an adoption life cycle: awareness, assessment, adoption, institutionalization, and continuous process improvement. Thus, customers in the awareness stage will require educational and consultancy services while those in the assessment stage may need domain, organizational, and economic assessment services. A reuse program which is truly driven by customer needs will be able to assume additional roles and tasks as required and phase out of activities which its constituents have outgrown.

References

1. M. Griss, "Software Reuse at Hewlett-Packard," presented at First International Workshop on Software Reusability, Dortmund, Germany, July 1991.
2. J. Tirso, "Presentation on The IBM Reuse Program," presented at Fifth Annual Workshop on Software Reuse, Palo Alto, CA, Nov. 1992.

8

IDENTIFYING ORGANIZATIONAL REUSE POTENTIAL AND APTITUDE

This chapter examines the organizational elements and traits that characterize effective reuse programs. By carefully analyzing such programs, we can identify common factors which contribute to and ultimately determine the success level of a reuse program. Such information will enable organizations considering reuse to determine where and how resources should be expended.

We begin by presenting a model for identifying organizations with reuse potential and aptitude for establishing reuse programs. This model is based upon data obtained from numerous interviews and case studies of software reuse. After discussing the factors for identifying reuse potential, we present the findings of several reuse assessments which measure an organization's aptitude for exploiting reuse. Finally, we conclude by discussing several examples within the context of the model.

8.1 Reuse Potential and Aptitude Model

Based upon research which began in 1990, we present a reuse potential and aptitude model which helps an organization identify its potential for reuse success. We believe that *to achieve reuse success, an organization must possess both the reuse potential and the ability to mine this potential.*

Reuse potential represents the latent redundancies and opportunities within and across domains which, when combined with the proper organizational ability, can become actual reuse. *Reuse aptitude* refers to the requisite ability or capacity to mine this reuse potential. The likelihood of reuse success is minimal without one or the other. For example, an existing lode of potential reuse cannot be tapped if the organization does not possess or cannot acquire the capability to mine this potential reuse. On the other hand, an organization that has the capability and is eager to reuse cannot do so if such opportunities do not exist.

Lack of reuse success may be traced to three possible combinations:

1. lack of reuse potential with adequate reuse aptitude;
2. lack of reuse aptitude with adequate reuse potential;
3. lack of both reuse aptitude and potential.

Fig. 8–1 illustrates the four possible scenarios under which organizations can be categorized. Given that an organization can succeed in only one of the four possible scenarios, it is important that we carefully examine an organization's reuse potential and aptitude before embarking on a reuse program.

Success naturally means different things to different people. In this model, reuse success describes those programs that achieved quality and productivity improvements and positive net present values through reuse.

Based on a qualitative evaluation of their abilities to successfully create and reuse assets in accordance to their targeted reuse potential, three programs were selected for the model's baseline. Their quality and productivity improvements from reuse ranged from 24% to 126%. All the reuse projects had a positive net present value. Net present value takes the value of reuse benefits and subtracts associated costs, taking into account the time value of money. Essentially, a positive net present value indicates that the benefits derived from a reuse program more than cover its costs taking into account the cost of capital. Reuse success may be further defined on a continuum. For example, an organization that falls short of mining a targeted reuse potential but still achieves a net positive gain may be defined as subop-

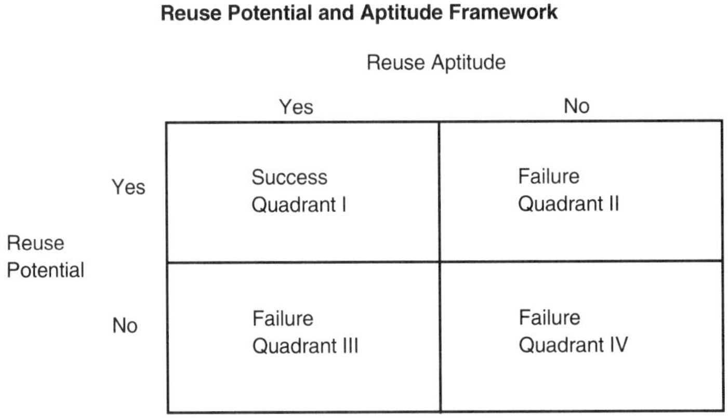

Reuse Potential and Aptitude Framework

Reuse Aptitude

	Yes	No
Yes	Success Quadrant I	Failure Quadrant II
No	Failure Quadrant III	Failure Quadrant IV

Reuse Potential

FIGURE 8–1   Reuse potential and aptitude framework.

timal compared to an organization that fully mines its targeted reuse potential and achieves the same net positive gain.

8.2   Reuse Potential

As we defined earlier, reuse potential is the latent redundancy which, using the proper methods, may be tapped for increased productivity, improved quality, and economic gain. In selecting an organization for a reuse program, or assessing one's own organization for its suitability for reuse, it would be useful to identify at the organizational level whether the entity possesses high reuse potential. Further detailed technical analysis for reuse potential can then be pursued later. We describe a set of high-level organizational traits which may be used to gauge reuse potential in organizations.

Stable Domain.   A stable domain promotes the understanding of the domain as well as the availability of artifacts for domain analysis. This stability also prevents the early obsolescence of reusable assets, providing a greater chance to amortize the reuse production costs over a greater number of reuses. If a portion of the domain was not stable, this may in fact serve as an incentive to productize and reuse the portion that was stable. Biggerstaff advocates the choice of a narrow domain [1].

Nonconstraining Performance Requirements and Memory Size.   Reusability does not necessarily mean that there will be a degradation in performance or that more memory will be required. However, under certain circumstances, depending upon a variety of factors, tradeoffs among reusability, performance, and memory may be necessary.

In products where performance requirements must be upheld or memory is limited, tradeoffs between these resources and reusability may be unavoidable. For example, performance standards for some real-time products are stringent and, therefore, firmware may need to be customized for the product (i.e., not written to be reusable for other products). On the other hand, in several instances, software developed to be reusable actually performed more effectively because reuse afforded more attention to optimizing the performance of the asset. Also, in some cases, reusable software required more memory. Consequently, the decision became a tradeoff between adding more memory or making the firmware less general.

Multiple-Product Family Members.   Shared commonality among planned future products is a good indicator of the number of potential consumers for a reusable asset. This is beneficial for a producer because there would be many consumers over which the cost of reuse would be amortized. A producer is a creator of reusable assets and the consumer is someone who uses them to create other software.

High Internal Redundancy. High internal redundancy indicates the potential for reuse within the product(s). The greater the redundancy within the product, the greater the number of opportunities over which to amortize the cost of reuse.

Identifying and exploiting redundancy within a product or across multiple family members is similar to a concept applied in manufacturing called "group technology." Group technology is a "complexity reducing philosophy that suggests the elimination of unnecessary variety where sameness occurs" [2]. A group technology approach to reuse was applied to a Hewlett-Packard software project which resulted in a 25% savings in total project cost [3].

Many Successive Releases. A high number of successive releases can indicate a potential for one form of reuse called "carry-over reuse." Carry-over reuse occurs when a software asset is used in a similar capacity in a subsequent version of the same system. It is not a distinct or new use of an asset [4].

It is important to note that the targeted reuse potential (the reuse potential that the organization seeks to pursue) is not necessarily the same as the total reuse potential available in a domain. For example, organizations may choose certain reuse opportunities over others because they provide a greater return relative to the effort to produce and consume, fit organizational scheduling constraints, or coincide with the strategic intent of the organization.

An organization which possesses some or all of these five traits must then carefully examine its capability for exploiting reuse potential. The factors that determine this capability are discussed below.

8.3   Reuse Aptitude

Reuse aptitude refers to the requisite ability or capacity to exploit the reuse potential characterized by the five properties described. In order to determine this aptitude, we examined three reuse programs to identify specific reuse areas and issues that contributed to the success of the program. An organization can determine its aptitude by assessing its performance in these important areas.

The data from which these areas were identified were collected through a set of organizational reengineering for reuse assessments (ORRA). An ORRA is an analytical and diagnostic method that collects both qualitative and quantitative data on software development with reusable assets. It benchmarks the participating organization in six areas:

1. management;
2. personnel;
3. economics and metrics;
4. technology;
5. process;
6. reusable assets and products.

The chart shown in Fig. 8–2 compares the respondents' ratings of how important an area is to software reuse to how well the organization has performed in the area. The chart is based on responses to more than 60 standardized questions answered by the target organization staff during the ORRA. From 13 interviews conducted in the three reuse programs, a benchmark "importance of area to reuse" rating was created and is based on the following scale: 5 = extremely important; 4 = very important; 3 = important; 2 = not so important; 1 = not important.

Our findings identified three areas which were considered critical success factors (extremely important) for reuse:

1. *Support from Managers* (mean score: 4.45).

   Support from managers was considered critical to the success of the reuse program. This was because such support provided both tangible benefits such as allocation of resources for producing reusable assets and establishment of the reuse infrastructure, and less tangible benefits such as the endorsement of reuse as a strategy for software development.

2. *Maintenance of Reusable Assets* (mean score: 4.55).

   Maintenance of the reusable assets was also rated as extremely important. This was because in addition to all the activities associated with traditional maintenance, this activity also ensured that the assets remained reusable.

Example of Reuse Needs Analysis Results

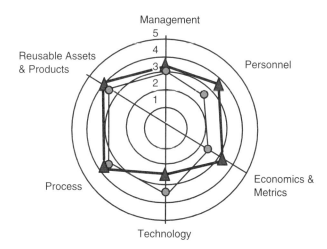

▲ Importance Rating
  5 = Extremely Important
  4 = Very Important
  3 = Important
  2 = Not So Important
  1 = Not Important

◉ Performance Rating
  5 = Excellent
  4 = Good
  3 = Average
  2 = Poor
  1 = Deficient

FIGURE 8–2   Example of reuse needs analysis results.

3. *Producer Testing* (mean score: 4.45).
   Producer testing was also regarded as extremely important because it in-creased the likelihood that the assets were of high quality and functioned in multiple contexts.

Additional important areas included:

Support to Consumers (mean score: 4.36).
Support to consumers such as helping them with their inquiries, was considered very important because it increased the likelihood and frequency of asset reuse.
Determining the Extent of Commonality (mean score: 4.36).
Determining the extent of commonality within projects, across projects, and with future projects (domain analysis) was regarded as very important since it enabled the reuse programs to identify the assets to produce.
Quality of the Assets (mean score: 4.36).
Having high-quality assets was very important because this prevents con-sumers from encountering difficulties in reusing the assets and propagating de-fects through the reuse of these assets.
Process to Inform Users of a Defect (mean score: 4.20).
Having a process to inform users of defects in the assets was considered very important because this prevented the propagation of defects and ensured that consumers are provided with an updated asset.
Configuration Management (mean score: 4.18).
Configuration management is very important because the creation of new ver-sions, offsprings, and combinations of assets requires tracking and management.
Interface Standards (mean score: 4.00).
Interface standards were very important because they facilitated interoperabil-ity between the assets.

Areas considered to be less important included:

Classification Scheme (mean score: 1.50).
The classification scheme was not rated as very important, either because there were not many assets or greater emphasis was placed on consumer training.
Library Metrics (mean score: 1.70).
Library metrics, such as the number of hits and misses, were considered to be unimportant.
Library Search Scheme (mean score: 1.73).
The library search scheme (e.g., keyword) was rated as "not so important" even by the consumers of a reuse program that possessed several hundred components.

We now examine the most important success factors in each of the six organizational categories.

Management

- Support from Managers (mean score: 4.45).
  (previously described).

Personnel

- Organizational Structure (mean score: 3.90).
  The organizational structure was considered very important because it determined the reporting relationships and impacted the reuse responsibilities.
- Incentives to Design for Reuse (mean score: 3.64).
  Incentives to design for reuse was deemed very important because it required extra effort (in the case where the producer is the consumer) or needed to be a part of the engineer's job description.
- Design with Reuse Training (mean score: 3.36).
  Training on design with reuse was important because it facilitated understanding what assets were available and how to reuse them.

Economics and Metrics

- Economic Metrics (mean score: 3.58).
  Economic metrics were considered very important because they determined the value of reuse.
- Productivity Metrics (mean score: 3.45).
  Productivity metrics were important since they track the output level for a specified level of input resources.
- Quality Metrics (mean score: 3.45).
  Quality metrics were also deemed very important since they kept track of the defect density of the assets.

Technology

- Configuration Management (mean score: 4.18).
  (previously described).

Process

- Producer Testing (mean score: 4.55).
  (previously described).
- Maintenance of Reusable Assets (mean score: 4.45).
  (previously described).
- Support to consumers (mean score: 4.36).
  (previously described).
- Process to inform users of a defect (mean score: 4.20).
  (previously described).

- Interface Standards (mean score: 4.00).
  (previously described).

Reusable Assets and Products
- Quality of the assets (mean score: 4.36).
  (previously described).

An organization with a high aptitude for reuse either shows a high level of performance or possesses the resources needed to attain such a level within the important areas described above.

8.4 Case Studies

To illustrate the application of the reuse potential and aptitude model, we present several examples. The first example is the San Diego Technical Graphics (STG) Division of Hewlett-Packard (HP) which develops, enhances, and maintains firmware for plotters and printers. Among STG's goals were lowering development costs by reducing duplication and providing consistent functionality across products. They developed a reusable asset of 20,000 noncomment source statements in size and successfully reused it 16 times between 1990 and 1994 [5].

We first apply the reuse potential framework to STG (Fig. 8–3). The fact that the underlying algorithms and domain architecture were not expected to change for quite some time contributed to the stability of the domain. As STG expected, the initial version of the reusable asset displayed some performance degradation, but

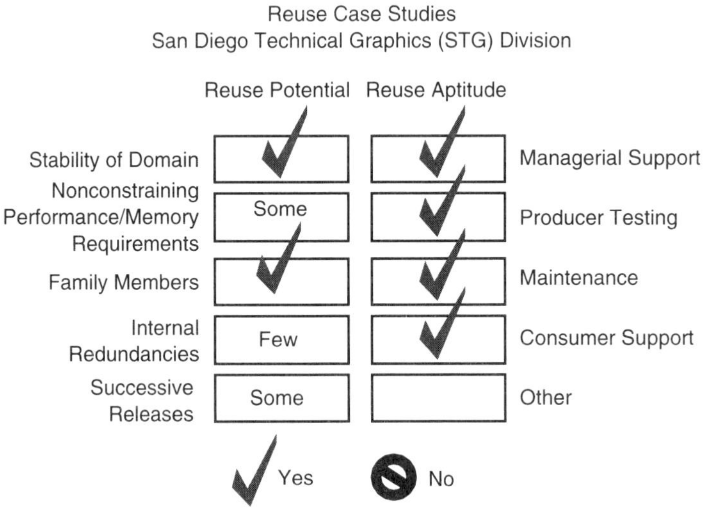

Reuse Case Studies
San Diego Technical Graphics (STG) Division

Reuse Potential   Reuse Aptitude

Stability of Domain	✔	✔	Managerial Support
Nonconstraining Performance/Memory Requirements	Some	✔	Producer Testing
Family Members	✔	✔	Maintenance
Internal Redundancies	Few	✔	Consumer Support
Successive Releases	Some		Other

✔ Yes   🚫 No

FIGURE 8–3   Case study: San Diego Technical Graphics Division of Hewlett-Packard.

this issue was quickly remedied in subsequent efforts at optimizing its performance. Although the reusable asset required more memory than a nonreusable version, its size was well within the memory constraints of the product. While there was some internal redundancy to be exploited and some successive releases expected, the greatest benefit of creating the reusable asset was clearly in the *many* product family members that required the functionality provided by the asset. From this analysis, it is clear that high reuse potential existed.

The STG reuse project also had the earmarks of success. Because the managers recognized that reuse improved productivity and enhanced consistency, the reuse project enjoyed strong managerial support at multiple levels. In the area of maintenance, STG specifically had a process for "evolving" the reusable asset both to correct defects and meet consumers' needs. In fact, additions of functionality were specified by a language committee. Producer testing was performed rigorously with a test suite when the asset was first created and whenever changes were made. At STG, consumer support was considered to be crucial. Each consumer project had one individual designated as a consumer support person. More difficult inquiries were forwarded to the producer group. Overall, STG had reuse potential, and high competency in several key areas. The organization would therefore be classified into quadrant I of Fig. 8–1.

Another organization, which we shall call "Organization S," recognized the reuse potential across multiple product family members, and in high internal redundancies (Fig. 8–4). The domain was stable, no significant memory or performance requirements that would inhibit reuse existed, and there were few successive releases. Unfortunately, the organization's low reuse aptitude doomed the reuse pro-

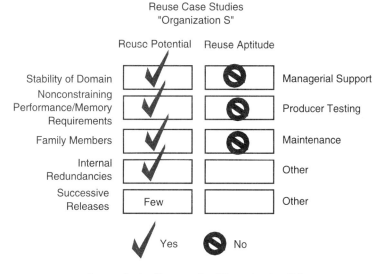

FIGURE 8–4   Case study: "Organization S."

ject to failure. Managerial support was not secure. A call was made for the submission of assets regardless of whether they were designed for reuse or not. Neither the submitters nor the librarian were responsible for maintaining the assets. It was not required that the assets be tested by the producer prior to submission. Since the goal was to build up the repository to a certain mass, the emphasis was on submitting assets, not necessarily on the suitability for reuse of the assets. It was incorrectly assumed that when the repository reached a certain critical mass, consumers would flock to reuse its contents. Organization S's reuse project, which no longer exists, would be designated as a Quadrant II type (see Fig. 8–1).

Our third illustration is the Manufacturing Productivity (MP) section of HP's Software Technology Division, which produces large-application software for manufacturing resource planning. This organization enjoyed a stable domain, performance, and memory requirements which did not constrain reuse, multiple product family members, some successive releases, and very high internal redundancies (Fig. 8–5). The reuse project at MP received excellent support from managers. This support was in the form of allocating engineers' time to design for reuse and encouraging reuse activities. Producer testing was done by collaborating with a consumer project for intensive testing of the newly developed asset. There were some concerns, however, with maintenance of the reusable assets because the assets were not "owned" by a single maintainer. For example, a consumer who detected a defect would usually implement the fix as well.

MP created and deposited one reusable asset which we will call "Asset F" into the repository. Although each reuse of the asset saved the consumer 1.5 engineering days, the organization had experienced a net loss of 31.5 engineering days by

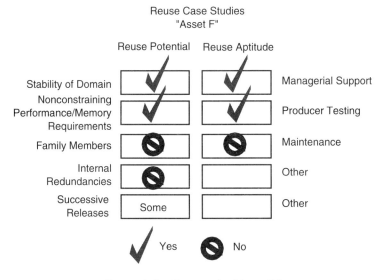

FIGURE 8–5   Case study: "Asset F."

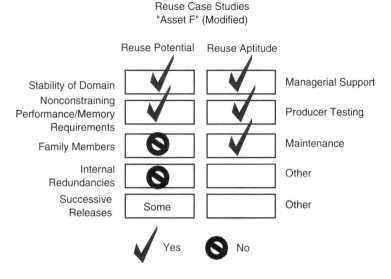

FIGURE 8–6   Case study: "Asset F" (modified).

producing the asset. The reason for the loss was that there were fewer reuses than expected and maintenance costs were higher than expected. In this instance, MP had overestimated Asset F's reuse potential and the organization's capability of maintaining the asset. Thus the experience of Asset F falls into Quadrant IV of Fig. 8–1. It should be noted, however, that although the creation of Asset F resulted in a net loss, the overall reuse program at the MP section was very successful.

Lastly, if the maintenance techniques of the MP section were not an issue, the lack of reuse potential for Asset F would still have resulted in a net loss for producing the asset. Reuse capability would not have been an inhibitor, but the lack of reuse potential would have been an obstacle to Asset F's success (Fig. 8–6). This modified scenario would be classified in Quadrant III of Fig. 8–1.

Fig. 8–7 summarizes the case studies.

Reuse Case Studies

| | | Reuse Aptitude | |
		Yes	No
Reuse Potential	Yes	Success Quadrent I *STG*	Failure Quadrant II *"Org S"*
	No	Failure Quadrant III *"Asset F" (modified)*	Failure Quadrant IV *"Asset F"*

FIGURE 8–7   Case study summary.

Summary

In the model described in this chapter, we emphasize the necessity of having both the potential for reuse and the aptitude to maximize the chances for success. Based on interviews with those involved with successful reuse programs and the results of reuse assessments, we identified several indicators of reuse potential: stable domain, nonconstraining performance requirements and memory size, multiple product family members, high internal redundancy, and many successive releases.

The top three factors identified as critical for a successful reuse program are: 1) support from managers; 2) maintenance of reusable assets; and 3) producer testing. An organization that can achieve a high level of performance in these and other important reuse areas is considered to have a high aptitude for reuse. Organizations lacking in important areas should strengthen their capabilities in these areas before implementing reuse.

Based upon our experiences with successful reuse programs, we have found that an organization can increase its likelihood of reuse success by focusing its effort and resources on these critical areas.

Note

A previous version of this chapter was presented and published as a paper at Reuse 95, Making Reuse Happen—Factors for Success, sponsored by Asset Source for Software Engineering Technology, held Aug. 14–17, 1995, in Morgantown, WV.

References

1. T. J. Biggerstaff, "An Assessment and Analysis of Software Reuse," in *Advances in Computers*, vol. 34, M. C. Yovits, Ed., New York, N.Y.: Academic Press, 1992.
2. U. Wemmerlov and N. L. Hyver, "Group Technology," in *Handbook of Industrial Engineering*, G. Salvendy, Ed. New York, N.Y.: John Wiley & Sons, 1992, pp. 464–488.
3. M. Griss, "Software Reuse at Hewlett-Packard," presented at First International Workshop on Software Reusability, Dortmund, Germany, Nov. 1991.
4. M. Ogush, "Terms in transition: a software reuse lexicon," *Crosstalk: The Journal of Defense Software Engineering*, pp. 41–45, Dec. 1992.
5. W. C. Lim, "Effects of reuse on quality, productivity, and economics," *IEEE Software*, vol. 11, pp. 23–30, Sept. 1994.

8-A

A Survey of Prior Research on Reuse Success Factors

What are the critical factors that enable a reuse program to succeed? A number of researchers have explored these issues to identify such factors. In the following appendix, we summarize the work of these researchers and their findings below.

Biggerstaff. Biggerstaff [1] identified eight properties that foster successful reuse:

1. narrow domains;
2. well-understood domains and architectures;
3. slowly changing domain technology;
4. intercomponent standards;
5. economies of scale in market;
6. economies of scale in technologies;
7. infrastructure support;
8. reuse implementation technology.

Like Incorvaia *et al.,* he found that the breadth of the target domain for reuse has a greater impact on productivity and quality improvement than other factors. Choosing a narrow domain results in a significantly larger payoff than choosing one so broad it spans several application areas. Well-understood domains and architectures are preferred for reuse because, as a domain becomes better understood, several architectural archetypes emerge from the domain. Such archetypes may be harnessed for reuse so that they need not be developed from scratch each time an application is developed. Domains with slowly changing technologies minimize the chances for obsolescence. Biggerstaff believes that 80% of reuse success can be attributed to the choice of domain.

Intercomponent standards allow two components to "plug" together, thereby avoiding additional effort to build "interface" software. Multiple reuses of an asset or multiple applications of a reuse technology (e.g., generator) amortizes the cost of the investment and results in economies of scale. Biggerstaff states that there are economies of scale in the technology itself, i.e., there are greater productivity gains in reusing larger reusable components. Having a well-defined and mature software development infrastructure that can support reuse technologies offers the best payoff. Finally, the choice of an enabling technology to implement reuse will affect the success of a reuse approach. He concludes, "Reuse success is not the result of one technology or one process model or one culture . . . [but rather] it is a result of many different mixtures of technologies, process models, and cultures."

Davis.   Davis [2], in describing the software productivity consortium (SPC) work on domain assessment, identifies five factors which affect reuse potential:

1. quality and availability of existing software assets;
2. the level of standardization in the domain;
3. the stability of the domain;
4. commonalities and variations between assets;
5. market needs.

In his work with the SPC [3], he found that more reuse is likely to occur if high-quality reusable assets and domain expertise are available. Standardization limits the amount of variation and customization of an asset, thereby increasing the opportunities for its reuse. With stability, developer and end-user needs are easier to predict. Consequently, reusable assets which possess a longer life may be created. Providing for possible and potential variabilities in the systems to be built from reusable assets increases the number of reuse instances over which the reuse investment may be recouped.

Also developed at the SPC, the reuse capability model (RCM) [3] facilitates the institutionalization of reuse by baselining an organization's current reuse capabilities and then identifying the critical success factors for improvement. The critical success factors are categorized into four major groups: management, application development, asset development, and process and technology. The model described in this chapter is similar to the RCM in its notions of reuse opportunities and capabilities, but differs both in implementation and in the set of factors used in identifying such opportunities and capabilities.

Frakes and Fox.   Frakes and Fox [4] describe their findings from a survey of 16 common questions on reuse. Although the survey was not designed specifically to identify reuse success properties, its results yield insights on the impact of various factors on software reuse. From their analysis, they conclude that an organization attempting to improve systematic reuse should concentrate on:

1. educating personnel on reuse;
2. helping developers understand the economic feasibility of reuse;
3. instituting a common development process;
4. ensuring the availability of high-quality assets to developers.

Frakes and Fox did *not* find evidence that one language supported reuse better than another; computer aided software engineering (CASE) tools or repositories promote reuse; reuse increased with more engineering experience; legal problems were an impediment; there was any relationship between organization size and level of reuse; there was any relationship between measurement of reuse and the level of reuse; or that respondents were discouraged by reuse due to a lack of quality of assets.

Incorvaia.   Incorvaia *et al.* [5] examined the results of six case studies to determine common traits shared by these successful reuse programs. They formulated and tested a set of hypotheses regarding factors which are necessary for the success of reuse by collecting case study data through interviews and literature review. The six case studies were performed within five organizations: Digital Equipment Corporation; BTG, Inc.; the United States Army; Raytheon Company; and Hartford Insurance. They found four success factors common to all of the organizations:

1. practice of reuse in narrow, well-defined domains;
2. upper management support;
3. cultural acceptance and integration of reuse into the organization;
4. reusable software subjected to standards prior to its use or addition to the repository.

The team also found that factors such as the chosen implementation language, use of a centralized repository, and the use of advanced software engineering methods may aid reuse, but were not critical to its success. From their research of the five organizations, the team concluded that there was no particular correct approach to reuse. Rather, each organization must identify the approach appropriate to its culture.

Sonnemann. Sonnemann [6] investigated the relationship between software reuse, productivity, and quality, as well as many of the theories proposed by the literature to provide greater software reuse capability. He used a questionnaire and statistically analyzed 99 projects from 83 organizations, 5 countries, and 22 different domains. His 560 paper report summarizes the state-of-the-practice (102 findings) and result of over 100 relationship comparisons. His analysis showed that software reuse is predictive of productivity and quality. However, a product-line approach and software architecture are higher predictors of productivity and quality than software reuse. This study also found no relationship between software reuse capability and the library approach (the strategy of collecting a large set of components from previous projects and making them available to other projects). Based on the results of this research, the top individual predictors of software reuse capability are:

1. product-line approach;
2. software architecture—standardizes interfaces and data formats;
3. common software architecture across the product-line;
4. design for manufacturability approach;
5. software reuse process;
6. domain engineering;
7. commonality across products;
8. strong influential individual(s) in senior management who advocate(s) and support(s) developing a software reuse capability;
9. management understands software reuse issues;
10. leading edge reuse technology;
11. kind of software artifacts (requirements, design, code, documentation, test cases, and data) reused.

His analysis demonstrated that many success factors behave significantly different. In some cases, software reuse capability steadily increases with increased levels of a success factor. While other success factors only make a difference going from the low to medium or medium to high software reuse capability groups. Many of the relationships are dynamic and will change as an organization's software reuse capabilities increase. He also performed some preliminary multivariate analysis to better understand the interactions of applying combinations of success factors and found some multiplier effects and reverse correlations.

References

1. T. J. Biggerstaff, "An Assessment and Analysis of Software Reuse," in *Advances in Computers*, vol. 34, M. C. Yovits, Ed., New York, N.Y.: Academic Press, 1992.

2. T. Davis, "Adopting a policy of reuse," *IEEE Spectrum*, vol. 31, pp. 44–8, June 1994.
3. "Reuse adoption guidebook," Software Productivity Consortium, Herndon, VA, SPC-92051-CMC, Version 01.00.03, Nov. 1992.
4. W. B. Frakes and C. J. Fox, "Sixteen questions about software reuse," *Communications of the ACM*, vol. 38, pp. 75–87, 112, June 1995.
5. A. J. Incorvaia, A. M. Davis, and R. E. Fairley, "Case studies in software reuse," presented at Fourteenth Annual International Computer Software and Applications Conference (Cat. No.90CH2923-1), 1990.
6. R. M. Sonnemann, "Exploratory study of software reuse success," Ph.D. dissertation, Dep. Engineering, George Mason University, Fairfax, VA, 1996.

SELECTING PILOT PROJECTS

Having identified reuse potential at the organizational level, we now focus our efforts on identifying pilot projects. From the corporate reuse program perspective, the choice of a pilot project(s) is important because the pilot:

- serves as a test site for proposed reuse practices;
- upon completion, may serve as a showcase for wide deployment of reuse throughout the corporation;
- may determine the scope and extent of allocated resources for reuse.

A number of approaches may be used to identify reuse pilot projects. One method is to publicize a request for candidates for pilot projects. The benefits of this approach are that it opens the opportunity for consideration from interested candidates and expedites the process of locating suitable candidates. Another approach identifies potential pilots from existing relationships with projects that have expressed early support and interest in reuse. The benefit of this approach is that it does not require the more lengthy process of the first alternative, and the corporate program usually already has some familiarity with the candidate projects.

The corporate reuse program and candidate pilot projects should share some common goals, such as the success of reuse for the pilot project. However, the corporate reuse program has a particular interest in capturing the information and methodology in the success of the pilot project so that the knowledge can be used in proliferating reuse across the corporation. The corporate reuse program must demonstrate how it can add value to the pilot project and either convince the pilot project to expend or provide the resources to help document the experience and perform other activities that they otherwise would not do if they pursued the reuse effort for their own purposes.

9.1   Criteria for Selecting Pilot Projects

In the last chapter we covered the items which help us identify reuse potential and capability. In addition to those factors that help us make an "initial cut," we still need to consider issues of *similarity* and *diversity.*

When choosing a pilot project, the *similarity between the pilot project and future candidates for reuse* should be considered. The greater the similarity between future projects and the pilot project, the greater the chances of convincing the former to practice reuse. For example, firmware projects would respond favorably to a firmware pilot project success, and analytical instrument projects to successes in the same or similar domain.

Diversity also plays a role in pilot project choice. For example, if a corporate entity is funded by many divisions or projects, it may have an obligation not to provide the majority of its services to a minority of its constituents. Consequently, in its choice of pilot projects, the corporate reuse program may need to ensure that its diverse constituents are represented in its choice of reuse pilot projects.

We will now discuss examples of factors that may be considered in the context of similarity and diversity in the choice of pilot projects:

Domain.   If the potential for reuse on future projects in a particular domain is substantial, then choosing a pilot project(s) in that domain would certainly be beneficial. However, this choice must be balanced by the need for diversity. For example, if the potential for reuse in the corporation appears to be approximately two-thirds analytical instrumentation and one-third medical instruments, all things being equal, there certainly should be consideration in placing pilot projects in both (vertical) domains.

Reuse Emphasis.   The area of focus of a particular project may also be a factor in choosing a pilot. For example, there may be a need for one pilot project to focus on reuse processes and another on reuse metrics and cultural change.

Adoption Stage.   The adoption stage refers to an organization's state in the reuse institutionalization process. For example, some pilot proposals may be a first-time concerted effort and others may be an improvement in the existing program. The stage where a potential pilot project currently is determines the type and nature of its activities. For example, a first-time reuse effort may have a larger education component to its program.

Geographical.   By geographical we mean both the value of having a pilot project in diverse geographical regions (in order to pilot a project with the local customs and culture, etc.) if there is sufficient reuse potential in those regions, as well as reuse pilots whose scopes span geographical regions. The latter would be a learning process in managing reuse projects that entail potential differences in time zones, culture, etc. Roland Martin [1] of Hewlett-Packard, for example, describes the challenges of conducting reuse across continents.

Corporate Impact if Successful.   A mapping of the likelihood of success versus the impact if successful should also be considered. By preparing gross estimates of net benefit for each potential pilot project and estimating the likelihood of successfully implementing reuse, we can obtain a risk/reward measure. (Fig. 9–1) The risk/reward grid helps us position each prospective reuse pilot project. We would expect rewards to be commensurate with risk.

First-order estimates for the reward axis are made on the basis of expected value, alignment with corporate and business strategy, and intangibles. Similar estimates can be made for the risk axis with a technology risk assessment based on the work of Cash [2]. Furthermore, we can obtain a risk/reward measure at the corporate level by considering the ease and risks of implementing the reuse solution from each pilot project.

Risk/Reward Tradeoff for Three Pilot Projects

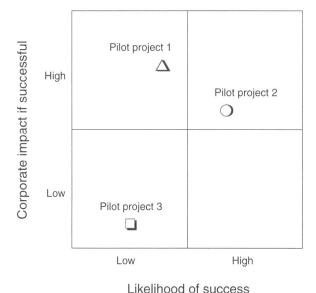

FIGURE 9–1   Corporate impact factor in choosing a reuse pilot project.

Summary

The choice of a pilot project is important because it will serve as a test site for proposed reuse practices, may be used to showcase reuse for corporate-wide deployment, and may determine the scope and allocation of resources for reuse. While the corporate reuse program and the pilot project may share the common goal of having the pilot project succeed, the corporate reuse program may have the additional goal of capturing and documenting the knowledge gained from the pilot project so that reuse can be proliferated throughout the corporation. Both similarity and diversity of pilot projects should be take into consideration. Examples of factors in the choice of a pilot project include domain, geography, reuse emphasis, adoption stage, and, if successful, the corporate impact.

References

1. R. Martin, "Software Reuse Across Continents," presented at The Fourth Annual Workshop on Software Reuse, Reston, VA, Nov. 1991.
2. J. I. Cash, F. W. McFarlan, and J. L. McKenney, *Corporation Information Systems Management.* Homewood, IL: Richard D. Irwin, 1992.

10

REUSE INVESTIGATION

Regardless of an organization's type or size, a thorough investigation into the feasibility, potential effectiveness, and role of reuse is an important first step in implementation. The investigative process which we will describe in this section will help organizations better understand the advantages and disadvantages of reuse, maximize reuse potential, and identify where within the organization reuse has the highest chance of succeeding. In order to perform such an investigation, it is important to discuss some motivations for reuse and introduce tools that will help us make the right decisions.

First, we need to identify and define the qualitative and quantitative benefits and costs of software reuse. This will be covered in chapter 11. Understanding these elements and evaluating them properly will help us determine the applicability of reuse to our needs. To determine whether the benefits justify the costs of reuse, we introduce a reuse cost justification model (chapter 12), which utilizes well-established economic techniques. This model helps us to identify tradeoffs between various benefits and costs, distinguish between high return and less promising projects, and prioritize among multiple reuse endeavors. Another helpful tool for our investigation is the reuse assessment (RA), an analytical tool for evaluating reuse potential and measuring reuse progress (chapter 14). These tools, the cost justification model and the RA, together with the costs and benefits of reuse, form the foundation for deciding whether and where reuse is implemented.

Progressive organizations with the resources to look beyond reuse simply as a means of "optimizing" software development among its portfolio of products should investigate how reuse can be utilized for competitive advantage and entering new markets. Chapter 13 discusses this forward-thinking approach and its many important implications. It stresses that the organization should take a strategic view, determine what its goals are in the broad context of the industry, the company, and its businesses and products. Then, based on this assessment, the organization should evaluate the applicability of reuse against other strategic alternatives in addressing these needs. Only then will the appropriate solution be chosen for the appropriate problem.

Since the scope of reuse in an organization plays such a significant role in defining the issues and activities required for successful reuse implementation, we distinguish reuse at seven levels. Note that the issues defined in Fig. 10–1 for each level pertain to each succeeding level as well.

Scope of Reuse

1) *Personal reuse* is practiced by the individual software engineer. Over time, the engineer typically accumulates a personal library of routines primarily for his or her own use.

2) *Intraproject reuse* describes reuse within a project. This usually involves designating one or more engineers to create the reusable assets (typically a function library) for the other project members to reuse.

3) *Interproject reuse* is the practice of reuse across multiple projects. Reuse at this level highlights the issues of coordination and organization among several groups, and often requires steering committees and new job classifications. In addition, issues related to funding and having projects in disparate geographical locations may arise.

4) *Enterprise-wide reuse* characterizes reuse throughout an enterprise. This may require support and coordination of multiple levels of management in multiple organizations.

5) *Interenterprise reuse* describes reuse across enterprises. An example of this is the practice of reuse across several different companies. Issues that are raised at this level include copyright, pricing, and enterprise proprietary issues.

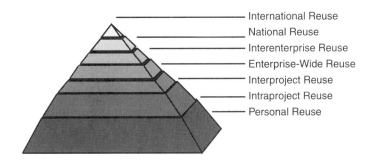

FIGURE 10–1   Scope of reuse.

6) *National reuse* is the reuse of assets on a national basis. At this scope, management issues are of utmost importance.

7) *International reuse* describes the reuse of assets across countries. Prominent issues raised at this level include issues of language, international copyright laws, and even greater management issues.

Although this book is focused primarily on personal, intraproject, interproject, and enterprise-wide reuse, we will be discussing interenterprise, national, and international reuse in chapter 27.

This section is intentionally written so that organizations of different sizes and reuse efforts of various scopes may choose to use those concepts most applicable to their situation. Organizations of different sizes and resources may wish to utilize the tools in the sequence most appropriate for their needs. Large organizations such as corporations may wish to decide on reuse as a strategy, then identify those suborganizations with the highest reuse potential, and, finally, conduct detailed assessments for each project identified to determine its feasibility for reuse. Limited resources may not permit large organizations to conduct reuse assessments for all suborganizations prior to deciding on reuse. Smaller organizations, such as individual projects, that are considering implementing reuse, may wish to conduct a reuse assessment prior to making a decision. Once the desired reuse projects or organizations have been chosen, their success or performance as a result of reuse can be measured by conducting a reuse assessment at various stages of the project. Subsequent reuse data can be compared with baseline data and used to improve the reuse process.

In order to specify more precisely the benefits, costs, and effects of reuse for different kinds of entities, we categorize organizations into three major types. Although these organizations share many common concerns (such as increased productivity and quality), their priorities and objectives often differ. We identify some of these unique issues here.

Commercial organizations engage in the sale of software products or products which include or rely upon other software in a competitive marketplace. Usually a major objective of commercial organizations is shortening the time it takes to deliver a product from the concept stage to the market.

In-house information systems are organizations within a larger entity that provide and support in-house systems. Their major goals include cost reduction, cost efficiency (since the operation is usually a cost center), and user responsiveness.

Government contractors describe organizations that provide software development and support services to government agencies. Required to create and submit competitive bids for contracts, these organizations are concerned with accurate forecasting and timely delivery of a project within budget constraints.

11

BENEFITS AND COSTS OF SOFTWARE REUSE[1]

An investigation into the feasibility of reuse for an organization first requires careful consideration of its benefits and costs. Cost/benefit identification and proper evaluation provide the basis upon which reuse decisions on many different levels should be made. These include an organization's decision whether or not to pursue a reuse program, a corporation's decision of selecting which of its organizations are the best candidates for reuse, or a project's decision of whether or not to reuse a particular asset. A good understanding of reuse benefits and costs can help organizations make informed decisions about reuse, resulting in a more efficient and successful reuse program.

In this chapter, we identify and discuss in detail the benefits and costs of implementing reuse. Some are readily quantifiable and can be directly translated into real dollars. Others that are more intangible may not be quantifiable, but are, nonetheless, equally important in the analysis. Certain benefits and costs are trade offs. For example, we may choose higher performance at the expense of less generality. We will present a method of analyzing these tradeoffs later in this chapter. The concepts and ideas presented here will be used extensively in the cost justification analysis in the following chapter, as well as throughout our discussions of deciding on and implementing reuse.

[1]Portions reprinted, with permission, from Wayne C. Lim, "Effects of reuse on quality, productivity, and economics," *IEEE Software,* vol. 11, no. 5, pp. 23–30, Sept. 1994. Copyright 1994 IEEE.

11.1   Reuse Benefits

The benefits of reuse will be presented in two parts. In part one, we will analyze the qualitative benefits that are a direct result of reuse (primary benefits), and in part two, we will discuss how some of those benefits translate directly into dollars in the form of cost savings, costs avoided, and increased revenue (economic benefits). Among the primary benefits of implementing software reuse are those shown in Fig. 11–1.

Improved software quality is achieved because the assets have been tested and subjected to multiple uses. Productivity increases when reuse requires less input for the same or greater level of output. Time-to-market is shortened when reuse occurs along the critical path of the development project. When assets are reused among multiple applications, consistent functionality, e.g., graphical user interfaces, may be achieved. The risk of cost and schedule overruns is reduced when the functionality is already available in the form of easy-to-utilize reusable assets. The availability of reusable assets allow for prototyping and early validation of user requirements. Finally, reuse enables the leveraging of technical skills and knowledge, capturing this expertise in reusable assets, which may be used by less experienced or specialized personnel. We now discuss the improved software quality, higher productivity, and competitive advantages that can be achieved from reuse in greater detail.

Improved Software Quality.   Software quality is improved through reuse from the perspective of both the consumer (the user of reusable assets in the development of software products) and the end-user (customer of the software product). Fig. 11–2 depicts the factors of software quality as adapted from Cavano and McCall [1]. Many of the factors are interrelated such that changes in one can positively or negatively affect another.

We examine several of these factors to see exactly how reuse can help consumers enhance software quality in their end products. Functionality—the extent to which a program fulfills its users' objectives—may be improved because reused components can be used to quickly create prototypes. These prototypes help end-users clarify their requirements so that the consumers can better fulfill them. Cor-

Reuse Benefits

- Improved software quality.
- Increased development productivity.
- Shortened time-to-market.
- Consistent application functionality.
- Reduced risk of cost and schedule overruns.
- Allows prototyping for validating user requirements.
- Leveraging of technical skills and knowledge.

FIGURE 11–1   Reuse benefits.

Software Quality Factors

1. Functionality	Extent to which a program fulfills the user's mission objectives in terms of its feature set and capabilities.
2. Correctness	Extent to which the software is free from design and coding defects.
3. Usability	Friendliness and ease of use to learn, operate, prepare input, and interpret output of a program.
4. Reliability	Extent to which a program can be expected to perform dependably and with the absence of failure.
5. Performance	Efficient use of system resources; adequate response time.
6. Supportability	Ease in which the program is maintained; cost of ownership.
7. Localizability	Effort required to modify a program in order to meet the needs of the regional user.
8. Flexibility	Effort required to modify an operational program.
9. Integrity	Extent to which access to software or data by unauthorized parties can be controlled.
10. Testability	Effort required to test a program to ensure it performs its intended function.
11. Portability	Effort required to transfer a program from one hardware configuration and/or operating environment to another.
12. Interoperability	Effort required to couple one program to another.

FIGURE 11–2   Software quality factors. Adapted from J. P. Cavano and J. A. McCall, "A framework for the measurement of software quality," ACM Software Quality Assurance Workshop, pp. 136–137, Nov. 1978.

rectness, the extent to which software is defect free, may be improved since the reusable assets have been tested and reused in a variety of situations. In addition, prototyping with reusable assets will enable detection and resolution early in the software life cycle, contributing to correctness. Usability can also be enhanced. For example, when several software products reuse the same user interface scheme, terms and conventions would be used consistently (e.g., the same function key would bring up the "help" menu on each product). This shortens the learning curve and increases productivity for end-users who own several of these products.

Supportability may also be improved if the maintenance engineers are familiar with the reusable assets. This is particularly true when maintenance of the reusable assets is handled by a separate organization, thereby reducing the burden on the maintainers of the system. In the case of very-high-quality reusable assets, the maintainers of the system can narrow their search to the unique code portion of the system when isolating the cause of a defect. Localizability may be improved when reusable assets are used interchangeably to provide the necessary functionality for a given region (e.g., unit of measure, regional tax rate). Flexibility can also be enhanced by reuse, when modification to a system entails only changes to parameters on a reusable asset or when easy integration of additional assets into the system adds functionality. Reuse also contributes to interoperability. For example, when a component that contains an error message handling routine is reused by several systems, these systems can expect standard data representations and protocols.

Although they may not be aware of how reuse improves software quality in the products they use, end-users benefit from all of the aforementioned software qualities. In particular, they will see the results of increased reliability, maintainability, correctness, and flexibility in the form of less down time and fewer and faster turnaround times on maintenance or enhancement requests.

Because reusable assets are used multiple times, the defect fixes from each reuse accumulate, resulting in a higher quality asset. The time and effort originally spent on the development and debugging of many similar software modules can be expended on a single module that is used multiple times. Because these costs can be amortized over a greater number of usages, an organization can afford to invest more time and greater effort in producing higher quality and more reliable software. We illustrate this point mathematically in Fig. 11–3.

Data provided by the Manufacturing Productivity (MP) section of the Software Technology division at HP indicates that the defect density rate for reused code is approximately 0.9 defects/KNCSS compared to 4.1 defects/KNCSS for new code [2]. Use of reused code in conjunction with the new code (68% reuse) resulted in approximately 2.0 defects/KNCSS rate for the product, a 51% reduction in the defect density compared to new code. If the effects of generated code were considered as well, a total defect density reduction of 76% compared to new code would be achieved.

The San Diego Technical Graphics Division (STG) in HP has also reported a positive experience with reusable code. This division estimates a defect density rate for reused code of 0.4 defects/KNCSS and a rate of 1.7 defects/KNCSS for new code. A released product with approximately 30% reuse resulted in a defect density rate of about 1.3 defects/KNCSS (Fig. 11–4).

Higher Productivity.   Higher productivity is achieved through reuse because the software product life cycle now requires less input to obtain the same output. This may be accomplished in a number of ways. For example, reuse can reduce the labor cost input by encouraging personnel specialization (e.g., software engineers who specialize in user interfaces). Because of their experience, specialized personnel working on their particular aspect of development usually accomplish the task more efficiently than nonspecialized personnel. Furthermore, productivity is increased simply because fewer software assets need to be created from scratch. For example, if reusable assets have already been documented and tested, these activities for the final product are reduced. Since the reusable assets are of higher quality, less time and effort will be spent fixing defects, thus increasing productivity. Reuse can also improve the maintainability and reliability of the software product, thereby reducing labor input in the maintenance phase.

Fig. 11–5 illustrates some of the benefits reported by organizations that have implemented reuse.

In general, software reuse improves productivity by reducing the amount of time and labor needed to develop and maintain a software product. Another project

How Software Reuse Affords Higher Reliability

The cost of debugging software is economically justified when it does not exceed the expected loss due to failure of the software.

Let: c_d = cost of debugging;
        t = anticipated lifetime of software product (or combined lifetimes of all copies of product);
        f = relative frequency with which a code component is executed;
        E = tf = number of times the code will be executed;
        p = probability that code component contains a fault;
        r = fp = reliability; or the probability of code causing a product failure;
        c_f = cost per failure of code component.

The break-even point (when the cost of debugging equals the expected loss due to failure) when the code component is used in one product is

$$C_d = Epc_f.$$

If the code component has the potential to be reused in N products, then the total number of executions of the component would be

$$E_{total} = \sum_{i=1}^{N} E_i.$$

Thus, the break-even point when the code component is used in N products is

$$C_d N = E_{total}\, pc_f.$$

Because $E_{total} \geq E$, it must be true that $C_d N \geq c_d$. The more a piece of code is executed, the greater the expenses for debugging the code that can be justified since it is amortized over multiple usages. Reuse affords more debugging which decreases p, the probability that the code component contains a defect, and thereby improves r, the reliability of the product.[2]

A Simple Example

Suppose we had a code component that will be used in a single product. Assume:

    c_f = \$1000;
    E = 100 000 executions;
    p = 0.001.

Then: c_d = Epc_f
        = 100 000 × .001 × \$1000
        = \$10 000.

We would conclude that expenditures of up to \$10K for debugging would be cost-justified. On the other hand, if the component can be potentially reused in three products where the component will be executed 100K, 200K, and 300K times, respectively, with c_f = \$1000 and

p = .001, then
     $Er = Epi$ = 100K + 200K +300K = 600K
     C_d (3) = 600K × .001 × \$1000 = \$60K

Thus, a six-fold increase in debugging costs would be justified.

    FIGURE 11–3   How software reuse affords higher reliability.

[2]Adapted from M.D. Lubars, "Affording higher reliability through software reusability," ACM SIGSOFT Software Engineering Notes, vol. 11, no. 5, Oct. 1986, p. 39.

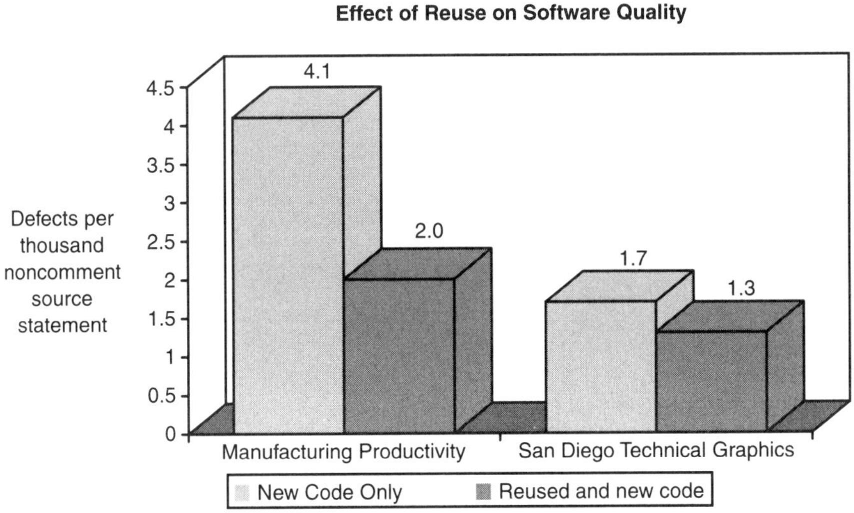

Effect of Reuse on Software Quality

FIGURE 11–4   Effect of reuse on software quality.

in the MP section at HP reported a productivity rate of 0.7 KNCSS/engineering month for new code. Use of reused code with the new code (38% reuse) resulted in a productivity rate of 1.1 KNCSS/engineering month, a 57% increase in productivity (Fig. 11–6).

A firmware division within HP has been tracking the reuse ratio and the productivity rates in the development of their products. As shown in Fig. 11–7, by 1987, several products had already exceeded their 1990 productivity goal of 2.0 KNCSS/engineering month with greater than 70% reuse, as well as their projected productivity rates. It should be noted that the reuse ratio calculation (shown at the bottom of Fig. 11–7) used in this division includes leveraged code as well.

Reported Reuse Benefits

AT&T	50% decrease in time-to-market for 40–90% reuse.
Raytheon Missile Systems	1.5 times increase in productivity from 40–60% reuse.
GTE Data Services	$1.5 M in cost savings in 1988 for 20–50% reuse.
SofTech	Ten to 20 times increase in productivity for reuse of greater than 75%.
DEC	Increase of 25% in productivity.

FIGURE 11–5   Reported reuse benefits. *Sources:* M. Griss, Hewlett-Packard Company; and T. Startsman and T. Zysk, "Case study: making the transition at DEC," *Object Magazine,* vol. 3, no. 1, p. 58, May-June 1993. Note: For additional sources showing productivity and quality increases due to reuse, see [3], [4], and [5].

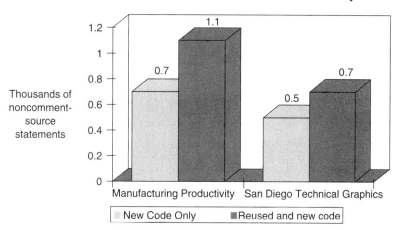

Effect of Reuse on Software Productivity

FIGURE 11–6   Effect of reuse on software productivity.

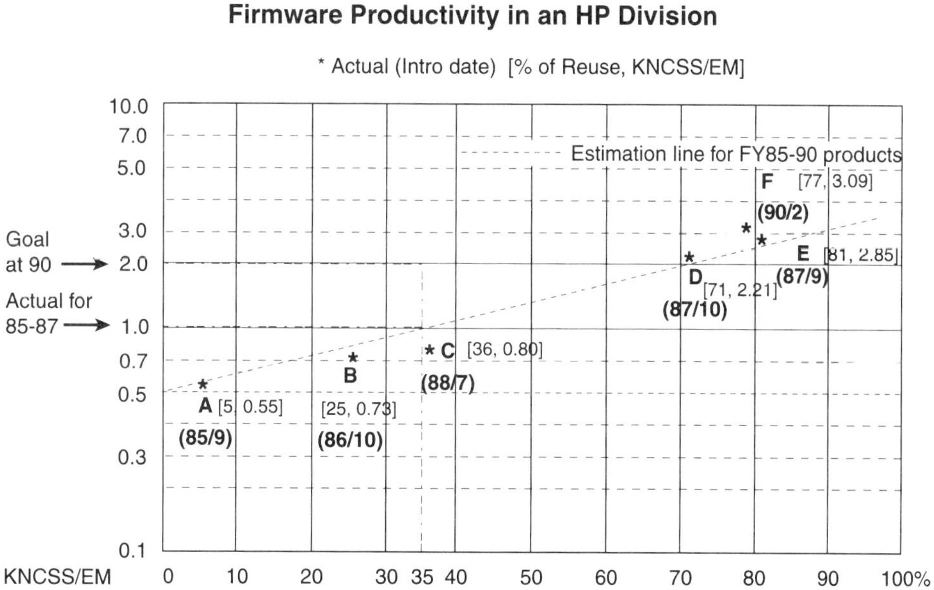

Firmware Productivity in an HP Division

* Actual (Intro date) [% of Reuse, KNCSS/EM]

FIGURE 11–7   Firmware productivity in an HP division.

The Tradeoff Between Quality and Productivity.   Software engineering, like many other processes, is subject to the economic reality of the limited resources available (e.g., labor, time, capital) as input that are capable of producing alternative outputs necessitates a choice between the outputs. Every organization must decide how to allocate limited software engineers, technical knowledge, and other resources to the production of a certain set of outputs. For simplification, let us examine the choice between quality and productivity as outputs. These will be used to illustrate the problem of choosing between two outputs, but the same analysis can be applied to any choice of outputs, such as between more functionality and longer time to market.

Suppose the resources of the organization were fully and efficiently employed in creating the outputs. Fig. 11–8 denotes the efficient tradeoff of software quality for productivity. The concave curve as viewed from the origin in the figure is called a production–possibility frontier and depicts the organization's menu of choices for quality and productivity. An organization that is on this production–possibility frontier is considered efficient. The concavity of the production–possibility frontier is due to the law of increasing relative costs: in order to obtain equal extra amounts of one output, ever-increasing amounts of the other output must be foregone. If the organization is inefficient, i.e., the organization is inefficiently organized or some resources are left idle, then the organization would not be on the production–possibility frontier, but rather, within the region bounded by the x-axis, y-axis, and the production–possibility frontier (x-axis and y-axis are inclusive).

Let us illustrate how an organization may choose between two outputs: suppose that a software project is currently on the production–possibility frontier at a

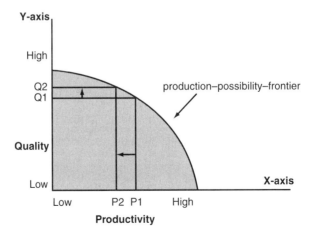

FIGURE 11–8   Tradeoff between quality and productivity.

quality level designated by Q1 and a productivity rate of P1. Let's further suppose that the manager of the software project decides to remove defects until a quality level of Q2 is achieved. However, in order to achieve Q2, time must be spent to fix these defects, and this time translates into an overall lower productivity rate of P2. The key point here is that within certain limits, tradeoffs between quality and productivity can be a conscious decision on the part of the manager.

Let us now note what impact reuse can have upon quality and productivity. In Fig. 11–9, suppose our software project is currently on the production–possibility frontier, PP1, at a quality level designated by Q1 and a productivity rate of P1. As we saw previously, if an organization invests in software reuse, it would enable the organization to achieve higher levels of quality and productivity. Graphically, this would extend the production possibility frontier outward (northeast), as denoted by PP2. The project may now choose to be at point R1 along the new production–possibility frontier, PP2. In this case, it chooses to allocate the "gain" that results from reuse in achieving a higher level of quality, namely Q2. Or, the project may choose to be at point R2. In this event, it chooses to spend the "gain" that it receives from reuse in achieving increased productivity. (In some situations, reuse may result in a quality level that is greater than Q1. This level serves as a floor in that any deliberate decision to tradeoff quality for productivity cannot result in a quality level below this floor.) Or, the project may choose some point along PP2 that is between R1 and R2, such as R3. Such a point would result in the project displaying both increased quality and productivity that it otherwise would not.

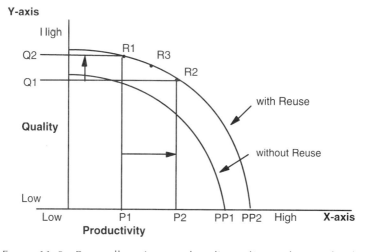

Reuse Allows Increased Quality and/or Productivity Levels

FIGURE 11–9   Reuse allows increased quality and/or productivity levels.

We have seen that within certain limits, outputs of the software engineering process can be a conscious decision on the part of the project team. They can decide how much of one output to forgo for another. We can also see the effect that software reuse can have on this mix of possible choices.

Competitive Advantages.   Software reuse provides advantages to an organization that competes in the marketplace by improving software quality, increasing productivity, and leveraging unique personnel skills. The first two have already been discussed in the previous sections. Leveraging unique personnel skills is a form of personnel specialization. Unique personnel skills refer to specialized expert knowledge that has served as a competitive advantage for the organization in the past. Just as "expert systems" attempt to capture expertise so that it may be shared across the organization, software reuse leverages unique personnel skills in the form of reusable assets. Reuse enables experts to concentrate on creating assets which may then be reused by less specialized personnel.

Unlike those provided by, for example, a commercially available software productivity tool, the competitive advantages offered by software reuse to an organization can be sustainable in the long term. To understand why, let us examine what constitutes a sustainable competitive advantage. One of the reasons that certain advantages are not sustainable may be ascribed to the "fallacy of composition". This fallacy states that what is considered to be true of a part is declared true for the whole as well. An example given by the Massachusetts Institute of Technology economist Paul Samuelson [6] is: "For everybody to stand on tiptoe to watch a parade does no good, even though one person may gain a better view by so doing." Applying this to our earlier example indicates that while early adopters of a software productivity tool will benefit from a competitive advantage initially, this advantage will not be sustainable once the use of the tool becomes the industry norm. This is especially true if the tool or its underlying technology is available to competitors through vendors, consultants, or even former employees. Eventually, adopting the tool becomes a necessity for all competitors who wish to remain in the market. On the other hand, sustainable competitive advantages are those which an organization's competitors cannot replicate in the short term. As Michael Miron [7] of McKinsey & Co. points out, sustainable advantages most likely come from leveraging the organization's existing business strengths, such as economies of scale or the leveraging of unique institutional skills.

Economies of scale refers to the unit-cost savings that can be achieved at higher output levels. For example, an auto assembly line may not be worth building if only a few automobiles are to be produced. However, if many automobiles are to be produced, creating an assembly line will lower the unit cost. Related to economies of scale are economies of scope. Achieving lower costs by producing a variety of products subject to economies of scale is a form of economies of scope. For example, utilizing the same assembly line to produce several different automobile models takes advantage of the economies of scope. Another example is the steel company that produces a variety of steel products by using the same furnace to produce molten steel which is then poured into different molds to produce different products [8].

Unlike the actual production of automobiles in which many of the same models are produced and are thus subject to economies of scale, the development of software is subject to economies of scope. Organizations that produce a large number of products or systems that share commonality would gain a greater advantage from reuse than an organization producing a smaller number of products or systems. An example Michael Porter [9] of the Harvard Business School uses to illustrate the sharing of development activities is "the multi-business company that manufactures small electric motors which are then used in fans, hairdryers, and cooling systems for electronic equipment." Likewise, reusable assets can be created for common use among a variety of products.

L. M. Ericsson in Sweden is an example of a company that has utilized modular, reusable software to become a successful global competitor [10]. In order to introduce electronic switching systems to countries with smaller telephone systems in the 1970's, Ericsson introduced a series of modular software packages that were designed to be reused and configured to the needs of each country. Fig. 11–10 shows that before exploiting reuse, the investment needed to develop software for these electronic switching systems to fit the requirements of each country made the systems prohibitively expensive. By sharing activities subject to economies of scale, Ericsson was able to amortize development costs quickly.

The competitive advantage provided by unique personnel skills is sustainable to the extent that the knowledge or individual(s) possessing these skills remain with the organization. Software reuse helps the leveraging of unique expertise by allowing this knowledge to be shared throughout the organization in the form of reusable assets created by individuals with these expert skills. It may also lessen the impact of departures by these experts from the organization because their expertise is partially captured in well-documented reusable assets which can continue to be used by others.

Realizing Economies of Scope Through Software Reuse

	Representative Systems	New Modules Required	Existing Modules Used
Year 1	Sodertaije, Sweden	57	0
Year 2	Orleans, France	22	57
Year 3	Abo, Finland	0	77

FIGURE 11–10 Realizing economies of scope through reuse. *Source: A Framework for Swedish Industrial Policy* (Liberfolag: Stockholm, 1978), used by permission of The Boston Consulting Group.

11.2   Economic Benefits

We will now discuss how these primary benefits, namely, higher quality, increased productivity, and competitive advantages translate directly into economic benefits. These benefits come in four forms: reduced costs, avoided costs, increased profit, and other opportunities. Fig. 11–11 depicts the relationships between qualitative and quantitative benefits. Let us now look at each of these in more detail.

Cost Reduction.   A major economic benefit of employing reuse is a reduction in the costs required to design, develop, and maintain a software product. Because software development and maintenance are labor-intensive, most of the reduction results from savings in labor costs. These savings are realized through the leveraging of personnel expertise, a shorter software development life cycle, and reduced maintenance effort.

The need to leverage personnel expertise has been fueled by the limited supply of software engineers and the increased demand for software. Barry Boehm [11] has calculated this shortfall between supply and demand. Boehm observes that the supply of software engineers is increasing at about 4% per year whereas the demand for software is rising by at least 12% per year. Because software engineers' productivity is increasing at only about 4% a year, a deficit of roughly 4% a year is estimated. This has serious implications for the future considering that estimates of the shortage in 1983 exceeded 100,000 software personnel.

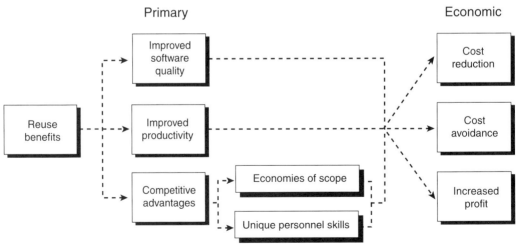

FIGURE 11–11   Qualitative and quantitative benefits.

Software reuse enables an organization to utilize its personnel more effectively because it leverages the expertise of experienced and specialized software engineers. Reuse allows these people to concentrate on creating assets which may then be reused by less-experienced and less-specialized personnel. In fact, such personnel, called "workproduct assemblers," can integrate the reusable software assets to create a final product, thus reducing the workload of more experienced engineers. Employing reuse has helped Raytheon Missile Systems, Bedford, MA make more efficient and productive use of software engineers [12]. Within just four months, eight of the company's software engineers entirely rewrote a large manufacturing system by utilizing reusable code techniques. Thus, leveraging personnel expertise through reuse can result in a significant labor cost reduction.

Cost reduction may also result from a shortened software development life cycle. High-quality software assets have relatively low defect densities because they have been rigorously tested and previously used. Consequently, a significant amount of engineer time normally spent fixing defects on freshly coded software during the development life cycle can be saved. Engineer time is also productively used when the time required to retrieve and integrate reusable assets is less than the time necessary to create the asset from scratch. In addition, Thomas Standish [13] observes from Boehm's research that "since economic analysis indicates that the cost of software is an exponential function of software size, halving the size of the software which must be built much more than halves the cost of building it." The result of shortening the software development life cycle is a savings in engineer time which may then be used to improve other aspects of the product or on new projects.

Increased productivity from reuse, however, does not necessarily result in shortened time-to-market. Shortened time-to-market refers to the time it takes to deliver a product to market from time of conception. For example, when reuse does not occur along the critical path of a software development project, increased productivity may result, but not necessarily shortened time-to-market.

There are numerous examples that illustrate how reuse reduces the development effort. Don Leavitt [14] reports one particular case at the Raytheon Company's Missile Systems Division where a major inventory system normally estimated to require 126 man-months of development effort took only 36 man-months. This was achieved in a reuse development environment where the software developed averaged 65% reusable code.

Reuse reduces maintenance costs by producing quality software and increasing the productivity of the maintenance team. Maintenance costs have been shown to constitute 50% or more of the total software effort [15]. Several studies have shown that the further along the software life cycle that a defect is detected and fixed, the more costly the fix [16]. Reuse can lower maintenance costs by preventing user requirement defects early in the life cycle through prototyping. This enables the engineer to avoid fixing these defects later, and, in many cases, in the maintenance phase. Reuse also helps reduce maintenance costs by enabling a reliable, low defect density software product to be developed. Less effort is required in the maintenance phase simply because there are less defects to fix. In addition, previous experience and familiarity with reusable assets by maintenance engineers will facilitate the maintenance effort. Highly reliable software assets also reduce the effort of isolating the cause of defects by narrowing the search to focus on that portion of the product which is not created from reusable assets. The productivity of the maintenance team is improved because any fix to a reusable asset would be propagated to all software products that incorporate that asset. Modifications to the system are also easier in instances where only parameters need to be changed on a reusable component or where integrating an additional reusable component into the system is required in order to add functionality. Moreover, since reuse implies that all assets are well-documented for potential users, this further reduces maintenance costs. In some organizations, maintenance of reusable assets is handled by a separate team, thus reducing the burden on system maintainers.

Cost Avoidance. In addition to reduced costs, avoided costs are also an economic benefit resulting from reuse. Although both are monetary benefits, it is important to understand the distinction between reduced costs and avoided costs. Avoided costs are those that would have been incurred if reuse were not implemented. Avoided costs come in two forms. The first, additional resource costs, refer to those inputs into the software product life cycle that would have been necessary if reuse were not employed. For example, suppose a labor force of ten software engineers was working at full capacity and three more engineers were needed to match the projected workload. If reuse is implemented which enables the current ten engineers to handle the projected workload, then the cost of the three engineers has been avoided. If reuse increases productivity to a level where only eight engineers are needed, the cost has been reduced by two engineers, and that of three engineers has been avoided.

Second, by shortening development schedules, reuse enables certain penalty costs to be avoided. For example, missing a market window or deadline may result in a severe financial penalty. In some cases, this penalty is an opportunity cost, i.e., revenues forgone for not having the product on the market earlier. We will discuss opportunity costs in the next section. In other cases, it may have a more immediate and tangible impact such as a drop in the price of the company's stock. An example is the Lotus Development Corporation's missed deadlines in releasing an upgraded version of their spreadsheet program [17]. The effects of these missed deadlines were reflected in the company's stock prices.

Increased Profit. Another type of economic benefit resulting from reuse is a potential increase in profits realized through shortened time-to-market and customer-perceived quality software. These benefits are most relevant to commercial or market-driven organizations. Not only does reuse reduce and avoid costs, but it may also potentially increase profits by allowing organizations that employ reuse to meet market windows of opportunity that they would otherwise miss. Bringing a product to market before competitors in certain instances enables a firm to obtain a greater market share, and thus, greater profits. Furthermore, having a higher quality product in the market that truly fulfills customer needs may lead to increased revenues.

Malcolm Rix [18] describes the decrease in time-to-market for eight different products at one HP division (Fig. 11–12). The percent reuse for the January 1986

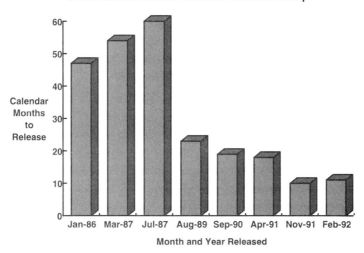

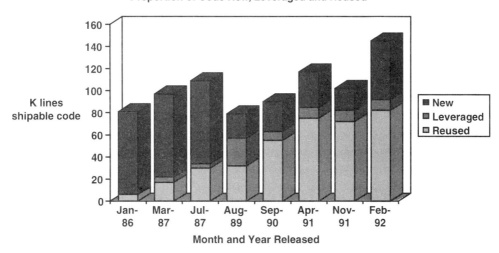

FIGURE 11–12 Effect of reuse on time-to-market: Common Firmware Group. *Source*: M. Rix, Presentation and poster: "Case study of a successful firmware reuse program," Palo Alto, CA: 5th Annual Workshop for Instituting Reuse, Oct., 1992.

product was negligible. Each released product thereafter had an increasingly higher percent of reuse. The February 1992 product comprised about 57% reuse. The data clearly indicates that products with higher reuse resulted in a shorter time-to-market.

AT&T experienced a similar effect of reuse on time to market. In ten software systems ranging from 75,000 to 545,000 lines of code, some system deliveries have been more than halved. AT&T predicts that as they gain more experience in software reuse, improve the software system design process, and increase the size of the reusable assets, delivery of software systems in less than six months will become the norm [19].

At the San Diego Technical Graphics Division, the use of a reusable asset is estimated to shorten the development time-to-market for a product by approximately 15 engineering months. This project required only 21 calendar months for development compared to an estimated 36 calendar months had the reusable asset not been used (Fig. 11–13).

Other Opportunities.   Lastly, software reuse may also provide opportunities to pursue other endeavors with the newly available resources saved through reuse. For example, if a project normally requires ten engineering months to complete but with reuse requires only eight, the remaining two engineering months can be employed to pursue other projects.

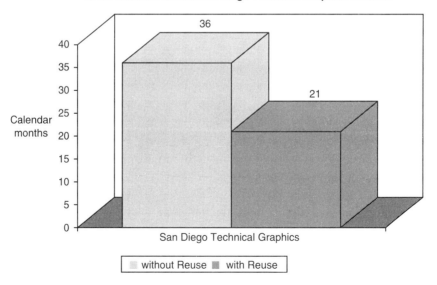

FIGURE 11–13   Effect of reuse on time-to-market: San Diego Technical Graphics.

11.3 Reuse Costs

We now examine the costs of implementing reuse. Aside from the expenses incurred in the creation, development, and maintenance of reusable software assets, reuse costs also include possible performance degradation, risk of obsolete assets, and additional security considerations. Let us examine each of these in more detail.

In some cases, where reusable software assets are more general than their nonreusable counterparts, their use in highly specialized applications may result in overall performance degradation. For example, portions of a reusable asset may be in a "ready-to-process" mode even though they may not be needed. This affects product performance features such as speed, efficiency, resource consumption, throughput, and response time. In certain applications where performance is critical, predominantly "tailored" code may still be appropriate. Another consideration in certain situations is the additional memory that may be required to accommodate reusable assets. Thus, before creating a reusable asset, the tradeoffs between reusability and performance and memory needs to be carefully weighed within the context of the application.

Second, an inherent risk is assumed when reusable software assets are stockpiled. Changes in technology and/or strategy may impact the value of the assets in a reuse library. For example, a major strategic shift by the organization or a rapid technological change can render the assets obsolete. For this reason, a reuse plan should take into consideration technological and strategic factors and recognize that reusable software assets have their own limited life cycle. Organizations in industries where new technologies continually replace old methods should recognize this fact and incorporate it into their reuse plan.

In some instances, software that is reusable may also pose a security risk. The modules may contain information that an organization desires not to reveal. This information may simply be proprietary designs or it may be more revealing, such as the scheme for a missile system. One aerospace company encountered such a predicament when they wanted to make a reusable software engineering system available to all their engineers, but were concerned that some modules would reveal the nature of their work with the U.S. Department of Defense. The problem was solved by providing an access code to those engineers who needed to retrieve sensitive reusable modules for their task.

The bulk of the costs incurred from implementing reuse stem from the development and maintenance of reusable assets, tools, and one or more libraries. Such costs are included in the cost–benefit analyses described in the next chapter. These costs can be categorized into initial costs and recurring costs. Initial costs are one-time expenses needed to start a software reuse program. They include the costs of investigating reuse; acquiring and creating reuse tools; hiring and educating personnel; determining which reusable assets to create; and producing the assets. Recurring costs are ongoing expenses necessary to maintain software reuse. These include the costs of tools and reusable asset maintenance, user support, and publicity of the reuse program.

The expenses associated with implementing reuse include the cost of the initial investigation, the development of reuse tools, hiring reuse personnel, educating the organization about reuse, and creating and maintaining reusable assets. These are defined below.

Investigation.   These costs are incurred to determine whether the organization can benefit from and support software reuse from a technological and strategic standpoint. It includes an assessment of the reuse tools, training, and policies necessary to implement reuse.

Tools.   These expenses include the creation and maintenance of a reusable software library (if appropriate) and the support of reuse tools. The library serves as a repository for the software assets. When the library is populated with many assets, it also becomes necessary to have a cataloging mechanism. More details are available on reuse tools in chapter 24.

Reuse Personnel.   Reuse will create the roles of producer and consumer among development engineers. Other new roles created by software reuse are library administrators who oversee and maintain the software reuse library, and workproduct assemblers, who integrate the reusable software components into a final product. Additional information regarding reuse personnel is presented in chapter 16.

Education.   Education costs are those resources used to attain managerial and engineering support, awareness, and acceptance. Costs include the expense of instructing engineers and assemblers how to create and incorporate reusable software into their products, and training the library administrator to run and maintain the reuse library.

Reusable Assets.   Creating and maintaining reusable assets is a major cost in reuse. Techniques for creating reusable assets range from obtaining existing assets which are then retrofitted to be "reusable," to creating these assets from scratch expressly for reuse. Maintenance of reusable assets requires significant resources. However, this cost is less than the sum of the maintenance costs of the multiple assets that would be incurred if reusable software was not implemented.

11.4   Economic Costs of Reuse

In this section, we will focus on the costs of creating and consuming reusable assets. Techniques for creating reusable assets range from obtaining existing assets which are then made "reusable" to creating these assets from scratch intentionally for reuse.

The relative cost to produce is the cost to produce a reusable asset divided by the cost to produce a nonreusable version. The relative cost to reuse is the cost to reuse an asset divided by the cost to produce a nonreusable version. Tracz [20] indicates that the cost to produce reusable assets relative to that of producing non-reusable assets ranges from 130–300%. Lenz [21] describes his experience at IBM which yields data showing this relative cost to be 200%. Tracz [22] later published data to indicate that the relative cost to produce is 120–125%. Card [23] describes the relative cost to reuse in the Flight Avionics domain to be 20%. Margono [24] cites experience with software reuse in the Air Traffic Control Advanced Automation System showing that the relative cost of creating reusable code is about twice that of creating a nonreusable version. Integration costs (cost to reuse) ranged from 10% to 20% of the cost of creating a nonreusable version. Favaro [25] cites findings that the relative cost of producing a reusable component ranged from 120% to 480% of the cost of creating a nonreusable version. Integration costs ranged from 10% to 63% of the cost of creating a nonreusable version. Experience at the San Diego Technical Graphics division has shown that the cost of creating reusable firmware is 111% of the cost of creating a nonreusable version. Integration costs were 19% of the cost of creating a nonreusable version. At the HP Test & Measurement Division within the instruments firmware domain, the relative cost to create was 181% and the cost to reuse was 44%. Fig. 11–14 summarizes these findings.

Even within a given domain, the additional effort required to create a reusable asset over a nonreusable one can vary over a wide range and, as such, may not be captured in a single metric expressed as a percentage of the effort to create a nonreusable asset. For example, an analysis of 24 reusable assets at the Manufacturing Productivity section of HP indicates that the size of the effort to create a nonreusable asset explained very little of the variance in the size of the additional effort required to make a reusable asset ($R^2 = 0.02424$) (see Fig. 11–15). This suggests that there may be other factors which affect the additional level of effort required to make an asset reusable besides the estimated effort required to create a non-reusable version (i.e., the additional effort required to make assets reusable is unlikely to be proportionate to the development effort to create a nonreusable version).

Fig. 11–16 shows the percent increase in engineering months by life cycle phase (except maintenance) in creating a reusable software asset at STG. Definitions of each phase are as follows:

Investigation: initial analysis of user requirements and product risks and benefits;

External Design: detailed analysis of user requirements and definition of the product external view;

Internal Design: translation of external design into detailed design of system and modules;

Code: coding through unit testing;

Test: integration and system test through alpha and beta test;

Repair: repair of defects discovered during test phase.

The data shows that the most significant increases were in the investigation and external design phases. This is because the producer of the asset required a greater

Range of Producer and Consumer Costs

	Tracz 1988	*Lenz 1988*	*Tracz 1988*	*Card 1986*
	(a)	(b)	(c)	(d)
Relative cost to produce reusable code	120 to 125%	200%	130 to 300%	N/A
Relative cost to reuse	N/A	N/A	N/A	20%
	Air-traffic-control system 1992	Menu and forms management system 1990	Graphics firmware 1994	Instrument firmware 1994
	(e)	(f)	(g)	(h)
Relative cost to produce reusable code	200%	120 to 480%	111%	181%
Relative cost to reuse	10 to 20%	10 to 63%	19%	41%

Note: The relative cost to produce is the cost to produce a reusable asset divided by the cost to produce a nonreusable version. The relative cost to reuse is the cost to reuse an asset divided by the cost to produce a nonreusable version.

FIGURE 11–14   Range of producer and consumer costs. *Sources:* (a) W. Tracz, "Software reuse maxims," *Sigsoft Software Engineering Notes,* vol. 13, Oct. 1988, pp. 23–31. (b) M. Lenz, "Software reuse through building blocks," *IEEE Software,* vol. 4, July 1987, pp. 34–42. (c) W. Tracz, "Software reuse myths," *Sigsoft Software Engineering Notes,* vol. 13, Jan. 1988, pp. 17–21. (d) D. Card, et al., "An empirical study of software design practices," *IEEE Transactions on Software Engineering,* vol. 12, Feb. 1986, pp. 264–271. (e) J. Margono and L. Lindsey, "Software reuse in the air traffic control advanced automation system," Software Reuse and Re-engineering Conference, National Institute for Quality and Productivity, Apr. 1991. (f) J. Favaro, "What price reusability," Ada Lett. (USA), *Ada Letters,* vol. 11, Spring 1991, pp. 115–124. (g) W. C. Lim, "The effects of reuse on quality, productivity, and economics," *IEEE Software,* vol. 11, Sept. 1994, pp. 23–30. (h) J. Mueller, Hewlett-Packard, 1994.

amount of time to understand the multiple contexts in which the asset would be reused. Margono [26] also cites additional costs by life cycle phase in producing reusable code. He found that analysis and top-level design required 10% more than normally incurred in that phase (15% more for complex components), in the detailed design phase, 60% more, and in the code and unit test phases, 25% more.

Fig. 11–17 shows the relative cost to reuse by phase at the San Diego Technical Graphics Division. In this case, most of the effort to reuse were incurred early in the life cycle. This is because of the effort required to understand how the asset fulfilled the system requirements.

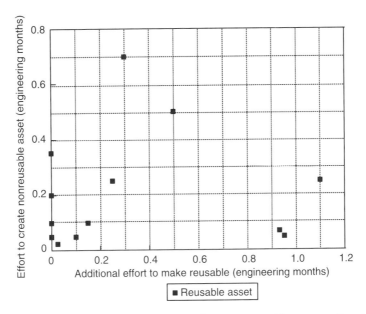

FIGURE 11–15   Additional effort to make asset reusable versus effort to create a nonreusable asset.

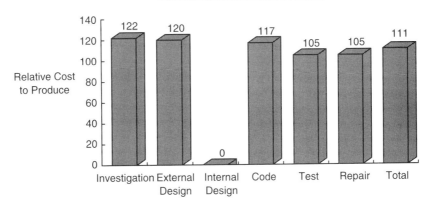

FIGURE 11–16   Producer costs: Hewlett-Packard San Diego Technical Graphics division.

. . . costs which pay off handsomely for the consumer.

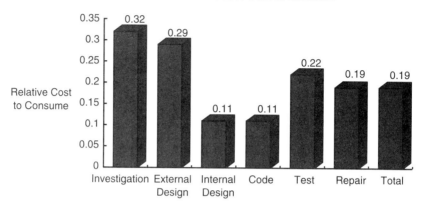

FIGURE 11–17   Consumer costs: Hewlett-Packard San Diego Technical
Graphics division. *Source*: J. Cassidy, Hewlett-Packard.

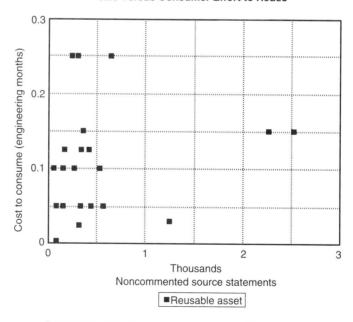

FIGURE 11–18   Size versus consumer effort to reuse.

Is there a relationship between the consumer effort to reuse and the size of the reusable asset? An analysis of 21 reusable assets in the Manufacturing Productivity section of HP indicates that the size of a reusable asset explained very little of the variance in the consumer effort to reuse ($R^2 = 0.02685$) (Fig. 11–18). This suggests that there may be other factors affecting the level of effort required to reuse an asset, other than size of the asset.

11.5   Economic Savings from Reuse

An important aspect of software reuse is the economic return that the organization receives for its efforts. Barnes, Bollinger, Durek, Gaffney, and Pfleeger have done pioneering research in the area of reuse economics. Gaffney and Durek [27] present a relative cost model that describes development with reuse as a proportion of a baseline project. Barnes, Bollinger, and Pfleeger [28], [29] determine the cost/benefit by subtracting producer investment costs of making assets reusable from the consumer development costs saved net of adaptation costs. Lim uses the well-established net present value (NPV) method, which is illustrated in the next chapter [30]. NPV takes the estimated value of reuse benefits and subtracts from it associated costs, taking into account the time value of money [31]. This NPV-based model contributes to the field of reuse economics by recognizing the potential increased profit from shortened time-to-market and accounting for risk. It is also meant to be applied over the entire software life cycle including the maintenance phase. An economic analysis may be performed for a reuse project or a given reusable asset. We begin with economic analyses at the project level.

Fig. 11–19 summarizes the economic information on two reuse programs at HP, the Manufacturing Productivity Section, and the San Diego Technical Graphics division. Their respective net present values cannot be directly compared because of the differences in the time horizon.

The economic analysis for the MP reuse project was calculated over a ten year horizon (see Fig. 11–20). By creating reusable assets periodically as the opportunity arose, MP pursued an incremental investment strategy. The reuse project required approximately 26 engineering months as startup costs for six products (see Figs. 11–19 and 11–20). These startup costs included training for the engineers. Since no reuse-specific tools were purchased, engineers' time constituted the majority of the expenses. Startup expenses were \$0.3M and ongoing expenses were approximately \$0.7M resulting in gross expenses of \$1.0M. The gross savings during this period was \$4.1M. The return on investment was 310%. An NPV analysis indicated a savings of \$1.6M. The break-even point since starting the reuse project occurs in the second year for MP.

The analysis for the STG reuse project was conducted over an eight year time horizon and includes a projection of costs and benefits for the final year (see Fig. 11–21) The STG reusable asset was created within three years and used by development projects in subsequent years. Startup resources required were \$1.3M and on-

Reuse Program Economic Profiles

Organization	Manufacturing Productivity	San Diego Technical Graphics
Time horizon	1983–1992 (ten years)	1987–1994 (eight years) (1994 data estimated)
Startup resources required	26 engineering months (startup costs for six products) $0.3 million	107 engineering months (three engineers for three years) $1.3 million
Ongoing resources required	54 engineering months (one-half engineer for nine years) $0.7 million	99 engineering months (one to three engineers for five years) $1.3 million
Gross cost	80 engineering months ($1.0 million)	206 engineering months ($2.6 million)
Gross savings	328 engineering months ($4.1 million)	446 engineering months ($5.6 million)
Return on investment (savings–cost)/cost	310%	115%
Net present value	125 engineering months ($1.6 million)	75 engineering months ($0.9 million)
Break-even year (recoup startup costs)	Second year (for first product)	Sixth year

FIGURE 11–19   Reuse program economic profiles.

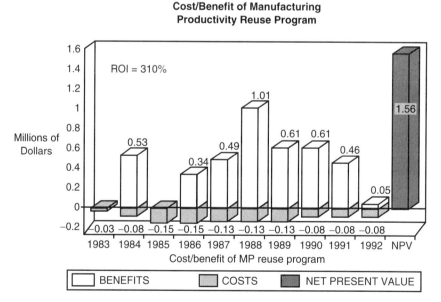

FIGURE 11–20   Economic analysis of manufacturing productivity reuse program.

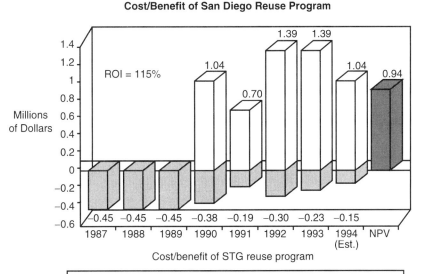

FIGURE 11–21   Economic analysis of San Diego reuse program.

going expenses were also approximately $1.3M resulting in gross costs of $2.6M (see Figs. 11–19 and 11–21). Gross savings resulting from reuse was $5.6M. The return on investment was 115%. The net present value of this reuse investment was $0.9M. Recovery of asset creation costs occurs on the fourth reuse of the asset which occurs in the fifth year. In the sixth year, the STG reuse project breaks even with the seventh reuse of the asset.

An economic analysis may also be conducted for reusable assets. Such an analysis was conducted for 15 reusable assets from MP (see Fig. 11–22) and the results indicated the savings that a consumer receives from reuse of a asset ranged from 0.2 to 4.0 engineering days. The assets ranged in size from 58 to 2257 non-commented source statements.

Likewise, an economic analysis from the perspective of the producer was done for the same reusable asset. Here, the analysis attempts to answer the question "Is it worthwhile for me as a producer to create this reusable asset?." This economic analysis was conducted for the same 15 reusable assets and is shown in Fig. 11–23. The economic gain/loss that the producer provided to the organization ranged from a gain of 43.3 engineering days to a loss of 31.5 engineering days. The 31.5 engineering day loss was the result of fewer reuses and higher maintenance costs than expected. These figures do not include overhead costs.

The results of an analysis from the perspective of the STG consumer at the asset level are shown in Fig. 11–24. In the first year, the time required for the con-

Although each reuse of an asset can result in consumer savings. . .

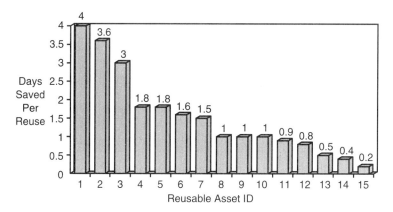

Hewlett-Packard Manufacturing Productivity Section
Value to consumer

FIGURE 11–22   Value to consumer: Manufacturing Productivity.

. . . not all assets are worth producing.

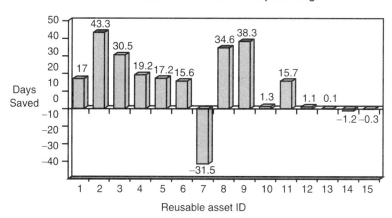

Hewlett-Packard Manufacturing Productivity Section
Value provided by producer

FIGURE 11–23   Value provided by producer: Manufacturing Productivity.

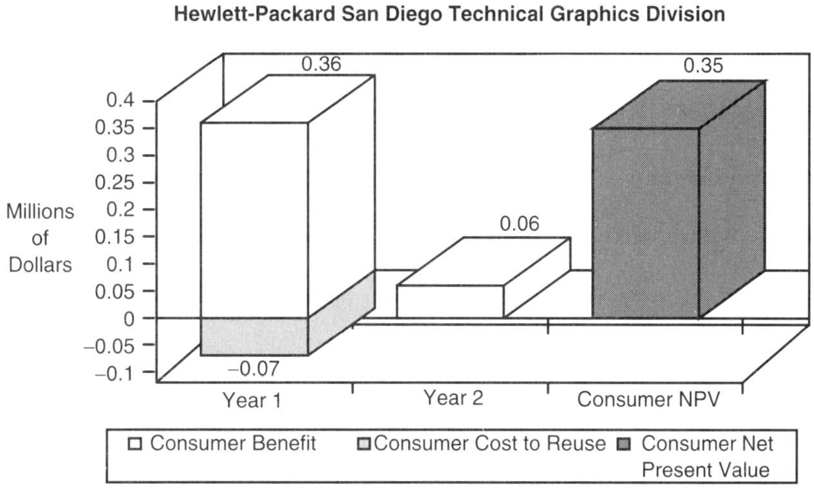

Hewlett-Packard San Diego Technical Graphics Division

FIGURE 11–24   Consumer gain from reusing asset.

sumer to understand, adapt, and integrate the reusable asset translates to $.07M. The savings to the consumer in the initial year from not having to create the functionality that the reusable asset provides is $.36M. In the second year, the consumer avoids having to repair defects that he would have had otherwise had he created the functionality from scratch. This cost avoidance is $0.06M. Taking into account the time value of money, the net value received by a consumer with each reuse of this asset is $.35M.

11.6   Economic Analysis for Future Assets

An analysis can also be performed to determine the economic viability for assets under consideration to be made reusable. Fig. 11–25 displays the results of such an analysis for four potential MP assets. Such an analysis is useful because the results serve as a decision support system in deciding which assets are economically worthwhile to create and the sequence in which they should be created. In our example, all four assets are economically worthwhile to create since their net present values are positive. The number of reuses to achieve break-even (recovery of creation costs) ranges from one to eight times. An economic ranking of these assets suggests that producers create the assets in the following sequence: 1, 2, 4, and 3. In prioritizing the creation of reusable assets, producers should also take into consideration the schedules of the consumer projects.

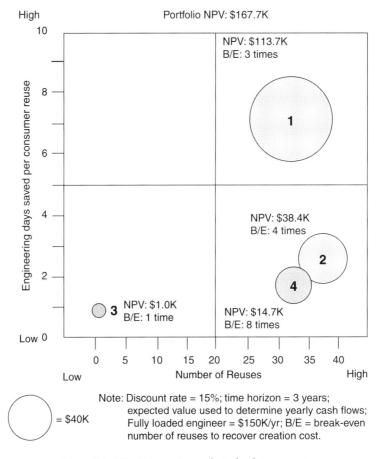

FIGURE 11–25   Economic analysis for future assets.

Summary

The primary benefits that an organization derives from implementing software reuse are improved software quality, higher productivity, and competitive advantages. Software quality factors that may be improved by reuse include functionality, correctness, usability, reliability, supportability, flexibility, localizability, and interoperability. Higher productivity is achieved through reuse because the software product life cycle requires less input to obtain the same output. Because resources are scarce, the decision to improve one factor may be made at the expense of another.

In some cases, software reuse can enable improvements in both factors simultaneously by expanding the universe of possible choices between the factors.

Reuse offers competitive advantages through economies of scope and leveraging of unique personnel skills. Reuse translates into economic benefits through cost reduction, cost avoidance, and a potential increase in revenues. Cost reduction is achieved by reuse through leveraging personnel expertise and reducing the development and maintenance effort. Cost avoidance occurs when reuse mitigates the need for additional resources and penalties for lateness are not incurred. A potential increase in profits is realized through shortened time to market, customer-perceived quality software, and the use of newly freed-up resources. The costs in reuse take the form of possible performance degradation, risk of obsolete assets, additional security considerations, and all the tangible expenses incurred in implementing reusable software assets.

Data collected at HP indicate reuse can improve quality and increase productivity significantly. However, these benefits are offset by costs associated with reuse. While the overall economics for two reuse projects have been positive, economic analysis for one of these projects indicates that creating some of the assets has resulted in an overall economic gain while a few have resulted in a loss. Performing cost–benefit analyses for potential assets helps determine which assets should be created or reengineered to be reusable.

References

1. J. P. Cavano and J. A. McCall, "A Framework for the Measurement of Software Quality," presented at The ACM Software Quality Assurance Workshop, 1978, pp 133–139.
2. A. Nishimoto, "Evolution of a Reuse Program in a Maintenance Environment," presented at 2nd Irvine Software Symposium, Irvine, CA, Mar. 1992.
3. Y. Kim and E. A. Stohr, "Software reuse: issues and research directions," presented at Proceedings of the Twenty-Fifth Hawaii International Conference on System Sciences (Cat. No. 91TH0394-7), 1991.
4. W. B. Frakes, T. J. Biggerstaff, R. Prieto-Diaz, K. Matsumura, and W. Schaefer, "Software reuse: is it delivering?," *13th International Conference on Software Engineering (Cat. No. 91CH2982-7)*, pp. 52–9, 1991.
5. C. McClure, *The Three Rs of Software Automation*. Englewood Cliffs, N.J.: Prentice-Hall, 1992.
6. P. Samuelson, *Economics*, 10th ed. New York, N.Y.: McGraw Hill, 1976.
7. M. Miron, J. Cecil, K. Bradicich, and G. Hall, "The Myths and Realities of Competitive Advantage," in *Datamation*, Oct. 1988, pp. 71–82.
8. B. R. Binger and E. Hoffman, *Microeconomics with Calculus*. Glenview, IL: Scott Foresman, 1988.
9. M. E. Porter, *Competitive Strategy*. New York, N.Y.: The Free Press, 1980.

10. T. Hout, M. E. Porter, and E. Rudden, "How Global Companies Win Out," *Harvard Business Review*, vol. 60, pp. 98–108 : Charts, Sept.–Oct. 1982.

11. B. W. Boehm and T. A. Standish, "Software technology in the 1990s: using an evolutionary paradigm," *Computer*, vol. 16, pp. 30-7, Nov. 1983.

12. R. G. Lanergan and D. K. Dugan, "A successful approach to managing, developing and maintaining software," in *Proceedings of Trends & Applications 1982. Advances in Information Technology*, May 1982, pp. 84–91.

13. T. Standish, "Software Reuse," presented at ITT Workshop on Reusability in Programming, Newport, RI, Sept. 1983.

14. D. Leavitt, " Reusable Code Chops 60% Off Creation of Business Programs," in *ComputerWorld*, vol. 13, Oct. 1979, pp. 1–2.

15. R. Grady and D. Caswell, *Software Metrics: Establishing a Company-Wide Program*. Englewood Cliffs, N.J.: Prentice-Hall, 1987.

16. B. Martens, "The User's Role in Acceptance Testing," presented at Sixth International Conference on Testing Computer Software, May 1989.

17. J. Schwartz, "Hard Times for Software," in *Newsweek*, Apr. 1989, pp. 42.

18. M. Rix, "Case study of a successful firmware reuse program," Palo Alto, CA: 5th Annual Workshop for Institutionalizing Software Reuse, Oct. 1992.

19. R. P. Beck, S. R. Desai, R. P. Radigan, and D. Q. Vroom, "Software reuse: a competitive advantage," in *ICC 91. International Conference on Communications Conference Record (Cat. No. 91CH2984-3)*, June 1991, pp. 1505–9.

20. W. Tracz, "Software reuse myths," in *SIGSOFT Software Engineering Notes*, vol. 13, Jan. 1988, pp. 17–21.

21. M. Lenz, H. A. Schmid, and P. F. Wolf, "Software reuse through building blocks," *IEEE Software*, vol. 4, pp. 34–42, July 1987.

22. W. Tracz, "Software reuse maxims," *SIGSOFT Software Engineering Notes*, vol. 13, pp. 28–31, Oct. 1988.

23. D. N. Card, V. E. Church, and W. W. Agresti, "An empirical study of software design practices," in *IEEE Transactions on Software Engineering*, vol. SE-12, Feb. 1986, pp. 264–71.

24. J. Margono and L. Lindsey, "Software Reuse in the Air Traffic Control Advanced Automation System," presented at Improving the Software Process and Competitive Postion via Software Reuse and Reengineering, Alexandria, VA, Apr. 1991.

25. J. Favaro, "What price reusability? A case study," *Ada Lett. (USA), Ada Letters*, vol. 11, pp. 115–24, Spring 1991.

26. J. Margono and T. E. Rhoads, "Software reuse economics: cost-benefit analysis on a large-scale Ada project," in *International Conference on Software Engineering*, May 1992, pp. 338–48.

27. J. E. Gaffney and T. A. Durek, "Software Reuse—Key to Enhanced Productivity: Some Quantitative Models," Software Productivity Consortium, Herndon, VA, Tech. Report SPC-TR-88-015, 1988.

28. B. H. Barnes and T. B. Bollinger, "Making reuse cost-effective," *IEEE Software*, vol. 8, pp. 13-24, Jan. 1991.

29. T. B. Bollinger and S. L. Pfleeger, "The Economics of Software Reuse," Contel Technology Center, Chantilly, VA Tech. Report CTC-TR-89-014, 1989.

30. W. C. Lim, "A Cost-Justification Model for Software Reuse," presented at 5th Annual Workshop for Institutionalizing Software Reuse, Palo Alto, CA, Oct. 1992.

31. R. Brealey and S. Myers, *Principles of Corporate Finance*. New York, NY: McGraw Hill, 1981.

12

A Cost Justification Model for Software Reuse

An economic cost/benefit analysis of software reuse provides valuable information which helps organizations decide whether or not reuse is a worthwhile investment. This chapter explains how to conduct such an analysis using well-established economic techniques. This analysis relies heavily upon the aspects of reuse that are quantifiable. Thus, because not all factors that enter into a decision *are* quantifiable, the cost/benefit analysis alone should not serve as the sole criterion in deciding whether or not to pursue reuse.

For this chapter, costs refer to *total* life cycle costs, or those incurred from investigating, designing, coding, testing, debugging, and maintaining the asset. Similarly, benefits include *total* life cycle costs saved. For commercial market organizations, benefits also include additional profits resulting from earlier completion of the product. A comparison of 17 economic models appears in Appendix 12-A.

12.1   The Producer and the Consumer: An Important Distinction

Software development in a viable software reuse infrastructure can be viewed from two perspectives: that of the *producer*, a creator of reusable assets, and that of the *consumer*, one who uses these assets in the creation of other software. In many organizations, a software developer may have both consumer and producer roles. This distinction between producers and consumers is important because the costs and benefits of each may differ. Thus, it is possible that reuse is economically feasible for the consumer but not for the producer.

Consumers incur the costs of locating, adapting, and integrating the reusable assets into their software. Benefits can be derived in two ways: from the reduction and avoidance of costs that accrue from not having to create and maintain all the equivalent functionality[1] provided by the assets, and from increased profit in completing the product and delivering it to the market earlier.

For producers, the costs consist of startup and ongoing expenses. Startup costs include the expense of creating a reusable asset or making an existing asset reusable, and the cost of setting up a library, if warranted. Maintaining the assets and library, as well as providing consumer support constitute ongoing costs. For this chapter, we will assume that the producer is a cost center, i.e., it does not explicitly charge for its assets or services. In this case, the benefit provided by the producers' activities is equal to the sum of the benefits that all of its consumers are receiving. We will discuss the case in which the producer explicitly transfers some or all of its costs to its consumers in chapter 18.

By using the producer–consumer distinction, we can analyze the costs and benefits of software reuse from the perspective of the consumer and the producer. Let us take a look at each of these in more detail.

The Consumer Perspective.   From the consumer viewpoint, the decision to reuse a given asset is economically feasible when the total cost of reusing the asset is less than the total cost of creating the equivalent functionality that will be used in the asset. It is important to keep in mind that these costs cover all relevant phases of the software development life cycle. Some consumer engineers err in their analysis by considering the costs and benefits of reuse in the coding phase only. In doing so, they may arrive at a different conclusion than one which takes into account costs and benefits across all phases of the life cycle.

Fig. 12–1 illustrates the components of the consumers' total gain/loss. At the lowest level, an economic gain/loss occurs each time a consumer reuses an asset. These economic gains/losses at the asset level may be summed up to determine the economic gain/loss at the consumer project level. If multiple projects constitute a product, then the economic gains/losses resulting from using reusable assets at the project level may be summed up to determine the economic gain/loss at the product level. The total gain/loss from software reuse for the consumers in the organization would be the sum of the gains/losses of the products as a result of using reusable assets.

As shown in Fig. 12–1, it is clear that a consumer's potential gain/loss from reuse is the sum of the benefits/costs less a wastage component. We define wastage as the time, effort, and resources expended on a failed attempt to implement reuse. For example, an unsuccessful library search for a specific asset constitutes wastage. Measuring and tracking wastage helps determine areas of weakness, such as lack of training or asset breadth, or the need for a more effective library searching mechanism.

---

[1]We use "equivalent functionality" rather than an entire reusable asset because the consumer may have had to create only a portion of the reusable asset if it had not been available for reuse.

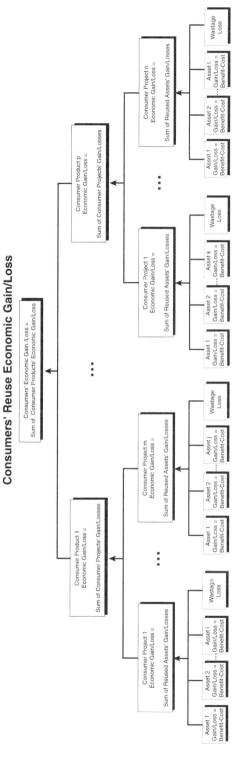

Figure 12–1 Consumers' reuse economic gain or loss.

The Producer Perspective. The producers' cost is the sum of the costs for creating and maintaining

1. reusable asset(s);
2. reuse library(ies);
3. reuse tool(s);
4. other reuse related processes or programs (e.g., training).

From the producer's perspective, a reuse program is economically feasible if the overall benefits enjoyed by the consumers reusing the assets exceed the producer's costs of creating and maintaining the set of assets and its accompanying infrastructure. Consequently, the benefit of a producer to the organization is measured by totaling all the benefits each consumer receives from reusing the producer's assets (see Fig. 12–2).

In addition to analyzing the total reuse program, the producer may also analyze reuse on an asset-by-asset basis. To estimate the benefits from each potential asset, the producer must estimate the number of reuses and the net benefit to the consumer resulting from each reuse. Producer asset costs are those costs which may be directly attributable to a reusable asset. They include mainly the creation and maintenance of the reusable asset. Creating a particular asset makes economic sense if its benefits outweigh its costs.

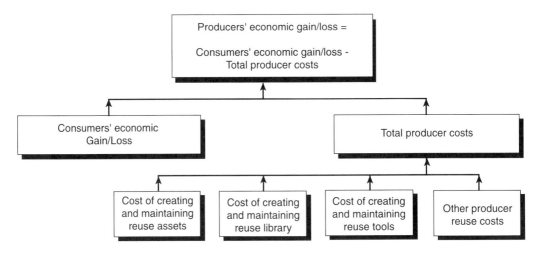

FIGURE 12–2   Producers' reuse economic gain or loss.

We now illustrate how the cost/benefit tradeoff can be analyzed more precisely using capital budgeting techniques. Capital budgeting is the evaluation of long-term investment proposals. Such a model will allow users to evaluate and to compare software reuse with other development strategies. In addition, the model can help users prioritize among assets being considered for development.

12.2   Net Present Value

While there are many existing models that accomplish this purpose, we believe that the well-established net present value (NPV) technique best serves our needs. NPV transforms the benefits and costs into positive and negative cash flows and expresses them in current dollars. In evaluating the reuse decision, the benefits will be the expected future differential cash *inflows* due to reuse and the costs will be the differential cash *outflows*. Differential cash flows represent the difference between an original cash flow and one that has changed as a result of a specific decision. This determination of an original cash flow is an important one which deserves further elaboration. The original cash flow for an organization represents what would have happened if reusable assets for an organization were not available. The size of this cash flow is determined in part by the *coordination efficiency* of the organization and whether the organization had been leveraging software.

Coordination Efficiency.   Coordination efficiency simply refers to how well reusable assets, when available, are reused within an organization. Let us illustrate this concept with an example. After surveying its projects, organization A determines that each project needs asset X in its software development work. Organization A decides to designate a producer to create a reusable asset X for all its projects to use. Let us suppose in this case that organization A is "coordination inefficient," i.e., had a producer not been designated to create a reusable asset, each project in the organization would have created its own individual asset X. Let us say that an organization B has also surveyed its projects and determined that an asset X is needed by all its projects. It too designates a producer to create a reusable asset X for all its projects to use. Organization B, however, is coordination efficient. If a producer had not been designated to create the reusable asset X, the projects would have convened and designated among themselves one producer to create such a reusable asset X. This reusable asset would, in turn, be reused by the other projects. Clearly, organization A, being more coordination inefficient would have a greater original cash inflow than organization B. This is because *every* project in organization A avoids having to create asset X when the reusable asset X is made available. In organization B, only *one* project avoids having to create asset X. Fig. 12–3 illustrates this concept.

If the organization had been leveraging software prior to reuse, the time and effort usually spent to leverage an asset would constitute the original cash flow. This time and effort to leverage represents what would have occurred if the reusable asset were not available.

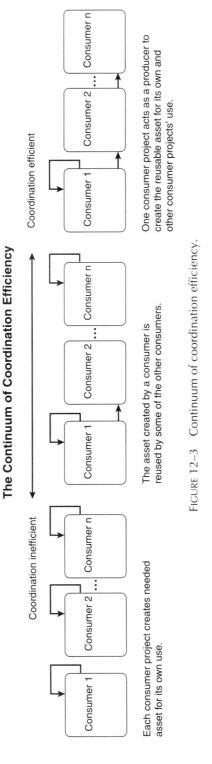

FIGURE 12–3   Continuum of coordination efficiency.

Cost Justification Model. Let us apply the NPV technique to evaluate whether or not an organization should implement a reuse program. Note that such an evaluation is from the producer perspective. For reuse to be economically feasible, total benefits should exceed total costs

(1)   producer costs < consumer benefits.

In monetary terms

(2)   cash outflow < cash inflow.

Cash *outflows* will typically include one-time startup costs (e.g., library, guidelines, asset creation) and ongoing costs (e.g., library and asset maintenance). Cash *inflows* result from reduced costs, avoided costs and increased profits. Reduced costs result when the cost to develop and maintain software using reuse is less than that of using the current method. Costs avoided are additional future costs which would have been incurred if the organization continued to use the current method, e.g., the cost of hiring more engineers. For commercial market firms, reuse may lead to a shortened time-to-market and thus, additional revenues and profits that the firm might not have otherwise received.

A probability is assigned to each time period to reflect the likelihood of receiving the net cash flow in that period. The net cash flow is multiplied by this probability to obtain the expected value for that time period. (Use of expected value in the NPV is sometimes referred to as the "expected NPV.") Each cash flow is then discounted to account for the time value of money. The discount rate, i, represents the incremental cost of capital to the organization, or the rate at which the organization would be charged to obtain funding for the proposal. If the organization is part of a corporation, this rate is usually called a "hurdle rate," i.e., an expected rate of return that a project is expected to achieve. This hurdle rate may be used as the discount rate.

We now present the cost justification model in detail. Due to the more quantitative nature of this material, readers may choose to skim or skip this section and continue with the example.

Model definitions:

1. **Costs reduced and/or avoided** through reuse from
   a) not having to create functionality of reusable assets;
   b) fewer defects;
   c) not having to hire additional personnel;
   d) reduced maintenance;
   e) other reduced or avoided costs.

Quantitative representation:

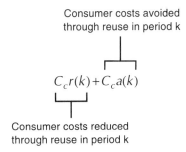

2. **Increased profit** through reuse from
   a) shortened time-to-market;
   b) added software capabilities (e.g., increased functionality);
   c) other drivers of increased profit.

Quantitative representation:

3. **Startup costs** with reuse from
   a) conducting a reuse investigation;
   b) creating or acquiring reusable assets;
   c) creating or acquiring reuse library;
   d) creating or acquiring reuse tools;
   e) creating or acquiring training;
   f) other startup and overhead costs.

   and **ongoing costs** from
   a) consumers' time to search, find, understand, adapt, and integrate reusable assets;
   b) maintenance of reusable assets;
   c) maintenance of reuse library;
   d) maintenance of reuse tools;
   e) training;
   f) other ongoing and overhead costs.

Quantitative representation:

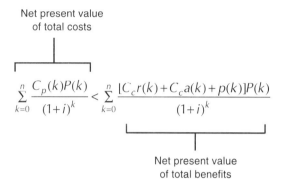

If a reuse asset or project is economically feasible, then the sum of its benefits should be less than the sum of its costs.

where

$C_p(k)$ Producer costs at time period k.
$C_c r(k)$ Consumer costs reduced at time period k.
$C_c a(k)$ Consumer costs avoided at time period k
$p(k)$ Increased consumer profit at time period k
$P(k)$ Probability of receiving net cash flow in time period k.
i interest rate by which cash flows are discounted.
n number of periods in time horizon.

Note: Data for consumer costs reduced and avoided is sometimes more easily collected as "savings per reuse" multiplied by the "number of reuses." A separate probability may be assigned to each type of cash flow for finer evaluation of the likelihood of occurance.

Subtracting costs from the benefits and rearranging the equation results in the net present value formula:

$$NPV = \sum_{k=0}^{n} \frac{[C_c r(k) + C_c a(k) + p(k) - C_p(k)]P(k)}{(1+i)^k}$$

If the NPV is positive, then reuse would be an attractive investment for the organization. However, if other software development strategies also have a positive NPV, but only one strategy may be pursued, then the strategy with the highest NPV should be selected, assuming all strategies have similar time horizons.

NPV Example.   A software company is considering starting a reuse program to reduce costs and increase profits. Their hurdle rate is 15% and their time horizon is six years. All costs are measured in terms of the cost of a fully loaded software engineer which we assume to be $100 000 per year.

End of year	0	1	2	3	4	5	6
(in thousands)							
PRODUCER—cash outlays							
Costs—Startup							
-Asset creation							
(two engineers)	200	0	0	0	0	0	0
-Library creation	50	0	0	0	0	0	0
(1/2 engineer)							
-Creation of other reuse							
tools (1/2 engineer)	50	0	0	0	0	0	0
-Training/marketing	100	0	0	0	0	0	0
(one engineer)							
Costs—Ongoing							
-Asset maintenance and							
creation (3/4–1 engineer)	0	100	100	100	75	75	75
-Library maintenance							
(1/2 engineer)	0	50	50	50	50	50	50
-Reuse tools maintenance							
(1/2 engineer)	0	50	50	50	50	50	50
-Marketing							
(1/2–1/4 engineer)	0	50	50	50	25	25	25
-Training							
(1/2 –1/4 engineer)	0	50	50	50	25	25	25
(a) TOTAL Costs with reuse	400	300	300	300	225	225	225
CONSUMER—cash inflows							
Benefits (in thousands)							
-Costs avoided	0	0	0	0	50	100	100
-Costs saved	0	325	350	425	350	350	340
-Increased profits	0	0	0	0	0	200	300
(b) TOTAL Benefits	0	325	350	425	400	650	740
(c) **Net cashflow**	−400	25	50	125	175	425	515
(Benefits − Costs, (b) − (a))							
(d) **Probability of occurrence**	100%	90%	80%	80%	75%	75%	75%

End of year	0	1	2	3	4	5	6
(e) **Adjusted net cashflow** (net cashflow × probability of occurrence, (c) × (d))	−400.00	22.50	40.00	100.00	131.25	318.75	386.25
(f) **Discount factor** $(1+i)^k$	1.00	1.15	1.32	1.52	1.75	2.01	2.31
(g) **Discounted net cashflow** (Adjusted net cashflow ÷ discount factor, (e)/(f))	−400	19.57	30.25	65.75	75.04	158.48	166.99

NET PRESENT VALUE: 116.07
[sum of discounted
net cashflows, (g)]

Since its NPV is positive, the proposal is an attractive candidate for investment.

12.3 Internal Rate of Return Method

Another evaluation method we can use is the internal rate of return (IRR) method. This technique tells us the break-even rate of return, or the rate that would equate the cash inflow to the cash outflow of the investment project. In calculating IRR, the NPV is set to zero and the discount rate is treated as the unknown variable. The formula used in the IRR method is shown below.

$$NPV = 0 = \sum_{k=0}^{n} \frac{[C_c r(k) + C_c a(k) + p(k) - C_p(k)]P(k)}{(1+IRR)^k}$$

The IRR is then solved through trial and error. If the IRR for the investment proposal is greater than the hurdle rate, then the proposal is an attractive candidate for investment by the organization. Of course, if the organization must choose among multiple software development strategies where the IRR also exceeds the hurdle rate, then the strategy with the highest IRR should be chosen, all else being equal.

IRR Example.   To calculate the internal rate of return for this proposal, we set the NPV to zero and solve iteratively for the interest rate i, using a trial and error process. From the NPV analysis, we know that at a rate of 15%, the NPV is positive. Thus, our first guess should be higher than 15%.

After a few more iterations, we find that the IRR of the proposal is about 21.6%. Since our hurdle rate is 15%, the proposal is an attractive investment for the organization. Because the IRR method is subject to many anomalies [1], we recommend using the NPV method.

End of year	0	1	2	3	4	5	6
Adjusted net cashflow (from (e) in NPV example)	−400.00	22.50	40.00	100.00	131.25	318.75	386.25
First guess: IRR = 20%							
Discount factor at 20%	1.00	1.20	1.44	1.73	2.07	2.49	2.99
Discounted net cashflow	−400	18.75	27.78	57.87	63.30	128.10	129.35
NPV at IRR = 20%	25.15 (too high)						
Second guess: IRR = 22%							
Discount factor at 22%	1.00	1.20	1.49	1.82	2.22	2.70	3.30
Discounted net cashflow	−400.00	18.75	26.87	55.07	59.25	117.94	117.14
NPV at IRR = 22%	−4.98 (too low)						

Correct guess: IRR = 21.6%

12.4 A Process for Conducting a Reuse Return-On-Investment Analysis

In our six-step process for conducting a reuse return-on-investment analysis (shown in Fig. 12–4), we advocate beginning with an understanding of the organization's goals and objectives. This is important because although a potential reusable asset may have a projected positive ROI, an impending change in strategic direction may render a potential reusable asset worthless. Furthermore, an organization's policies

A Process for Reuse Return On Investment Analysis

1. Understand the organization's goals and objectives
   - Strategic direction
   - Policy
2. Identify the decision to be made
   - e.g., whether to create a reusable asset or reengineer an existing asset for reuse
3. Identify the time horizon
   - Life of the asset and the application
   - Account for the maintenance phase if possible
4. Quantify the benefits and costs
   - Assess what baseline data is available
   - Proforma or historical
5. Conduct return-on-investment analysis
   - Determine return-on-investment
   - Break-even by number of reuses or time period
6. Utilize the results in consideration with other criteria
   - Intangible benefits
   - Strategic direction

Figure 12–4   A process for reuse return–on–investment analysis.

should also be taken under consideration since policies that discourage interproject reuse may affect the actual ROI.

In the second step, we frame the decision to be made. For example, is the decision whether to create a reusable asset or whether to reengineer an existing asset for reuse? Or, on a broader scale, is it to determine whether it is worthwhile to pursue a reuse program?

The third step is to identify the appropriate time horizon. Will it be over a two- or ten-year horizon? Will it take into account the life of the asset and the life of the software that will reuse the asset?

The fourth step is to quantify the costs and benefits. Although actual historical data would be most useful, in proforma ROI analyses, a combination of estimates, experience, and rules of thumb may also be used.

The fifth step is to conduct the ROI analysis. This analysis may include other economic measures such as break-even by number of reuses or break-even by number of days, months, or years.

The sixth step is to utilize the ROI results in consideration with other criteria. For example, a reason for pursuing reuse may be to increase usability and consistency in the target software. Such characteristics are much harder to quantify for a ROI analysis. Or, reuse may be done in order to gain experience before moving in a strategic direction. In such a case, reuse may not be economically warranted by a ROI analysis but may still make good business sense to pursue.

Summary

A cost justification analysis quantifies the costs and benefits of reuse and helps organizations decide whether or not reuse is a worthwhile investment. A given asset or reuse program is economically feasible if its benefits exceed its costs. A cost/benefit analysis can be viewed from two perspectives: that of the producer, a creator of reusable assets, and that of the consumer, a user of these assets in the creation of other software. It is possible for an asset to be economically feasible for the consumer but not for the producer.

Producer costs include those incurred from creating and maintaining a reuse program and reusable assets. In the case where the producer is a cost center (i.e., it does not explicitly charge for its assets or services), its benefits are simply those that are enjoyed by its consumers, namely, reduced costs, avoided costs, and in some cases, increased profits.

The net present value (NPV) method determines the present value of a stream of cashflows that results from creating an asset or establishing a reuse program. The internal rate of return (IRR) technique calculates the break-even rate of return that causes the NPV of the project to be zero. Both techniques can be used to determine the attractiveness of reuse as an investment compared with other software development strategies.

Reference

1. R. Brealey and S. Myers, Principles of Corporate Finance. New York, NY: McGraw Hill, 1981.

For Further Reading

1. J. Favaro, "What price reusability? A case study," *Ada Lett. (USA), Ada Letters*, vol. 11, no. 3, pp. 115–24, Spring, 1991.
2. S. L. Pfleeger and T. B. Bollinger, "The economics of reuse: new approaches to modelling and assessing cost," *Information and Software Technology*, vol. 36, no. 8, pp. 475–84, Aug., 1994.
3. M. Swanson and S. Curry, "Implementing an Asset Management Program at GTE Data Services," *Software Engineering: Tools, Techniques, Practice*, vol. 1, no. 2, pp. 4–13, July/Aug., 1990.
4. J. Poulin, *Measuring Software Reuse*, Reading, MA: Addison-Wesley, 1996.
5. R. J. Leach, *Software Reuse*, New York, NY: McGraw-Hill, 1996.
6. D. J. Reifer, *Practical Software Reuse*, New York, NY: John Wiley & Sons, 1997.

12-A

A SURVEY OF REUSE ECONOMIC MODELS[1]

This appendix is an excerpt from a report which baselines the state-of-the-art in reuse economic modeling by surveying and comparing 17 economic models and presenting conclusions and recommendations for further research [1]. The analyses indicate a great deal of commonality among the set of models. While this may indicate that researchers are arriving at similar models independently, it may also suggest that we should direct our efforts at forging new ground in reuse economics. Five areas for further research in reuse economics are recommended, and general guidelines for helping organizations decide on a suitable economic model are discussed.

12A.1 Introduction

Since the late 1980's, there has been a proliferation of reuse economic models. Such economic models are important because they serve to gauge the economic worthiness of pursuing reuse. We describe seven such models but include all 17 models in our analysis. (Descriptions of the remaining ten models are included in the original version of this paper. Contact information for the full report is available in [1].) Such a comparison is useful because it helps us understand the nature of the existing models, and enables us to baseline the state-of-the-art in reuse economic models so that we may focus future efforts on those areas in reuse economic model-

[1]Reprinted with permission from Wayne C. Lim, "Reuse Economics: A Comparison of Seventeen Models and Directions for Future Research," 4th International Conference on Software Reuse, IEEE Computer Society, Los Alamitos, CA, April 1996. Copyright 1996 IEEE.

ing which deserve further attention. While there have been earlier efforts at examining various economic models ([2], [3], [4]), we contribute here to the field of reuse economics by comparing a significantly greater number of models, relating each one at the level of detail of the data element (a data element is an operand within a model) and offering a matrix for identifying the data elements of each economic model. In addition, five areas for further research in reuse economics are recommended, and general guidelines for helping organizations decide on a suitable economic model are discussed.

12A.2   Methodology

We describe each model in the original author's terminology, translate each model using a common lexicon (Fig. 12–5), and map the data elements of the lexicon to those of each model. Whenever possible, we translate a model's original data element in terms of its constituent data elements found in the common lexicon. We examine the resulting matrix for the frequency of data elements occurring or constituting original data elements among the models. The methodology utilized here extends the procedure originated by Malan [2] by mapping the data elements to each model to determine the statistical aspects of each data element.

We identify five characteristics or features found in some of the reuse economic models and describe the circumstances under which each characteristic may be of use to an organization. Such a framework will assist the organization in deciding on an appropriate reuse economic model, or in the case of an organization choosing to build its own model, which characteristics to include.

12A.3   Reuse Economics Lexicon

To facilitate a detailed comparison of the reuse economic models, we created a lexicon of common data elements which will be used to translate each model (Fig. 12–5).

12A.4   Reuse Economic Models

We include descriptions and translations of only seven of the 17 models compared. The ten models which are included in the comparison analysis but which are not described here are [5], [6], [7], [8], [9], [10], [11], [12], [13], and [14]. Readers interested in the unabridged version of this appendix should contact [1].

Bollinger and Pfleeger (1990) [15]
Description.   Bollinger and Pfleeger describe a reuse economic model where the benefit is defined as the sum of the difference between the development cost

Reuse Economics Lexicon of Data Elements

Quantities

NP	Number of projects reusing assets.
N	Number of times the reusable asset is reused.
NA	Number of assets that require adaptation.
NWP	Number of assets.
r	Number of upgrades.

Consumer

Cc,wrp	Cost to create product/system without reuse.
Cc,rp	Cost to consumer to create product/system with reuse.
Cc,mwr	Cost to operate and maintain product or system created without reuse.
Cc,mr	Cost to operate and maintain product or system created with reuse.
Cc,wra	Cost to consumer to create nonreusable version of asset.
Cc,ra	Cost to consumer to reuse asset.
$Cc,r1$	Cost to search database.
$Cc,r2$	Cost to adapt asset.
$Cc,r3$	Cost to acquire reusable assets; includes external acquisition, generalization, searching, and retrieval.
$Cc,r4$	Cost to utilize assets; includes instantiation and asset-specific training.
$Cc,r5$	Cost to reuse; includes cost to identify, retrieve, understand, validate, integrate, and test an asset.
$Cc,r6$	Cost of incentive paid to original developer of a component when it is reused and/or incentive paid to current developer; includes royalties or fees.

Producer

Cp,r	Cost to producer to create asset for reuse.
Cp,l	Cost to add an asset to the library.
Cp,lm	Cost to maintain the reusable asset in the library; includes configuration management and change management.
Cp,wr	Cost to producer to create nonreusable version of asset.

Overhead

O	Overhead charges.
$O1$	Library overhead costs.
$O2$	Cost of domain engineering.
$O3$	Infrastructure cost including repository mechanisms.
$O4$	Infrastructure costs which include domain analysis, common architecture, and education.

Lines of Code

$RLOC$	Reused lines of code in product.
$RLOCL$	Reusable lines of code in library.
$PLOC$	Lines of code in product.
$WPLOC$	Lines of code in reusable asset.

Profit

P	Profit from increased revenues enabled by reuse.

Risk

p	Probability of receiving cashflow.

Time Value

i	Interest rate by which cash flows are discounted.
sk	Period at which a consumer starts to create product k.
fk	Period at which a consumer finishes creating product k with reuse.

fn,k	Period at which a consumer finishes creating product *k* without reuse.
sph	Period at which a producer starts creating upgrade *h*.
fph	Period at which a producer finishes creating upgrade *h*.
sch	Period at which a consumer starts incorporating upgrade.
fh	Period at which a consumer finishes incorporating upgrade *h* with reuse.
fn,h	Period at which a consumer finishes incorporating upgrade *h* without reuse.
M	Number of time periods under consideration.
mp	Number of periods taken to produce the reusable component.
Output	
S	Savings from reuse.
ROI	Return on investment.
Rel	Relative comparison (e.g., cost with reuse has to be less than cost without reuse).
NBE	Number of reuses to break-even.
Per	Develop with reuse expressed as a percentage of the resources to develop without reuse.
NBY	Number of years to break-even

FIGURE 12–5   Common reuse economics lexicon.

and the cost to adapt the asset across the number of times the asset is reused less the investment cost to make the asset reusable.

Comments.   Malan [2] observes that this model "estimates the net benefit of reuse from a multiproject perspective, taking into account the fact that the different activities may entail different amounts of new development and adaptation effort."

Model:

$$Benefit = \left[\sum_{i=1}^{n}(Development\ i - Adaptation\ i)\right] - Investment$$

where

Investment   total cost of resources applied specifically to making the product or set of products reusable;

Development$_i$ associated cost of building the product or products without any use of the equivalent reusable products (in the *i*th activity);

Adaptation$_i$ cost of finding, customizing, and integrating the reusable part (in the *i*th activity).

Translated model.

$$Benefit = \left[\sum_{i=1}^{n} (C_c, wrp_i - C_c, rp_i) \right] - (C_p, r_i - C_p, wr_i).$$

Gaffney and Durek (1988) [16]

Description. Gaffney and Durek provide a reuse economic model which presents the cost of developing software with reuse relative to that of developing software without reuse, the effect of reuse on productivity, and the number of reuses to achieve break-even. The relative reuse economic model takes the proportion of new code in the target application multiplied by the baseline cost for new code development only. This product is added to the product of the proportion of reused code in the target application multiplied by the relative cost of integrating reusable code and the amortized relative cost of creating reusable code.

Comments. One of the earlier models of reuse, the Gaffney and Durek model lends insight into the relationship among the proportion of reuse, cost, and productivity. Several simplifying assumptions have been made, e.g., all of the products that reuse the code have the same proportion of code, cost to integrate [2], and amortized cost.

Model:

$$C = R[b + \frac{E}{n} - 1] + 1, \ P = \frac{1}{C} \ \text{and} \ n_o = \frac{E}{1-b}$$

where

C cost of software development for a given product relative to all new code (for which $C = 1$);

R proportion of reused code in this product ($R \leq 1$);

b the cost relative to that for all new code of incorporating the reused code into the new product ($b \leq 1$);

E relative cost of creating reusable code ($E \geq 0$);

n number of uses over which code cost is to be amortized;

P relative productivity;

n_o number of reuses to break-even.

Translated model.

$$C = \left(\frac{RLOC}{PLOC}\right)\left[\left(\frac{Cc,ra}{Cc,wra}\right) + \left(\frac{\frac{Cp,r}{Cp,wr}}{N}\right) - 1\right] + 1$$

$$P = \left(\frac{Cc,wrp}{Cc,rp}\right)$$

$$NBE = \frac{\left(\frac{Cp,r}{Cp,wr}\right)}{1 - \left(\frac{Cc,ra}{Cc,wra}\right)} = \left(\frac{C,pr}{Cp,wr}\right)\left(\frac{Cc,wra}{Cc,wra - Cc,ra}\right).$$

Guerrieri *et al.* (1989) [17]

Description.   In the course of developing a strategy for populating a reuse library, Guerrieri *et al.* describe a financial model to evaluate and compute the profitability of a reusable asset. The cost to reuse is subtracted from the cost avoided through reuse and multiplied against the number of times the asset is reused per year. The maintenance cost is subtracted from this figure and discounted, resulting in a present value figure for the savings from reuse. Finally, this present value is divided by the cost to acquire or create the reusable asset. This model is the predecessor to the NATO model [12].

Model.   Guerrieri describes the use of an NPV-based "profitability index" for reusable components in the RAPID Center Library

$$PI = \frac{1}{C_A}\sum_{y=1}^{L}\frac{(A - C_R)N_y - C_{m,y}}{(1-i)^y}$$

where

L = Service Life   The estimated useful lifetime of the reusable component (i.e., how long we will maintain it in the library) in years, taking into consideration the application areas identified as well as any characteristics of the component itself that might limit its life.

N_y = Demand Distribution   Estimated number of times the component could be reused each year y of its service life L where $y = 1,2 \ldots L$.

A = Cost Avoided by Reuse   Estimated costs avoided each time the component is reused, i.e., what it would cost if a new component were developed for each application. Considers all development and maintenance costs, including design, coding, testing, quality assurance, documentation, maintenance, and configuration management. Note: since each project's life time is different, recurring costs such as maintenance are easier to handle if lumped together (as present value) with the one-time costs.

C_R = Cost to Reuse   Estimated cost incurred each time the component is reused, including identification and retrieval, familiarization, modification (if likely), and installation.

C_A = Acquisition Cost   Estimated cost to acquire the desired software component. This includes obtaining the raw material; developing the final, complete reusable software component with all documentation in accordance with our quality standards; and installing it in the library.

C_m = Maintainance Cost   Estimated cost to maintain the component in each year y of its lifetime, where y 1,2 . . . L.

i = Required Rate of Return   This number is normally a constant for an organization, and reflects the minimum level of profitability the organization expects for an investment. Also known as the discount rate, it is used to compute the present value of future cash flows and to compare investment alternatives. A discount rate typical of large engineering firms is 16%.

Translated model:

$$PI = \frac{1}{-Cp,r} \sum_{k=1}^{M} \frac{(Cc,wra - Cc,ra) \times N_k - Cp,lm_k}{(1+i)^k}.$$

Lim (1992) [18]
Description.   The Lim model calculates the value from reuse by taking the sum of the consumer costs reduced and avoided and the increased profit from reuse, less the producer costs. This figure is then multiplied by a probability which accounts for risk, and finally discounted to take into account the time value of money.

Comments.   The Lim model explicitly takes into account risk as well as increased consumer profit. Malan [2] observes that while the need to collect information from the maintenance phase is explicitly mentioned in the text, the model does not explicitly have a term for maintenance. In addition, Malan notes that discounting the entire cash flow implies that all cost and profit elements carry the same risks.

Model:

$$NPV = \sum_{k=0}^{n} \frac{[C_{c,r}(k) + C_{c,a}(k) + p_i(k) - C_p(k)]P(k)}{(1+i)^k}$$

where

$C_p(k)$ producer costs at time period k;
$C_{c,r}(k)$ consumer costs reduced at time period k;
$C_{c,a}(k)$ consumer costs avoided at time period k;
$p_i(k)$ increased consumer profit at time period k;
$P(k)$ probability of receiving net cash flow in time period k;
i interest rate by which cash flows are discounted;
n number of periods in time horizon.

Translated model:

$$NPV = \sum_{k=0}^{M} \frac{[Cc,wrp_k - Cc,rp_k + P_k - Cp,r_k]p_k}{(1+i)^k}$$

Malan and Wentzel (1993) [19]

Description.   Malan and Wentzel provide a detailed breakdown of the cost drivers of software reuse. The total savings are described as the sum of the expected consumer cost saved in product development, the consumer saving on product up-grades, and the aggregated incremental profit from new opportunities afforded by reuse, less the expected producer's development phase cost, the expected producer's cost to create upgrades, and overhead and setup costs. All costs are discounted. Malan notes that when expected rather than gross values are used, the model at a high level is essentially the same as Lim (1992).

Comments.   The paper includes a detailed discussion of the cost and benefits of reuse. The model described incorporates time value of money, risk, and profit from shortened time-to-market.

Model:

$$s = \left[\sum_{i=1}^{n} \left[\overline{C}_{Ni} - \overline{C}_{CRi} + \sum_{j=1}^{r} (\overline{C}_{NU_{i,j}} - \overline{C}_{CRU_{i,j}}) \right] \right] + \nabla \prod A - \left[\overline{C}_{PR} + \sum_{j=1}^{r} \overline{C}_{PRU_j} + \overline{A} \right]$$

where

$\overline{C}_{Ni}$ discounted total cost of producing product i with no reusability;
$\overline{C}_{CRi}$ discounted consumer cost to use the reusable comnent(s) in product i;

$\overline{C}_{Ni} - \overline{C}_{CRi}$ the discounted expected consumer cost saved in the development of product i;

$\overline{C}_{NU_{ij}} - \overline{C}_{CRU_{ij}}$ cost to produce upgrade j to product i without reuse less the consumers' cost to integrate the upgraded component(s) into product i;

$\nabla \prod A$ discounted aggregated incremental profit from new opportunities afforded by reuse;

C discounted expected producer's development phase cost;

$\overline{C}_{PRU_j}$ discounted expected producer's cost to create upgrade j;

$\overline{A}$ discounted overhead and setup costs.

Translated model:

$$
S = \sum_{k=1}^{N} \left[\begin{array}{c} \left[\displaystyle\sum_{j=sk}^{fnk} \frac{Cc, wrp_{k,j}}{(1+i)^j} - \sum_{j=sk}^{fk} \frac{Cc, ra_{k,j}}{(1+i)^j} \right] + \\ \displaystyle\sum_{h=1}^{r} \left[\sum_{j=sch}^{fnh} \frac{Cc, mwr_{h,j}}{(1+i)^j} \right] - \sum_{j=sch}^{fh} \frac{Cc, mr_{h,j}}{(1+i)^j} \end{array} \right] +
$$

$$
\sum_{j=1}^{M} \frac{P_{k,j}}{(1+i)^j} - \left[\sum_{j=1}^{mp} \frac{Cp, r_j}{(1+i)^j} + \sum_{h=1}^{r}\sum_{j=sph}^{fph} \frac{Cp, lm_{j,h}}{(1+i)^{j,h}} + \sum_{j=1}^{M} \frac{O_j}{(1+i)^j} \right].
$$

Margono and Rhoads (1992) [3]

Description. Margono and Rhoads calculate the amortized cost of producing a given reusable asset, the sum of the cost to reuse the asset N times, and the cost to develop the asset n times if the reusable version were not available.

Comments. As Malan [2] observes, the model expresses the savings (or loss) generated by reuse of the asset N times by incorrectly using the amortized producer cost of creating the asset. Using the correct term, i.e., the unamortized cost, results in: $S = C_N - (U_p L + C_C)$.

Model:

$$
C_p \frac{U_p L}{n}; C_c = nU_c L; C_N = nU_N L; S = C_N - (C_p + C_c)
$$

where

n potential number of consumers;

L estimated SLOC in the component;

U_p estimated unit cost for developing the component in terms of \$/SLOC;

U_C estimated unit cost of reusing code in terms of \$/SLOC;

U_N estimated unit cost of developing a line of nonreusable code.

Translated model:

$$S = N(Cp,wr) - \left[\left(\frac{Cp,r}{N} \right) + N(Cc,r) \right].$$

Poulin and Caruso (1993) [20]

Description.   Poulin and Caruso present a ROI model based on rigorously defined metrics. Both a project level ROI and a corporate level ROI model are presented. The project level ROI is defined as the cost avoidance for the initiating project plus the cost avoidance enjoyed by other projects benefiting from the reusable code written by the initiating project less the additional cost of writing reusable code to the initiating project. The corporate level ROI is the discounted net savings from reuse less corporate reuse startup costs. The model explicitly takes into account the savings in the maintenance phase as the cost avoided from not having to fix errors in newly developed code.

Model.   Project level ROI:

$$ROI = RCA + ORCA - ADC$$

Corporate level ROI:

$$NPV = -C_o + \sum_{i=1}^{n} \frac{R_i - C_i}{(1+k_o)^i}$$

where

RCA reuse cost avoidance for the initiating project;

$ORCA$ reuse cost avoidance for other projects benefiting from the reusable code written by the initiating project;

ADC additional development cost of writing reusable code to the initiating project;

C_o corporate reuse startup costs;

C_i costs in year i;

R_i revenue (savings) in year i;

n number of years for which revenues are to be considered;

K_0 cost of capital.

Translated model:

$$ROI = \left[\sum_{k=1}^{M} (Cc, wrp_k - CC, rp_k) + (Cc, mwr_k - Cc, mr_k) \right]$$
$$-(Cp, r - Cp, wr)$$
$$NPV = \sum_{k=0}^{M} \frac{(Cc, wrp_k - Cc, rp_k) - Cp, r_k)}{(1+i)k}.$$

12A.5   Comparing the Reuse Economic Models by a Common Lexicon

In Fig. 12–6, we construct a matrix mapping the reuse economic models against the data elements previously described. This matrix is especially useful for organizations planning on utilizing two or more models in the economic evaluation of their reuse efforts (as was done by [3] and [4]). It identifies the data elements (both common and unique) which need to be collected by the organization.

Analyses of this matrix indicate a great deal of commonality among the 17 economic models, i.e., the original data elements used in the 17 economic models may be defined using a smaller core set of data elements. Forty-three data elements were identified in our core set of data elements. The data elements most frequently utilized in our set of models examined were

1. cost to producer to create asset for reuse (15 models);
2. number of times the reusable asset is reused (12 models);
3. cost to create product/system without reuse (ten models);
4. cost to consumer to reuse asset (ten models);
5. cost to consumer to create nonreusable version of asset (eight models).

We found that these five data elements (which constitute 12% of the total data elements found in our core set):

- on average, account for 45% of the data elements used in a reuse economic model (high = 100.0%; low = 16.7%);
- on average, occur in 65% of the reuse economic models (high = 88.2%; low = 47.1%).

Eliminating four models which share a common genealogy of at least one author from our set of economic models ([5], [7], [9], and [12]) does not significantly alter the above results. In the reduced set of 13 economic models, the five data elements on average account for 44% of the data elements used, and occur in 63% of the reuse economic models.

Comparison of Reuse Economic Models by Data Element

	Bar '91	Bol '90	Bow '92A	Bow '92D	Gaf '92	Gaf '89	Fra '93	Gue '89	Kan '89	Lim '92	Mal '93	Mar '92	May '91	NAT '91	Pou '93	Ray '91	Sch '92	Instances
Quantities																		
NP																Y		1
N	Y	Y	Y		Y	Y		Y	Y		Y	Y	Y	Y			Y	12
NA													Y					1
NWP													Y					1
r											Y							1
Consumer																		
Cc,wrp	Y	Y		Y	Y	Y	Y				Y	Y			Y		Y	10
Cc,rp	Y	Y				Y				Y					Y			5
Cc,mwr				Y							Y				Y			3
Cc,mr				Y							Y				Y			3
Cc,wra			Y	Y	Y	Y	Y	Y	Y					Y				8
Cc,ra			Y	Y		Y		Y	Y		Y	Y	Y	Y			Y	10
Ccr1													Y					1
Cc,r2			Y	Y									Y			Y		4
Cc,r3							Y											1
Cc,r4							Y											1
Cc,r5			Y															1
Cc,r6			Y															1
Producer																		
Cp,r	Y	Y	Y	Y		Y	Y	Y	Y	Y	Y	Y	Y	Y	Y		Y	15
Cp,l		Y																1
Cp,lm		Y	Y					Y			Y			Y				5
Cp,wr	Y	Y				Y	Y					Y	Y		Y			7
Overhead																		
O											Y							1
O1													Y			Y	Y	3
O2					Y													1
O3							Y											1
O4				Y														1

Lines of Code

	C1	C2	C3	C4	C5	C6	C7	C8	C9	C10	C11	C12	C13	C14	C15	Total
RLOC			Y	Y										Y	Y	4
RLOCL			Y	Y											Y	2
PLOC			Y	Y										Y	Y	4
WPLOC								Y							Y	2
Profit																
P								Y	Y							2
Risk																
p								Y	Y							2
Time Value																
i								Y	Y		Y	Y				5
sk									Y							1
fk									Y							1
fn,k									Y							1
sph									Y							1
fph									Y							1
sch									Y							1
fh									Y							1
fn,h									Y							1
M						Y		Y	Y		Y	Y			Y	6
mp									Y							1
TOTAL	5	8	9	7	9	7	4	7	22	5	9	7	8	6	10	135

Comparison of Reuse Economic Models by Output

	C1	C2	C3	C4	C5	C6	C7	C8	C9	C10	C11	C12	C13	C14	C15	Total
S	Y	Y	Y	Y		Y	Y	Y		Y	Y	Y	Y			9
ROI	Y			Y		Y		Y	Y		Y			Y		5
Rel	Y	Y		Y	Y											4
NBE			Y	Y												2
Per			Y													1
NBY															Y	1

FIGURE 12–6   Comparison by data element.

12A.6   Commonalities and Variabilities

Further commonalities and variabilities may be found in our set of economic models. The economic models can be categorized into six types based on their outputs. The most common type of output by the models is savings from reuse (41%); followed by return on investment (23%); relative comparison (18%); number of reuses to break-even (9%); development with reuse expressed as a percentage of the resources to develop without reuse (4.5%); and number of years to break-even (4.5%). These percentages reflect the fact that some models have multiple outputs.

Most of the models (65%) do not indicate whether the producer or consumer bear the cost of producing the reusable assets. Three models ([7], [8], and [20]) explicitly indicate the producer project bears the cost of developing reusable software. In two of these models ([7], [8]), the consumers are charged for a portion of the infrastructure costs although they are not charged for the producers' cost of creating the assets.

Most of the models (71%) do not account for time value of money. Only five models ([17], [18], [19], [12], and [20]) take this aspect into consideration.

Only two of the models (12%) take into account increased profit from shortened time-to-market and risk from reuse ([18] and [19]).

Most models (65%) do not explicitly account for the maintenance phase. Some models take only the producer's maintenance costs and not the consumers' maintenance savings into consideration.

Many of the models (59%) do not account for the overhead costs of reuse. In the models that do, definitions of overhead range from only the reuse library to any investments in the reuse infrastructure such as tool purchases or domain modeling [8].

While the commonalities discussed in the previous section may indicate that researchers are arriving at similar models independently, it may also suggest that we direct our efforts at forging new ground in reuse economics. Five areas for further research in reuse economics are recommended.

12A.7   Recommendations for Further Research

Based on the 17-model analysis here and lessons drawn from experience, five particular areas are identified for further reuse economics research:

1) *Develop better data collection methods.* While we may develop the most elegant models, they are of little use if we cannot collect the appropriate data to the level of accuracy that we desire. We need to develop methods to collect the necessary data for use in the models.

2) *Collect data to identify the cost drivers.* An area that is still relatively unidentified are the cost drivers of software reuse. We are just beginning to collect data on the additional cost to create reusable software by life cycle phase, cost to reuse, and so forth. Our understanding of the areas that consume most of our resources in reusing software is sparse. We do not know whether the current data el-

ements in our reuse economic models capture 70%, 80%, or 90% of the costs and benefits that result from reuse. This is important as it will help us identify the key data elements that should be explicitly expressed in our models.

3) *Collect data to identify the cost savings.* While there has been some data collected on cost savings, we need to continue identifying these savings at a finer level of granularity. Doing so will enable us to obtain a better understanding of the cost/benefit tradeoff of various methods and technologies for reuse.

4) *Apply economic models.* While 17 models were examined in this study, only some of them explicitly indicate that they have been applied. We need to apply and analyze the results from these models for their validity. We also need to apply them in order to test their practicality in the field, and assure that they are not simply theoretical models.

5) *Link cost prediction to cost return on investment models.* Eventually, there should be an evaluation and linkage of cost prediction models (e.g., COCOMO-type) to reuse ROI models so that we may be able to predict our costs with reuse to some level of accuracy as well as determine our return on investment so that we can decide which reuse strategy, if any, to pursue.

12A.8   Deciding on an Economic Model

When deciding which economic model to use, it is important to understand the characteristics of the reuse program on which the model is to be applied. We discuss several distinguishing features of economic models which will help determine the most suitable model to use. In Fig. 12–7, we map these features to our set of economic models. Although models which possess all features may be the most detailed, they are also the most difficult to implement because of the very large number of data elements that need to be collected. In deciding which model to use or create, the user should take into consideration not only the model's features, but the tradeoff between the amount of data required and the level of detail desired in the model.

The time value of money takes into account the saying that "a dollar today is worth more than a dollar tomorrow." It accounts for the fact that most investments have an alternative use, and therefore an alternative rate of return. Generally, if the reuse program is expected to be a long-term effort, then taking into account the time value of money is desirable.

Uncertainty or risk refers to the likelihood that a cash flow in a given year will actually occur. For example, we may be more certain of the reuses of a given asset in the current and next year but increasingly uncertain of its reuses in subsequent years. One of the ways to account for this uncertainty is to assess a likelihood of occurrence for the cash flow, e.g., 75% chance that there will be two reuses in the next year. This probabilistic assessment is multiplied against the cash flow to obtain the expected value of the cash inflow from reuse savings for that year. Such an uncertainty or risk feature is desirable in an economic model if the respondent ex-

Comparison of Reuse Economic Models

Model	Time Value of Money	Risk	Increased Profit	Maintenance Phase	Overhead Costs
Barnes and Bollinger (1991)	N	N	N	N	Y[1]
Bollinger and Pfleeger (1990)	N	N	N	N	Y[2]
Bowes (1992) Acquisition	N	N	N	Y[3]	Y[4]
Bowes (1992) Direction Level	N	N	N	Y	Y[5]
Frazier (1993)	N	N[6]	N	N[6]	Y[7]
Gaffney and Cruickshank (1992)	N	N	N	N	Y[8]
Gaffney and Durek (1988)	N	N	N	N	N
Guerrieri, et al, (1989)	Y	N[6]	N	Y[3]	N
Kang and Levy (1989)	N	N	N	N	N
Lim (1992)	Y	Y	Y	N[6]	N[6]
Malan and Wentzel (1993)	Y	Y	Y	Y	Y
Margono and Rhoads (1992)	N	N	N	N	N
Mayobre (1991)	N	N	N	N	Y[9]
NATO (1991)	Y	N	N	Y[3]	N
Poulin & Caruso (1993)	Y	N	N	Y	N
Raymond and Hollis (1991)	N	N	N	N	Y[4]
Schimsky (1992)	N	N	N	N	Y[4]

1. Reuse investments defined as "any costs that do not directly support the completion of an activity's primary development goals but are instead intended to make one or more work products of that activity easier to reuse."

2. Investment is defined as "the total cost of resources applied specifically to making the product or set of products reusable."

3. Includes producer's maintenance costs only.

4. Includes library overhead costs only.

5. Explicitly includes domain analyses, common architectures, and education costs.

6. Mentioned in the text of the paper but not explicitly included in the model.

7. Explicitly includes "any investments in the reuse infrastructure, such as tool purchases or domain modeling."

8. Considers the cost of domain engineering "the set of activities that is involved in the creation of reusable software objects (RSOs) that can be employed in a number of specific software systems or application systems."

9. The database cost (DBC) includes database maintenance costs (system backup, configuration) and librarian activities (reworking reusable assets to make them visible to potential users, identifying users' needs, component purchases, etc.).

FIGURE 12–7   Comparison of reuse economic models.

pects there to be significant uncertainty and he or she is willing to assess a likelihood of occurrence for the cash flows.

Increased profit refers to the additional revenues net of costs (e.g., distribution costs, cost of goods sold, taxes) as a result of reuse. Such additional sales may be due to shortened time-to-market or additional features and functionality which results in greater sales of products and/or services. Several models have been suggested in estimating the increased profit from shortened time-to-market in general and from reuse in particular [2]. Such a feature in a reuse economic model is desirable only if the organization implementing reuse is a commercial entity and where reuse results in additional revenues of significance.

Economic models which take into account the maintenance phase recognize that reuse has effects which extend beyond the development phase. Indeed, since the maintenance phase accounts for approximately 80% of the costs over the life of a system, the economics of this phase should not be overlooked. Organizations which expect a long system life cycle would desire an economic model which takes into account the maintenance phase.

Overhead costs account for the costs associated with the reuse library, architecture, training, management, etc. Essentially, these items are indirect costs. While some reuse economic models account for overhead costs beyond the library, most do not. Reuse programs which incur and wish to account for costs beyond that of a reuse library would desire this feature in their economic model.

Note

A previous version of this appendix was presented and published as a paper at The Fourth International Conference on Software Reuse, held April 23–26, 1996, in Orlando, Florida. The economic model version presented in this book is an adaptation of [18] and takes into account the time value of money, risk, increased profit, maintenance phase and overhead costs.

References

1. "A Survey of Reuse Economic Models," Lombard Hill Group, Corporate Report No: LH-12001, For more information, contact www.lombardhill.com or reuse@hotmail.com.
2. R. A. Malan, "Software Reuse: A Business Perspective," Hewlett Packard, Palo Alto, CA, Hewlett-Packard Technical Report, Feb., 1993.
3. J. Margono and T. E. Rhoads, "Software reuse economics: cost-benefit analysis on a large-scale Ada project," *International Conference on Software Engineering*, pp. 338–48, May, 1992.
4. B. Stevens, "Linking Software Re-Engineering and Reuse: An Economic Motivation," *CASE Trends*, pp. 24–36, Mar., 1993.
5. B. H. Barnes and T. B. Bollinger, "Making reuse cost-effective," *IEEE Software*, vol. 8, no. 1, pp. 13–24, Jan., 1991.
6. R. J. Bowes, T. R. Huber, and R. O. Saisi, "Informal Technical Report for the Software Technology for Adaptable, Reliable Systems (STARS) Acquisition Handbook—Final," Central Archive for Reusable Defense Software (CARDS), DSD Laboratories, Inc. for Air Force Materiel Command, Hanscom AFB, MA, Oct. 30, 1992.
7. R. J. Bowes, T. R. Huber, and R. O. Saisi, "Informal Technical Report for the Software Technology for Adaptable, Reliable Systems (STARS) Direction Level

Handbook—Final," Central Archive for Reusable Defense Software (CARDS), DSD Laboratories, Inc. for Air Force Materiel Command, Hanscom AFB, MA, Nov. 20, 1992.

8. T. Frazier, "Economics of Software Working Group," *2nd Annual West Virginia Reuse and Education and Training Workshop*, Oct. 25–27, 1993.

9. J. E. Gaffney, Jr. and R. D. Cruickshank, "A general economics model of software reuse," *International Conference on Software Engineering*, pp. 327–37, May, 1992.

10. K. C. Kang and L. S. Levy, "Software methodology in the harsh light of economics," *Information and Software Technology*, vol. 31, no. 5, pp. 239–50, June, 1989.

11. G. Mayobre, "Using Code Reusability Analysis to Identify Reusable Components from the Software Related to an Application Domain," *4th Annual Workshop on Software Reuse*, Nov. 18–22, 1991.

12. NATO, "Standard for Management of a Reusable Software Component Library," NATO Communications and Information Systems Agency, Aug. 18, 1991.

13. G. E. Raymond and D. M. Hollis, "Software reuse economics model," *WADAS '91/Summer SIGAda Meeting. Eighth Annual Washington Ada Symposium/Summer SIGAda Meeting Software: Foundation for Competitiveness. Proceedings*, pp. 141–55, June, 1991.

14. D. Schimsky, "Software Reuse—Some Realities," *Vitro Technical Journal*, vol. 10, no. 1, pp. 47–57, Summer, 1992.

15. T. B. Bollinger and S. L. Pfleeger, "The Economics of Software Reuse," Contel Technology Center, Chantilly, VA, Tech. Report CTC-TR-89-014, Dec. 13, 1989.

16. J. E. Gaffney and T. A. Durek, "Software Reuse—Key to Enhanced Productivity: Some Quantitative Models," Software Productivity Consortium, Herndon, VA, Tech. Report SPC-TR-88-015, Apr., 1988.

17. E. Guerrieri, L. A. Lashway, and T. B. Ruegsegger, " An Acquisition Strategy for Populating a Software Reuse Library," *National Conference on Software Reusability*, July 19–20, 1989.

18. W. C. Lim, "A Cost-Justification Model for Software Reuse," *5th Annual Workshop for Institutionalizing Software Reuse*, Oct. 26-29, 1992.

19. R. A. Malan and K. Wentzel, "Economics of Reuse Revisited," Hewlett-Packard Laboratories, Palo Alto, CA, Technical Report, HPL-93-31, Apr., 1993.

20. J. S. Poulin and J. M. Caruso, "A reuse metrics and return on investment model," *Proceedings Advances in Software Reuse. Selected Papers from the Second International Workshop on Software Reusability (Cat. No. 93TH0495-2)*, pp. 152-66, Mar. 24–26, 1993.

DECIDING ON REUSE
AS A STRATEGY

The decision to implement reuse within many organizations is usually made without any formal analysis of whether reuse is the proper development strategy to pursue. Although such an analysis is by no means a prerequisite for practicing reuse, a rigorous investigation of its potential relative to alternatives will help ensure its proper prioritization among the organization's strategic initiatives. We introduce in this chapter the concept of strategy-driven reuse, the deliberate choice and implementation of reuse as a software development strategy for the purpose of gaining competitive advantage. Because of this benefit, commercial organizations with the appropriate resources and capabilities should consider strategy-driven reuse.

Most organizations will progress through several levels of reuse before reaching the strategy-driven level. We begin this chapter by describing the three levels of reuse that typically (but not necessarily) precede strategy-driven reuse. (For further reading on other models, see Appendix 13-A.) We will then spend the remainder of this chapter expanding this concept and discussing the decision process important to choosing reuse as a competitive software engineering strategy.

13.1   Levels of Reuse

Ad Hoc.   Whether or not they recognize it, most organizations already practice some degree of reuse (Fig. 13–1). Often, these reuse efforts are short-term solutions that are unplanned and scattered across different groups. Called ad hoc reuse, this activity is primarily directed at reuse of code. It begins when a software engineer recognizes functional similarities between code he had previously written and code he needs for a current project. Overtime, he may store repeatedly used rou-

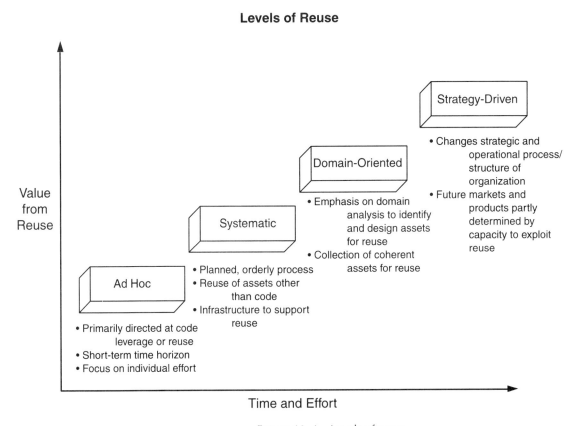

FIGURE 13–1   Levels of reuse.

tines in a personal library and share them with fellow engineers in the group. Currently, most organizations practice reuse at the ad hoc level.

Systematic Reuse.   Unlike ad hoc reuse, systematic reuse is not driven by spontaneous demand but rather by a careful and well-coordinated planning process. It is typically preceded by a detailed assessment by the organization to determine what types of assets are needed. Resources are specifically allocated for the establishment of a reuse program, which may include the creation and management of reusable assets, a central library, review boards, software standards, and reuse metrics. Such an undertaking usually requires the hiring of additional software engineers, managers, and perhaps, a librarian. A concentrated effort is made to spread awareness of the assets throughout the organization.

Domain-Oriented Reuse. Domain-oriented reuse is a specialized form of systematic reuse which focuses on identifying and designing assets within the context of existing and future business areas. Domains, or areas of specialization, are analyzed to create a definition of functions, objects, data, and their relationships. This analysis, called a domain model, helps an organization decide how reuse should be implemented. By analyzing each domain, organizations can identify areas of commonality to determine where reusable assets can add the greatest value. Like systematic reuse, domain-oriented reuse is a carefully planned process with resources specifically allocated for this purpose. The difference lies in the latter's emphasis on domains and domain analysis.

Each of the reuse utilization levels described above focuses on identifying and reusing assets for existing and future products. Efforts are aimed at ways of exploiting reuse among the organization's set of current and future software products. For some organizations, reuse at the systematic or domain-oriented levels is sufficient. However, for those in highly competitive environments, strategy-driven reuse can potentially offer the organization a competitive advantage.

Strategy-Driven Reuse. The final level of reuse, strategy-driven, encompasses a broader view of the organization and its strategic direction. As we defined earlier, strategy-driven reuse is the choice and implementation of reuse within the context of how the organization intends to compete in the marketplace (see Fig. 13–1). For a commercial market organization, this forward-thinking strategy influences which businesses or product lines it ought to pursue in order to best take advantage of reuse. Under the preceding three levels, products are decided first, followed by an appropriate reuse strategy for the development of those products. Strategy-driven reuse incorporates both decisions into one. Future products are determined in part by their capacity to exploit reuse. Managers ask themselves, "What businesses/product lines shall I enter that will enable me to exploit reuse?" In this case, reuse is not relegated to "automating" software development, but rather, changes the fundamental strategic and operational process of the organization.

Let us further clarify this distinction with an example. Suppose two firms, A and B, manufacture portable ovens. Both intend to compete in the marketplace as the lowest-cost producer. Firm A manufactures both toaster ovens and microwave ovens. In an effort to exploit economies of scope (reuse), the engineers in firm A examine its two products for commonality and discover that parts of the chassis are similar. Through the sharing of design and manufacturing costs, total production costs drop 10%.

Firm B chooses a strategy-driven approach, carefully analyzing its manufacturing and reuse capabilities to determine potential new product lines. A combined effort by the engineering, marketing, and strategic planning departments leads to a deliberate decision to manufacture portable heaters, a product that uses the same heating elements as those used in toaster ovens. By entering this market, firm B can lower its total production costs by 25%. Through economies of scale in manufacturing and design, this cost reduction will make firm B the lowest-cost producer of toaster ovens *and* portable heaters. Potential competitors would be at a cost disadvantage unless they also diversified their product lines and businesses. This example illustrates how a firm can maximize design cost amortization and economies of scale by carefully choosing the product lines and/or businesses in which it competes.

Strategy-driven reuse attempts not only to optimize reuse among existing product lines, but also to maximize reuse in the context of the organization's goals and strategy by deliberately entering businesses that take full advantage of reuse. Consequently, strategically implementing reuse is not confined to the engineering laboratory, but rather, is the result of an alliance between the engineering, marketing, and strategic planning functions of the organization. Strategy-driven reuse must be an explicit goal of the entire organization. As shown in Fig. 13–2, there are three levels of emphasis for software reuse: cost reduction, reuse-enabled, and strategy-driven.

Most organizations practice at the lowest level: cost-reduction reuse. At this level, efforts are focused on how reuse can reduce software development and maintenance costs (via higher productivity and quality) for the organization.

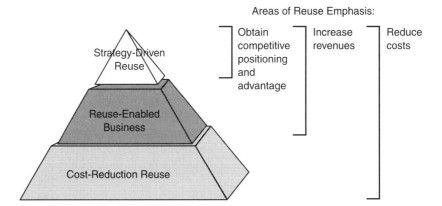

Organizational Emphases for Reusing Software

Strategy-Driven Reuse: "How can we obtain competitive positioning by entering markets and/or creating new products through reuse?"
Reuse-Enabled Business: "How can we reduce the time-to-market for our products and what new products can we develop with our reusable assets?"
Cost-Reduction Reuse: "How can we reduce the development and maintenance costs of our products through reuse?"

FIGURE 13–2   Organizational emphases for reusing software.

At the next level are those organizations that have utilized reuse not only as a cost-cutting tool but also as a means of increasing revenues, i.e., reuse as a business enabler. An organization utilizes reusable assets to 1) shorten the time-to-market, capture a greater share of the marketplace, and realize revenues earlier than would have been possible without reuse; or 2) create new products and/or add functionality to existing products to generate profits that would not have occurred without reuse. For example, a software asset designed by one organization to be reusable was intended for a product line X. The functionality provided by the reusable asset was subsequently offered as an option on product line Y. Since then, the majority of the purchasers of product Y have chosen the option. A significant portion of product line Y sales have been attributed in part to the functionality provided by the reusable asset. Note that with reuse-enabled business, cost-reduction can still occur.

The next level is strategy-driven reuse in which organizations enter markets and/or create new products driven by intent to utilize reuse for the purpose of obtaining a competitive position in the market. The organization does not implement reuse after the products have been decided upon, but rather incorporates reuse into their decision of which businesses to enter and which product lines to pursue. Reuse is used for competitive positioning and advantage. Because reuse potential exists when similar but not matching systems are desired, pursuing markets or product lines where this potential can be exploited enables the organization to obtain a strategic cost advantage across multiple markets or product lines. Some organizations have obtained a competitive position within a market by developing a reusable core in its product and allowing its clients to "customize" the product to their needs. By doing so, the organization differentiates itself from its competitors through "mass customization" [1] of its products. Mass customization is the combining of processes or tasks to "tailor-make" a product or service to the unique tastes of the consumer. Finally, reuse frees up resources that the organization can utilize for competitive advantage such as adding features to the product or bolstering its product support. We illustrate strategy-driven reuse with several real-life examples.

- L.M. Ericsson of Sweden developed and utilized modular, reusable software that could be combined to meet the diverse needs of international telephone systems. By utilizing reusable software in such a manner, Ericsson was able to quickly amortize development costs and "compete globally in small systems" [2].

- One multinational organization first identified the markets where it wanted to offer systems. They deliberately identified a core set of common software and designed this set to be reusable across the systems offered. They also designed another set of software to enable the systems to be customized for a given market. By doing so, the organization straddled multiple markets and acquired a strategic cost advantage over the competitors in each of those markets.

- Another organization in the video instruments industry was exploring opportunities in a new market. Initial market analyses indicated that the market size was not sufficient to justify the required investment to launch the product. However, after examining a closely related market, it was determined that products which could potentially be sold in the two markets could share functionality that could be provided by reusable software. A decision was made to pursue the market opportunities in both markets.

A manager who is strategy-driven will determine whether reuse is or can be an appropriate software engineering strategy. This decision should be made in a broad context that starts with an analysis of the goals and needs of both the organization and the industry in which it competes. After this analysis has been done, alternative business and product strategies are evaluated and one is chosen on the basis of how well it fulfills these needs. Different software development strategies are then considered in the context of the industry, the organization, and the chosen product or business strategy. The choice of a software development strategy is made only after these goals and needs are understood. As we shall see, this decision process is actually a decision cycle (see Fig. 13–3). Typically, several iterations through the cycle are necessary in order to determine the optimal strategy. Let us now analyze each step of the decision cycle in more detail.

13.2   Competitive Software Engineering—A Process for Deciding on a Software Development Strategy

Any strategic plan begins with an assessment of an organization's needs, goals, and competition. Competition clearly plays a definitive role in driving organizational goals and needs. For example, a Department of Defense contractor may seek to lower costs in order to effectively compete for a contract. A commercial software vendor may desire to shorten the time-to-market for its product in order to establish itself in the marketplace before its competitors do. An in-house MIS department may want to avoid a backlog of applications programming in order to prevent losing internal customers to external application developers. Competition does not limit itself to the organization's product. It may also include, for example, vying to hire the best or highly specialized software engineers. Because competition so heavily influences a firm's goals and needs, it should be an explicit and integral part of formulating a software engineering strategy.

Competitive software engineering is an integrated approach to software development that is attuned to the competitive demands of the marketplace. A strategy that is based on competitive software engineering acknowledges external competition, recognizes organizational assets, and provides a plan to align the organization's resources as a formidable weapon against this competition. This approach will enable us to formulate a software development strategy that will provide competitive advantage.

**Decision Cycle for Formulating a Competitive
Software Engineering Strategy**

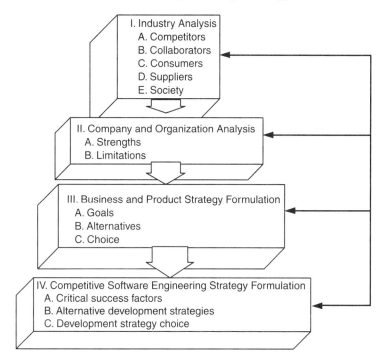

FIGURE 13–3   Competitive software engineering strategy decision cycle.

Fig. 13–3 outlines the flow of analysis in formulating a competitive software engineering strategy. We begin with a complete analysis of the firm's position in its industry and in society. The results of this analysis are then incorporated into the company's assessment of strengths and weaknesses. From this assessment, potential business and product lines are investigated and chosen. Finally, a suitable competitive software engineering strategy to fulfill the above objectives is formulated. We will illustrate this process with an example of a company, Firm 1. Firm 1 produces financial management software for personal investors.

13.3   Industry Analysis

Competitors.   An integral part of formulating a competitive software engineering strategy is to determine who existing and potential competitors are and what strategies they are employing. Understanding a competitor's strategy will help the organization position itself vis a vis the competition. For example, if a competitor's strategy for dominance in the market is low-cost production, can reuse help the organization achieve lower costs than its competitors by straddling multiple markets?

Through its industry analysis, Firm 1 determines that Firm 2 is the current leader in the market that Firm 1 is considering entering. Firm 2 differentiates itself from the competition by emphasizing its product's superior analytical features.

Questions to consider:
- Who are my existing and potential competitors?
- What are their strategies?
- How are they differentiating themselves?
- Given the above, where can I best position my firm?

Collaborators.   Collaboration can be a form of competition when it enables the participants to be in a better position vis a vis their competition. Forming an alliance with another organization may be desirable because it enables resources to be pooled and development costs of expensive technologies to be amortized more quickly. Such an alliance may allow sharing operations that are subject to economies of scale, such as sales personnel or distribution channels. Collaboration can also affect the choice of a software development strategy. For example, a partnership between two firms to create software products which share data may potentially benefit from standardization of data structures and protocols that can be supported through reuse. Or, an alliance can exploit commonality between each partner's software product by sharing reusable assets and thereby lowering the cost of software development. In our example, Firm 1 identifies another firm with whom it may potentially collaborate by making its own personal financial software compatible with the collaborating firm's product.

Questions to consider:
- Does my firm have existing alliances that could provide a competitive advantage?
- Are there potential alliances that should be investigated?
- Who are my competitors' existing and potential collaborators?

Consumers.   Defining and understanding the consumer market and its trends is essential in formulating a competitive software engineering strategy. A firm may wish to appeal to a certain segment of the market by emphasizing certain features in their software products. For example, if product reliability is important for the targeted market segment, the organization should choose a software development strategy that will maximize reliability in its products. Firm 1 commissions an extensive marketing study on the concerns and priorities of potential consumers of a personal financial software package.

Questions to consider:
- What is the consumer market or market segment my firm should target?
- What are their needs and wants?

Suppliers. Suppliers provide raw materials needed to create a software product. In a software organization, these materials include hardware, software tools and environments, and, of course, labor. The availability and cost of supplies will affect the firm's choice of products and its software development strategy. For example, scarcity of specialized software engineers may limit the range of products a firm wishes to offer. Thus, a software development strategy must be chosen that takes into consideration this scarce resource. Such is the case with Firm 1, whose most valuable resource is the professionals who possess both an engineering and a financial background. Since the supply of such individuals is limited, Firm 1 chooses a strategy that will leverage the expertise of the engineers in their employ.

Questions to consider:
- What supplies are required for my firm's potential products?
- What are their costs and availability?
- How does this information affect my choice of a product and software development strategy?

Society. Society refers to the legal, regulatory, institutional, social, and political factors and trends that impact a business or product [3]. Examples include the acceptance of software standards, establishment of research consortiums, and the intellectual property laws that affect software. Because Firm 1's proposed personal financial software package calculates the capital gains tax on the sale of securities, the firm needs to keep abreast of federal and state tax developments that may impact its product.

Questions to consider:
- What legal, regulatory, institutional, social or political factors and trends impact my business or product?
- Which existing or new products will thrive within the current or future societal environment?

13.4 Company and Organization Analysis

Strengths. An honest assessment of an organization's strengths is a vital part of strategy formulation. Specifically, a firm needs to identify and capitalize on its core competencies, or "the collective learning in the organization" [4]. A software reuse development strategy may help leverage organizational core competencies. For example, if an organization is particularly skilled at developing firmware that handles sample analysis for mass spectrometers, this expertise may be exploited by making the firmware reusable for other spectroscopic instruments. One of Firm 1's strengths is its expertise in creating and maintaining one of its existing products, a financial management package for nonprofit agencies.

Questions to consider:
- What are my organization's greatest strengths and how can they be used to gain competitive advantage?
- What strengths would be most difficult for a competitor to emulate or supplant?

Limitations. Recognizing limitations and weaknesses impacts the choice of a business and software engineering strategy. Identifying these weaknesses will enable the organization to either choose not to compete in that business or to take steps toward fortifying the area of weakness. Firm 1's lack of proper distribution channels is a major obstacle to increasing its current market share. Thus, it needs to open new avenues of distribution and strengthen its current channel relationships.

Questions to consider:
- What are my firm's limitations and where do the greatest weaknesses lie?
- Are these weakness in areas where strength is critical?
- Can reuse or another software development strategy turn these weaknesses into strengths?

13.5   Business and Product Strategy

Goals. Only after analyzing industry factors and identifying the company's areas of competence and weaknesses will the organization be in the proper position to determine its goals. In establishing a set of goals, an organization needs to consider reasonableness, timeliness, and achievibility. The goal should be well-defined and explicit so that the firm's success or failure can be measured accordingly. Examples of organizational goals are:

- attain a 20% compound annual growth rate in revenues for the next three years;
- reduce costs by 20% in the upcoming fiscal year;
- achieve a 15% return on equity.

After examining the industry and itself, Firm 1 establishes a long-term goal of becoming the market leader in personal financial software, and a short-term objective of attaining a 15% compound annual growth rate in revenues within five years.

Questions to consider:

- What are my organization's achievable goals in the context of its strengths, weaknesses and its industry position?
- How will I know when these goals are achieved?

Business and Product Strategy Alternatives. The business strategy dictates how the organization intends to accomplish the goals defined in the previous step. All the available strategies should be examined (and compared with the current strategy if there is one) to determine the strategy with the highest probability of meeting its objectives. Firm 1 is weighing the following business/product strategies: emulate the current market leader's strategy of emphasizing certain analytical features; market its product as a "no-frills," low-cost personal financial software package; or stress its product's user-friendliness and compatibility with a collaborator's individual income tax software product.

Questions to consider:

- What strategies are available that will best meet the organization's goals?
- What strategies are my competitors pursuing and have they been successful?

Business and Product Strategy Choice. Once each alternative has been identified, its potential feasibility, likelihood of success, and expected payoffs must

Risk/Reward Tradeoff for the Three Strategies

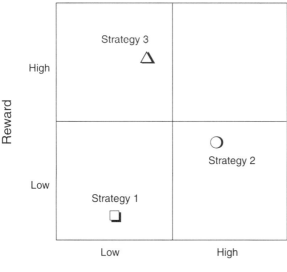

FIGURE 13–4 Risk/reward tradeoffs.

be carefully assessed. A strategy can then be chosen based on the risk/reward trade-off. Firm 1 concludes that if it emulates the current market leader's strategy, it can, at best, carve out only a 10% market share in five years. If it pursues the low-cost strategy, it can achieve a 25% market share in five years. The market survey results that Firm 1 commissioned reveal that consumers are concerned with "ease of use" and a product's ability to enable the user to construct "what if" income tax scenarios. Armed with this information, Firm 1 examines the third potential strategy of differentiation by emphasizing its product's user-friendliness and compatibility with a popular personal income tax software package. With this strategy, Firm 1 predicts that it can capture at least 40% of the market in five years. Fig. 13–4 summarizes these strategies and their risk/reward payoffs. Firm 1 determines that the best choice given these alternatives is strategy 3.

Question to consider:

- What is the likelihood of success and potential reward for each alternative strategy?

13.6   Competitive Software Engineering Strategy Formulation

Critical Success Factors.   Once a business strategy has been chosen, a plan must be mapped out to best ensure its successful implementation. Identifying critical success factors (CSFs), elements or processes which must occur to achieve success, is an important step in formulating this plan. Examples of business-critical success factors are extensive distribution channels, outstanding field installation support, and excellent on-line product support. Product quality critical success factors depend largely upon the application and emphasis of the software application. Examples of product quality critical success factors are shown in Fig. 13–5 [5]. Firm 1's product quality critical success factors, given their chosen strategy, are usability and interoperability.

Question to consider:

- What are the critical success factors for my chosen business or product strategy?

Alternative Development Strategies.   We now come to the final steps in this process: the investigation and selection of software development strategies that will fulfill the established goals and satisfy the CSFs within the framework of the chosen business strategy. Such strategies (for software development) include reuse, performance modeling, and prototyping. Every step of the decision process from industry analysis onward will affect the choice of a software development strategy. For example, trends in the industry for greater interoperability may emphasize the use of standards in the development strategy. Or perhaps the organization's core competencies may be the focus of the development strategy. Some strategies to address CSFs are shown in Fig. 13–6.

Examples of Software Product Quality Critical Success Factors

	Emphasis of Software Product	Product Quality Critical Success Factors
✚	• Life sustenance (Heart monitoring system)	• Reliability • Correctness • Testability
✈	• Long life cycle (Aviation control system)	• Supportability • Flexibility • Portability
🕐	• Real-time application (Stock quotation system)	• Performance • Reliability • Correctness
🚫	• Processing of classified information (National security information system)	• Integrity
✊	• Interrelating systems (University registration and tuition billing systems)	• Interoperability

FIGURE 13–5 Software product quality critical success factors. *Source*: Adapted from: J. Vincent, et al., *Software Quality Assurance*, Prentice-Hall, Upper Saddle River, N.J., 1988, p. 22.

Questions to consider:

- What are the alternative software development strategies appropriate for my organization?
- How will each strategy satisfy the CSFs?

Development Strategy Choice. The final step in the decision process is to choose the best development strategy(ies) for the organization given the analysis in each step shown in Fig. 13–3. The development strategy choice should be made on the basis of

1. its expected cost/benefit;
2. how well it addresses the critical success factors;
3. how well it fits the current organization;
4. its risk/reward tradeoff.

Sometimes the choice(s) will be obvious. More often, however, a particular strategy will not be able to address all issues. Thus, the advantages and disadvan-

Examples of Strategies to Achieve
Product Quality Critical Success Factors

Product Quality Critical Success Factor	Possible Strategies
• Functionality	• Prototyping • Quality Function Deployment
• Correctness	• Formal Methods • Reuse
• Usability	• Training • Prototyping
• Reliability	• Formal Methods • Reuse
• Performance	• Performance Modeling
• Supportability	• Documentation • Modularization
• Localizability	• Late Binding • Parameterization
• Flexibility	• Modularization • Standardization
• Integrity	• Passwords • Privileged Accounts
• Testability	• Modularization • Simplification
• Portability	• Conditional Compilation • Modularization
• Interoperability	• Standardization

FIGURE 13–6 Strategies to achieve product quality critical success factors.

tages of each strategy must be weighed carefully, and tradeoffs made in accordance to the organization's priorities.

After having carefully evaluated these factors, Firm 1 chooses to pursue reuse and training as its software development strategies. Reuse capitalizes on the firm's software assets which are already used in the firm's existing financial management package. Reuse also aids interoperability of the personal financial software with its collaborator's individual income tax software product and promotes usability by sharing its partner's user interface. Usability will also be enhanced by a developing a self-tutorial training module as part of the software package. With these strategies, Firm 1 will be able to reduce its costs, command a large market share, and thereby achieve a higher annual growth rate.

Question to ask:
- Which of the feasible alternative software development strategies best meet the company/organization's goals?

Recall that the decision process for formulating a competitive software engineering strategy is iterative. Each step of the process is not necessarily independent of the others. For example, the choice of reuse as a development strategy may affect the business or product strategy alternatives or the organizational goals or both.

Firm 1, recognizing the potential reuse opportunities, revisits its product strategy and decides to expand its current product line as part of its new strategy. Among the new products is a software package which certified financial planners can use to analyze their clients' financial status. This new strategy will help Firm 1 fulfill its short- and long-term goals.

We have shown in this chapter the overall process for deciding on reuse as a strategy. This type of analysis is suitable for large corporations as well as small in-house engineering laboratories. Large firms that have decided on reuse (or some development strategy) will need to identify groups within the firm that are potential candidates for reuse. In the next section, we will discuss a process that will help an organization make that determination.

Summary

Organizations practice reuse at different levels. Those at the three lower levels, ad hoc, systematic, and domain-oriented, attempt to optimize reuse among existing and planned products or domains. Organizations at the strategy-driven level obtain competitive advantage and positioning by incorporating reuse into their decisions about which markets to enter and which products to develop.

To determine whether or not reuse is the proper software development strategy to pursue, we utilize concepts in competitive software engineering, an integrated approach to software development that is attuned to the competitive demands of the marketplace. First, a framework is established by identifying and analyzing the organization's goals, strengths, and limitations, its market, and its competitive environment. Based on these analyses, possible business or product strategies are formulated and one or more are chosen that help achieve the organization goals. Finally, a development strategy is chosen. Following this choice, each step of the decision cycle should be reevaluated to ensure that it is consistent with the chosen development strategy.

References

1. B. J. Pine, B. Victor, and A. C. Boynton, "Making mass customization work," *Harvard Business Review*, vol. 71, pp. 108–111, Sept.–Oct. 1993.
2. T. Hout, M. E. Porter, and E. Rudden, "How Global Companies Win Out," *Harvard Business Review*, vol. 60, pp. 98–108 : Charts, Sept.–Oct. 1982.
3. M. E. Porter, *Competitive Strategy*. New York, N.Y.: The Free Press, 1980.
4. C. K. Prahalad and G. Hamel, "The Core Competence of the Corporation," *Harvard Business Review*, vol. 68, pp. 79–91 : Charts, May–June 1990.
5. J. Vincent, A. Waters, and J. Sinclair, *Software Quality Assurance*. Englewood Cliffs, N.J.: Prentice-Hall, 1988.

13-A

A SURVEY OF REUSE AND MATURITY MODELS

13A.1 Introduction

Multiple models for software reuse have been developed since the Software Engineering Institute's (SEI) introduction of the Capability Maturity Model (CMM). A reuse maturity model is a set of stages through which an organization progresses. Each stage possesses a certain set of characteristics and brings the organization to a higher level of workproduct quality and productivity.

A maturity model specifies progressively higher levels to which organizations could aspire so that the resulting outcome would be increased quality, productivity and other desired outcomes in the organizations' output. Because of the widespread interest in the CMM, some organizations have been attempting to determine the relationship of reuse to that model. Other organizations have developed reuse maturity models that are independent of CMM. In this appendix, we review the SEI CMM, discuss its relationship with reuse, and survey several reuse maturity models.

13A.2 The Capability Maturity Model

As detailed below, the CMM was developed by Watts Humphrey. The model consists of five levels with each level building upon the previous one. A mature process indicates that the set of activities to develop software are linked and managed to consistently yield high-quality software within cost and schedule constraints.

Level 1. Initial

Characteristics:

- ad hoc;
- little formal structure;
- methods and tools not integrated.

Level 2. Repeatable

Characteristic:

- process appears to be under control except to meet evolving needs.

Level 3. Defined

Characteristics:

- software engineering base;
- few quality/productivity metrics;
- qualitative success.

Level 4. Managed

Characteristics:

- development products scrutinized;
- formal quality control function.

Level 5. Optimizing

Characteristics:

- development process scrutinized;
- statistical quality control;
- continuous quality improvement.

Source: Watts Humphrey "Characterizing the software process: A maturity framework," *IEEE Software*, vol. 5, no. 2, Mar. 1988.

13A.3   Reuse and the Capability Maturity Model

Researchers and practitioners have not agreed on the relationship between reuse and the CMM. Draft C of the CMM (version 2) contains an Organization Software Asset Commonality key process area at level 4 that addresses reuse.

Reuse can be practiced at multiple levels in the CMM. However, the benefits of reuse progressively increase as we practice reuse at higher levels of the CMM. The practice of reuse at the lower levels may not result in a net benefit. For example, an organization that practices reuse at the lower levels with a defect-prone software development process will propagate reusable assets with defects. Some benefit may be experienced from not having to create similar functionality, (which may be equally defect-ridden), and having to fix a defect only once. However, this benefit is offset by the likelihood that the reuse process itself is equally unsystematic and, therefore, the fixes may not be done or delivered properly.

Reuse implemented at the higher levels, however, will result in propagating high-quality assets. Both the development and reuse processes would be more systematic. Reuse will further improve the quality of the software asset by affording greater resources to be invested in the design and testing of the assets. In summary, some benefits can be achieved through reuse in a disorderly process but greater benefits can be attained at higher levels.

A study done by Mike Cusumano, *et al.* [1] of software factories in Japan show that reuse can and is being done successfully without being at level 5. They found that "successful companies (in Japan) don't necessarily implement practices in the SEI order of Level 1, then Level 2, etc." Cusumano notes that "companies we had visited had, for the most part, made software reuse an integral part of their development process. Yet SEI's model relegates software reuse to level 5. The model's implicit message is 'after you do everything else, consider implementing software reuse.' Many of the Japanese companies established different priorities because they had validated features of their production process. That is, they had measured the payoff of software reuse."

13A.4   A Survey of Reuse Maturity Models

In this section, we survey several reuse maturity models [2]: the Bassett model, the Bollinger model, the Cusumano model, the Koltun and Hudson model, the Griss model, and two Software Productivity Consortium models.

Bassett.   Paul Bassett [3] describes five maturity levels through which organizations evolve:

Level 1: Unaware.   The great majority of organizations are at this level, where what little reuse is practiced depends on individual developers pulling a design they used last week out of their desks.

Level 2: Latent.   These organizations are building systems by reusing vendor-supplied architectures implicitly. While they are not yet designing their own components, they are still achieving 70–80% reuse. (Percent reuse = the source code produced by common components/total source code = [approx.] work avoided due to reuse.)

Level 3: Project.   Beyond the vendor-supplied component architectures, developers at the project level create components for reuse within individual projects, achieving 80–90% reuse.

Level 4: Systematic. These organizations have institutionalized reuse to the point that at least 40% of the developers routinely use a common component architecture across projects. At this point, hard-core resistance to reuse begins to crumble. Reuse ranges from 90–95%.

Level 5: Cultural. The entire organization reflects the reuse culture. Reuse levels routinely exceed 95%.

Bollinger. Although not a maturity model, Terry Bollinger [4] describes a reuse scale which he developed and utilized to categorize software:

5- Commercial	Software that cannot only be reused, but sold.
4- Corporate	Software that can be used throughout a corporation.
3- Project	Software that can be used throughout a project.
2- Personal	Software that one person (author) can easily reuse.
1- Maintenance	Software that can be maintained at reasonable cost.
0- Throw-away	Software that is easier to rewrite than to maintain.

Cusumano. After analyzing a number of reuse programs in Japan, Michael Cusumano concluded that reusability can be placed along a continuum which ranges "from no reuse, because of no commonality in applications or stability in program architectures and functions, to various degrees of accidental or ad hoc reuse and then to systematic reuse, with categorizations of software going beyond application domain libraries to indexing software modules and designs by functional content [1]."

He describes a "reusability spectrum" with the following four reuse levels:

Level 1: None
> No commonality among projects;
> No stability in program architectures and functions;
> No design planning or management for multiple projects;
> No reuse support tools and libraries;
> No reuse promotion organization and incentives;
> Little or no measurable reuse.

Level 2: Some
> Some commonality among projects;
> Some stability in program architectures and functions;
> No design planning or management for multiple projects;
> No reuse support tools and libraries;
> No reuse promotion organization and incentives;
> Occasional but still ad hoc or accidental reuse.

Level 3: More
> Much commonality among projects;
> More stability in program architectures and functions;
> Some design planning or management for multiple projects;
> Reuse support tools and libraries;

No reuse promotion organization and incentives;
More frequent but not maximum reuse.

Level 4: Most
Much commonality among projects;
More stability in program architectures and functions;
Design planning or management for multiple projects;
Reuse support tools and libraries;
Reuse promotion organization and incentives;
Systematic and maximum reuse.

Koltun and Hudson.   Koltun and Hudson [5] of the Harris Corporation developed a reuse maturity model "to assess organizational processes instrumental to achieving high levels of reuse." Inspired by the SEI Maturity Model, Koltun and Hudson created the reuse maturity model to emphasize the processes needed to implement reuse and to deal with both technology and business issues. The Reuse Maturity Framework consists of five stages of reuse maturity:

Level 1: Initial/chaotic;
Level 2: Monitored;
Level 3: Coordinated;
Level 4: Planned;
Level 5: Ingrained.

The characteristics of each stage are described in Fig. 13–7. Koltun and Hudson break down each stage into further detail by investigating different aspects of reuse and, within each aspect, how reuse at each stage may appear. Fig. 13–8 summarizes these aspects and describes each reuse maturity level and the key events that may be necessary to progress to each succeeding level.

Cusumano *et al.* applied the Koltun and Hudson model to organizations in Japan and found the organizations to span from Level 2 to 4 [6]. They note several areas which they consider to be deficiencies with the model. For example, under the dimension of "legal, contractual, accounting considerations," treating software as a key capital asset is not necessarily conditional on having first developed a royalty scheme.

Griss.   Martin Griss's study of several projects within HP suggests a SEI-like process maturity model [7]:

1. No Reuse—Characterized by apathy, lack of knowledge, belief that reuse is not a significant part of solution.

Reuse Maturity Framework					
Dimensions of maturity	1. Initial/Chaotic	2. Monitored	3. Coordinated	4. Planned	5. Ingrained
Motivation/ culture	Reuse is discouraged	Reuse is noted indifferently reinforced, rewarded	Reuse is incentivized	Reuse is indoctrinated	Reuse is "the way we do business"
Planning for reuse	Nonexistent	Grassroots activity	Targets of opportunity	Business imperative	Part of a strategic plan
Breadth of reuse involvement	Individual worker	Work group	Department	Division	Enterprise
Responsibility for making reuse happen (advocacy + day-day-today management)	Individual initiative (personal goal; as time allows)	Shared initiative	Dedicated individual	Dedicated group	Corporate group (for visibility not control) with division liaisons
Process by which reuse is leveraged	Development process chaotic; unclear where reuse comes in	Reuse questions raised at design reviews (after the fact)	Design emphasis placed on reuse of off-the-shelf parts	Focus on developing families of products	All software products genericized for future reuse
Reuse inventory (assets)	Salvage yard (no apparent structure to collection)	Catalog identifies language-and platform-specific parts	Catalog organized along application-specific lines	Catalog includes generic data processing functions	Planned activity to acquire or develop missing pieces in catalog
Classification activity	Informal, individualized ("in the head," "in the drawer")	Multiple independent schemes for classifying parts	Single scheme, catalog published periodically	Some domain analyses performed to determine catagories	Formal, complete, consistent, timely classification
Technology support	Personal tools, if any	Lots of tools, e.g., configuration management, but not specialized to reuse	Classification aids and synthesis aids	Electronic library separate from development environment	Automated support integrated with development system
Metrics	No metrics on level of reuse, payoff, or cost of reuse	Number of lines of reused code factored into cost models	Manual tracking of reuse occurrences of catalog parts	Analyses performed to identify expected payoffs from developing reusable parts	All system utilities, software tools, and accounting mechanisms instrumented to track reuse
Legal, contractual, accounting considerations	Inhibitor to getting started	Internal accounting scheme for sharing costs, allocating benefits	Data rights and compensation issues resolved with customer	Royalty scheme for all suppliers and customers	Software treated as key capital asset

FIGURE 13–7   Koltun and Hudson's Reuse Maturity Framework. *Source:* P. Koltun and A. Hudson, "A Reuse Maturity Model," 4th Annual Workshop on Reuse, Herndon, VA, Nov. 1991.

Koltun and Hudson's Five Stages of Reuse Maturity

	Initial/Chaotic	Monitored	Coordinated	Planned	Ingrained
C h a r a c t e r i s t i c s	• Reuse is individualized, uncoordinated, unmonitored, etc. • High reliance on people reuse. • Frequent resistance to reuse. • Costs of reuse are "feared". • Short-term thinking.	• Managerial awareness of reuse activities, but little active promotion of reuse. • Costs of reuse known. • Basic definitions of reuse are agreed upon. • Reuse is viewed as a set of single point opportunities. • Individual achievements are rewarded. • General-purpose analyzers, configuration management tools, etc., combined to assess reuse levels.	• Organization responsible for reuse. • Product line domain analyses performed. • A key business strategy. • Part of annual operating plan objectives. • Investments made in reuse, payoffs expected. • Reuse tactics worked out. • Payoff of reuse is "known" and understood for a given domain. • Shared understanding of all the activities needed to support reuse. • Standardization on components. • Tools customized to support reuse.	• Life cycle view of reuse. All costs associated with a component's development and all savings from its reuse are reported. • Have all the data needed to decide which components to build/acquire. • Synergistic processes are in place to support and encourage reuse. • Reuse occurs across all functional areas.	• Corporation-wide view. • A discriminator in business success. • "The way we do business." • Outstanding successes have occurred. • All major obstacles to reuse have been removed. • All definitions, guidelines, standards, command media, are in place, enterprise-wide • Domain analyses performed across all product lines. • Fully integrated with development and reporting systems.
Motivation for advancement to next stage:		Recognition of competitive pressures	Technology support becomes available	Multi-year commitment; larger benefits sought five-year vision of where to target	Enhance competitive advantage; build leadership position.
Necessary Travel event:		General manager demands periodic progress reports	Specific annual operating plan objectives are set.	Business planning activity addresses life cycle costing.	Insitutionalization and acculturation.

FIGURE 13–8   Koltun and Hudson: Five Stages of Reuse Maturity. *Source:* P. Koltun and A. Hudson, "A Reuse Maturity Model," 4th Annual Workshop on Reuse, Herndon, VA, Nov. 1991.

2. Leverage—Characterized by cloning, scavenging source code of one product to create next; improved development cost and time-to-market, but proliferating copies lead to maintenance nightmare.

3. Ad hoc/opportunistic reuse—Selected modules extracted from leveraged systems, declared as frozen for reuse; however, as several products develop, increasing amounts of control are needed to ensure that gratuitous changes and redundant maintenance are not performed.

4. Systematic/managed reuse—Involves the introduction of a formal process, organizational changes to separate producers from users, establishment of a librarian and reuse management. Start of "develop for reuse" guidelines, workproduct certification guidelines.

5. Domain-specific reuse—Focus on formal design and development "for" and "with" reuse. Producers will invest in domain analysis, architectures, and increased coverage of entire product family. Users will design and build products within the constraints of the family design.

Software Productivity Consortium-1.   The Software Productivity Consortium [8] has developed a five-level reuse maturity model in conjunction with their Reuse Library Prototype (RLP 01.00):

Level 1: Ad hoc reuse

This level relies on individual initiative to reuse components between projects. Components are simple parts, consisting of fragments of requirements, design, test, and code, as available. The parts are rarely organized into complex structures, have unknown quality, and provide incompatible interfaces. Reuse libraries, if established, have inconsistent structure and management policies. Reuse of a part generally requires rework and risk.

Level 2: Repeatable reuse

This level represents the establishment of a repeatable process that formalizes the communication between the reusable component developer(s) and the reusers, making the risk of reusing a component known. Components are stored in a reuse library system with known and enforced policy and procedures. Components are complete, having the design, test, and implementation documentation necessary to understand and reuse the part. There should be no need to engage the original developer for explanation. Parts are of a known quality level and are determined by a defined quality evaluation process. Parts can be reused in a similar project context without reuser inspection or modification. Interfaces between parts are not necessarily consistent.

Level 3: Portable reuse

This refinement of repeatable reuse addresses the portability of reusable components to specific ranges of context. This is primarily due to the adoption and enforcement of coding styles to remove host development and target environment system dependencies. The parts are of a high-quality level but may still have inconsistent interfaces.

Level 4: Architectural reuse

This refinement of portable reuse addresses the ability to design large architectural components for reuse. Components are building blocks of standard architectures with consistent interfaces. Behavior is parameterized for a wide range of contexts, supporting families of components.

Level 5: Systematic reuse

This fully integrated, reuse-oriented development process considers reuse throughout the development life cycle. Reusable components are built as a side effect of the development process. Components and structures are highly parameterized, making innovative uses possible with minimum modification.

Software Productivity Consortium-2.   The Software Productivity Consortium [9] also issued a "risk-reduction growth implementation model." Each stage does not represent a step on a capability scale, but rather, portrays a key characteristic of that stage:

1. Opportunistic—Individual projects develop a reuse strategy (i.e., how reuse will be practiced in the project). The project staff supports the reuse strategy and resources are committed to enact the strategy. Reuse activities are defined in the project's software and specialized reuse tools, automated or nonautomated, are used where advantageous to support the defined reuse activities. The product developers identify potential reusable assets throughout the project life cycle; the assets reused could be requirements, designs, code, architectures, systems, etc. Current developer needs are identified and used as a basis for acquiring or developing reusable assets. Similarities between needs are identified and used to target assets for multiple use.

2. Integrated—A standard reuse process is defined and integrated with the organization's standard software development process. The organization's structure, policies, procedures, etc., support the standard process. Tools are tailored to support the standard process. The management and staff are actively involved in defining and implementing the standard process. Anticipated developer needs are identified and used as a basis for acquiring or developing reusable assets. Similarities between assets and between architectures of assets are identified and used to develop adaptable assets and architectures of assets to meet multiple needs.

3. Leveraged—A product line reuse strategy is developed to maximize the benefits of reuse over sets of related products; product pricing and funding strategies take into account the expected costs and benefits over the product line. Performance of the standard reuse process is measured and analyzed to identify weaknesses, and plans are established to address the weaknesses. Reuse tools are integrated with the software development environment. Current customer needs are identified and used as a basis for acquiring or developing reusable assets. Transformation relationships between needs and their corresponding solutions are identified and used to enable broad spectrum reuse where reuse of early life cycle assets re-

sult in the reuse of subsequent life cycle assets without the need for additional analysis.

4. Anticipating—Management creates new business opportunities which take advantage of the organization's reuse capability and reusable assets. High-payoff assets are identified. Customers needs are anticipated and used as a basis to acquire or develop reusable assets to meet those needs. New technologies are identified which will meet or drive customer needs, and are inserted into the organization's product lines. The effectiveness of reuse technologies is measured and used to determine the most effective technology for a given situation. The organization's process has sufficient flexibility to rapidly adapt to new product environments.

References

1. M. A. Cusumano, "Systematic" Versus "Accidental" Reuse in Japanese Software Factories," Massachusetts Institute of Technology, Alfred P. Sloan School of Management, Cambridge, MA, Working paper WP# 3328-BPS-91, Sept. 9, 1991.
2. "A Survey of Reuse Maturity Models," Lombard Hill Group Corporate Report No: LH-RMM001, (Report-In-Progress), For more information, contact www. lombardhill.com or reuse@hotmail.com.
3. P. G. Bassett, "To Make or Buy? There is a Third Alternative," in *American Programmer*, vol. 8, E. Yourdan, Ed., Nov. 1995.
4. T. Bollinger, "Building a Winning Corporate Software Portfolio," presented at Informatics '93, Apr. 1993.
5. P. Koltun and A. Hudson, "A Reuse Maturity Model," presented at 4th Annual Workshop on Software Reuse, Herndon, VA, Nov. 1991.
6. M. Cusumano, *Japan's Software Factories*. New York, N.Y.: Oxford University Press, 1991.
7. M. L. Griss, "Software Reuse: Objects and frameworks are not enough," in *Object Magazine*, Feb. 1995, pp. 77–87.
8. "Reuse Library Prototype, version 01.00," Software Productivity Consortium, Herndon, VA, Nov. 1990.
9. "Reuse adoption guidebook," Software Productivity Consortium, Herndon, VA, SPC-92051-CMC, Version 01.00.03, Nov. 1992.

14

CONDUCTING A
REUSE ASSESSMENT

Reuse assessments are systematic tools for analyzing and understanding an organization's current practices and future potential for reuse. Assessments may be designed generally with questions to ascertain the state and environment of reuse in the organization, or specifically with benchmark data to perform a diagnosis on a particular issue. Such tools are useful because they support the decision maker in deciding whether or not to proceed with reuse and, if so, what areas should be prioritized [1]. A survey and description of reuse assessments developed by other practitioners and researchers appears in Appendix 14-A.

14.1 Organizational Reengineering for Reuse Assessment (ORRA)

The ORRA is an analytical and diagnostic tool for collecting both qualitative and quantitative benchmark data on software development with reusable assets. The assessment benefits the reuse program by analyzing the management, personnel, metrics, technology, process, and reusable asset aspects of the reuse infrastructure; qualitatively identifying further reuse opportunities; benchmarking the costs/benefits of reusable assets, the level of reuse in the target system, the productivity, quality, and time-to-market with and without reuse; and offering a set of recommendations for improving the organization's reuse program.

Data is collected from all appropriate levels of the organization. These may include, for example, managers from the project to executive level, software engineers, and support staff. If a reuse infrastructure has already been established, we may wish to distinguish these roles further with producer, consumer, or support distinctions, e.g., producer manager, reusable asset support engineer, etc. The data is collected at the organization site via group or person-to-person interviews.

An ORRA is conducted once near the beginning of a proposed reuse effort to establish the proper reuse infrastructure and/or baseline a reuse program, and periodically, during an organization's ongoing reuse effort, to identify opportunities for improvement.

14.2   The Assessment Process

The actual steps in the ORRA process are shown in Fig. 14–1. They are:

1. identify target organization;
2. coordinate tasks with pilot project to undergo assessment;
3. gather initial information and deliver preliminary questionnaire and metric worksheets;
4. conduct assessment interviews;
5. analyze data and present findings;
6. create and deliver ORRA report to organization.

The time commitment for participants in group interviews is typically two days. The group interview is facilitated by a reuse champion and an assistant. For organizations choosing to conduct interviews one-on-one, the time commitment is 3.5 to 4 hours for each participant depending upon the type and number of ques-

Software Reuse Assessment Process

1. Pilot project identified.

2. Agreement signed with pilot project to collect metrics, undergo assessment, etc.

3. Initial information gathering for overview (e.g., organizational charts, demographic data) and delivery of preliminary questionnaire and economic metric worksheets.

4. Conduct assessment interviews and review economic metric worksheets.

5. Analyze data, create and present reuse assessment report for assessed organization.

6. Compile and incorporate feedback into questionnaire and economic metric worksheets. Begin at Step 3 for next assessment of the same organization.

FIGURE 14–1   The ORRA process.

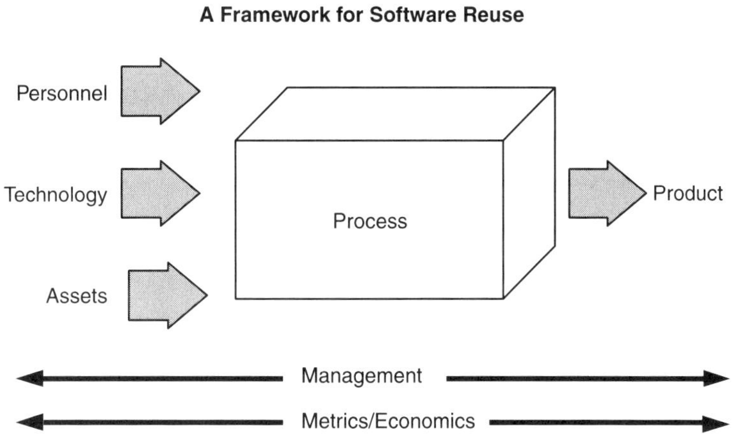

A Framework for Software Reuse

FIGURE 14–2   Framework for software reuse.

tionnaires to be completed. An average ORRA process requires approximately two-and-a-half to three weeks.

To better understand the issues that an ORRA addresses, we provide in the following section several examples illustrating some results from an ORRA. Unless otherwise noted, the data shown is hypothetical but representative of actual data from past assessments. By revisiting the example questions answered by the assessment, we now sample the kinds of analysis and information that the reuse assessment can provide us.

To determine the areas that an organization should focus on for reuse success, we develop a framework for software reuse to help identify major factors affecting reuse (Fig. 14–2). In this framework, personnel, technology, and assets are inputs to a process the output of which is a product. This process itself is managed, monitored through metrics, and has an economic outcome. This model serves as the basis for depicting the six major areas that affect software reuse as shown in the diagram in Fig. 14–3.

To fill in the framework, we assess respondents' ratings of the importance of reuse to a specific area and compare that rating with the organization's performance in the area. We accomplish this through reuse needs and reuse gap analyses.

14.3   Reuse Needs Analysis

A reuse needs analysis identifies which of the six reuse areas (management, personnel, economics and metrics, technology, process, and reusable assets and products) in the organization warrants further attention. Using hypothetical data, the chart in Fig. 14–3 compares the respondents' ratings of how important an area is to software reuse [from "not important" (1) to "extremely important" (5)] to how well the organization has performed in this area [from "deficient" (1) to "excellent" (5)]. (This

Example of Reuse Needs Analysis Results

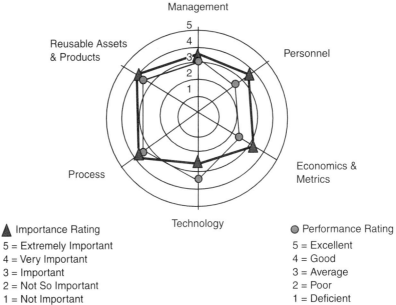

Importance Rating
5 = Extremely Important
4 = Very Important
3 = Important
2 = Not So Important
1 = Not Important

Performance Rating
5 = Excellent
4 = Good
3 = Average
2 = Poor
1 = Deficient

FIGURE 14–3   Example of reuse needs analysis results.

diagram was presented previously in chapter 8 to illustrate the results of a reuse needs analysis.) Ideally, an organization would prefer that its rating match its performance. In other words, an organization would like to be performing well in areas which are important. While excellent performance in unimportant areas is commendable, it may also indicate that resources may be better spent elsewhere.

The data shown here is based on responses to more than 60 standardized questions answered by the target organization staff during the ORRA process.

Following is a sample set of questions asked for the personnel area. Each respondent is asked to rate each subarea on their importance to reuse as well as how well their project is likely to perform in each subarea given their set of resources and constraints.

How important is training on the use of the reuse library to the reuse program?
How well is training on the use of the reuse library likely to be performed?

How important is training in designing *for* reuse to the reuse program?
How well is training in designing *for* reuse likely to be performed?

How important is training in designing *with* reuse to the reuse program?
How well is training in designing *with* reuse likely to be performed?

The information from this analysis provides an overview of the target organization and summarizes quantitative findings of the reuse needs analysis. For example, in this data, the largest gap between the organization's performance and importance ratings is in the economics and metrics area. Thus, it may be prudent to shift resources from the technology area to the economic and metrics area to maximize reuse effectiveness.

Available but not shown in Fig. 14–3 are the "importance of area to reuse" and "organizational performance" benchmark ratings, two indexes that reflect average ratings by experienced and successful reuse programs. The benchmark ratings allow an organization to compare its ratings to those of experienced reuse programs.

Further information on the organization's status within each of the six areas of software reuse is analyzed and included in the final analysis reports. For example, in Fig. 14–4, more detailed ratings are provided for a subset of the management category, the overall investigation. Shown are the ratings for two of the eight questions that constitute the overall investigation subcategory. The horizontal bars across the vertical bars represent the benchmark importance and performance ratings by experienced reuse programs.

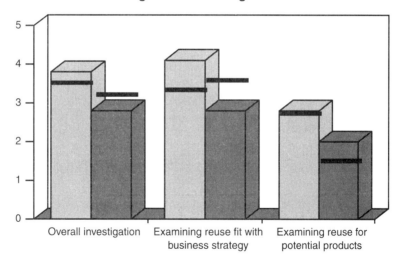

FIGURE 14–4   Example of detailed ratings.

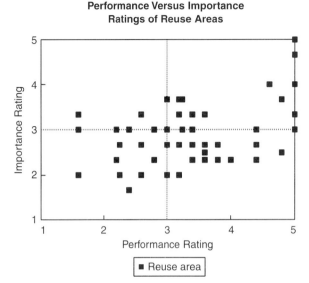

FIGURE 14–5   Reuse gap analysis.

14.4   Reuse Gap Analysis

Gap analysis is useful as a tool to identify reuse areas which require attention and additional resources. As shown in Fig. 14.5, the performance rating of a given area is mapped against its importance rating. For example, the reuse areas in the northwest quadrant of the matrix are areas which are rated highly in importance but rated low in terms of current performance. These are the areas on which an organization's efforts should be focused, in order to migrate them to the northeast quadrant.

14.5   Reuse Potential

The ORRA also helps an organization qualitatively determine its potential for reuse. As we defined earlier in chapter 8, reuse potential is the latent redundancy which, with the proper methods, may be tapped to increase productivity, improve quality, and achieve economic gains. As part of the ORRA, interviews which determine the extent that an organization possesses the traits (for more information, see chapter 8) shown in Fig. 14–6 may be conducted to qualitatively identify the reuse potential. Further detailed technical analysis for reuse potential can then be pursued later.

Traits Used to Identify Reuse Potential

Stable domain
Nonconstraining performance requirements and memory size
Multiple product family members
High internal redundancy
Many successive releases

FIGURE 14–6   Reuse potential traits.

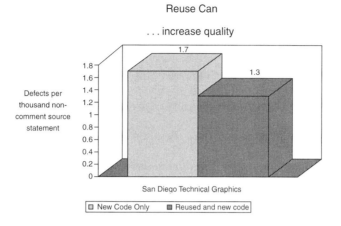

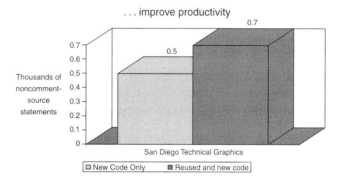

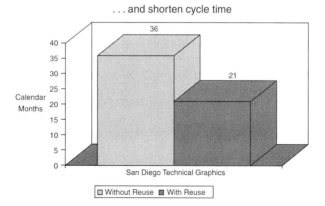

FIGURE 14–7   Measuring improved quality, increased productivity, and shortened time-to-market.

14.6   Reuse Metrics

Analyzing the improved quality, increased productivity, and shortened time-to-market of a certain level of reuse helps the organization to understand the impact of reuse as well as to obtain further support and resources for reuse. Since determining these factors is easier after the implementation of reuse, this analysis is usually conducted during the organization's ongoing reuse effort.

  If data is available from the organization, the ORRA calculates the improved quality, increased productivity, and shortened cycle time from reuse. For example, we determined for the HP San Diego Technical Graphics division reuse program that quality had improved by 24%, productivity had increased by 40%, and the time-to-market had been reduced by 42% through software reuse for a 31% level of reuse (Fig. 14–7).

14.7   Baselining and Analyzing the Process for Reengineering

An ORRA analysis can help baseline an organization's current processes, identify critical paths and compare activities' processing and cycle times. A functional flowchart can depict and map the current process. Fig. 14–8 [2] shows an example of a request to add a feature to a reusable asset. Rectangles refer to activities and dia-

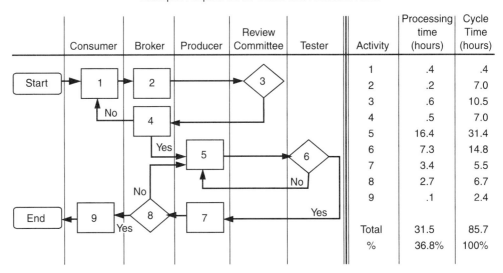

Baselining and Analyzing the Process for Reengineering

Example: Request for a Feature in a Reusable Asset

					Activity	Processing time (hours)	Cycle Time (hours)
					1	.4	.4
					2	.2	7.0
					3	.6	10.5
					4	.5	7.0
					5	16.4	31.4
					6	7.3	14.8
					7	3.4	5.5
					8	2.7	6.7
					9	.1	2.4
					Total	31.5	85.7
					%	36.8%	100%

FIGURE 14–8   Baselining and analyzing the reuse process for reengineering. Adapted from: H.J., Harrington, *Business Process Improvement*, New York, N.Y.: McGraw-Hill, 1991, p. 103.

monds to decision points. The elongated circle depicts the start or end of a process. The steps shown in the figure are as follows:

Step 1. Consumer identifies feature desired for a given software asset and submits request.

Step 2. Broker receives request and collects such requests for next meeting of the review committee.

Step 3. Review committee convenes and considers the request.

Step 4. Broker receives the approved/disapproved request from the review committee, informs the consumer, and forwards the work order to the producer.

Step 5. After receiving the work order to add the feature to the reusable asset, the producer investigates, designs, and codes the feature.

Step 6. Independent tester performs testing on reusable asset.

Step 7. Producer updates documentation on the reusable asset.

Step 8. Broker receives the asset from the producer, verifies the asset, updates the library documentation, and installs the asset into the library.

Step 9. Consumer receives the reusable asset with the added feature.

Improvements include, for example, informing the consumer if and when the review committee approves the request.

Baselining the organization's processes enables us to examine the current flow of activities and identify bottlenecks. It also allows us to analyze them for reengineering opportunities such as running processes in parallel and combining steps.

14.8   Cost/Benefit Analysis

Conducting a cost/benefit analysis from using or producing reusable assets enables an organization to understand the economic impact of implementing reuse (Fig. 14–9). Although a pro forma (projected) economic analysis can be performed prior to implementing reuse, it is usually easier to perform a cost/benefit analysis after the collection of data.

ORRA also collects information on development with and without reuse. From this data, we can identify the additional producer effort by phase to produce reusable assets (Fig. 14–10) as well as the consumer effort saved by reusing assets relative to that of using traditional methods (Fig. 14–11).

14.9   Product Software Quality Factors

Through an ORRA, we can also analyze the impact and importance of software quality factors among end-users and consumers and compare these results against those of producers.

For example, consumers are asked to rate the importance of the SQF to the end-user of a product. In order to determine how well the producers understood

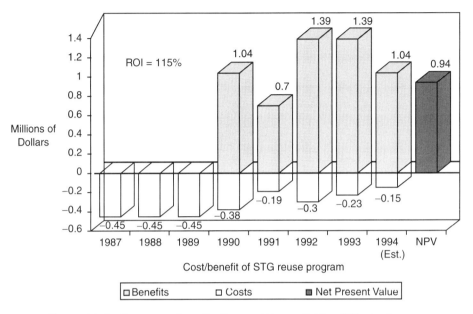

FIGURE 14–9   Reuse cost/benefit. *Source*: Wayne C. Lim, "Effects of reuse on quality, productivity, and economics," *IEEE Software*, Sept. 1994. Copyright 1994 IEEE.

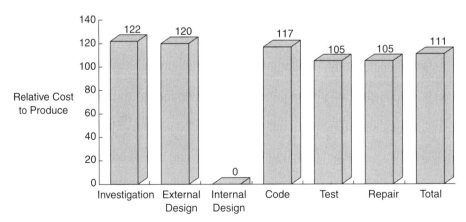

FIGURE 14–10   Relative cost to produce. *Source*: Wayne C. Lim, "Effects of reuse on quality, productivity, and economics," *IEEE Software*, Sept. 1994. Copyright 1994 IEEE.

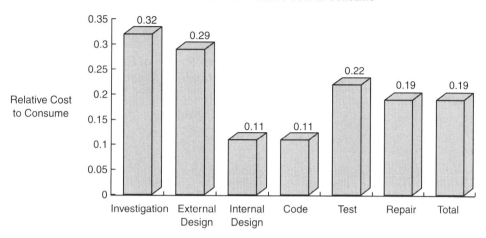

FIGURE 14–11   Relative cost to consume. *Source*: J. Cassidy, Hewlett-Packard.

end-users' needs and priorities, producers were also asked to rate how important the SQFs were to end-users.

Example results showing mean values for the consumers and producers are shown in Fig. 14–12. The consumer rankings are overlaid onto the producer rankings. As is evident from the chart, the perceptions of importance coincide well in general, with the greatest differences being in integrity and interoperability. A close match between the consumer and producer scores indicate a common understanding of end-users' needs and is the first step in determining whether consumers and producers are in concert to address the end-users' needs.

In the case where the producer has consumers who address multiple end-users with significantly differing needs, we obviously expect to see greater score differences. In this situation, more emphasis should be placed on analyzing the producers' perceptions of the consumers' needs.

Consumer ratings of the impact of reuse is overlaid onto the consumer ratings of importance of the software quality factors to the product in Fig. 14–13. The factors where importance exceeds impact most are in performance, localizability, and integrity. Flexibility and portability are the two areas where reuse impact exceeds importance. This chart contrasts the consumers' perception of how much impact reuse is having upon those areas that are considered important to them. This analysis is useful as a starting point for a producer and consumer group discussion on how reusable assets can be created or utilized to address some of the important but as yet under-addressed SQFs.

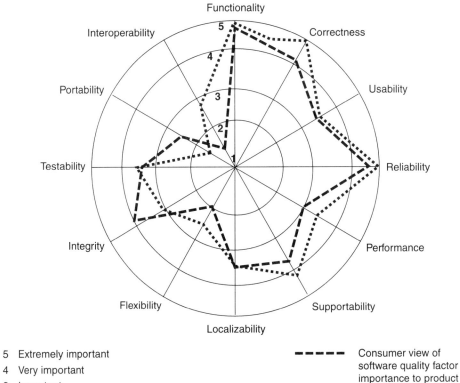

FIGURE 14–12   Consumer versus producer rating of reuse software quality factor importance to product.

Consumer Rating of Reuse Impact Versus
Importance of Software Quality Factor to Product

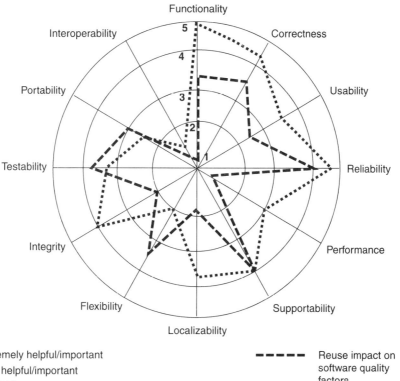

5 Extremely helpful/important
4 Very helpful/important
3 Helpful/important
2 Not so helpful/important
1 Not helpful/important

- - - - - Reuse impact on
software quality
factors

· · · · · · · · · Software quality factor
importance to product

FIGURE 14–13   Consumer rating of reuse impact versus importance of
software quality factor to product.

FAILURE	CAUSE
No Attempt to Reuse	
	Poor management
	Lack of education XX
	No economic incentive XXX
	No success model XX
	Not invented here X
	Unrealistic time constraints XXX
	More fun to write X
	Non-egoless programming
	Legal problems
	Utility of reuse unclear X
	Other _____
Part does not exist	
	No economic incentive X
	Novel technology
	Other _____
Part is not available	
	No import organization
	Part cannot be scavenged X
	Part not designed for reuse XXX
	Part cannot be found
	Part is proprietary
	Source code missing
	Other _____
Part is not found	
	Insufficient representation XX
	Poor search tools
	Other _____
Part is not understood	
	Insufficient representation XX
	Poor education XX
	Part too complex XX
	Other __
Part is not valid	
	Poor testing
	Insufficient information X
	Lack of standards X
	Other _____
Part cannot be integrated	
	Language incompatibilities XXXX
	Improper form
	Nonfunctional specs
	Other _____

FIGURE 14–14 Frakes's reuse failure modes. *Source*: W. Frakes, "An Empirical Framework for Software Reuse Research," in Third Annual Workshop: Methods and Tools for Reuse, Syracuse, NY, 1990.

14.10   Frakes's Reuse Failure Modes

Respondents can identify those factors that impede reuse in their organization by utilizing Frakes's Reuse Failure Model [5]. "The table summarizes a set of failure modes for software reuse and some possible causes for these failures. Each of these causes might also have causes, and thus the table summarizes only the first level of analysis." For further information on the Reuse Failure Model, see [3] and [4]. In Fig. 14–14, each "X" represents one response for that category.

Summary

The ORRA benchmarks organizations that are considering or currently conducting reuse. The assessment benefits the organization by:

- Identifying reuse improvement opportunities in six major reuse areas: management, personnel, metrics and economics, technology, process, and reusable asset and product.
- Qualitatively evaluating the potential for reuse.
- Benchmarking the level of reuse, the reuse process, the improved quality, productivity and shortened time-to-market resulting from reuse.
- Determining the reuse economics.
- Documenting the additional producer effort by phase to create reusable assets.
- Identifying differences in producer and consumer perceptions.

The ORRA is an important tool for providing guidance in reuse planning.

References

1. W. C. Lim, "Software Reuse Assessments and Economics," presented at Reuse Bay Area Roundtable, Palo Alto, CA, June 1993.
2. H. J. Harrington, *Business Process Improvement.* New York, N. Y.: McGraw-Hill, 1991.
3. W. B. Frakes and C. J. Fox, "Software reuse survey report," Software Engineering Guild, Sterling, VA, 1993.
4. W. Frakes, "A Survey of Software Reuse," presented at Proceedings of the First International Workshop on Software Reusability, Dortmund, Germany, June 1991.
5. W. Frakes, "An Empirical Framework for Software Reuse Research," presented at Proceedings of the Third Annual Workshop: Methods and Tools for Reuse, Syracuse, N.Y., 1990.

A SURVEY OF REUSE ASSESSMENTS

In this appendix, we review several reuse assessments: the Aharonian question-naire; the Central Archive for Reusable Defense Software (CARDS) Franchise Plan; Durek assessment; Frakes survey; Freeman questionnaire; Prieto-Diaz assessment; the Software Technology for Adaptable Reliable Systems (STARS) Reuse Strategy Model (RSM), the Software Productivity Consortium Reuse Capability Model; and the United States Army Information Systems Software Center (USAISSC) Reuse Technology Assessment [1].

Reuse assessments can be classified into two major categories: general ques-tionnaire and diagnostic assessment. A general questionnaire is more qualitative, re-lying on commentary from respondents to assess results. A diagnostic assessment is more quantitative in that responses are recorded numerically on a scale and ana-lyzed statistically. The latter assessment facilitates benchmarking, which may be rel-ative to its own or other organizations' results.

Examples of General Questionnaires. The CARDS [2] Franchise Plan and Prieto-Diaz [3] assessment present examples of questions to be asked in the context of describing how reuse may be implemented. The Aharonian questionnaire, Durek assessment, and Freeman questionnaire provide questions that an organization should ask of itself in considering reuse.

Examples of Diagnostic Assessments. The Frakes survey provides a bench-mark against which answers from an organization may be compared. During the process of a software productivity consortium reuse capability model assessment, respondents' answers are compared and evaluated. By contrast, the RSM assesses the current state of reuse practice and identifies an initial goal set based on an absolute benchmark called "scale values."

Aharonian Questionnaire. Aharonian presents a set of questions that may be used in assessing an organization for reuse [4]. The set of questions covers a broad range of areas including economics, management, technology transfer, training, legal issues, politics, tradition, and technology. How well a company is able to answer the questions is indicative of its preparedness to benefit from reuse. Examples of topics and questions include:

Ignoring existing resources
- Do you consider software reuse to apply only to reusably written software, or to software that already exists?

Economics
- Do the company's programmers have incentives to reuse software?

Management
- Are the company's managers given the financial and administrative resources to establish software reuse programs?

Avoiding the not-invented-here syndrome
- Is software being used from all sources, or is the company or command being parochial?

Legal
- What channels should be used to obtain public domain software from government agencies and laboratories that refuse or are unable to release their software?

Technical
- Will object-oriented approaches to software reuse for real-world problems be practical?

CARDS Franchise Plan. The Central Archive for Reusable Defense Software (CARDS) Franchise Plan is meant to be used as a tool to "develop a detailed, tailored implementation plan which will prepare the organization to begin the process of software reuse."[2] The franchise plan describes steps for establishing a reuse infrastructure:

1. obtain management commitment for reuse;
2. develop an organizational assessment to identify the current state and the potential for reuse;
3. perform a requirements/implementation study to identify the requirements for implementing reuse;
4. outline a reuse implementation plan to identify the steps for establishing a reuse infrastructure.

Example questions include:

Processes
- Is the domain under consideration mature and stable?
- Will the domain form a key part of an organization's future "business"? Is there competition within the domain? Are there opportunities for strategic or short-term partnerships for development?
- Is the size of the market (now and future) for systems in the domain stable and growing?

Reuse capability
- Is reuse done on an individual, team, or organizational level?
- Is there an organization unit responsible for developing a reuse action plan?
- Is there a formal or informal way of identifying reuse opportunities?
- Is planning for reuse part of the project planning cycle?
- Is data on the investment in reuse maintained?
- Are reusable assets created by an independent development team? If yes, how many people are involved and what are their roles?

Durek Assessment. Durek describes an analysis where five areas are analyzed in detail to determine the feasibility for reuse [5]. The areas include business environment, requirements volatility, organizational readiness, availability of domain knowledge, and economic reuse impact. Examples of detailed factors to examine in each of these areas follow:

Business environment
- expected value of awards;
- financial incentives;
- explicit contractual requirements.

Requirements volatility

- predictable requirements variation;
- size and complexity of variation;
- frequency of change.

Organizational readiness

- previous successful attempts;
- acceptance of standards;
- understanding of impacts of reuse by developers, managers, and customers.

Availability of domain knowledge

- domain analyst expertise;
- stable set of well-documented core requirements;
- security or proprietary restrictions on data access.

Economic reuse impact

- economic benefits within project;
- productivity and breakeven measures;
- return on investment.

Freeman Assessment.   Freeman presents a 15-question reusability assessment to assist organizations in analyzing its software development efforts [6]. These questions include:

- Is there a program library (other than the normal mathematical routines) in your organization?
- Are there economic or organizational incentives to reuse code?
- Are there disincentives?

Frakes's Assessment.   Frakes and Fox conducted a software reuse survey of 113 individuals from 29 organizations [7]. The survey consists of 27 quantitative questions pertaining to the types and levels of reuse activities in the organization, the level of reuse practiced personally by the engineer and the organization, attitudes towards reuse, and impediments to reuse. Examples of the question follow:

- What percent of the life cycle objects your organization creates are typically composed of reused parts?
- What percent of life cycle objects you personally create are composed of reused parts?
- What percentage of the parts you reuse are from external sources?

The reuse survey results help benchmark the reuse activities of organizations, compare its activities and performance to that of other organizations in the survey, and determine what impediments to reuse in an organization exist and how they should be handled.

Prieto-Diaz Assessment. Prieto-Diaz proposes that an assessment report be created as part of a strategy for implementing an incremental reuse program [3]. In addition to an implementation plan, he suggests that the assessment report should include a feasibility analysis, domain suitability assessment, and cost/benefit analysis. Examples of the types of questions for each type of analyses are:

Feasibility analysis
- Does the organization have enough resources (financial and human) to implement a reuse program?
- Does the organization want to do it?
- Is management committed to implementing a reuse program?

Domain suitability
- Is the domain mature and well understood or is it new and not well understood?
- Is the domain stable or rapidly changing?
- Is the domain very technology dependent?

Cost/benefit analysis
- How much does it cost (cost schedule)?
- Is it worth doing?
- What alternatives exist for implementing a reuse program?

The Software Technology For Adaptable, Reliable Systems (STARS) Reuse Strategy Model. The reuse strategy model (RSM) "consists of a method for gauging the current state of reuse practice with concurrent identification of goals that support transition to a state closer to the STARS vision." [8] The STARS vision is to "have institutionalized a disciplined architectural and engineering-based approach to the development and evolution of software-intensive systems." [9] The RSM differs from its peers in that it analyzes not the efficiency of the reuse practice, but the characteristics of what types and levels of reuse are practiced and supported. It assesses the extent of a transition from traditional software development "to domain-specific, reuse-based development both with respect to engineering and management practice and the infrastructure supporting those practices." [8] Intended to be used as a project planning support tool, the method benchmarks the current reuse practice, designs a set of objectives which are then reexamined in the light of resource and time constraints, and provides conceptual notions of possible metrics for measuring progress toward those objectives.

As shown in Fig. 14–15, the RSM has five dimensions and 34 indicators. The five dimensions, shown in row 1 are domain stability, organization readiness, experience with domain-specific knowledge, usage of technology for reuse processes, and business climate and reuse management. The elements in the column directly beneath each dimension depict the associated indicators for that particular dimension.

A set of discrete values measures progress in a particular dimension. Associated with each value is a goal and questions which help organizations determine if

Reuse Strategy Model (RSM) Indicators by Dimension

1. Domain Stability	2. Organization Readiness	3. Experience with Domain-specific Knowledge	4. Usage of Technology for Reuse Processes	5. Business Climate and Reuse Management
1.1 Domain age	2.1 Motivation for reuse	3.1 Experience with building of systems within this domain	4.1 Domain modeling technology used	5.1 Costing/pricing
1.2 Domain volatility	2.2 Scope of planning for reuse	3.2 Experience with domain model	4.2 Asset development technology used	5.2 Legal
1.3 Domain model(s) existence	2.3 Identification of reuse opportunities	3.3 Experience with reference or standard architecture	4.3 Asset management technology used	5.3 Contractual 5.4 Domain management
1.4 Standard or reference architecture existence	2.4 Management commitment to reuse	3.4 Experience with set of domain components	4.4 Asset qualification technology used	
1.5 Supported off-the-shelf components available	2.5 Level of reuse advocacy	3.5 Effectiveness of domain asset set	4.5 Asset classification/cataloging technology used	5.5 Domain support
	2.6 Awareness/commitment to process	3.6 Effectiveness of domain asset classifications	4.6 Asset identification/retrieval technology used	5.6 Domain learning
	2.7 Reuse accountability/effectiveness measurement		4.7 Asset Tailoring/integration technology used	
	2.8 Training for reuse		4.8 Integration of tools with processes	
	2.9 Reuse process improvement			

FIGURE 14–15   STARS reuse strategy model. *Source*: M. Davis, "Reuse Strategy Model: Planning Aid for Reuse-based Projects," The Boeing Company, Seattle, WA, July 31, 1993, p. 13.

the goal has been or is being met, and suggested metrics to help measure progress toward that goal. For instance, the domain model(s) existence indicator on the "domain stability" dimension has five scale values. The goal for transitioning from the lowest scale value:

domain model does not exist

to the next higher value is:

Goal: Completed domain modeling effort with domain model, vocabulary, and taxonomy.

The question that would indicate that the transition was already in progress is:

Transition Question: Are there any ongoing domain modeling efforts results of which are available to the organization?.

The metric that would monitor whether progress is being made is:

Metric: Status reports about the progress in domain modeling show definition of a domain model, taxonomy, and vocabulary and representation of the information in a computer processable form or show validation of the domain model, taxonomy, or vocabulary by domain experts.

The Software Productivity Consortium Reuse Capability Model. The reuse capability model (RCM) developed by the Software Productivity Consortium (SPC) is a tool to help organizations understand its current reuse processes and identify and prioritize areas needing improvement. In the RCM, an organization's process is assessed with respect to four groups: application development factors, asset development factors, management factors, and process and technology factors [10]. As shown in Fig. 14–16, associated with each group of factors are goals and questions designed to determine how well the goals are met and the impact on reuse of meeting those goals.

The team assesses their organization against each goal in two ways:

1) The extent the organization meets the specified goal on a scale of one—not satisfied, two—partially satisfied, three—fully satisfied.
2) The expected impact on the organization's reuse capability from fully satisfying the stated goal on a scale of one—no positive impact, two—low positive impact, three—moderate positive impact, four—high positive impact.

SPC Reuse Critical Success Factors

Management Factors	Application Development Factors	Asset Development Factors	Process and Technology Factors
Organizational commitment	Asset awareness and accessibility	Needs identification	Process definition and integration
Planning and direction	Asset identification	Asset interface and architecture definition	Measurement
Costing and pricing	Asset evaluation and verification	Needs/solution definition	Continuous process improvement
Legal/contractual constraints	Application integrability	Similarity/variation definition	Training
		Asset value determination	Tools support
		Asset reusability	Technology innovation
		Asset quality	

FIGURE 14–16   SPC reuse critical success factors. *Source*: Software Productivity Consortium Reuse Capability Model, Reuse Adoption Guidebook, Software Productivity Consortium, Herndon, VA, Ted Davis, SPC-92051-CMC, Version 02.00.05, Nov. 1993.

For example, the set of questions associated with organizational commitment under management factors are:

- Management commits to defining, implementing, and improving the organization's approach to reuse and demonstrates its commitment to the staff.
- Management commits funding, staffing, and other resources to define, implement, and improve the organization's approach to reuse.
- The staff supports the organization's approach to defining, implementing, and improving the organization's approach to reuse.
- Management structures its organization, policies, procedures, and standards to a standard reuse process supporting multiple product development efforts.

The assessment is administered in a focus group with individuals representing the major functions of the organizations, and SPC staff as facilitators.

Related to and usually conducted with the RCM is the domain assessment model which evaluates "the reuse opportunities in a business area."[11] Similar to the RCM, the domain assessment examines the domain in four areas: market potential for products, existing domain assets, commonalities and variabilities, domain stability, and standardization in the domain.

United States Army Information Systems Software Center (USAISSC) Reuse Technology Assessment.   The Army Reuse Center developed and distributes the USAISSC Reuse Technology Assessment. The purpose of the USAISSC Reuse Tech-

Comparison of Reuse Assessments

Reuse Assessment	Type	Purpose	Scale	Benchmark	Number of Questions	Areas Covered
Aharonian	Questionnaire	Assess readiness of organization to benefit from software reuse.	Yes or no	None	161	Existing resources, economics management, avoiding the not-invented-here syndrome, legal, technical
Central archive for reusable defense software (CARDS)	Representative questions	Help organizations develop a reuse implementation plan.	Yes or no	None	Representative questions	Representative questions provided for determining the domain and technology infrastructure, and critical success factors.
Durek	List of issues to be examined	Feasbility assessment to define and qualify the domain	None	None	List of 21 issues	Five major areas: business environment, requirements volatility, organizational readiness, availability of domain knowledge, and economic reuse impact
Frakes	Questionnaire	Benchmark reuse efforts and compare with efforts in industry	Varies	Yes	27	Percent of life cycle objects reused, attitudes towards reuse, and problems in reusing.
Freeman	Questionnaire	Reusability analysis for the organization	Yes or no	None	15	Life cycle, work-products, library, applications, language, economics, incentives/disincentives, designs, test plans, and competitive advantage.

FIGURE 14–17 Comparison of reuse assessments.

Reuse Assessment	Type	Purpose	Scale	Benchmark	Number of Questions	Areas Covered
Organizational Reeingeering for Reuse assessment (ORRA)	Questionnaire	1) Benchmarks the organization's current reuse practices; 2) qualitatively evaluates the potential for reuse; 3) identifies the organizational reuse areas for improvement.	Scaled and open-ended	Yes, baseline data from experienced reuse programs	63	Management, personnel, economics and metrics, technology, process, and reusable assets and products.
Prieto-Diaz	Representative questions	Feasibility analysis, domain suitability analysis and cost/benefit analysis.	Varies	None	Representative questions	Availability of resources, management commitment, domain maturity, and economics.
Software technology for adaptable, reliable systems (STARS)	Questionnaire	Characterizes the type of reuse practiced and supported.	Yes	Yes, scale provides an absolute comparison	34	Domain stability, organization readiness, experience with domain-specific knowledge, usage of technology for reuse processes, and business climate and reuse management.
Software Productivity Consortium (SPC)	Questionnaire	Assess process with respect to reuse and establish priorities for improvement	Yes	Yes, respondents' answers are compared to each other.	Reuse Capability: 59 questions. Domain assessment: 31 questions.	Application development factors, asset development factors, management factors and process and technology factors
United States Army Information Systems Software Center) (USAISSC	Questionnaire	Identify and evaluate reuse expertise and capabilities	Varies	None	42	System description, system hardware and software requirements, reuse training; reuse policies; activities, inhibitors/motivators, and repository usage.

FIGURE 14–17 (cont.)   Comparison of reuse assessments.

nology Assessment is to "identify and evaluate reuse expertise and capabilities within the USAISSC software development center." [12] The responses to the questionnaire were used to identify "existing reuse policies and procedures; reuse education and technology transfer; reuse tools and capabilities; and reuse initiatives" [12].

The questionnaire covers general areas such as system description, system hardware; and software requirements, and reuse-specific areas such as the types of reuse training received and desired; reuse policies; activities, inhibitors/motivators; and repository usage.

Comparison.   Fig. 14–17 compares the reuse assessment tools discussed in this appendix and their main features.

Summary

A reuse investigation will enable an organization to understand the benefits and costs of reuse, its alignment and influence upon business strategy, and, in the case of large organizations, identify suborganizations with high reuse potential. In this section, we introduced some tools and techniques used to determine whether, how, and where reuse is implemented. These include a cost justification model, which allows us to conduct a return-on-investment analysis on the implementation of software reuse for a particular organization; the reuse assessment, a framework for determining potential reuse success and measuring reuse progress; and a set of system and product characteristics and good organizational practices, which is used to help identify organizations that have the most potential for reuse. The application of these tools is dependent upon the reuse scope of an organization and whether an organization is commercial, an in-house information system division, or a government contractor. If appropriate, an organization with the adequate resources should consider strategy driven reuse, a proactive strategy that may lead to competitive advantage.

References

1. "A Survey of Reuse Assessments," Lombard Hill Group Corporate Report No: LH-RA001, (Report-In-Progress), For more information, contact www.lombardhill.com or reuse@hotmail.com.
2. R. M. Armstrong, "Informal Technical Report for the Software Technology for Adaptable, Reliable Systems (STARS): Franchise Plan Central Archive for Reusable Defense Software (CARDS)," DSD Laboratories, Inc. DRAFT-STARS-VC-B010/001/00, Feb. 28, 1994.
3. R. Prieto-Diaz, "Making software reuse work: an implementation model," *SIGSOFT Software Engineering Notes*, vol. 16, pp. 61–8, July 1991.
4. G. Aharonian, "Starting a Reuse Effort at Your Company," *ReNews—The Electronic Software Reuse Newsletter*, vol. 1, Sept. 1991.

5. T. Durek, "Strategies and Tactics for Software Reuse," in *Improving the Software Process and Competitive Postion via Software Reuse and Reengineering*. Alexandria, VA: The National Institute for Software Quality and Productivity, May 1991.

6. P. Freeman, "Reusable Software Engineering Tutorial," Irvine, CA: University of California at Irvine, 1987.

7. W. B. Frakes and C. J. Fox, "Software reuse survey report," Software Engineering Guild, Sterling, VA, 1993.

8. M. Davis, "Reuse Strategy Model: Planning Aid for Reuse-based Projects (for Software Technology for Adaptable, Reliable Systems (STARS))," The Boeing Company, Seattle, WA, July 31, 1993.

9. "Informal Technical Report for the Software Technology for Adaptable, Reliable Systems (STARS): STARS Reuse Concepts, Volume I—Conceptual Framework for Reuse Processes (CFRP)," Version 2.0, STARS-UC-05159/001/00, Nov. 13, 1992 1992.

10. "Reuse Adoption Case Study Workbook," Software Productivity Consortium, Herndorn, VA SPC-92051-CMC, Nov. 1992.

11. T. Davis, "Adopting a policy of reuse," *IEEE Spectrum*, vol. 31, pp. 44–8, June 1994.

12. "Reuse Technology Assessment Report (for Army Reuse Center)," CACI, Inc., Document No: PD295, Contract No. DAEA26-87-D-2001, Jan. 14, 1994.

15

A REUSE VISION AND MISSION STATEMENT

A *reuse vision* describes the state that an organization desires to attain and provides a common target for the participants (e.g., the producer, broker, and consumer suborganizations) that make up the total organization. A reuse *mission statement* articulates an organization's or participant's purpose while a vision defines an organization's direction. While participants may share a common vision, a mission statement should still be created for each participant since each has a distinct role in ensuring reuse success; the statement is also critically important because it specifies what participants are collectively attempting to achieve and the exact role of each suborganization. The statement helps suborganizations align their efforts to achieve the common goal of reuse. Furthermore, it can foster motivation and team spirit among the participants.

15.1 Creating a Vision and Mission Statement

Conceiving an appropriate vision and mission statement is an iterative process. A preliminary mission statement should be prepared early in the reuse adoption process. Mission statements are "living documents"—as the organization moves forward, the initial statement will be revisited and refined as necessary when more information becomes available or conditions change.

The organization benefits not only from the statements that are produced, but also from the clarity achieved by participants as they define their vision and mission. Actively involved participants are more likely to truly understand the vision, "buy into" it, and feel ownership of the statements.

The characteristics of an effective vision and mission statement depend in part on the organization. However, it should always specify the desired state of the organization and is also often inspirational. It should specify the purpose and responsibilities of the suborganization, describes tasks to be accomplished; often, it specifies how these accomplishments will support the organization in achieving its vision.

15.2   Examples of Reuse Vision and Mission Statements

In this section, we present examples of reuse vision and mission statements from the U.S. Department of Defense, IBM, and the U.S. Army Reuse Center.

Reuse Vision

U.S. Department of Defense.   A software reuse vision and strategy document prepared by the U.S. Department of Defense (DoD) Reuse Executive Steering Committee says that "reuse principles, when integrated into its acquisition practices and software engineering process, (will) provide a basis for dramatic improvement in the way software-intensive systems are developed and maintained over their life cycle [1]." The document further states that:

> "The vision of the DoD Software Reuse Initiative is to drive the DoD software community from its current 're-invent the software' cycle to a process-driven, domain-specific, architecture-centric, library-based way of constructing software. The strategy to realize this vision is based on systematic reuse: where opportunities are predefined and a process for capitalizing on those opportunities is specified [1]."

To support this, the document also outlines 10 elements to realize the vision.

Reuse Mission

IBM.   IBM has a flourishing corporate-wide internal reuse program. As a byproduct of its internally developed reuse expertise, it now offers some of its training materials to others on the external market. The IBM internal reuse program mission is:

> "To be the industry leader in providing and applying reuse technology and methodologies by developing tools, processes, and parts for internal use with market potential [2]."

U.S. Army Reuse Center.   The U.S. Army Reuse Center (ARC), Fort Belvoir, VA, is a primary resource for reuse within the Department of the Army. The ARC was "established to support the development of reliable, high quality systems while reducing the time and resources required to develop and maintain those systems [3]." Their statement follows:

> "The mission of the Army Reuse Center is to develop, implement, maintain, and administer a total reuse program that will support the entire software development life-cycle [3]."

To achieve this mission, the ARC provides an automated library system of more than 1400 reusable design, code, and document components. Domain analysis, reuse engineering, user indoctrination and training, library population, and customer support are also offered.

Summary

A reuse vision and mission statement provides direction and purpose to an organization seeking to implement reuse. Creating such statements is an iterative process and should begin early in the reuse adoption process. Participants in the creation of such statements acquire a better understanding of their vision and purpose.

References

1. J. Piper, "DoD Software Reuse Vision and Strategy," *Crosstalk: The Journal of Defense Software Engineering*, no. 37, pp. 2–8, Oct., 1992.
2. "IBM Reuse Program Poster," The 5th Annual Workshop on Institutionalizing Software Reuse, Palo Alto, CA, Oct. 26–29, 1992.
3. "Army Reuse Center literature," Army Reuse Center, Fort Belvoir, VA, 1993.

16

STAFFING FOR SOFTWARE REUSE

16.1 Introduction

Selecting, educating, and motivating an appropriate staff is critical to establishing an effective reuse infrastructure. In fact, personnel issues such as improper training and lack of incentives are often cited as major inhibitors to reuse [1]. Thus, an appreciation and understanding of personnel issues specific to reuse and the implications of staffing decisions is crucial in managing a successful reuse program.

In this chapter, we will discuss the key issues in staffing for reuse, which include the selection, roles, responsibilities, motivation, and education of personnel. We will begin by identifying the different roles important to a reuse team and discussing the scope of responsibilities and the skills required to perform those roles effectively. Large organizations will often have one or more individuals in each role; smaller organizations may have just one or two individuals who must be responsible for all roles. What is important is that each function is recognized and that responsibility for assuming the role is borne by someone within the organization, project, or lab. We will also present several examples of reuse staffing in various companies.

Next, we will discuss incentive programs that help motivate software personnel to create, use, maintain, and promote reusable workproducts. We will investigate some inhibitors to reuse and suggest ways to resolve them. Finally, we will present a framework for educating and training reuse personnel, including a set of core topics and skills, and an example reuse curriculum.

223

16.2   Creating an Effective Reuse Environment

As with any innovation, introducing reuse into an organization precipitates many changes. Being aware of these developments will help an organization defend itself against undesirable consequences and exploit desirable ones.

An inevitable consequence of reuse for software developers is increased specialization of labor. Just as workers on Henry Ford's automobile assembly line specialized in a particular task, software personnel will gain considerable expertise in smaller and more defined areas of software development as software assets become more standardized through reuse. As happened in the automobile industry, this will lead to greater efficiency and productivity for each individual.

Reuse can also stratify job levels and stretch the ends of the engineering job spectrum by creating new positions. For example, reuse introduces a new level of workers called "workproduct assemblers." These are staffers who specialize in integrating reusable workproducts into systems or subsystems. Naturally, these assemblers need expertise in integration and design. However, extensive knowledge of each individual workproduct is not necessary. Thus, reuse has the potential of having highly experienced engineers concentrate on developing reusable assets, which are then reused by workproduct assemblers.

We can also view this as a further movement toward bringing programming to the end-user. An example of this is the use of financial spreadsheet software by end-users. For general applications, end-users do not necessarily need specialized knowledge to define their requirements and program spreadsheets. However, more technically sophisticated spreadsheets, e.g., those with macros, may require the expertise of a financial spreadsheet specialist.

Wald suggests that systems characterized by bureaucracy and multiple reporting levels tend to value short-term results to the detriment of long-term benefits [2]. Software reuse can be a victim of this myopia if changes in the software development culture and in the mindset of the participants are not made.

Traditionally, programmers are trained to write and not to reuse [3]. Software development personnel are often assessed in terms of production quantity rather than effectiveness or efficiency. The "not-invested-here" (NIH) syndrome results from this kind of training and fear of competition, job loss, and the inferior work of others. Likewise, managers fear that increased productivity and efficiency may lead to staff reductions, and are reluctant to raise their costs for the benefit of others. Thus, a change in culture, not just behavior, must take place in order for reuse to be successful in the long-term. Reuse needs to be integrated into the standard programming process of the organization.

Change in attitude or mindset is very different from change in behavior. This distinction is often overlooked in organizations seeking to implement change. Organizations concentrate on modifying behavior through reorganization, new job and task descriptions, and incentive programs. In reuse, this may mean a new title, new requirements to reuse at least some library workproducts, or small cash awards for library contributions. Using only mechanisms like these may bring immediate results, but will have little long-term impact.

Long-term benefits are realized only when participants' attitudes toward reuse are changed. This can be accomplished through proper education and training, visible management support, regular communication of progress, and involvement of participants in planning for reuse. Behavior modification mechanisms *should* be used, but in conjunction with attitude modification programs. Once a reuse mindset has been established, there is often much less need for external motivators and incentives to encourage reuse.

16.3 Roles and Responsibilities

We now discuss the key roles necessary for implementing reuse. These functions can be fulfilled by a single person or an entire team, depending upon the scope, size, and experience of the organization.

Reuse Champion.   Many authors agree that the role of reuse champion is critical to the success of a reuse program [4]. Modesto Maidique concludes that "new ideas either find a champion or they die [5]." A champion is one "who is committed to the innovation and who enthusiastically supports and promotes it" [6]. This person must understand and believe in the reuse effort to the extent that his or her enthusiasm infects everyone within the organization. The reuse champion has responsibility for educating others on the concept of reuse, its long-term benefits, its inhibitors, and the motivation behind its implementation. Other responsibilities include:

- building and spreading support throughout the organization at all levels;
- setting the direction for the reuse effort and implementation;
- communicating successful reuse efforts throughout the organization;
- helping resolve organization-wide issues inhibiting the implementation of reuse.

Domain Analyst.   The domain analyst defines the borders of an application domain and identifies the common features, operations, objects, and structures in systems within this domain. He or she works with the domain expert to analyze the variants, properties, and concepts, and to understand their relations and the contexts in which they apply. Based on this knowledge, the analyst develops a domain model or framework to help determine the suitability of potential reusable workproducts within the domain.

Domain Expert.   The domain expert supports the domain analyst by providing detailed information about the application domain, existing systems and components, and their relations with the domain. He or she is expected to possess in-depth knowledge of the domain, be fluent in its terminology, and keep abreast of changes and new trends within the domain.

Domain Workproduct Manager.   The domain workproduct manager serves as a coordinator between the domain analyst, the domain expert, the reusable work-product consumers, and the librarian. He or she communicates consumer needs to the analyst and helps to ensure that the needs are understood and met. The domain workproduct manager is expected to have complete knowledge of the application domain and to manage all its workproducts and the domain analysis process.

Reuse Engineers.   We define three types of reuse engineers as follows:

>   The *producer engineer* creates reusable workproducts from scratch and reengineers existing workproducts to be reusable. He or she is responsible for maintaining these workproducts and helping users to understand workproduct functionality, features, limitations, and applicability. He is also responsible for testing workproducts and ensuring that quality standards are met.
>
>   The *broker engineer* assesses, certifies, classifies, adds, and deletes assets from the reuse library, while also maintaining the operational aspects of the reuse library.
>
>   The *consumer engineer* uses reusable workproducts in the creation of other workproducts. He or she is responsible for searching the reuse library for potential reusable workproducts and communicating project needs to the producer engineer. Together with the producer engineer, the consumer engineer integrates reusable workproducts and is responsible for additional engineering or modifications made necessary by this integration.

Reuse Analyst.   The reuse analyst works with the producer engineer and consumer engineer to determine reusability requirements. He or she should be familiar with each stage of the product development process and with domain models. The reuse analyst is responsible for evaluating and helping to restructure software components for reuse.

Reuse Economist/Metrician.   The reuse economist/metrician is responsible for the development and implementation of cost models and reuse metrics. He or she tracks reuse performance and progress by collecting and analyzing economic data and metrics. Through the use of these evaluations, the reuse economist helps reuse teams prioritize among projects.

Librarian. The reuse librarian manages and maintains the inventory of reusable workproducts. Additional responsibilities include:

- ensuring that all workproducts meet quality, documentation, and other established standards;
- communicating new workproduct additions or deletions to all reuse personnel;
- assisting users in workproduct searches;
- developing and maintaining a component classification system;
- collecting metrics on and tracking workproduct use;
- actively seeking and gathering reusable workproducts throughout the organization;
- communicating and matching consumer engineer needs with producer engineer capabilities and availability.

A librarian is sometimes referred to as a broker.

Reuse Manager. The reuse manager provides a leadership role by managing and coordinating the entire reuse effort. He or she helps to define reuse objectives and to develop and utilize metrics, assessments, and reviews to ensure fulfillment of reuse goals. The manager also promotes reuse by educating others on the reuse concept, communicating reuse objectives and benefits, establishing educational and ongoing training for reuse personnel, and providing incentives to reuse. The reuse manager should ensure that problems are identified and resolved quickly, as well as controlling project schedules, allocating resources, and managing personnel.

Other reuse roles which may be desirable include a *reuse council, asset manager,* and *reuse architect.* The reuse council provides guidance and consultation on the development of reusable assets. This team (or individual) may also allocate reuse resources and help resolve any conflicts among reuse projects. The asset manager establishes and controls workproduct quality standards and is responsible for making sure all assets are maintained. The reuse architect designs a general framework for reuse and component interfaces.

Several organizations have defined reuse personnel roles to suit their needs. For example, the Grenoble Networks Division of Hewlett-Packard has seven roles in its reuse program: domain analyst, reverse engineering analyst, reuse manager, domain expert, domain engineer, librarian, and asset manager. In its initial reuse program, these seven roles were filled by six staff members (Fig. 16–1). As the program expanded, the roles were filled by more personnel (Fig. 16–2). The Myers Corner Laboratory at IBM utilizes a centralized staffing structure which minimizes overhead by giving the reuse champion, called the *site coordinator,* responsibility for reuse across all sites [7]. This structure is illustrated in Fig. 16–3.

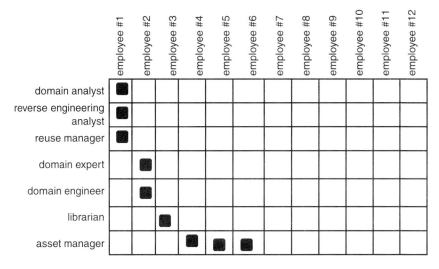

FIGURE 16–1   Reuse program early stage distribution of roles. *Source:* G. Mayobre, Hewlett-Packard Grenoble Networks Division.

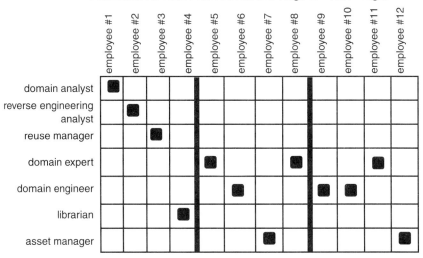

FIGURE 16–2   Reuse program mature stage distribution of roles. *Source:* G. Mayobre, Hewlett-Packard Grenoble Networks Division.

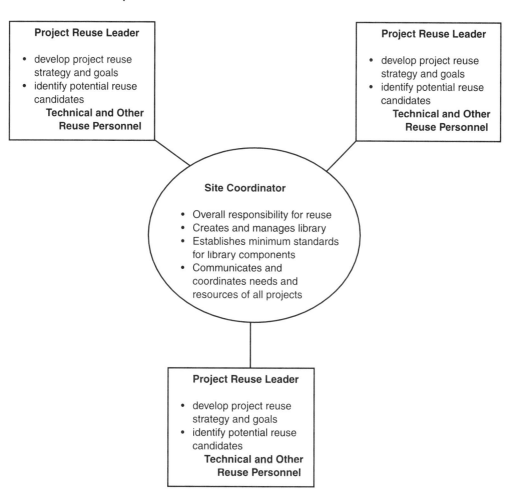

FIGURE 16–3   IBM staffing structure. *Source:* J. R. Tirso, "Establishing a software reuse support structure," in *International Conference on Communications Conference Record (ICC 91),* June 1991, vol. 3, pp. 1500–1504.

The site coordinator assumes most of the functions of a reuse librarian. Working closely with the site coordinator are project reuse leaders, responsible for developing reuse strategy and goals and identifying potential reuse candidates. These leaders function as reuse managers for all other reuse personnel. The project reuse leaders, the site coordinator, and other management representatives form what is called the *reuse review board,* which reviews all assets submitted for possible addition into the library.

The organizational structure of the asset management program (AMP) at GTE Data Services (GTEDS) is also centered around the reuse library (called the asset library) [8]. As shown in Fig. 16–4, all reuse activities are performed by various interacting groups, each consisting of reuse personnel with similar responsibilities. The *identification and qualification group* identifies and procures new assets for the library. The *development and maintenance groups* consist of producer engineers, analysts, and domain specialists. They are responsible for producing and maintaining assets. The *help support group* provides training and assistance for reuse personnel. Finally, all groups are overseen by the *asset management group*, which sets reuse policy, controls the budget, and promotes reuse.

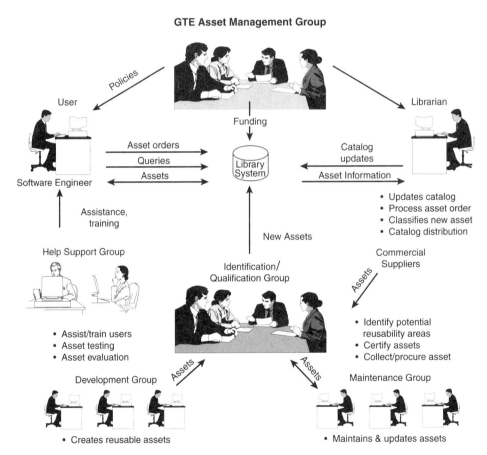

GTE Asset Management Group

User
Librarian
Policies
Funding
Software Engineer

Asset orders
Queries
Assets

Library System

Catalog updates
Asset Information

• Updates catalog
• Process asset order
• Classifies new asset
• Catalog distribution

Assistance, training

New Assets

Help Support Group

Identification/ Qualification Group

Commercial Suppliers

Assets

• Identify potential reusability areas
• Certify assets
• Collect/procure asset

• Assist/train users
• Asset testing
• Asset evaluation

Development Group
Assets
Assets
Maintenance Group

• Creates reusable assets

• Maintains & updates assets

FIGURE 16–4   GTE asset management group. *Source:* R. Prieto-Diaz, "Implementing faceted classification for software reuse," *Communications of the ACM,* vol. 34, no. 5, p. 93, May 1991.

16.4   Motivation and Incentives

Implementation of a new technology such as reuse requires a complex process of change. As mentioned earlier in this chapter, a complete change in attitude among reuse personnel is important for long-term success. Most people are creatures of habit and are resistant to change unless convinced through education and management support that the change is not only necessary but beneficial [9]. However, once committed, many require no additional motivation or incentives to implement change.

Unfortunately, for many personnel facing these challenges, a change in mind-set often comes slowly. For this reason, incentives for promoting reuse play an important role in the change process. According to Isoda:

> "For the software reuse activities to succeed, it is important to create an encouraging atmosphere in the organization. An award system is very helpful in doing this because it demonstrates top management support of the reuse activities ... The reuse awards symbolize organizational recognition of effort, devotion, and ideas of distinguished software engineers [10]."

A range of incentives are being used to encourage both individual and team contributions of reusable assets and use of reusable components. These include group- and company-wide recognition, cash bonuses, special events and dinners, and company products.

Managers at IBM's Myers Corner Laboratory encourage reuse by giving quarterly awards to programming teams that reused the most software from a reuse library [7]. In addition, a library contributor earns points each time his or her software or a part thereof is reused outside the team, as well as for each thousand lines of code (KLOC) saved by the reuse of her software. Multiple authors of a single reusable asset are given points according to their contribution to the asset. When authors reach a predetermined plateau, they receive public recognition and a financial award. Organizations such as GTE and NASA Ames provide small cash awards ($25 and $50, respectively) while Hartford rewards reusers with a special dinner.

Although financial awards are often used as incentives, research and empirical studies of high-technology professionals reveal that financial rewards are less important than rewards relating to job content, such as participation in important and challenging work, and opportunity for advancement and career development [11].

In a study by Couger on motivating factors, job content ranked highest among analysts and programmers, followed by opportunity for achievement, opportunity for advancement, pay and benefits, and recognition [12]. Based upon these and other findings, although financial awards and recognition may be part of a reuse program, more attention should be paid to job content, making work more challenging and meaningful to reuse personnel.

Earlier in this chapter, we discussed skill specialization as a consequence of reuse. Although specialization often brings about increased productivity and efficiency, it can also result in work monotony, which in turn reduces motivation. Since the lack of motivation and incentives are among the most often cited inhibitors to reuse [1], considerable attention should be paid to identifying motivations that support the development and use of reusable assets.

Communicating how reuse contributes to job enrichment and presenting it as an opportunity rather than a burden can help foster the change in attitude needed for its successful implementation. Humphrey suggests involving personnel in planning for reuse so "they can better understand the change, see why and what to expect [9]." Equally valuable is visible management commitment to reuse. In his study of four reuse programs, Prieto-Diaz found "unconditional and extensive management support" to be a key factor in all successful reuse programs [13].

16.5   Reuse Training and Education

Proper education and training of reuse personnel is one of the most important means of communicating a reuse purpose and goals. Without it, personnel cannot be expected to implement or carry out a reuse program. Some researchers believe that the limited success of reuse can be partly attributed to its neglect in current software engineering education [14]. Often cited excuses for not implementing reuse include [15]:

"We have no reusability skills."
"I don't believe reusability works."
"Reusable software destroys creativity."
"Reuse of software cannot be efficient."
"We have no reusability plan."
"Introduction of reusable software will eliminate my job."

These kinds of statements are evidence of a lack of understanding and uncertainty about reuse. These obstacles can be overcome by educating personnel on the organizational objectives of reuse. A short discussion on what reuse encompasses, why it is important, what its costs, benefits, and impact are, and how management will support reuse, would be appropriate for employees on all levels. Regular communication throughout the organization regarding reuse progress on all levels will emphasize the importance and legitimacy of reuse as a software development technology. *Concept training must occur before tool training* [6].

All reuse personnel should have a formal software engineering education or equivalent engineering experience. They should be proficient at software analysis and development and be familiar with object-oriented programming methods. In addition, each reuse specialist should possess some expertise or experience in his or her specialization. For example, domain analysts, experts, and managers should have experience in domain analysis; librarians, expertise in metrics and tools; and economists, knowledge of cost/ benefit modeling and metrics. Managers need to be educated on the costs of reuse and expected impact, both positive and negative [16]. They should be made aware of potential inhibitors to reuse and educated on how they can be overcome. Programmers should be trained on writing reusable software and modifying existing practices to maximize reuse. All reuse personnel should be educated on identifying reuse opportunities.

As with any high technology, two main aspects of reuse should be emphasized:

- *managerial issues:* economic, organizational, and legal issues as well as metrics and resource management;
- *technical issues:* tools and techniques for creating, developing, and using reusable assets, and implementing and maintaining a reuse library.

A single individual will rarely be well-versed in both managerial and technical issues; however, the reuse team should be comprised of people trained to address problems in both areas. Bott claims "It would be a mistake to see the problems of software reuse in purely technical terms [17]." He believes that the cumulative effect of nontechnical obstacles often outweigh the technical problems. In a recent experiment, Smart *et al.* found that software development personnel untrained in software reuse cannot properly assess the worth of reusing a candidate asset [18]. Furthermore, the staff was confused with respect to distinguishing important and trivial features important to a reuse decision.

All reuse personnel, managers and programmers alike, should have some exposure to both organizational and technical reuse issues. An effective education program for reuse should include courses that integrate both areas but at different levels appropriate for particular personnel.

A core curriculum in reuse should include the following topics.

Topic Area	**Helps Answer**
Overview	
• Reuse definition and terminology	- Why reuse?
	- What can be reused?
• Organizational objectives and goals	- What are the benefits and costs of reuse?
	- What is the impact of reuse on software quality and productivity?
	- What are the limits of reuse?
	- What are some legal aspects that need to be addressed?

Managerial Issues

- Planning and organizing for reuse

    - What organizational practices best support reuse?
    - What are the inhibitors to reuse and how can they be overcome?
    - What incentives and motivators can be utilized to encourage reuse?
    - What staffing is needed?

- Development and use of economic models for reuse

    - What elements are important in measuring the economic impact of reuse?
    - How can benefits and costs to reuse be quantified?
    - How do we determine whether or not the creation of a reusable asset is economically worthwhile?

- Development and use of reuse metrics

    - Which metrics should be employed to measure reuse progress?
    - How should these metrics be defined and tracked?

Technical Issues

- Design for Reuse

    - What are the tools and techniques needed to create reusable assets?
    - What features make an asset reusable?
    - What is required for an asset to be reusable?
    - What are the tools and techniques for modifying existing assets to make them reusable?
    - How do we examine existing assets for reusability?

- Design with Reuse

    - How do we develop and maintain a system using reusable assets?
    - How do we integrate new components with reusable components?

- Library Management

    - What are the tools and skills needed for library management?
    - How should the library be organized for search efficiency?

| | - What are the means by which library assets are classified, catalogued, and maintained? |

* Domain Analysis

- What product characteristics maximize reuse?

- How do we identify common domain characteristics within and outside of product lines?

- How are projects assessed for reuse potential?

Ideally, hands-on exercises should be incorporated into all technical and managerial courses that involve modeling. Use of case studies and examples of actual systems created from reusable workproducts is invaluable. In larger organizations where programming courses are taught, introductory reuse concepts and topics should be integrated wherever appropriate. This will help expose a larger audience of programmers and analysts to reuse early in their careers.

Summary

The selection, education, and motivation of appropriate staff can have a significant impact on establishing an effective reuse infrastructure. The roles in a reuse program include: reuse champion, domain analyst, domain expert, domain asset manager, reuse engineers, reuse analyst, reuse economist/metrician, librarian, and reuse manager. A change in attitude and culture is important for long-term reuse success. Education and training are some of the means for achieving this cultural change as well as for communicating the goals and purpose of the reuse initiative.

References

1. W. Tracz, "Software reuse: Motivators and inhibitors," in *Digest of Papers. COMPCON Spring '87, 32nd IEEE Computer Society International Conference. Intellectual Leverage*, Cat. no. 87CH2409-1, 1987, pp. 358–363.
2. E. Wald, *STARS Reusability Guidebook, Version 4.0*, U.S. Department of Defense, 1986.
3. G. Oddy, "Software reuse at G-MRC," in *1st International Workshop on Software Reusability*, July 3–5, 1991, pp. 30–35.
4. J. Tirso, "Championing the cause: Making reuse stick," in *5th Annual Workshop on Institutionalizing Software Reuse*, Oct. 26–29, 1992.
5. M. A. Maidique, "Entrepreneurs, champions, and technological innovation," *IEEE Engineering Management Review*, vol. 12, no. 1, pp. 24–40, Mar. 1984.

6. J. L. Wynekoop and J. A. Senn, "CASE implementation: The importance of multiple perspectives," in *Proceedings of the 1992 ACM SIGCPR Conference*, Cincinnati, OH, 1992.

7. J. R. Tirso, "Establishing a software reuse support structure," *ICC 91, International Conference on Communications Conference Record*, Cat. no. 91CH2984-3, 1991, vol. 3, pp. 1500–1504.

8. G. Jones and R. Prieto-Diaz, "Building and managing software libraries," in *Proceedings COMPSAC 88: 12th International Computer Software and Applications Conference*, Cat. no. 88CH2611-2, 1988, pp. 228–236.

9. W. S. Humphrey, *Managing for Innovation: Leading Technical People*. Englewood Cliffs, NJ: Prentice-Hall, 1987.

10. S. Isoda, "An experience of software reuse activities," in *Proceedings of the 15th Annual International Computer Software and Applications Conference*, Cat. no. 91CH3023-9, 1991, pp. 8–9.

11. M. A. Y. Von Glinow, *The New Professionals: Managing Today's High-Tech Employees*. Cambridge, MA: Ballinger, 1988.

12. J. D. Couger, "New challenges in motivating MIS personnel," *Journal of Information Systems Management*, vol. 6, no. 4, pp. 36–41, Fall 1989.

13. R. Prieto-Diaz, "Making software reuse work: An implementation model," *SIGSOFT Software Engineering Notes*, vol. 16, no. 3, pp. 61–8, July 1991.

14. G. Sindre, E. A. Karlsson, and T. Stalhane, "Software reuse in an educational perspective," in *Software Engineering Education. SEI Conference 1992 Proceedings*, 1992, pp. 99–114.

15. *Creating Reusable Ada Software*, EVB Software Engineering, Inc., Frederick, MD, 1987.

16. J. Tirso, "The IBM reuse program," in *4th Annual Workshop on Software Reuse*, Nov. 18–22, 1991.

17. M. F. Bott and P. J. L. Wallis, "Ada and software re-use," *Software Engineering Journal*, vol. 3, no. 5, pp. 177–183, Sept. 1988.

18. P. F. Smart, S. N. Woodfield, D. W. Embley, and D. T. Scott, "An empirical investigation of the effect of education and tools on software reusability," in *7th Annual International Phoenix Conference on Computers and Communications. 1988 Conference Proceedings*, Cat. no.TH0188-3, pp. 224–228.

17

ORGANIZATIONAL STRUCTURES FOR SOFTWARE REUSE

The reuse organizational structure refers to the formal system of working relationships that permits both the division of labor and coordination of tasks for individuals and groups to achieve the common goal of reuse. Effective implementation of reuse can often be traced to an organization's structure and how well that structure supports the organization's reuse strategy and process. In this chapter, we describe a framework of organizational forms for software reuse and their advantages and disadvantages. The choice of an appropriate organizational structure depends upon the reuse strategy, current environment factors, critical success factors, and the nature of the organization itself; the proposed reuse organizational structure should be examined in this context. Previous work in reuse organizational structures is reviewed in Appendix 17–A.

The ideal reuse organization is both *effective* and *efficient*:

A reuse organization is *effective if it facilitates the contribution of individuals in the attainment of software reuse.* The alignment of individuals toward a common goal is often referred to as "the principle of unity of objective." It assumes that the organization will clearly define its reuse objective, that this objective is measurable, and that it is communicated to all participants.

A reuse organization is *efficient if it facilitates reuse while minimizing undesirable consequences and costs.* In this case, efficiency encompasses not only the financial aspect, but also the satisfaction of the individual and group.

Organizations seeking to implement reuse should be careful to choose a structure based upon these two principles of effectiveness and efficiency. In some cases, gains in efficiency may result in an undesirable sacrifice in effectiveness and vice versa. For example, an organization where reuse is centralized may be able to lower the costs of producing reusable assets. However, the centralized department may be so far removed from its consumer projects that the specific needs of the projects may not be met, resulting in reusable assets with little or no value to the consumers. Choosing an organizational structure that strikes the appropriate balance between effectiveness and efficiency requires a thorough understanding of the advantages and disadvantages of each structure, which we will discuss later in this chapter.

We will begin by discussing a continuum of possible organizational structures for reuse. We will then examine three major archetypes and discuss their advantages and disadvantages. Finally, we will illustrate these structures by examining several reuse organizations in the industry.

17.1   Organizational Structures for Reuse: A Continuum

A wide range of structural forms exists for software reuse. Each has its particular advantages and disadvantages which may be accentuated by the particular circumstances of the project.

Fig. 17–1 illustrates a continuum of structural forms which may be adopted by organizations to support reuse [1].

At one end of the continuum is the functional form, which is organized around the "inputs" to the software engineering task. Examples of inputs are software testing, coding, and documentation. Thus, an organization with a pure functional form would have a separate testing department, coding department, and so forth (Fig. 17–2).

The Range of Organizational Alternatives

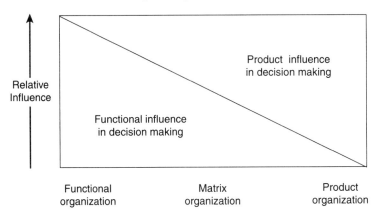

FIGURE 17–1   Range of organizational alternatives. *Source:* Adapted from J. R. Galbraith, "Matrix organization designs," *Business Horizons,* vol. 14, no. 1, p. 37, Feb. 1971.

Functional Organization

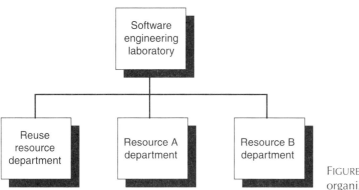

FIGURE 17–2 Functional organization.

The decision making process in such an organization is highly influenced by its inputs. At the other end of the continuum is the project or product form which is structured around the "outputs" of the task such as a spreadsheet product. For example, teams consisting of members, each with responsibility for providing various resources for accomplishing the software engineering task, focus on a particular market or product (Fig. 17–3).

Project Organization

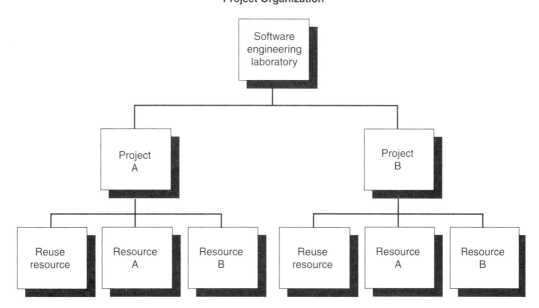

FIGURE 17–3 Project organization.

Organizations that assume a structure closer to the functional end of the continuum are more centralized and tend to provide a more functional influence, i.e., influence from the point of view of the function (the testing department, for example) in decision making. They also tend to develop highly qualified reuse technical skills and high efficiency. In organizations that assume a structure toward the product organization end, there is greater product influence (i.e., influence from the point of view of the product or market) in decision making. Reuse personnel are more familiar with the particular product and its specific problems. They are more involved with the entire project as opposed to being dedicated to only one aspect.

Halfway between each extreme lies the matrix structure, which is a combination of the functional structure and the project structure. It is characterized by having functional departments the personnel of which reside or have indirect reporting obligations to projects (Fig. 17–4).

Matrix Organization

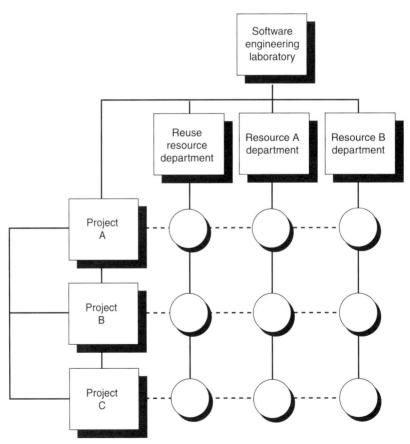

FIGURE 17-4 Matrix organization.

A matrix structure may be appropriate for an organization which is not able to utilize full-time reuse personnel for its projects, but desires its reuse specialists to be involved with its consumers to the level associated with product structures. It should be noted that these three structures are archetypes from which an appropriate reuse organizational structure may be derived. In practice, organizational structures tend to be hybrid structures, i.e., combinations of these archetypes.

Communication and coordination between different units within the same organization can be achieved through an "integration mechanism." Integration mechanisms are "the hierarchy, standard rules and procedures, and planning and information systems" [2] that may be used to facilitate coordination between different parties. Galbraith [3] describes lateral integrating mechanisms in order of increasing complexity:

- Direct information contacts among managers in lateral positions;
  Lateral managers agree to share information to facilitate coordination and communication.
- Creation of a liaison role between independent groups;
  A subordinate is designated to serve as a liaison between groups.
- Creation of a task force/steering committee;
  Representatives from each of the groups meet until the task is completed or periodically in the form of a task force/steering committee.
- Creation of a temporary coordinating manager;
  A manager is temporarily assigned the duty of overseeing coordination among the groups.
- Creation of a permanent coordinating manager;
  A manager is permanently assigned the duty of overseeing coordination among the groups.
- Establishment of the matrix organization form;
  Personnel are assigned to functional departments but reside or have indirect reporting obligations to projects.

Fig. 17–5 depicts how the lateral integrating mechanisms serve to bridge communication and cooperation within each archetypal organizational form. For example, communication among Resource A personnel is facilitated with the functional organization because they reside under a single department. Communication and coordination between Resource A and B personnel, however, is more difficult: each resides under its own department. In order to improve coordination between Resource A and B, we could utilize one or more of the lateral integrating mechanisms mentioned earlier. Our choice of integrating mechanisms ranges from "direct information contacts" to the more complex "establishment of the matrix form." Likewise, communication among Resource A and B on project A is facilitated through the

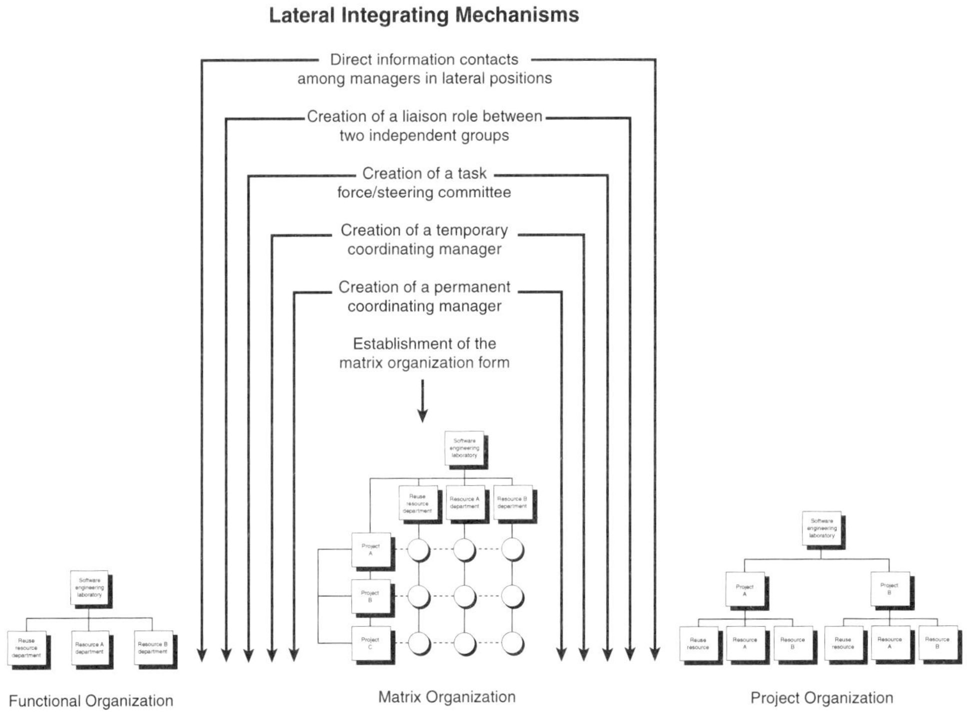

Lateral Integrating Mechanisms

FIGURE 17–5   Lateral integrating mechanisms.

project organization, but not between, for example, Resource A on project A and Resource A on project B. In order to facilitate coordination between Resource A personnel on separate projects, any of the lateral integrating mechanisms may be utilized.

Walton [4] describes two companies that utilize integrating mechanisms in their reuse organizations. The first is Logica, where there are software teams concerned with the development and maintenance of the reusable assets and other software teams using the assets. A steering committee oversees the entire process and defines policy and standards. The steering committee, in this case, serves as an integrating mechanism and a bridge between all the teams.

Another approach described by Walton is the one used by British Telecom, which utilizes a liaison group that promotes and coordinates standard practices.

17.2   Reuse Functional Organization

The functional organization is highly centralized and, as Schermerhorn [5] observes, appropriate for stable environments and stability-oriented strategies. It also tends to work well in smaller and less complex organizations. Its advantages are as follows:

- Reuse personnel have a more global and objective perspective of consumers' and end-users' interests and needs.
- Common software reuse tasks can be combined.
- Strong dedication of reuse personnel to reuse activities is fostered.
- Development of reuse standards and a consistent methodology is supported.
- Greater reuse specialization is encouraged.
- An environment conducive to high efficiency is created.

Another key advantage of the functional organization is the centralization of all reuse activities, which results in the consolidation of certain tasks that may have otherwise been duplicated under a decentralized project structure. Moreover, such an organization, with its more global view, will be better positioned to serve the needs of many diverse consumers and end-users. Such a structure also reinforces the development of consistent reuse standards and methods. A decentralized structure, on the other hand, may encourage proliferation of incompatible standards and methods.

In addition, there are personnel advantages that stem from having a functional reuse organization, including the facilitation of the exchange and proliferation of ideas, an increase in the overall level of technical skill, and simplified training. It also provides an opportunity for personnel to fully develop their specialized skills.

Disadvantages are as follows:

- Reuse personnel tend to be further removed from understanding the local consumers' and end-users' needs.
- Reuse-related problems may have to be resolved at the top of the reuse department hierarchy.
- Response to interdepartmental problems may be slow.
- Accountability for total product or system delivery may be reduced.

Among the disadvantages of the functional reuse organization is that it is further removed from the local consumer and end-user and thus may have a lesser understanding of consumer and end-users' needs. There may also be a delay in or lack of responsiveness to reuse problems as the problems are "floated" up the hierarchy for resolution. Difficult or vague communication across departments may also impede responsiveness. Finally, accountability for the entire product or system may be reduced as compared with an organizational structure where a team of individuals hold responsibility for a given product.

17.3   Case Studies of Reuse Functional Organizations

Nippon Telegraph and Telephone Corporation.   Organized reuse efforts at the Nippon Telegraph and Telephone Corporation [6] are highly centralized and consist of 1) a reusability committee, 2) a support group, and 3) a tool development group. These three groups support various software development projects in their reuse efforts (Fig. 17–6).

The reusability committee is comprised of representatives from each participating software development group. Responsibilities of the committee include the establishment of guidelines and standards for reusable assets, validation checklists,

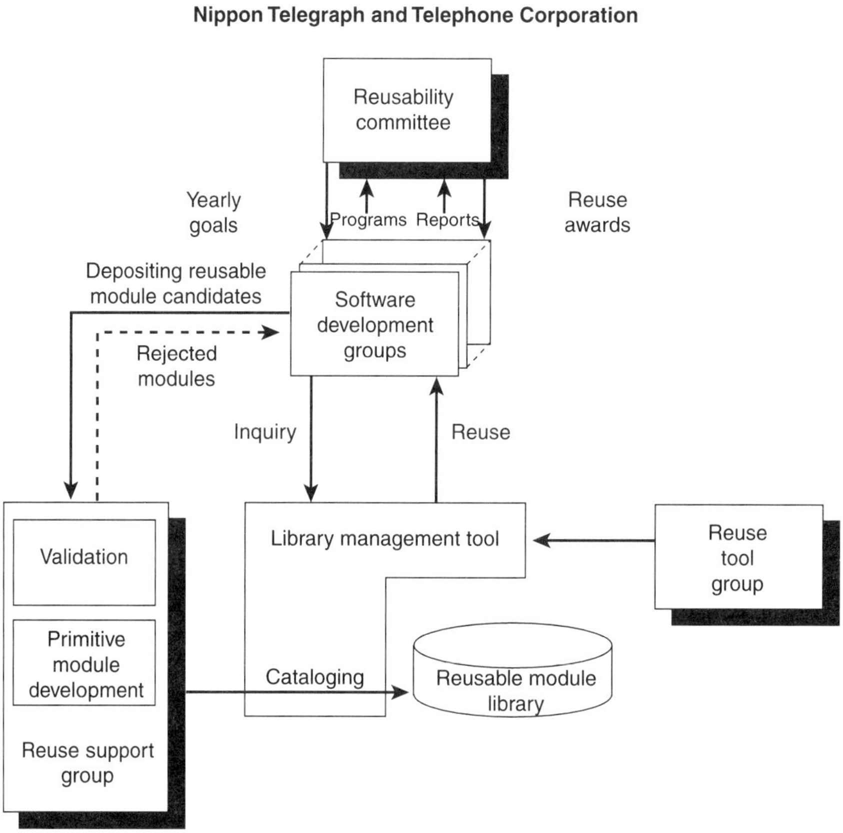

Nippon Telegraph and Telephone Corporation

FIGURE 17–6   Nippon Telegraph and Telephone Corporation reuse organizational structure. *Source:* S. Isoda, "Experience report on software reuse project: Its structure, activities, and statistical results," *Proceedings of the International Conference on Software Engineering*, no. 14, p. 321, 1992.

and reuse incentives. The reuse support group spearheads the reuse effort by providing recommendations to the reusability committee, providing reports to upper management, and overseeing the development and maintenance of a reuse library. The reuse tool development group is responsible for developing the library management tool.

The reuse support group is centralized and is an example of a functional group serving as a resource to projectized software development groups. The reusability committee is an example of a lateral integrating device wherein members of the software development groups convene to discuss reuse issues that are of common concern across the groups.

San Diego Technical Graphics Division of the Hewlett-Packard Company. A functional organizational structure is utilized at San Diego Technical Graphics Division of the Hewlett-Packard Company (Fig. 17–7). Producers are in a separate organization than the consumers. In fact, the consumers are predominantly outside the producer's organization.

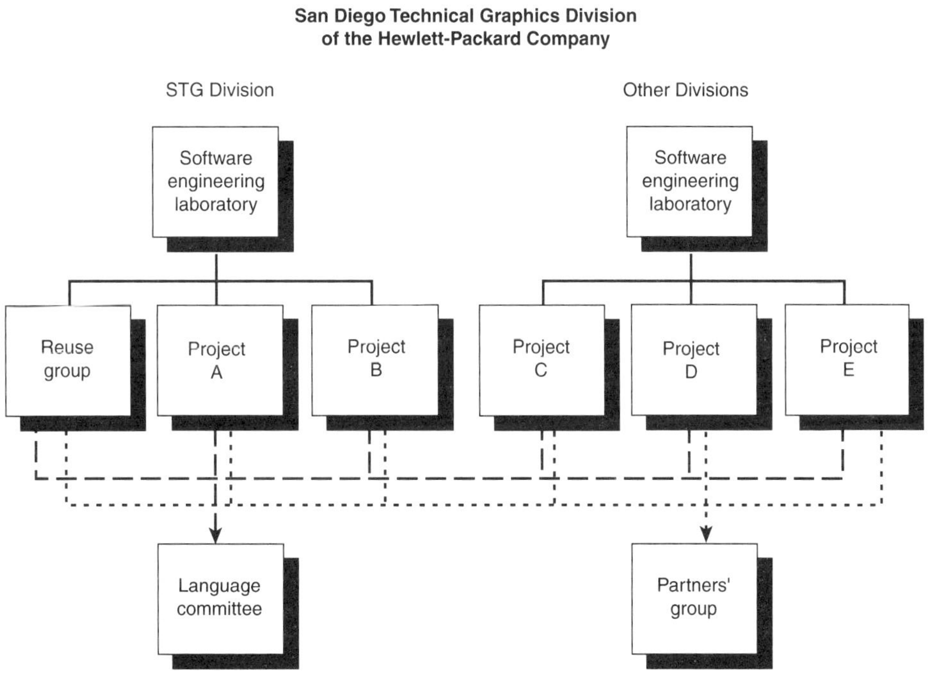

FIGURE 17–7   San Diego Technical Graphics Division reuse organizational structure. *Source:* J. Cassidy, Hewlett-Packard San Diego Technical Graphics Division.

The lateral integrating mechanisms between the producer and consumer groups are the Reusable Workproduct Language Committee and the Partners Group, where coordination and information on reuse is disseminated. The Reusable Workproduct Language Committee meets to discuss external issues, e.g., what features ought to be incorporated into the reusable assets. Fifteen representatives from participating organizations meet every six weeks. In addition, feedback from marketing is used as part of the process to determine which reusable software features to incorporate. A Partners' Group, the membership of which consists of implementors/acceptors, communicate (primarily via phone) to determine how features will be implemented.

Toshiba. Toshiba [7] is another example of a functional organization. As shown in Fig. 17–8, consumers utilize parts (maintained in a "parts center") that are produced in a "parts manufacturing department," in much the same way as a manufacturing production.

The integrating mechanism used by Toshiba is a "software parts steering committee." The committee gathers, selects, and authorizes the creation, update, and discard of reusable modules. The authorized requests are delivered to the parts

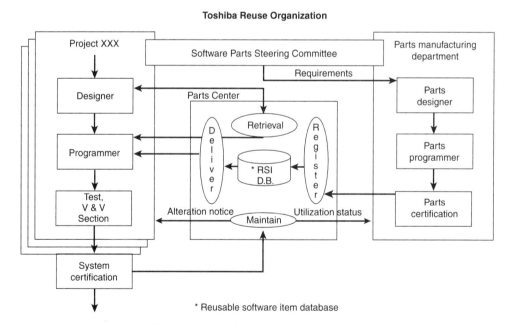

FIGURE 17–8 Toshiba reuse organizational structure. *Source:* Y. Matsumoto, "A software factory: An overall approach to software production," *IEEE Tutorial: Software Reusability*, Peter Freeman, Ed., Los Alamitos, CA: IEEE, 1987, p. 173.

manufacturing department and fulfilled. When new parts are developed, each part is evaluated according to pre-established criteria. Parts which meet or exceed the standards are then transferred to the parts center. Identification of the parts, which includes a description of its attributes and a keyword, are then registered into a reusable software item database. The actual part is stored separately. The parts department not only registers and stores parts, but also provides services such as retrieval, delivery, maintenance, and publication of registered parts.

17.4 Reuse Project Organization

The reuse project organization is highly decentralized (Fig. 17–3) and, as Schermerhorn [5] points out, is appropriate for rapidly growing organizations, or those facing an unstable environment requiring quick responses to changing problems and opportunities.

Advantages of a reuse project organization are as follows:

- Reuse personnel are more attuned to local consumers' and end-users' needs.
- Many reuse-related decisions can be resolved at the project level, thereby relieving higher levels of the organization.
- Response time to interfunctional problems is shortened.
- Attention to and accountability for the product and/or system is increased.

The main advantage of the project structure is the increased understanding and accommodation of particular reuse needs of a project by reuse personnel. For example, a producer who is part of the project team will tend to have a greater understanding of the project domain and be more sensitive to the needs of that particular project. Because reuse-related issues can be resolved at a local level, response time is shortened. Interfunctional issues may also be resolved in a more timely manner because all the members are situated on the same project. Finally, the project structure focuses attention and accountability on the total product or system. Responsibility for a given project clearly lies with the team of individuals involved.

Disadvantages of a reuse project organization include:

- The global perspective of all consumers' and end-users' interests and needs may be reduced.
- Greater potential for duplication of reuse tasks exists.
- Reuse personnel may be reassigned to other software development activities.
- Maintenance of shared resources (e.g., the reuse library) may be more difficult.
- The environment may create inconsistencies in reuse standards and methods.
- The development of sufficient depth of reuse expertise may be slowed.

Because reuse personnel report to the project manager, it is more difficult to obtain an objective global view of multiple consumers' and end-users' needs. For example, a producer engineer, whose job is to create reusable assets for all projects, but who reports to a local project manager, may tend to produce assets which are optimized only for the needs of his manager's project. A decentralized organization structure can potentially also make the maintenance of shared resources difficult. For example, the lack of direct responsibility for maintenance of the reuse library may result in its neglect. In addition, reuse standards may diverge when each project gradually modifies the reuse standards for their particular needs, thereby reducing the assets' reusability for other projects. Finally, a project structure may not facilitate the sharing of ideas and experiences among the reuse personnel, resulting in insufficient depth of reuse expertise.

17.5   Case Study of a Reuse Project Organization

Software Technology Division of the Hewlett-Packard Company.   The Manufacturing Productivity section (MP section) of the Software Technology Division within the Hewlett-Packard Company utilizes a project organizational structure (Fig. 17–9). Both producers and consumers are distributed among the projects. In fact, engineers have both producer and consumer roles. The integrating mechanism is a "Shared Components Council" consisting of representatives from all the projects. Information regarding defects, potential reusable assets, and other reuse issues is shared during periodic meetings. The reuse repository is centralized and maintained by a librarian.

17.6   Case Study of a Reuse Hybrid Organization

Air Traffic Control Advanced Automation System.   The air traffic control advanced automation system (AAS) was an effort intended to replace the existing air traffic control (ATC) computer systems [8], [9]. It had a hybrid organizational structure that consisted of both a functional and a project organization. Because of its size and complexity, the advanced automation system was divided into six subsystems, which in turn contained 16 identified software configurations called "computer software configuration items" (CSCIs).

Each CSCI was used in one or more AAS systems and can have one or more operational units (OUs) or functional groups (FGs), which are collections of computer software components (CSCs) (Fig. 17–10). A reuse working group (RWG), which consisted of two chairpersons and a number of representatives from each OU/FG, promoted software reuse across AAS.

To address the problems of having limited domain experts and creating reusable components that are general enough to be reused across AAS systems yet specific enough to address individual project needs, AAS had reusable components created both by the RWG and each OU/FG. The RWG handled components which

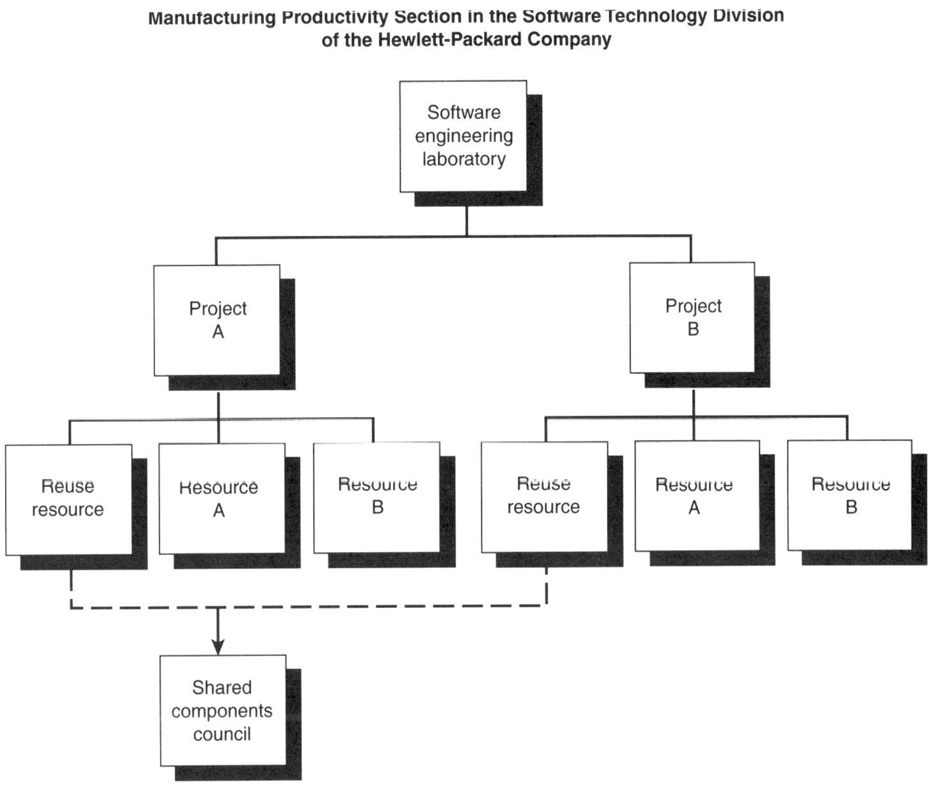

**Manufacturing Productivity Section in the Software Technology Division
of the Hewlett-Packard Company**

FIGURE 17–9   Hewlett-Packard Manufacturing Productivity section reuse organizational structure. *Source:* A. Nishimoto, Hewlett-Packard Manufacturing Productivity section.

were more general and did not require specific domain knowledge. The OU/FG created components which required more expertise in a specific domain.

17.7   Reuse Matrix Organization

The matrix organization is a combination of the functional and project forms and, according to Schermerhorn [5], is appropriate for organizations pursuing growth strategies in dynamic *and* complex environments. It is most appropriate when there is "outside pressure for dual focus, pressure for high information processing capability, and pressure for shared resources [2]." In a matrix organization, reuse personnel are part of a central reuse department, but they are assigned to a cross-functional team consisting of members from various resource departments working on a given project.

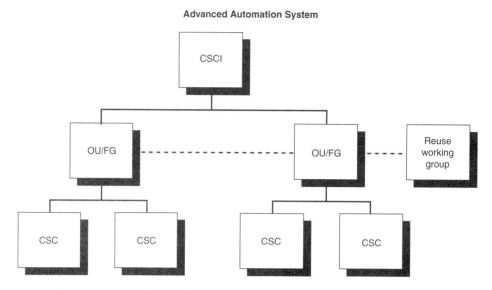

FIGURE 17–10   Advanced automation system reuse organizational system.
Source: Adapted from J. Margono and L. Lindsey, "Software reuse in the
air traffic control advanced automation system," in *Improving the Software
Process and Competitive Position via Software Reuse and Re-engineering
Conference*, The National Institute for Software Quality and Productivity,
Alexandria, VA, Apr. 29–30, 1991.

Advantages of a reuse matrix organization are as follows:

• Both local consumers' and end-users' needs, as well as the larger picture of global reuse across many projects, is acknowledged.
• Reuse-related decisions are relegated to the cross-functional team.
• Reuse resources are used by projects as needed.
• Communication with other reuse personnel is facilitated.

In a matrix structure, the reuse specialist is intimately familiar with the reuse needs of a project, yet able to address global reuse issues as well. For example, the reuse producer engineer assigned to project A will be acutely aware of project A's needs and, because he reports to the reuse department, will be able to create assets that balance the needs of many projects with his own. Reuse-related decisions may be resolved at the cross-functional team level and need not be pushed up the reuse department hierarchy. This increases response time and lessens the burden at the top of the reuse department. The advantage of the matrix structure over the project structure is that a given project may not be able to utilize a full-time reuse specialist, or the project may be of short duration. Finally, the matrix structure encourages camaraderie among reuse personnel: the reuse specialists are allied with their colleagues and report to a manager who is a reuse specialist. Some reuse specialists may view that their professional advancement may be served better by belonging to such a group.

Disadvantages of a reuse matrix organization include:

- Potential conflict between allegiance to both a project and the reuse department exists.
- Roles may conflict.
- Reward system may conflict.
- A high level of coordination is required.

Among other disadvantages of the matrix structure is the inherent ambiguity that results from reporting to two managers. It violates the unity of objective principle. For example, a producer may experience a conflict of interest between a need to design the workproduct to optimize the requirements of the project and of optimizing the workproduct to meet the needs of other projects. A properly designed managerial support system and individuals who can tolerate ambiguity will work best in this type of organizational structure. In addition, there may be a conflict of roles: the role of reuse personnel within the department may differ from that within the project. There may also be a conflict within the reward system. The producer, for example, may be rewarded by the project manager for the number of reusable assets created or procured for his project whereas the reuse department manager may reward the producer for workproducts that are appropriate for *all* the projects.

Successful establishment of the matrix structure entails changing the management control systems to accommodate the new structure. For example, the profit reporting mechanism and reward structure must comply with the multidimensional nature of the organizational structure. Because functioning in a matrix structure is inherently more complex, the personnel involved must develop his or her career based on a multifunctional perspective, act in a participatory manner, and have the ability to prioritize activities.

17.8   Case Studies of Reuse Matrix Organizations

GTE [10] is an organization that has utilized both a functional reuse group and a matrix organization. As shown in Fig. 17–11, the Asset Management Group sets the policies and manages the program budget.

A Help Support Group provides training for software development groups on the use of the library, standards, and guidelines. A Identification/Qualification Group assesses and validates the reusability of assets before inclusion in the library and identifies assets that should be created which have high reuse potential.

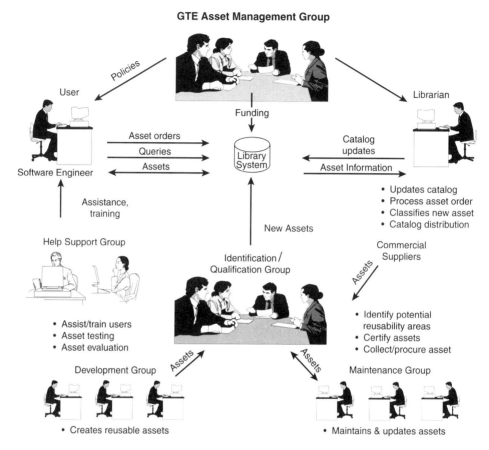

FIGURE 17–11   GTE reuse organizational structure. *Source:* R. Prieto-Diaz, "Implementing faceted classification for software reuse," *Communications of the ACM*, vol. 34, no. 5, p. 93, May 1991.

Organized as a matrix, the Development and Maintenance Groups are "regular" product development groups but also produce assets as identified by the Identification/Qualification Group. Assets may be submitted by development groups either within the AMP organization or external development groups.

17.9   Test and Measurement Group of the Hewlett-Packard Company

Another example of a hybrid functional and matrix structure is the Hewlett-Packard Test and Measurement Group's (TMG) proposed organizational structure (Fig. 17–12).

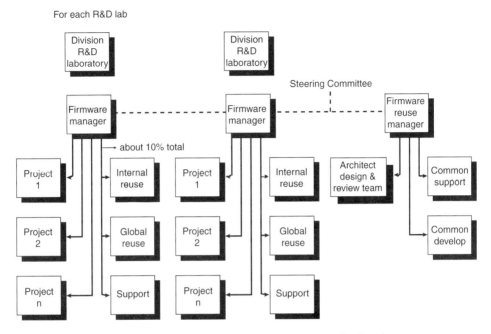

FIGURE 17–12   Test & Measurement Group reuse organizational structure.
Source: J. Mueller, Hewlett-Packard Test and Measurement Group.

The proposed approach is to allocate 10% of its firmware resources to address the following: 1) internal reuse to benefit the project; 2) "global" reuse to benefit the entire group of projects; and 3) a formal support organization that would include, for example, a software reuse library. Overseeing much of this would be a steering committee consisting of members from each of the division R&D laboratories. A functional structure would be utilized by the firmware and reuse managers within their own groups. A matrix structure would coordinate the software development of assets for global reuse.

The TMG hybrid organization for reuse is analogous to the federal, state, and local government structure. The basic philosophy that underlies the government system (and the TMG method) is that decisions should be handed down to the lowest organization level with the necessary information and resources to handle them. Consequently, local governments are best positioned to identify and deal with local issues and problems. Likewise, for TMG, the creation of unique and reusable software that requires much expertise may be best handled locally where information is most complete. Reusable software that may be used across several local areas under the same "state" may be best handled at the "state" level. Only from the viewpoint of the state (or its functional equivalent) can the appropriate information be available to analyze the best solutions to reuse issues at this level. These stratified levels of component development (local, state, federal) may be drawn analogously to an organization's own hierarchical structure. For example, Hewlett-Packard is organized as follows: project, laboratory, division, group, and corporate.

17.10   The Horizontal Reuse Organization

Another form of organization being explored is the horizontal or flat organization [11]. In such a organization, work is structured around a number of key or "core" business processes. These processes flow from the supplier to the employee to the customer. Such organizations recognize and optimize these processes which deliver value to the customer. In addition, emphasis is given to team, not individual, performance, employees are encouraged to be competent in multiple areas, and managers own processes, not departments. Fig. 17–13 depicts the transformation from a vertically based reuse organization to a horizontal reuse organization. In this case, the three reuse processes of reuse, produce reusable assets, broker reusable assets, and consume reusable assets, are the processes upon which work is structured. The design of a reuse organization around core processes has been the subject of investigation at Hewlett-Packard [12].

Summary

An effective and efficient reuse organizational structure contributes to software reuse while minimizing undesirable consequences and costs. There are three archetypes: the functional, project, and matrix forms. Other hybrid structures are formed by combining features of these three. Each of these three structures has its advantages and disadvantages, which are accentuated by the particular circumstances of the reuse effort. Integrating mechanisms, such as a steering committee, must be carefully selected to facilitate coordination and communication between different groups within a given organizational structure. The appropriate organizational form and integrating mechanisms for a reuse organization should be chosen based on reuse strategy, the current environment, and the organization's unique characteristics and culture.

Acknowledgments

The author wishes to thank Jack Cassidy, Sadahiro Isoda, Johan Margono, Yoshihiro Matsumoto, Joe Mueller, Alvina Nishimoto, and Ruben Prieto-Diaz for discussing and providing permission to describe the organizational structures used in their reuse efforts. A version of this chapter was published as "Choosing an organizational structure for reuse," *Reuse 95*, Morgantown, WV.

Transformation from the Vertical Reuse Organization ...

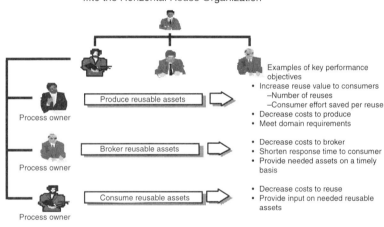

...to the Horizontal Reuse Organization

FIGURE 17–13   The horizontal reuse organization. *Source:* Adapted from F. Ostroff and D. Smith, Redesigning the Corporation: The Horizontal Organization, *The McKinsey Quarterly*, no. 1, p. 150–151, 1992.

References

1. J. R. Galbraith, "Matrix organization designs," *Business Horizons*, vol. 14, no. 1, pp. 29–40, Feb. 1971.
2. A. C. Hax and N. Majluf, "Organization design," in *Management Handbook: Operating Guidelines, Techniques, and Practices*, P. Mali, Ed. New York, NY: Wiley, 1981.
3. J. R. Galbraith, *Designing Complex Organizations*. Reading, MA: Addison-Wesley, 1973.

4. P. Walton, "Software reuse: Management issues," in *1st International Workshop on Software Reusability*, July 3–5, 1991, pp. 100–106.

5. J. Schermerhorn, *Management for Productivity*. New York, NY: Wiley, 1984.

6. S. Isoda, "Experience report on software reuse project: Its structure, activities, and statistical results," in *Proceedings International Conference on Software Engineering*, 1992.

7. Y. Matsumoto, "A software factory: An overall approach to software production," in *IEEE Tutorial: Software Reusability*, P. Freeman, Ed. Los Alamitos, CA: IEEE Computer Society Press, 1987, pp. 155–178.

8. J. Margono and L. Lindsey, "Software reuse in the air traffic control advanced automation system," presented at *Improving the Software Process and Competitive Position via Software Reuse and Reengineering*, Alexandria, VA, 1991.

9. G. M. Bowen, "An organized, devoted, project-wide reuse effort," *Ada Letters*, vol. 12, no. 1, pp. 43–52, Jan./Feb., 1992.

10. R. Prieto-Diaz, "Implementing faceted classification for software reuse," *Communications of the ACM*, vol. 34, no. 5, pp. 88–97, May 1991.

11. F. Ostroff and D. Smith, "The horizontal organization," *McKinsey Quarterly*, no. 1, pp. 148-168, 1992.

12. J. Navarro, "Organization design for software reuse," in *5th Annual Workshop on Institutionalizing Software Reuse*, Oct. 26–29, 1992.

17–A

A SURVEY OF PRIOR RESEARCH ON REUSE ORGANIZATIONAL STRUCTURES

Prior research has been done in the area of software reuse organizational structures.

Basili *et al.* [1] describe a reuse organization that is flexible and able to learn from its own experiences. They describe an organizational framework which consists of two separate organizations: a *project organization* and an *experience factory*. The goal of the project organization is to deliver applications required by the customer. The experience factory has the responsibility of monitoring and analyzing project trends, developing and packaging experience, and supplying these reusable assets to the projects.

Bongard *et al.* [2] describe the *project-oriented, component-management oriented,* and *production-line oriented* organizational structures and their implications for reuse. The project-oriented organization consists of project teams which are responsible for both development *with* reuse and *for* reuse. In the component management-oriented organization, the project teams produce the reusable components, but a separate team manages the components with the aid of a repository. The primary responsibilities of the component management team are to determine the type and ensure the quality of the reusable assets in the repository. In the production line-oriented organization, project teams do not produce reusable assets, but rather separate teams are established to create assets within specific domains (e.g., user interface, database).

Kruzela [3] describes the management structures of three reuse organizations: Toshiba Fuchu Software Factory, GTE, and NTT Software Laboratories. He concludes that they have the following in common: 1) strong management support; 2) reuse that is planned from the start of projects; 3) production of reusable components separated from their use; 4) repository of components with a dedicated sup-

257

port staff; 5) training of programmers in the use of the repository; and 6) an incentive to promote reuse in the organization.

Fafchamps [4] of Hewlett-Packard describes her findings of reuse producer-consumer models in terms of four archetypes: lone producer, nested producer, pool producer, and team producer. In the lone producer model, an individual handles multiple project teams' needs. In the nested producer model, each project team has a reuse member dedicated to providing reuse expertise. In the pool producer model, two or more project teams collaborate to both produce and share reusable components. In the team producer model, a dedicated reuse producer team is afforded the same organizational level and recognition as the project teams.

Lavoie *et al.* [5] describe three approaches to organizing programming teams to benefit from reuse based on the work of Adele Goldberg. The first approach, *distributed responsibility*, entails that each project team "design with reuse" and "design for reuse." Although this approach requires the least change in organizational structure, it can also prevent the team from delivering the product. In the second approach, *independent reuse teams* are established, separate from those teams responsible for delivering applications. The responsibility of the reuse teams is to recondition existing assets into reusable ones. The drawback to this approach is that some assets are not worth reconditioning and would be more worthwhile if they were created reusable. The third approach is to establish a *dedicated reuse team* the members of which work closely with the project teams to guide them in both reusing and creating assets for reuse. The reuse team member supports the project by bringing knowledge of available reusable assets and coaches the project team members on how to create reusable assets.

Moad [6] describes the use of a *reuse brigade*. Similar to a division between applications engineers and systems software developers, a reuse brigade focuses on the creation and use of reusable assets while project teams focus on delivering the applications.

Navarro [7], also of Hewlett-Packard, is conducting research on applying business process reengineering principles on reuse organizational structures at Hewlett-Packard Laboratories. This includes identifying core processes and their relationships to the personnel roles in the organization, mapping the information flows, determining process discontinuities and problems, and then identifying several design alternatives for creating a "flexible software factory."

References

1. V. R. Basili, G. Caldiera, and G. Cantone, "A reference architecture for the component factory," *ACM Transactions on Software Engineering and Methodology*, vol. 1, no. 1, pp. 53–80, Jan., 1992.
2. B. Bongard, B. Gronquist, and D. Ribot, "Impact of reuse on organizations," *REBOOT*, Sept. 4, 1992.

3. I. Kruzela, "Successful management structures for reuse," in *Integrated Software Reuse: Management and Techniques*, P. Walton and N. Maiden, Eds. Brookfield, VT: Ashgate, 1993.

4. D. Fafchamps, "Organizational factors and reuse," *IEEE Software*, vol. 11, no. 5, pp. 31–41, Sept. 1994.

5. D. Lavoie, H. Baetjer, W. Tulloh, and R. N. Langlois, "Component software: A market perspective on the coming revolution in solutions development," *Distributed Computing Monitor*, vol. 8, no. 1, pp. 3–19, Jan. 1993.

6. J. Moad, "Cultural barriers slow reusability (programming)," *Datamation*, vol. 35, no. 22, pp. 87–92, Nov. 15, 1989.

7. J. Navarro, "Organization design for software reuse," *5th Annual Workshop on Institutionalizing Software Reuse*, Oct. 26–29, 1992.

18

FINANCE AND ACCOUNTING FOR A REUSE PROGRAM

18.1 Introduction

For our purposes, finance and accounting address the acquisition and management of financial resources necessary to implement reuse. In order to avoid confusion in this chapter, we will use the term "reusable workproducts" to refer to "reusable assets" since the term "asset" is commonly used in finance and accounting to refer to any valuable resource.

Finance is primarily concerned with procuring capital to acquire tangible assets such as a reuse library, reusable code components, or intangible assets such as technical expertise.

Accounting is "the process of recording, classifying, reporting and interpreting the financial data of an organization [1]." Types of accounting include managerial, financial, and cost accounting. Managerial accounting measures change in segments of a business, with managers receiving information specific to their area of responsibility rather than the entire business. Financial accounting is the measurement of economic changes that occur in the business as a whole. Cost accounting provides for the timely determination of product/system costs.

18.2 The Role of Finance and Accounting in Software Reuse

Finance and accounting are essential elements in funding, measuring, and tracking an economically viable reuse program. *Finance* includes deciding among alternatives for the initial and ongoing funding of a reuse effort. In addition, techniques used in finance allow us to calculate the sustainable growth rate for a reuse program using internally generated funds. *Accounting* concerns the measurements taken in a reuse endeavor. Some metrics are used to measure the economic changes in the reuse program, while others are intended as decision support and management control systems for managers.

A *management control system* is a set of policies that ensures resources are procured, and effectively and efficiently utilized from strategy development to implementation, while also ensuring that managers and engineers work together to achieve the organization's goals. For example, a reuse management control system (RCMS) links participant rewards and incentives to the goals and objectives of the reuse program and the organization itself.

18.3   Finance

A reuse effort may be viewed from three perspectives. The first perspective is *producer–broker* (Fig. 18–1). For example, a suborganization may be established to produce and broker reusable workproducts. This suborganization would want to identify means of reducing costs in creating and maintaining reusable workproducts. Another example is a company that creates, brokers, and licenses reusable workproducts on the external market.

The second perspective is *broker–consumer* (Fig. 18–2). For example, software development projects which recognize redundancy and the need for reusable workproducts may designate a contractor, whose responsibility it will be to contract with an internal or external producer organization, to develop the reusable workproduct. The contractor acts as a broker representing the interests of the consumer projects.

The third perspective is from the stand-alone *broker* point-of-view (Fig. 18–3). A stand-alone broker is independent and does not align itself with either a producer or consumer. In such a case, the broker acts as an intermediary, identifying and fulfilling the needs of consumers by contracting for reusable workproducts from producers.

Throughout this chapter, we will explore reuse issues from these various perspectives.

Budgeting for a Software Reuse Program

A budget is a set of pro forma financial statements that show anticipated financial results. In every case, the budget begins with a forecast of the demand for reusable workproducts. Such demand determines the producer time and effort required, cash flows, and financing requirements.

Producer–Broker Combination

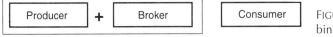

FIGURE 18–1   Producer–broker combination.

Broker–Consumer Combination

FIGURE 18–2 Broker–consumer combination.

Forecasting Demand for Reuse

Indicator Methods.   Indicator methods use proxies that serve as an indication of demand for reusable workproducts. For example, the number of similar software systems demanded by end-users is one indicator of demand.

Historical Analysis Methods.   Although not always a good indicator of the future, some organizations use historical trends to project reuse trends. For example, some reuse programs use Caldiera and Basili's metric (ratio of number of static calls to a module divided by the number of calls to the average system module) to identify reusable components.

Judgmental Methods.   Some organizations forecast levels of reuse based on experience with the organization's end-users, consumers, and products.

The applicability of any method depends on the characteristics of the organization. Furthermore, any indicator by itself may exclude other factors which affect the demand for reuse.

Calculating the Level of Financing Needed for a Reuse Program

Once we have forecasted the demand for reusable workproducts, we estimate the desired level of resources to address the demand. This estimate is usually based on experience or comparable data from other companies [2]. We then identify the cost–benefit of the proposed reuse program, as outlined in Chapter 12. Finally, by comparing the desired level of resources to the resources currently available, we can determine the level of financing required for the proposed reuse program.

Stand-alone Broker

Producer	Broker	Consumer

FIGURE 18–3 Stand-alone broker.

Financing Example.   A suborganization of a large corporation is considering establishing a reuse program. (In our example, we use the term "producer group" synonymously with "reuse program.") After estimating the benefits to the consumer and producer costs over a five-year period, the suborganization is ready to determine its financing needs for the reuse program.

End of year	1	2	3	4	5
Producer Costs (in thousands)					
Startup					
-Reuse management	−100				
-Workproduct creation	−300				
-Library creation	−50				
-Tools creation	−50				
-Training/marketing	−100				
-Other	0				
Total Startup Costs:	−600				
Ongoing					
-Reuse management	0	−100	−100	−100	−100
-Workproduct maintenance	0	−250	−250	−250	−250
-Library maintenance	0	−50	−50	−50	−50
-Tools maintenance	0	−25	−25	−25	−25
-Training/marketing	0	−25	−25	−25	−25
-Other	0	0	0	0	0
Total Ongoing Costs:	0	−450	−450	−450	−450
Total Startup and Ongoing Costs	−600	−450	−450	−450	−450
Consumer Benefits (in thousands)					
Number of reuses	0	16	26	30	35
Benefit per reuse:	50	50	50	50	50
-Total Benefits	0	800	1300	1500	1750

If the producer group does not charge for its services or products, the startup costs in the first year and the ongoing costs in each successive year would be the amount of financing required each year. If the producer group intends to recoup its startup and ongoing costs and become financially self-sustaining, it may charge for its services and products. Each consumer may be charged an amortized portion of startup and ongoing costs.

Predictions regarding the number of consumers become increasingly uncertain as organizations attempt to estimate further into the future. As a result, organizations may consider charging early consumers a greater portion of the amortized cost for developing the reusable workproducts. This reduces the risk that the reuse investment will not be recovered by the amortization scheme [3]. Accelerated methods such as sum-of-years digits or double declining balance may be utilized [4]. The sum-of-years digits method determines the yearly amortized amount by multiplying the total original value by the number of years remaining in the life of the asset and then dividing by the sum of the digits from 1 through the last year of the life of the asset. The double declining balance method calculates the annual amortized amount as twice the current book value divided by the total years of economic life. Some producer groups may want to levy a charge for their products and services so that they can pursue more reuse opportunities or become a profit center.

The amount of annual financing required can be determined with a *statement of cash flows*. This provides useful information about a reuse program's cash receipts and cash payments over a specified period of time.

As an example, let us say the consumer has agreed to pay the reuse program 50% of the value for using a reusable workproduct (estimated to be $50,000 per reuse) and the reuse program's initial cash balance is $500,000. Assume that the reuse program will finance itself through corporate funding. To determine the amount of financing needed, the reuse program needs to determine the difference between cash inflow and outflow.

End of year	1	2	3	4	5
Statement of Cash Flows					
Cash flows from startup activities					
Cash paid for startup costs	−600	0	0	0	0
(a) Net cash provided by startup activities	−600	0	0	0	0
Cash flows from operating activities					
Cash from consumers	0	400	650	750	875
Cash paid for ongoing costs	0	−450	−450	−450	−450
(b) Net cash provided by operating activities	0	−50	200	300	425
Cash flows from financing activities					
(c) Current cash balance	500	0	0	200	500
Net cash balance (a+b+c)	−100	−50	200	500	925
Additional funding required	100	50	0	0	0

In the first two years, funding is required in the amounts of $100,000 and $50,000, respectively. In the third, fourth, and fifth years, funding is no longer required since the reuse program has a positive net cash balance of $200,000, $500,000, and $925,000, respectively.

We now describe various means of acquiring funding for a reuse program, beginning with the producer–broker perspective. The producer–broker is seeking ways to cover its initial and ongoing costs from creating and maintaining reusable workproducts.

Methods for Funding a Reuse Program

A range of methods is available for the initial and ongoing funding of a software reuse program. Subsidized funding is needed when the reuse program is expected to provide only a portion of the initial or ongoing funds. Some reuse programs may be expected to furnish an increasingly greater percentage of the total funding as the program progresses.

Initial Funding.   Initial funding for a reuse program can be critical. In many cases, the funding is for a pilot which may determine how or whether reuse will be proliferated to the rest of the organization. In some progressive organizations, a mechanism may already be established to fund and allow pilot projects to experiment with new techniques and technologies.

Grant.   In the case of grant funding, an initial sum of money is provided to finance a startup reuse program without expectation of repayment. The goal of the party providing this seed money is usually to obtain proof-of-concept on software reuse. Such grants may be provided by corporate entities that wish to test the viability of software reuse and encourage its proliferation.

Investor.   *Investors* who provide seed money or resources expect to receive a return on their investment. They become owners in the reuse venture, i.e., their investment (which may be in the form of personnel, equipment, or capital) in the venture is considered their equity. If the venture does not succeed, the investors may recover only a portion (if any) of their equity investment. If the venture does succeed, they may receive a significant return on their equity.

Often, as was the case at Hewlett-Packard, multiple organizations will contribute resources and share ownership. In such cases, the initial funding may resemble venture capital funding.

Loan.   Another funding alternative is to secure a loan which is then repaid from the reuse program's net revenues. Bollinger and Pfleeger [5] describe their concept of a bank that provides reuse investment loans in the form of capital or resources enabling projects to build reusability into workproducts. The bank would charge the consumer projects an amortization bill to gradually collect on their loans.

Barter.   Another method is *barter* or the exchange of one item of value for another. For example, two or more organizations may each agree to develop useful
products based on different techniques for software improvement. One may focus
on reuse, another on walkthroughs, with other organizations given leads for improvement efforts in other areas. Such a cooperative effort took place at Hewlett-
Packard.

Ongoing Funding.   *Ongoing funding* refers to long-term financing of a reuse
program wherein investment, loan, and barter alternatives are usually available.
Grants are rarely available since these are usually offered to demonstrate the viability of reuse.

Assume the reuse organization decides to fund its program by charging for its
products and services. We describe in the next section a framework for high-level
versus low-level revenue collection.

High-Level Versus Low-Level Revenue Collection.   A range of alternatives
exists for revenue collection. An organization can, however, use multiple strategies.
Several factors should be taken into consideration including administration costs;
equitableness in matching costs to those who benefit; the nature of existing cost systems; and the culture of the organization. For example, in some organizations,
charging at the high level of the organization may be culturally acceptable while
charging for each reusable workproduct is not. However, both methods fulfill the
same goal: obtaining resources from participating organizations. In this section we
examine the administrative cost and equitableness of each method.

In our framework for revenue collection, the alternatives range from a high-
level charge (e.g., a flat fee charge-per-organization per-year) to a more administra-
tively complex low-level charge (e.g., charge-per-workproduct) method (Fig. 18-4).
For the former, the administrative costs are low, but it may be difficult to identify an
appropriate, equitable flat fee to charge. For the latter, the scheme results in a more
equitable allocation of costs to those who benefit, but the increased effort to identify
and charge individual consumers results in higher administrative costs. We hope
the use of information technologies and other techniques may devise new methods
which are both equitable and low in administrative costs.

Charge at the High Level of the Organization.   At one extreme is the flat fee
to an organization. An analogy is the public library, for which each taxpayer pays a
fee (through taxes) allowing him or her to use the library an unlimited number of
times. If each taxpayer receives equivalent value from the library, the benefits relative to the costs (assume that each person is taxed the same amount) are equitable
and the administrative costs of funding the library remain low. Where most taxpayers uses the public library infrequently yet still bear the same costs as those who use
it frequently, the funding mechanism becomes inequitable. Another analogy is the

Tradeoff Between Cost of Tracking Reusers and Equitableness

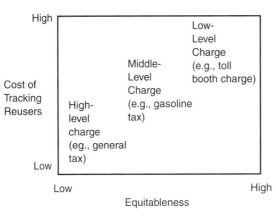

FIGURE 18–4   Tradeoff between cost of tracking reusers and equitableness.

funding of public roads through taxation: not all taxpayers use the roads with the same frequency.

In the context of software reuse, suborganizations may be charged an annual flat fee to utilize the reuse library and receive supporting services. The cost of administering such a fee is low since each organization is billed a flat fee once a year.

When the benefit received from reuse is approximately equivalent to the fee charged of each suborganization, equitableness *and* low administrative costs are achieved. However, where the benefit received from reuse proves to be small relative to the cost, an alternative charging method should be considered.

To illustrate, let us say that a simple flat fee charge per year is levied upon three consumer suborganizations to fund a reuse program. One year later, metrics indicate that one suborganization accounts for over two-thirds of total workproduct reuse in the organization, suggesting that two suborganizations are subsidizing reuse for the third. Assuming that all the organizations are fully exploiting their reuse opportunities, such a flat fee charge per year system is inequitable for two of the three organizations.

In deciding whether to change to a more equitable system such as charge per reuse, we must consider the magnitude of the imbalance compared with the cost of implementing a system that is more "fair."

Charge at the Middle Level of the Organization.   An example of a charge that more closely matches those who benefit with the costs is the gasoline tax, which is designed to assign the costs of building and maintaining a highway infrastructure to the individuals who use it most. The gasoline tax costs more to collect—more effort is needed to collect from every gasoline distributor—however, it is more equitable than a tax that charges *all* taxpayers for the highway infrastructure.

In software reuse, an analogous example is a program which charges at the middle (e.g., division) level of the organization. This more closely matches the costs of the reuse program to those who benefit, because only those middle-level suborganizations benefiting from reuse will bear its costs.

Charge at the Low Level of the Organization.   Under this method, the consumer is charged at the workproduct level. For example, the consumer is charged once for the reusable workproduct, and then has unlimited use of it. An analogy is the charge for a videotape rental. Renters are charged to possess a videotape for a specified period of time. They may then use the videotape many times within that period. The administrative costs are high: the video store must track and bill each rental. However, equitableness is high as well: those who benefit are charged accordingly. Another analogy is the toll charge for crossing a bridge or using a portion of a highway. While there are greater costs in establishing the system for monitoring and collecting fees (e.g., purchasing and maintaining toll booths and paying toll collectors), and greater inconvenience for the user, the system is fair.

The following illustrates a case where a charge-per-workproduct may be appropriate.

In year 1, three consumer suborganizations A, B, and C have the option of participating in a reuse program. The cost of the reuse program is $300,000. All three consumers elect to participate, so the total cost for the program is divided evenly among them under the flat fee method (i.e., $100,000 each). Each suborganization has the choice of whether to participate in the reuse program at the beginning of each year.

At the end of year 1, the three consumers A, B, and C receive an annual benefit of $200,000, $150,000, and $150,000, respectively, by participating in the program. Under the current flat fee method of charging, each had been charged $100,000 annually. The net benefit to each consumer then, is $100,000, $50,000 and $50,000, respectively.

Year 1

Consumer	Benefit	Flat fee charge	Net benefit
A	$200,000	$100,000	$100,000
B	$150,000	$100,000	$50,000
C	$150,000	$100,000	$50,000

At the beginning of year 2, the cost of the reuse program for the coming year is esti-mated to remain at $300,000. The benefits to consumers A, B, and C for the coming year are estimated to be $200,000, $75,000, and $75,000, respectively. Each con-sumer suborganization will be charged $100,000 under the flat fee method. The re-sulting net benefit is expected to be $100,000, −$25,000, and −$25,000, respec-tively for each consumer suborganization.

Year 2			
Consumer	*Benefit*	*Flat fee charge*	*Net benefit*
A	$200,000	$100,000	$100,000
B	$75,000	$100,000	−$25,000
C	$75,000	$100,000	−$25,000

Under the flat fee method, consumers B and C would elect not to participate in the reuse program. If consumer A elects to participate, the suborganization would incur a loss since it would have to bear all the costs of the reuse program.

Possible Year 2 Scenario If Consumer A Bears All Costs:			
Consumer	*Benefit*	*Flat fee charge*	*Net benefit*
A	$200,000	$300,000	−$100,000

However, under a charge-per-workproduct method, the benefits can match the costs such that all consumers benefit.

Possible Year 2 Scenario with Low-Level Charge Method:			
Consumer	*Benefit*	*Charge per workproduct*	*Net benefit*
A	$200,000	$172,000	$28,000
B	$75,000	$64,000	$11,000
C	$75,000	$64,000	$11,000

If administrative costs are not excessive, a charge-per-workproduct method is preferable to the flat fee method: each consumer organization would bear a portion of the cost that is commensurate with the benefit received from the reuse program. Each consumer would also have an incentive to participate in the reuse program. This example can be applied to any high and lower level in the organization.

Following are general rules for identifying an appropriate reuse chargeback system.

General Guidelines for Identifying an Appropriate Chargeback System. A higher level flat fee charge should be considered when there are many reusable workproducts of small granularity and users are numerous and difficult to identify. The administrative cost of charging a flat fee to a division (which consists of many consumers) for access to a suite of reusable workproducts is generally lower than charging on a per-workproduct basis.

A low-level charge-per-workproduct system should be considered when the granularity of the reusable workproduct is large and utilized by a few easily identifiable consumers. Such a system would offer lower administrative costs and greater fairness.

These guidelines are also applicable when we are deciding whether to:

1. charge a site license: unlimited use of the workproduct;
2. charge only when workproduct is used in a product/application;
3. charge only when a product is shipped or a system is delivered with the reusable workproduct.

If there are many small workproducts, a site license charge is simpler. Charging only when a consumer utilizes a workproduct requires more effort to track, but more closely matches the benefit of reuse to its cost. Finally, charging only when a product is actually delivered with a reusable workproduct is a conservative approach which attempts to charge a consumer only when the workproduct adds value. (Of course, billing arrangements will need to be made when a consumer uses a workproduct not meant to be shipped with the product but rather, as part of the development process such as test data.)

As we move from site license to "charge when a product is shipped," the accounting/tracking becomes more cumbersome but equitableness increases.

Alternative Mechanisms for Charging

Transfer prices are charges that one suborganization levies upon another for the use of a product or service. Some transfer prices closely reflect the value of the benefit received by the consumer; others are modest and serve more as an incentive to the producer to create reusable workproducts.

Transfer prices appear under different titles: awards, barter, contributions (tithes), payments, royalties, and taxes. However, they all serve a similar function by allocating a portion of the benefits from reusing the workproduct to cover the cost of creating and maintaining the workproduct.

In the next section, we enumerate different types of transfer prices.

Awards.   At Motorola's Israel facility, software reuse is encouraged through a cash award program [6], [7]. To encourage software engineers to submit reusable workproducts into the repository, a $100 cash bonus is provided to the engineer for each workproduct approved and accepted into the database. In addition, each time a workproduct is reused, an award proportionate to the benefits is divided between the producer and the consumer. The producer receives 40% and the consumer 60% of this award (Fig. 18–5).

Some awards are not meant as much to cover the cost of producing than to serve as an incentive to produce. For example, the Hartford Insurance Group rewards individuals who submit a reusable workproduct to the library with imprinted coffee mugs. Each submission becomes a candidate for Best Productivity Suggestion of the Month, an award which pays $300 [8]. Another example is the monetary award that the NASA Cosmic Repository provides for submittal of reusable workproducts [9]. Pacific Bell promoted its library by offering coffee mugs and screwdrivers to contributors [8].

Isoda [10] reports that at the Nippon Telegraph and Telephone Corporation, three types of awards were presented to groups or individuals who distinguished themselves in the following ways: high-deposition group award, high-reuse-ratio group award, and highly-utilized-module award for a producer. The awards were accompanied by a modest cash award. The logic is that larger payments could encourage counterproductive behavior such as deliberate redundant coding. As such, the award is not meant to have an economic meaning but rather a sociological one.

Barter.   As already discussed, barter is the exchange of goods or services. For example, two organizations at Hewlett-Packard each agreed to develop a reusable workproduct for reuse by the other.

Savings in $	Award (% of savings)	Maximum award(s) in $
250–500	12.0	60
501–1000	10.0	100
1001–2500	7.5	187.50
2501–50,000	5.0	2500

FIGURE 18–5   Motorola reuse award amounts. *Source:* R. Joos, "Software reuse at Motorola," *IEEE Software,* vol. 11, no. 5, p. 45, Nov. 1994.

Contributions. Also known as tithes, contributions are distinguished from payments by the fact that they are voluntary. Usually, this takes place when several organizations contribute resources in the form of personnel, equipment, and capital to create a producer entity. Subsequent "fine-tuning" may be done to ensure a closer matching of benefits to costs. At Hewlett-Packard, several divisions pooled their resources to support an effective reuse effort.

Payments. Payments are explicit charges to consumers for use of a reusable workproduct. A payment may be for a license to use the workproduct, for each use of the workproduct, or for each shipment of a product which includes the workproduct. The latter two forms of payment are sometimes called *royalties.*

Royalties. Royalties are payments that are made to the owner of the reusable workproduct each time the workproduct is utilized.

Cox [11] has suggested royalty payments in software reuse similar to those in the music industry. He suggests monitoring the *use* of software and distributing payments to the owners of that software based upon usage. The analogy that he draws upon is the system that the American Society of Composers, Authors, and Publishers (ASCAP) and the Broadcasting Musicians Institute (BMI) use to administer fees to television and radio companies whenever their music is played on the air. Cox points to the efforts of the Japanese Electronics Industrial Development Association (JEIDA) as an example of this type of revenue collection occurring in the computer industry.

GTE Data Services' Asset Management Program instituted a program which paid programmers $50 to $100 cash for each workproduct accepted into the library. Royalties were paid to the producers of these workproducts each time the workproducts were reused [8], [12].

Wolff [13] advocates a royalty rate expressed as a percentage of new development costs that are avoided through reuse. Wolff suggests this royalty plus the cost to reuse should not exceed half of the cost of new development to ensure the consumer's savings are high enough to motivate reuse.

Taxes. A tax is "a sum levied upon members of an organization to defray expenses" [14]. The tax may be charged at various levels of the organization to fund the reuse program. The Hewlett-Packard Corporate Reuse Program is one reuse endeavor funded through taxation of the organizations that it serves.

Methods of Contracting for Reuse Workproducts

In the previous section, we took the viewpoint of the producer–broker. The producer–broker seeks to cover its investment costs through the funding techniques already described. In the broker–consumer combination, consumers identify the need for reusable workproducts and then empower the broker to contract a producer to create this workproduct. One of the goals of the broker–consumer combination is to minimize the costs of contracting with a producer.

There are several alternatives available for the terms of the contract. Among the alternatives available are:

1. actual cost plus a markup;
2. budgeted costs without any markup;
3. budgeted cost plus a markup;
4. prices negotiated by the managers.

These alternatives are discussed in detail in Setting the Transfer Price on page 278.

Growth Rate for a Self-Sustaining Reuse Program

The sustainable reuse growth rate (SRGR) refers to the growth rate which the reuse program can finance from internally generated funds *assuming all ratios remain unchanged.*

The SRGR can be calculated as follows:

SRGR = (Reuse Revenues − Reuse Expenses)/(Reuse Revenues) × (Reuse Revenues)/(Book Value of Assets) × (Book Value of Assets)/(Beginning Equity).

Example:

In year one, let:

Consumer benefit = $1,300,000
Percentage of consumer benefit received by producer = .50
Reuse Revenues = $650,000
Reuse Expenses = $450,000
Book Value of Assets = $600,000
Beginning Equity = $500,000
Assuming all ratios remain unchanged, then

SRGR = ($650K − $450K)/($650K) × ($650K)/($600K) × ($600K/$500K) = .40.

The reuse program can accommodate a 40% annual growth rate from internally generated funds. Consequently, in the following year, $1,820,000 [i.e., $1,300,000 x (1.40)] worth of value can be provided to the consumer with funds generated from the current year assuming consumer demand is at least at that level in the following year.

18.4 Accounting

In this section, we describe reuse management control systems, revenue, profit and cost centers and their implications for reuse organizations. We also discuss the choice of an appropriate transfer price, implications of excess capacity for reuse producers, and managerial, financial, and cost accounting for reuse. For those interested in further information on revenue, profit, and cost centers and transfer prices for reuse, a good source is Malan [3].

A Reuse Management Control System

A reuse management control system (RMCS) is a set of policies designed to ensure that resources are acquired and used efficiently, from reuse strategy development through implementation. The organization's goals and key success factors should be considered in the creation of an RMCS. A primary objective is to attain *goal congruence:* to ensure that managers' and engineers' goals are aligned to the organization's goals. A successful RMCS provides employees incentive to strive toward reuse for the organization. Furthermore, employees must believe that the RMCS measures their performance accurately.

In designing an RMCS, several key questions should be asked, including:

1. Will the critical elements of the reuse operation be monitored?
2. What are the right measures to use?
3. Will managers be motivated by the system?

The RMCS also assists in long-range planning by aligning planning with budgeting. Finally, the resource allocation system should explicitly state its evaluation criteria which should reinforce corporate goals. For commercial companies, an effective RMCS will maximize overall company profits, maximize each division's profits, and identify each profit center's contribution to overall profits.

An important aspect of the RMCS is the design of the *responsibility center* in reuse. A responsibility center is the location where responsibility for certain activities lies. In our case, we will be examining the various forms of responsibility centers and their implication for the producer. We will consider the broker as part of the producer in this discussion.

In measuring the performance of responsibility centers, we look for *efficiency* (amount of output per unit of input), *effectiveness* (whether the outputs meet objectives), and whether the form of the responsibility center is consistent with overall goals.

A responsibility center can take one of three forms, as follows.

The first is as a *cost center* where the center has responsibility for costs compared to budget, but not for the value of its output. The cost center is generally used for organizational entities where measuring output is difficult, e.g., research and development organizations.

The second is as a *revenue center* where the center has responsibility for revenues compared to budget but not for the cost of producing goods or services. The revenue center is used for suborganizations such as sales offices.

The third is as a *profit center* where the center has responsibility for revenues earned as well as expenses incurred. A profit center requires more record keeping and transfer prices play an important role.

The Producer as a Cost Center. The cost center model for the producer group is used by many organizations and may be appropriate for reuse programs in certain situations. For example, a reuse program attempting to obtain proof-of-concept in a startup situation may use a cost center model.

A cost center designation is also appropriate when the producer organization is organizationally situated outside the profit centers which are its consumers and provides relatively equal benefits to each of the profit centers. Under these circumstances, there is no conflict with the management control system.

However, suppose a producer organization is a cost center which resides within a profit center, but some of its consumers do not reside within that profit center. In this case, the profit center is penalized because it bears costs of reuse the benefits of which are being enjoyed by consumers in a different profit center. One way to rectify this situation is by having external consumers reimburse the producer organization for its *cost* without a profit.

For producer groups that are cost centers, measuring them according to how well they stay within budget may be difficult, if not arbitrary, unless there is a basis for determining the budget.

The Producer as a Revenue Center. The revenue center model is rarely appropriate for producer groups. It makes little sense to measure revenue only without considering the cost of producing the reusable software that generated the revenue.

The Producer as a Profit Center. The profit center model offers an incentive to the producer to proactively provide benefits (which translate to revenues) *and* hold costs down. There are several implications. For example, imagine a consumer has funded a profit-center producer to develop a reusable workproduct. Let's say this producer group would not have created such a workproduct for its own use. Since the producer could be deploying its resources to make a profit elsewhere, merely covering costs would reduce the producer's overall performance. In this case, the consumer should cover the producer's *opportunity* cost, i.e., the return that the producer would have received if it had pursued the next best opportunity available to it.

When the profit center producer is also a consumer of the reusable workproduct it creates, the producer's opportunity cost in expending the incremental effort needed to make the workproduct reusable by others should be considered. In one organization, several consumers identified the need for a common workproduct. They designated one profit center consumer to create the workproduct. That organization expended more effort to create a reusable version than would have been required to build a product solely for its own use. Although the other consumer organizations reimbursed the designated producer for the additional effort to make the workproduct reusable, they should have reimbursed the producer for its *opportunity cost*—the return the producer would have received by employing that additional effort to its next best opportunity.

The profit center model has many advantages. Producer groups (even if they are currently cost centers) should consider being evaluated as a profit center.

Implications of Responsibility Centers for Reuse.   Consumers typically are (or reside in) cost or profit centers. As such, they are subject to financial measures which gauge their performance.

When a producer *and* its consumers reside in the same responsibility center (Fig. 18–6), no conflict exists with the financial management control system. The costs borne by the producer and the benefits enjoyed by its consumers both impact the bottom line of the same responsibility center.

However, when the consumers (especially a significant number) reside outside the responsibility center (Fig. 18–7), a conflict exists. The responsibility center where the producer resides incurs the cost of production, while the benefits of reuse are enjoyed by consumers in another responsibility center. Although such reuse adds value to the corporation, the management control system penalizes the producer for creating reusable workproducts and discourages reuse with consumers in other responsibility centers.

Such a management control system offers an incentive to the producer to create and optimize reusable workproducts only for consumers residing in its own responsibility center, and not for others. Since a number of reuses must occur before the producer breaks even, reuse is discouraged and the number of reusable workproducts created is less than optimal for the corporation.

Several alternatives are available to remedy this. Top-level management might verbally endorse and offer some sort of recognition for producing and reusing. However, the existing management control system would mitigate the response to this endorsement: the staff is still subject to measurements which discourage reuse. More effectively, transfer prices might be added to the management control system, allowing one suborganization to levy charges upon another for reuse. The producer can cover its costs and the consumer enjoys a portion of the benefits. These transfer prices promote behavior which is consistent with the interests of the organization.

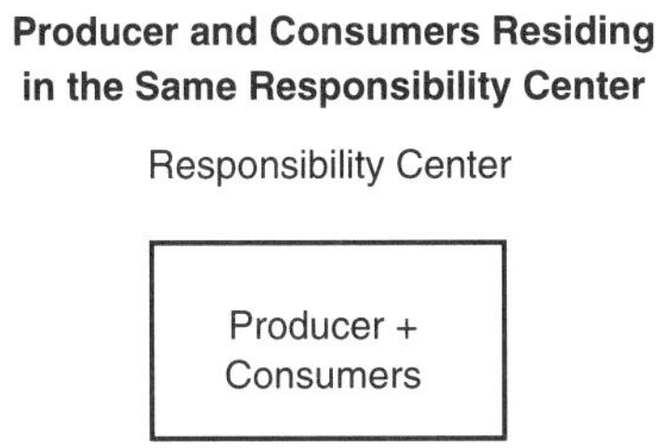

**Producer and Consumers Residing
in the Same Responsibility Center**

Responsibility Center

Producer +
Consumers

Figure 18–6   Producers and consumers residing in the same responsibility center.

**Producer and Consumers Residing
in Different Responsibility Centers**

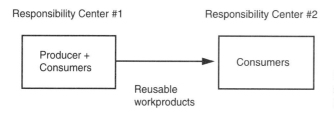

Responsibility Center #1   Responsibility Center #2

Producer +   Consumers
Consumers

Reusable
workproducts

FIGURE 18–7 Producer and consumers residing in different responsibility centers.

The financial metrics by which the producer and consumer are measured
should offer them an incentive to produce and consume, respectively, optimizing
the value of reuse to the organization as a whole.

In short, problems occur when there is inter-responsibility center reuse because those who benefit from reuse do not bear its costs. Producer cost centers
need to be reimbursed for its costs and producer profit centers need to be compen-
sated for its forgone costs and profits through transfer prices.

Setting the Transfer Price. Producers are unwilling to settle for a transfer
price lower than their cost to build and maintain workproducts, just as consumers
will not accept a price higher than what it would cost them to create and maintain
the workproduct themselves. (For the sake of simplicity, other reuse benefits such as
time-to-market savings and new market opportunities are not considered.)

In the case of the broker–consumer combination, consumers identify a common need and ask their broker to procure an appropriate workproduct. If it is not
available externally, the producer decides whether it should be created in-house or
contracted to an external organization. If the workproduct is available or can be developed externally, the broker asks for a price quote. If the workproduct is to be developed internally, a transfer price must be identified to cover the cost of developing it (Fig. 18–8).

In the case of the producer–broker combination, the producer creates a
workproduct which is brokered to consumers. In such a case, the broker must
identify the transfer price to charge the consumer for using the workproduct (Fig.
18–9).

Where the broker is an independent entity, two separate transfer prices may
be required. One transfer price is incurred to procure the workproduct from the producer and another to charge the consumer for its use (Fig. 18–10).

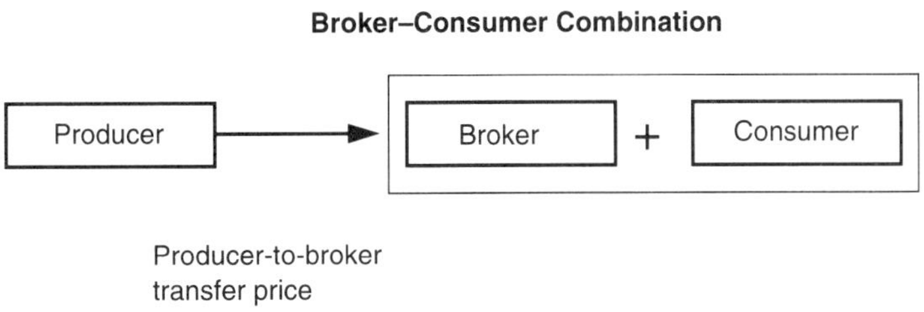

Broker–Consumer Combination

Producer ⟶ Broker + Consumer

Producer-to-broker
transfer price

FIGURE 18–8   Broker-consumer combination.

Setting the Producer to Broker Transfer Price.   The following examples explore the implications of several pricing policies for the transfer price from an internal producer to the broker (i.e., producer to broker transfer price).

1. **Transfers could be made at actual cost plus a markup for the producer.**
   Advantages:
   From the perspective of the producer, such a pricing policy ensures a profit.
   Disadvantages:
   This pricing policy does not offer incentives to the producer group to keep costs down. The producer group would generate more profit if they allowed their costs to rise. Such a policy allows cost inefficiencies to be passed on to consumers.

2. **Transfers could be made at budgeted costs without any markup.**
   Advantages:
   This pricing policy offers incentives to producers to restrain costs because they cannot pass on cost inefficiencies and would keep the benefits if they lowered costs.

Producer–Broker Combination

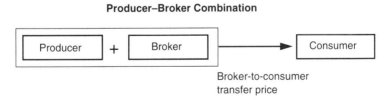

Producer + Broker ⟶ Consumer

Broker-to-consumer
transfer price

FIGURE 18–9   Producer-broker combination.

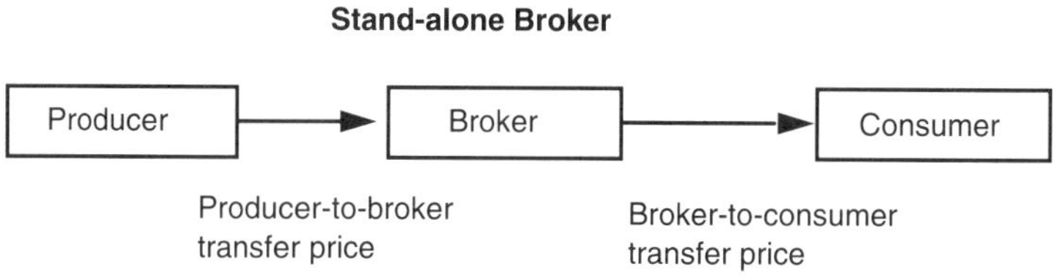

Stand-alone Broker

| Producer | → | Broker | → | Consumer |

Producer-to-broker   Broker-to-consumer
transfer price   transfer price

FIGURE 18–10   Stand-alone broker.

Disadvantages:

The producer group would receive no profit under this policy. This is out of line with the profit center concept. (Consumers, of course, would welcome this approach.) Identifying the budgeted cost may be difficult.

3. **Transfers could be made at budgeted cost plus a markup.**

Advantages:

This pricing approach allows producers to secure a profit and offers them an incentive to restrain costs since markups are applied on the basis of budgeted cost.

Disadvantages:

Identifying the budgeted cost may be difficult.

4. **Transfers could be made at market prices.**

Advantages:

This pricing policy provides the freedom to buy or sell externally instead of within the organization. If enough external organizations are available to competitively determine a market price, this price is generally the best bench-mark. The difference between the market price and internal cost (when the market price is greater than the internal cost) is the *contribution margin*.

Disadvantages:

Market prices may not be representative and may include sales commission costs which would not be borne by an internal price.

5. **Transfers could be made at prices negotiated by the managers.**

Advantages:

Problems that arise with the use of market prices can be alleviated with this pricing policy. If the consumer group is dissatisfied with an internal price, they can purchase the reusable asset in the external market.

Disadvantages:

The negotiated transfer price may be skewed by the negotiation skills of the producer and consumer groups.

How Excess Capacity Affects the Producer's Transfer Price. When a producer organization is operating at excess capacity and is approached with a bid for creating a reusable workproduct, it should consider pricing the workproduct between its variable cost (a variable cost is an expense that varies in direct proportion to the number of reusable workproducts created) and the market price.

We illustrate this with an example.

Consumer group A of company XYZ is planning to create a family of software products to sell in the marketplace. They have identified a reusable workproduct that they can use across this family of software products. Since consumer group A can choose to have this reusable workproduct created in-house or externally, they have asked their broker to obtain price quotes for both. The broker receives a price quote of $50,000 from an external software development group.

The in-house producer group is operating at excess capacity (i.e., some producer engineers are idle). Their variable cost in creating the workproduct is $40,000. Realizing that they have excess capacity, the producer manager identifies a transfer price of $45,000, which is less than what they would have charged if they were at full capacity, but more than their variable cost. By doing so, the internal producer group wins the bid, obtaining work for their excess capacity and some profit for both the producer group and the company that may otherwise be lost to an external organization.

Setting the Broker-to-Consumer Transfer Price. One form of the broker-to-consumer transfer price is the amortized cost to *procure* the workproduct. Other methods for setting the transfer prices from the broker to consumer may be found in Chapter 20.

Administering the RMCS. In administering the RMCS, we should examine the way management uses the information that is collected, identify the system's strengths and weaknesses, and assess the cost of the system relative to its benefits.

Once the system is in place, it should be continuously monitored for its alignment with company goals, including nonquantitative goals such as customer satisfaction. Also examine its impact on managers' behavior and whether managers' authority matches their responsibility.

Accounting Implications For Reuse

Understanding accounting concepts enables us to judiciously use appropriate tools for managing software reuse. For example, Frazier [15] describes the use of an accounting concept, T-accounts, to track the benefits of software reuse. In this section, we explore similar tools in managerial, financial, and cost accounting which will help us manage and make better decisions in reuse.

Managerial Accounting

Reuse Volume–Cost–Benefit. Reuse volume–cost–benefit analysis is a technique for examining the relationship between the number of reusable workproducts created (reuse volume), costs, and benefits. This information is useful for planning and budgeting. Let us begin with some definitions.

Variable or *direct* costs. These are expenses that vary in direct proportion to the number of reusable workproducts created. An example of a variable cost is the cost of software engineers' time to create and maintain reusable workproducts.

Contribution margin. In our context, this is the difference between the total value provided by a reusable workproduct to consumers and the cost incurred in creating and maintaining it. The term *contribution* refers to the amount remaining after expenses are deducted from the value provided to cover other costs or to produce a profit.

Fixed or *indirect* costs. Certain costs are incurred regardless of the number of reusable workproducts created. (More accurately, these costs do not vary over a *range* of the number of workproducts created.) These are designated *fixed costs* and are usually necessary to provide the capacity for the operation. An example is the cost of training consumers to use the reuse repository.

Because costs have different characteristics, producers should employ various strategies to manage them. For example, assume producers have prioritized the creation of reusable workproducts by each workproduct's contribution margin, and that the reuse infrastructure has excess capacity (i.e., producer engineers are underutilized and the reuse library has capacity). Then, the producers should continue to create reusable workproducts until the value provided by the next reusable workproduct is equal to or less than the cost of creating and maintaining that workproduct (in economic terms, when *marginal value equals marginal cost*).

If we have an approximation of the average contribution margin of a typical reusable workproduct, we can estimate the break-even number of reusable workproducts needed to cover our variable and fixed costs.

Fig. 18–11 applies the volume–cost–benefit concept to software reuse. The total fixed cost line shows an expense of $200,000. A variable cost line depicts the cost at each number of reusable workproducts. The sum of the fixed and variable costs provides us with a total cost line. The total benefit at any volume is shown by the benefit line.

At the break-even point, total benefits equal total costs. At this volume, the reuse program has covered its total costs and every additional reusable workproduct developed contributes a positive net benefit to the organization. When the reuse program is operating below break-even, the program costs more than the benefits it provides.

Reuse volume–cost–benefit analysis is most useful when the costs and benefits (cost and contribution margin) are relatively the same for all workproducts; many workproducts will be created, and the objective is to estimate the number of workproducts required to break even.

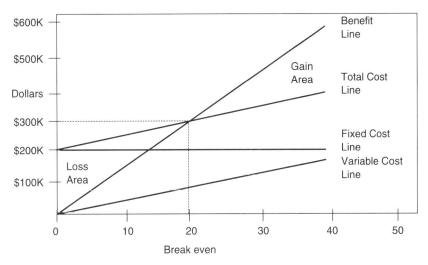

FIGURE 18–11   Volume–cost–benefit chart.

Cost Behavior.   Fixed costs may be further categorized into two types: *discretionary costs* and *committed costs.* Discretionary costs are those that may be eliminated with managerial discretion. Committed costs are those which can only be eliminated by ceasing operation.

An example of a discretionary fixed cost is the publication of a directory of reusable workproducts available from a repository. Such a directory is beneficial but not essential for the reuse program to operate (assuming the repository has an on-line search mechanism).

A *committed fixed cost* is the minimum cost that a reuse program must incur in order to operate. When a reuse program cannot operate without a reuse repository, the repository is considered a committed fixed cost.

Discretionary costs are distinguished from committed fixed costs when we examine daily operations and make decisions.

A *separable fixed cost* is directly attributable to a segment under consideration.

A cost that is related to multiple segments is called a *joint fixed cost.* For example, if a support engineer was responsible for multiple sets of workproducts, his salary would be considered a joint fixed cost.

Such distinctions are necessary in order to analyze whether to discontinue supporting a reusable workproduct or a suite of reusable workproducts.

Deciding Whether to Carry a Reusable Workproduct Suite.   Following are income statements of domain-specific suites of reusable workproducts (Fig. 18–12). An income statement shows us the financial results of operations over a specified period of time. (In this example, we ignore the amortized cost to create the reusable workproducts.) We can use these income statements to analyze the relative benefit of each suite.

The reusable workproduct suite margin is the difference between the contribution margin from the reusable workproduct suite and the related avoidable fixed costs. If the reusable workproduct suite margin is positive, the producer group's profits would drop by this amount if the producer eliminated it. If the reusable workproduct suite margin is negative, the profits would increase by that amount if the suite was eliminated. Comparable analyses can be performed for individual reusable workproducts to determine whether a reusable software suite should be replaced with a new one.

(in thousands)	GUI	Instrumentation	Error Handling	Total
-Benefits	$2400	$1800	$1300	$5500
-Cost of Creation	$1050	$900	$700	$2650
-Cost of Maintenance	$240	$180	$130	$550
-Other Variable Costs	$150	$120	$90	$360
Total Variable Costs	$1440	$1200	$920	$3560
Contribution Margin	$960	$600	$380	$1940
Separable-discretionary fixed costs:				
Salaries	$80	$65	$40	$185
Other	$30	$15	$10	$55
Total separable-discretionary fixed costs	$110	$80	$50	$240
Reusable workproduct suite margin	$850	$520	$330	$1700
Committed and fixed costs:				
Repository				$455
Salaries of training staff				$140
Salaries of remaining staff				$410
Other				$500
Total committed and joint fixed costs				$1505
Net Benefit				$195

FIGURE 18–12   Income statements of four reusable software product lines. *Source:* From *Managerial Accounting,* 3rd ed. by Louderback and Dominiak. Copyright © 1982 PWS-Kent Publishing. Used by permission of South-Western College Publishing, a division of International Thompson Publishing, Inc., Cincinnati, OH 45227.

Types of Costs in Decision Making.   A *sunk cost* is any cost that will not change regardless of a decision under consideration. Sunk costs can be ignored in making such a decision.

An *opportunity cost* is the benefit forgone by choosing one alternative over another. For example, if the organization has only one support engineer who can support one set of reusable workproducts, then choosing to support one set of products means abandoning support for the others. The benefit that would have been provided by supporting the other suite is the opportunity cost.

Complementary Effects.   Complementary effects concern the impact that demand for one product has on another. Eliminating a reusable workproduct from the repository may change the demand for complementary workproducts. Therefore, careful analysis should be performed before a workproduct is added or eliminated.

Although one workproduct within a suite may not itself be economically justified, carrying it may be prudent since it completes the suite of workproducts (full-line). (Sometimes this is the attraction of toolkits: you may never or rarely use certain components in the kit, but those components are available when you need them.) Such a workproduct is called a *loss-leader*. Although the organization loses money on the loss-leader, it is kept in the belief that the demand for the full set of workproducts will result in a gain that will more than offset the loss-leader.

Financial Accounting

Cost–Benefit Analyses.   Cost–benefit analysis is a fundamental aspect of financial accounting. Such an analysis compares the cost of an activity to its benefits. If the benefits outweigh the costs, the activity is deemed a worthwhile endeavor from a financial perspective. We applied a cost–benefit analysis to workproducts in Chapter 11 and demonstrated how to perform a similar analysis to a reuse program in Chapter 12.

The "Rule of Three" Revisited.   One of the heuristics circulating among the reuse community is the "Rule of Three" [16], [17]. The Rule of Three is as follows

1. analyze three systems to generate reusable software;
2. use the software three times before realizing a savings.

In the early stages of a new methodology, using a heuristic such as the Rule of Three is understandable. However, as the methodology matures, we need to validate such heuristics based on empirical data. We will examine the second of the two statements in the Rule of Three.

An analysis was performed on 15 reusable workproducts from the Manufacturing Productivity section at Hewlett-Packard. As shown in Fig. 18–13, the number of reuses to break even (i.e., cover the variable cost to create the reusable workproduct) ranged from 0.1 to 24 reuses. The average number to break even was 4.7 reuses. For this set of workproducts, the second part of the Rule of Three did not hold.

Favaro [18] describes an analysis of reusable workproducts using an economic model developed at the Software Productivity Consortium [19]. These reusable workproducts were classified by increasing order of complexity as: *monolithic, polylithic, graph, menu,* and *mask* types.

As part of the analysis, Favaro identified the *payoff threshold value*—the break-even number of reuses for a component. For monolithic components, the cost of creation was recovered after nearly two reuses. For polylithic components, the cost of creation was recovered after about three reuses. However, as components of greater complexity and size are reused, the break-even number of reuses increases. For example, a graph component break-even number of reuses was about five, a

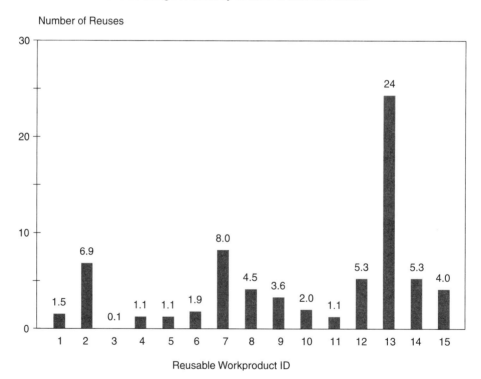

Number of Reuses to Break Even
Manufacturing Productivity Section of Hewlett-Packard

FIGURE 18–13   Number of reuses to break even.

menu component required approximately seven reuses, and the most complex form of a mask component needed nearly 14 reuses. In summary, the minimum number of reuses for a component to break even ranged from 1.33 to 12.97 [20].

Favaro's analysis indicates it is sometimes necessary to reuse a workproduct more than three times before a saving is realized. The break-even number is influenced by many factors (e.g., the cost to create the reusable workproduct, the benefit received by the consumer per reuse, and experience of the consumer). This makes it unlikely that we will arrive at a general number of reuses to break even which will hold true in all cases.

Reuse Financial Statements.   Earlier in this chapter, we demonstrated the use of a *statement of cash flows* to determine the amount of funding required for the reuse program. Other financial statements which may be useful include the *income statement* and the *balance sheet*. The income statement shows us the financial results of operating a reuse program over a specified period. In the reuse program context, a yearly income statement is a listing of the revenues received by the producer group, minus the amortized start-up costs, less ongoing expenses at the end of the year.

The simplified reuse income statement shown below depicts the second year of the example we used earlier in this chapter. Although there is a negative cash flow of $50,000 expected in year two, a financial net loss of $140,000 is expected when amortization is taken into consideration.

A balance sheet (or statement of financial position) is a snapshot in time which informs us of the reuse program's *assets* (equipment, reusable components, etc.), *liabilities* (for example, a loan to start the reuse program), and *equity* (capital provided by an investor).

End of year	2
Reuse Income Statement	
(a) Consumer Benefit	800
(b) Percent of Consumer Benefit	0.5
(c) Revenue Received (a × b)	400
(d) Less amortization on cost to create reusable workproducts	−90
(e) Contribution Margin (c + d)	310
(f) Less expenses	−450
(g) Net Gain/Loss (e + f)	−140

The simplified reuse balance sheet shown below depicts the second year of our earlier example.

End of year	2
Reuse Balance Sheet	
Assets	
–Reuse Workproduct Inventory	
(book value)	600
Accumulated amortization	–90
–Cash	0
Total Assets:	510
Liabilities:	0
Equity:	510
Total Liabilities and Equity:	510

The reuse program may choose to utilize other tracking tools for managing the program, and we include such examples to emphasize the fact that the reuse program should be operated as a business within the organization.

Cost Accounting. Cost accounting focuses on assigning costs to products. In *full* or *absorption* costing, overhead costs are fully allocated to the reusable workproducts.

In deciding whether to create a particular candidate reusable workproduct, the ongoing costs of an existing reuse library/infrastructure should *not* be allocated to candidate reusable workproducts. We illustrate how absorption costing can lead to the wrong decision with the following example.

A manager at a brokerage firm must decide whether to hire an additional stockbroker. "It's simple," he thinks. "If the benefits are greater than the cost of hiring him, I should hire him." In determining the costs, he calculates the portion of the cost for office space, lighting, and heating that will be utilized by the additional stockbroker and adds these to the salary, benefits, phone lines, and computer costs. Since the costs exceed benefits, the manager decides not to hire the additional stockbroker.

The manager, however, is mistaken in his analysis. He does not realize that the office space, heating, and lighting are *fixed* costs. They would be incurred regardless of whether the additional stockbroker is hired, so they should not be considered in the analysis. Costs which are directly attributable to the action of hiring the additional stockbroker are *direct* costs, and should be considered in the decision. If the benefits from hiring the additional stockbroker exceed the direct costs, the broker would be providing a contribution margin to defray the indirect costs, and should be hired.

How to Treat Indirect Costs in Deciding Whether to Create a Reusable Workproduct. In deciding whether to create a particular candidate reusable workproduct, the ongoing costs of an existing reuse library/infrastructure should not be allocated to candidate reusable workproducts. Rather, compare the candidate's contribution margin to other potential reusable workproducts. To determine whether to establish or continue a reuse program, perform a cost–benefit analysis which includes both fixed and variable costs.

18.5 Finance and Accounting Issues by Scope of Reuse

As the scope of reuse broadens beyond a single organization, enterprise, or even nation, financial and accounting issues become more complex. In Fig. 18–14, we outline some major financial and accounting issues by scope of reuse.

Finance and Accounting Issues by Scope of Reuse

1. *Personal Reuse* is practiced by the individual software engineer. Over time, the engineer typically accumulates a personal library of routines primarily for his own use. Every individual is responsible for producing and maintaining his or her own set of workproducts.

   Financial issues:
   * Determine the economic worthiness of producing or reengineering a workproduct for reuse.

   Accounting issues:
   * None

2. *Intraproject Reuse* describes reuse within a project. This usually involves designating one or more engineers to create the reusable workproducts (typically a function library) for the other project members to reuse. A project policy must be established on reuse to address the following contractual issues.

   Financial issues:
   * Address all the financial issues outlined in previous levels.
   * Identify the level of funding required to support reuse.

   Accounting issues:
   * Effort expended for developing and reusing software must be accounted for and tracked.

3. *Interproject Reuse* is the practice of reuse across multiple projects. Reuse at this level highlights the issues of coordination and organization among several groups and possibly geographical locations.

   Financial issues:
   * Address all the financial issues outlined in previous levels.
   * Identify the appropriate funding and pricing methods.

   Accounting issues:
   * Address all the accounting issues outlined in previous levels.

FIGURE 18–14 Finance and accounting issues by scope of reuse.

(continued)

- Design and implement a reuse management control system with transfer prices if necessary.

4. *Enterprise-wide Reuse* characterizes reuse throughout an enterprise. For our purposes, organizations which fall under this category include commercial companies and organizational units within the government (e.g., the Air Force). Reuse at this level requires support and coordination of multiple levels of management in multiple organizations. Depending upon the size of the enterprise, a broker may be required to match the supply and demand needs of enterprise constituents.

Financial issues:
- Address all the financial issues outlined in previous levels.

Accounting issues:
- Address all the accounting issues outlined in previous levels.
- Establish appropriate accounting guidelines and policies on the enterprise-wide use of shared workproducts.

5. *Interenterprise Reuse* describes reuse across enterprises. This includes the practice of reuse across several different companies.

Financial issues:
- Address all the financial issues outlined in previous levels.

Accounting issues:
- Address all the accounting issues outlined in previous levels.
- Revenues from the sale or licensing of reusable workproducts appear on the corporation's financial statements.

6. *National Reuse* is the reuse of workproducts on a national level. At this scope, management issues are of utmost importance.

Financial issues:
- Address all the financial issues outlined in previous levels.

Accounting issues:
- Address all the accounting issues outlined in previous levels.
- Understanding which reusable workproduct lines should be carried (managerial accounting) and determining product costs (cost accounting) are of greater importance.

7. *International Reuse* describes the reuse of workproducts across countries.

Financial issues:
- Address all the financial issues outlined in previous levels.

Accounting issues:
- Address all the accounting issues outlined in previous levels.
- Understand varying accounting conventions for offices in different countries.

FIGURE 18–14   *(continued)*

Summary

Finance and accounting for software reuse address the acquisition and management of financial resources necessary to implement reuse.

Finance is concerned with procuring capital to operate a reuse program. A budget is a set of pro forma financial statements which show the anticipated results for a future period. In every case, the budget begins with a forecast of the demand for reusable workproducts. Three techniques are available for forecasting the demand for reuse: indicator, historical analysis, and judgmental methods.

Use of a cash flow statement is helpful in determining the level of funding required for a reuse program. Initial funding for a reuse program may be provided as a grant, investment, loan, or barter. Ongoing funding may be in the form of an award, barter, contribution, payment, royalty, or tax. The choice of an appropriate method for charging is affected by a number of factors including the costs of administering the method; equitableness in matching costs to those who benefit from reuse; the nature of existing cost systems; and the culture of the organization.

A reuse management control system (RMCS) is a set of policies designed to ensure that resources are acquired, utilized effectively and efficiently from reuse strategy development to implementation.

References

1. P. H. Walgenbach, N. E. Dittrich, and E. I. Hanson, *Principles of Accounting*, 2nd ed. New York, NY: Harcourt Brace Jovanovich, 1980.
2. W. C. Lim, "Effects of reuse on quality, productivity, and economics," *IEEE Software*, vol. 11, no. 5, pp. 23–30, Sept. 1994.
3. R. A. Malan, "Software reuse: A business perspective," Hewlett-Packard, Palo Alto, CA, Hewlett-Packard Tech. Rep., Feb. 1993.
4. C. Collier and W. Ledbetter, *Engineering Economic and Cost Analysis*. New York, NY: Harper & Row, 1988.
5. T. B. Bollinger and S. L. Pfleeger, "The Economics of software reuse," Contel Technology Center, Chantilly, VA, Tech. Rep.CTC-TR-89-014, Dec. 13, 1989.
6. R. Joos, "So much for motherhood, apple pie, and reuse," in *5th Annual Workshop on Institutionalizing Software Reuse*, Oct. 26–29, 1992.
7. R. Joos, "Software reuse at Motorola," *IEEE Software*, vol. 11, no. 5, pp. 42–47, Sept. 1994.
8. E. J. Joyce, "Reusable software: Passage to productivity?," *Datamation*, vol. 34, no. 18, pp. 97–102, 1988.
9. W. Tracz, "The design and analysis of reusable software," UCLA Extension Department of Engineering, Los Angeles, CA, June 13–15, 1987.
10. S. Isoda, "Experience report on software reuse project: Its structure, activities, and statistical results," in *Proceedings International Conference on Software Engineering*, 1992.
11. B. Cox, "What if there is a silver bullet? And what if the competition builds it first?," *ReNews: The Electronic Software Reuse and Re-engineering Newsletter*, vol. 2, no. 3, Nov. 1992.
12. R. Prieto-Diaz, "Making software reuse work: an implementation model," *SIGSOFT Software Engineering Notes*, vol. 16, no. 3, pp. 61–68, July 1991.
13. F. Wolff, "Long-term controlling of software reuse," *Information and Software Technology*, vol. 34, no. 3, pp. 178–184, Mar. 1992.

14. *Merriam Webster's Collegiate Dictionary.* 10th ed., Springfield, MA: Merriam, 1997.

15. T. Frazier, "Economics of software working group," in *2nd Annual West Virginia Reuse and Education and Training Workshop,* Oct. 25–27, 1993.

16. W. Myers, "Hard data will lead managers to quality," *IEEE Software,* vol. 11, no. 2, pp. 100–101, Mar. 1994.

17. W. Schafer, R. Prieto-Diaz, and M. Matsumoto, *Software Reusability.* West Sussex, England: Ellis Horwood, 1994.

18. J. Favaro, "What price reusability? A case study," *Ada Letters,* vol. 11, no. 3, pp. 115–124, Spring 1991.

19. B. Barnes, T. Durek, J. Gaffney, and A. Pyster, "Cost models for software reuse," in *Software Productivity Consortium,* Reston, VA, SPC-TN-87-012, June 1987.

20. J. Margono and T. E. Rhoads, "Software reuse economics: Cost–benefit analysis on a large-scale Ada project," in *International Conference on Software Engineering,* May 1992, pp. 338–348.

REUSE METRICS

19.1 Introduction

The effects of measurement are humorously depicted in the following story about a Russian nail factory.

As part of a new decree from the centralized government, a Russian nail factory was informed that its performance would be measured on the basis of the number of nails that it produced. The factory immediately chose to produce tacks, and plenty of them.

After officials visited the factory and decided that their choice of measurement was not appropriate, the factory was informed that its performance would be measured on the basis of weight, not the number of nails produced. Soon after, the factory changed its product line to extremely heavy spike nails. The lesson? People tend to gravitate towards that upon which they are measured.

19.2 Goals of Chapter

The goals of this reuse metrics chapter are to provide an overview of reuse metrics and to describe a methodology for determining effective reuse metrics. A review of the literature and examples of reuse metrics utilized in industry are provided in Appendix 19–A.

19.3 The Rationale for Reuse Metrics

A reuse metric defines a way of measuring some attribute of developing software with reusable assets. Not limited to code, these metrics also measure the reuse infrastructure, the underlying foundation or basic framework that supports reuse, including the library, process, and other elements.

Reuse metrics provide valuable information to help organizations determine whether they are achieving their reuse goals. This information helps identify areas which may need greater attention as well as areas which are doing particularly well. Such metrics can be collected on an ongoing basis in order to provide continuous feedback on the impact of software reuse in the organization. The rationale for measuring reuse can be categorized into three areas: *benchmarking, incentives*, and *decision making*.

Benchmarking.   Metrics serve as a guide or benchmark, providing the means for determining an organization's current status of reuse in both an absolute and relative sense. In an absolute sense, metrics measure progress toward set goals; in a relative sense, they reveal where an organization stands compared to others.

Incentives.   If carefully and deliberately chosen, metrics serve as incentives to elicit the desired behavior from personnel. IBM, for example, has recognized this capability of metrics and deliberately selected measurements to motivate its employees to embrace reuse [1].

Decision Making.   The information provided by reuse metrics facilitates management decision making by helping to determine if the reuse program is progressing as planned, how it compares to other technologies, which areas of the reuse program are successful, and which require additional attention.

19.4   Goal–Question–Metric Paradigm

Because Appendix 19–A deliberately covers a broad range of reuse metrics, your organization may not require all the metrics discussed. You should understand the needs and goals of your organization in order to identify an appropriate critical set of reuse metrics. One method that may be useful in identifying appropriate reuse metrics is the "goal–question–metric" paradigm.

Basili and Rombach describe the use of the "goal–question–metric" paradigm in identifying software metrics [2]. They suggest first identifying the goal for which information is to be collected (e.g., "Improve software productivity through reuse"). Associated with the goal are a set of questions that would help clarify whether the goal has been achieved (e.g., "What is productivity without reuse?", "What is productivity with reuse?"). Appropriate metrics may then be formulated to help address the questions (e.g., "Thousands of noncomment source statements (KNCSS) of new code/user engineering days," "KNCSS of reused code/user engineering days").

Essentially, the metrics are *data* which, when used to answer the questions, become *information*. These questions, in turn, map our progress toward the goals. Following the paradigm ensures that metric information collected will address relevant questions and clarify whether goals have been achieved. The Department of Defense Software Reuse Initiative [3] is one example of an organization that has utilized the goal–question–metric methodology in identifying appropriate reuse metrics.

At Hewlett-Packard, one organization considered the constraints or resource limitations in the goal–question–metric process and identified criteria for pursuing one goal, question, or metric over another (Fig. 19–1).

Fig. 19–2 shows a case study in identifying reuse metrics using the goal–question–metric paradigm. The case study organization had three major organizational goals: improving quality, reducing cycle time, and leveraging experience or unique expertise. Appropriate questions and metrics were identified which helped determine whether the goals were being met.

19.5   The Dashboard of Metrics

Meyer has suggested identifying a critical set of metrics for use on a "dashboard" [4]. Analogous to the dashboard of an automobile, such metrics would provide the user with measurements specifically relevant to his or her needs.

For example, a driver need only know if his or her battery is discharging; he or she can determine later (through other measurements) whether this is due to a defective alternator, bad battery, or other reason. Likewise, in metrics measurement, users having a "dashboard" of essential metrics at their disposal would allow them to gauge the essential aspects of their job. When an item requires attention, the user can then examine other metrics which shed further light on the situation.

Reuse Metrics Case Study

One Hewlett-Packard project established criteria for pursuing one goal, question, or metric over another. Example criteria were (in order of priority):

1. the organization has a strong need to manage progress toward the associated goal;
2. the information needed to manage progress is not currently available;
3. having answers to the associated assessment question would significantly improve the organization's ability to manage progress toward the goal;
4. the cost/benefit of implementing the metric is acceptable to the organization.

FIGURE 19–1   Reuse metrics case study. *Source:* P. Collins and B. Zimmer, "Evolutionary metrics adoption method for reuse," in *7th Annual Workshop for Institutionalizing Software Reuse,* St. Charles, IL, Aug. 28–30, 1995.

A Case Study in Identifying Reuse Metrics

I. Goal: Improve software quality through reuse

Questions to be addressed:
1. What is quality without reuse?
2. What is quality with reuse?

Suggested Metrics:
1. Defects of new code/KNCSS
2. Defects of reused code/KNCSS
3. Defects of new and reused code/KNCSS

II. Goal: Shorten the cycle time (the time that is required to deliver a system) through reuse

Questions to be addressed:
1. What is the cycle time without reuse?
2. What is the cycle time with reuse?

Suggested Metrics:
1. Estimated time it would have taken to deliver system without reuse (using historical data)
2. Actual time required to deliver system with reuse

III. Goal: Leverage experienced or unique expertise through reuse

Questions to be addressed:
1. Without reuse, how many projects and at what level of involvement are experts able to contribute per unit of time?
2. With reuse, how many projects and at what level of involvement are experts able to contribute per unit of time?

Suggested Metrics:
1. Without reuse, the number of projects and level of involvement (qualitative) that experts were able to contribute per unit of time.
2. With reuse, the number of projects and level of involvement (qualitative) that experts were able to contribute per unit of time.

FIGURE 19–2   A case study in identifying reuse metrics for an organization.

The goal–question–metric approach provides a mechanism to consider the perspective of the appropriate party in the definition of the goal. This may be from an *organizational* perspective (Fig. 19–3), a *personnel hierarchy* perspective (Fig. 19–4) (i.e., engineer, senior engineer, project manager, section manager, lab manager), or another perspective. For example, the productivity metric might be measured differently for different audiences. An engineer who is responsible for producing reusable assets would find the measure of his or her productivity useful. A reuse project manager would like to know the aggregate average productivity of his or her reuse producer engineers. A lab manager would like to gauge the overall productivity of the engineers producing the systems/products in his or her lab.

In defining metrics for each managerial and engineering level, it is important to provide appropriate *information*. To use a simple example from a commercial organization, lab managers are concerned about reducing the cost of software development. Marketing managers want to increase sales volume and generate higher revenues. Both of these managers report to a division manager who is most concerned with—and should be presented with—the profit margin. Profit margin is a "derived" metric from both the cost and revenue metrics (i.e., profit = revenues – costs). Again, the derived metric should be sufficient to alert us to potential problem areas, which may then be investigated further.

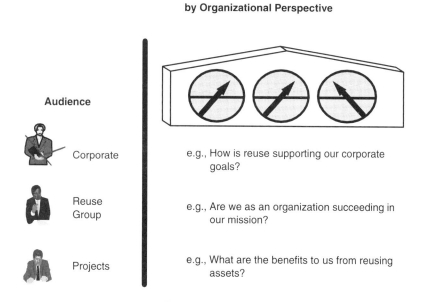

FIGURE 19–3   Dashboard by organizational perspective.

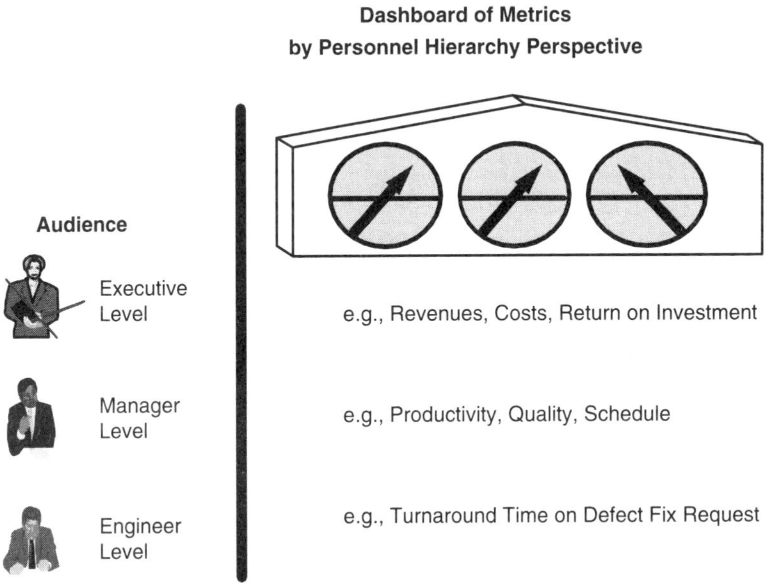

**Dashboard of Metrics
by Personnel Hierarchy Perspective**

Audience

Executive
Level   e.g., Revenues, Costs, Return on Investment

Manager
Level   e.g., Productivity, Quality, Schedule

Engineer
Level   e.g., Turnaround Time on Defect Fix Request

FIGURE 19–4   Dashboard by personnel hierarchy perspective.

19.6   Key Considerations in Measuring Software Reuse

"(The) developer needs to ascertain what sort of reuse is meant. Is it the number of times the code is incorporated into other code? The number of times the code is executed? A combination, the number of times the incorporating code is executed? A figure of merit reflecting the value or utility or saving rather than being a simple count of uses?"—P.A.V. Hall [5]

Among the key considerations in measuring reuse are the *amount* of reuse, the *value* of reuse, and the *unit of measure*. To identify appropriate metrics, first ask "What is our goal in measuring?" Too often, managers fail to ask this question.

Amount of Reuse.   The question of "how much" reuse addresses one of the primary goals of measurement, which is to provide a snapshot of where we stand relative to our goals and other organizations. Consequently, we need consistent measures across organizations so that the metrics may be compared. We need standard ways of counting, e.g., how to count macros, include files, subroutines, templates, functions, and the references to any of them (with their respective binding times). For example, we need to consider whether to count each subroutine or the number of times the subroutine is invoked.

Organizations that set a specific percentage improvement goal for reuse should be careful about how they intend to use this metric. While the goal appears simple and clear, it may be misleading and problematic for use in a reward system. For example, suppose project team Y is highly productive while project team Z typically lags behind, with lower productivity. A goal specifying a certain increase in reuse will penalize project Y, since for the equivalent amount of effort, project Z will show a substantially greater improvement. Furthermore, project Y may have already successfully exploited its reuse potential, whereas project Z may not have.

Value of Reuse. If the goal is to measure the value that software reuse provides to an organization, then the value must be defined and understood before an appropriate metric can be selected. Are we measuring the value that a reusable asset provides to an organization's normal practices? In other words, what is our baseline?

Establishing a clearly defined baseline is especially important for instituting incentives to reuse. For example, suppose we are measuring the benefit that two organizations, A and B, receive from reusable asset X. Organization A has three applications that could use asset X and organization B has four. We wish to measure the effort saved from the introduction of this reusable asset. If organization A did not have access to reusable asset X, its projects would have created the equivalent functionality of X three times for use in its application programs. Organization B, however, is more "coordination efficient," and would have recognized the redundancy in asset X among its projects. One project would have developed the equivalent functionality of X and three other projects would have reused the code.

If the total size of each organization's applications are equivalent, the "amount of reuse" metric (reuse percent) would indicate that organization A and organization B received the same value from reuse. However, the value of the reusable asset is clearly greater for organization A (the reusable asset saves it the effort of creating approximately 3X lines of code) than it is for organization B (the reusable asset saves it the effort of creating approximately 1X lines of code).

If the goal is to measure the value of reuse in terms of effort saved from the introduction of reuse, then the concept of differential effort is more appropriate than simply measuring reuse percent increase. Differential effort is simply the change in effort expended relative to a specified baseline as a result of taking a specific action, in this case, reuse. From this example, it is clear that a particular reusable asset can contribute a different value to different development projects, even if the number of reuses and the costs to procure and reuse are the same.

Unit of Measure. The choice of a unit of measure should be appropriate to the entity being measured. For example, calendar time can be measured in days, months, years, etc. Measuring software, however, is more complex.

Two widely used means of measuring software are lines of code (LOC) and function points (FP). While LOC are relatively easy to collect, issues relating to the use of an LOC metric must be clearly defined. These metrics include the treatment of nonexecutable statements and the handling of multiple lines on a single statement. For a discussion on the inconsistencies that can arise when measuring lines of code, see Jones [6] and Conte [7]. We will be using the KNCSS form of lines of code measure throughout this chapter.

Function points are used to measure program size and, consequently, development effort. Introduced by Albrecht [8], they are used to value a project based on the number of input data items, on-line inquiries, output screens or reports, master files, and interfaces to other systems. An appropriate weight, which depends on a subjective assessment of the complexity of the item, is applied to the count of each of these items. The FP value is computed using the sum of these weighted counts, several constants, and the sum of 14 complexity adjustment values. One of these complexity adjustments takes into consideration whether the code is designed to be reusable.

Pfleeger and Bollinger [9] note that "the function point method accommodates *producer* reuse (that is, code that is designed to be reused), but not *consumer* reuse (that is, components from previous projects that are reused on this project)." While FP counting may represent a more accurate measure, it may require more training [10]. Banker and Kaufmann [11] describe the use of function points on a two-year reuse project at the First Boston Corporation. For further information on function points, see Dreger [12].

19.7 Reuse Metrics

Before we examine some reuse metrics, let us review some definitions.

- Assets: Products or byproducts of the software development process, including code, design, and test plans.
- Producers: Software developers who create reusable assets.
- Consumers: Software developers who use these assets in the creation of other software.

Reuse metrics measure many aspects of software reuse, including:

- quality, productivity, and time-to-market metrics;
- reuse economic metrics;
- reuse library metrics;
- reuse process metrics;
- reuse product metrics;
- reuse asset metrics.

Primary metrics such as quality, productivity, and time-to-market serve as inputs to reuse economic models. All the other metrics contribute to primary metrics. Fig. 19–5 shows several examples of metrics and how they relate in a metric framework.

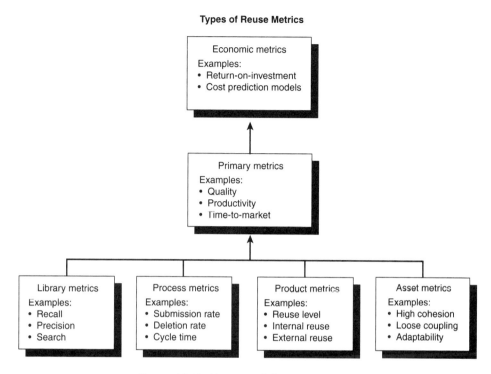

FIGURE 19–5   Framework for reuse metrics.

We offer a framework for reuse metrics (Fig. 19–5) and illustrate each category with examples in Appendix 19–A.

1. Quality, Productivity, and Time-To-Market Metrics

    a) Quality: Measures the defect density of new assets versus reused assets. (The defect density may be in lines of code, function points, or any other appropriate unit.)

1. Metric:	Defects/KNCSS of new asset.	
	Defects/KNCSS of reused asset.	
Benefit:	Enables comparison of defect density level for reused as-sets to new assets. May be used for estimating potential quality improvement for a given level of reuse.	
2. Metric:	Defects/KNCSS of product development without reuse	
	Defects/KNCSS of product development with reuse	
Benefit:	Determines level of defect density before and after incor-porating reuse on development projects. Includes defects	

that occur as a result of integrating reusable assets with new assets.

b) Productivity: Measures the consumer productivity rate in the creation of new assets and the use of reused assets. Measures the producer productivity rate in creating reusable assets.

3. Metric: KNCSS of new asset/consumer engineering days (or appropriate unit of measure).
KNCSS of reused asset/consumer engineering days (or appropriate unit of measure).

Benefit: Will enable a comparison between the efficiency in creating new assets versus the effort expended in using them.

4. Metric: KNCSS of reused asset/producer engineering days (or appropriate unit of measure).
KNCSS of nonreusable asset/producer engineering days (or appropriate unit of measure).

Benefit: Used to estimate the additional effort required to create reusable assets.
Usually, the effort to create the nonreusable asset must also be estimated.

5. Metric: KNCSS of nonreusable asset/producer engineering days (or appropriate unit of measure) to reengineer a nonreusable asset into a reusable asset.

Benefit: Used to estimate effort required to reengineer nonreusable assets into reusable assets.

c) Time-To-Market: Measures the time elapsed in delivering the product/system to the customer. For commercial companies, shorter time-to-market measures are important because reduced cycle time typically increases profit. Since increased productivity does not necessarily result in shortened time-to-market, time-to-market should be explicitly measured.

6. Metric: Time-to-market without reuse (in an appropriate unit of time).
Time-to-market with reuse (in an appropriate unit of time).

Benefit: Will determine whether reuse shortens time-to-market for product/system. Can be used to help estimate increased profit due to shortened time-to-market. May identify need to create and reuse assets on critical path of product/system.

2. Reuse Economic Metrics

The goal of reuse economic metrics is to measure the cost–benefit aspects of software reuse. Within this category, there are three types of economic metrics: reuse value, return-on-investment, and cost prediction.

a) Value Metric: Reuse value metrics are used to compute the worth provided by the reusable assets to the consumer. See Appendix 19–A for examples from First Boston and IBM.

b) Return-On-Investment Metrics: Return-on-investment metrics are collected for the purpose of measuring the magnitude of the benefits relative to the costs. Some return-on-investment models take into account factors such as risk and cost of capital (i.e., cost of funds for the reuse program); models include those that use net present value, internal rate of return, and payback methods. See Appendix 12–A for examples of reuse economic models.

c) Cost Prediction Metrics: Cost prediction metrics are incorporated in a model which predicts the decrease in cost or increase in productivity if reuse is implemented. See Appendix 19–A for examples of models in this category.

3. **Reuse Library Metrics**

If your organization utilizes a software reuse library, the following metrics may be useful for measuring the efficiency and effectiveness of your reuse library. The first two metrics of *recall* and *precision* are applicable if your organization has many reusable assets and wishes to measure the efficiency and effectiveness of the search scheme. Use of the other library metrics is less dependent on the number of assets.

a) Recall metric: The number of relevant items retrieved divided by the number of relevant items in the database [13].

  Metric: Number of relevant reusable assets retrieved/total number of relevant reusable assets in database/library.

  Benefit: Indicates the efficiency of the library search scheme. Total relevant reusable assets usually must be estimated.

b) Precision metric: The number of relevant items retrieved divided by the total number of items retrieved [13].

  Metric: Number of relevant reusable assets retrieved/total number of reusable assets retrieved

  Benefit: Indicates effectiveness of the library search scheme. A low precision percentage may indicate that the search scheme is too broad, requiring human discrimination of the retrieved assets.

c) Search metric:

  Metric: Number of library searches/consumer or unit of time.

  Benefit: Indicates number of searches for information from library by consumers.

d) Volume metric:

  Metric: Number of reusable assets in library.

Benefit: Indicates the size of task in library management. May be used with asset metrics (size in lines of code, memory required) to project capacity utilization of the library.

e) Usage metric:

Metric: Number of reusable assets used from library/consumer or unit of time.

Benefit: Indicates the volume of assets used. May be used with asset metrics (consumer savings from reuse of a given asset) to determine overall savings per unit of time.

4. Reuse Process Metrics

a) Producing Reusable Assets (PRA): The activities in PRA include 1) analyzing domain; 2) producing assets; and 3) maintaining and enhancing assets. Examples of PRA metrics include domain analysis and acceptance rate metrics.

   1. Domain Analysis Metrics

      Domain analysis metrics aid in the process of identifying commonalties and variabilities in the domain of interest. See Appendix 19–A for examples.

   2. Acceptance Rate: Rate of approval for reusable assets submitted to library.

      Metric: Number of reusable assets accepted/number of reusable assets submitted (may be over appropriate unit of time).

      Benefit: Indicates the rate at which new reusable assets are being accepted. A low acceptance rate may indicate a need, for example, to train producers on design/coding standards.

b) Brokering Reusable Assets (BRA). BRA activities include 1) assessing assets for brokering; 2) certifying assets; 3) adding assets; and 4) deleting assets. Examples of BRA metrics include submission rate, deletion rate, and cycle time metrics.

   1. Submission Rate: Rate of submission for reusable assets to library.

      Metric: Number of reusable assets submitted, divided by unit of time (or per person).

      Benefit: Indicates the rate at which new reusable assets are being submitted. A low submission rate may indicate a lack of incentive to submit, near fulfillment of a comprehensive set of assets for the domain, or other reason(s).

   2. Deletion Rate: Rate of deletion of reusable assets from library.

      Metric: Number of reusable assets deleted divided by unit of time.

      Benefit: Indicates the rate at which reusable assets are purged from library. A high deletion rate may indicate change in the domain or a lack of usage. The reasons for purging should be tracked.

3. Cycle Time: Time required for turnaround on a reusable asset request or defect fix.

    Metric: Elapsed time for reusable asset creation or defect fix.

    Benefit: Indicates the speed in which consumer/customer needs are satisfied. A short cycle time for a reusable asset defect fix may reflect the benefit of having maintainers more familiar with reusable assets than with new assets.

c) Consuming Reusable Assets (CRA). The activities in CRA include 1) identifying system and asset requirements; 2) locating assets; 3) assessing assets for consumption; and 4) integrating assets.

User Satisfaction: Measures of user satisfaction in terms of quality of assets, turnaround time, etc.

Metric: Ratings of software quality factors of reusable assets.

Benefit: Indicates whether producers are fulfilling user needs and desires.

5. Reuse Product Metrics

Reuse product metrics gauge the characteristics of the final product or system.

a) Reuse Percent Metric: Used to approximate the amount of effort saved as a result of reuse (i.e., this metric only approximates "effort avoided by reusing/total effort without reuse"). Also known as the "reuse level" metric.

Metric: KNCSS of reused asset divided by KNCSS of total assets.

Benefit: Approximates the amount of effort saved as a result of reuse.

Use of the reuse percent metric alone to measure the benefit from reuse is not sufficient for the following reasons [14].

1. A product/system with high-percentage reuse does not necessarily have a high or even positive net benefit.

The reuse percent level is used by some to approximate the amount of effort saved. A high reuse percentage, however, does not mean that the time and effort expended to achieve that level is justified, i.e., it may cost more than it is worth to achieve. First, the consumer cost to reuse must be measured; in the case where the consumer cost exceeds the benefit, there is a net loss. Second, although the consumer may be experiencing a net gain (consumer benefits less consumer costs), the producer may be experiencing a net loss (sum of consumers net gain/loss less producer cost). Even if the reuse percent metric is high, the organization could still be experiencing an economic loss from reuse.

2. The reuse percent does not necessarily reflect effort saved from reuse.

Example:

(Reused lines of code)/(total lines of code = new and reused lines of code) = 50/100 = 50%; but if only a portion would have been created by the consumer, e.g., (avoided lines of code)/(new and avoided lines of code) = 32/82 = 39%, then the reuse percent metric does not reflect the effort saved.

The reuse percent does not necessarily reflect the effort that was saved from reuse. For example, reuse of an asset may account for 50% of a product when the unit of measure is lines of code reused divided by new and reused lines of code. However, if the consumer would have actually only created a portion of the reusable asset had it not been available, then the 50% reuse level inflates the gains from reuse.

The difference between reused and avoided lines of code may be due to:

a) additional lines of code to make the asset reusable;
b) extra lines of code to incorporate the asset into the application;
c) "unactivated" code, i.e., code which is in a "ready-to-process" mode but never used;
d) our selection of an easily collected metric without fully considering what constitutes "avoided" effort in the organization (see the section "Coordination Efficiency" on page 137).

Let us examine the first three factors further. In using the reuse percent metric, the gains from reuse may be inflated because of the way in which additional code to make the asset reusable, incorporate the reusable asset into the application, or "unactivated" code is accounted (see boxed text accompanying Fig. 19–6).

Not having a benchmark of current organizational practices that enables us to determine what effort is actually avoided through reuse can lead to a misleading reuse percent metric. For example, some managers have used KNCSS of subroutines/total KNCSS of product or (KNCSS of subroutines x number of times called)/total KNCSS of product. The problem with both measurements is that they do not necessarily indicate the effort avoided.

For example, if the effort in creating new code is avoided twice when a subroutine is called twice, then the first metric misses this avoidance. The second measurement can overestimate the savings from reuse. For example, if the subroutine is called ten times by ten engineers, but only five engineers would have coded the asset and the other five would have reused the asset, then only the effort of coding the asset five times has been avoided. This is another example of the "coordination efficiency" mentioned earlier.

3. Differing definition of reuse impacts reuse percent metric.

Example:

Product/systems which include carryover reuse in their calculations may have very high reuse percent levels.

How the Reuse Percent Metric Can Exaggerate Reuse Benefits

In this example, we use lines of code as our unit of measure. However, this analysis is applicable to other units of measure as well (e.g., function points, objects).

Let T be the total lines of code in a system/product if it were developed from scratch. If we utilize reusable code during development, the system/product will consist of lines of code developed expressly for the system/product (new code, N), lines of code reused (code which need not be developed, i.e., avoided lines of code, A), and lines of code added to make a nonreusable component reusable, incorporate a reusable component to the application, or provide alternative functionality which is not used (R). So, let:

T = total lines of code in system/product if it were developed from scratch
N = lines of new code.
A = lines of code avoided by reusing.
R = lines of code added to make a nonreusable component reusable, incorporate a reusable component to the application, or provide alternative functionality to the component which is not used.

(As an example of the latter, consider a utility which handles input in a month/day/year format. Let us add lines of code to the utility enabling it to process input in either a day/month/year or year/day/month format. Now consider an application which has a screen edit that will only allow data to be entered in a month/day/year format. When the application uses this utility, the lines which were added to provide the alternative functionality, i.e., input in day/month/year or year/day/month format, are in a "ready-to-process" mode but never used.)

Since A expresses the lines that have been avoided by reusing, (A/T) is a closer approximation of effort saved than (A+R)/(T+R). However, most organizations use (A+R)/(T+R) because it is more easily collected.

The percent error of the reuse percent metric due to counting lines that make the component reusable, incorporate a reusable component to the application, or add alternative functionality which is not used may be expressed as follows:

$$\text{Percent Error} = [(A+R)/(T+R) - (A/T)]/(A/T).$$

Let

$$A = mT, \text{ where } 0 < m \le 1$$
$$R = nT, \text{ where } 0 \le n < 1$$
$$\text{and } 0 < m+n \le 1$$

where

m is the percent of total lines avoided by reusing
n is the percent of total lines that are added to make a nonreusable component reusable, incorporate a reusable component to the application, or provide alternative functionality to the component which is not used.

FIGURE 19–6   Reuse percent metric error.

(continued)

With substitution,

$$\text{Percent Error} = [(mT+nT)/(T+nT)-(mT/T)]/(mT/T)$$
$$= [((m+n)/(1+n))-m]/m$$
$$= (1/m)[(m+n)/(1+n)]-1.$$

For example, if 20% of the total lines are lines added to make a nonreusable component reusable, incorporate a reusable component to the application, or provide alternative functionality to the component which is not used (i.e., n=20%) and 25% of the total lines are lines that have been avoided by reusing (i.e., m=25%), then the percent error between the reuse percent metric (A+R)/(T+R) and the more accurate ratio (A/T) is 50%. We can see in the figure below all values of m and n that would result in a 50% error when (A+R)/(T+R) is used instead of (A/T).

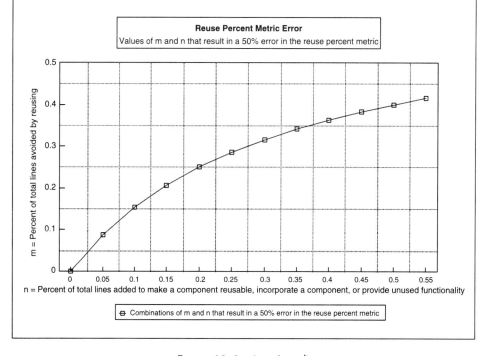

Reuse Percent Metric Error
Values of m and n that result in a 50% error in the reuse percent metric

FIGURE 19–6   *(continued)*

Finally, one must ask whether the reuse percent level includes "carryover" reuse. Carryover reuse is the moving of code from one version to the next. While there are benefits of practicing carryover reuse, it does have implications for reuse measurement. Products which include carryover reuse in their calculations tend to have very high reuse percent levels compared to those which do not.

b) External Reuse Level: Measures the amount of existing assets from outside the project (or unit of organization) to create new software.

  Metric: Number of parts from external sources/total parts in the system [15].

  Benefit: Measures level of reused assets from external source. By measuring the external reuse level, we can tell 1) whether the project is reusing assets that have already been created externally before being created for the project (which would presumably be more cost effective if there is no charge for use of the external reusable asset); 2) whether a low level of external reuse may be an indication that the external assets do not match the requirements of the project or there may be some impediment (e.g., "not invented here syndrome") to reusing external parts.

c) Internal Reuse Level: Measures the amount of existing assets from within the project (or unit of organization) to create new software.

  Metric: Number of nonexternal parts used more than once divided by total parts in the system [15].

  Benefit: Measures level of reused assets from internal source. If the product is not a new or unique program to the organization, a low level of internal reuse may warrant further investigation.

d) Black Box Reuse Level: Black box reuse is employing existing assets (as is) in the software product development process, preserving asset integrity [16].

  Metric: Number of black box KNCSS/total KNCSS.

  Benefit: Measures the level of unmodified lines of code, which is the most desired form of reuse.

e) White Box Reuse Level: White box (or leverage) reuse means starting with existing assets in the software development process and modifying as needed to meet specific system requirements [16].

  Metric: Number of white box KNCSS/total KNCSS.

  Benefit: Measures the level of modified lines of code, which may be more costly than black box reuse.

f) Carryover Reuse Level: Carryover software occurs when one version of a software component is taken to be used, as in a subsequent version of the same system. Carryover reuse appears to be more widely practiced than other forms of reuse.

  It is distinguished from black box reuse because it does not represent a distinct or novel usage of the same components [16].

  Metric: Number of carryover KNCSS of assets divided by total KNCSS of assets.

  Benefit: Measures and encourages carryover reuse separately from black box reuse.

Carryover reuse is measured separately because it is fairly widespread when creating new versions. If carryover reuse is bundled with black box reuse, unrealistically high and misleading levels of reuse can result. IBM [1] also recognizes this and thus does not count "unchanged base instructions from prior releases of the product" (i.e., carry over reuse) in either changed source instruction (CSI) or reused source instructions (RSI). Nippon Telephone and Telegraph (NTT) also measures carryover reuse separately.

Commenting on the practice of carryover reuse, Wegner [17] observes that:

> "Reuse of a component in successive versions of an evolving program appears to be a more important source of increased productivity than reuse of code in different applications. Components are rarely portable between applications, and even if they are, the incremental benefit of using a component in two applications is only a factor of two. But the number of versions of a system over its lifetime can number in the thousands."

g) Reuse of Asset from Library: Identifies whether the asset reused originated from the reuse library.

Metric: Reuse library KNCSS/total KNCSS.

Benefit: When used with the reuse percent metric, a low reuse of asset from library percent may suggest that the projects are reusing or leveraging assets which have not passed the library entry criteria or are not supported by the librarian.

6. Reuse Asset Metrics

a) Size metric: Measures the size of a reusable asset.

Metric: KNCSS of reusable asset.

Benefit: Provides a measure useful for capacity and resource planning.

b) Number of reuses for each asset:

Metric: Number of reuses divided by unit of time.

Benefit: Measures the frequency of use for the asset. A low frequency may indicate that the asset needs to be reengineered to be more reusable or that opportunities for reusing the asset are diminishing.

c) Reusability metrics: Measure the reusability of an asset based on characteristics that support reusability. Such ratings may be subjective assessments by consumers (e.g., 1=excellent, 2=good, 3=average, 4=deficient, 5=poor). Some have devised ways to collect reusability metrics via automated tools [18]. See Appendix 19–A for a list of reusability characteristics enumerated by Hall and Wald.

Benefit: Identifies characteristics that producer can emphasize to meet user needs.

19.8 A Process for Identifying an Appropriate Set of Metrics

Six-Stage Reuse Measurement Process. A systematic, yet flexible measurement process will enable us to identify and implement a set of reuse metrics which are appropriate to the target organization's needs. Such a process enables us to identify consistent and carefully designed metrics. The six-stage reuse measurement process (adapted from Berns [19]) is as follows:

1. define and clarify goals;
2. identify reuse questions;
3. identify reuse metrics;
4. gather reuse metrics;
5. examine reuse metrics;
6. act on basis of reuse metrics.

Stage 1. Define and Clarify Goals. As part of establishing a reuse metrics program, the needs and goals of the organization, as well as the context in which reuse metrics will be defined, must be clearly defined. Since each organization's products/services or emphases may differ, this implies that a different set of metrics may be appropriate for different organizations, even within the same company. For example, one organization may emphasize the need to have systems created quickly for their users while another that maintains large transaction and back office systems may focus on keeping costs down. In some cases, identifying goals by level of management may be appropriate.

In their discussion of the use of the goal–question–metric paradigm, Basili *et al.* [2] suggest first identifying the goal for which information is to be collected (e.g. "improve software productivity through reuse"). Identifying the goals for the organization is accomplished through a series of brainstorming sessions. The discussion usually begins with a focus on the client goals and needs, end-user goals, the organization's goals, and then, if appropriate, any suborganization's goals. This approach begins by focusing on the client, because the organization's ultimate goal is adding value the client will recognize. In turn, the client organization that supplies the systems to end-users should be attuned to their needs.

Stage 2. Identify Reuse Questions. The purpose of this stage is to identify question(s) that relate to each goal and that will help to formulate appropriate metrics. Associated with the goal are a set of questions that help clarify whether the goal has been achieved (e.g. "What is productivity without reuse?" and "What is productivity with reuse?").

Stage 3. Identify Reuse Metrics. At this stage, we identify the metric or set of metrics that will allow us to answer the questions asked in Stage 2. Appropriate metrics may be formulated to help address the questions (e.g., "KNCSS of new code/consumer engineering days," and "KNCSS of reused code/consumer engineering days"). A list of possible metrics are identified and then shortened to highlight the key issues associated with the question. Participants should identify relevant attributes for each metric. These may include the unit of measure; the source of the metric; the proposed collection method; the party responsible for collecting the metric; the frequency that the metric will be collected and presented; the baseline that the metric will be compared to; the type of format that the metric will be presented; and the purpose for which the metric will be used, i.e., "What action can the metric elicit?" Following are the questions that should be asked of each metric.

Why? Why am I measuring this? What is my goal? Will this information lead me to take action? Will I be able to relate this to a baseline and determine its outcome? Can I tell whether the results are good, bad, or neutral?

Who? Who will be using this information? The metric should be targeted and relevant to this individual. Is the individual an engineer, project manager, laboratory manager, division manager, or a committee composed of several of these categories? Is his/her role a producer or consumer of reusable software?

When? When in the software development life cycle do I measure this? Do I measure this pre-release or post-release?

Where? Should the measurement take place within organizational boundaries (e.g. project, laboratory, etc.), or domain boundaries (e.g., analytical instrument firmware)?

What? What units do you count? Lines of code, function points, time, defects? What do you count? For example, do you count the number of subroutines used in a program or the number of times the subroutine is called?

How? How will these metrics be collected? Will they be collected from the engineers on-line? Via a reuse assessment?

Stage 4. Gather Reuse Metrics.   The collection of reuse metrics will identify areas of the reuse program that are successful and those which are problematic. The measurement frequency and purpose of the metrics will determine the channel or mechanism by which they are collected. For example, if the goal of the metrics data is to be used to assess the feasibility of reuse and/or survey the reuse program participants, then collection administered in the form of a reuse assessment at appropriate intervals may be desired. On the other hand, if the data will be used for immediate process control such as level of defects, then a more frequent collection schedule would be necessary.

Stage 5. Examine Reuse Metrics.   At this stage, we analyze reuse metrics for trends, comparisons, tracking, and decision making. Both problem areas and successes should be examined and documented. The analysis can help answer the questions posed in stage 2 and determine the priority of problematic issues and whether or not other metrics must be collected. From this information, recommendations and solutions can be proposed.

Stage 6. Act on the Basis of Reuse Metric Findings.   The purpose of this stage is to garner support from management to implement an action plan. This support should include not only funding but time and personnel as well. If necessary, stages 4 through 6 may be repeated.

19.9   Recommended Minimal Set of Reuse Metrics

The role of a corporate reuse program requires an enterprise perspective on reuse activities. Consequently, it is desirable for a corporate reuse program to identify a core set of reuse metrics that may be consistently collected across divisional reuse programs, and then aggregate and compare. This core set of reuse metrics, however, is not meant to cover all the goals and needs of divisional reuse programs. Divisional reuse programs should undergo the reuse metrics process to identify additional metrics which should be collected in addition to this core set.

At Hewlett-Packard, the corporate reuse program has identified a recommended minimal set of reuse metrics [20] for divisions considering reuse. With the goal of measuring the impact of software reuse and the extent of its worth, we suggest collecting the following metrics.

1. Reuse primary metrics
   a. quality;
   b. productivity;
   c. time-to-market.
2. Costs of the reuse program
   a. cost of creating and maintaining reusable assets;
   b. cost of creating and maintaining reusable library;
   c. other reuse costs.
3. Reuse level metric: Used to approximate the amount of effort saved as a result of reuse.
   KNCSS of reused assets/KNCSS of total assets
4. Number of reusable assets.
5. Size of reusable assets: minimum, maximum, mean.

We found the above core set of metrics to be the minimum necessary for measuring the impact of reuse and monitoring its progress throughout the divisions of Hewlett-Packard.

19.10   Reuse Metrics by Scope of Reuse

Measurement of reuse changes as the scope of reuse broadens. For example, measuring reuse increases in formality as we move from personal reuse to a broader scope. In Fig. 19–7, we outline some of the major financial and accounting issues by scope of reuse.

Metric Issues by Scope of Reuse

1. *Personal reuse* is practiced by the individual software engineer. Over time, the engineer typically accumulates a personal library of routines primarily for his or her own use. Given this, each individual is responsible for producing and maintaining his or her own assets for use by him or herself.

   Metric issues:
   - Track characteristics of reuse assets for individual use.

2. *Intraproject reuse* describes reuse within a project. This usually involves designating one or more engineers to create the reusable assets (typically a function library) for the other project members to reuse. A project policy on reuse must be established to address the following metric issues.

   Metric issues:
   - If a reuse library is established, determine metrics for its usage.
   - Identify appropriate reuse process, product, and asset metrics which correspond to the new roles of the engineers.

3. *Interproject reuse* is the practice of reuse across multiple projects. Reuse at this level highlights the issues of coordination and organization among several groups and possibly geographic locations.

   Metric issues:
   - Address all metric issues outlined in previous levels.
   - Ensure that methods for collecting reuse metrics are consistent across all projects.
   - Identify reuse metrics which measure the reuse of assets across projects and, if necessary, appropriate transfer prices (see chapter 18).

4. *Enterprise-wide reuse* characterizes reuse throughout an enterprise. For our purposes, organizations which fall under this category include commercial companies and organizational units within the government (e.g., the Air Force). Reuse at this level requires support and coordination of multiple levels of management in multiple organizations. Depending upon the size of the enterprise, a broker may be required to match the supply and demand needs of enterprise constituents.

   Metric issues:
   - Address all metric issues outlined in previous levels.
   - Provide greater emphasis on process metrics for managing the increased complexity for enterprise-wide reuse.
   - Establish standard metric collection guidelines and policies on the enterprise-wide use of shared assets
   - May require staff dedicated to the collection of reuse metrics across the enterprise.

5. *Interenterprise reuse* describes reuse across enterprises. This includes the practice of reuse across several different companies. At this level, significant legal issues of ownership, rights, licensing, and proprietary information must be addressed.

   Metric issues:
   - Address all metric issues outlined in previous levels.
   - Consider establishing a team dedicated to collecting reuse metrics.

FIGURE 19–7   Metric issues by scope of reuse.

(continued)

- Identify appropriate reuse metrics in order to properly package and support the reusable assets for interenterprise reuse.

6. *National reuse* is the reuse of assets on a national level. At this scope, management issues are of utmost importance. The previous level of interenterprise reuse may allow individual contracts with other companies. At this level, the appropriate legal mechanisms must be considered for widespread distribution of reusable assets.

   Metric issues:
   - Address all metric issues outlined in previous levels.
   - Identify appropriate reuse metrics in order to properly package and support the reusable assets for national reuse.

7. *International reuse* describes the reuse of assets across countries. Prominent issues raised at this level include language, international copyright laws, location and extent of jurisdiction, and individual nation laws, policies, and methods of recourse.

   Metric issues:
   - Address all metric issues outlined in previous levels.
   - Identify appropriate reuse metrics in order to properly package and support the reusable assets for international reuse.
   - Have localization specialists tailor the metrics information for reusable assets.

FIGURE 19–7   *(continued)*

Summary

A reuse metric defines a way of measuring some attribute of developing software with reusable assets. Not limited to code, reuse metrics also measure the reuse infrastructure—the underlying foundation or basic framework that supports reuse such as the library, process, and other elements.

The rationale for measuring reuse can be categorized into three areas: benchmarking, incentives, and decision making. Metrics serve as a guide or benchmark, providing the means for determining an organization's current status of reuse in both an absolute and a relative sense. If carefully and deliberately chosen, metrics serve as incentives to elicit desired behavior. Information provided by reuse metrics improves management decision making. It helps to determine whether the reuse program is progressing as planned, how it compares to other technologies, which areas of the reuse program are successful, and which require additional attention.

One method that may be useful in identifying appropriate reuse metrics is the goal–question–metric paradigm. Under this method, the goal for which information is to be collected is identified first, followed by the set of questions that would help clarify whether the goal has been achieved, and then the set of metrics which will address the questions. The idea of a "dashboard" of metrics is to tailor and provide a set of measurements to a user which are highly relevant to his or her needs. A framework for reuse metrics is provided which includes quality, productivity, and time-to-market metrics, reuse economic metrics, reuse library metrics, reuse process metrics, reuse product metrics, and reuse asset metrics. A six-step process to identify an appropriate set of metrics is presented as follows: define and clarify goals;

identify reuse questions; identify reuse metrics; gather reuse metrics; examine reuse metrics; and act on basis of reuse metrics.

References

1. J. S. Poulin and J. M. Caruso, "A reuse metrics and return on investment model," in *Proceedings Advances in Software Reuse, Selected Papers from the 2nd International Workshop on Software Reusability,* cat. no. 93TH0495-2, Mar. 24–26, 1993, pp. 152–166.
2. V. R. Basili and H. D. Rombach, "Tailoring the software process to project goals and environment," in *Proceedings of the 9th International Conference on Software Engineering, cat. no. 87ch2432-3,* 1987, pp. 345–357.
3. "Department of defense software reuse initiative reporting metrics and measures," Defense Information Systems Agency, Joint Interoperability and Engineering Organization, Center for Information Management, April 11, 1996.
4. C. Meyer, "How the right measures help teams excel," *Harvard Business Review*, vol. 27, no. 3, pp. 95–97+, May/June 1994.
5. P. A. V. Hall, "Software components and reuse-getting more out of your code," *Information and Software Technology*, vol. 29, no. 1, pp. 38–43, Jan./Feb. 1987.
6. C. Jones, "How not to measure programming productivity (part 1)," *Computerworld*, vol. 20, no. 2, pp. 65–76, Jan. 13, 1986.
7. S. Conte, H. Dunsmore, and V. Shen, *Software Engineering Metrics and Models.* Menlo Park, CA: Benjamin/Cummings, 1986.
8. A. Albrecht, "Measuring application development productivity," in *IBM Application Development Symposium*, Oct. 1979.
9. S. Pfleeger and T. B. Bollinger, "A reuse-oriented survey of software cost models," Contel Technology Center, Chantilly, VA, CTC-TR-90-002, Jan. 1990.
10. C. F. Kemerer, "Reliability of function points measurement: A field experiment," *Communications of the ACM*, vol. 36, no. 2, pp. 85–97, Feb. 1993.
11. R. D. Banker and R. J. Kauffman, "Reuse and productivity in integrated computer-aided software engineering: an empirical study," *Management Information Systems Quarterly*, vol. 15, no. 3, pp. 375–401, Sept. 1991.
12. B. Dreger, *Function Point Analysis.* Englewood Cliffs, NJ: Prentice-Hall, 1989.
13. W. B. Frakes and P. B. Gandel, "Representing reusable software," *Information and Software Technology*, vol. 32, no. 10, pp. 653–664, Dec. 1990.
14. W. C. Lim, "Tutorial: Does your reuse program measure up?: Assessments, economics, and metrics," in *4th International Conference on Software Reuse,* Apr. 23–26, 1996.
15. R. Prieto-Diaz and W. Frakes, "An introduction to software reuse," *National Technological University Advanced Technology and Management Program,* Feb. 3, 1992.

16. M. Ogush, "Terms in transition: A software reuse lexicon," *Crosstalk: The Journal of Defense Software Engineering*, no. 39, pp. 41–45, Dec. 1992.

17. P. Wegner, "Capital-intensive software technology," *IEEE Software*, vol. 1, no. 3, pp. 7–45, July 1984.

18. G. Caldiera and V. R. Basili, "Identifying and qualifying reusable software components," *Computer*, vol. 24, no. 2, pp. 61–70, Feb. 1991.

19. A. Berns, "Informal technical report for the software technology for adaptable, reliable systems (STARS): Metrics concept report," HGO Technologies, Inc., STARS-VC-B019/004/00, Mar. 31, 1994.

20. W. C. Lim, "Software Reuse Assessments and Economics," presented at *Reuse Bay Area Roundtable*, Palo Alto, CA, 1993.

For Further Reading

1. F. Britoe Abreu and R. Carapuca, "Candidate metrics for object-oriented software within a taxonomy framework," *Journal of Systems and Software*, vol. 26, no. 1, pp. 87–96, July 1994.

2. V. R. Basili, L. C. Briand, and W. L. Melo, "How reuse influences productivity in object-oriented systems," *Communications of the ACM*, vol. 39, no. 10, pp. 104–116, Oct. 1996.

3. B. Boehm, "Measuring and modeling software reuse," in *Applied Software Measurement (ASM) 93 Conference*, Nov. 11, 1993.

4. Y.-F. Chen, B. Krishnamurthy, and K.-P. Vo, "An objective reuse metric: Model and methodology," AT&T Bell Laboratories, Murray Hill, NJ 07974.

5. P. Devanbu, S. Karstu, W. Melo, and W. Thomas, "Analytical and empirical evaluation of software reuse metrics," in *Proceedings of the 18th International Conference on Software Engineering*, cat. no. 96CB35918), Mar. 25–30, 1996, pp. 189–199.

6. W. Frakes and C. Terry, "Reuse level metrics," in *Software Reuse: Advances in Software Reusability International Conference*, Nov. 1–4, 1994.

7. M. Hitz, "Measuring reuse attributes in object-oriented systems," in *OOIS '95. 1995 International Conference on Object Oriented Information Systems Proceedings*, Dec. 18–20, 1996, pp. 19–38.

8. A. E. Nieder, "Qualifying software components: Reusability metrics, software reuse, and re-engineering," in *National Symposium: Improving the Software Process and Competitive Position via Software Reuse and Re-engineering*, Apr. 1991.

9. S. L. Pfleeger, "Measuring reuse: A cautionary tale," *IEEE Software*, vol. 13, no. 4, pp. 118–127, July 1996.

10. S. L. Pfleeger, "Reuse measurement and evaluation," *American Programmer*, vol. 8, no. 11, pp. 25–30, Nov. 1995.

11. J. Poulin, *Measuring Software Reuse*. Reading, MA,: Addison-Wesley, 1997.

12. W. J. Salamon and D. R. Wallace, "Quality characteristics and metrics for reusable software (preliminary report)," National Institute of Standards and Technology, Gaithersburg, MD, NISTIR 5459, May 1994.
13. M. Sarshar, "Reuse measurement and assessment," in *Systematic Reuse: Issues in Initiating and Improving a Reuse Program. Proceedings of the International Workshop on Systematic Reuse,* Jan. 8–9, 1996, pp. 52–63.

19-A

A SURVEY OF REUSE METRICS

19A.1 Examples of Reuse Metrics by Category

Quality, Productivity, and Time-To-Market Metrics

Both Nortel and Hewlett-Packard have invested significant effort in collecting quality, productivity, and time-to-market metrics. According to Fraser, Nortel (formerly Bell Northern Research, Ltd.) measures productivity gains, the number of reusable components, and component quality. Nortel makes these measurements toward the end of the development life cycle, during the postmortem phase, via an on-line questionnaire [1]. Hewlett-Packard's Corporate Reuse Program measures quality, productivity, and time-to-market elements associated with reuse programs at the divisional level [2].

Reuse Economic Metrics

In the following section, we review a series of reuse economic metrics.

Value Metrics

First Boston Reuse Value Metric. Banker *et al.* have attempted to define a rigorous method for calculating *reuse value*. Their approach seeks to go beyond simply counting objects by weighting the level of reuse based on what it costs to program each type of object. Banker's formula is as follows:

$$\text{Reuse Value} \; = \; 1 \; - \; \frac{\sum\limits_{j=1}^{J*} Cost_j}{\sum\limits_{j=1}^{J} Cost_j}$$

where
Cost = Average cost for building object *j*, calculated in person-days;
J = Number of object occurrences found in an application meta-model hierarchy;
J* = Quantity of unique objects built to support the application.

By using this metric, managers and developers can estimate what percentage of development costs they have saved through reuse [3].

IBM Reuse Cost Avoidance (RCA).   Poulin and Caruso of IBM seek to clearly define reuse metrics while at the same time distinguishing savings attributable to reuse from those generated by other software engineering methods. The result is a comprehensive return on investment (ROI) model which delivers credible business justification for reuse programs [4]. Poulin and Caruso have three goals for their reuse metrics program:

1. to quantify reuse;
2. to promote reuse;
3. to standardize the way reused components are counted.

They stress the measurement of *planned reuse*. Poulin and Caruso point out that planned reuse maximizes cost and productivity gains because it allows developers to maintain only one "base product." They utilize a rigorous definition of reuse, excluding reuse wherever an asset is used within the same organization that developed it.

Following is the data needed to measure reuse with Poulin and Caruso's metrics. A detailed description of each appears in [4].
IBM's formula for quantifying reuse savings in development is as follows: [4]

Development Cost Avoidance (DCA) = RSI x (1−.2) × (New Code Cost).

IBM's estimate of the relative cost of reuse is 0.20.
IBM's formula for quantifying maintenance savings is as follows:

Service Cost Avoided (SCA) = RSI × (defects per KLOC) × (cost to fix per defect).

Adding the results of both formulas gives the total savings associated with reuse as follows:

IBM Data Measurements

Shipped Source Instruction (SSI): Lines of code in product source files.

New and Changed Source Instructions (CSI): Lines of code that have been created or changed for a new product release.

Reused Source Instruction (RSI): Lines of code included in source files, though not written for the product, i.e., reused components that are completely unchanged.

Source Instructions Reused By Others (SIRBO): Lines of code in the current product that other products later reuse.

Software Development Cost: An average development cost that can be used as a baseline for estimating costs avoided by reuse.

Software Development Error Rate: An average cost that can be used as a baseline for estimating error-related costs avoided by reuse.

Software Error Repair Cost: An average maintenance cost that can be used as a baseline for estimating maintenance costs avoided by reuse.

$$\text{Reuse Cost Avoidance} = \text{DCA} + \text{SCA}.$$

IBM Reuse Value Added (RVA). IBM has also developed the reuse value added (RVA) metric, a separate metric designed to help management promote reuse throughout the organization [4]. In the RVA metric, an organization that neither creates nor uses reusable assets scores 1, while an organization that has doubled its productivity through consuming or creating reusable components scores 2. Of course, the higher the score, the more effective the organization. RVA is calculated as follows:

$$\text{Reuse Value Added (RVA)} = ((\text{SSI} + \text{RSI}) + \text{SIRBO})/\text{SSI}.$$

Return-On-Investment (ROI) Metrics
Appendix 12–A presents 17 reuse economic models.

Cost Prediction Metrics
No less than eight cost prediction metrics have been developed, each with its own strengths:

- Aykin (AT&T) Model;
- Balda and Gustafson Reuse Cost Estimation Model;
- Banker and Kauffman Model;
- Conte, Dunsmore, and Shen Model;

- Hunt (Texas Instruments) Model;
- Jensen Model;
- Londeix Model;
- Pfleeger Cost Model.

These metrics are described as follows.

The Aykin (AT&T) Model.   Aykin begins with the COCOMO (Constructive Cost Model [9]), seeking to compare software development costs when reuse is employed, and when it is not [5]. COCOMO calculates the effort in person months and product duration in months. The difference in cost (presumably, a savings) represents the benefit of reuse. Once Aykin has quantified the benefit of reuse, he can estimate ROI.

In the COCOMO formula, the organic mode indicates the staff has extensive experience. The semidetached mode notes that the staff has an intermediate level of experience. Aykin provides formulas for both COCOMO's organic and semidetached modes as follows:

Organic:	$PM = 2.4(KDSI)^{1.05}$	(1)
	$TDEV = 2.5(PM)^{0.38}$	(2)
Semidetached:	$PM = 3.0(KDSI)^{1.12}$	(3)
	$TDEV = 2.5(PM)^{0.35}$	(4)

where

KDSI = Thousands of source code instructions;

PM = Person-months;

TDEV = Time needed to develop the software.

COCOMO can reflect the impact of adapted reusable components if one calculates an equivalent number of delivered source instructions (EDSI), as in the following formula:

$$EDSI = (ADSI)\ AAF/100$$

where

ADSI (Adapted DSI) = Number of delivered source instructions adapted from existing software;

AAF = Adaptation adjustment factor.

We now must calculate Aykin's adaptation adjustment factor (AAF) as follows:

$$AAF = 0.40(DM) + 0.30(CM) + 0.30(IM)$$

where

DM = percent of adapted software's design that must be modified;

CM = percent of adapted software's code that must be modified;

IM = percent of effort required to integrate modified code in the overall project, as compared with typical integration effort.

In contrast with some models, Aykin attempts to take feasibility analysis, planning, inventory and documentation into account, using another term he calls the *conversion planning increment (CPI)*. Aykin's model contains six levels of conversion planning:

0 None;

1 Simple conversion schedule, test, and acceptance plan;

2 Detailed conversion schedule, test, and acceptance plan;

3 Add basic analysis of existing inventory of code and data;

4 Add detailed inventory, basic documentation of existing system;

5 Add detailed inventory, detailed documentation of existing system.

Working with this CPI, one can estimate an equivalent number of delivered source instructions (EDSI) for inclusion in other COCOMO formulas:

$$CAF = AAF + CPI$$
$$EDSI = (ADSI)\ CAF/100$$

where CAF stands for conversion adjustment factor.

Aykin next presents a hypothetical case study, using the following parameters:

Products	5;
Developers	100;
Developer cost	$10,640/month;
Development tool cost	$9000 +$100/user;
Shared library hardware cost	$20,000;
Average size of software product	50,000 lines of code.

Using the COCOMO formulas, he establishes a baseline: without reuse, the cost of developing these five products will be $7,763,475.

Now Aykin reflects the usage of a new software development tool designed to promote reuse. This tool adds greater complexity, so he uses the equations associated with COCOMO's semidetached model. He arrives at a cost of $12,761,085.

He determines the cost of the five products with the new software development tool. Because of the greater complexity brought on when the new tool is utilized by the projects, we use the semidetached equations (3) and (4). The cost of the five products is estimated to be $12,761,085. Clearly, in the first year (before the benefits of reuse begin) costs have risen substantially.

Now, Aykin assumes that in the second year, 10% of code will be reused, and that this will increase by 10% per year until the fifth year, after which it will remain constant at 50%. He then builds in additional conversion planning costs as follows:

- Training ($100,000);
- User interface design/style guide ($106,400);
- Prototyping user interfaces ($42,560);
- Cost of software development tool ($19,000);
- Cost of shared library hardware ($20,000);
- Cost of shared library maintenance ($139,065).

Now, Aykin can present year-by-year cash flows. The values in Fig. 19–8 assume annual discounting at 8%.

Not surprisingly, reuse raises costs early in the process but lowers them later. By the sixth year, the company has begun to save money. In the meantime, the time required to build software (TDEV$_{existing}$ versus TDEV$_{new}$) has been reduced.

The Balda and Gustafson Reuse Cost Estimation Model. Balda and Gustafson [6] object to the COCOMO model for several reasons. They believe it oversimplifies the process of designing reusable components, excludes factors known to affect software cost, and reflects the traditional waterfall model that is in-applicable to many reuse projects.

As Balda and Gustafson put it, COCOMO requires order-of-magnitude estimates of software cost even before requirements are known, as per the following formula:

$$PM = \alpha(KDSI)^{\beta}$$

where

PM = Person-months of effort;
α = Complexity coefficient;
β = Complexity exponent;
KDSI = Thousands of delivered source instructions (estimate).

α and β are derived from Fig. 19–9.

Balda and Gustafson seek to refine the measurement of PM through a detailed set of assumptions, and by setting a value for γ, the relationship between effort needed to develop unique code versus reusable code. Their formula is

$$PM = \alpha N_1^{\beta} + 20\gamma\alpha N_2^{\beta} + \gamma\alpha N_3^{\beta}$$

Present value of the cost of development of the existing and the new systems

Year	Reuse %	Cost of Existing	Cost of New	Total Present Value Existing	Total Present Value New
1	0	$7,763,475	$13,049,045	$7,188,202	$12,082,111
2	10	$7,763,475	$7,233,817	$13,844,605	$18,283,662
3	20	$7,763,475	$6,579,985	$20,007,251	$23,506,854
4	30	$7,763,475	$5,935,205	$25,713,406	$27,869,230
5	40	$7,763,475	$5,298,933	$30,997,227	$31,475,684
6	50	$7,763,475	$4,671,173	$35,889,769	$34,419,457
7	50	$7,763,475	$4,671,173	$40,419,756	$37,145,086

FIGURE 19–8   Sample year-by-year cash flows in Aykin model. *Source:* N. Aykin, "Software reuse: A case study on cost-benefit of adopting a common software development tool," in *Cost-Justifying Usability,* R. Bias and D. Mayhew, Eds. Orlando, FL: Academic, 1994, p. 196.

Values α and β are unchanged from the traditional model. The critical value γ ranges from .0909 to .1739, depending on project specifics. In addition

N_1 = Thousands of lines of unique code developed;

N_2 = Thousands of lines of code developed for reuse;

N_3 = Thousands of lines of unchanged reused components.

The 20γ modifier in the formula reflects the fact that it usually requires more effort to write code for reuse while the γ modifier reflects the fact that it usually requires less effort to reuse code that already exists than to create it from scratch.

Deriving values for the basic COCOMO formula

Complexity level	Coefficient(α)	Exponent(β)
Application	2.4	1.05
Utility	3.0	1.12
System	3.6	1.20

FIGURE 19–9   Deriving values for the basic COCOMO formula. *Source:* D. M. Balda and D. A. Gustafson, "Cost estimation models for the reuse and prototype software development life-cycles," *SIGSOFT Software Engineering Notes,* vol. 15, no. 3, p. 44, July 1990.

The Banker and Kauffman Model. Banker and Kauffman [7] describe two models that have been introduced at a leading investment bank (First Boston) and retailer (Carter Hawley Hale). These models are as follows:

- An integrated computer-aided software engineering (ICASE) object reuse estimation model;
- An ICASE development productivity estimation model, used with an ICASE development toolset, high-productivity systems (HPS).

The object reuse estimation model uses the following formula:

$$NEW\_OBJECT\_PCT = \alpha_0 + \alpha_1 \times LOG \,(MATURITY) + \alpha_2 \times LOG \,(APPLICATION) + \varepsilon.$$

In this formula

      NEW_OBJECT_PCT = Unique objects divided by total objects;

      MATURITY =

         e if the project is a Year 2/HPS Version 2 Project

         1 if it is a Year 1/HPS Version 1 Project;

      APPLICATION =

         e if the project creates an on-line, real-time application

         1 if it creates a batch application;

      $\alpha_0, \alpha_1, \alpha_2$ each model parameters that must be estimated;

      ε represents a normally distributed error term.

The development productivity estimation model uses the following formula:

$$LOG \,(FUNCTION\_POINTS) = \beta_0 + \beta_1 \times LOG \,(PERSON\_DAYS) + \beta_2 \times LOG \,(NEW\_OBJECT\_PCT) + \beta_3 \times LOG \,(MATURITY) + \beta_4 \times LOG \,(APPLICATION) + LOG \,(\xi).$$

In this formula:

      FUNCTION_POINTS = Chosen output metric for measuring the size of the final software product;

      PERSON_DAYS = Chosen input metric for development effort;

      OBJECT_REUSE = Unique objects divided by objects used;

      MATURITY =

         e if the project is a Year 2/HPS Version 2 Project

         1 if it is a Year 1/HPS Version 1 Project;

      $\beta_0, \beta_1, \beta_2, \beta_3, \beta_4$ each model parameters that must be estimated;

      ξ represents a log-normally distributed error term.

Banker and Kauffman went on to sample 20 projects, deriving model parameters from them. They interpreted the results as follows:

- on-line real-time projects lent themselves to reuse more than batch applications;
- less new code was needed for applications in their second year;
- the HPS toolset in use did in fact enable First Boston and Carter Hawley Hale to increase reuse;
- for each 1% additional reuse, productivity rose 1.92%;
- smaller projects lent themselves to greater productivity;
- in the second year, users increased their productivity with the CASE tools by 1.49 times.

Conte, Dunsmore, and Shen's Equivalent Size Measures. Cost estimation models like COCOMO obviously require inputs, and Conte, Dunsmore, and Shen [8] have reviewed approaches to creating equivalent size (S_e) measures that reflect reuse but can be used successfully in standard cost estimation models, in place of existing size measurement terms. They note that any measurement of size—whether counted in lines of code, token count or function count—must reflect:

S_n for new code;
S_u for reused or adapted code.

In considering what functions to use, Conte, Dunsmore, and Shen disregard differences between reused and revised (leveraged) code. One approach they identify is Boehm's:

$$S_e = S_n + (a/100)S_u$$

The critical term here is *a*, the adjustment factor. Boehm calculates it using the following formula:

$$a = 0.4(DM) + 0.3(CM) + 0.3(IM) \text{ where}$$

DM = percent of adapted software design that must be modified;
CM = percent of adapted software code that must be modified;
IM = percent of effort required to integrate modified code in the overall project, as compared with typical integration effort.

Keep in mind that *a* cannot be allowed to exceed 100, the point at which it would be no easier to adapt used code than to create new code.

Conte, Dunsmore, and Shen point out that IM must be determined subjectively in advance, and that the formula assumes we have "before-and-after" information for calculating CM and DM. They further note the absence of corroboration for this approach, beyond the original COCOMO studies [9].

The Hunt (Texas Instruments) Model.   At Texas Instruments, Hunt [10] reported on a study of defect prediction led by Dr. John Hedstrom, which led to the development of the Software Sigma Predictive Engine. This engine, which has been translated into a spreadsheet, allows developers to predict levels of software defects based on either historical data within a specific project or across all projects designed by a team or organization.

Using the Software Sigma Predictive Engine requires an organization to capture detailed defect data, especially where (and when) defects were detected, and where they originated. This data is plotted and incorporated in the predictive engine, along with the quality goal, typically measured in sigmas (fault density). Developers are also asked to "guesstimate" how many defects slip through the detection process completely.

Given information like this, the engine can make a preliminary maintenance cost estimate for maintenance. To accommodate reuse, the engine can be reseeded with another round of information, based on the results from the first round. This can, for example, help maintainers understand how many remaining defects they may have to fix during the reuse process.

As Hunt points out, approaches like these can not only predict defect levels in reusable software, but can be incorporated into estimates of how many reuses will be needed to break even. She adds that the model might even be able to identify how many errors will occur in each part of the development process—ideally helping developers reduce those errors, identify them when they are most easily fixed, or at a minimum, account for them in the budgeting process.

The Jensen Model.   Jensen [11] points out that the only way to estimate software development cost correctly is to begin with an accurate size estimate, but that standard approaches to estimating size are insufficient to account for reuse because they do not reflect added integration and testing costs that can be associated with reused components.

As a result, Jensen has devised a new formula that reflects effective size with reuse:

$$S_e = \{S_{new} + S_{old}(0.4F_{des} + 0.25F_{imp} + 0.35F_{test})\}(1 + F_{res}) = S_{en} + S_{en}F_{res}$$

where

S_e = Effective size;
S_{new} = Lines of code needed to create new functionality;
S_{old} = Existing lines of code to be used "as-is" or modified;

F_{des} = Effort needed to engineer, reengineer, and design modifications, compared to effort needed to develop the same software from scratch;

F_{imp} = Effort needed to code and unit test modifications, compared to effort needed to code and test equivalent new software;

F_{test} = Effort needed to integrate and test modifications, compared to effort needed to integrate and test equivalent new software;

F_{res} = Effort needed to reverse engineer and integrate a reusable component, compared with software development effort ignoring component integration; the closer F_{res} is to 0, the more reusable the component is.

In using these metrics, Jensen finds that component integration efforts can significantly increase the cost of reusable components and that even slight changes to the internals of a reusable component can dramatically increase the cost of a project. He concludes that reusable components can only achieve their promised benefits if they have black box characteristics, i.e., if their contents can remain completely invisible to the developers reusing it.

The Londeix Model. Londeix [12] seeks to quantify how much source code is actually being reused and how much is changing. He posits a reused source code of size S_i, containing a procedure of size S_p. This procedure can be modified in three ways:

1. by adding new code (size S_n);
2. by deleting part of the initial source code (size S_d);
3. by revising part of the initial source code (size S_c).

To see what percentage of the reused process source code S_i remains unchanged, calculate

$$S_i - (S_c + S_d).$$

Fig. 19–10 shows the Londeix effort allocation table for assigning relative effort to each stage of the development process, when code is being developed from scratch, when it is being reused unchanged, and when it is reused with changes.

Londeix ultimately arrives at the following formula to determine the equivalent size of reused code S(equ):

S (equ) = 43% S_i (code base)

+ 6% S_p (modified procedures)

+ 100% S_n (code added)

+ 51% S_c (code revised)

– 49% S_d (code deleted).

Comparison between full development and development with reused code

Type of Development	Higher Level Specification/ Design	Specification	Design	Code	Unit Test	Higher Level Test	Total
Full development	8	9	16	17	25	25	100%
Re-use—no change	8	2	4	4	6	25	49%
Re-use with change							
Code base, S_i	8	2	4	4	—	25	43%
Procedure modified, S_p	—	—	—	—	6	—	6%
Added code, S_n	8	9	16	17	25	25	100%
Changed code, S_c	—	7	12	13	19	—	51%
Deleted code, S_d	−8	−2	−4	−4	−6	−25	−49%

FIGURE 19–10   Londeix effort allocation table. *Source:* B. Londeix, *Cost Estimation for Software Development.* Reading, MA: Addison-Wesley, 1987, p. 131.

With this size estimate in place, managers can more effectively estimate the effort required to build software using reusable components.

The Pfleeger Cost Model.   Pfleeger [13] seeks to reflect reuse in more accurate estimates of cost and productivity. Pfleeger's formula is

$$P_{actual} = P_{avg} \times f(X_1, X_2,..., X_n).$$

In this formula

P_{actual} = A project's actual productivity;

P_{avg} = The product of its actual productivity;

$f(X_1, X_2,..., X_n)$ = An adjustment function, *f*, reflecting a series of cost factors as inputs.

Pfleeger's model seeks to give managers the flexibility to incorporate whatever cost factors make sense in a given project, rather than limiting them to predefined factors. For example, a manager might identify political or technical constraints that would never be found in a standard model.

Once a cost factor is identified, a cost multiplier is created for it, reflecting

- percentage of the project affected by the cost factor (between 0 and 1);
- actual cost associated with the factor, including associated costs such as training;
- number of projects that can contribute to amortizing the added cost. For example, if a special cost factor is established to reflect purchase of a new de-

sign tool, the manager can estimate how many projects will benefit from use of the tool

Pfleeger distinguishes between the few projects that can share *project-specific* or *application-specific* components and cost factors, and the broader range of projects that can benefit from a reuse component's presence in a reuse library.

Assume you must write highly secure code that will be shared by three related applications. This code can be made highly reusable across the three applications, but not all the code may be appropriate for wider reuse. Therefore, you may only amortize the cost of reuse across the three projects. Now, imagine that some code modules within the component that are not security related *can* be reused more broadly. Those modules may be amortized over a wider set of projects.

This model has several advantages:

- it allows the production of reuse components to be considered as a cost factor;
- it can reflect the existence of a reuse library;
- it can (and should) reflect more than one project, making it easier to analyze long-term tradeoffs and identify how many reuses are really necessary for a component to be profitably developed;
- it can reflect reuse of noncode elements (e.g., requirements, design, and test data).

After productivity is computed, effort can be derived relatively easily, since productivity is the ratio of functionality (size) to effort.

Conclusions from Reuse-Oriented Survey of Cost Estimation Models.
Pfleeger and Bollinger [13] review existing software cost models and conclude the following:

1. First and foremost, the models often do not deliver accurate results.
2. The models use highly subjective parameters to the extent that they may render the model invalid.
3. Most models are surprisingly organization-specific and very difficult to use in other organizations than the ones for which they were created.
4. It is doubtful whether all cost factors have been taken into account, and equally doubtful whether they have been represented appropriately in the model's formulas.
5. Most models use historical data that does not take into account new technologies, methods, or tools.

6. Many models attempt to estimate process-related costs from product-related characteristics. It is not clear which process variables have the most impact on cost.

7. Most of the models are least helpful when they are needed most: early in development. Few of them offer adequate feedback to improve estimates as development progresses.

Pfleeger and Bollinger recommend that cost models reflect the following characteristics:

1. Consumer and producer activities should be estimated separately, since the cost factors associated with each are dissimilar.

2. Broad-spectrum reuse must be emphasized more in cost modeling, and these models must be made more sophisticated to reflect its subtleties.

3. Models must do a better job of reflecting reuse across multiple projects. If they cannot do so, managers will not be able to justify initial investments in reuse.

4. Models should help managers and users identify work products that may lend themselves especially well to reuse, so reuse programs and software systems may be structured more effectively.

A more detailed evaluation of software cost models can be found in Kemerer [14], [15].

Reuse Library Metrics

We now move from cost estimation models to metrics that relate to reuse libraries. Such metrics include recall, precision, search, volume, and usage metrics. In this section, we provide examples of precision and usage metrics.

Browne *et al.* [16] describe a precision of retrieval metric intended to measure how effectively useful components can be retrieved from a reuse library. Browne's formula is as follows:

$$P = NC_r/NC_t$$

where

NC_t = Number of components retrieved in *all* queries;
NC_r = Relevant queries retrieved;
P = Precision of retrieval.

Bieman [17] suggests measuring the number of times objects of a particular class are created for a new system, compared with the number of times particular class objects are referenced in that system.

Reuse Process Metrics

We now move to metrics related to the production, brokering, and consumption of reusable assets.

Caldeira and Basili Methodology. Caldeira and Basili [18] offer a metric that may be valuable in domain analysis. In attempting to understand what makes a component reusable, they identify three primary attributes as follows:

- usefulness;
- cost to reuse;
- component quality.

Next, they identify four software metrics that can be used to project these three attributes as follows:

- volume (V);
- cyclomatic complexity (C);
- regularity (R);
- reuse frequency (RF).

We will examine each in the following:

Volume: According to Halstead, volume corresponds to the minimum number of bits that are needed to code the information in a module. Halstead's formula is

$$V = (N_1 + N_2)\log_2 (\eta_1 + \eta_2)$$

where

η_1 = Number of operators in the program;
N_1 = Total of all usage of all operators;
η_2 = Number of unique operands defined/used;
N_2 = Total of all usage of all operands.

Where volume is extremely small, the cost to reuse (extract, adapt, integrate) a component may be higher than the cost to build it from scratch. When volume is extremely high, the component may be too error-prone to be reused.

Cyclomatic Complexity: Cyclomatic complexity is a classic measure of the maximum number of independent paths in a program or component

$$C = e - n + 2$$

where

$$e = \text{Number of edges;}$$
$$n = \text{Number of nodes.}$$

As complexity increases, testing costs increase as well, making modules more difficult to qualify. However, once again, modules with very low complexity may not be worth the overhead involved in reuse.

Regularity: In regularity, we seek to compare how long a component is expected to be, and how long it actually is

$$r = (\eta_1 \log_2\eta_1 + \eta_2 \log_2\eta_2)/(N_1 + N_2).$$

Another way of looking at regularity is to say that it measures readability and nonredundancy. When regularity is close to 1, a component has been designed and implemented well.

Reuse Frequency: In measuring reuse frequency, we seek to understand how likely a component is to be reusable. Reuse frequency is the proportion of static calls to a component compared with the average number of static calls to a system module. As reuse frequency increases, components are expected to be more reusable

$$RF = \frac{n(C)}{\frac{1}{M} \sum_{i=0}^{M} n(S_i)}$$

where

M = Number of system modules;
$n(C)$ = Static calls to component C;
$n(S_i)$ = Static calls to system module S_i.

Hewlett-Packard Grenoble Networks Division. Mayobre's [19] work at Hewlett-Packard focused on metrics that help users select the right reusable software assets from within a domain. He reviews three methodologies that can be used to retrieve the most appropriate reusable assets as follows:

- Caldeira and Basili (discussed earlier).
- *Domain Experience Based Component Identification Process (DEBCIP)* which uses a standard decision graph to help domain experts identify components with exceptionally high reuse potential. To perform DEBCIP effectively, one must first carefully define domain bounds and models. It can also be challenging to define specification distances that quantify how much software must be

adapted in order to be reused. Therefore, this parameter is often viewed as suggestive rather than definitive.

- *Variant Analysis Based Component Identification Process (VABCIP)*, which uses code metrics, is also based on domain experience, and utilizes code metrics to estimate how closely existing software resembles needed software. VABCIP seeks to identify components that would cost less to reengineer than to build from scratch.

Reuse Product Metrics

We now move to measurements of internal, external, and overall reuse levels.

Banker, Kauffman, and Zweig Metrics.   Banker, Kauffman, and Zweig [20] report on experiences using the reuse percentage metric at a leading retailer (Carter Hawley Hale) and a major investment bank (First Boston). Reuse percentage seeks to measure object calls: the proportion that represents reuse versus the proportion that does not. The reuse percentage formula is

$$\text{Reuse Percentage} = (1 - (\text{Number of New Objects Built/Total Number of Objects Used})) \times 100$$

where

Number of New Objects Built = Objects created from scratch for the application;

Total Number of Objects Used = Objects that would be needed if there were no reuse.

Each time an object is reused, it is counted as another instance of reuse, so one object can be counted many times.

Banker *et al.* [3] also define two related metrics: *new code percent* and *reuse leverage*.

New Code Percent: In the following formula, Banker *et al.* identify the portion of a project's software that was developed from scratch:

New Code Percent = Number of New Objects Built/Total Number of Objects Used.

Reuse Leverage: The term "leverage" refers to the extent that new objects are used. In the following formula, they measure the average number of times objects are used within a system:

Reuse Leverage = Total Number of Objects Used/Number of New Objects Built.

Imagine that a system contains 600 objects; 200 had to be created from scratch. Reuse leverage is 600/200, or 3. In other words, the average object has been reused three times.

IBM Reuse Percent. IBM's reuse percent metric seeks to identify what percentage of lines of code—and, by extension, effort—was saved by reuse [4]. IBM measures reuse percent in three situations as follows:

- first version of a product;
- next release of a product;
- organization-wide.

For first releases and organization-wide measurements, IBM's reuse percent formula is

$$\text{Reuse Percent} = \text{RSI}/(\text{RSI} + \text{SSI}) \times 100\%.$$

For follow-up releases, IBM uses the following formula:

$$\text{Reuse Percent} = \text{RSI}/(\text{RSI} + \text{CSI}) \times 100\%.$$

Components are only considered reused if they are completely new to the product. In these formulas

RSI = Software used by the organization but maintained elsewhere;

SSI = Software developed and maintained by the organization;

CSI = Software that is new or changed in a new product release.

Nippon Telegraph and Telephone Corporation. According to Isoda [21], the Nippon Telegraph and Telephone (NTT) Corporation uses the following reuse ratio metric:

$$\text{Reuse Ratio} = \text{Reused Module Size}/\text{Developed Program Size}.$$

By tracking reuse ratio over four years, Isoda found an increase in reuse from 3% in the first year to 12% in the second year and 16% in the fourth year, as shown in Fig. 19–11.

Prieto-Diaz and Frakes. Prieto-Diaz and Frakes [22] propose two formulas for calculating external and internal reuse as follows:

External Reuse = Parts from external sources/Total parts;
Internal Reuse = (Non-external parts used > 1)/Total parts.

First Boston and Carter Hawley Hale. Banker *et al.* [3] describe the *external reuse percent metric* as follows:

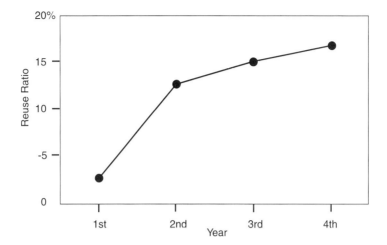

FIGURE 19–11   Tracking reuse ratios at NTT. *Source:* S. Isoda, "Experiences of a software reuse project," *Journal of Systems Software*, vol. 30, p. 175, 1995.

External Reuse Percent = (Objects Owned by Other Systems)/(Total Objects Used).

The authors note that external reuse involves objects contained in the repository, but owned, developed, maintained, and tested by someone other than the developer using the object. They also note that external reuse is highly dependent on the quality of the repository's indexing system: if users cannot find relevant objects, they cannot use them.

Banker *et al.* define *internal reuse percent* as

Internal Reuse Percent = 100% – New Code Percent – External Reuse Percent.

Internal reuse percent calculates how often an object recurs in a software application, compared to the total number of objects used in that application. The first occurrence of each object is excluded.

Banker *et al.* [20] evaluated a wide variety of projects at First Boston and found that 85% of reuse was internal. They further found that reuse was driven by a "pool of familiar code, rather than by the entire pool of reuse candidates." In general, developers reused components within the same project rather than searching for components created for previous projects.

Nippon Telegraph and Telephone.   At NTT, Isoda [21] tracked reuse of assets stored in a repository for three years, and compared this reuse to assets stored outside the repository. In addition, focusing on those assets stored in the repository, he compared usage of modules deposited by the consuming project, versus usage of modules deposited by other projects. He used the following formulas:

Ratio of Modules from outside the repository = (lines of code of modules from outside the library)/(total reused lines of code);

Ratio of Modules deposited by the project = (lines of code of modules deposited by the project)/(total reused lines of code);

Ratio of Modules deposited by other projects = (lines of code of modules deposited by other projects)/(total reused lines of code).

Over time, he found that developers became more likely to use modules deposited by other developers in connection with other projects. While at first 90% of reuse came from modules developed for the same project, this dropped to 30% by the end of the fourth year. Incidentally, in this respect, Isoda's results were quite different from Banker's [20].

Reuse Asset Metrics

Next, we consider metrics related to reuse assets, including size metrics, number of reuses for each asset, sources, and characteristics of reuse modules. Once again, we begin with Isoda's comprehensive research at NTT.

Nippon Telegraph and Telephone.   Isoda [21] tracked trends in the size of reusable modules over three years and found that, on average, modules grew significantly as developers became familiar with the reuse process. By year 4, average module size was roughly 600 lines–approximately twice what Isoda found in year 2. Since reusing larger modules can dramatically increase reuse ratios, Isoda found this information extremely valuable.

Isoda next measured trends in *average reuse frequency* (the total number of module reuses divided by the number of modules in the repository). He found that this, too, increased over time, from 18% in year 2 to 28% in year 4. Finally, he evaluated the *active module ratio*—the percentage of modules in the repository that were reused at least once in a year. He found this remained stable at around 20%. He concluded that the approach of deleting modules that go unused for three years does, in fact, make sense.

Hall.   Hall *et al.* [23] sought to identify the subjective characteristics that developers can use to identify promising reuse candidates. They list eight characteristics which may be used as reusability metrics as follows:

Application Independence: The software implementation is independent of database system, system libraries, microcode, computer architecture, and algorithms.

Document Accessibility: The software and related products provide an easy access to software documents, software source listing, and selective use of the software program's components.

Functional Scope: The software provides scope of functions required to be performed, i.e., function specificity, function commonality, and function completeness.

Generality: The function performed by the software module is utilized in several applications.

Modularity: The software has been partitioned into logical independent parts.

System Clarity: The software and its documentation provide a clear description of program structure in the most noncomplex, easily understandable, and modifiable manner.

Self-Descriptiveness: The software and its documentation contain information regarding its objectives, assumptions, constraints, inputs, processing, outputs, components, etc.

Simplicity: The software lacks complexity in organization, language, and implementation techniques, and is constructed in the most understandable manner.

Wald. Wald [24] found 16 common characteristics of highly-reusable software components, which she calls *parts*.

Understandable: The part can easily be understood.

Primitive: Developers do not need to understand the underlying implementation to reuse the part.

Complete: All the information a developer needs to use a part is built into the part.

Loosely Coupled: To the extent practical, the part limits dependencies on other parts.

Highly Cohesive: All relevant information is contained within the part.

Abstract: The part can extract information it needs and disregard information it does not need.

Information Hiding: Implementation details are effectively hidden from developers.

Reliable: The part should be unlikely to fail.

Modifiable: It should be easy to change the part to work in a new application.

Localization: Within the part, information is organized logically.

Uniform: The part works consistently with other parts; for example, it follows the same conventions they do.

Efficiency: The part's spatial and temporal behaviors are defined clearly.

Environment-Independent: The surrounding environment is irrelevant to the part's behavior.

Simplicity of Interface: The part connects with other parts through a clear, simple interface.

Protection against Incorrect Usage: A rigid part interface enforces external assumptions.

Error handling: The part includes built-in capabilities for handling abnormal situations or errors.

Balance Between Generality and Specificity: Through the use of parameters and other methods, it should be easy to tailor the part as needed.

Lowell. Lowell identifies five attributes of reusable components: generality, hardware independence, modularity, self-documentation, and software system independence [25]. He says reusable components can be identified both through walkthroughs and via the use of static analyzers.

References

1. S. Fraser, "Pragmatic approaches to software reuse at BNR, Ltd.," in *4th Annual Workshop on Institutionalizing Software Reuse*, Nov. 18–22, 1991.
2. W. C. Lim, "Effects of reuse on quality, productivity, and economics," *IEEE Software*, vol. 11, no. 5, pp. 23–30, Sept. 1994.
3. R. D. Banker, R. J. Kauffman, C. Wright, and D. Zweig, "Automating output size and reuse metrics in a repository-based computer-aided software engineering (CASE) environment," *IEEE Transactions on Software Engineering*, vol. 20, no. 3, pp. 169–187, Mar. 1994.
4. J. S. Poulin and J. M. Caruso, "A reuse metrics and return on investment model," in *Proceedings Advances in Software Reuse. Selected Papers from the 2nd International Workshop on Software Reusability,* cat. no. 93TH0495-2, Mar. 24–26, 1993, pp. 152–166.
5. N. Aykin, "Software reuse: A case study on cost–benefit of adopting a common software development tool," in *Cost-Justifying Usability*, R. Bias and D. Mayhew, Eds. Orlando, FL: Academic, 1994, pp. 177–202.
6. D. M. Balda and D. A. Gustafson, "Cost estimation models for the reuse and prototype software development life-cycles," *SIGSOFT Software Engineering Notes*, vol. 15, no. 3, pp. 42–50, July 1990.
7. R. D. Banker and R. J. Kauffman, "Reuse and productivity in integrated computer-aided software engineering: an empirical study," *Management Information Systems Quarterly*, vol. 15, no. 3, pp. 375–401, Sept. 1991.
8. S. Conte, H. Dunsmore, and V. Shen, *Software Engineering Metrics and Models.* Menlo Park, CA: Benjamin/Cummings, 1986.
9. B. Boehm, *Software Engineering Economics.* Englewood Cliffs, NJ: Prentice-Hall, 1981.
10. D. A. A. Hunt, "Estimating the cost of software reuse with predictive defect data," in *Reuse '96 Conference*, 1996.
11. R. W. Jensen, "Estimating the cost of software reuse," *Crosstalk: The Journal of Defense Software Engineering*, vol. 10, no. 5, pp. 2–8, May 1997.
12. B. Londeix, *Cost Estimation for Software Development.* Reading, MA: Addison-Wesley, 1987.
13. S. Pfleeger and T. B. Bollinger, "A reuse-oriented survey of software cost models," Contel Technology Center, Chantilly, VA, CTC-TR-90-002, Jan. 1990.
14. C. F. Kemerer, "An empirical validation of software cost estimation models," *Communications of the ACM*, vol. 30, no. 5, pp. 406–429, May 1987.

15. C. F. Kemerer, "Reliability of function points measurement: A field experiment," *Communications of the ACM*, vol. 36, no. 2, pp. 85–97, Feb. 1993.

16. J. C. Browne, T. Lee, and J. Werth, "Experimental evaluation of a reusability-oriented parallel programming environment," *IEEE Transactions on Software Engineering*, vol. 16, no. 2, pp. 111–120, Feb. 1990.

17. J. Bieman, "Deriving measures of software reuse in object oriented systems," Colorado State Univ., Ft. Collins, tech. rep. CS-91–112, July 1991.

18. G. Caldiera, "Domain factory and software reusability," in *Software Engineering Symposium: New Frontiers for Software Maintenance*, May 1991.

19. G. Mayobre, "Using code reusability analysis to identify reusable components from the software related to an application domain," in *4th Annual Workshop on Software Reuse*, Nov. 18–22, 1991.

20. R. D. Banker, R. J. Kauffman, and D. Zweig, "Repository evaluation of software reuse," *IEEE Transactions on Software Engineering*, vol. 19, no. 4, pp. 379–389, 1993.

21. S. Isoda, "Experiences of a software reuse project," *Journal of Systems Software*, vol. 30, pp. 171–186, 1995.

22. R. Prieto-Diaz and W. Frakes, "An introduction to software reuse," in *National Technological University Advanced Technology and Management Program*, Feb. 3, 1992.

23. F. Hall, R. A. Paul, and W. E. Snow, "R&M engineering for off-the-shelf critical software," in *Annual Reliability and Maintainability Symposium, 1988 Proceedings*, cat. no. 88CH2551-0, pp. 218–26, Jan. 1988.

24. E. Wald, *STARS Reusability Guidebook, Version 4.0*, U.S. Department of Defense, STARS, 1986.

25. J. A. Lowell, *Measuring Programmer Productivity*. New York, NY: Wiley, 1985.

MARKETING REUSABLE SOFTWARE

20.1 Reuse Marketing Defined

Marketing is traditionally viewed in the context of an organization's relationships with external constituents. In our case, we examine and stress the importance of *internal marketing* for reuse. Ouellette defines internal marketing as "simply creating an awareness of your value . . . and a focus on providing solutions to problems". [1] While this chapter focuses on internal marketing, the concepts described may also be utilized by an organization that is marketing reuse externally.

Although sometimes mistakenly used as a synonym for selling and promoting, marketing is actually a broad concept. The essence of *reuse marketing* is the exchange of an asset of value (e.g., information, design assets, code assets, support) intended to satisfy the organization's needs and desires. This may be an exchange for funding or, in some organizations, validation that the reuse organization is performing its job properly. All of the activities that expedite this exchange are considered reuse marketing.

The marketing concept as applied to reuse is that the key to achieving the reuse organization's goals lies in accurately identifying the needs and desires of the target organizations and delivering the desired value. To truly understand the target organization's needs, a reuse program must also understand the needs of the organization's customers, the end-users. For example, understanding the end-users' needs would enable the reuse program to anticipate the demand for a reusable asset.

In the broadest sense, reuse marketing encompasses not only the reuse organization's products and services, but also 1) the idea of utilizing existing assets to increase productivity and quality; 2) a change in behavior of the engineers in producing and consuming reusable assets; and 3) a belief that reuse is effective.

Reuse marketing targets not only the direct consumers of reusable assets, but also the organization's high-level managers who provide the funding, consumer project managers who must factor reuse into their schedules, and others whose area of responsibility is impacted by reuse.

We define marketing in the context of software reuse. Reuse marketing is an integrated set of activities to identify, price, distribute, and promote the reuse products and services to present and potential consumers. These activities are market-oriented, interrelated, and do not cease until the consumer is satisfied.

Very little has been written on marketing in the context of software reuse. EVB Software Engineering, Inc., enumerates some of the issues in reuse marketing including defining the target market and determining the needs of the market [2]. Wentzel observes that if reuse organizations are to succeed, their programs should be operated systematically as a business [3]. Reuse marketing would be an essential aspect of any such business.

In this chapter, we examine the elements traditionally known in marketing as the "four Ps" as applied to software reuse: product, price, place (distribution), and promotion. This chapter was also influenced by the works of Stanton [4].

20.2   The Importance of Reuse Marketing

Whenever we attempt to persuade someone to perform some activity, whether it is donating to the reuse library, reusing assets, or even accepting the reuse concept, we are engaging in marketing.

Broadly defined, the marketing function may include: 1) a reuse visionary trying to market the reuse concept to the organization and generate managerial support; 2) a reuse manager providing a reuse library prototype to generate proof of concept; and 3) reuse educators trying to teach and make interesting the concepts of reuse to their audience.

Under the reuse marketing concept, the reuse program devotes its activities to determining the consumer's desires and then satisfying them. This, of course, is tempered by the fact that sometimes the consumer is not aware of what he wants. The reuse marketing concept is also a reorientation of the perspective regarding "what business the reuse program is in." When asked "What business are you in?" a reuse manager will usually answer, "We supply reuse components and services." These managers need to begin thinking in terms of the benefits they market and the needs they are satisfying (Fig. 20–1).

Under the reuse marketing concept, a reuse program determines the consumers' and end-users' desires and then attempts to develop products and/or services that will satisfy them.

Reuse marketing requires a consumer rather than a reuse program perspective. It is important to satisfy the consumer because the satisfied consumer 1) returns to

What business are you in?

Production-oriented answer	Market-oriented answer
"We develop reusable assets."	"We offer savings in time and effort."

FIGURE 20–1   A reorientation in perspective.

the reuse program for more assets and services; 2) speaks favorably of the reuse program to others, thereby generating new consumers; and 3) will consider other products and services offered by the reuse program.

The reuse program should be designed to maximize the consumers' opportunity to complain. In this way, the reuse program will learn about its performance and ways to improve. Listening is not adequate, however; the reuse program must also respond constructively to the complaints. Albrecht and Zemke report that:

> "Of the customers who register a complaint, between 54 and 70 percent will do business with the organization if the complaint is resolved. The figure goes up to a staggering 95 percent if the customer feels that the complaint was resolved quickly. Customers who have complained to an organization and had their complaints satisfactorily resolved tell an average of five people about the treatment they received."
> [5]

Although Albrecht and Zemke's study was of external businesses, similar dynamics are likely to occur within an organization.

Recognizing the importance of understanding the reuse market, a market study [6] was commissioned to provide the Central Archive for Reusable Defense Software (CARDS) program with information on current software development and maintenance practices in the military services. The two major goals of the survey were to characterize how software development and maintenance were being performed and to identify the level of reuse knowledge held by managers and their subordinates.

20.3   The Market

The cardinal rule of marketing is to understand your markets. Consequently, a solid reuse marketing program starts with a thorough investigation of the market demand for the reuse product or service.

We define the reuse market as a place where producers, consumers, and their agents interact. Through their interaction, reuse products or services may be offered and exchanged for funding. The term "market" may also be used to refer to the aggregate demand by consumers for reuse products or services. For the purpose of this book, the market shall be defined as the consumers with needs to satisfy. As mentioned earlier, we will focus on the market within an organization although many of these concepts are also applicable to the external market.

Market Segmentation

In analyzing the internal market for reuse, the reuse program should decide whether it is advantageous to segment the internal market as a cluster of smaller parts, differentiated in such a fashion that each cluster may be treated in a relatively homogeneous way. In the production-oriented view, reusable assets are created and an attempt is made to reach as many consumers as possible. In the market-oriented view, the needs of each segment are identified and products or services are developed to address them. The market for reuse may consist of submarkets that are significantly different from one another. These differences may be traced to distinctions based on the applications that will reuse the assets, motives for reusing assets, or other factors.

Criteria for Effective Segmentation.   Market segmentation is the activity of partitioning the market such that each segment responds to a marketing effort in a similar fashion. Two principles help in the process of segmentation.

1. The characteristics used for segmenting must be quantifiable and the data should be available.

The basis for segmentation may include, for example, vertical domains: analytical instruments, manufacturing software, or horizontal domains: graphical user interfaces, error handling, etc. Further segmentation might be based on platform, language, etc. We may segment the market to a level of granularity such as reusable graphical user interfaces for analytical instruments written in a particular language. In each case, however, the producer group should weigh the cost to the benefit of segmenting the market further.

2. In segmenting the market, care must be taken to ensure that each segment is economically worthwhile.

The reuse program should not develop too wide of a variety of reusable assets. Usually, the limits of economies of scope prevent this type of proliferation. Information which would help us make this determination may include: number of systems/products to be built; reuse consumer benefit from each reuse; and the cost to create the reusable assets.

Influences on the Market

Influence of Reference Groups.   An understanding of reference group theory from sociology and the way it influences consumer behavior is useful. A reference group is a set of people who influence an individual's behavior and values. As such, reuse champions should consider the following:

1. Who influences the decision to reuse?
2. Who makes the decision to reuse?
3. Who will actually reuse?

Different people may be involved or one person may be responsible for all three.
Finally, different concerns may be held at different levels of the organization.
The reuse champion needs to understand and address the concerns at each level.

Reuse Stakeholder Analysis

Chief Executive Officer, Chief Operating Officer:
Concerns: Can you increase market share and shareholder value?
Measures: Increased market share and share price.

Group Level Manager:
Concerns: Can you lower the costs and increase the revenues of my group?
Measures: Increased profitability, reduced costs, improvements in quality, productivity, and time-to-market for products in the group.

Division Manager/Department Manager:
Concerns: Can you keep my development cost down and help deliver my product? Can you help me spend less on maintenance projects and more on "star" projects?
Measures: Reduced costs, meet milestones.

Project Manager:
Concerns: Can you help me meet deadlines with my limited resources? Don't expect me to provide extra resources to make my software reusable.
Measures: Finished on time within budget at a certain level of quality.

Engineers:
Concerns: Can you free up my time so that I can do more interesting work? Can you reduce the pressure to meet deadlines and require me to fix fewer defects?
Measures: Less tedious programming; meeting deadlines; fewer defects to fix.

Adoption and Diffusion.   If the reuse concept and methodology are perceived as being new by a person, then by definition, reuse is an innovation for him. The reuse adoption process is the series of activities through which the innovation is accepted by the individual.

Rogers identifies five characteristics which influence an individual's adoption rate [7]. We discuss them in the context of adopting reuse.

1. *Relative advantage* is the perceived advantage of the innovation to the existing method or system. The reuse champion must demonstrate and convince the target organization that reuse is preferable over the existing software development method.

2. *Compatibility* is the extent that the innovation is compatible with the existing culture, beliefs, and attitudes of the organization. The reuse champion must assess the organization's culture, its compatibility with the reuse concept, and whether cultural change is achievable and warranted.

3. *Complexity* is the degree to which the innovation is difficult to comprehend and utilize. Reuse education and attention to usability are key tactics for mitigating complexity and increasing comprehension.

4. *Trialability* is the extent to which the innovation may be sampled on a trial basis and produce positive net benefits. Stanton observes that "a central home air-conditioning system is likely to have a slower adoption rate than some new seed or fertilizer, which may be tried on a small plot of ground." [4] On this note, the reuse champion should consider advocating reuse pilot projects and the incremental introduction of reusable assets.

5. *Observability* is the degree to which an innovation's benefits can be readily seen. For example, Stanton notes that "a weed killer that works on existing weeds will be accepted sooner than a preemergent weed killer." [4] Consequently, the reuse champion should endeavor to collect and communicate metrics and information on the benefits experienced by reuse projects.

Psychological and Sociocultural Influences.   Stanton defines an attitude as "a person's enduring favorable or unfavorable cognitive evaluation, emotional feeling, or action tendency toward some object or idea." [4] Attitude changes toward software reuse implies this: How can the reuse program create a sense in which consumers perceive that their needs will best be served by software reuse? Following the above definition of attitude, Stanton suggests it involves changing one of more of three factors: evaluation, feeling, and action tendency. Specifically, consumers' cognitive evaluation of software reuse may change if relevant and persuasive data regarding reuse is provided. Consumers' emotional feelings also might change with an "emotionally appealing" message. An incentive to consumers to try something may change their "action tendency." For example, a reward to induce consumers to change their actions—at least long enough to try the reuse repository—may result in longer term benefits.

Characteristics of the Internal Reuse Market

Several traits characterize the internal market for reusable software.

Derived Demand. The consumer demand for reusable software is derived from the end-user demand for different (but similar) products or systems into which reusable assets are incorporated. The fact that reusable software demand is derived implies that it is subject to the fluctuations of primary, or end-user, demand. For example, weakened demand for end-user products due to the economy may render the creation of particular reusable assets undesirable, or worse, result in a net loss. Such a net loss is due to the fact that there are not enough reuse instances to amortize the creation costs. Reuse programs which keep abreast of end-user demand may obtain a sense of the future demand for reusable assets.

Limit on the Size of the Market. If the reuse program is constrained to developing assets for internal consumers, a limit is imposed on the number and type of reusable assets which can be feasibly created. Assets which are created and marketed to both internal and external consumers are subject to more reuse instances, which cover the creation costs more effectively. An organization may wish to stratify the assets that they utilize at several levels: those which they create and supply to both internal and external markets (presumably, licensing the use of these assets will not result in a competitive disadvantage); those which they market only internally in their own organizations (these assets either are unique enough that only the internal market would want them or they provide certain competitive advantages such that the organization does not want to license them externally); and those that the organization licenses to use internally (e.g., Booch components, Rogue Wave reusable components).

20.4   The Product

Product Planning and Development

In the marketing view, a product is a collection of tangibles and intangibles that would satisfy consumers' needs and desires. Intangibles would include items such as warranties and guarantees. This definition highlights the idea that a consumer is seeking not just a reusable asset, but rather a bundle of tangibles and intangibles that serve to satisfy his needs and desires.

Product planning for a reuse program includes all activities which allow the program to identify the products and services it will develop. Product development embraces the activities of product research, design, and engineering. The combination of the two includes decision making in:

1. Under which domains should the reuse program offer reusable assets and services?
2. What types of reusable assets and services should be developed?
3. Which assets should the reuse program specifically offer?
4. What should be provided with the reusable assets (e.g., service, warranty)?
5. For profit center-based reuse programs, how should the asset or services be priced?

Innovation in Reuse Products and Services. The value of a reuse program lies in its ability to continuously satisfy the needs and desires of its consumers. As a consequence, innovation in reuse products and services serves an important role in the reuse program.

Assets Have Life Cycles. Products generally follow a five stage life cycle of: introduction, growth, maturity, decline, and abandonment [4]. Similarly, reusable assets undergo a life cycle where the demand for the asset grows, declines, and then becomes obsolete. As an asset becomes obsolete, it must be revitalized or pruned from the list of offerings. The decline and ultimate abandonment of a reusable asset can be due to 1) a diminishing need for the asset (e.g., end-user products/systems no longer being developed; changes in platform or language) or 2) a superior reusable asset is developed which supplants the original.

Considerations for Adding a New Asset or Suite of Assets. Following are some considerations to use when determining whether a proposed new asset or suite of assets should be added to a reuse organization's offering.

1. Is there sufficient demand for the asset?
2. Will it fit in with existing producer and broker capabilities?
3. Will it fit from an economic point of view?
4. Will it be cleared from a legal standpoint?
5. Will management have adequate resources to manage the new asset?
6. Will the new asset be in line with the reuse program's objectives?

Deciding on a Product-Mix Policy

The policies associated with the reuse program's offering of products and services is its product-mix.

Product Mix and Product Line. A reusable asset product line is a set of assets having comparable traits and being intended for similar uses. The product mix consists of all the products the reuse organization offers. This mix can vary in breadth (number of product lines) and depth (the variety within a product line). For example, reusable graphical user interfaces (GUIs) may be a product line and the assortment of such GUIs the depth. The reuse program should examine the worth of carrying a full assortment within a product line which would attract consumers who otherwise would not reuse. Not unlike having the full range of screwdriver sizes available, some organizations contend that consumers are more likely to visit the repository if the full range of reusable assets is available.

20.5 The Price

In this section, we discuss a way to determine a price that a producer–broker combination may charge its consumers for a reusable asset. This is applicable where consumers have agreed to pay the producer–broker for use of the asset or for commercial enterprises that desire to sell reusable assets in the marketplace. While there are additional considerations when setting external instead of internal prices, the basic methodology remains the same. Before determining an actual price, however, the meaning and importance of pricing should be understood, and the goal of pricing should be determined.

What Is a Price? A price is an offer for a set of goods or services. Prices are important because they are a factor in determining which assets will be produced and who will get how many of these assets.

Price Elasticity. Market demand is determined in part by the price of the reusable asset or service. However, there are situations in which demand remains strong in spite of price increases. In these cases, we say the demand is relatively inelastic. For example, if certain reusable assets contain proprietary techniques not found elsewhere (or ones unlikely to be duplicated), then there is no substitute for the asset. In this case, demand will likely be inelastic.

Consumers tend to be less price sensitive when:

- the asset is relatively unique;
- there are no viable substitutes;
- the cost of the asset is low relative to the consumer's development budget;
- the cost of the asset is low relative to the total cost of the development project;
- the asset will be used in conjunction with assets previously purchased.

Pricing Goals and Determination. Before determining the price, a reuse program should identify its pricing goals.

Examples of pricing objectives for internal reuse programs include:

- Consumers share a portion of the producer costs. This may be a portion of the variable costs or all variable costs and a portion of the fixed costs.
- Consumers cover all producer costs, both variable and fixed.
- Consumers cover all producer costs and provide a profit to the producer.
- Achieve a rate of return equivalent to or exceeding the next best alternative use of the funds. This method emphasizes the most efficient use of capital. If the reuse program cannot achieve such a rate of return, alternative use of the capital should be considered.

Examples of pricing objectives for external reuse programs include [4]:

- Achieve target return on investment or on net sales.
- Maintain or improve share of the market.
- Meet or prevent competition.
- Maximize profits.

Methods for Setting Prices

Several basic methods are available for setting prices.

Pricing Based on Cost-Plus.   In cost-plus pricing, the price is set at the total cost of the reusable asset plus a specified profit. For example, let us say the variable cost to develop ten reusable assets is $150,000 and fixed costs are $50,000. The total amount is $200,000. Let us also say that each asset has one consumer buyer. The producer desires a profit of 10% or $20,000. Given that the cost plus the profit is $220,000, each asset would be sold at $22,000 a piece to meet the target profit.

The advantage of the cost-plus system is that it may be easily applied. The disadvantage, however, is that this technique does not account for the differences in behavior of fixed and variable costs in relation to the quantity sold. For example, let us say that the producer created and sold only six of the reusable assets. Revenues would be $132,000. Since the variable cost of creating the assets is $90,000 and fixed cost is $50,000, the producer would experience a net loss of $8,000.

Pricing Based on Variable Cost.   Variable cost pricing sets the price which will recoup the variable costs, but not the fixed costs. This type of pricing may be used if the producer engineers have excess time available, to encourage consumers to try reusable software, or when the sale of one asset would generate sales of other related assets.

Pricing Based on Consumer Benefit.   Establishing a price according to the benefit realized by the consumer is another technique.

Price Per Reuse for a Single Asset.   Let us start by assuming that a reusable asset is large-grain and that the consumer will be charged on a per reuse basis. By understanding the value of reusing to the consumer, the producer can establish a ceiling for the price as the consumer will not pay over the value that he/she would receive from reuse of the asset. Furthermore, by predicting the number of reuses and costs of creating and maintaining the asset, the producer can set a floor for the price as any price below this floor (given the expected number of reuses) will result in a loss for the producer.

As an example, Fig. 20–2 depicts the situation if a consumer project were to create the asset from scratch. The asset would require 580 person days at a cost of $.36M. Maintenance costs would require 2,320 person days at a cost of $1.47M. By reusing a given asset, the consumer would require 112 person days to integrate the reusable asset at a cost of $.07M. Consumer maintenance costs with the reusable asset would require 1160 person days at a cost of $.72M. The benefit to the consumer would be $1.04M. (There are actually more benefits; some, such as increased profit from shortened-time-to-market are economically tangible, and others, such as ease-of-use, are less tangible.) The figure of $1.04M constitutes the ceiling to the price for the consumer.

The total costs for the producer in creating and maintaining this reusable asset are $2.6M. It is anticipated that there will be three reuses. Consequently, if the total costs are to be recovered from the three reuses, each consumer would be charged $.87M. This constitutes the floor to the price that the producer would want as a minimum.

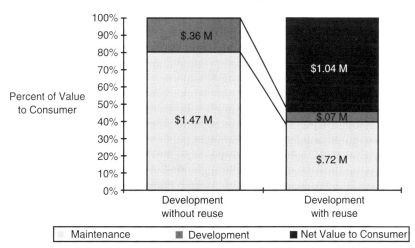

FIGURE 20–2   Pricing based on consumer benefit.

In this case, the difference between the ceiling and the floor is $.17M. The price should be lowered or raised accordingly in order to meet objectives. For example, the price may be lowered in order to provide an incentive for the consumer to try the asset or to match or undercut the price of a competitor's reusable asset. The price may be raised to the first several consumers so that recovery of the cost of creation and maintenance is accelerated. This technique considers value to the consumer, cost to the producer, and alternatives in the marketplace.

Price for Use of a Suite of Reusable Assets.   This method may also be used to ascertain the cost for a suite of reusable assets. In this case, an estimate must be made of the benefit that the consumer will derive from reuse of the assets. The price must then be less than this level of benefit but, when aggregated across all consumers, more than the cost of developing the assets.

For example, EVB Software Engineering, Inc. [8], licenses its library of reusable software assets, Generic Reusable Ada® Components for Engineering (GRACE) in source form on a CPU basis. The price for the license to use the reusable assets varies according to the number of users. The GRACE license is priced so that it constitutes less than half of the costs avoided by the licensee.

20.6   Distribution

The channel of distribution refers to the route taken to exchange the title to, or license to use, a reusable asset as it moves from the producer to the consumer. Such a channel includes the producer, the consumer, and any brokers involved in the process.

Separate from the channel of distribution for the title is the channel for the "movement" or transfer of the asset from the producer to the consumer. The routes for each may differ. For example, a consumer may order and obtain an asset from a broker. The license to use the asset, however, may be delivered from the producer to the consumer.

Since the transfer of title for assets developed within an organization is not a significant issue, we will discuss only the channels of distribution for the transfer of the reusable asset.

Channels of Distribution

The choice of a channel of distribution for transfer of the asset depends on a number of factors, including the geographical locations, time zones, and preferences of the consumers. For our purposes, the channel refers to the medium for distributing not only reusable assets, but also the training, accompanying support services, and other reuse-related items.

When the scope of reuse is confined within the enterprise or corporation, the channels of distribution are internally focused. For example, the internal networks of a corporation may be utilized for reusable asset distribution. If the scope of reuse extends beyond the limits of the enterprise, then the channels of distribution transform to a more external and commercial focus.

When reuse is practiced by the individual software engineer, his/her reusable assets may simply reside in the account on the development system. Any sharing of software assets is informal and may be done on the local network. When reuse is intraproject practiced in the same location, the distribution channel for the reusable assets is the local network. For example, the Manufacturing Productivity section of the HP Software Technology Division maintains reusable assets under a revision control system that is managed by a release account manager. When a request by a software engineer for a particular asset is approved, the release account manager dispenses a copy of the asset to the consumer's account.

If the reuse effort encompasses multiple geographic locations, the choice of a channel of distribution needs to take into consideration along with access to the assets from distributed sites and possibly different time zones. For example, several in-house corporate reuse programs the consumer projects of which are geographically distributed across the globe have enabled their consumers to obtain copies of assets via an intranet or the file transfer protocol (FTP), a technique for transferring files. Another reuse organization sends the reusable assets via e-mail to the user's Internet address.

Stockwell and Krause describe the use of Internet information access tools, Gopher and Wide Area Information Servers (WAIS), as the foundation of a network information discovery and retrieval system used at the MITRE Corporation's Center for Advanced Aviation System Development (CAASD) [9]. Borrowing both technology and software from the Internet community, Stockwell and Krause argue that these are "cost-effective building blocks for implementing distributed, heterogeneous libraries." Organizations such as ASSET [10] and CyberSource Corporation [11] have established World Wide Web sites on the Internet for the sale and purchase of reusable assets.

The Role of the Broker

Because of the amount and types of assets created by producers, keeping track of the assortment of assets may be difficult for consumers. Brokers fulfill a need by collecting, proactively commissioning the creation of reusable assets in some cases, and distributing these assets to the consumers.

As discussed in chapter 18, brokers may align themselves with the producer (e.g., a commercial company offering reusable assets), the consumer (e.g., a set of consumers who have joined together to create or acquire assets), or be a standalone entity (e.g., ASSET).

The function that brokers perform adds value in the form of time and place. The producer creates *form value* by developing or reengineering existing assets into reusable assets. Because the consumer may not immediately need the reusable asset, the broker provides *time value* by providing the asset when the consumer requires it. Finally, the broker usually aids with *place value* by distributing it to the location where the consumer needs the asset.

20.7   Promotion

The Promotion Program

By our definition, reuse promotion is the activity of assisting the growth and development of reuse. Reuse promotion consists of effectively communicating information and persuading the audience. An effective reuse promotion coordinates the reuse message, literature, and other materials for the appropriate audience.

Internal Marketing Techniques

Marketing reuse and the reuse program *internally* within the organization is an often overlooked yet important aspect. Ouellette recognizes the importance of internal promotion for creating an awareness of value and to obtain strategic support [1]. Although written in the context of marketing an information systems department within an organization, many of his concepts are also applicable to reuse programs.

Ouellette suggests 12 ways to conduct *internal* marketing [1].

1. Brochures

   Publishing a brochure facilitates communication. Such a brochure may, for example, address frequently asked reuse questions.

2. Newsletters

   Publishing a newsletter can be an effective way to publicize timely information on reuse. Ensure that the newsletters appear regularly and on time.

3. Management Reports

   Such reports are annual or semi-annual and include a state-of-the-program message. Include information such as an overview of accomplishments, future directions, and industry trends.

4. 5/15 Reports

   Such reports are called "5/15 reports" because they should only require five minutes to read and 15 minutes to write. These reports are "brief, monthly updates" to keep consumers aware of your activities.

5. Publications

   Have the company or organization magazine feature an article about the reuse program. Such an article can highlight "recent changes, success stories, and upcoming plans." Attempt to obtain coverage in external publications or write an article for publication in trade journals.

6. Walk-In Center

   Offer a walk-in center where consumers can read and obtain literature and watch demonstration on reuse.

7. Presentations

   Offer to provide an overview to consumer and other organizations of the reuse program and the benefits of reuse.

8. Brown Bag Seminars

Issue a general invitation for company employees to join the reuse program staff for a presentation of your services and capabilities during the lunch hour.

9. House Calls

Schedule meetings with managers for one-on-one dialogue about what the reuse program is and how it can help them.

10. Client Coordinators

Appoint members of the reuse program to be client coordinators (account managers) for different areas of the corporation. The client coordinators develop a thorough understanding of the clients' business and their needs.

11. Technology/Productivity Fair

Instead of waiting for consumers to come to the walk-in center, the technology/productivity fair brings the exhibits and information to the consumers. Such an activity allows attendees the opportunity of a hands-on demonstration of reuse tools and library.

12. The Success Story

When the reuse program has had, for example, a successful pilot, educate people with the details. Be careful not to overstate the success and temper it with any experiences from failures.

20.8 Marketing Issues by Scope of Reuse

As the scope of reuse broadens beyond a single organization, enterprise, or even nation, these marketing issues become more complex. For example, if we engage in reuse at the interproject level, we would need to promote awareness and identify appropriate channels of distribution such as e-mail or FTP. However, if we pursue national reuse, significant additional issues such as marketing promotion of the reusable assets as a product and the appropriate distribution channels need to be identified. In Fig. 20–3, we outline some of the major marketing issues by scope of reuse.

Marketing Issues by Scope of Reuse

1. *Personal Reuse* is practiced by the individual software engineer. Over time, the engineer typically accumulates a personal library of routines primarily for his own use. Given this, each individual is responsible for producing and maintaining his or her own assets.

Marketing issues: None

2. *Intraproject Reuse* describes reuse within a project. This usually involves designating one or more engineers to create the reusable assets (typically a function library) for the other project members to reuse. A project policy needs to be established on reuse to address the following marketing issues.

Marketing issues:

  • Ensure that other engineers within the group are aware of the assets available for reuse.

FIGURE 20–3 Marketing issues by scope of reuse.

(*continued*)

- Package and support the reusable assets to the appropriate degree necessary for intraproject reuse.

3. *Interproject Reuse* is the practice of reuse across multiple projects. Reuse at this level highlights the issues of coordination and organization among several groups and possibly geographic locations.

   Marketing issues:
   - Address all of the marketing issues outlined in previous levels.
   - May require a person dedicated to promoting awareness of reusable assets across all projects.
   - Identify the appropriate channel of distribution for the reusable assets (e.g., e-mail, intranet).
   - Identify the appropriate transfer price if profit and loss boundaries are crossed.
   - Package and support the reusable assets to the appropriate degree necessary for interproject reuse.

4. *Enterprise-wide Reuse* characterizes reuse throughout an enterprise. For our purposes, organizations which are in this category include commercial companies and organizational units within the government (e.g., Air Force). Reuse at this level requires support and coordination of multiple levels of management in multiple organizations. Depending on the size of the enterprise, a broker may be required to match the demand and supply needs of enterprise constituents.

   Marketing issues:
   - Address all of the marketing issues outlined in previous levels.
   - Establish standard marketing guidelines and policies on the enterprise-wide use of shared assets.
   - May require persons dedicated to promoting awareness of reusable assets across the enterprise.
   - Package and support the reusable assets to the appropriate degree necessary for enterprise reuse.

5. *Interenterprise Reuse* describes reuse across enterprises. This includes the practice of reuse across several different companies. At this level, significant legal issues of ownership, rights, licensing, and proprietary information need to be addressed.

   Marketing issues:
   - Address all of the marketing issues outlined in previous levels.
   - Establish team dedicated to promoting reusable assets in other enterprises.
   - Identify the appropriate price for the reusable assets and services.
   - Identify the appropriate channel of distribution for the reusable assets (e.g., tape, e-mail, FTP).
   - Package and support the reusable assets to the appropriate degree necessary for interenterprise reuse.

6. *National Reuse* is the reuse of assets on a national level. At this scope, management issues are of utmost importance. The previous level of inter-enterprise reuse may allow individual contracts with other companies. At this level, the appropriate legal mechanisms need to be considered for widespread distribution of the reusable assets.

   Marketing issues:
   - Address all marketing issues outlined in previous levels.
   - Establish a team dedicated to promoting reusable assets nationwide.
   - Identify the appropriate channel of distribution (e.g., retail, mail-order, Internet) for the reusable assets.
   - Package and support the reusable assets to the appropriate degree necessary for national reuse.

FIGURE 20–3   *(continued)*

7. *International Reuse* describes the reuse of assets across countries. Prominent issues raised at this level include language, international copyright laws, location and extent of jurisdiction, and individual nation laws, policies, and methods of recourse.

Marketing issues:
- Understand applicable international marketing needs in software reuse.
- Have localization specialists tailor and promote reusable assets.
- Identify the appropriate channels of distribution for the reusable assets which are appropriate for international reuse.

FIGURE 20–3   *(continued)*

Summary

Reuse marketing is an integrated set of activities to identify, price, distribute, and promote the reuse products and services to present and potential consumers. Under the reuse marketing concept, a reuse program determines consumer and end-user desires and attempts to develop solutions that will satisfy them. Consequently, a solid reuse marketing program begins with an understanding of the market. This is followed by an examination of the elements traditionally known in marketing as the "four Ps" as applied to software reuse: product, price, place (distribution), and promotion.

References

1. L. P. Ouellette, "How to market the IS department internally: Gaining the recognition and strategic position you merit," *Journal of Systems Management*, vol. 43, no. 11, pp. 6–11, Nov. 1992.
2. "Creating reusable Ada software," EVB Software Engineering, Inc., Frederick, MD, 1987.
3. K. Wentzel, "Software reuse—It's a business," in *5th Annual Workshop on Institutionalizing Software Reuse*, Oct. 26–29, 1992.
4. W. J. Stanton, *Fundamentals of Marketing.* New York, NY: McGraw-Hill, 1981.
5. K. Albrecht and R. Zemke, *Service America!* Homewood, IL: Dow-Jones-Irwin, 1985.
6. L. G. Meheran, "Informal technical report for software technology for adaptable reliable systems (STARS) market study (Interim) central archive for reusable defense software (CARDS)," DSD Laboratories, Inc., under contract to Unisys Corporation, Reston, VA, STARS-VC-B001/000/00, Dec. 23, 1993.
7. E. M. Rogers, *Diffusion of Innovations.* New York, NY: Free Press, 1983.
8. "What managers need to know about GRACE," EVB Software Engineering, Inc., Frederick, MD, 1987.

9. T. Stockwell and M. Krause, "Internet information discovery and retrieval tools—Cost effective building blocks for asset libraries," in *3rd Annual Workshop for Institutionalizing Software Reuse*, Nov. 2–4, 1993.

10. C. Lillie, private communication, 1997.

11. "The reusable software market" (http://components.software.net), CyberSource Corporation, San Jose, CA, 1997.

CHAPTER

21

LEGAL AND CONTRACTUAL ISSUES OF SOFTWARE REUSE[1]

21.1   Introduction

Reusing and leveraging software assets brings to the forefront a host of legal and contractual issues regarding rights, liabilities, and obligations. Although seemingly peripheral to the activities of reuse, these issues, if ignored, may have adverse ramifications that can inhibit reuse. This chapter is meant to provide a general overview of legal and contractual issues of software reuse; readers with specific legal questions, however, should consult a lawyer.

Participants in the reuse process should be aware of the potential legal and contractual risks of reusing assets and how to minimize the risks while at the same time protecting individual and organizational works and rights. These participants include consumers, producers, and brokers. Consumers should ensure that their reuse or modification of assets will not infringe upon any legal or contractual rights of the producers. In addition, the allocation of responsibility and means of recourse in the event of asset defects must be clearly stated and understood.

Producers of reusable software wish to retain ownership of their work, to recoup their investment costs, and/or receive recognition for their efforts. If they be-

[1]This chapter is an expanded version of a previously published paper and is printed with the permission of W. C. Lim. "Legal and contractual issues in software reuse," *Proceedings of the 4th International Conference on Software Reuse*, Orlando, FL, Apr. 23–26, 1996, pp. 156–164, Copyright 1996 IEEE.

lieve that they will not be able to retain adequate ownership rights, they will have less incentive to produce reusable assets. As with consumers, producers who create reusable assets by reengineering existing assets should ensure that the rights of other producers are not violated.

Liability risks from providing defective assets or deficient information regarding assets are a major concern for brokers of reusable software. Other issues include brokering assets which are subsequently reused illegally and preventing illegal access to proprietary assets by providing adequate security in the management of an asset repository.

The key to successful reuse within the legal context is to strike the appropriate balance in allocating these risks among all parties so that reuse can be encouraged and not encumbered by legal problems. This chapter explores the legal and contractual aspects of reuse. We begin with a brief definition of terms used in the chapter and an overview of the issues that must be addressed at each level of reuse. We will then describe the intellectual property tools available for software protection and the advantages and disadvantages of each, followed by a discussion of the legal implications for common software reuse and leverage activities. Finally, we will examine contractual issues in reuse, including those relating to work with U.S. Government agencies.

21.2 Definitions

It is important to distinguish between the terms *legal* and *contractual*. *Legal* is defined as "deriving authority from or being founded on law." [1] *Contractual* refers to a contract which is "a binding agreement between two or more persons or parties." [1] For example, if a contract is made between two parties in the same company and is broken, they may seek recourse through whatever mechanism the company policy provides (e.g., an arbitration panel). If a contract is made between two parties in different companies and is broken, they may seek recourse through the legal system.

21.3 An Overview of Legal and Contractual Issues

As the scope of reuse broadens beyond a single organization, enterprise, or nation, these contractual and legal issues become more complex. For example, if we engage in reuse at the company-wide level, we would need to clarify the internal policies with regard to who will correct a reusable asset if a defect is detected and who will be liable if a defect damages an external customer. However, if we pursue intercompany reuse, significant additional issues such as disclosure of proprietary information and infringement of copyrights must be addressed. Formal agreements regarding licensing, warranty, and intellectual property issues must be created. In Fig. 21–1, we outline some of the major legal and contractual issues by scope of reuse.

Legal and Contractual Issues by Scope of Reuse

1. *Personal Reuse* is practiced by the individual software engineer. Over time, the engineer typically accumulates a personal library of routines primarily for his own use. Given this, each individual is responsible for producing and maintaining his or her own assets for use by him or herself.

   Legal issues: None

   Contractual issues: None

2. *Intraproject Reuse* describes reuse within a project. This usually involves designating one or more engineers to create the reusable assets (typically, a function library) for the other project members to reuse. A project policy on reuse must be established to address the following contractual issues.

   Legal issues: None

   Contractual issues:
   - Designate who will produce and maintain reusable assets, what will be created, and when the assets will be available.
   - Assign responsibility for correcting a reusable asset if a defect is detected.
   - If leveraging will be allowed, designate responsibility for the leveraged assets.

3. *Interproject Reuse* is the practice of reuse across multiple projects. Reuse at this level highlights the issues of coordination and organization among several groups and, possibly, geographic locations.

   Legal issues: None

   Contractual issues:
   - Address all of the contractual issues outlined in previous levels.
   - If a broker function is required, determine responsibility for screening and qualifying the assets before use.
   - Fairly allocate the risks and rewards among all projects to encourage reuse. For example, there is little incentive for a project that has traditional product development responsibilities and deadlines to provide assets to another if it faces the prospect of having to provide maintenance support for these assets while impeding its own product development effort. On the other hand, a potential consumer project may not have any incentive to reuse if little or no support is provided on the reuse of assets with minimal documentation.

4. *Enterprise-wide Reuse* characterizes reuse throughout an enterprise. For our purposes, organizations which fall under this category include commercial companies and organizational units within the government (e.g., Air Force). Reuse at this level requires support and coordination of multiple levels of management in multiple organizations. Depending upon the size of the enterprise, a broker may be required to match the demand and supply needs of enterprise constituents.

   Legal issues: None

   Contractual issues:
   - Address all of the contractual issues outlined in previous levels.
   - Establish standard guidelines and policies on the enterprise-wide use of shared assets.

5. *Interenterprise Reuse* describes reuse across enterprises, including the practice of reuse across several different companies. At this level, significant legal issues of ownership, rights, and licensing and proprietary information must be addressed.

   Legal issues:
   - Determine who owns the reusable software and what ownership rights, if any, are exclusive.
   - Determine the conditions under which users are allowed the rights to reuse assets.

FIGURE 21–1   Legal and contractual issues by scope of reuse.

(continued)

Contractual issues:
- Address all of the contractual issues outlined in previous levels.

6. *National Reuse* is the reuse of assets on a national level. At this level, management issues are of utmost importance. The previous level of interenterprise reuse may allow individual contracts with other companies. At this level, the appropriate legal mechanisms must be considered for widespread distribution of the reusable assets.

Legal issues:
- Address all legal issues outlined in previous levels.
- Provide protection of intellectual property rights for widespread distribution of reusable assets.

Contractual issues:
- Address all contractual issues outlined in previous levels.

7. *International Reuse* describes the reuse of assets across countries. Issues raised at this level include language, international copyright laws, location and extent of jurisdiction, and individual nation laws, policies, and methods of recourse.

Legal issues:
- Understand applicable international intellectual property laws and regulations of software reuse.

Contractual issues:
- Address all contractual issues outlined in previous levels.

FIGURE 21–1   *(continued)*

21.4   Legal Issues

Intellectual property law refers to the legal framework of ownership. It "provides property rights of a sort in the intellectual products of the mind." [2] These laws are intended to encourage the development and distribution of innovative works for public benefit. Some view intellectual property laws as an impediment to the reuse of software, i.e., if software were "free" to be copied, there would be greater reuse. Others view intellectual property laws as a necessity for reuse. Since the cost of replication is negligible relative to the cost of creation, there is an economic motivation for consumers to copy the assets without payment to the producers. Laws which offer protection to producers also provide them with a means of recouping investment costs and obtaining financial gain.

Society benefits from this in two ways. The first is when the reusable software is made available via licensing or sale. The second is when the term of exclusive rights expires and the reusable software is made available to the public to be used and duplicated [2].

Intellectual property protection for owners of software is available in the form of copyrights, trade secrets, and patents. Copyright law protects the expressions of ideas contained in original works of authorship from unauthorized duplication, use, and exploitation. Trade secrets law protects proprietary information which provides a competitive business advantage [3]. Patents protect innovative and useful products and processes [3]. If a reusable asset cannot be protected or can no longer be protected under any of the above means, then it is within the public domain and available for all to use. When a work is within the public domain, "no one holds rights to exclude members of the public from using, altering, replicating, sharing, or commercially exploiting copies or versions of the work that they have legitimately obtained." [2]

Means by which reusable software may enter the public domain include: 1) not qualifying as protectable subject matter; 2) eligible parties qualified to establish a claim of ownership choose not to do so or fail to do so within the allowable time constraints or under established guidelines; or 3) intellectual property protection for the reusable software expires [2].

Copyrights

Copyrights apply to "expressions of ideas embodied in original works of authorship" and provide the owner with the exclusive right to reproduce, publish, and sell the work [3]. Copyright protection "for an original work of authorship" does not extend to any idea, procedure, process, system, method of operation, concept, principle, or discovery regardless of the form in which it is described, explained, illustrated, or embodied in such work [4]. Clearly eligible for copyright protection is source code, object code, "program manuals and documentation, such as design notes, file note specifications, flowcharts, and digitally stored information." [5] Also deemed protectable under copyright by a number of U.S. court decisions is a computer program's structure, sequence, and organization [5].

Copyright Requirements. Before reusable software can qualify for copyright protection it must meet all of the following criteria: 1) originally created with no parts copied by the parties seeking the copyright; 2) fixed in a tangible medium of expression (sufficiently stable in its embodiment so that it can be perceived); and 3) considered nonutilitarian work (works are considered to be utilitarian if they do more than just convey information or display an appearance) [2].

Author Ownership of Copyrights. Copyrights can be claimed by the producer of reusable software except in situations where authorship and ownership of the assets belong to the company rather than the employee who produced it. If the company hires a contractor (not an employee) to produce reusable software, and the company wishes to retain the copyright, they must enter into a specific agreement with the contractor specifying transfer of copyright [4]. (For dealings with the U.S. Government, see the "Reuse Contractual Issues with Government Agencies" on page 373.)

Issues of copyright ownership arise when independently copyrighted reusable software are utilized together. For example, if two software engineers each create a subroutine with the intention of merging them together as part of a single program, they co-own the program and share the copyright. However, if the two software engineers create subroutines which are reused and integrated into a single program, then this program is considered a collective work. The software engineers own only their respective subroutines and do not share in the copyright of the whole program [4].

Ownership Rights of Copyright Holder. A copyright owner has exclusive rights to the copyrighted work and can prevent others from

1. reproducing the copyrighted asset;
2. preparing "derivative works" based upon the copyrighted asset;
3. distributing copies of the copyrighted asset "to the public by sale or other transfer of ownership, or by rental, lease, or lending." [2]

An owner may also sell, license, or surrender a copyright and/or exclusive rights. Exceptions and limitations to the above rights include reproduction of the copyrighted asset for archival purposes only or reproduction or adaptation of the asset if necessary in using it in conjunction with a machine. "Fair use" situations may also place limitations on exclusive rights. Examples of fair use include the use and distribution of copyrighted works for comment, criticism, and scholarly discussion [2].

Obtaining Copyrights. For works created after March 1, 1989, a copyright notice is no longer required to be placed on a work for it to be protected. However, registration with the Copyright Office is required in order to sue for infringement [2]. To prove an infringement of copyright, it must be shown that either the copyrighted work was in fact copied, or that the "accused infringer's work adopts a substantial portion of the copyrighted work." [4]

For personal authors, copyrights last for the life of the author plus 50 years. For corporate authors, copyrights expire 100 years after creation or 75 years after first publication, whichever comes first [2].

Advantages of Copyrights [6]. There are particular advantages in utilizing copyrights as a means of protection for reusable software:

- A copyright is relatively easy and inexpensive to obtain.
  Copyright is automatically conferred when the work is fixed in a tangible form. Formal copyright registration is quick and inexpensive.
- A copyright facilitates dissemination of works.
  The copyright was developed for works meant for proliferation. As long as the infringer can be identified, a preliminary injunction and rights may be claimed.
- A copyright provides a long period of protection.
  The duration of copyright protection is quite long and will often surpass that of the life of a reusable asset.

Disadvantages of Copyrights [6].
- Uncertainty with respect to forms and scope of material.

With software reuse, there may be uncertainty regarding what forms and activities fall within the bounds of copyright law. For example, can both graphical displays and the programs written to generate them be protected under copyright?

- Difficulty in enforcing rights.
  With wide dissemination of reusable assets, prevention of unauthorized duplication is extremely difficult.

Trade Secrets. A trade secret is "any formula, device, process, or information which gives a business an advantage over its competitors." [7] A wide range of software assets can be protected under trade secrets; these include but are not limited to algorithms, techniques, software tools, methodologies, components, and information. To be considered a trade secret, however, the asset must serve as a source or have the potential to be a source of competitive advantage [2].

Trade Secret Rights. A trade secret owner may enforce confidentiality by prior agreement with another party. The owner also has the right "not to be deprived of the trade secret by trespass, fraud, coercion, bribery, or other improper means." [2] A trade secret has the potential to be of unlimited duration. However, if a party chooses to protect an innovation as a trade secret and this innovation is independently discovered and patented by another party, the original party may have to seek a license to utilize the innovation.

Advantages of Trade Secrets [6]

- Application to a broad scope and range of subject matter.
  Trade secrets can apply to idea and expression as well as direct and indirect products of software reuse.
- Immediate protection.
  Similar to copyrights but unlike patents, trade secret protection is available immediately upon creation.
- Long duration of protection.
  A trade secret has the potential to be of unlimited duration so long as it is maintained as a secret.

Disadvantages of Trade Secrets [6]

- Lack of protection against independent development.
  If a similar innovation is independently developed, there is no protection against disclosure or use by the other party.
- Not suited for wide distribution.
  Trade secret protection is not well-suited for reusable assets meant for wide distribution. If a subject matter suitable for patent but only protected by trade

secret is illegally made public, the owner can only seek a course of action against the party who made it public. He cannot prevent the public from utilizing the secret.

Patents. "Patent protection is awarded for products and processes that are novel, non-obvious, and useful." [3] Patents are "for inventions or discoveries of any new and useful process, machine, or composition of matter, or any new and useful improvement thereof." [5] Patents are generally offered for the following: 1) processes, 2) machines, 3) manufactures, and 4) compositions of matter. Patents accompanying software have generally been under the category of "processes." In the past, such patents have been awarded for inventions relating to operations control and monitoring, data/file management, compiler, and application programs [5].

The inventor must ensure that the invention is useful, has not been previously developed and/or documented by others, and is "non-obvious" to persons skilled in the field to which the invention applies. This last criteria ensures that the invention is not simply a small improvement of an existing work. The inventor must apply for a patent within one year of the date of the first public or commercial use of the invention. Once awarded, a patent protects its owner against unauthorized use of the invention by others [2]. Patents last for 17 years from issuance, after which the invention becomes public domain.

Advantages of Patents [6]

- Protection against independent development.
  If the innovation is independently developed, the patent holder has the right to exclude others from using the innovation in certain ways.
- Wide scope and breadth of protection.
  Unlike copyrights, which apply only to a specific form of expression, patent rights can be extended to include the protection of the underlying algorithm as well as different expressions of that algorithm. Patent protection can also extend to the environment in which a program is used.
- Holder of patent need not prove copying.
  Unlike the case with copyrights, holders of patents do not need to prove copying in a patent suit.
- Appropriate for wide distribution.
  Unlike trade secrets, patents are useful for widespread dissemination of assets.

Disadvantages of Patents [6]

- Uncertainty and difficulty in meeting patent criteria.
  It is often difficult to know what inventions can be patented and often even more difficult to show that an innovation, although valuable, is both novel *and* non-obvious.

- Lag in protection.
  Patent protection cannot be provided until the patent is granted. It is not uncommon for the patent application process to take more than two years from filing to approval. During this waiting period, the applicant is not protected against exploitation of his invention by others.
- Higher cost.
  To obtain and maintain a patent requires payment of higher fees (generally a few thousand dollars, not including attorney fees) than that of a copyright.
- Overseeing infringement can be difficult.
  Similar to the case for copyrights, policing infringers can be difficult.

It is not uncommon for software to fall under the protection of more than one of the above intellectual property tools. Trade secret protection may be used in conjunction with copyright protection, especially when the secret has been documented. However, trade secret protection cannot be used with a patent because of the need to disclose information in patent registration [2]. As is the case for intellectual property protection for software in general, there is no certainty with regard to laws pertaining to reusable software. Because software is both a written document, which is usually protected by copyright, as well as an invented process, which is traditionally protected by patent, there has been difficulty in determining which combinations of intellectual property protection is most efficient comprehensive [2].

The three types of protection discussed thus far are relevant mainly for producers of reusable software. Consumers and brokers have different concerns which also need to be addressed.

Before using or brokering reusable software, consumers and brokers must know or determine its origins. If the software was developed internally, consumers should investigate whether or not contractual agreements with respect to reusing and modifying the software exist. For externally obtained software, consumers and brokers must obtain or negotiate a license to reuse [8].

Publicly available software may also carry licensing requirements or restrictions which should be investigated before reuse. Much of this analysis and documentation may be performed by a reuse librarian or repository administrator. The establishment of standard procedures and guidelines for information to accompany reusable components will facilitate reuse activity and minimize risks of legal and contractual infringement. In addition, a repository administrator should consider investigating a component's origins and searching for relevant copyrights and patents as part of the process of evaluating repository additions.

21.5 Implications of Intellectual Property for Software Reuse Activities

We now examine specific reuse activities and the issues and implications of intellectual property.

Reproduction and Reuse.   As discussed previously, a copyright owner has exclusive rights to reproduce a work except in cases of fair use and machine compatibility. Given the exclusivity of these rights, only the copyright owner can reproduce and/or authorize others to copy a reusable asset. In the cases where authorized owners of a copy of the assets wish to allow a third party to reuse the assets, permission must be obtained from the copyright holder.

Since the reuse of assets essentially involves reproducing all or part of an asset, such activity without prior authorization violates copyright law. The courts have ruled in several cases involving copyright violations wherein the unauthorized reuse of portions of software that make up a larger program constitutes infringement of the copyright holder's rights.

Modification.   The copyright owner also owns the right to create derivative works based upon the copyrighted work. Consequently, unless a consumer has obtained a license to modify the reusable asset, doing so infringes upon the rights of the copyright owner, except in the cases set forth under the Computer Software Copyright Act enacted by the U.S. Congress in 1980. Under this Act, the owner of a copy of a program may change or authorize another to change the program if the modifications are essential in its use with a machine and if the changes serve no other purpose [5].

Sookman [5] suggests that the owner of an authorized copy of software who has the right to translate the program to another language probably has the right to adapt a program for use in different operating environments.

Use of Standards to Facilitate Reuse.   The creation and use of software development standards to facilitate reuse is technically protected by copyright. However, because the difference between an unprotectable idea and its protectable expression in the development of software is not well delineated, no general rules of thumb exist to determine whether a copyright has been violated. In the case of standards, individual evaluations are necessary to determine whether the standard is protected and, if so, whether the right of use for that standard can be acquired [9].

21.6   Contractual Issues

Potential contracts between consumers, producers, and brokers to reuse can be established at two levels. At the first level, intraproject, interproject, and enterprise-wide reuse usually require agreement terms within one company or organization. In these cases, an organizational policy should be identified to fairly allocate the risks and responsibilities to all contractual parties. Producers need adequate protection against liability due to misuse of an asset and consumers require some assurance of the quality of a reusable component. Balancing these needs is the key to creating an effective policy that facilitates reuse.

At the second level of contractual agreements, specifically those between companies, the possibility of a license agreement between parties should be considered in addition to all of the previously discussed issues. Producers can grant consumers permission to reuse software through licensing, although they may need to provide adequate warranties that protect the consumer from certain risks of reuse. These warranties serve as incentives for consumers to purchase or reuse the assets.

As an example, contracts governing software reuse activity may cover the following:

1. the party responsible for correcting a reusable asset if a defect is detected;
2. the party assuming liability for damages to an external customer caused by a defect found in a reused asset;
3. all parties indemnified from losses caused by an asset resulting in damage to an external customer;
4. the extent and limits of each liability;
5. the parties responsible for maintaining a reusable asset;
6. the parties responsible for correcting defects for assets which have been leveraged;
7. the supporting materials which will be delivered and level of support provided with the reusable assets;
8. the warranty coverage, if any, which will be provided with the reusable assets and the parties which will be responsible for coverage of those warranties;
9. the rights that the producer retains and the rights that will be provided to the broker or consumer.

Wald [10] provides an example of a contractual agreement outlining producer and consumer obligations as follows:

1. A developer of reusable parts shall be responsible for guaranteeing that his part meets its original specification. In cases of failure of the software part, his liability will usually be limited to replacement of the defective part. It should be noted, however, that different parts in the library may have different warranty levels. The parts developer will have no liability for subsequent use or misuse of his part (i.e., there will be no third party liability).
2. A user of reusable parts shall be responsible for the product that he has developed, within the limits of any warranties which may exist from the original developers of the incorporated parts.

To be complete, the above agreement should also state who assumes responsibility for maintenance, defect repair, damage to external customers caused by a defect, and who retains rights of ownership.

We now discuss some legal issues from the perspective of the participants in software reuse. Further discussion may be found in [11].

Producers.   In some cases, producers may wish to establish an agreement with a repository for royalty payments based on the frequency with which their contributions are used. Potential problems could arise in situations where a consumer borrows a library component, studies and learns its design, and then returns it without actually reusing it. An agreement should state whether or not royalties should be paid in such cases [12].

Consumers.   The main concerns of a consumer focus on an asset's quality and usability. Some of these concerns can be abated by requiring producers to adhere to explicit guidelines and standards in creating reusable software. Consumers also need protection against infringement suits filed by third parties (different than the providers of an asset) whose rights have been violated by reuse of an asset. Such protection may be provided by the producer or broker [12].

Brokers.   Major contractual concerns for brokers focus on software component title and rights transfers. In order to provide effective service, brokers need to be granted either full rights to reusable assets or rights to authorize consumers to use, copy, leverage, and/or improve them. Brokers can be held liable for unauthorized access to proprietary software and failure to provide critical and accurate information [12].

End-users.   The concerns of an end-user are protection from damages arising from software that was created from defective assets or assets that are accompanied with misinformation. Another concern is the purchase of software which is later determined to have been made from assets which infringe on a third party's rights.

Licenses.   A license issued by an owner grants permission to perform specific functions and to modify products in ways explicitly stated in the licensing agreement. A license is limited in duration, and at the end of its term all rights revert back to the owner. A license does not transfer ownership but may authorize some rights of ownership such as reproduction.

In the case of software reuse from the producer's perspective, at least two licenses may be necessary. The first license provides consumers with permission to utilize the reusable assets in some specified fashion. This may include the conditions under which the reusable software can be used, copied, and modified. Such a license would also cover the transfer of the reusable asset to a third party. For example, EVB Software Engineering, Inc. [13], licenses the use of its reusable software on a CPU basis as well as on a site license basis. EVB's license allows consumers to incorporate its reusable software into their own software. In fact, the consumer may deliver the EVB reusable software as part of the product, even in source form. The consumer is restricted from selling or providing the components at no cost to someone who does not already hold a valid EVB license.

The second license allows another party to "broker" the reusable assets. This agreement stipulates the conditions under which the broker may provide rights to consumers of the reusable assets. The fact that a license must be for a limited term may be advantageous for both the producer and broker. If the useful life of a software asset is relatively short due to rapid changes in technology, a broker will wish to market an asset and pay its accompanying royalties only when it is in demand. On the other hand, should the asset be a success, the broker may want an option to buy ownership of the asset. A license agreement can provide for both stipulations [14]. The producer, having retained ownership of the asset, can modify and remarket it, or sell or license it to another broker.

Warranties. A warranty is a guarantee that goods sold to a purchaser are as represented. A warranty will protect the consumer from certain risks involving deficiencies in, and information about, the reusable software. For example, EVB Software Engineering, Inc., warrants that if a consumer detect any errors in its reusable software, they will correct the errors at no cost to the consumer [13].

In certain cases, the warranty may be tailored to the consumer. In considering a warranty, a consumer should understand exactly [15]

1. what is being protected by the warranty;
2. what remedies are available for exercising the warranty;
3. how long and under what conditions the warranty is effective;
4. how cost-effective the warranty is.

DSD Laboratories, Inc. [15], has outlined an analysis tool for producers and brokers to assess whether warranty coverage should be included with reusable assets. See Fig. 21–2.

Reuse Contractual Issues with Government Agencies. Several additional issues warrant consideration in contractual relationships with U.S. Government agencies. Depending upon the relationship, the U.S. Government has established a set of rules governing reuse activities. For example, a software contractor can copyright any software written under a government contract for use outside government work except for specially designated works. This software can be sold outside the government market, in which case the contractor may have to reimburse government funds used to develop the reusable software. The contractor may even sell the reusable software to another government contractor, as long as the government

	Software component developed to be reusable, or modified for reuse	Existing software component identified reusable "as is"	Commercial software component
Software component characteristic requiring warranty consideration	• Reusable assets should perform to the level described in supporting documentation. -Developers of reusable components should support this concept.	• Same as for new and/or modified software, but: -Original developer may not be willing to warrant for reuse. -Any existing warranty may be exclusive of or voided by reuse elsewhere.	• Typically, only the standard commercial warranty will be offered. -May be sufficient. -Commercial vendor may consider extended coverage.
Remedies required	• Fix the software component to perform at documented levels. • Consequential damages possible if user adequately tested component prior to reuse, but defect not detectable. Consider use of liquidated damages.	• Same as for new and/or modified software but: -conditions above still apply.	• Consequential damages typically excluded. • Performance to documented levels warranted.
Warranty duration	• Some reasonable period after delivery - typically not more than 1 to 2 years. -Software may not change, but a prudent business person would not commit to longer periods.	• Same as for new and/or modified software.	• Commercial limits -90 days to 1 year typical.
Cost/benefit analysis results	• What is the added warranty cost over the warranty period? • What is the likelihood that the component will be reused in the warranty period? • What is the likelihood that a failure can be discreetly identified? • What are the administration costs?	• Same as for new and/or modified software, but: - Also assess whether reuse warranty costs necessarily duplicate any existing warranty costs.	• Included in commercial off-the-shelf (COTS) price. • Usually difficult to analyze added cost for extra coverage. - Commercial pricing protection.

FIGURE 21–2 Analysis tool for assessing warranty effectiveness/applicability. *Source:* R. J. Bowes, T. R. Huber, and R. O. Saisi, *Informal Technical Report for the Software Technology for Adaptable, Reliable Systems (STARS) Acquisition Handbook—Final,* Central Archive for Reusable Defense Software (CARDS), DSD Laboratories, Inc. for Air Force Materiel Command, Hanscom AFB, MA, Oct. 30, 1992, p. 55.

does not pay twice for the same software. This criteria also holds if a contractor reuses software originally written under an Air Force contract for a Navy contract [8].

The federal government also receives full copyright privileges for any software developed under contract unless it was developed with a contractor's private funds, at a time different from that under contract, and is not essential to the performance of the contract software. Contractor-owned software that is reused in government contract work must be identified in advance if the contractor wishes to retain ownership. However, these ownership rights are not exclusive. Current Federal Acquisition Regulations (FAR) give the government the right to allow other government support service contractors access to and use of any software produced under government contract (regardless of whether or not it was developed with private funds) [8]. Conversely, contract developers may reuse government software for government purposes without a license.

The complexity of rules governing software developed under government contract and the inconsistencies in regulations among defense and nondefense agencies discourage government contract work in software reuse. A clear and more comprehensible policy, as well as adequate incentives, need to be established before widespread reuse in government contract work can occur.

Foucher [16] discusses a reuse acquisition checklist created by the Reuse Acquisition Action Team and ACM SIGAda Reuse Working Group which can be used for planning to include reuse considerations and to facilitate communications between technical and procurement personnel on requirements that must be translated into a request for proposal. The goal of the checklist is to ensure that reuse is considered as an integrated part of overall software development/engineering efforts, and to encourage implementation of effective planned reuse. A copy of the checklist appears in [15].

The CARDS Acquisition Handbook [15] is a guidebook to "assist . . . in incorporating software reuse into all phases of the acquisition life cycle." The document discusses acquisition/reuse plans, RFPs, evaluation and selection of contractors, and contract management. Included are considerations for reuse license agreements, choosing a contractor, and contract language for an award fee in software reuse.

It is necessary for software developers to attain a minimum level of understanding regarding legal and contractual reuse issues because under both the Department of Defense and FAR, if there is any conflict between the developer's standard licensing agreement terms and the requirements of the government, the government usually wins [8].

21.7 Conclusion

The legal and contractual aspects of reuse will become more important as reuse increases in scope. Participants in the reuse process would do well to stay informed of the potential legal and contractual risks of software reuse and the means of mitigat-

ing such risks. Successful reuse in the legal and contractual context rests upon allocating risks among participants so that reuse can be encouraged and not encumbered by legal problems.

Summary

Reusing and leveraging software assets brings to the forefront a host of legal and contractual issues with regard to rights, liabilities, and obligations. Intellectual property
protection for owners of software is available in the form of copyrights, trade secrets,
and patents. It is not uncommon for software to fall under the protection of more than
one of these intellectual property protection tools. In the context of software reuse, the
copyright owner of a reusable asset has the exclusive right to reproduce and modify
that asset. Potential contracts between consumers, producers, and brokers to reuse
can be established at two levels. At the first level, intraproject, interproject, and enterprise-wide reuse usually require agreement terms within one company or organization. At the second level of contractual agreements, specifically those between companies, the possibility of a license agreement between parties should be considered.

References

1. *Merriam Webster's Collegiate Dictionary*. 10th ed., Springfield, MA: Merriam,
   1997.
2. P. Samuelson and K. Deasy, "Intellectual property protection for software,"
   Software Engineering Institute, Carnegie-Mellon University, Pittsburgh, PA, SEI
   Curriculum Module SEI-CM-14-2.1, July 1989.
3. "Intellectual property issues in software," National Academy Press, National
   Research Council (U.S.). Steering Committee for Intellectual Property Issues in
   Software, Washington, D.C, 1991.
4. G. Miller, "Intellectual property and liability issues with software reuse," in
   AIAA Aerospace Design Conference, Feb. 18, 1993.
5. B. Sookman, "Intellectual property rights and software reuse: A Canadian and
   U.S. perspective, Part I," *Canadian Computer Law Reporter*, vol. 7, no. 1,
   Dec. 1989/Jan. 1990.
6. D. Bender, *Computer Law-Software Protection..* New York, N.Y.: Times Mir-
   ror Books, 1992.
7. M. Roberts, "Intellectual property," Harvard Business School, Boston, MA, 9-
   384-188, Aug. 1984.
8. *Reuse Adoption Guidebook*, Appendix D: Summary of legal/contractual reuse
   issues, Software Productivity Consortium, Herndon, VA, SPC-92051-CMC,
   Version 01.00.03, Nov. 1992.
9. B. Sookman, "Intellectual property rights and software reuse: A Canadian and
   U.S. perspective, Part II," *Canadian Computer Law Reporter*, vol. 7, no. 2,
   Feb. 1990.

10. E. Wald, *STARS Reusability Guidebook, Version 4.0*, U.S. Department of Defense, STARS, 1986.

11. C. A. Will and J. Baldo, *Workshop on Legal Issues in Software Reuse*, 1991.

12. B. Sookman, "Confronting legal liability in the reuse of computer software," presented at *Workshop on Legal Issues in Software Reuse*, 1991.

13. *What Managers Need to Know About GRACE*, EVB Software Engineering, Inc., Frederick, MD, 1987.

14. T. D. Harris, *The Legal Guide to Computer Software Protection: A Practical Handbook on Copyrights, Trademarks, Publishing, and Trade Secrets.* Englewood Cliffs, N.J.: Prentice-Hall, 1985.

15. R. J. Bowes, T. R. Huber, and R. O. Saisi, *Informal Technical Report for the Software Technology for Adaptable, Reliable Systems (STARS) Acquisition Handbook—Final*, Central Archive for Reusable Defense Software (CARDS), DSD Laboratories, Inc. for Air Force Materiel Command, Hanscom AFB, MA, Oct. 30, 1992.

16. D. Foucher, "Contract considerations for software reuse," presented at *Tri-Ada '92: Industry, Academia and Government*, 1992.

For Further Reading

1. K. Copeland, "An incentive program for contractors who reuse software," presented at *AIAA Aerospace Design Conference*, 1993.

2. W. J. DeVecchio, "Legal barriers to reuse and liability," in *Software Productivity Consortium*, Herndon, VA, video, 1990.

3. *Creating Reusable Ada Software, Legal Issues*, EVB Software Engineering, Inc., Frederick, MD, 1987.

4. T. Huber, "Findings of the CARDS sponsored software reuse legal workshop," in *6th Annual Workshop for Institutionalizing Software Reuse*, Nov. 2–4, 1993.

5. T. R. Huber, "Reducing business and legal risks in software reuse libraries," in *Software Reuse: Advances in Software Reusability—International Conference*, Nov. 1–4, 1994, pp. 110–117.

6. B. Hulbert, "Overview of recent developments in copyright protection for software," in *4th Annual Workshop on Institutionalizing Software Reuse*, Nov. 18–22, 1991.

7. M. A. Lemley and D. O'Brien, "Encouraging software reuse," *Stanford Law Review 255*, vol. 49, no. 50, 1997.

8. T. Syms and C. L. Braun, "Software reuse: customer vs. contractor point-counterpoint," presented at *Ada: The Choice for '92. Ada-Europe International Conference Proceedings*, Athens, Greece, 1991.

9. W. Tracz, "Software reuse: Principles and practice," University of California, Irvine, CA, Feb. 26–28, 1990.

10. W. Tracz, "Legal obligations for software reuse," *American Programmer*, Mar. 1991.

MANUFACTURING REUSABLE SOFTWARE

Manufacturing offers insights that can be used to manage software reuse programs. In this chapter, we compare manufacturing to software development, discuss the way manufacturing strategy links manufacturing to the goals of the business, and describe manufacturing techniques that match the process to the product.

We will also examine manufacturing methods and concepts such as group technology, flexible manufacturing systems, and mass customization. We will show how leading organizations are applying these concepts to software development and reuse. Finally, we will discuss the idea of software factories and the role of reuse in these factories. This chapter is informed by the works of Sasser *et al.* [1] and Mayer *et al.* [2].

22.1 Analogy of Manufacturing to Software Development

Software development has long been the domain of highly skilled and creative personnel; a similar situation existed in early manufacturing.

Software production has been likened to a cottage industry where "efforts to treat software construction as a more conventional manufacturing process have had too little time to mature." [3] Using manufacturing as an analogy, Aranow observes that many software organizations have invested in pieces of machinery as opposed to building a software factory [4].

Cox describes the implications of a software industrial revolution, "transforming programming from a solitary cut-to-fit craft, like the cottage industries of colonial America, into an organizational enterprise like manufacturing is today." [5] He cites gunsmithing in the United States, which evolved from craft-oriented production to a new paradigm based on interchangeable parts.

Using an analogy to hardware, Cox also describes the idea of a *software IC*. He observes that hardware engineers build systems from generic, reusable, silicon chips, each with its own technical specification sheets. Hardware engineers have defined a unit of granularity which allows them to create and assemble a solution instead of developing one from scratch. A software IC draws upon this idea and can be used for assembling software systems.

Wegner notes the similarities between technologies used in industrial and software production and the way terms like "software tools" and "software factory" reveal industrial models that can be used for software production. He observes that software technology is becoming progressively less labor-intensive and more capital-intensive as it matures. Industrial technology underwent a similar transformation. Wegner writes:

> "Machine tools of the industrial revolution and software tools such as compilers are both (considered) reusable resources. Moreover, any reusable resource may be thought of as a capital good whose development cost may be recovered over its set of uses. Thus, it seems reasonable to identify the notion of capital goods with that of reusable resources and the notion of capital with that of reusability." [6]

We acknowledge differences between software development and industrial manufacturing. For example, in manufacturing a product is designed and then produced in the quantity desired. In software, the system is designed and production occurs when the software is replicated. Furthermore, the majority of the cost in manufacturing a product is in production. Conversely, in software development, the majority of the cost is in design; replication costs are almost negligible. One implication of the different cost structures in manufacturing and software development is this: manufacturers design products to minimize production costs whereas software developers have a greater incentive to minimize design costs.

In spite of these differences, we can still gain insight by examining and applying the lessons learned in industrial manufacturing to the *development* stage of the software life cycle.

22.2   Manufacturing Strategy

Manufacturing strategy is an integrated set of principles that determines the use of resources, the method by which a product is manufactured, and the organization of an infrastructure to support manufacturing. More importantly, manufacturing strategy aligns these activities to business goals.

Manufacturing Strategy Techniques.   A *learning curve* maps the relationship between labor hours-per-unit to cumulative units produced. An *experience curve* is a variation of the learning curve in that it depicts the relationship between cost-per-unit to cumulative units produced. Learning and experience curves may be identified in both producing and reusing software. From our experience at Hewlett-Packard, as the cumulative number of reusable assets produced increases, producers gain experience and can produce assets in less time and with less effort. Similarly, as consumers reuse more assets, the time required to reuse them decreases.

A good manager plans to capitalize from the experience curve, taking into consideration its effects in capacity planning, resource utilization, and strategic planning.

Matching Production Processes to the Product.   In the early days of manufacturing, each product was created as though it were unique. With the maturing of manufacturing processes, a product could be created through a spectrum of available processes.

In manufacturing, production processes may differ in several aspects. However, one element that is always critical is understanding the extent of *variability* in the product that will be produced. At one extreme are *project processes* which allow for high tailorization, and at the other, *continuous processes* which capitalize on economies of scale. *Economies of scale* are reductions in unit costs that occur as the amount of output increases. Both product manufacturing and service delivery can be considered in light of this spectrum.

The Range of Alternative Manufacturing Methods.   When highly customized products are to be developed, specific *project processes* must be carefully developed and coordinated. Custom products are likely to require variable amounts of time and effort in the planning, design, and production phases. Consequently, the ordering and scheduling of tasks become critical success factors. Examples of such projects are building world-class race cars and developing one-of-a-kind satellites.

Compared to project processes, *batch processes* are suitable for situations with low production volumes, limited standardization among the products being manufactured, and great similarity in the tasks required to create the product. Batch processes offer less variation and capitalize upon the commonality in the products. Because of the small volume, use of assembly lines is not economically justified. Examples of batch processes include the manufacture of Rolls Royces, musical instruments, and book binding.

Continuous processes and *line flows* (which includes assembly lines) are suitable for creating products in large volumes. For such products, standardization is essential. There is significant division of labor, worker tasks are often narrowly defined and activities are partitioned into simple techniques. Each step of the process is closely coupled with the next and work-in-process is continuously flowing to the next station. Examples of continuous processes and line flows include paper manufacturing and fast-food preparation.

Managers can choose from this menu of manufacturing alternatives. More than one of them can usually be employed to build a given product. However, each of the processes bear attributes that make them more suitable for different circumstances, and no single alternative is likely to be suitable for every situation. For example, a line flow is unlikely to be appropriate for creating customized products. A project process is not well-suited for a commodity product. A manufacturing process should be chosen on the basis of how well it serves the organizational strategy, target market, and product.

Continuous processes and line flows capitalize upon economies of scale. Economy of scale refers to the unit cost savings that can be achieved at higher output levels. Achieving lower costs by producing a variety of products subject to economies of scale is a form of *economies of scope*. An example is the steel company that produces a variety of steel products by using one furnace to produce molten steel that is subsequently poured into molds to produce different products [7]. This is analogous to the software development technique of building reusable assets that can be used in multiple products.

Just as there is a spectrum of manufacturing techniques, there is a spectrum of software development techniques, from traditional methods to systematic reuse. Moving from one extreme to the other requires changes in virtually every element of the system, including human, physical, informational, and monetary elements (Fig. 22–1).

Mapping Products to Processes.   Manufacturing strategy alternatives may be identified from the relationship between a *product* life cycle and *process* life cycle. A new product is usually characterized by a limited market size, frequent product changes, and little standardization. A mature product is highlighted by greater standardization and the peaking of market volume.

The traits of the process appropriate to each phase of the product life cycle can be identified. A project process is most appropriate for a new product because of its flexibility. A specialized process that offers high quality and some variability may be best suited for mid-life products. Finally, a highly automated and dedicated process is appropriate for a mature, standardized product which must be produced dependably at the lowest cost possible. A mapping of the product life cycle to the spectrum of processes is shown in Fig. 22–2.

This matrix enables the manufacturing strategist to map the organization's products to manufacturing strategies, determine their appropriateness, and realign each product to the appropriate manufacturing strategy if necessary.

We can map the software development process to the software product in a similar fashion. Using Fig. 22–2 again, we can depict the process and technologies corresponding to general purpose, specialized, and dedicated processes on the vertical axis and the life cycle of the product/domain on the horizontal axis. For products and domains that are relatively new or changing, the process most appropriate would be a general purpose or "crafted" solution. The domain may be entirely novel or simply new to the organization and its engineers.

The Process Spectrum

Traditional Software Development   <———>   Systematic Software Reuse

As we move along the spectrum from traditional software development to systematic software reuse, we note the following.

The People System

- Labor content per dollar value of the software product decreases as more automated tools and reusable assets are utilized.
- Greater emphasis for software engineers to specialize in assembling or producing reusable assets.
- Training times decline as consumer engineers assemble reusable assets rather than develop specialized software.

The Physical System

- Software tools and equipment become less general purpose and more dedicated to support reuse.
- Greater capital utilization than labor utilization on software tools and reusable assets in the creation of software.

The Information and Decision Systems

- Long-term issues such as planning, coordination, and long-range forecasting for the production and consumption of reusable assets become more important than day-to-day operating considerations.
- Greater emphasis on quality control, especially for reusable assets.

The Monetary System

- The cost structure of software development tends to have a higher proportion of fixed costs and lower proportion of variable costs.
- Control of capital expenditures become increasingly important.

FIGURE 22–1   The process spectrum. Adapted from W. E. Sasser, K. B. Clark, D. A. Garvin, M. B. W. Graham, R. Jaikumar, and D. H. Maister, *Cases in Operations Management*, Homewood, IL: Irwin, 1982, pp. xvii–xix.

Domains that are dynamic but have some stable elements are candidates for specialized processes. Software tools utilized include component libraries and templates. Software products in domains that are very mature can utilize a dedicated process. Organizations are typically required to provide a greater upfront investment for these technologies and processes, but incur a lower cost to generate the applications. Examples include generators and transformation systems.

Multiple software development strategies may be used to develop a single software product. For example, at the Manufacturing Productivity section of Hewlett-Packard, an application was developed using a generator for extremely stable portions and reusable templates and components for other portions.

Product Life Cycle to Spectrum of Processes Mapping

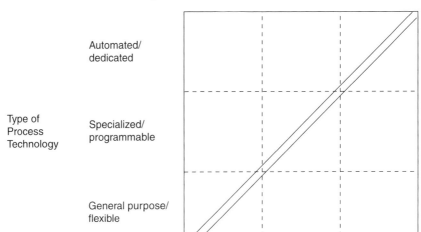

FIGURE 22–2   A mapping of product life cycle to spectrum of processes. *Source:* R. J. Mayer, K. K. Agarwal, and S. Beckman, "Manufacturing strategy," in *AMA Management Handbook,* W. K. Fallon, Ed. New York, NY: AMACON, 1983, pp.4–10.

22.3   Manufacturing Concepts

In this section, we discuss the following techniques and concepts which are used to control the costs in manufacturing, and describe their application in software reuse: group technology, flexible manufacturing systems, mass customization, and the factory concept.

Group Technology

The purpose of *group technology* in manufacturing is to utilize economies of scope by identifying and exploiting similarities in parts to be manufactured, and the sequence of machines that are necessary for the processing of those parts. Parts are classified into families on the basis of characteristics such as size and geometry. The machines that are used to process the part families are situated in proximity to each other in "machine cells."

Wemmerlov and Hyer [8] highlight three ways group technology benefits are achieved:

- by performing similar activities together, less time is wasted in changing from one unrelated activity to the next;
- by standardizing closely related items or activities, unnecessary duplication of effort is avoided;
- by efficiently storing and retrieving information related to recurring problems, search time is reduced and the need to solve the problem again is eliminated.

The similarity of group technology to software reuse is striking. Although there are differences between software reuse and group technology, the two technologies share the philosophy of rationalization.

As early as the 1920s, product standardization and optimal routing paths were used by the Jones and Lamson Machine Company to build machine tools. Such approaches were refined over the years and given various names such as "part family manufacturing."

Group technology can be traced back to the 1940s and 1950s when a group of Russian scholars focused on sequencing similar items in order to decrease manufacturing setup time. From Russia, the practice of group technology spread to Europe, Japan, and the United States. European journals published in the 1960s contained articles which highlighted the design of group technology classification systems. Group technology continues to be the subject of both scholarly research and industrial practice.

Wemmerlov and Hyer [8] identify four important principles that serve as a foundation for group technology:

- *Classification* serves as the basis for forming families and establishing standardization, organizes information for better or faster decisions, and reduces costs since there are fewer errors.
- A *family* is a group of parts that possesses common traits which are pertinent for various purposes such as identifying all parts that require processing by a specific machine.
- *Simplification* reduces variety and is an result of classification and family identification.
- *Standardization* is the "selection of preferred items," including manufacturing procedures, terminology, and part features.

Group Technology Applied to Software Reuse.   Several organizations have researched or applied group technology to software reuse. The University of Southern California (USC) System Factory Project has recognized the similarities of large-scale software systems to the development of large structural, electrical, and mechanical systems. Its research objective is to tap the potential of applying group and flexible manufacturing system technologies to software development [9].

At Hewlett-Packard, a real-time database software project applied group technology to perform a reuse-oriented early design review. As a result of this review, the final code size was reduced by 25%, and the time required in detailed design, implementation, and unit testing by 40%. The project experienced an overall saving of 25% in total project cost as a result of the reuse review [10].

Cluster Analysis. One of the means for family identification in group technology is cluster analysis, which is "concerned with grouping of objects into homogeneous clusters (groups) based on the object features." [11]

Some researchers have utilized cluster analysis for the purpose of reuse classification. For example, Maarek and Kaiser describe the use of conceptual clustering to classify software components. Taxonomies of software components are created "by using a classification scheme based on conceptual clustering, where the physical closeness of components mirrors their conceptual similarity." [12] The objects are gathered into clusters where they are more "similar" to each other than to the members of other clusters.

Cluster analysis was applied to software reuse at the Manufacturing Productivity (MP) section of the Software Technology Division of Hewlett-Packard to solve a problem concerning the maintenance of reusable assets called "utilities." [13]

The MP section produces large application software for manufacturing resource planning. The MP reuse program began in 1983 and continues to the present. The original motivation for pursuing reuse was to increase the productivity of the engineers to meet critical milestones [14]. MP has since discovered that reuse also eases the maintenance burden and supports product enhancement.

Reuse was practiced in the form of reusable assets (application/architecture utilities and shared files) and generated code. Total code size for the 685 reusable assets was 55,000 lines of noncommented source statements (KNCSS).The reusable assets were written in Pascal and SPL (the systems programming language for the HP3000 Computer System). The development and target operating system was the multiprogramming environment (MPEXL). The utilities at MP are many (685 utilities) and small in size (lines of code range from 14 to 619 KNCSS). In manufacturing systems software developed by MP, a transaction constitutes a cohesive set of activities used for inventory management and is a subunit of the manufacturing systems software.

Within each transaction, calls are made to the appropriate utilities as required, and are contained in an include file specific to the transaction. However, this has led to a proliferation of different include files since each transaction is usually created by a different engineer. When a utility is modified, all the include files that contain this utility must be identified and updated with the new version, which has resulted in a tremendous amount of effort.

To reduce the effort required for future updates, a cluster analysis was conducted on the use of utilities by transactions. First, a 13 by 11 matrix was created by designating the rows as transactions and the columns as utilities (Fig. 22–3). A "1" indicates that a transaction makes a call to the particular utility and a "0" indicates that a transaction does not make a call to the particular utility.

```
Input Matrix: (rows are transactions; columns are reusable assets)
1 0 1 0 0 0 0 0 0 0 0
0 0 1 0 0 0 0 1 0 0 1
0 0 1 0 0 0 0 1 0 0 0
0 0 0 0 0 0 0 1 0 0 1
0 0 1 0 0 0 0 0 0 0 1
0 0 1 1 0 0 0 0 0 0 1
0 0 1 0 0 0 0 0 0 0 0
0 1 0 0 1 0 1 0 0 0 1
0 1 0 0 1 0 1 0 0 0 0
0 1 0 0 1 1 1 0 1 1 1
0 1 0 1 1 1 1 0 1 1 1
0 1 0 1 0 0 1 0 0 0 1
0 1 0 1 1 0 1 0 0 0 1

Columns (Reusable assets):
1=Adj summary-qty
2=Autobofill
3=check'store'um
4=invalid-fld-check
5=potency-inv-qty
6=prep'for'pcm
7=print-document
8=report-neg-qty
9=send'to'pcm
10=update'pcm'buff
11=write-stock-file

Rows (Transactions):
1=adjhand
2=issalloc
3=isseu
4=issord
5=issunp
6=issbo
7=move
8=recinloc
9=recinsp
10=recwo
11=recrun
12=recpopt
13=recpoit
```

FIGURE 22–3   Input matrix.

The matrix is then used as an input file to a clustering algorithm provided by Dr. Andrew Kusiak of the University of Iowa.

The output solution, as shown in Fig. 22–4, reorders the reusable assets into "clusters." The results suggest that we place utilities (depicted by the columns) 1, 3, and 8 into a single include file for transactions 1 to 7.

Utilities 2, 5, 6, 7, 9, and 10 should be placed into another include file for transactions 8, 9, 10, 11, 12, and 13.

Utilities 4 and 11 can either be placed in both include files, or a separate one may be created for them.

Benefits of Cluster Analysis for Reuse.   Cluster analysis is useful in the creation of include files with specified utilities that would reduce the effort required to maintain the files. In our example with the MP section, prior to cluster analysis, 13 individual include files were maintained—one for each transaction. By utilizing cluster analysis, we were able to identify the commonalties and differences within the 13 include files and specify a core set of two include files. By reengineering the 13 include files into two, the number of files can be reduced by 85%.

Cluster analysis also has applications in software reuse. It may be used to identify "families of systems" that share the same features. For example, we can apply cluster analysis to a matrix where the columns represent the features of software systems/products and the rows represent the software systems/products. The analysis would cluster the features to the software systems/products, thereby helping to identify families of systems which share common features. This information may be useful in determining specific reusable assets to create.

Flexible Manufacturing Systems

A flexible manufacturing system (FMS) is a "self-contained grouping of machinery (e.g. machine tools, robots) that can perform all the operations in the manu-

Cluster Analysis Solution (rows are transactions; columns are reusable assets)

```
                            1 1
          1 3 8 2 5 6 7 9 0 1 4
    1     1 1
    2     1 1               1
    3     1 1
    4       1               1
    5     1                 1
    6     1                 1 1
    7     1
    8         1 1   1       1
    9         1 1   1
   10         1 1 1 1 1 1 1
   11         1 1 1 1 1 1 1 1 1
   12         1     1       1 1
   13         1 1   1       1 1
```

FIGURE 22–4   Cluster analysis solution. *Source:* Andrew Kusiak, University of Iowa.

facture of a number of parts with similar processing requirements." [15] Flexible manufacturing systems can easily adapt to different parts, minimizing the setup time required to change between parts. They can lower labor costs, improve productivity and quality, and reduce work-in-process inventories.

Flexible Software Factories. Cusumano observes that flexible software factories were the result of "recogniz(ing) that combinations of efficiency and flexibility allowed them to meet various and changing customer needs more effectively than maximizing one dimension." [16] The flexible software factory offered medium variety, lower volume, and required medium skills.

Basili identifies the desirable features of FMS as "modular architecture, integration of heterogeneous methods and tools, configuration and reconfiguration capabilities, and wide automation under human control." He is seeking to capture these features in his "component factory." [17]

As mentioned earlier, the USC System Factory Project is attempting to tap the potential of flexible manufacturing system technologies to software development [9].

Griss [10] describes research being conducted at the Hewlett-Packard Laboratories into the "flexible software factory." This factory offers a framework for designing and equipping a software development organization's infrastructure to efficiently produce, consume, and support domain-specific software kits. Both an organization's business and technical styles must be considered when identifying appropriate processes and kits.

Navarro, also of Hewlett-Packard Laboratories, defines a flexible software factory as an entity that develops software through the use of reusable software kits which consist of components, frameworks, documentation, etc. [18]. He observes that a flexible software factory possesses the following traits which allow it to improve and adapt to dynamic conditions:

- understands its core process(es), the key processes critical to its success, and their relationship to key business goals;
- designs the organization as a system to control and improve its core process(es), focusing on the customer to guide decisions;
- adapts to change work activities as business conditions warrant;
- supports concurrent execution of work, maintaining alignment across organizational boundaries;
- learns from and reuses experience, creating a growing base of organizational competencies.

Mass Customization

Mass customization provides a product or service that dynamically changes according to the customer's needs and desires through the interaction of independent processes. These processes or tasks, called *modules*, are placed together in the right combination and sequence to "tailor-make" a product or service to the unique tastes of the consumer. In mass customization, two critical aspects are as follows:

1. minimizing the cost and increasing the ease by which processes interact to satisfy a customer's request;
2. broadening employees' capabilities in order to make possible a wider range of customization.

While organizations have traditionally been forced to choose between "providing large volumes of standardized goods or services at a low cost, or . . . mak(ing) customized or highly differentiated products in smaller volumes at a high cost, continuous process improvement and mass customization allows an organization to achieve low costs, high quality, and the ability to make highly varied, often individualized customized products." [19] Well-known practitioners of mass customization include Motorola, Bell Atlantic, and Hallmark.

Software reusability embodies some of the concepts and objectives of mass customization. Shared goals include the creation of a product on-demand by the customer through the linkages of modules that satisfy the customer's desires. Software reuse also strives to achieve low cost and high quality while offering varied, customized products.

22.4   The Software Factory

Japanese Software Factories.   While the term "software factory" was first coined and applied by several American companies—in particular the System Development Corporation and IBM in the 1960s—it was the Japanese companies, especially Fujitsu, NEC, Hitachi, and Toshiba, which rigorously applied their experience in manufacturing and production to software development [16].

There is no universally accepted definition of a software factory. Software factories have sometimes been described simply as facilities that use a production approach. Some suggest that a software factory is a philosophy; others believe it exhibits certain characteristics. Those characteristics may include planned economies of scope, a division of labor, the sharing of standard parts and processes across a family of products, and possibly the use of computer-aided software engineering tools.

Japanese firms view the problems of developing software less as finding the appropriate technology solutions than systematically matching the proper process to the given product. This led to the application of factory techniques to software development.

Hitachi, which opened its software factory in 1969, is considered a leader in this area. Standardization was no accident, as company policy dictated that Hitachi establish standardized procedures for engineering, manufacturing, and administration. While the company displayed incremental improvements in productivity and quality, it found that it had underestimated the difficulty of applying factory methods to software development—particularly in reusability and process standardization.

After establishing a software factory in 1977 to create real-time control software for industrial applications, Toshiba's approach to software development emphasized the reuse of components. Four policies were instituted [16]:

1. standardization in the development process;
2. reuse of standard inputs;
3. raising the average level of worker performance through tools and other types of support;
4. ongoing training.

In 1976, NEC formed a distributed software factory network. The company believed that not all end-users wanted state-of-the-art products: products made through standardized methods and tools would serve the needs of some market segments

Fujitsu sought information and help from its United States counterparts in establishing software factories. Many of the company's facilities sought to achieve high levels of standardization, control, and integration. Kobayashi [20] describes the Fujitsu software factory as a concept in which the organization adapts itself according to the social needs of the workforce and the division of labor so that experience may be accumulated quickly—resulting in higher quality and productivity.

Cusumano [16] notes that Japanese companies have recognized the appropriateness of the factory approach to large-scale and similar projects. The common elements of the software factory approach for managing across a series of projects are:

• commitment to process improvement;
• product process focus and segmentation;
• process quality analysis and control;
• tailored and centralized process R&D;
• skills standardization and leverage;
• dynamic standardization;
• systematic reusability;
• computer-aided tools and integration;
• incremental product/variety improvement.

Other Software Factories.   Basili describes a *component factory* that is an example of the more general notions of an experience and domain factory [17]. An *experience factory* is an organization that examines and synthesizes experience, stores it, and, upon request, provides it to various projects. A subdivision of the experience factory is the *domain factory*. The domain factory specifies the process for developing the application, creates the environment to support the process, and continuously monitors and improves both the process and environment.

The component factory, another subdivision of the experience factory, develops and packages software components. The "critical features" of a component factory are flexibility and continuous improvement. Flexibility means being capable of adjusting configuration with minimal impact. Continuous improvement means the factory benefits from reusing its experience base and matures toward higher quality levels.

The USC Software Factory Project began in 1981 and has been conducting exploratory and applied research on large software systems [9]. This research has encompassed both the organizational and technological dimensions of software engineering. While software reuse has not been an explicit research topic at the USC Software Factory Project, reuse techniques that have been of interest in the context of a software factory include "domain analysis and modeling, formal development methods, reverse software engineering, module interconnection formalisms, software process reuse, representations for reasoning about reuse, group technology, and flexible manufacturing systems." [9]

Bellcore implemented a software factory with the goal of improving the software development process and the ability to manage complexity [21]. At the core of this factory is the development of the capability to reuse assets such as designs, architectures, components, tools, and experience during the software development life cycle. Particular emphasis has been placed on the ability to reuse across organizational, project, and/or domain boundaries.

The Eureka Software Factory project mission is to "establish the technical and economic foundations for software factory engineering in Europe." [23] It views its mission as being accomplished when there is effective *management control* and *evolution control* over the software development process. Management control is established when schedules, costs, and outcomes can be estimated and corrected if necessary. Evolution control is achieved when development tools and methods are available and continuously improve. These tools and methods would be supported by compatible products and services.

Humphrey argues that software development should follow a similar, yet different path from that of the traditional factory paradigm [22]. Early factories structured work into well-defined, repetitive tasks that could be assigned to workers. While that may have been appropriate for then, Humphrey warns that today's workers require a measure of empowerment, dislike detailed orders, desire some choice in their assignments, and wish their concerns to be heard by management. These early factory practices are no longer effective, even in the domain for which they were created. Software development managers should bypass such ineffective methods in their effort to create software factories, and focus on the techniques that have been proven to work.

Summary

Manufacturing strategy is an integrated set of principles that determines the use of resources, the method by which a product is manufactured, and the organization of the infrastructure to support manufacturing. Lessons learned in manufacturing can be applied to software development, for example, choosing an appropriate software development process to match the stage of the product or domain life cycle. Manufacturing concepts such as group technology, cluster analysis, flexible manufacturing systems, and mass-customization have been applied to software development. Software factories are among the best examples of software manufacturing.

References

1. W. E. Sasser, K. B. Clark, D. A. Garvin, M. B. W. Graham, R. Jailkumar, and D. H. Maister, *Cases in Operations Management*. Homewood, IL: Irwin, 1982.
2. R. J. Mayer, K. K. Agarwal, and S. Beckman, "Manufacturing strategy," in *AMA Handbook*, W. K. Fallon, Ed. New York, NY: AMACON, 1983.
3. P. Bassett and J. Giblon, "Computer aided programming, part I," in *SOFTFAIR. A Conference on Software Development Tools, Techniques, and Alternatives Proceedings*, 1983, pp. 9–20.
4. E. Aranow, *Software Reuse: Because the Waters are Rising*, The Reuse Group, 1997.
5. B. J. Cox, "There is a silver bullet (reusable software components)," *Byte*, vol. 15, no. 10, pp. 209–218, 1990.
6. P. Wegner, "Capital-intensive software technology," *IEEE Software*, vol. 1, no. 3, pp. 7–45, 1984.
7. B. R. Binger and E. Hoffman, *Microeconomics with Calculus*. Glenview, IL: Scott Foresman, 1988.
8. U. Wemmerlov and N. L. Hyver, "Group technology," in *Handbook of Industrial Engineering*, G. Salvendy, Ed. New York, NY: Wiley, 1992, pp. 464–488.
9. W. Scacchi, "Notes on software reuse in the USC system factory project," working paper, Univ. Southern California, Los Angeles, 1991.
10. M. L. Griss, "Software reuse: From library to factory," *IBM Systems Journal*, vol. 32, no. 4, pp. 548–566, 1993.
11. A. Kusiak and W. S. Chow, "Decomposition of manufacturing systems," *IEEE Journal of Robotics and Automation*, vol. 4, no. 5, pp. 457–471, Oct. 1988.
12. Y. Maarek and G. Kaiser, "Using conceptual clustering for classifying reusable Ada code," in *Using Ada: ACM SIGAda International Conference*, Dec. 9–11, 1987.
13. W. C. Lim, "Applying cluster analysis to software reuse," in *7th Annual Workshop on Institutionalizing Software Reuse*, Aug. 28–30, 1995.
14. A. Nishimoto, "Evolution of a reuse program in a maintenance environment," presented at *2nd2 Irvine Software Symposium*, Irvine, CA, 1992.

15. C. Young and A. Greene, "Flexible manufacturing system," American Management Association, New York, NY, 1986.

16. M. Cusumano, *Japan's Software Factories.* New York, NY: Oxford Univ.Press, 1991.

17. V. R. Basili, G. Caldiera, and G. Cantone, "A reference architecture for the component factory," *ACM Transactions on Software Engineering and Methodology,* vol. 1, no. 1, pp. 53–80, Jan. 1992.

18. J. J. Navarro, "Characteristics of a flexible software factory: organization design applied to software reuse," presented at *38th Annual IEEE Computer Society International Computer Conference (Compcon '93),* San Francisco, CA, 1993.

19. B. J. Pine, B. Victor, and A. C. Boynton, "Making mass customization work," *Harvard Business Review,* vol. 71, no. 5, pp. 108–111, Sept./Oct. 1993.

20. K. Kobayashi, "Fujitsu software factory approach," in *Proceedings COMPCON Fall '84. The Small Computer Revolution,* cat. no. 84CH2070-1, Sept. 16–20, 1984, p. 132.

21. J. Eng, "Implementing a software factory at Bellcore," in 5th *Annual Workshop on Institutionalizing Software Reuse,* Oct. 26–29, 1992.

22. W. S. Humphrey, "Software and the factory paradigm," *Software Engineering Journal,* 1991.

23. M. Gera, B. Hirsch, B. Holtkamp, J.-P. Moularde, G. Samuel, and H. Weber, *Eureka Software Factory CoRe,* Nov. 25, 1992.

23

REUSE PROCESSES

Reuse processes and tools are the techniques and instruments that facilitate software reuse. *Reuse processes* include methods used for producing, brokering, and consuming reusable assets. *Reuse tools* (covered in chapter 24) encompass mechanisms such as reuse libraries, object-oriented programming, and application templates. Techniques and tools have been among the most heavily researched areas in software reuse to date.

Reuse processes are sets of procedures used in producing, brokering, and consuming reusable software. An organization that wishes to promote reuse should understand its current processes, envision the desired reuse processes which fulfill its reuse goals and needs, and then reengineer its existing processes.

When used properly, tools can amplify the capability to achieve reuse. However, tools by themselves are not adequate to produce sustainable reuse [1], [2]. Processes and tools must support and be considered in the context of the reuse infrastructure.

This section will provide an overview of the basic reuse processes and tools. The processes are described at a level independent of the approach employed (e.g., object-oriented analysis and design, structured analysis and design).

23.1 Definitions

First, we will define some reuse concepts and related software engineering terms. Fig. 23–1 adapts Frakes and Terry's [3] faceted framework for existing forms of software reuse. The major facets include development scope, modification, approach, domain scope, and management. *Development scope* indicates whether a reusable

Development Scope	Modification	Approach	Domain Scope	Management
Internal (Private)	White Box (Leveraged)	Generative	Vertical	Systematic (Planned)
External (Public)	Black Box (Verbatim)	Compositional	Horizontal	Ad hoc (Unplanned)
	Gray Box	Carry Over		

Notes:
1) Adapted from W. Frakes and C. Terry, "Software reuse and reusability metrics and models," Virginia Tech, Falls Church, VA, TR-95-07, May 4, 1995.
2) Synonyms are indicated in parentheses.

FIGURE 23–1   Existing forms of software reuse

asset originated from within or outside a project. *Modification* describes the extent to which an asset has been altered. *Approach* comprises the various technical methods for implementing reuse. *Domain scope* indicates whether reuse occurs within or across a family of systems. *Management* covers the extent to which reuse is practiced systematically.

Internal.   *Internal reuse* is "avoiding redundant implementation of functionality within a single project by careful design and inspection at early stages such that selected components are identified for distinct uses within the project (system or subsystem)" [4]. Frakes and Terry quantify this type of reuse by defining the internal reuse level as "the number of lower level items in the higher level item which are not from an external repository divided by the total number of lower level items in the higher level item" [3]. Internal reuse is also known as *private reuse*, which Fenton defines as the "degree to which assets within a product is reused within the same product" [5].

External.   *External reuse* is the reuse of assets produced in one project and consumed by another [4]. Frakes and Terry define external reuse as "the number of lower level items from an external repository in a higher level item divided by the total number of lower level items in the higher level item" [3]. External reuse is sometimes called *public reuse*, which Fenton defines as "the proportion of a product which was constructed externally" [5].

White Box.   *White box*, also known as *leveraged reuse*, is by far the most common type of reuse and begins with existing assets in the software development process, modifying them as needed to meet specific system requirements [4]. White box reuse requires separate maintenance of each modified version. The majority of reuse programs, including software factories, use white box reuse [6].

Black Box. *Black box reuse*, also known as *verbatim reuse*, employs existing assets without modification of the software product development process, thereby preserving asset integrity [4]. Under black box reuse, setting parameters is one means of instantiation. Typically, the consumer need only understand the asset interface and functionality, not the implementation details. Although generally more expensive to develop and maintain, this form of reuse avoids the propagation of variants and thus, in some situations, may be more cost-effective in the long term.

Gray Box. *Gray box reuse* occurs when the "reuse component itself is not modified, but the variant is achieved by a specialization technique that creates a new component" [7]. An example is object-oriented programming where a subclass can inherit the characteristics of a super class. The derived asset, however, must be maintained separately.

Generative. *Generative reuse* is a form of reuse "accomplished via the use of application generators to build new applications from high level descriptions" [4]. Under this approach, a software tool utilizes reusable assets and automates the identification, selection, modification, and incorporation of these assets.

Compositional. *Compositional reuse* is "the construction of new software products (or systems) by assembling existing reusable (assets)" [4]. Well-established collections of reusable assets, efficient library systems, and standard interfaces are associated with compositional reuse [6]. Most of the assets under compositional reuse are code assets [6].

Carry Over. *Carry over reuse* is "software that occurs when one version of a software component is taken to be used as is in a subsequent version of the same system" [4], and is commonly practiced today.

Vertical. *Vertical reuse* is "reuse within the same application or domain" [6]. An example of a vertical domain is a class of systems such as order inventory or command and control. Because horizontal reuse tends to be of smaller granularity, larger payoffs are expected from vertical reuse defined within narrow domains.

A form of vertical reuse is *product line reuse*. A product line is a collection of systems or products having comparable traits and being intended for similar uses. The product mix consists of all the products the organization offers. This mix can vary in breadth (number of product lines) and depth (the variety within a product line). Product line reuse rations the resources required to develop a product line by capitalizing on its commonality.

Horizontal. *Horizontal reuse* generally consists of general, low-level assets common across multiple domains. Examples of horizontal reuse include user interfaces, classes of error-handling messages, and mathematical algorithms.

Systematic. *Systematic reuse* is "the planned reuse of (assets) with a well-defined process and life cycles, with commitments for funding, staffing, and incentives for production and use of reusable workproducts" [4]. Systematic reuse allows an organization to efficiently and effectively tap the potential of reuse. Reuse maturity models are intended to guide an organization through the process of implementing systematic reuse.

Ad Hoc. *Ad hoc reuse* is unplanned and opportunistic and does not realize the full potential of reuse. It is performed with little or no planning or commitments to produce, broker, or consume assets. In essence, ad hoc reuse is merely a "salvage expedition" searching for reusable components when the opportunity arises.

Additional Software Engineering Terms Defined.   Additional software engineering terms used in the context of software reuse include *reengineering* and *reverse engineering*. Reengineering means examining and altering a software system or component to reconstitute it in a new form [8]. In the course of reengineering, components from the previous system may be reused in the new form. Reverse engineering involves analyzing a system to determine its components and interrelationships in order to either create a higher level or another type of representation [8]. The process of reverse engineering may identify useful reusable components.

23.2   Producing, Brokering, and Consuming Assets

Reuse processes refer to the series of activities that contribute to the goal of reusing software. In this chapter, we present an overview of basic reuse processes and illustrate differences between the traditional waterfall software development life cycle and reuse producer and consumer processes. While we will discuss reuse processes using the traditional waterfall method as a basis for comparison, reuse has been applied to other paradigms such as the spiral model [9]. Previous work involving reuse processes is summarized in Appendix 23–A.

Experience has shown that successful reuse involves more than simply creating a repository, having engineers deposit assets, and hoping that other engineers will reuse those assets. A reuse support infrastructure is also essential. This infrastructure should define a *process* for reuse.

In its simplest form, the process of reuse consists of four major activities, as shown in Fig. 23–2:

managing the reuse infrastructure (MRI);
producing reusable assets (PRA);
brokering reusable assets (BRA);
consuming reusable assets (CRA).

These activities involve three categories of participants. *Producers* create assets with the specific goal of reusability. *Brokers* act as intermediaries, providing a repository and support for reusable assets. *Consumers* use reusable assets to produce software products and/or additional reusable assets.

Managing the reuse infrastructure (MRI) involves establishing rules, roles, and goals that support reuse. It includes designating conventions and standards; approving additions, deletions, and changes to the library; commissioning component construction; coordinating schedules and resources; and aligning reuse goals to business goals. MRI also includes establishing and awarding incentives, interpreting metrics data, and implementing economic models. In short, MRI is planning and driving the reuse process.

Producing reusable assets (PRA) involves developing, generating, or reengineering assets with the specific goal of reusability. Two major elements of PRA are domain analysis and domain engineering. *Domain analysis* consists of identifying, collecting, organizing, analyzing, and representing the commonality and variability among systems in an application domain and software architecture. It involves studying existing systems, underlying theory, emerging technology, and development theories within the domain of interest. *Domain engineering* consists of building components, methods, and tools and their supporting documentation to solve the problems of system/subsystem development. To build these elements, software

The Reuse Process

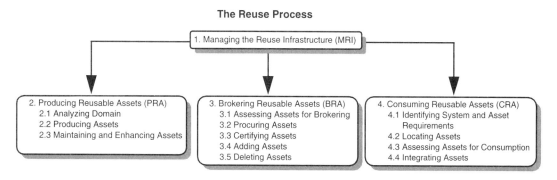

FIGURE 23–2   The reuse process.

engineers must apply their knowledge of the domain model and software architectures. A *domain model* represents the requirements in the domain by describing the functions, constraints, and structure within the domain.

Brokering reusable assets (BRA) aids the reuse effort by qualifying or certifying, configuring, maintaining, and promoting reusable assets. It also involves classifying and retrieving assets in the reuse library.

Consuming reusable assets (CRA) is the process of building systems with reusable assets. Consumers utilize the library and associated tools to learn about the reusable assets available to them; identify and retrieve needed components; integrate the components into their system; and provide feedback and component requests to the librarian. CRA is also known as *application engineering.*

23.3 Tradeoffs in Software Reuse

Several tradeoffs must be considered in the implementation of reuse. These are as follows.

High Versus Low Levels of Abstraction.   Prieto-Diaz observes that software representations at lower levels of abstraction are less reusable than those at higher levels (e.g., analysis and design) [10]. Implementation decisions greatly reduce the reusability of lower level assets. Karimi observes that since the coding phase accounts for only 15% of the software development effort, a greater gain can be achieved by reusing higher level assets [11]. Bollinger and Pfleeger note that use of assets from earlier in the life cycle results in the use of subsequent associated assets downstream [12].

However, Gaffney and Durek [13] and Balda and Gustafson [14] both argue that use of higher level assets still requires developing the subsequent assets. Malan notes this discrepancy and suggests that the mode of reuse and level of modification needs to be explicitly considered when evaluating the costs associated in reusing higher level assets [7]. Prieto-Diaz believes that the reusable components are at an optimal level of reuse when they are at a medium level of abstraction [10].

Large Versus Small Components.   Experts debate the optimal size of a reusable code asset. Some argue that small components are easier to write and use because they are not very complex, while others prefer large, subsystem-type components that are more self-contained and offer a larger payoff [15].

Belady notes that the larger a component is, the less likely it can be widely reused: either the component will have been too tailored to a specific application, or it will be so general that it contains many unused capabilities [16]. In the former case, the components may subtly encode very specific information about the operating system, the run-time library, underlying hardware, the packaging of data and interfaces, etc. [17]. In either case, reuse would likely be inefficient. Belady suggests that the best choice must be a product of experience and experimentation [16].

Sage also notes that as the size of the asset increases, the more difficult it is to reuse [18]. The smaller the size of the asset, the more frequently it can be reused. However, the benefits of small size can be offset by the effort required to manage more components. Sage believes the optimal size is a function of intended use, environment, and other factors.

Prieto-Diaz observes that smaller components are usually easier to reuse than larger components. However, this is offset by the fact that more time and effort is saved by reusing larger components. He concludes that optimally reusable code is of medium size [10].

Tracz summarizes the tradeoffs in software reuse [19]:

Component Size Versus Reuse Payoff
The greater the component size, the greater the payoff from its reuse.

Component Size Versus Reuse Potential
The greater the component size, the less likely it is to be reused without modification.

Component Specificity Versus Reuse Payoff
The more specific a component is, the greater the payoff is for reusing it.
The more specific a component is, the more likely a greater effort will be required to reuse it.

Component Specificity Versus Reuse Potential
The more specific a component is, the less likely it is to be reused without modification.
The more general a component is, the more likely it is to be reused without modification.

We will now discuss each of the four major reuse processes in greater detail.

23.4 Managing the Reuse Infrastructure

As previously mentioned, MRI involves planning the reuse effort and driving the reuse process. This includes identifying standards; commissioning the development of components; coordinating schedules; obtaining resources; establishing incentives; and implementing metrics and economic models. Although sometimes delegated to the BRA or PRA function, another role of MRI is to scout for assets. Scouting for assets means proactively identifying internal and external assets that would be candidates for reuse by the targeted consumers. An effective reuse program keeps abreast of available reusable assets, continually provides feedback to external producers, and stimulates the production of needed assets.

If scouting for assets is delegated to producers, they will drive decisions about acquiring reusable assets. Brokers would then serve primarily as a repository and distribution mechanism. In a broker-centric model, however, brokers play a proactive role in driving "make versus buy" decisions about reusable assets.

23.5 Producing Reusable Assets

Reusable assets can be created either by prefabrication or retrofitting. In either case, the production of the reusable asset is preceded by domain analysis (DA).

Analyzing Domain.   In this section, we define DA and explain its role in the production of reusable software. In Appendix 23–B, we describe and compare several DA methods.

What Is Domain Analysis?   DA is an evolving technique with no universally accepted definition or agreed-upon methodology. However, we can examine various definitions of DA in use today. Wartik notes that "domain analysis is concerned with knowledge acquisition, and also with methods to make use of that knowledge" [20]. Prieto-Diaz states that "domain analysis is a process by which information used in developing software systems is identified, captured, and organized with the purpose of making it reusable when creating new systems" [21]. Bailin emphasizes the quest for identification of commonality in his definition: "domain analysis (is) the formulation of the common elements and structure of a domain of applications" [22].

Prieto-Diaz observes that under the traditional waterfall model, the role of the system designer is to create a specific design from the end-users' requirements, and the task of the system analyst is to develop a model of an existing system [23]. In both cases, the focus is on a single model for a specific system. DA, by contrast, attempts to create a domain model which generalizes all systems within a domain. Consequently, DA is at a higher level of abstraction than systems analysis. Durek describes this process as finding a canonical solution instead of a point solution [24]. Arango notes that this form of modeling is not specific to DA, but rather has traditionally been done in requirements analysis, data modeling, systems analysis, and object-oriented analysis [25]. He also observes that, in fact, most DA authors have utilized representations and principles from those practices. What sets DA apart from the other practices is its focus on classes of applications instead of a single system.

While many reuse efforts have applied DA informally (and usually without realizing that the activity that they are performing is DA), a formalized process provides greater consistency, and consequently greater success, in reusability. The resulting assets from a domain analysis possess the functionality necessary for applications developed in that domain. A survey of domain analysis approaches may be found in Appendix 23–B.

Producing Assets.   *Producing assets* consists of developing reusable assets from scratch and/or reengineering assets with the specific goal of reusability. The assets produced are those identified by the DA and include both components and architectures. The *architecture* is the structure and relationship among the constituent components. As Kendall notes, rather than collecting and attempting to integrate random components, it is more effective to begin with an architectural starting point [26]. Such a reusable architecture defines the reusable assets, the interfaces, and the method for governing software execution.

Having identified the set of assets that have a high number of future reuse instances, two approaches are available for producing these assets: prefabricating and retrofitting.

Prefabricating.   One approach is to "build" reusability into assets when they are created. This approach has been variously called "design for reuse" and "a posteriori reuse." [27] This requires an understanding of the contexts in which the asset will be reused, which in turn will aid in understanding what is required to make the asset reusable. We shall use the term "prefabricate" to emphasize the fact that the motivation for this approach stems from the goal to preplan and intentionally engineer reusability into the asset the first time that it is created.

Life Cycle for Prefabricating.   To understand prefabrication, it is necessary to understand the phases of the software life cycle. We will define them as follows:

Investigation: initial analysis of user requirements and product risks and benefits.

Design: consists of external and internal design. External design is the detailed analysis of user requirements and definition of the product external view. Internal design is the translation of external design into the detailed design of system and modules.

Code: coding through unit testing.

Test: integration and system test through alpha and beta test.

Repair: repair of defects discovered during test phase.

Maintenance and enhancement: changing the software system/product after it has been delivered.

We will now describe the life cycle for prefabricating reusable assets.

Investigation.   Instead of conducting activities normally associated with this phase for a single system/product (also known as a "point" solution), the producer engineer performs them for a family of systems/products. For example, user requirements are collected for a family of existing and planned systems/products and then analyzed for commonality. This process was described earlier as "domain analysis."

A *risk assessment* is traditionally performed in this phase. Let us use a commercial software organization as an example, where such a risk analysis includes an analysis of both marketing and technical risks. The marketing analysis includes the projected number of products planned, market size, market penetration, and other uncertainties (e.g., the likelihood of competitors' products entering the market) all leading to an estimate of the number of products which may be sold. The technical analysis includes, for example, experience of the engineers, novelty of the product, and novelty of the technology. This assessment aids in the decision of whether to proceed with the development of the product.

Whereas a risk and benefit assessment may have been performed for a single product/system in traditional software engineering, performing such an assessment for multiple products and systems is more complex. The producer team must assess the likelihood that the consumer group(s) will require the reusable asset when the consumers themselves face great uncertainty. The producer must then decide whether a reusable asset is worth creating given the expected number of reuses. Producers must consider the needs of all their consumers and incorporate those needs into the design of the reusable asset.

If an asset is deemed worthwhile, it is produced. However, a consumer project that planned to utilize the asset in the future may decide to abort their product due to a shift in market demand. If multiple consumer projects abort, the producer group will have developed an asset that loses money. (In this scenario, the risk is borne by the producer. It is possible, however, to create a contract that assigns risk to the consumer or shares it between the consumer and producer.)

Design.   The design phase consists of both *external design* (the detailed analysis of user requirements and definition of the product external view) and *internal design* (the translation of the external design into a detailed design of the system and modules).

Existing designs should be examined for potential reuse. Design guidelines (e.g., standardizing interfaces, generalizing routines, and isolating environment-specific aspects of the design) have been created to aid the producer engineer in creating reusable assets. See Appendix 23–C for a survey of reusability guidelines which includes design guidelines.

Code.   The coding phase is the series of activities from coding through unit testing. Techniques which support reusability (e.g., parameterized procedures and code templates) should be utilized, and developers should emphasize good coding style. A number of coding guidelines have been created to enhance reusability. See

Appendix 23–C for a survey of reusability guidelines. Unit testing is covered in the next section.

Test. The test phase includes the integration and system test through alpha and beta test. For our purposes, we cover points in this section which apply to unit testing. In our definition, this phase also includes the repair of defects discovered during the test phase.

Testing reusable software is inherently more complex, because the testing plan must take into account all the contexts in which the software will be reused.

Reusable assets are afforded greater unit testing than nonreusable assets are. As discussed in chapter 11, Lubars emphasizes that the maximum amount of testing for a reusable asset is the amount of testing that would have been expended if consumers had created nonreusable versions of the asset independently. If many similar defects are found in common among nonreusable versions of the software, each unit of effort spent on testing reusable versions will have a larger payoff. These savings would be offset if the reusable version is more error-prone than its nonreusable counterpart, perhaps due to greater complexity. Of course, developers should not "test in," but rather "design in" quality for the reusable assets early in the life cycles.

As with all software testing, it may not be feasible to test every path (e.g., with a pathflow coverage tool). With reusable code, the number of paths may increase resulting in an even greater combinatoric explosion.

Regression test suites can simplify testing of reusable assets. At the Manufacturing Productivity section of Hewlett-Packard, automated test cases are stored in the repository along with the reusable code.

Many of the points emphasized for unit testing hold true for integration and system testing as well. In system and integration testing of reusable assets, the emphasis is on examining the interfaces, glue code, and the way the assets operate together.

Maintaining and Enhancing Assets. See *below*.

Retrofitting. The second approach is to examine existing assets, evaluate the feasibility of reengineering them for reuse, and if viable, doing so. This set of activities has been called *salvaging, scavenging, mining, leveraging,* or *a priori* reuse.

Caldiera and Basili present a model and metrics for extracting components for existing systems [28]. The metrics help identify potential reusable components. The process consists of two phases: identification followed by qualification.

Maintaining and Enhancing Assets. Maintenance involves changing the software system/product after it has been delivered. These changes are done to perform *perfective maintenance* (enhancing the performance or other attributes), *corrective* *maintenance* (fixing defects), or *adaptive maintenance* (accommodating a changed environment) [29].

Bollinger [12] suggests that maintenance is essentially "reuse-by-replacement," whereby a new system, similar in functionality, is developed by extensively reusing parts from a predecessor system. The new system serves as a successor for the old system. The relationship of reuse to maintenance is recognized by Basili [30] and Rombach [31].

A producer will perform maintenance to repair faults in the reusable assets and to improve the asset's reusability and other attributes. Essentially, he is performing traditional adaptive, corrective, and perfective maintenance, but with a greater emphasis on maintaining reusability.

These reusable code assets usually evolve over the life of the systems/products utilizing them. When these assets are enhanced, fixed, or replaced, the consumers are notified of the changes, and in many cases for active projects, will require integration of the newer versions of the assets.

Verification and Validation.   At one time, verification and validation (V&V) were seen as activities to be conducted near the end of the software life cycle, but current thinking is that they should be performed *throughout* the life cycle [32]. In software reuse, V&V are intended to demonstrate that the reusable asset will perform without fault under its intended conditions. Specifically, *verification* is the process of determining whether software development requirements have been fulfilled. *Validation* is the process of determining the correctness of the asset relative to the preceding phase in the software development life cycle. As such, testing may be considered as a part of V&V [32].

Bullard *et al.* [32] examined the use of three traditional V&V methods in the context of software reuse: simulation, static analysis, and mutation analysis. *Simulation* is the testing of the reusable asset in a variety of application environments. Major disadvantages of this technique include the need for a multitude of applications and the difficulty of characterizing such potential application environments by a set of well-understood parameters.

Static analysis is the verification of the reusable asset by inspecting the reusable asset without actually executing it [32]. Such methods include walkthroughs, and code and design reviews. The main advantage of static analysis is that it does not require a plethora of potential application environments. The major disadvantage of static analysis is that, in many cases, it can only detect the possibility of a reuse error. Many such errors involve component interaction between reusable assets which are harder to detect through static methods.

In *mutation analysis*, "mutation operators" are created to introduce errors into the software component. A test data set's capability of detecting the introduced errors is measured. This capability is used to gauge the test data set's ability in detecting true errors in the original software component [33]. The advantage of this method is that there is a measure of the capability of the test data to detect errors. The disadvantage is that it is difficult to construct the mutation operators. Further information on V&V in software reuse may be found in [32]–[34].

Changes to Traditional Life Cycle Activities. We now discuss the life cycle for *creating* reusable assets in contrast to the traditional software product/system development life cycle.

Investigation. For the producer, the investigation phase differs in the following ways from traditional software development processes:

- more time may be needed to understand the multiple contexts in which the software will be reused;
- producers should recognize that creating specification assets complete with downstream assets can result in significant benefits for consumers when they reuse these assets.

Design. For the producer, the design phase differs in the following ways from traditional software development processes:

- more design time may be required;
- producers must adhere to reusability design guidelines;
- increased documentation will be required;
- existing designs may be evaluated as candidates for reuse.

Code. For the producer, the coding phase differs in the following ways from traditional software development processes:
- more coding time may be required;
- producers must adhere to reusability coding guidelines;
- increased documentation will be required;
- existing code may be evaluated as candidates for reuse.

Test. For the producer, the testing phase differs in the following ways from traditional software development processes:

- more testing time may be required;
- existing test plans and test cases should be examined as candidates for reuse;

- reusable test assets (e.g., test suites) are typically created;
- reuse guidelines should be incorporated in walkthroughs.

Maintenance.   For the producer, the maintenance phase differs in the following ways from traditional software development processes:

- consumers must be informed of any fixes and/or enhancements;
- producers must understand the impact of a reusable asset fix requested by a consumer on other consumers of the asset.

23.6 Brokering Reusable Assets

Assessing Assets for Brokering.   Potential assets from both external and internal sources should be assessed before they are ordered.

Once potential assets are identified, brokers examine them, reviewing several factors. These include the following:

- Should the assets be purchased or acquired?
- What type of documentation and on-line support is available?
- Can the assets be modified?
- Are there licensing restrictions?

If the assets cannot be cost-effectively acquired from external sources, the broker may commission the assets to be produced in-house.

Procuring Assets.   Once the broker has assessed available external and internal reusable assets, he or she can determine whether to purchase or license the asset, purchase and reengineer the asset to match the consumers' needs, produce the asset in-house, or reengineer an existing in-house nonreusable asset to meet consumer needs.

Certifying Assets.   Reusable assets from both external and internal sources should be certified before they are accepted into the repository. Certification involves examining an asset to ensure that it fulfills requirements, meets quality levels, and is accompanied by the necessary information.

Once an asset is certified, the next step in the process is to accept the asset. For an internal producer, this is the actual "signoff" and acceptance of the asset by the consumer. For an external producer, this includes agreeing to the terms of the license and payment by the consumer.

Adding Assets.   Adding an asset involves formally cataloging, classifying, and describing it. To catalog the asset is to enter the item onto a list with other reusable assets. When the number of assets is large, a classification scheme (see chapter 24) may be necessary. This is a "systematic arrangement in groups or categories according to established criteria" [35]. The asset must also be described so that consumers can understand and identify whether it is appropriate for their needs. Such descriptions are comprised of information elements and are shown to the consumer according to a display scheme (see chapter 24).

Adding assets also includes the actual placement and storage of the asset in a repository. In some cases, such as at Toshiba [36] and at one Hewlett-Packard division, the actual storage of the asset is kept separate from its description.

Deleting Assets. The broker should examine the inventory of assets and delete those which are not worth continuing to carry or have been superseded by other reusable assets. Pruning the repository makes it easier for the broker to manage and for the consumer to search.

23.7 Consuming Reusable Assets

CRA involves using these assets to create systems and products, or to modify existing systems and products. A description of the types of assets which may be reused is available in chapter 2.

Identifying System and Asset Requirements. In this phase, end-users' needs are translated into system requirements. Requirements for assets are also determined as part of this analysis. In *reuse-enabled businesses*, system requirements are determined in part by the availability of reusable assets, i.e., a mental inventory of assets is conducted and the system is designed around these assets whenever possible. In *strategy-driven reuse*, a deliberate decision is made to enter certain markets or product lines in order to economically and strategically optimize the creation and use of reusable assets which fulfill multiple system requirements.

Locating Assets. Consumers then locate assets which meet or closely meet their requirements, using the reuse library, directory, or other means.

Assessing Assets for Consumption. Consumers next evaluate the assets, asking questions like these: What is the history of the asset? Can the asset be used as is? Would the asset require modification? Is the asset worth modifying not only from a development perspective but also from a long-term maintenance perspective? Would modification eliminate support from the broker group? If the asset is externally produced, what are the licensing restrictions, if any? What type of support is provided?

If a suitable asset cannot be found externally, the consumer must determine whether a reusable version should be requested from the producer group. In some circumstances, it may be more viable to create a nonreusable version for the project at hand.

A modified asset may be valuable to other projects as well. Consequently, the consumer should consider submitting a request for a modification of the reusable asset which would be supported by the broker group.

Adapting/Modifying Assets.   In this phase, the asset is adapted to the particular development environment. If modification is necessary, the consumer should carefully document the changes.

Black Box Reuse Versus White Box Reuse.   As briefly discussed earlier, black box reuse uses existing assets "as is" in the development life cycle, preserving the integrity of the asset, and thus requiring maintenance of a single base. Conversely, white box reuse necessitates the maintenance of additional versions, resulting in a need for greater resources, which in turn decreases the likelihood of economic feasibility. In addition, the difficulty in predicting the impact of modifying an asset may lead to unexpected and more expensive defect fixes later in the system life cycle.

Several studies have concluded that white box reuse is cost-effective only with a low level of modification to the asset. Cusumano and colleagues performed an extensive study of software reuse in Japan [37]. One of the companies in the study found that if more than 20% of the code in a module must be modified in order to fulfill new software requirements, it is more cost-effective to build the module from scratch than to reengineer the existing module. Tracz reports this figure to be 30% of code [19].

Later, Morrison and colleagues found even stronger evidence against leverage as a cost-effective strategy [38]. In this study, a Japanese company constructed a "make versus modify cost curve" and determined that the costs of modifying existing code always exceeded the cost of creating it from scratch. (In the reports, it was not clear whether or not the maintenance portion of the life cycle was taken into account.) This information suggests that either a very low level of modification (20–30%) or no modification (effectively, black box reuse) is acceptable for white box reuse. When we consider retrofitting pre-existing software for reuse, this suggests a break-even point at an even lower level of modification or no modification since creating reusable software requires more effort.

Given the state of information on leveraging, various corporations have taken different positions on the recognition and measurement of white box reuse. IBM has taken the position of recognizing white box components but not including them in its reuse measurements [39].

Integrating/Incorporating Assets.   Next, the reusable assets are incorporated with new assets created for the application.

Changes to Traditional Life Cycle Activities.   We will now discuss the life cycle for *consuming* reusable assets in contrast to the traditional software product/system development life cycle.

Investigation.   For the consumer, the investigation phase differs in several ways from traditional software development processes.

- More time is spent locating and understanding potential reusable assets.
- The consumer's risk/benefit assessment must consider reusable software. Risk may be mitigated if the functionality of the product/system is already available. However, the assessment should also consider the risk if consumer engineers are not experienced with reusing the assets.
- Reuse of requirements should be encouraged, as this may lead to reuse of associated assets (e.g., designs, code, test) further downstream in the life cycle.
- Decisions about which market to enter and which features to provide can be affected based on the reusable assets available.
- Estimates of the effort required and the time to market should take into account reusable software. Consequently, a product which may not have been justified without reuse, may be justified with reuse.
- Tradeoffs between user requirements and available components may be necessary.
- Certain design decisions may be made earlier in the life cycle to take advantage of reusable assets.
- More time may be available for innovation.
- There may be a greater opportunity to prototype.

Design.   Asset-centered design should be practiced in this phase. By this, we mean that the consumers need to be aware of available assets and the extent to which these assets match the desired functionality. The consumers then should examine whether the design may be modified to match the assets rather than vice versa. Reuse of designs should be encouraged as this could lead to reuse of associated assets (e.g., code, test) further downstream in the life cycle.

In the Manufacturing Productivity section of the Hewlett-Packard Software Technology Division, design walkthroughs were held to both ensure that reusable assets were being utilized in the design and also to identify assets which should be created to be reusable.

Code.   During the coding phase, the consumer utilizes tools to facilitate the reuse of code. This phase emphasizes retrieving, assembling, gluing, or integrating assets together.

In the Manufacturing Productivity section of Hewlett-Packard, code walkthroughs included an examination of proper reuse and potential usage of reusable assets. Error categories specifically related to reuse were used at the code walkthrough.

Maintenance.   Maintenance should be reduced for consumer projects because consumers must maintain only the unique portions of the product/system. Defects detected in the reusable portions of the system are submitted to the maintainer of the reusable software. Once fixes are made, consumers then incorporate the new release of the reusable asset into their products and systems. In a case where consumers know they are using very high-quality reusable assets, they can first examine the unique portions of their system (new and "glue" code) when isolating the cause of a defect.

Summary

Reuse processes are the series of activities that contribute to the goal of reusing software. In its simplest form, the process of reuse consists of four major activities: managing the reuse infrastructure (MRI), producing reusable assets (PRA), brokering reusable assets (BRA), and consuming reusable assets (CRA).

MRI involves establishing reuse rules, roles, and goals. PRA involves developing, generating, or reengineering assets with the specific goal of reusability. BRA involves qualifying, certifying, configuring, maintaining, and promoting reusable assets. CRA involves using reusable assets to build or improve systems or products. Consumers utilize the library and associated tools to understand the reusable assets available to them; identify and retrieve needed components; integrate the components into their system; and provide feedback and requests to the librarian.

References

1. W. B. Frakes and C. J. Fox, "Sixteen questions about software reuse," *Communications of the ACM,* vol. 38, no. 6, pp. 75–87, 112, June, 1995.
2. A. J. Incorvaia, A. M. Davis, and R. E. Fairley, "Case studies in software reuse," presented at the 14th Annual International Computer Software and Applications Conference (cat. no. 90CH2923-1), 1990.
3. W. Frakes and C. Terry, "Software reuse: Metrics and models," *ACM Computing Surveys,* vol. 28, no. 2, pp. 415–35, June, 1996.

4. M. Ogush, "Terms in transition: A software reuse lexicon," *Crosstalk: The Journal of Defense Software Engineering,* no. 39, pp. 41–45, Dec., 1992.

5. N. Fenton, *Software Metrics: A Rigorous Approach.* London, England: Chapman & Hall, 1991.

6. R. Prieto-Diaz, "Status report: Software reusability," *IEEE Software,* vol. 10, no. 3, pp. 61–66, 1993.

7. R. A. Malan, "Software reuse: A business perspective," Hewlett Packard, Palo Alto, CA, Hewlett-Packard technical report, Feb., 1993.

8. E. J. Chikofsky and J. H. Cross, II, "Reverse engineering and design recovery: A taxonomy," *IEEE Software,* vol. 7, no. 1, pp. 13–17, Jan., 1990.

9. "Informal technical report for the STARS program, application engineering with domain-specific reuse course description," Electronic Warfare Associates and Azimuth, Inc., STARS-AC-04102B/001/00, Mar. 6, 1993.

10. R. Prieto-Diaz, "A software classification scheme," Ph.D. dissertation, Dept. of Information and Computer Science, Univ. of California, Irvine, CA, 1985.

11. J. Karimi, "An asset-based systems development approach to software reusability," *Management Information Systems Quarterly,* vol. 14, no. 2, pp. 179–98, June, 1990.

12. T. B. Bollinger and S. L. Pfleeger, "The economics of software reuse," Contel Technology Center, Chantilly, VA, tech. report CTC-TR-89-014, Dec. 13, 1989.

13. J. E. Gaffney and T. A. Durek, "Software reuse—Key to enhanced productivity: Some quantitative models," Software Productivity Consortium, Herndon, VA, tech. report SPC-TR-88-015, Apr., 1988.

14. D. M. Balda and D. A. Gustafson, "Cost estimation models for the reuse and prototype software development life-cycles," *SIGSOFT Software Engineering Notes,* vol. 15, no. 3, pp. 42–50, July, 1990.

15. G. Gruman, "Early reuse practice lives up to its promise," *IEEE Software,* vol. 5, no. 6, pp. 87–106, Nov., 1988.

16. L. A. Belady, "Evolved software for the 80s," *Computer,* vol. 12, no. 2, pp. 79–82, Feb., 1979.

17. T. Biggerstaff and C. Richter, "Reusability framework, assessment and directions," *IEEE Software,* vol. 4, no. 4, pp. 41–49, July, 1987.

18. A. Sage, *Software Systems Engineering.* New York, NY: John Wiley & Sons, 1990.

19. W. Tracz, "The design and analysis of reusable software," UCLA Extension Department of Engineering, Los Angeles, CA, June 13–15, 1987.

20. S. Wartik and R. Prieto-Diaz, "Criteria for comparing reuse-oriented domain analysis approaches," *4th Annual Workshop on Software Reuse,* Nov. 18–22, 1992.

21. R. Prieto-Diaz, "Domain analysis: An introduction," *SIGSOFT Software Engineering Notes,* vol. 15, no. 2, pp. 47–54, April, 1990.

22. S. Bailin and J. Moore, "The KAPTUR environment: An operations concept," CTA, Inc., Rockville, MD, 1989.

23. R. Prieto-Diaz, "Domain analysis for reusability," in *Proceedings of COMP-SAC 87. The 11th Annual International Computer Software and Applications Conference* (cat. no. 87CH2447-1), pp. 23–29, Oct. 7–9, 1987.

24. T. Durek, "Strategies and tactics for software reuse tutorial," presented at Improving the Software Process and Competitive Postion via Software Reuse and Reengineering, Alexandria, VA, 1991.

25. G. Arango, "Domain analysis methods," in *Software Reusability*, W. Schafer, R. Prieto-Diaz, and M. Matsumoto, Eds. West Sussex, England: Ellis Horwood Ltd., 1994, pp. 17–49.

26. R. C. Kendall, "An Architecture of Reusability in Programming," ITT Programming, Hartford, CT, May, 1983.

27. G. Mayobre, "Reuse-oriented software development at Grenoble Networks Division," in *Hewlett-Packard Software Engineering Productivity Conference Proceedings*, Aug., 1992.

28. G. Caldiera and V. R. Basili, "Identifying and qualifying reusable software components," *Computer*, vol. 24, no. 2, pp. 61–70, Feb., 1991.

29. "IEEE Standard Glossary of Software Engineering Terminology," IEEE, Inc., New York, NY, IEEE Standard 729–1983, 1983.

30. V. R. Basili, "Viewing maintenance as reuse-oriented software development," *IEEE Software*, vol. 7, no. 1, pp. 19–25, Jan., 1990.

31. H. D. Rombach, "Software reuse: A key to the maintenance problem," *Information and Software Technology*, vol. 33, no. 1, pp. 86–92, Jan.–Feb., 1991.

32. C. K. Bullard, D. S. Guindi, W. B. Ligon, W. M. McCracken, and S. Rugaber, "Verification and validation of reusable Ada components," Software Engineering Research Center, Georgia Institute of Technology, Atlanta, GA, 1988.

33. D. S. Guindi, W. B. Ligong, W. M. McCracken, and S. Rugaber, "The impact of verification and validation of reusable components on software productivity," *Proceedings of the 22nd Annual Hawaii International Conference on System Sciences. Vol.II: Software Track* (IEEE cat. no. 89TH0243-6), vol. 2, pp. 1016–1024, Oct. 19–21, 1989.

34. J. Krone, "The role of verification in software reusability," Ph.D. dissertation, Dept. of Computer and Information Science, Ohio State Univ., Columbus, OH, 1988.

35. Merriam Webster's Collegiate Dictionary. Springfield, MA: Merriam, 1997.

36. Y. Matsumoto, "A software factory: An overall approach to software production," in *IEEE Tutorial: Software Reusability*, P. Freeman, Ed. Los Alamitos, CA: IEEE Computer Society Press, 1987, pp. 155–178.

37. M. Cusumano, "Software reuse in Japan," Technology Transfer International, Inc., Colorado Springs, CO, 1992.

38. J. Morrison, "Software manufacturing in Japan," National Technological University Advanced Technology & Management Program, Dec. 3, 1992.

39. J. S. Poulin and J. M. Caruso, "A reuse metrics and return on investment model," *Proceedings Advances in Software Reuse. Selected Papers from the 2nd International Workshop on Software Reusability* (cat. no. 93TH0495-2), pp. 152–66, Mar. 24–26, 1993.

A Survey of Reuse Processes

In the following appendix, we review several reuse processes including Beckman *et al.*, Biggerstaff and Richter, Boldyreff, Cohen, Goldberg and Rubin, McCain, Prieto-Diaz and Freeman, Redwine and Riddle, STARS, and Wade. Familiarity with the range of different reuse processes will help you design processes appropriate for your needs.

23A.1 Beckman *et al.*

Beckman *et al.* of the Jet Propulsion Laboratory at the California Institute of Technology identify the steps that a potential consumer must perform in order to reuse [1]:

1. locating;
2. understanding;
3. retrieving;
4. validating;
5. adapting.

With the steps of this process in mind, Beckman *et al.* developed a tool called the "encyclopedia of software components," which helps consumers reuse assets.

23A.2 Biggerstaff and Richter

Biggerstaff and Richter state that to operate successfully, four fundamental reuse process issues must be addressed [2]:

1. finding components;
2. understanding components;
3. modifying components;
4. composing components.

23A.3   Boldyreff

Boldyreff of the University of Durham describes a six-step reuse process which addresses both the identification of reusable concepts and their use in new applications [3]:

1. recognition;
2. decomposition/abstraction;
3. classification;
4. selection/retrieval;
5. specialization/adaptation;
6. composition/deployment.

23A.4   Cohen

Cohen describes the work at the Software Engineering Institute in developing a model of the software reuse life cycle [4],[5]. The process includes:

1. Constructing Design Methods: With domain analysis (DA) as an input, reusable assets such as components and architectures are created.
2. Collecting Control Methods: Existing libraries and new resources are assessed to create a reusable software library.
3. Creating Catalog Attributes: A database of projects and project software is created.
4. Classifying Facets in a Knowledge Base: A retrieval mechanism is developed after analyzing the applications and facets.
5. Considering Test Suite Benchmarks: Tests are developed and evaluated; benchmark data is maintained.
6. Automating Composition: An environment of composition tools (e.g., CASE, reengineering tools) is utilized to develop applications.

23A.5   Goldberg and Rubin

Goldberg and Rubin have identified the steps in producing and reusing components [6]:

1. Define: Specify the type of artifacts that should be reusable and the means to reuse them.
2. Identify: Determine the specific artifacts that are to become reusable assets.
3. Acquire: Build, purchase, or contract the creation of the reusable assets.
4. Certify: Establish and adhere to guidelines which determine acceptability of a reusable asset.
5. Classify: Select and apply a method and notation for organizing and labeling the reusable assets.
6. Store: Select a method for storing and retrieving the reusable assets.
7. Communicate: Identify methods for generating awareness and interest among potential reusers.
8. Locate: Select a method for finding assets in the library.
9. Retrieve: Select a method for obtaining a copy of the asset from the library.
10. Understand: Select a method which would reveal the purpose of the asset, and its analytic, design, or operational characteristics to the reuser.
11. Use: Select a method for integrating an asset into the new context.
12. Maintain: Select methods for extending, updating, and repairing the assets in the library.
13. Update Reusers: Choose a method for updating systems that use modified assets.

23A.6   McCain

In early work on software development methods for reuse, McCain [7] of IBM describes a ten-step process for developing reusable components:

1. perform DA for the current specification component;
2. reuse existing software if available;
3. define current specification reusable objects;
4. define current specification reusable abstractions;
5. define abstract interface specification for reusable abstraction;
6. define abstraction constraints implied by abstract interface specification;
7. perform constraint analysis;
8. redefine abstract interface;
9. implement current specification component and reusable components;
10. continue refinement.

23A.7   Prieto-Diaz and Freeman

Prieto-Diaz and Freeman note that code reuse involves three steps [8]:

1. accessing the code;
2. understanding the code;
3. adapting the code.

They note that code accessibility is supported by a classification scheme: understanding depends upon the consumers' experience and characteristics of the software and adaptation depends on the difference between the requirements and the capabilities of the reusable asset, as well as the skills of the engineer.

23A.8   Redwine and Riddle

Redwine and Riddle [9] note that for reuse to be successful, it must occur in the context of an overall process. They detail the reuse activities involved in the practice of reuse:

1. Selection: Identifying potentially reusable assets through query-based search or browsing.
2. Adaptation: Modifying the assets as needed to meet project requirements.
3. Assembly: Editing and integrating the assets as well as creating new assets as needed.
4. Cataloging: Classifying and storing the assets as well as library maintenance operations.
5. Assessment: Validating and verifying.

23A.9   STARS

The Software Technology for Adaptable, Reliable Systems (STARS) program has developed the Conceptual Framework for Reuse Processes (CFRP) to "define a context for considering reuse-related software development processes, their interrelationships, and their composition and integration with each other and with non-reuse-related processes to form reuse-oriented life-cycle process models" [10]. The model consists of two major processes: *reuse management* and *reuse engineering*. The reuse management process concentrates on the steps of planning, enacting, and learning for reuse. The reuse engineering process identifies steps for creating, managing, and utilizing reusable assets. The steps in the STARS process are included in the table below.

23A.10   Wade

Wade describes a seven-step reuse process utilized by the Federal Aviation Administration Advanced Automation System (AAS) that identifies and assigns responsibility for the production of a given reusable asset [11]. A reuse working group (RWG) composed of representatives from consumer organizations drives the process and conducts informal domain analyses. After an informal DA is performed, the reuse process begins with the following:

1. identification of candidate reusable assets;
2. assignment of a potential asset to, whenever possible, an individual that has a vested interest as a consumer of the reusable version of the asset;
3. development of an informal specification by the assignee and "completion of an informal specification sign-off sheet (that) contains the signatures of at least two" consumers who expect to reuse the asset;
4. development of formal specifications and inspection of the specification with a RWG representative;
5. implementation and inspection of the resulting code with a RWG representative;
6. unit test of the reusable code, usually with more stringent requirements;
7. maintenance of the reusable code by the RWG.

The process is highly iterative and several steps may be repeated when issues are identified.

In the table below, we present our framework of reuse processes mapped (to the best of our understanding) against other previously published reuse processes. Because several processes described in this appendix (McCain and Wade) are at a lower level, they are not included in the table.

Comparison of Reuse Processes

Lim [12] 1998	Beckman [1] 1991	Biggerstaff [2] 1987	Boldyreff [3] 1989	Cohen [5] 1988	Goldberg [6] 1995	Prieto-Diaz [8] 1987	Redwine [9] 1988	STARS [10] 1992
Producing Reusable Assets				Construct				**Asset Creation**
Analyzing Domain			Recognition		Define/Identify			Domain Analysis and Modeling
Producing Assets			Decomposition/Abstraction					Software Architecture Development/Application Generator Development
Maintaining & Enhancing Assets					Maintain/Update Reusers			Asset Evolution
Brokering Reusable Assets								**Asset Management**
Assessing Assets				Consider				
Procuring Assets				Collect	Acquire			Asset Acquisition
Certifying Assets					Certify			Asset Acceptance
Adding Assets			Classification	Catalog/Classify	Classify/Store/Communicate		Cataloguing	Asset Cataloging/Asset Classification/Asset Description/Asset Installation

Consuming Reusable Assets								**Asset Utilization**
Deleting Assets								
Identifying System & Asset Requirements								Asset Requirements Determination
Locating Assets	Locating	Finding	Selection/Retrieval		Locate/Retrieve	Accessing	Selection	Asset Identification
Assessing Assets for Consumption	Understanding/Retrieving/Validating	Understanding		Consider	Understand	Understanding	Assessment	Asset Selection
Adapting/Modifying Assets	Adapting	Modifying	Specialization/Adaptation	Customize	Use	Adapting	Adaptation	Asset Tailoring
Integrating/Incorporating Assets	Composing	Composing	Composition Deployment	Compose	Use		Assembly	Integration of Assets with Application

References

1. B. Beckman, W. V. Snyder, S. Shen, J. Jupin, L. V. Warren, B. Boyd, and R. Tausworthe, "The ESC: A hypermedia encyclopedia of reusable software components," Jet Propulsion Laboratory, California Institute of Technology, Pasadena, CA, Sept. 3, 1991.

2. T. Biggerstaff and C. Richter, "Reusability Framework, Assessment, and Directions," *IEEE Software*, vol. 4, no. 4, pp. 41–49, July 1987.

3. C. Boldyreff, "Reuse, software concepts, descriptive methods and the Practitioner Project," *SIGSOFT Software Engineering Notes*, vol. 14, no. 2, pp. 25–31, April 1989.

4. S. Cohen, "Process and products for software reuse and domain analysis," Software Engineering Institute, Pittsburgh, PA, 1990.

5. S. Cohen, "Application-based search and retrieval," in *Tri-Ada 88*, Oct. 24–27, 1988, pp. 237–249.

6. A. Goldberg and K. Rubin, *Succeeding with Objects*. Reading, MA: Addison-Wesley, 1995.

7. R. McCain, "A software development methodology for reusable components," in *Proceedings of the 18th Hawaii International Conference on System Sciences 1985*, vol. 2, pp. 319–324.

8. R. Prieto-Diaz and P. Freeman, "Classifying software for reusability," *IEEE Software*, vol. 4, no. 1, pp. 6–16, Jan. 1987.

9. S. T. Redwine and W. E. Riddle, "Software reuse processes," in *Software Productivity Consortium*, Herndon, VA, SPC-TN-88-006, Mar. 1988.

10. *Informal Technical Report for the Software Technology for Adaptable, Reliable Systems (STARS): STARS Reuse Concepts, Volume I—Conceptual Framework for Reuse Processes (CFRP)*, Prepared for Electronic Systems Division, Air Force Systems Command, USAF, Hanscom AFB, MA, Version 2.0, STARS-UC-05159/001/00, Nov. 13, 1992.

11. D. M. Wade, "Designing for reuse: A case study," *Ada Letters*, vol. 12, no. 3, pp. 92–98, May–June, 1992.

12. W. C. Lim, *Managing Software Reuse*. Englewood Cliffs, NJ: Prentice-Hall, 1998.

23-B

A Survey of Domain Analysis Approaches

Domain analysis (DA) has relationships with other areas such as knowledge acquisition and modeling. Prieto-Diaz highlights these associations with several examples involving expert systems creation and robot vision modeling [1]. Wartik and Prieto-Diaz offer a partial genealogy of DA approaches in the figure below [2]. In this appendix, we discuss and contrast several DA approaches based on the work of Wartik and Prieto-Diaz [3] and Arango [4].

23B.1 Descriptions of Domain Analysis Methods

Feature Oriented Domain Analysis (FODA).   Developed at the Software Engineering Institute, the FODA method is based on the features that a class of systems exhibit [5]. A feature is a distinguishable aspect of a system which is apparent to the user. Features which are both common and unique to all systems within a domain are identified by domain analysts.

FODA comprises three activities: *context analysis, domain modeling*, and *architecture modeling*. In context analysis, domain analysts, domain experts, and users interact to scope the boundaries of the domain. A context model is developed which is used in domain engineering. In domain modeling, models are developed with the end-user, developer, and requirements analyst in mind. For the end-user, a feature model is created which identifies the common and variable capabilities of the applications in a domain. For the developer, an entity–relationship model is developed which identifies the objects and the way they interact. Data flow and finite-state machine models are developed which cater to the requirements analyst's view of application functionality within the domain. In architecture modeling, high-level

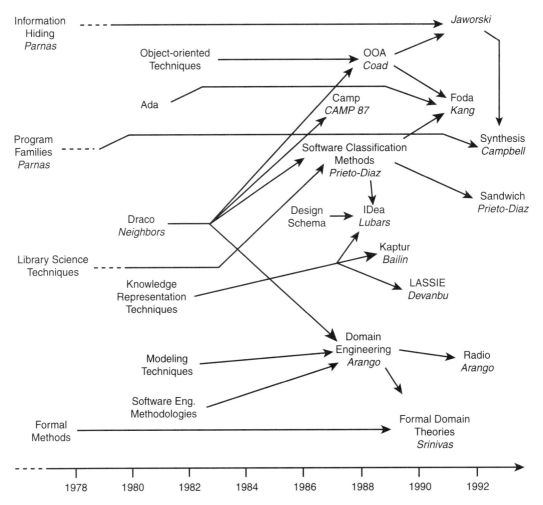

Figure 23–3   Geneology of domain analysis approaches. Adapted from S. Wartik and R. Prieto-Diaz, "Criteria for comparing reuse-oriented domain anaysis approaches," *International Journal of Software Engineering and Knowledge Engineering,* vol. 2, no. 3, p. 417, Sept. 1992.

design specifications solutions to domain problems are defined. Use of this method is illustrated in the windows management systems domain.

Jaworski.   Jaworski at the Software Productivity Consortium developed a DA approach which utilizes the object-oriented analysis techniques of Coad [6] to identify and describe the entities (objects) and their operations in a domain at the requirements level [7]. This four-step DA process provides a *domain definition, feasibility analysis, knowledge base*, and *canonical requirements*. A domain definition outlines the boundaries of the domain. A feasibility analysis determines the cost benefit of creating reusable assets in the domain. A knowledge base is created which contains relevant artifacts useful to developers. Canonical requirements, also known as *generic* requirements, are used to specify reusable components. This method has been used in the Satellite Operations Control Center, job management systems, and automobile cruise control domains.

KAPTUR.   Moore and Bailin present a DA method originally developed for NASA control centers which emphasizes a life cycle approach [3], [8], [9]. Their DA approach recognizes system development as an ongoing process, and consequently, strives to be a continuing process. To develop a generic domain model, Moore and Bailin analyzed seven control center systems.

The authors identify two perspectives in reuse-based development:

the *demand* side of reuse: the viewpoint of the system developer who creates new systems;

the *supply* side of reuse: the viewpoint of the domain developer who identifies commonly used artifacts.

On the supply side of reuse, models of existing systems are created with information from existing documentation, source code, and interviews with users. These models reveal which assets are likely to be reusable on future projects.

The DA method consists of five steps:

1. existing systems are examined and described in common terms;
2. a "strawman" generic model is constructed;
3. the reasons for differences among systems and between these systems and the generic model are examined and documented;
4. the generic model, issues, and rationales are reviewed with domain experts;
5. the reusable parts of the generic model are identified, as well as alternatives; possible reasons for choosing between them are documented.

Lubars.   Lubars describes intelligent design aid (IDeA), a design environment which focuses on the reuse of abstract software designs in the form of design schemas [10]. Such schemas are design solutions and are represented as dataflow diagrams. The software engineer is assisted by the IDeA environment during the development of software designs.

In the IDeA approach, DA involves examining an application domain to identify the operations, data objects, properties, and abstraction to formulate solutions for problems within the domain. Domain engineering is the construction of design schemas, property hierarchy constraints, a data type lattice, and rules which allow IDeA to aid in the development of designs in the application domain.

Lubars presents a seven step process (certain steps are repeated as necessary) for DA [10]:

1. identify the domain-oriented operations and data objects for solving a particular problem in the application domain;

2. extend the set of domain-oriented operations and data objects by considering other solutions to the given problem in the application domain;

3. group related domain-oriented operations and data objects into common abstractions;

4. extend the set of domain-oriented operations and data objects by considering other types of problem solutions within the application domain;

5. group related domain-oriented operations and data objects into common abstractions, as identified in steps 1–4;

6. extend the set of domain-oriented operations and data objects by considering other problem solutions in related application-domains;

7. group related domain-oriented operations and data objects into common abstractions, as identified in steps 1–7.

Neighbors. Neighbors is credited for introducing the term *domain analysis* in his doctoral dissertation at the University of California at Irvine [11]. He defines it as "the activity of identifying the objects and operations of a class of similar systems in a particular problem domain" [12]. In contrast to systems analysis, which is concerned only with a specific system, DA involves examining all systems in a domain. The Common ADA Missiles Project (CAMP) project implemented Neighbors' ideas into practice and concluded that DA was the most difficult aspect of establishing a software reusability program [1].

Prieto-Diaz. Prieto-Diaz proposes a DA technique for which tools to support the process can be developed [1]. The essential steps of his DA technique are as follows.

1. Prepare Domain Information
   1.1 define DA approach;
   1.2 bound domain;
   1.3 define domain;
   1.4 select knowledge sources;
   1.5 define domain requirements.

2. Analyze Domain
   2.1 identify common features;
   2.2 select specific functions/objects;
   2.3 abstract functions/objects;
   2.4 define specific relationships;
   2.5 abstract relationships;
   2.6 do classification;
   2.7 define domain language.
3. Produce Reusable Workproducts
   3.1 select reusable candidates;
   3.2 encapsulate reusable workproducts;
   3.3 define reusable guidelines;
   3.4 create domain standards.

Simos.   Simos presents a reuse method based on "intelligent libraries" of reusable components which are modified to suit specific application areas [13]. He describes this type of repository as an *organon*, a combination of knowledge, components, and generative tools. Simos envisions a repository that would support users in identifying and choosing reusable assets as well as configure requested components.

Simos' DA phases are as follows:

1. domain selection and scoping;
2. analysis of existing systems;
3. feature analysis;
4. separate selectability tradeoff analysis;
5. selection of appropriate technologies;
6. phased implementation plan.

In the first step, domain selection and scoping, the lines of the business are examined for maturity, stability, and commonality that would indicate high payback potential. In the second step, analysis of existing systems, Simos emphasizes the value to be gained from 1) examining multiple systems rather than generalizing a single system and 2) examining a set of systems not coming from a common predecessor but preferably rather from systems in the same domain but developed independently. Doing this would uncover logical rather than historical commonalities.

In the third step, feature analysis, application-dependent features are identified and isolated in order to abstract logical interdependencies between features. The resulting features may be represented as a linear sequence if they are dependent upon each other, and as a lattice if they are independent. In the fourth step, separate selectability tradeoff analysis, a tradeoff analysis is made, quantifying the costs and benefits associated with maintaining sets of features deemed most useful.

In the fifth step, selection of appropriate technologies, a choice is made from constructive and generative techniques. In the sixth step, phased implementation plan, the model produced can be implemented using a phased approach, starting with a minimum set of features which are then increased gradually with succeeding "builds".

Synthesis. Wartik *et al.* note that Synthesis is in some ways a variation of Jaworski's DA method but with a greater emphasis on program families rather than object-oriented analysis [3].

Synthesis consists of DA activities and precedes the domain engineering process [14]. Completion of the Synthesis activities results in a *domain definition* and a *domain specification*. The domain definition identifies the boundaries of the domain. It consists of a decision model, product requirements, process requirements, and product design.

The decision model outlines the set of decisions that developers must make to develop an application within the domain. *Product requirements* identify the common and unique behavior exhibited by the applications in the domain. *Process requirements* describe the series of activities through which an application can be developed and validated using the decision model. *Product design* specifies the architecture of each asset and maps the decision model to the reusable asset. Synthesis has been applied to a number of domains including the communication control systems domain.

Vitaletti and Guerrieri. Vitaletti and Guerrieri describe a DA process proposed for the Reusable Ada Products for Information system Development (RAPID) program [15]. The RAPID DA process consists of three iterative phases:

1. DA preparation;
2. domain analysis;
3. DA product generation.

DA preparation consists of specifying the domain, collecting domain-specific information, and establishing a domain information database. In defining the domain, the scope of the application domain is identified by "a sponsor's directive," the business area, or the extent of commonality within an application area. In gathering information on the domain, data is acquired from documents, similar systems, and interviews with experts. Information collected regarding the domain is stored into a database.

In the DA phase, functional decomposition, abstraction, and interface definition is performed. Specific objects and related characteristics are specified and grouped together in the functional decomposition activity. Object abstractions are then culled from these groups. Next, the interfaces between abstractions are identified and classified.

The DA product generation phase produces "a version of the domain model, reusable product encapsulations, recommended classification scheme terms, and recommended candidate reusable components." A domain model is developed which illustrates the common structure within the applications using a minimum set of components and interfaces. Recurring abstractions are identified and incorporated in the model. Using this model, templates are created from which code can be instantiated. A classification scheme is developed to locate and characterize the reusable assets. After abstractions and/or requirements are prioritized and compared to other applications with similar requirements, candidate reusable components are recommended.

23B.2   How Do the Domain Analysis Methods Compare?

Given the number of DA approaches available, engineers are unclear on which are best suited for their needs. Wartik and Prieto-Diaz [3] and Arango [4] have compared various DA approaches to answer this question.

Wartik and Prieto-Diaz' Survey of Domain Analysis Methods.   Wartik and Prieto-Diaz observe that there is general agreement that DA is "the analysis of some area, leading toward some predetermined goal [3]." They state that at a minimum, a DA method must identify the opportunities, i.e., what assets may be potentially reusable. Ideally, the DA method would inform the engineer which asset most closely matches his or her needs and how to modify it if necessary.

Wartik and Prieto-Diaz [3] compared six DA methods: Jaworski [7], Synthesis, Prieto-Diaz [1], feature-oriented DA (FODA) [5], Lubars [10], and KAPTUR [8]. The first three were developed in whole or in part at the Software Productivity Consortium. The remainder were developed at the Software Engineering Institute (SEI), Microelectronics and Computer Technology Corporation (MCC), and CTA Incorporated, respectively. Wartik and Prieto-Diaz essentially conducted a domain analysis on DA methods with the goal of identifying their common and unique aspects.

Wartik and Prieto-Diaz [3] developed a set of criteria for comparing DA methods based on the contextual factors discussed earlier. The table on page 432 depicts the criteria used to study the differences among the DA methods.

Summary of Domain Analysis Comparison Criteria

Criterion	Meaning	Choices
Definition of "Domain"	What a domain encompasses, how that influences what is considered a domain, and how organizations satisfy business goals accordingly.	• Application area • Business area
Determination of Problems in the Domain	The approach used to arrive at the set of problems that make up a domain.	• Problem-oriented • Solution-oriented • Problem/solution-oriented
Permanence of DA Results	Whether products of DA evolve.	• Permanent • Mutable
Relation to the Software Development Process	Constraints on process models imposed by DA.	• Prerequirements, dependent • Prerequirements, independent • Meta-process
Focus of Analysis	The fundamental concept on which analysts focus during analysis.	• Objects and operations • Decisions
Paradigm of Problem Space Models	The fundamental concept emphasized by the problem space model the analysts derive.	• Generic requirements • Decision model • Both
Purpose and Nature of Domain Models	Intended uses of the products of DA.	• Repository • Software specification • Process specification
Approach to Reuse	Strategies for exploiting the reusable components generated during DA and implementation.	• Opportunistic • Systematic
Primary Product of Domain Development	Most significant product resulting from domain implementation, guiding how other products will be used.	• Reuse library • Application engineering process

Source: S. Wartik and R. Prieto-Diaz, "Criteria for comparing reuse-oriented domain analysis approaches," *International Journal of Software Engineering and Knowledge Engineering,* vol. 2, no. 3, p. 409, Sept. 1992.

The following table describes the way each approach handles each criterion [3].

Comparison of Domain Analysis Methods

	Synthesis	Prieto-Diaz	FODA	Lubars	KAPTUR
Definition of "Domain"	Business area	Application area	Application area	Application area	Application area
Determination of Problems in the Domain	Problem-oriented	Problem/Solution combination	Problem-oriented	Solution-oriented	Solution-oriented
Permanence of DA Results	Mutable	Permanent	Permanent	Permanent	Mutable
Relation to the Software Development Process	Meta-process	Prerequirements, independent	Prerequirements, independent	Meta-process	Prerequirements, independent
Focus of Analysis	Decisions	Objects and operations	Decisions	Objects and operations	Decisions, objects and operations
Paradigm of Problem Space Models	Decision model	Generic requirements	Decision model and generic requirements	Generic requirements	Generic requirements
Purpose and Nature of Domain Models	Process specification	Software specification	Software specification	Software specification	Process specification
Approach to Reuse	Systematic	Opportunistic	Opportunistic	Opportunistic	Systematic
Primary Product of Domain Development	Application engineering process	Reuse Library	Reuse Library	Reuse Library	Reuse Library

Source: S. Wartik and R. Prieto-Diaz, "Criteria for comparing reuse-oriented domain analysis approaches," *International Journal of Software Engineering and Knowledge Engineering,* vol. 2, no. 3, p. 418, Sept. 1992.

Arango's Survey of Domain Analysis Methods.   Arango [4] surveyed eight published DA methods: McCain [16], Prieto-Diaz [11], Simos [13], FODA [5], Synthesis [14], Lubars [10], Vitaletti and Guerrieri [15], and KAPTUR [8]. He concludes the approaches are "functionally equivalent," i.e., there is much greater commonality than uniqueness. Furthermore, he notes that many of the techniques employed in DA have roots in systems analysis, data modeling, or knowledge representation. DA adds value by integrating known methods to optimize the reuse of assets when creating applications within the domain.

Arango compares the eight DA methods using a "common process." The common process summarizes the commonalities in the methods using five generic activities: *domain characterization, data collection, data analysis, taxonomic classification*, and *evaluation* [4]. Each of the activities is described in greater detail as follows.

Domain characterization and project planning consists of:

Business analysis:
  Investigate the worththiness of pursuing reuse by examining the business objectives, return-on-investment, etc.
Risk analysis:
  Understand the risks involved with reuse implementation.
Domain description:
  Identify the boundaries of the domain.
Data identification:
  Determine the availability and accessibility of data on the domain.
Inventory preparation:
  Identify documentation, applications, and other sources of information.

Data collection consists of:

Abstraction recovery:
  Understand the structure and behavior of implemented applications to recover abstractions.
Knowledge elicitation:
  Obtain knowledge through methods such as interviewing, questionnaires, etc.
Literature review:
  Understand the domain through the review of existing literature and documentation.
Analysis of context and scenarios:
  Analyze the context and developing scenarios.

Data analysis consists of:

Identification of entities, operations, and relationships:
  Model the entities, operations, and relationships in the domain with the purpose of creating reusable asset descriptions.
Modularization:
  Modularize information usually using object-oriented analysis or functional decomposition.

Analysis of similarity:
  Identify commonalities which may suggest consolidation.
Analysis of variations:
  Identify variations for encapsulation or parameterization opportunities.
Analysis of combinations:
  Identify combinations which may suggest typical structural patterns or behaviors.
Tradeoff analysis:
  Evaluate tradeoffs between the way reusable assets may be partitioned and how requirements for different applications within the domain might be satisfied.

Taxonomic classification consists of:

Clustering:
  Cluster descriptions which are similar.
Abstraction:
  Develop abstract descriptions for the most relevant common features in the descriptions within each cluster.
Classification:
  Classify new descriptions into existing clusters.
Generalization:
  Organize abstractions into hierarchies.
Vocabulary construction:
  Construct a vocabulary (domain language) for the particular problem domain.

Evaluation consists of:

Evaluation:
  Evaluate DA process and/or products.

Arango has found that the DA approaches differ by [4]:

1. emphasis on certain data acquisition means over others; some methods, for example, strongly advocate reverse engineering existing applications over other means;
2. approach to subsidiary modeling; object-oriented techniques versus functional and data decomposition;
3. overlapping subsets of software engineering notations—dataflow diagrams, structure diagrams, object-oriented analysis notations, entity–relationship modeling notations, finite-state machines, and statecharts;

Summary of Commonalities in Domain Analysis Approaches

DA steps	McCain	Prieto Diaz	Simos	Kang et al.	Jaworski et al.	Lubars	Vitaletti & Guerrieri	Bailin
Domain characterization phase								
Business analysis	X	X	X	X	X		X	X
Risk analysis	Y	Y	Y	X	X		X	Y
Domain description	Y	X	X	X	X		X	X
Data identification	Y	X		X	X	X	X	X
Inventory preparation		Y	Y	Y	Y		Y	Y
Data collection phase								
Abstraction recovery	Y	X	X	X	X	X	X	X
Knowledge elicitation	Y	X	X	X	X	X	X	X
Literature review	Y	X	X	X	X	X	X	X
Analysis of context and scenarios			X	X	X	X	X	X
Data analysis phase								
Identification of entities, operations, and relationships	X	X	X	X	X	X	X	X
Identification of decisions				X	X			X
Modularization	X	Y	X	X	X	X	X	X
Analysis of similarity	X	X	X	X	X	X	X	X
Analysis of variation	X	X	X	X	X	Y	Y	X
Analysis of combinations	X	Y	X	X	X	Y	Y	X
Tradeoff analysis	X		X	X	X	Y	Y	X
Taxonomic classification								
Clustering	Y	X	X	X	X	X	X	X
Abstraction	X	X	X	X	X	X	X	X
Classification	X	X	X	X	X	X	X	X
Generalization	Y	X		X	X	X	X	X
Vocabulary construction		Y	Y	Y	Y		Y	Y
Evaluation		Y	Y	X	Y	Y	Y	X

Note: "X" indicates when a DA method *explicitly* makes a recommendation to pursue the activity. "Y" indicates that the method *implicitly* suggests the activity.

Source: G. Arango, "Domain analysis methods," in *Software Reusability*, W. Schafer, R. Prieto-Diaz, and M. Matsumoto, Eds. West Sussex, England: Ellis Horwood, 1994, pp. 38–39.

4. different groupings of the same activities under different names; for example, authors collect slightly different subsets of equivalent activities under labels such as "gather data" or encapsulate abstractions;

5. same names with slightly different meanings; for example, "feature" in FODA does not have the same meaning in the methods of Simos or Bailin.

References

1. R. Prieto-Diaz, "Domain analysis for reusability," in *Proceedings of COMP-SAC 87, The 11th Annual International Computer Software and Applications Conference*, cat. no. 87CH2447-1, Oct. 7–9, 1987, pp. 23–29.

2. S. Wartik and R. Prieto-Diaz, "Criteria for comparing reuse-oriented domain analysis approaches," *International Journal of Software Engineering and Knowledge Engineering*, vol. 2, no. 3, pp. 403–431, Sept. 1992.

3. S. Wartik and R. Prieto-Diaz, "Criteria for comparing domain analysis approaches (draft)," in *Software Productivity Consortium*, Herndon, VA, 1991.

4. G. Arango, "Domain analysis methods," in *Software Reusability*, W. Schafer, R. Prieto-Diaz, and M. Matsumoto, Eds. West Sussex, England: Ellis Horwood, 1994, pp. 17–49.

5. K. Kang, S. Cohen, J. Hess, W. Novak, and A. S. Peterson, "Feature-oriented domain analysis (FODA) feasibility study," Software Engineering Institute, Pittsburgh, PA, Tech. Rep. CMU/SEI-90-TR-21, Nov. 1990.

6. P. Coad, "OOA—object-oriented analysis," Object International, Inc, Austin, TX, 1989.

7. A. Jaworski, F. Hills, T. Durek, S. Faulk, and J. Gaffney, "A domain analysis process," in *Software Productivity Consortium*, Herndon, VA, 1990.

8. S. Bailin and J. Moore, "The KAPTUR environment: An operations concept," CTA, Inc., Rockville, MD, 1989.

9. J. M. Moore and S. Bailin, "Domain analysis: Framework for reuse," in *Domain Analysis and Software Systems Modeling*, R. Prieto-Diaz and G. Arango, Eds. Los Alamitos, CA: IEEE Computer Society Press, 1991, pp. 179–203.

10. M. Lubars, "Domain analysis and domain engineering in IDeA," in *Domain Analysis and Software Systems Modeling*, R. Prieto-Diaz and G. Arango, Eds. Los Alamitos, CA: IEEE Computer Society Press, 1991, pp. 163–178.

11. R. Prieto-Diaz, "Domain analysis: An introduction," *SIGSOFT Software Engineering Notes*, vol. 15, no. 2, pp. 47–54, April 1990.

12. J. Neighbors, "Software construction using components," Ph.D. dissertation, ICS Department, Irvine, CA, 1984.

13. M. Simos, "The growing of an organon: A hybrid knowledge-based technology and methodology for software reuse," in *Domain Analysis and Software Systems Modeling*, R. Prieto-Diaz and G. Arango, Eds. Los Alamitos, CA: IEEE Computer Society Press, 1991, pp. 204–221.

14. G. Campbell, "Synthesis reference model," in *Software Productivity Consortium*, Herndon, VA, 1990.

15. W. Vitaletti and E. Guerrieri, "Domain analysis within the ISEC RAPID Center," in *Proceedings of 8th Annual National Conference on Ada Technology*, Mar. 5–8, 1990, pp. 460–470.

16. R. McCain, "A software development methodology for reusable components," in *Proceedings of the 18th Hawaii International Conference on System Sciences 1985*, vol. 2, pp. 319–324.

For Further Reading

1. J. A. Hess, W. E. Novak, P. C. Carroll, S. G. Cohen, R. R. Holibaugh, K. C. Kang, and A. S. Peterson, "A domain analysis bibliography," Software Engineering Institute, Carnegie Mellon University, Pittsburgh, PA, Tech. Rep. CMU-SCI-90-SR-3, July 1990.

2. R. Prieto-Diaz and G. Arango, *Domain Analysis and Software System Modeling.* Los Alamitos, CA: IEEE Computer Society Press, 1991.

23-C

A Survey of Reusability Guidelines

Many reusability guidelines have been developed for producing reusable assets, including design, code, and general guidelines. Although some guidelines are language-specific, the underlying concepts may be applicable to other languages as well.

Basic design and coding practices are certainly also important in creating reusable software. Modularity and packaging design guidelines may be found in [1]–[3].

While guidelines may enhance reusability in a general context, they do not necessarily address reusability issues associated with specific contexts, such as the particulars of a given domain, language, or operating system that may be leveraged in designing an asset for greater reusability.

23C.1 Ada Guidelines

Ada was created with the intention of increasing the reuse of software. Since its inception, a number of Ada reusability guidelines have been developed, including [4]–[8].

Following is a summary of the STARS [7] reusability coding guidelines which may be used as a checklist during code development.

Ada Coding Guidelines Summary [7]

Design:

      make cohesion high within each component;
      make coupling low;
      document each interface thoroughly;
      isolate compiler, operating system, and machine dependencies;
      make all dependent components reusable.

Comments:

      make each comment adequate, concise, and precise;
      document each subprogram with a subprogram specification comment block.

Declarations and Types

General:

      avoid anonymous types;
      try to use limited private types;
      use range constraints on numeric types;
      avoid predefined and implementation defined types;
      explicitly specify the precision required;
      use attributes instead of explicit constraints.

Arrays:

      explicitly declare a type to use in defining discrete ranges
      do not hard code array index designations.

Names:

      use descriptive identifier names;
      keep identifier names less than 80 characters long;
      do not overload names from package STANDARD.

Statements:

      use explicitly declared types for integer ranges in the loop statement;
      use elseif for nested if statements;
      avoid using the when others clause as a shorthand notation.

Subunits:

      use named constants for parameter defaults;
      use named parameters if there is more than one parameter;
      make components complete;
      write each module so it has high cohesion;
      use information hiding;
      only put in the specification those declarations that must be seen externally;

only use compilation units that are really needed;
use private and limited private types to promote information hiding;
use descriptive named constants as return values.

Exceptions

Design:

never use the when others construct with the null statement;
avoid pragma suppress;
handle exceptions as close to where they are first raised as possible;
embed potential elaboration exceptions in a frame.

Propagation:

do not propagate an exception beyond where its name is visible;
do not propagate predefined exceptions without renaming them.

Usage:

do not execute normal control statements from an exception handler.

Documentation:

document all exceptions which will be propagated;
clearly list in subprogram specification comment blocks all the conditions that reuse exceptions for each operation.

Parameters:

be sure that out parameters cannot be undefined.

Implementation Dependencies

Design:

isolate implementation dependencies;
avoid optional language features.

Pragmas:

avoid using pragmas;
if pragmas are used, isolate and thoroughly document them.

I/O:

encapsulate I/0 uses into a separate I/0 package;
do not rely on NEW_PAGE;

document implementation dependent procedures;
close files before a program completes;
do not input or output access types.

Source: R. W. Ekman, "STARS reusability guidelines," IBM Systems Integration Division, Gaithersburg, MD, contract F19628-88-D-0032, Apr. 30, 1990, pp. 2–3.

Berard [9] describes ten guidelines for increasing reusability in Ada as follows.

Ada Reusability Guidelines [9]

1. meaningful mnemonics;
2. attributes;
3. named parameters;
4. fully qualified names;
5. precise, concise comments;
6. subunits and separate compilation;
7. packages;
8. generics;
9. isolated machine dependencies;
10. isolated application specific dependencies.

Berard further observes that reusability is *decreased* when using the following:

1. literal constants;
2. use clauses;
3. default values for discriminants, record field values, and formal parameters;
4. optional language features such as pragmas, unchecked-deallocation, and unchecked-conversion;
5. anonymous types;
6. predefined and implementation-defined types;
7. attention to underlying implementation;
8. restrictive modules;
9. assumptions about garbage collection.

Source: E. Berard, "Creating reusable Ada software," in *National Conference on Software Reusability and Maintainability*, Sept. 10–11, 1986.

St. Dennis of Honeywell lists characteristics that make Ada components reusable [10]–[12]. He states that these measurable characteristics form the underlying basis for guidelines for writing reusable software. They define reusability in terms that can be understood and followed by software developers, and provide a means to control reusable software development. Some of these reusability characteristics are also applicable to other languages.

Ada Reusability Guidelines [12]

1. interface is both syntactically and semantically clear;
2. interface is written at appropriate (abstract) level;
3. component does not interfere with its environment;
4. component is designed as object-oriented, that is, packaged as typed data with procedures and functions that act on that data;
5. actions based on function results are made at the next level up;
6. component incorporates scaffolding for use during "building phase;"
7. separate the information needed to use software, its *specification,* from the details of its implementation, its *body;*
8. component exhibits high cohesion/low coupling;
9. component and interface are written to be readable by persons other than the author;
10. component is written with the right balance between specificity and generality;
11. component is accompanied by sufficient documentation to make it findable;
12. component can be used without change or with only minor modifications;
13. insulate a component from its host/target dependencies and assumptions about its environment; isolate a component from format and content of information passed through it which it does not use;
14. component is standardized in the areas of invoking, controlling, terminating its function, error-handling, communication, and structure;
15. components should be written to exploit domain of applicability; components should constitute the right abstraction and modularity for the application.

Source: R. J. St. Dennis, "Reusable Ada software guidelines," in *Proceedings of the 20th Hawaii International Conference on System Sciences 1987,* vol. 2, p. 515.

Baker notes that Ada uses the notion of generic program units to support generalization and reusability [13]. By noting in the specification of the program unit which parameters can be designated at compile time, engineers can use a general purpose unit while still tailoring it for their needs.

Gargaro and Pappas [14] discuss guidelines for creating reusable code when the methodology being used does not address reusability. They propose a set of three criteria to follow when creating reusable code. In order to be reusable, they suggest that a program must:

1. be transportable;
2. have an orthogonal (context-independent) composition;
3. be independent of the Ada runtime system.

23C.2   C and C++ Guidelines

Ogush [15] of Hewlett-Packard has developed C guidelines for reuse. Following is a brief description of these guidelines.

C Reusability Guidelines [15]

1. minimize the size of global name space;
2. reduce the possibility of name conflicts;
3. have cohesive and loosely coupled modules;
4. create generic functions;
5. encapsulate data structure access;
6. use consistent memory allocation policies;
7. use consistent exception handling policies.

Source: M. Ogush, "Design for reuse: Guidelines and principles," University of California at Irvine, Irvine Research Unit in Software, in *Re-Bay Area Round Table Meeting,* Palo Alto, CA, Jan. 8, 1993.

Chen and Lee present a method based on the object interface to produce reusable C++ components, and a five-step approach for constructing applications from reusable C++ components [16]. They also describe the results of a controlled study demonstrating how software reuse improves quality and increases productivity. To quantify the experiment's results, several metrics were collected. These included lines of source code, effort, Halstead's size metric, program volume, program level, estimated difficulty, McCabe's complexity, and Dunsmore's live variable.

23C.3   Modula-2 Guidelines

Oktaba [17] describes a four-step process for creating reusable software in Modula-2. He states that Modula-2 possesses several features that promote the design of reusable software: separate compilation of modules, import lists, opaque types, procedure types, and open arrays. Shammas [18] also describes another approach to creating reusable modules with Modula-2.

23C.4   General Guidelines

Rubin and Lim describe general guidelines in designing code to be reusable [19]:

The Modularization Rules [19]

1. Each component should perform a single logically distinct operation.

   In general, if this rule is followed, each component will consist of only a few executable statements, if written in any high-level programming language. If any component includes as much as a page of program code, it almost certainly can be divided into smaller functional components. This does not mean that it should be made into more subroutines, but only that the separate functions can be clearly identified and annotated.

2. Components should isolate all separate design decisions.

   Every future design or implementation or resource change should change only one component, if at all possible. This is a very important attribute for transportability: the changes in resources between different computer systems should require rewriting only a limited set of system interface components.

3. Every component should interact with the external system in such a way that its internal implementation can be totally redesigned without affecting the outer system.

   This rule also implies a hierarchical structuring of the components. Most of the "internal" mechanism of a component will be provided by calls to lower-level components, but the control of that "mechanism" will be in the component at the top of that particular subtree in the whole system. Thorough modularization of every internal processing subsystem will allow the reuse of much of it, even when major changes are made.

4. Only the minimum required data items should be passed between components.

   Any component should have access to no more data than is necessary for it to perform its function. Using this rule also aids in locating optimal component boundaries. There will be places in any program where there are minima in the amount of data that is necessary to transfer. (Note: on a logical basis, one item of data may be very large, such as an input file to a compiler.)

5. If a component raises any errors, the state of the system should be unchanged (except for the error indication) from that when the component was first called, unless absolutely necessary, at which point the changed state will be announced or explained.

   This rule, proposed by Parnas, imposes severe constraints on the designer. Fortunately, the most direct approach to achieving this condition is to identify all functions that may cause an error and isolate each one in a separate component. The purpose of this rule is to avoid irreversibility. If a component cannot detect the error until after it has changed the system state, then it should either restore the state prior to returning or inform the calling component how the state has been changed.

6. Use appropriate data structures to achieve efficient processing.

   The efficiency of a data structure may be based on an analysis of the processing necessary to perform the task, or on a need to minimize memory usage. These two criteria often conflict (e.g., a tree structure takes more memory than an array for the same amount of data, but may reduce processing steps dramatically for a large enough data set).

7. Use the minimum number of standard data structures at component interfaces.

   This rule appears to conflict with the previous rule. It is necessary to reach a compromise between the efficiency that may be gained by tricky special-purpose data structures and the advantage of well-understood standard data structures for ease of maintenance. Another argument for a small number of standard data structures is reusability: it is difficult to reuse a component that passes any unusual data structure at its input/output interface. When special data structures are used, they should be fully encapsulated (see the next rule). This is the best way to resolve the dilemma of efficiency versus maintainability.

8. Separate components should be provided for access and manipulation of each data structure type used in the design.

   This rule provides two useful advantages. One is that a particular data structure, say a queue, will be accessed in a uniform way throughout the system. This will add to the reliability of the system. The second is that the system is not affected if the data structure is modified or recoded for any reason.

The Reusability Rules

1. Replace constants with parameters wherever appropriate.

   All numerical constants should be in the form of symbolic parameters. The parameters can be set at compile time, or at run time, depending on the usage of the component and the facilities available in the programming language. The parameters should be independent of each other; any dependent parameters should be expressed as a function of the independent parameters. The significance and limitations of all parameters must be explained in the documentation for the component. The component must, of course, work correctly for all allowed values of any of the parameters.

2. Design components to accept a variable number of parameters.

   Many generalized functions that can be designed will utilize only some of the possible input parameters for some of their cases. In Ada, for example, not all parameters need be included in the input argument list. In FORTRAN, other provisions can be made to specify how many arguments should be used in any invocation of the subroutine.

3. Design each component to be general purpose.

   Given any set of system requirements, it will usually be possible to design many of the functional level components of the system to a higher degree of generality than the minimum necessary to meet the requirements. In many cases, this approach will produce simpler components than would be designed specifically to fit narrowly stated requirements. The specificity is supplied by the choice of parameters and the use of control tables. The effective application of this rule requires that the designer develop a strong, simple, underlying structure for the overall system and for each of its major subsystems. This approach will not only provide optimal reusability, but will also minimize system integration problems.

4. Detailed documentation must be included with every component.

   The reusability of components depends on both the actual capabilities coded into the component and how well they are understood by each potential user. A functional abstract should be included with every component, explaining what the component is designed to do, and the limitations of its parameterization. A design, written in a machine-independent design notation should also be provided to aid in converting the component to other programming languages or operating systems.

5. Each component must be correct in all respects.

   Correctness is obviously the sine qua non of any software. In the case of reusable components, the requirement of correctness takes on additional meaning. The code must not only be logically correct in and of itself, as any ordinary program component should be, but it must be correct in two other ways. It must perform correctly, or at least produce a reasonable output, for all possible values of all its parameters. If any parameter values could cause malfunction, or are unacceptable for any reason, the design and documentation should specify the allowable limits. Another problem of correctness is that each reusable component must be able to execute correctly within unknown software environments. This requires that the interface to the reusable component be rigorously defined. Where feasible, the component itself should verify that any input data is acceptable and within its own processing capabilities. Finally, correctness must be judged, not by whether a processing failure occurs within the software, but whether it does not do what a user (or external application system) may reasonably expect it to do.

Source: S. Rubin and W. C. Lim, "Guidelines for modularization and reusability," in *Hewlett-Packard Software Engineering Productivity Conference*, Aug. 1987.

Durek [20] describes a set of reuse guidelines utilized by the Federal Aviation Administration for the AAS project as follows.

Federal Aviation Administration AAS Reuse Guidelines [20]

In general, an object-oriented design approach promotes reuse. The following list highlights some of the key ideas that promote reuse. (Memory and performance should also be considered when designing for reuse.)

    a) A reuse package should contain all operations that would naturally be performed on an object at a given level of abstraction. This makes the package extensible and truly reusable because even though an operation may not be needed now, it may be needed in the future.

    b) Reusable packages should provide basic building blocks that are general so that higher level packages can build higher level abstractions. These higher level abstractions may also be reusable.

    c) Packages should have a small interface (i.e., a moderate number of procedures/functions). This will promote understanding and maintainability, and will reduce compilation dependencies. Some more specific guidelines on what operations to put into a package specification are as follows.

1. If the package contains a private abstract type, it should contain the following operations:
       a) operations to create and initialize objects of the abstract type (create);
       b) operations to access and to change the value of each attribute of the type (selectors and constructors);
       c) operations to assign objects of the implemented type and to test for equality.

2. If the abstract type is a composite, then the following operations should also be provided:
       a) operations to add and delete objects from the collection;
       b) an iterator, which allows each element to be visited;
       c) functions to obtain information about the object as a whole (such as its size).

3. After defining a sufficient set of operations, additional operations can be defined if they are needed by one or more users.
       a) use private or limited private types, where appropriate, to hide the implementation details from the users;
       b) use generics, where appropriate;
       c) make the software target-independent where possible;
       d) create "families" of reusable components where the interfaces are identical or similar (e.g., Booch's stack packages).

Source: Software Technical Note (STN), FAA No. DTF01-88-C-00042 as presented in T. Durek, *Strategies and Tactics for Software Reuse Tutorial Improving the Software Process and Competitive Position via Software Reuse and Reengineering,* Alexandria, VA, 1991.

McCain [21] enumerates the characteristics of reusable software components and notes that a software asset can be reused even if it does not possess all of the characteristics.

Characteristics of Reusable Software [21]

1. Component is applicable to multiple users.

   If a software component is needed only in a unique application for which it is developed, the component is clearly not reusable. Conversely, potential reuse can be maximized by developing components that have a substantial domain of applicability. Note that references to component "users" are intended, in general, to apply to other software entities requiring the services of the component to function properly, not end-users of the overall software product under development.

2. Component is usable.

   Component usability is a prerequisite for component reusability. If a component is not constructed to satisfy the user's needs in a highly usable manner, the component may have limited reuse even if it has a significant domain of applicability. Major factors contributing to the usability of the component are as follows:

   • specification precision;
   • user knowledge proximity;
   • interface abstractness;
   • functional cohesion.

   The component implementation should have a significantly smaller impact on the usability of the component than the above factors.

3. Interfaces are completely and accurately specified.

   All interfaces should be explicitly defined with a formalized specification that is separate from the implementation itself. The specification should include all information which must be provided to use the component, including procedural parameters, tailoring options, end-user-supplied code.

4. Component has minimum dependency on other components.

   Component users should be able to utilize the component with minimum dependencies on other components. Whenever possible, data and code related to the implementation of the component function should be encapsulated within the component itself. The usage of global data should be substantially restricted. If dependencies on other components are unavoidable, they should be well-understood by all potential users.

5. Component user requires minimum knowledge of the internal implementation of the component.

   Whenever possible, the user should view the component as a "black box" regardless of the component structure (e.g., procedure, function, frame, template, etc.). He/she should only have to understand the required interface (as defined via the formal specification) to use the component. Furthermore, the interface definition should conceal any knowledge about component data representation or implementation.

6. Reasonable changes to the component are isolatable.

   In general, all desirable instantiations of a component cannot be anticipated and certainly not implemented. To ensure optimum reuse of the component, it is highly desirable that the component be flexibly built to accommodate reasonable implementation or requirement changes. If a component's interfaces are sufficiently abstract, modification to the component implementation should have a minimal impact on the interfaces.

Source: R. McCain, "A software development methodology for reusable components," in *Proceedings of the 18th Hawaii International Conference on System Sciences 1985*, vol. 2, pp. 319–320.

Wirsing describes six requirements for the design of reusable components: generality, modularity, levels of abstraction, transformability, operators on components, and retrievability [22].

Edwards lists a set of language-independent principles to be used when designing for reuse. This list was developed by a working group which began at the Workshop for Institutionalizing Software Reuse in 1992 [23]. Edwards cautions that these principles are intended to be language-independent and thus are not meant for practicing programmers. Rather, the target audience includes university researchers and technology transfer organizations.

Design for Reuse Language Independent Principles [23]

1. separate interfaces and implementations;
2. identify and encapsulate commonality and variability;
3. focus on composability:
   a. minimize contextual requirements;
   b. use standardized interfaces.
4. focus on optimization;
5. do not allow the user of an interface to break the abstraction;
6. separate *client* information (specification) from *implementor* information (body); and separate *variable* information (parameters) from *fixed* information;
7. common part shall be able to incrementally grow;
8. design and implement common policies for:
   - resource management (memory, disk space, etc.);
   - error handling;
   - persistence;
   - concurrency;
   - development process (prototyping, testing, monitoring);
   - coding standards/practices.
9. control aliasing;
10. postpone binding time;
11. design for correctness;
12. use black box reuse;
13. minimize name space clutter;
14. specify interfaces in abstract, implementation-neutral form;
15. extension by addition;
16. define who is responsible for preconditions to operations;
    two competing alternatives are:
    a. the receiver is responsible for handling bad messages;
    b. the sender is responsible for ensuring preconditions.
17. design for testability;
    - self-check;
    - printing.
18. provide a reuse descriptor as part of the design (for classification, search, etc.);

19. design components as though they were products;
20. layer control and synchronization on top of functionality;
21. program without side-effects;
22. use only functions, and use call by value rather than call by address;
23. use generic ADTs and encapsulate specifications (i.e., interfaces) separately from implementations;
24. use pre- and post-conditions to specify semantics for each function;
25. do not consider control-flow;
26. provide DFDs, DD, and psuedo-code as documentation;
27. reverse engineer the design if necessary to ensure it is consistent with the implementation;
28. program defensively;
29. use black box functions;
30. verify and validate code extensively;
31. prototype as much as possible;
32. give signatures (types) for functions and ADTs;
33. encapsulate as much as possible;
34. use tools as much as possible (source code control, lint, make, etc.);
35. provide extensive documentation;
36. reuse library functions as much as possible;
37. use lots of (run-time testable) assertions in addition to pre- and post-conditions.
38. give axioms whenever possible (in addition to signatures/types for functions and ADTs).

Source: Design-for-Reuse: A Set of Language Independent Principles, S. Edwards, Ed. Columbus, OH: Ohio State University, 1992.

Bowen discusses design considerations for reusable software [24]. Using the Rome Air Development Center framework, he states that reuse is generally intended to mean adaptation of existing software. Consequently, he adds three additional quality factors: *portability, flexibility,* and *expandability.* Designing an asset with these four factors results with a higher level of reusability.

Moore and Bailin [25] describe some of the methods to enhance reusability as follows.

Systematic Reusability-Enhancing Methods [25]

- isolate replaceable features;
- ensure self-containment;
- parameterize;
- enrich;
- abstract and specialize;
- restructure;
- test and validate.

Source: J. M. Moore and S. Bailin, "Domain analysis: Framework for reuse," in *Domain Analysis and Software Systems Modeling,* R. Prieto-Diaz and G. Arango, Eds. Los Alamitos, CA: IEEE Computer Society Press, 1991, p. 191.

References

1. B. Meyer, "Principles of package design," *Communications of the ACM,* vol. 25, no. 7, pp. 419–28, July 1982.

2. H. Weber and H. Ehrig, "Specification of modular systems," *IEEE Transactions on Software Engineering,* vol. SE-12, no. 7, pp. 784–798, July 1986.

3. D. L. Parnas, "A technique for software module specification with examples," *Communications of the ACM,* vol. 15, no. 5, pp. 330–336, May 1972.

4. C. Ausnit, C. Braun, S. Eanes, J. Goodenough, and R. Simpson, "Ada reusability guidelines," Softech, Inc., Waltham, MA, AD-A161 259, April 1985.

5. M. F. Bott, A. E. Elliot, and R. G. Gautier, "Ada reuse guidelines," Macclesfield, U.K., Alvey Eclipse Project Report, 1985.

6. C. Braun and J. Goodenough, "Ada reusability guidelines," Softech, Inc., Waltham, MA, 3285-2-208/2, April 1985.

7. R. W. Ekman, "STARS reusability guidelines," IBM Systems Integration Division, Gaithersburg, MD, contract F19628-88-D-0032, April 30, 1990.

8. "STARS Q9 baseline Ada library reusability guidelines," Unisys Corporation, Reston, VA, contract F19628-88-D-0031, May 5, 1989.

9. E. Berard, "Creating reusable Ada software," *National Conference on Software Reusability and Maintainability,* Sept. 10–11, 1986.

10. R. St. Dennis, "A guidebook for writing reusable source code in Ada," Honeywell, Inc., Minneapolis, MN, CSC-86-3:8213, May 1986.

11. R. St. Dennis, P. Stachour, E. Frankowski, and E. Onuegbe, "Measurable characteristics of reusable Ada software," *ACM SIGAda ADA Letters,* vol. 6, no. 2, pp. 41–50, Mar./Apr. 1986.

12. R. J. St. Dennis, "Reusable Ada software guidelines," in Proceedings of the *20th Hawaii International Conference on System Sciences 1987,* vol. 2, pp. 513–520.

13. F. T. Baker, "Ada and software engineering," *IEEE Potentials,* vol. 7, no. 1, pp. 9–12, Feb. 1988.

14. A. Gargaro and T. L. Pappas, "Reusability issues and Ada," *IEEE Software,* vol. 4, no. 4, pp. 43–51, July 1987.

15. M. Ogush, "Design for reuse: Guidelines and principles," University of California at Irvine, Irvine Research Unit in Software, *Re-Bay Area Round Table Meeting,* Palo Alto, CA, Jan. 8, 1993.

16. D.-J. Chen and P. J. Lee, "On the study of software reuse using reusable C++ components," *Journal of Systems and Software,* pp. 19–36, 1993.

17. H. Oktaba and R. Berber, "Crafting reusable software in Modula-2," *Byte,* vol. 12, no. 10, pp. 123–128, Sept. 1987.

18. N. C. Shammas, "Creating reusable modules (capsule editors customize modules in Modula-2)," *Byte,* vol. 11, no. 1, pp. 145–150, Jan. 1986.

19. S. Rubin and W. C. Lim, "Guidelines for modularization and reusability," in *Hewlett-Packard Software Engineering Productivity Conference,* Aug., 1987.

20. " Software technical note (STN), FAA No.DTF01-88-C-00042," in *Strategies and Tactics for Software Reuse Tutorial, presented at Improving the Software Process and Competitive Position via Software Reuse and Reengineering,* T. Durek, Ed. Alexandria, VA: The National Institute for Software Quality and Productivity, 1991.

21. R. McCain, "A software development methodology for reusable components," in *Proceedings of the 18th Hawaii International Conference on System Sciences 1985,* vol. 2, pp. 319–324.

22. M. Wirsing, "Algebraic description of reusable software components," *CompEuro 88—System Design: Concepts, Methods, and Tools,* cat. no. 88CH2548-6, 1988, pp. 300–312.

23. *Design-for-Reuse: A Set of Language Independent Principles.* S. Edwards, Ed., Columbus, OH: Ohio State University, 1992.

24. T. P. Bowen, "Design considerations for (reusable software)," in *Proceedings of COMPSAC 85, The IEEE Computer Society's 9th International Computer Software and Applications Conference,* cat. no. 85CH2221-0, 1095, pp. 203.

25. J. M. Moore and S. Bailin, "Domain analysis: Framework for reuse," in *Domain Analysis and Software Systems Modeling,* R. Prieto-Diaz and G. Arango, Eds. Los Alamitos, CA: IEEE Computer Society Press, 1991, pp. 179–203.

REUSE TOOLS

In our broad definition, *reuse tools* are instruments that facilitate the reuse of assets; included in this definition are reuse libraries, application templates, and generators. While reuse tools by themselves are not sufficient to ensure success in a reuse program, they can facilitate the production, brokering, and consumption of reusable assets.

24.1 Reuse Library

A *reuse repository* or *library* is the mechanism to store reusable assets. Libraries range from simple repositories to more elaborate libraries which provide tiered information display schemes (progressively more detailed information is provided at each level), metric collection, and aids to support the consumer in locating a desired reusable asset. Such aids range from a simple keyword in context mechanism to a taxonomy specifically created for a particular domain.

Some organizations have successfully implemented reuse without an elaborate library. An example of this is the Hewlett-Packard San Diego Technical Graphics Division, which has emphasized large-scale reuse and has created a set of only a few reusable assets.

The importance of libraries depends on the following factors [1].

1. Libraries are less important in organizations where there is a low personnel turnover rate. Information regarding the availability and functionality of reusable assets is generally available from the producers or even the consumers of the assets. Low turnover rates may partially explain how Japanese

companies are able to successfully utilize simple descriptions of their reusable assets.

2. Libraries are less important in organizations which rely more heavily on generative methods. Although generative methods may entail the use of a repository, the selection, adaptation, and integration of reusable assets are largely automated and require little or no human intervention.

3. Representation techniques are less important where there is only a small set of reusable assets because searching is relatively easy. Frakes informally defines a representation as "something that stands for something else" and notes that representations are created because some operations may be more easily performed on them than on the items being represented. Large collections are beginning to emerge; for example, IBM's library contains more than 1200 components. These large libraries will require more emphasis on representation techniques.

We now examine approaches for representing reusable assets, information elements and display schemes, configuration management, and entry and exit criteria for the library.

Representation Method. A representation method in software reuse is an approach that enables a mapping of reusable assets to corresponding objects depicting the assets. These objects are easier to manipulate and grasp conceptually. Frakes uses this example: it is usually easier to sort a set of bibliographic records by author than to sort the same number of books by author [1].

Next, we examine several representation methods: keyword, classification schemes (enumerated and faceted), attribute–value, semantic nets, hypertext, frames, and rules.

Keyword. Vocabulary used in representation methods can be controlled or uncontrolled. A *controlled* vocabulary places limits on the terms and/or the combination of those terms that may be used to describe the reusable assets. An *uncontrolled* vocabulary has no such restrictions [1].

In the *free text keyword* method, terms are mechanically identified from the documentation and/or body of the reusable software (see Fig. 24–1). Since this method can be completely automated, it is inexpensive compared to methods which require human judgment. However, keywords provide less information about the relationships between terms [2].

vertebrates
respiration
reproduction

FIGURE 24–1   Example of keywords.

Classification Scheme. When there are numerous reusable assets in the repository, a *classification scheme* may be useful. This is a plan of "systematic arrangement in groups or categories according to established criteria." [3]

All indexing is a form of classification. Frakes provides the example of using the term "sort" to index a reusable asset. Since this reusable asset will be associated with all other reusable assets described by the term "sort," such indexing can be considered class labeling [2]. There are two main classification schemes: *enumerated* and *faceted*.

Enumerated. Enumerated classification involves dividing a subject area into mutually exclusive and usually hierarchical classes [1]. An example is the Dewey Decimal System, widely used in libraries (see Fig. 24–2).

Frakes [1] observes that the advantage of such systems lies in their hierarchical structures. Users can easily identify the relationships among terms and adjust searches for greater specificity or generality by progressing up or down the hierarchy. A disadvantage is that creating these systems requires a thorough, costly analysis of the subject area. Such systems also only provide one view of the relationship between terms. Finally, modifications are difficult, particularly in dynamic domains since they require a total restructuring of the system.

Example of Enumerated:
Physiology:
    Respiration
    Reproduction
Water animals:
    Physiology of water animals
        Respiration of water animals
        Reproduction of water animals
Land animals:
    Physiology of land animals
        Respiration of land animals
        Reproduction of land animals
Invertebrates:
    Physiology of invertebrates
        Respiration of invertebrates
        Reproduction of invertebrates
    Water invertebrates
        Physiology of water invertebrates
          Respiration of invertebrates
          Reproduction of invertebrates
Land invertebrates:
    Physiology of water invertebrates
        Respiration of invertebrates
        Reproduction of invertebrates.

FIGURE 24–2 Enumerated classification example. *Source:* R. Prieto-Diaz and P. Freeman, "Classifying software for reusability," *IEEE Software,* vol. 4, no. 1, p. 8, Jan. 1987.

Example of Faceted:
<by process facet>
    physiology
    respiration
    reproduction
<by habitat facet>
    water animals
    land animals
<by taxonomy facet>
    invertebrates
    vertebrates

FIGURE 24–3   Faceted classification example. Source: R. Prieto-Diaz and P. Freeman, "Classifying software for reusability," *IEEE Software*, vol. 4, no. 1, p. 8, Jan. 1987.

Faceted.   Under a faceted classification system, multiple perspectives or facets of a subject area are identified. For example, reusable assets in a subject area might be defined with the following facets [1]: 1) action which is performed, 2) object upon which they operate, and 3) environment in which they operate (see Fig. 24–3).

The advantage of faceted classification is that an indexer can identify facets as needed. Not all facets need to be identified at the inception of the classification system. Such a system is also easier to modify since changes do not impact the other facets. The disadvantage is that such systems may quickly become enormous. Indexers may struggle through a plethora of facets before finding the right combination to locate the reusable asset they need [2].

A faceted classification method for software reuse was developed by Prieto-Diaz and Freeman [1] where each component is classified according to a sextuple consisting of <function, objects, medium, system type, functional area, setting>.

Attribute–Value.   For *attribute–value classification*, a reusable asset is both labeled and selected via its attributes. An attribute is a property or characteristic of the asset, e.g., the language in which the asset is written. As such, attribute–value is comparable to faceted classification [1] (see Fig. 24–4).

Example of Attribute–Value:
<by habitat attribute>
    land animals
<by taxonomy attribute>
    vertebrates

FIGURE 24–4   Attribute–value classification example.

Semantic Nets, Rules, Frames, and Hypertext.   Other types of representation methods used in reuse libraries include semantic nets, rules, frames, and hypertext. A *semantic net* is "a directed graph whose nodes correspond to conceptual objects and whose arcs correspond to relationships between those objects [4]". In a *rule-based system*, information about courses of action, in the form of "if-then rules" are integrated with facts about the object, events, and situations. For example, a rule might be used to identify an asset as follows [2]:

If algorithm needed IS a sort
AND sort speed required IS fastest
AND implementation language IS C
THEN sort to use IS quicksort.c

Frames are a means of representing knowledge by storing a list of the object's attributes with the object. For example, a frame on a book may include attribute information on the number of pages, physical dimensions of the book, etc. *Hypertext* is "a structure that allows a user to move from place to place in a body of text via links [2]". For example, a consumer reviewing the documentation of a reusable asset may highlight the name of a subroutine mentioned in the documentation and hypertext can "jump" to the documentation on the subroutine.

Comparison of Selected Representation Methods.   Frakes and Pole describe an empirical study of methods for representing reusable software [1]. Thirty-five subjects conducted searches in a UNIX tools database for reusable assets utilizing four representation methods: attribute–value, enumerated, faceted, and keyword. The subjects used a single reuse library system called Proteus which supported the multiple representation methods. Measures of effectiveness were given by the following metrics: *recall* (number of relevant items retrieved over number of relevant items in database); *precision* (number of relevant items retrieved over total items retrieved); and *overlap* (number of unique items found by the method). The methods were then rated by the subjects in terms of their preferred use and helpfulness in component understanding.

Some of the conclusions from the study were as follows.

- No significant differences in search effectiveness were found between the four methods (as measured by recall and precision).
- Although the methods were not significantly different in terms of recall and precision, each method found different items from the repository. Average pairwise overlap for the methods ranged from 72% to 85%.
- Significant differences in search times were found between all methods. The average difference between enumerated average (best) and keyword average (worst) was 18.4 minutes.

- Users preferred the methods about equally.
- The subject's level of programming and UNIX experience had no significant effect on search performance as measured by recall, precision, and search time.
- No significant differences between methods for helping subjects understand components were found.

While Frakes and Pole note that a single experiment is not adequate to establish results, they offer the following advice to practitioners based on their experiment.

- Represent your collection of reusable assets in as many ways as you can afford. No single method is sufficient for locating all relevant components for a given search. Having more representations increases the likelihood that relevant items will be found. Furthermore, individual users may prefer one method over another.
- If you must choose just one method and are primarily interested in searching effectiveness and cost–benefit, choose free text keyword. All methods are equally effective in terms of searching. However, since free text keyword does not require human indexers, it is the least expensive. Therefore, free text keyword is the best in terms of cost–benefit for searching effectiveness.
- If you must choose just one method and are primarily interested in search time, the enumerated method is best.
- Do not expect any of the methods to adequately support understanding of the components. The methods were rated equally for helping users understand components, and none of the methods did better than moderately well. Component understanding is an area where other techniques such as domain analysis may be needed.

Information Elements/Display Scheme. *Information elements* are the data required of each reusable asset to inform the potential consumer of its characteristics and allow the producers to maintain the assets. Such information elements are sometimes referred to as a *prologue*. Examples of information elements are available in Appendix 24–A.

The *display scheme* refers to the way information elements are presented to the consumer. For example, users of the repository may select progressively greater levels of information as they narrow the pool of candidate reusable assets. They may also selectively choose the information elements they wish to view.

Configuration Management. *Configuration management* comprises the procedures used to identify and define configuration items, manage the release and modification of these items, document change requests, and ensure correctness. A configuration item is a group of elements which may be hardware, software, or both [5].

Configuration management is important for software reuse because of the need to manage changes to the reusable assets. Reuse projects have utilized off-the-shelf tools such as PC-based version control tools and commercial configuration management tools. Some have developed in-house configuration management tools with features designed specifically for software reuse.

Sommerville [6] discusses additional configuration management problems that occur when reuse is practiced as follows:

1. How can the configuration management team keep track of systems which contain reused components from other teams?
2. Who is responsible for maintaining a component: the original developers or one of the consumers; or, are all reused components maintained independently? How are errors and omissions communicated to other users?
3. If a component is modified by a reuser and functionality added to it, should this enhanced component be available to other reusers and, if so, how do they find out about it?

Entry and Exit Criteria.   *Entry criteria* are the set of standards a reusable asset must meet or exceed in order to be accepted into the repository. *Exit criteria* are the standards a reusable asset must meet to be removed from the repository.

Certification Levels.   *Certification levels* are evaluations of reusable assets in meeting progressively more stringent criteria toward goals such as quality, completeness, etc. A survey of certification levels appears in Appendix 24–B.

Lockheed defines reusability certification procedures and metrics as "a set of documentation, coding, quality, and reusability checks that instill confidence in reusable software [7]". They are pursuing a certification strategy of identifying characteristics of assets that encourage reuse and then provide automated methods that ensure the reusable assets actually possess these characteristics.

Kitaoka describes the use of certification evaluations on an ADA reuse repository to "filter" the repository, eliminating redundant and outdated versions and ensuring consistency of form and content [8]. A *gatekeeper* function was established to compare submitted reusable code against repository standards, collect quality metrics, and examine the completeness of documentation.

Examples of Reuse Libraries.   Following are descriptions of example reuse libraries.

STARS.   The STARS reuse library was established to reduce development costs and increase product quality through the reuse of software assets. Such assets include code, technical reports, requirements, and design documents. The STARS Reuse Library consists of four primary functions: asset search, asset supply, asset problems/evaluation, and asset catalog [9].

Asset search locates assets contained in the reuse library. Consumers can customize and execute their searches based on specific facets. Having located an asset, consumers can view its attributes (e.g., name, producer, version). Extracting an asset involves duplicating a copy of the asset from the Library into the consumer's account. If consumers want to know when an asset in the Library is revised, they can "subscribe" to an asset.

New assets and revisions to existing assets in the library can be handled through the asset supply function. The librarian is notified of new assets to examine prior to accepting them into the library. Producers provide asset-specific *data* (e.g., asset name, producer, abstract, date, version);*elements* (e.g., language, pathname, file name); *dependencies*; and *object supply* (e.g., organizations, contracts). Consumers may generate problem reports or evaluation issues using the asset problem/evaluation function. The librarian is responsible for evaluating and selectively accepting new assets, identifying facet terms, updating the reuse catalog, and collecting problem reports [9].

Alvey ECLIPSE Program: The Software Component Catalog.   Developed as part of the Alvey ECLIPSE program, the software component catalog was created to store and retrieve reusable assets [6]. The catalog utilizes a knowledge representation method called *concept case frames* for retrieval. In concept case frames, an *n*-tuple is assigned to the component where both the function and the objects upon which the component acts are described. The catalog has been evaluated by a major aerospace company and deemed useful.

GTE.   Huff and Thomson discuss GTE's focus on not only supporting reuse via organizing software components into a library, but also on understanding and adapting the reusable assets [10]. To do this, the company utilizes knowledge of the application domain programming constructs and their relationships. By doing so, the domain knowledge shows how individual assets are related.

NEC America.   Diab [11] describes a software reuse repository system built by the software reuse group at NEC America. The repository stores reusable entities which include software modules or documents.

After logging on and receiving security clearance from the system, users may retrieve relevant reusable entities using a keyword or attribute searching method. They may ask for either a brief or detailed display of information about the items retrieved. If users decide to obtain the reusable entities, they can place an order for delivery via e-mail.

The repository allows the users to search for keywords or attributes. The keyword search method has features which enable the use of wild cards, a thesaurus, phrases, Boolean combinations, and stemming (e.g., adding "ing" to the keyword as a viable search term). In an attribute search, users may specify attributes (e.g., operating system, authors) which would identify the reusable entities of interest. The users may also retrieve entities by the dates that the items were created or registered into the repository.

The repository also allows the submission of reusable entities. The submitter is presented with an entity submittal form by the repository, and the librarian verifies the information regarding the reusable entities prior to registering them.

Information regarding the use of the repository is automatically captured and analyzed. Such information includes user name and ID, the keywords attempted by the users, the attributes utilized by the users, and which entities were examined in detail after a successful search.

NASA Encyclopedia of Software Components. The Encyclopedia of Software Components (ESC) is a catalog and retrieval system which utilizes hypertext, hypergraphics, and an encyclopedia metaphor [12]. The actual content of the ESC resides on distributed computers and consists of assets in various levels of granularity. An Encyclopedia Construction Kit is provided to users so that they may submit their own reusable software.

Browsing is supported by three functions: the *bookshelf* (which allows unstructured browsing); the *searcher* (which supports query style searching); and the *publisher* (which enables the addition of assets and rebuilding of the bookshelf and searcher) [13].

Westinghouse. ReuSE is an information asset management tool with hypertext capabilities [14] which was developed by Westinghouse. The tool possesses the following capabilities: library submittal, administration, browsing, and retrieval. Searching may be done via keywords, facets, or function. Furthermore, metric collection on library performance and usage, and configuration control is automated.

Reuse SoftBoard. Originally developed at the Software Productivity Consortium, the Reuse SoftBoard is a tool which serves as an automated library for reusable assets [15]. The library tool includes the capability to import, manage, classify, catalog, query, and export reusable assets.

Standards for Reuse Libraries. Emerging standards for reuse libraries have been proposed by the Reuse Library Interoperability Group (RIG) in the form of the uniform data model (UDM). The UDM offers a standard set of asset information, allowing different libraries to exchange assets [16].

Some of the reuse libraries discussed are summarized in Fig. 24–5.

Reuse Libraries

System	Organization	Method	Contents
ESC	NASA/JPL	Semantic Net/Hypermedia	Code, Documents, and other
ReuSE	Westinghouse	Hypertext/Keyword Faceted/Functional	Code, Documents, and other
Reuse SoftBoard	Software Productivity Consortium	Faceted/Hierarchical	Code and Documents
STARS Reuse Library	STARS	Faceted	Code and Documents
NEC Reuse Library	NEC America	Keyword/ Attributes	Code and Documents

FIGURE 24–5   Reuse libraries.

24.2   Application Templates

Application templates are patterns of standard commonly used parts that serve as software development aids. McParland defines application templates more narrowly as "generic specifications for specific types of application(s)" such as financial and inventory control [17]. Hofman describes them as "existing systems, built with the aid of computer-aided software engineering (CASE) tools, that are changed at the design level and thereby customized for a new organization's use." [18] These templates provide the skeleton data models and processes for applications, which software engineers adapt to meet their particular set of requirements. Accompanying these templates are assets such as analysis, design, and code that facilitate application development.

Since a generic stock inventory application template can be independent of the type of stock that is stored [17], these templates can be modified by engineers into working inventory control applications that handle automobile parts or hospital supplies. Application templates may also be industry-specific, providing the common functionality for a particular industry such as life insurance or pharmaceutical companies.

Oracle Corporation offers industry-specific templates that use business models to create applications for the pharmaceutical, healthcare, utility, electronics, oil and gas, public sector, and other industries [19]. Each industry template includes a *high-level enterprise model*, an *applications architecture model*, and an *implementation model*.. The high-level enterprise model depicts business operations by function and incorporates industry best practices and efficient operating procedures. The applications architecture model is the "blueprint for a system's software, hardware, and network structure." The implementation model defines the various building blocks of the application architecture and utilizes CASE frameworks to rapidly develop custom applications. In addition, Texas Instruments has templates for general ledger applications and Andersen Consulting provides templates for life insurance and policy administration [20].

Advantages of application templates: According to McParland [17], beyond the quality and productivity gains derived from asset reuse, an application template combines the benefits of purchasing a third-party application with the control and flexibility that comes with building one's own application [17].

Disadvantages of application templates. Lubars [21] warns that in order to make templates viable, the consumer must believe that locating and instantiating a template requires less effort than creating the application anew. He observes that the more complex the template, the greater value a consumer derives from reusing it. However, the more parameters that the consumer is required to set, the less likely the consumer will want to reuse the template [21].

24.3 CASE

Computer-aided software engineering (CASE) is "a system of automated software life cycle support aids that permit the generally accepted principles of software engineering to be used in a practical and coordinated manner" [22]. Through the reuse of code assets, CASE has shown to increase productivity by an order of magnitude, thereby resulting in significant cost reductions [23].

The fundamental concept behind CASE tools is the use of software assets such as domain knowledge and artifacts. With CASE, such assets enable reuse earlier in the software development life cycle. Oman notes that data dictionaries and code generators within CASE promote reuse [24]. The data dictionary serves as a central repository and facilitates the reuse of assets, while code generators associated with certain CASE tools produce source code for graphical models.

Extended Intelligence, Inc., offers Reuse Process Manager (RPM), a CASE-based tool which provides a configurable reuse based software development environment. The tool supports reuse engineering, corporate reuse program planning, template-based development, domain analysis, and reuse-based object-oriented development [25].

The general advantages and disadvantages of CASE tools will not be discussed since they vary greatly with various CASE tools.

24.4 Generators

Generators are software packages used to create systems or components from a higher level, nonprocedural language. They aim for reuse in a domain that is more narrow than a general-purpose programming language but broader than a specific application [26]. Generators synthesize programs from preexisting reusable assets including user interface generators, test-case generators, and SYSGEN programs used to generate operating systems.

Advantages of generators: The effort expended to optimize the output of the generated programs can be amortized over the generated systems. In addition, consumer effort is minimized since output is generated from high-level specifications directly to code.

Disadvantages of generators: Generators require compromises in time and space efficiency in order to increase their generality [27], and the producer cost to create the generator may be substantial.

24.5   Language-Based Systems

Language-based systems emphasize the notation used to depict the system and "express common functions in a terse and elegant form." [28] The broad variety of language-based systems range from general purpose languages, called *very high level languages* (VHLL), to languages for a specific purpose, called *problem oriented languages* (POL's). These systems are most amenable to domains where the problem space is well-understood.

Megaprogramming is the "practice of building software by components in a context of architecture conventionalization and reuse." [29] Dr. Gio Wiederhold [30] of Stanford University is overseeing a research effort called Compiling High-level Access Interfaces for Multisite Software (CHAIMS), which is directed at developing a very-high level (mega) programming language for software module composition.

A module interconnection language (MIL) is a notation, language, or other formalism for declaring the interfaces and interconnections for large components which can be easily integrated into operational systems [31]. Prieto-Diaz notes that MILs provide formal grammatical constructs for determining the module interconnection specifications needed to assemble a system [32]. As such, a MIL may be considered a structural design language because it describes the system modules and the way they are integrated to provide the functionality of the system [32].

As an example of a MIL, researchers at the University of Southern California developed the NuMIL language to define how source code modules may be integrated into subsystem families via well-defined interfaces [31].

Advantages of Language-Based Systems: Because they can shield users from implementation details relatively well, these systems may allow end-users to construct their own applications. They may also allow developers to perform enhancement and maintenance at a high level, reduce debugging, simplify maintenance, enhance consistency, and automatically generate documentation. Compared to generators which are succinct and powerful in their narrow domains, VHLLs are more generally applicable to software development [27].

Disadvantages of Language-Based Systems: As with generators, however, a significant upfront expense is required to create a language-based system. Consequently, such a system is justified only if it has many uses. In addition, Kim notes that it may be difficult to obtain agreement on the language to be used, and an adequate number of people to learn the language [28]. Krueger suggests that the run-time performance of systems written with VHLLs is typically poor [27].

24.6 Object-Oriented

Object-oriented (OO) languages are another approach to reusability. Objects are packages that contain a group of related data (variables) and methods (procedures) for operating on the data [33]. In OO programming, the recurrent use of common object types is done through the use of classes. A class is "a general prototype which describes the characteristics of similar objects" [33]. An object which is a part of a class is considered to be an instance of that class.

The properties of OO which support reusability include *inheritance, polymorphism*, and *information hiding*. Inheritance allows data and methods defined in upper classes to also be used in lower classes on the same branch in the hierarchy. Polymorphism enables different implementations to be hidden behind a common interface. Taylor provides the example of defining a different *print* method for each kind of document. A *print* message sent to each one allows the document to be printed out regardless of the method [33]. Finally, information hiding prevents other modules from accessing a module's internal details, forbids outside interference, and protects other modules from depending on details which may change [33].

In an empirical study comparing the use of an OO language to a procedural language, researchers at Virginia Polytechnic University determined that the OO paradigm promoted higher productivity than the procedural paradigm when reuse was employed and that the "object-oriented paradigm demonstrat(ed) a particular affinity to the reuse process." [34] Another study by Chen found that a development approach utilizing C++ reusable components results in higher productivity and increased quality compared with using a traditional approach [35].

Advantages of OO programming: The advantages of OO programming include the mechanisms that support, but do not necessarily guarantee, reuse. These include inheritance, polymorphism, and information hiding.

Disadvantages of OO programming: Biggerstaff notes that classes still tend to be small-grained components which do not possess the value of larger scale reusable components [36]. He further notes, however, that OO systems also enable the creation of *frameworks*, large scale reusable components. A framework is "a set of classes that taken together represent an abstraction of parameterized skeleton of an architecture [36]".

24.7 Parameterized Systems

Parameterized systems are based on the idea that a user can be provided a menu of choices through a questionnaire to develop an application suiting his or her needs. End-users can indicate on the questionnaire responses consisting of "yes," "no," and "do not care" to describe the traits of the desired applications [37]. The system then creates the program based on the end-user input.

In the 1960s, IBM created a system called the Application Customizer Service whereby a user could specify the function, field sizes, and report formats [38]. Such questionnaire approaches were also pursued at the Rand Corporation [39].

Advantages of parameterized systems: The advantages of parameterized systems are that they enable the user to specify and customize the application that they need.

Disadvantages of parameterized systems: It can be extremely difficult, however, to identify the possible variations users desire. Moreover, a comprehensive questionnaire may be unwieldy, and it may be difficult to incorporate changes and enhancements over time.

24.8 Software Architectures

Krueger defines reusable software architectures as "large-grain software frameworks and subsystems that capture the global structure of a software system design [27]". An architectural framework is a model in which components can be combined according to rules to produce a series of related applications. Corcoran notes that instead of merely piecing assets together, producers first uncover the skeleton commonly shared by a group of related products, which is then reused by the consumers [40]. Given the large scale of such architectures, substantial value can be gained by reusing them. Reusable architectures include [27] database systems, user interface architectures, and design frameworks.

Kendall contends that rather than collecting and attempting to integrate random components, a more effective approach requires an architectural starting point [41]. Such a reusable architecture defines the reusable assets, the interfaces, and the method for governing software execution.

Advantages of reusable architectures: Since high-level abstractions are used to create software, savings in time and effort are significant. Furthermore, reusable architectures may be composed to create higher level architectures or stand-alone to develop applications [27].

Disadvantages of reusable architectures: Creating reusable architectures is difficult [27]. Many architectures will be required for a general purpose library, with estimates ranging from 100 to more than 1500 [42].

24.9 Software Schemas

Software schemas are an extension to reusable software components, but their "emphasis is on reusing abstract algorithms and data structures rather than reusing code [27]".

Krueger uses the PARIS system developed by Katz as an example of software schema [43]. In the PARIS system, the schema is instantiated to produce source code. The PARIS system takes a problem statement provided by the engineer and identifies a suitable schema, which when instantiated, properly addresses the problem.

Advantages of Schemas: Krueger notes that automated tools can be utilized for selecting, specializing, and integrating when the basis for schemas are formal specifications [27] and that schemas allow engineers to work at a higher level of abstraction.

Disadvantages of Schemas: Krueger also notes, however, that formal specifications for schemas can be sizable and complex [27]. Even with the aid of automated tools, it may be difficult to select, understand, and utilize schemas.

24.10   Subroutine Libraries

Horowitz notes that subroutine libraries come in two forms: 1) those which contain a set of functions (or procedures) considered to be of general use to the computing community and 2) those which are combined to form solutions to problems in a single application area [44]. Examples of the latter include statistical libraries (e.g., Statistical Package for the Social Sciences) or numerical analysis libraries (e.g., International Mathematical and Statistical Libraries).

Advantages of subroutine libraries: Applications developed using subroutine libraries have been machine efficient. These domains tend to be well-understood and narrow domains.

Disadvantages of subroutine libraries: Subroutine libraries have been successful in several narrow areas, they have enjoyed only limited success in others. This is due in part to the inherent difficulty in creating usable and efficient parameter-based systems. Also, in many cases, the code is dependent upon the environment where it was developed. Finally, repository-related issues have impeded the use of small routines.

24.11   Transformational Systems

A *transformation* is the incremental conversion of specifications through a sequence of expansions into a working program. Horowitz defines it simply as "taking high-level operational specifications and transforming them into efficient programs." [44]

Horowitz notes that in transformational systems, the original programs are often stated utilizing a few mutually recursive procedures. The transformation system produces an efficient program by successively refining each function, possibly introducing new variables and data structures [44]. An example of a transformational system may be found in [45].

Advantage of transformational systems: Because transformational systems can use abstractions at a higher level than VHLLs, they can produce more efficient implementations than with VHLL compilers [27].

Disadvantage of transformational systems: Because such transformations may require human guidance, time and effort are required from the software developer [27]. However, an increasing amount of this effort is being automated.

Summary

Reuse tools are instruments which facilitate software reuse. One such tool is the reuse library and its integral parts: representation method, information elements/display scheme, configuration management, entry and exit criteria, and certification levels. Other tools include application templates, CASE tools, generators, and software architectures. Tools can amplify our capabilities to achieve reuse, but are not adequate by themselves to produce sustainable reuse.

References

1. W. B. Frakes and T. P. Pole, "An empirical study of representation methods for reusable software components," *IEEE Transactions on Software Engineering*, vol. 20, no. 8, pp. 617–630, Aug. 1994.
2. W. B. Frakes and P. B. Gandel, "Representation methods for software reuse," in *Proceedings TRI-Ada '89*, Oct. 23–26, 1989, pp. 302–304.
3. *Merriam Webster Collegiate Dictionary*. Springfield, MA: Merriam, 1997.
4. W. B. Frakes and P. B. Gandel, "Representing reusable software," *Information and Software Technology*, vol. 32, no. 10, pp. 653–664, Dec. 1990.
5. "IEEE standard glossary of software engineering terminology," IEEE, New York, NY, IEEE Standard 729–1983, 1983.
6. I. Sommerville, "Information systems factory study software reuse," University of Lancaster, Lancaster, U.K., Jan. 1, 1988.
7. S. Patel, A. Stein, P. Cohen, R. Baxter, and S. Sherman, "Certification of reusable components," in *5th Annual Workshop on Institutionalizing Software Reuse*, Oct. 26–29, 1992.
8. B. J. Kitaoka, "Establishing Ada repositories for reuse," in *Proceedings TRI-Ada 89*, Oct. 23–26, 1989, pp. 315–323.
9. "STARS reuse library user's guide," Science Applications International Corporation, Orlando, FL, contract F19628-88-D0032, May 1991.
10. K. Huff and R. Thomson, "Supporting understanding and adaptation in software reuse," presented at *1st International Conference on Software Reuse*, Dortmund, Germany, 1991.
11. M. Diab, "Software reuse repository," in *4th Annual Workshop on Institutionalizing Software Reuse*, Nov. 18–22, 1991.
12. "Encyclopedia of software components: The requirements document," Jet Propulsion Laboratory, California Institute of Technology, Pasadena, JPL D-7839, Oct. 1990.
13. L. Van Warren and B. C. Beckman, "System for retrieving reusable software," Jet Propulsion Laboratory, California Institute of Technology, Pasadena, Jet Propulsion Laboratory Technology Report, NPO-18435/7974, June 1993.

14. E. Beser, "A hypertext reusable library system white paper," Westinghouse Electronic Systems Group, Baltimore, MD, 1988.

15. J. Conlon, Atherton Technologies, Inc., Fremont, CA.

16. G. H. Anthes, "Users look for standards on reuse libraries," *Computerworld*, vol. 28, no. 21, p. 97, 1994.

17. P. McParland, "Application templates: Reusable design," in *Integrated Software Reuse: Management and Techniques*, P. Walton and N. Maiden, Eds. Brookfield, VT: Ashgate, 1993, pp. 109–111.

18. J. D. Hofman and J. F. Rockart, "Application templates: Faster, better, and cheaper systems," *Sloan Management Review*, vol. 36, no. 1, pp. 49–60, Fall 1994.

19. "Oracle consulting literature," Oracle Corporation, Redwood Shores, CA, 1993.

20. G. H. Anthes, "Software reuse plans bring paybacks," *Computerworld*, vol. 27, no. 49, pp. 73–76, Dec. 6, 1993.

21. M. D. Lubars, "Code reusability in the large versus code reusability in the small," *SIGSOFT Software Engineering Notes*, vol. 11, no. 1, pp. 21–28, Jan. 1986.

22. J. H. Manley, "Computer-aided software engineering (CASE) foundation for software factories," in *Proceedings IEEE Computer Society International Conference*, Sept. 1984, pp. 84–91.

23. R. D. Banker and R. J. Kauffman, "An empirical assessment of CASE technology: A study of productivity, reuse, and functionality," New York University, New York, NY, 1990.

24. P. W. Oman, A. J. Bowles, R. Mount, G. Karam, D. Kalinsky, M. Tervonen, V. Bundonis, H. Fischer, M. Fish, D. Longshore, and N. Akiha, "CASE: Analysis and design tools," *IEEE Software*, vol. 7, no. 3, pp. 37–43, May 1990.

25. "Reuse process manager (RPM)," Extended Intelligence, Inc., Chicago, IL, 1997.

26. P. Wegner, "Varieties of reusability," presented at *ITT Workshop on Reusability in Programming*, Newport, RI, 1983.

27. C. W. Krueger, "Software reuse," *ACM Computing Surveys*, vol. 24, no. 2, pp. 131–183, June 1992.

28. Y. Kim and E. A. Stohr, "Software reuse: Issues and research directions," in *Proceedings of the 25th Hawaii International Conference on System Sciences* cat. no. 91TH0394-7, 1991.

29. B. W. Boehm and W. L. Scherlis, "Megaprogramming" presented at *DARPA Software Technology Conference*, Los Angeles, CA, 1992.

30. G. Wiederhold, P. Wegner, and S. Ceri, "Toward mega programming," *Communications of the ACM*, vol. 35, no. 11, pp. 89–99, Nov. 1992.

31. W. Scacchi, "Notes on software reuse in the USC system factory project," University of Southern California, Los Angeles, CA, working paper, 1991.

32. R. Prieto-Diaz and J. M. Neighbors, "Module interconnection languages," *Journal of Systems and Software*, vol. 6, no. 4, pp. 307–334, Nov. 1986.

33. D. A. Taylor, *Object-Oriented Technology: A Manager's Guide*. Reading, MA: Addison-Wesley, 1992.

34. J. A. Lewis, S. M. Henry, D. G. Kafura, and R. S. Schulman, "On the relationship between the object-oriented paradigm and software reuse: An empirical investigation," *Journal of Object-Oriented Programming*, vol. 5, no. 4, pp. 35–41, July–Aug., 1992.

35. D.-J. Chen and P. J. Lee, "On the study of software reuse using reusable C++ components," *Journal of Systems & Software*, vol. 20, no. 1, pp. 19–36, Jan. 1993.

36. T. J. Biggerstaff, "An assessment and analysis of software reuse," in *Advances in Computers*, M. C. Yovits, Ed. New York, NY: Academic, 1992, vol. 34.

37. A. F. Cardenas, "Technology generation for automatic generation of application programs," *MIS Quarterly*, pp. 49–72, Sept. 1977.

38. R. D. Gordon, "The modular application customizing system," *IBM Systems Journal*, vol. 19, no. 4, pp. 521–541, 1980.

39. A. S. Ginsburg, H. M. Markowitz, and P. M. Oldfather, "Programming by questionnaire," in *Proceedings 1967 Spring Joint Computer Conference*, pp. 441–446.

40. E. Corcoran, "Soft Lego," *Scientific American*, vol. 276, no. 1, pp. 145–146, Jan. 1993.

41. R. C. Kendall, "An architecture of reusability in programming," *ITT Programming*, Hartford, CT, May 1983.

42. T. C. Jones, "Reusability in programming: A survey of the state of the art," *IEEE Transactions on Software Engineering*, vol. SE-10, no. 5, pp. 488–493, Sept. 1984.

43. S. Katz, C. A. Richter, and K. The, "PARIS: A system for reusing partially interpreted schemas," in *Proceedings of the 9th International Conference on Software Engineering*, cat. no. 87CH2432-3, Mar . 30–Apr. 2, 1987, pp. 377–389.

44. E. Horowitz and J. B. Munson, "An expansive view of reusable software," *IEEE Transactions on Software Engineering*, vol. SE-10, no. 5, pp. 477–487, Sept. 1984.

45. T. E. Cheatham, Jr., "Reusability through program transformations," *IEEE Transactions on Software Engineering*, vol. SE-10, no. 5, pp. 589–594, Sept. 1984.

24-A

A SURVEY OF INFORMATION ELEMENTS (PROLOGUES)

In this appendix, we survey several prologues which are used by organizations or recommended by experts in the field. A prologue is the set of information collected for a reusable asset and displayed (sometimes progressively disclosed) to the consumer as he searches for assets. Another survey of prologues is covered by Tracz [1].

24A.1 Braun and Ruegsegger

The following material is from C. L. Braun and T. B. Ruegsegger, *Software Reusability and Ada*, Softech, Inc., Waltham, MA, 1990, p. 11.

Functional Description

Suggested Outline

1. Functional Summary
   1.1 Component Function
   1.2 Scope of Reuse
2. Documentation References
3. Performance Characteristics
   3.1 Sizing
   3.2 Timing
   3.3 Others
4. Known Limitations
5. User Modification/Customization Provisions
6. Partial Reuse Potential
7. Special Design Considerations

8. Error Handling
9. What to Do If a Problem Occurs
    9.1 Troubleshooting
    9.2 Whom to Contact
  10. Examples of Use

24A.2 NATO

The following material is from *NATO Standard for Software Reuse Procedures,* vol. 3, NATO Communications and Information Systems Agency.

    Reuser's Manual
1. Introduction
      Purpose of the document
      Overview of the component
2. Function
      Operation
      Scope
3. Interfaces
      Reusable software component (RSC) specification
      External references and parameters
      Interfaces by class
4. Performance
      Assumptions
      Resource requirements
      Exceptions (how the RSC responds to incorrect inputs)
      Test results (any performance measurements)
      Known limitations
5. Installation
      How to instantiate the component (e.g., generic parameters)
      Interfaces (enumerate and use)
      Partial reuse provisions
      Modification provisions
      Diagnostic procedures (what to do if a problem occurs)
      Usage examples
6. Procurement and Support
      Source (if not in library)
      Ownership (any legal or contractual restrictions)
      Maintenance (what support is available; points of contact)
7. Reference (any available documentation)
8. Appendices (as appropriate)

24A.3   Frakes and Nemjeh

The following material is from W. B. Frakes and B. A. Nemjeh, "An information system for software reuse," in *Software Reuse: Emerging Technology*, W. Tracz, Ed., Los Alamitos, CA: IEEE Computer Society Press, 1988, pp. 147–148.

1. Module Prologue

   The following fields are suggested for a module prologue.
   - Module: The name of the module.
   - Abstract: A concise and short (less than 10 lines) synopsis of the module.

   Description: A concise description of what the functions contained in the file do. This description should written with an understanding that generic inquiries into the source database will be matched on the prose appearing in this section of the file.
   - Supporting Documents: References to supporting requirements or design documents should be given here.
   - Size: Number of functions in module, number of lines of code in module, and object code size for each machine on which the module runs.
   - Contents: List the functions appearing in the file in the order in which they appear, with brief description of each function.
   - Data: List the global data defined in the file with a brief description of each data item.
   - Environmental Requirements: List the hardware and software that the module requires (e.g., certain kinds of hardware, compilers software libraries, operating systems, tools, database, etc.) to function properly.
   - Documentation Quality: State the comment-to-code ratio for the module and the documentation standards used for the module.
   - Portability: List the machines on which the module will run.
   - Programming Standards: List the programming standards document used in the module.
   - Time in Use: State the amount of time the module has been used prior to being added to the reuse data base.
   - Reuse Statistics: List each project that has used all or part of the module, how the module was used, when the module was used, and the person who used the module.
   - Reuse Reviews: Comments from others that have reused all or part of the module. Comments should be related to the performance, functionality, modifiability, testability, and understandability of the module.

2. Function Prologue

   The following format is recommended for a function prologue.
   - Function: The name of the function.

- Author: Name, location, and phone number of developer who wrote the function.
- Date: Date the function was written.
- Abstract: A concise and short (less than 5 lines) synopsis of the function.
- Description: A concise overview of the function in terms of the processing it performs. In addition, the input, output, and transformational processing performed by the function should be described.
- Keywords: Useful and pertinent keywords that can be used for quick searches.
- Size: Number of lines of code in function and object code size for each machine the function runs on.
- Complexity: Number of acyclic execution paths through function, number of logical conditions in the function, and any other complexity metrics available for the function.
- Performance: Execution times required by function for different data sets.
- Inspection: State whether or not the function has been inspected or reviewed.
- Testing: Specify the types of testing that have been done on the function (unit test, integration test, system test), the statement or branch coverage achieved on the function, and the location of test suites for the function (if available).
- Usage: List the #include files necessary to call the function.
- Parameters: The parameters passed to the function with a description of each parameter should appear here. For pointer parameters, the object pointed to should be discussed. Finally, if the value of any parameter is changed by the function, the modification should be described.
- Externals: All of the global variables referenced in the function, along with how their values are modified should be described here.
- Macros: List the macros used by the function.
- Returns: The value returned by the function should be described here. The function should be declared "void" if it does not return a value.
- Calls: List the functions called by this function along with the modules in which the called functions appear.
- Called By: List the functions and their corresponding files which call this function.
- Modifications: For each change to the file, list the following information: Date, Author of Change, Description of Change, Reason for Change. The contents of this field is taken directly from the modification history maintained by the version control system in use.

24A.4   Hall, Paul, and Snow

The following material is from F. Hall, R. A. Paul, and W. E. Snow, "R&M engineering for off-the-shelf critical software," in *Annual Reliability and Maintainability Symposium, 1988 Proceedings*, Jan. 1988, p. 223.

An adequate documentation set for a reusable software candidate must provide the following engineering information:

1. Characteristics of the host processor.
   a. Program initialization;
   b. Module scheduling;
   c. Interrupt management procedures;
   d. Error management procedures;
   e. Input/output management procedures.
2. Operational conditions and the modes of system operation in which the software component is used.
3. Constraints such as memory capacity, execution time, and peripheral equipment availability.
4. Technical performance requirements, which include the required computational accuracy and special constraints.
5. A program-to-module (top to bottom) description of the functions to be performed by the software.
6. Functional flow charts from the program to module level.
7. Inputs required by the program, with signal source, signal format, accuracy, coordinate system, and data rate.

A comprehensive documentation set will supplement the engineering descriptive with additional design information. In order not to lose information that is needed to modify components for a new user environment, a complete design description will include design decisions, operational specifications, and user requirements. This information, usually captured in comment statements, is often missing from a finished product.

24A.5 Lim and Rubin

The following material is from W. C. Lim and S. Rubin, "Guidelines for cataloging reusable software," in *Hewlett-Packard Software Engineering Productivity Conference*, Aug. 1987.

Example of an Information Element Scheme

1. Keywords

The keywords are intended to be the principal access tool to anyone searching the library for a module designed to serve a specific purpose and its properties. The keywords are to be controlled by the software librarian and maintained in a thesaurus for library users.

Each keyword will be a descriptive term that identifies a broad functional scope or group of properties. To provide the maximum selectivity in searching, each keyword should be as independent of all the other keywords as the English language permits. Any single keyword will, therefore, describe a large family of module purpose or characteristics, but any combination of independent keywords will be a very narrow description of only those modules that satisfy all the characteristics named.

When a new module is submitted to the library, all its keywords should be selected from the thesaurus, unless the module has a unique characteristic that should be identified by a new keyword. The software librarian should determine whether the new term is useful, and add it to the thesaurus if it is accepted.

When new keywords are added, it will be necessary to periodically review their applicability to earlier entries in the library.

2. Module Name

Each module name should be the name by which the module is most commonly recognized. It need not be unique, although it would be preferable for each module to have a unique name. However, in the case of low-level functions, it is usual for the function name to stay constant, even though there may be several different versions available. Mathematical functions are good examples of this situation. An access request for, say, a Bessel function, should turn up all available versions of Bessel function modules.

3. Accession Number

The accession number should be a numbering system that provides a unique value for every module. It can then be an access path for those situations in which the user knows the number, such as looking up required subroutines for a higher level module, or for library maintenance operations.

4. Source of Module

This information element should identify the original source material from which the module version was obtained. It may be an internal project, an external vendor, or a published book or article. This would also be the place to indicate any special limitations on the reuse of the module, such as licensing restrictions.

5. Language

The programming language in which the module is coded should be given here. If the module is in the form of a design, rather than code, the design language used can be given. The information in this element will be a valuable indication to a potential user of the probable effort that may be necessary to produce a working version of the module in the target language.

6. Descriptive Abstract

The abstract should describe the purpose and usage limitations of the module. Enough information on the algorithmic method in the module should be included in the abstract to help the user determine whether the module is appropriate for the intended application. For example, several modules may perform a sorting function, but the form of the data interface and the sorting method used may be crucial to be effective in a particular system. Since it is difficult to be certain, on the basis of an abstract, that a module is exactly suitable, the descriptive abstract is best.

7. Input and Output Arguments

The input and output arguments of each module are the interface to the rest of the system. Therefore, a system designer will want to verify that any proposed module has the needed data interface for the intended usage. This element should include an exact definition of the data structure of each argument. It also serves the purpose of providing interface information to the engineer in the early design stages so that the reusable module may be incorporated into the system.

8. Cognizant Persons

The purpose of this information element is to provide an access path into the living human network that can provide important information about the module. It may be faster for the user to phone someone, or even to have a meeting with knowledgeable people, than to dig through the detailed specification and design documents to learn the essential facts he needs to decide whether the module suits his purposes. It will probably be necessary to periodically revise the information presented in this element, as people change responsibilities.

9. Other Modules Required

Many of the modules listed in the library will be programs or procedures that need lower-level modules, such as subroutine or task modules, for their execution. Since all modules should be kept as discrete library units, the required lower level modules need to be referenced in each citation. This element should include the names and accession numbers of all modules that are necessary for the execution of the principal module cited. This will include both internally called subordinate modules and separate but closely related modules. Exceptions to this may be made for common libraries of subroutines that are normally available on most systems, such as the standard mathematical functions.

10. Revisions

This is intended to provide references to prior or later revisions of the cited module. As modules may be revised to enhance, simplify, or even correct them, a new module citation should be entered for the revised module, because the original one may also still be useful. These references should be given as name, accession number, revision date, and a succinct statement of the nature of the revision. The date of creation of the principal module reference should be included here also.

Reference

1. W. Tracz, "Software reuse: Principles and practice," University of California at Irvine, Irvine, Feb. 26–28, 1990.

24-B

A SURVEY
OF CERTIFICATION LEVELS

In this appendix, we survey certification levels developed by several organizations. The certification levels of AdaNet, ASSET, CARDS, CSRO, DoD/CIM, DSRS, RAPID, JPL, and the proposed ROME framework are described. (The following organizations are related: DoD/CIM, RAPID, DSRS, and CSRO.) Most of the information has been obtained from the Component Certification, Validation, and Qualification Working Group of the *Proceedings for the Second Annual West Virginia Reuse Education & Training Workshop* held Oct. 25–27, 1993 [1]. Some organizations did not designate a name to their certification levels. In this case, names were provided by the working group and are shown in brackets.

24B.1   AdaNET Framework

Poore and Trammell describe the AdaNet framework [1]:

> *Phase 0: [As is]*
> *Phase 1: [Described]*
> Informational requirements met by supplier and/or AdaNET.
> *Phase 2: [Analyzed]*
> Reports generated by automated tools.
> *Phase 3: [Tested]*
> Functional testing using test cases provided by supplier or, if necessary, created by AdaNET.

24B.2   Asset Source for Software Engineering Technology (ASSET) Framework

Poore and Trammell describe the ASSET framework [1]:

> *Level 1: Documented*
> Supplier attests to having complied with ASSET's information requirements relative to the asset.
>
> *Level 2: Audited*
> ASSET confirms that all informational requirements have been met.
>
> *Level 3: Validated*
> ASSET uses or examines the asset according to the supplier's claims and finds no deficiencies or internal inconsistencies.
>
> *Level 4: Certified*
> ASSET conducts an independent, repeatable, formal evaluation according to a predetermined and published protocol and certifies the asset according to that protocol.

24B.3   Comprehensive Approach to Reusable Defense Software (CARDS) Framework

Poore and Trammell describe the CARDS framework [1]:

> *Identification*
> Proactive search for and location of candidate components.
>
> *Screening:*
> Accept/reject component based on key factors (e.g., platform, OS).
>
> *Evaluation:*
> - Qualification: Accept/reject component based on domain criteria.
> - Certification: Characterize component according to common criteria.
> - Adaptation: Modify component if needed.
> - Integration: Add to CARDS asset library model.

24B.4   Center for Software Reuse Operations (CSRO) Framework

Brechbiel [2] describes the certification levels for the Center for Software Reuse Operations:

Level 1.   Identifies the component as being approved for installation based on demand only. It has not been put through any testing or documentation processes. The depository-level components can be provided to users quickly but offer the lowest level of confidence in quality, thoroughness, or completeness.

Level 2. Meaning that the CSRO engineering staff has not performed any formal testing on the component to verify its functional performance; however, the component is known to have been fielded and therefore some level of confidence exists in its validity. Unguaranteed commercial off-the-shelf (COTS) software such as the Booch components fall into this category. In some cases, these fielded level components will have received some reengineering to reduce hardware or other system dependencies; while they offer a greater level of confidence than Level 1 they have not received testing required to assure quality testing or documentation.

Level 3. The product has gone through CSRO testing, but does not conform to all CSRO standards for documentation. These tested level components come with a test suite that include input files, component tests, and representative output files. They provide a thoroughly tested component that provides the user program with the capability to reproduce or validate those results.

Level 4. The product complies with all CSRO standards for both testing and documentation. COTS software may be certified if it is fully guaranteed and documented by the vendor. These Documented level components offer the highest level of assured as to quality, completeness, and reusability, but can require significant levels of time and effort to certify.

24B.5 Department of Defense/Corporate Information Management (DoD/CIM) Framework

Balfour [3] describes five levels of certification used at Department of Defense/-Corporate Information Management organization:

> *Level 1: Depository*
> No formal testing/documentation
>
> *Level 2: Reviewed*
> Some testing/documentation
>
> *Level 3: Tested*
> Test suites validated, some documentation
>
> *Level 4: Documented*
> Fully tested/documented meets all standards/guidelines
>
> *Level 5: Secure*
> (not currently used)

24B.6 Defense Software Repository System (DSRS) Framework

AdaMAT is a commercial code analyzer developed by Dynamics Research Corporation. Poore and Trammell describe the DSRS framework [1]:

Level 1: [As Is]

Level 2: [Analyzed]
Compiled, and analyzed with AdaMAT

Level 3: [Tested]
Functional testing using test cases provided by supplier or, if necessary, created by DSRS

Level 4: [Extended]
Re-user's manual added

24B.7 Jet Propulsion Laboratory (JPL) Framework

Beckman *et al.* [4] describe recommended certification levels for reusable software as follows:

A+	formally validated
A	exhaustively tested over the input domain
A-	tested on random inputs (Monte Carlo)
B+	packaged with test data and working test programs
B	extensively reused by programmers other than the author of the component (in n applications by k other programmers)
C	Extensively reused by the author of the component (in n applications for m years)
D	Used by the author in one application
F	Untested

24B.8 Rome Framework (proposed)

The primary certification level is based on asset criticality as specified by domain standards. The primary level sets the objectives for the evaluation. Poore and Trammell describe the proposed Rome framework [1]:

[P] 0: No evaluation

[P] 1: Implementation correctness

[P] 2: Design correctness

[P] 3: Operational correctness

The secondary certification level specifies the level of confidence that has been achieved in meeting the objectives of the primary certification level. The secondary level is the weighted average of domain values for a set of component attributes. This computed secondary level specifies the techniques for the evaluation.

[S] 0: Static quality & function analysis

[S] 1: Dynamic quality & function analysis

[S] 2: Dynamic function & static behavioral analysis

[S] 3: Dynamic behavioral & formal analysis

24B.9 Reusable Ada Products for Information Systems Development (RAPID)

Piper and Barner [5] enumerate the five levels of certification for the RAPID center (now called the Army Reuse Center):

> RAPID has five reusable software component (RSC) certification levels and each level is progressive to the next. Levels 1 through 5 are defined as follows.
>
> *Level 1:* Indicates the RSC has not been tested nor documented by the RAPID Center staff. But, an abstract, classification scheme, and metric analysis are prepared to install it on the RAPID Center Library (RCL). RSCs at this level are customer driven and would be placed in the RCL to meet immediate needs.
>
> *Level 2:* RSC has been reviewed by the RAPID Center staff and is expected to be reliable based on previous uses, even though testing of the RSC's functional performance has not been performed. The popular unguaranteed COTS software such as Booch-Wizard components and government software such as AdaSAGE apply in this category.
>
> *Level 3: A Level 3* RSC has been reviewed and tested by either the RAPID Center staff or the supplying vendor/developer. The test materials are provided with the RSC. However, the vendor/developer components are not required to comply with RAPID's stringent standards for reengineered components.
>
> *Level 4: A Level 4* RSC has been reviewed and approved by the the RAPID Configuration Control Board (RCCB), which monitors the process and approves an RSC for inclusion in the RCL, for compliance and/or deviations to RAPID standards of format, style, documentation, and complete test materials. COTS software such as EVB-GRACE's components that provide test scripts and reuser's manuals are classified at this level.
>
> *Level 5: A Level 5* RSC is presently defined as having been prepared for Level 4 and it has been cleared for security purposes.

References

1. J. Poore and C. Trammell, "Component certification, validation, and qualification working group," in *Proceedings for the 2nd Annual West Virginia Reuse Education and Training Workshop*, Oct. 25–27, 1993, pp. 57–72.

2. F. Brechbiel, "Framework for certification of reusable software components (draft)," Department of Defense Center for Software Reuse Operations (CSRO), Falls Church, VA, Sept. 1992.

3. B. Balfour, "Corporate information management, MIS reuse program," Marine Corps Ada Working Group, Nov. 18, 1991.

4. B. Beckman, W. V. Snyder, S. Shen, J. Jupin, L. V. Warren, B. Boyd, and R. Tausworthe, "The ESC: A hypermedia encyclopedia of reusable software components," Jet Propulsion Laboratory, California Institute of Technology, Pasadena, Sept. 3, 1991.

5. J. Piper and W. Barner, "The RAPID Center reusable software components (RSCs) certification process," U.S. Army Information Systems Software Development Center, Fort Belvoir, VA, 1991.

IMPLEMENTATION STRATEGY

The implementation, or technology transfer, of reuse is a critical aspect of achieving systematic reuse. Technology transfer is the *insertion of a technology into an organization.* A reuse program planned down to the smallest detail is of no value if this technology cannot be successfully transferred to those who would benefit. As shown in Fig. 25–1, even with sufficient planning, ineffective implementation can result in failure.

Personnel who develop reuse expertise on one project and then, as part of their career, migrate to other projects, informally transfer reuse knowledge. For example, at the Manufacturing Productivity section of the Software Technology Division at Hewlett-Packard, personnel who had gained experience in reuse techniques and then progressed to other projects as part of their career path proliferated reuse throughout the laboratory. Glynn [1] has the opinion that "technology is transferred effectively between groups of different specializations only if staff move with the technology." However, if we are to achieve systematic, organization-wide reuse, we cannot rely upon ad hoc approaches to diffusion and implementation. We must pursue formal and systematic implementation approaches to transfer reuse. This chapter examines some of the issues in transferring technology and examines several approaches to reuse implementation.

25.1 Maturation Transaction Model

Przybylinski et al. of the Software Engineering Institute describe a maturation transaction model (Fig. 25–2) which identifies the role of change agents as connections between producers and consumers of technology. Specifically, the change agents

Reuse Planning and Implementation

	Good	Bad
Effective	Success	Failure
Ineffective	Failure	Failure

Reuse
Implementation

FIGURE 25–1   Success and failure in reuse planning and implementation.

include *advocates* and *receptors* of the technology. The role of these change agents is to help "translate the meaning and implications of the technology to the potential user in the users' own terminology [2]". Such change agents have had a role in the successful implementation of reuse in some organizations. For example, Hewlett-Packard has had the benefit of a "Reuse Rabbi" to champion the reuse cause.

Revisiting the Technology Receptor

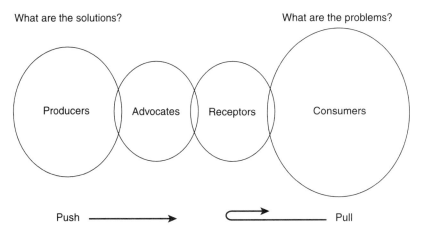

FIGURE 25–2   Advocates and receptors of technology. *Source:* S. M. Przybylinski, P. J. Fowler, and J. H. Maher, "Software technology transition tutorial," in *13th International Conference on Software Engineering,* May 12, 1991, p. 16.

25.2   Receptivity and Commitment

Our comprehension of the adoption of new technologies is aided by understanding how different individuals within organizations are receptive to and make commitments to new technology. Rogers [3] identified five classes of potential adopters (Fig. 25–3).

- *Innovators* are venturesome, cosmopolitan, usually possess technical expertise, and often control substantial financial resources as a "cushion" against potential losses from a failure in the innovations.
- *Early adopters* are respectable opinion leaders and serve as role models for other members in the society.
- *Early majority* deliberates for a period of time before adopting an idea and seldom hold a leadership position in the adoption of an innovation.
- *Late majority* approaches innovations with a skepticism and usually adopt in response to pressure from peers; does not adopt until most others have done so.
- *Laggards* are the last to adopt an innovation, are traditional, often isolated, and make decisions based on what has been previously done.

Przybylinski et. al. [4] note that "both individuals and groups make commitments to the adoption of new technologies in a regular pattern" (as follows and Fig. 25–4):

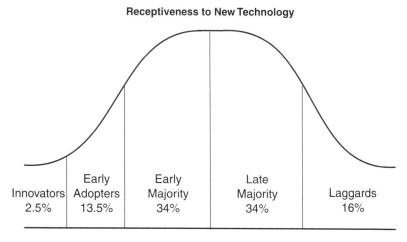

Receptiveness to New Technology

| Innovators 2.5% | Early Adopters 13.5% | Early Majority 34% | Late Majority 34% | Laggards 16% |

FIGURE 25–3   Adopter categories *Source:* E. M. Rogers, *Diffusion of Innovations.* New York, NY: Free Press, 1995, p. 262.

Commitment is a Phased Process

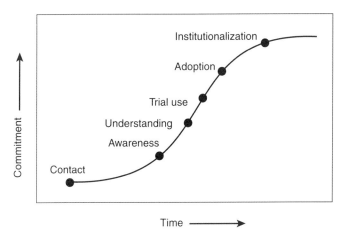

FIGURE 25–4   Commitment over time. *Sources:* S. M. Przybylinski, P. J. Fowler, and J. H. Maher, "Software technology transition tutorial," in *13th International Conference on Software Engineering,* May 12, 1991, p. 22; and D. R. Conner and R. W. Patterson, "Building commitment to organizational change," *Training & Development Journal,* vol. 36, no. 4, p. 19, Apr. 1982.

Contact—The transition target has had contact with the technology through some means, e.g., documents, briefings, marketing information, etc.

Awareness—That contact (or others) makes the target aware of the existence of the technology.

Understanding—The target understands the technology well enough to be conversant in the relevant details.

Trial use—The target agrees to use the technology for some purpose on a trial basis, e.g., a pilot project, prototype development, etc. This is often done to facilitate the "adoption" decision.

Adoption—The target agrees to use the technology more widely within their organization for an application that is related to the target's business purpose.

Institutionalization—The use of the technology is made part of the standard practices of the organization.

These two frameworks aid our understanding of how some individuals within an organization are more receptive than others and the phases by which this receptivity is translated into the actual adoption of new technology.

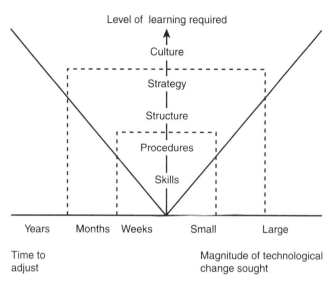

FIGURE 25–5   Time and magnitude of technological change. *Source:* P. S. Adler and A. Shenhar, "Adapting your technological base: The organizational challenge," *Sloan Management Review,* vol. 32, no. 1, p. 36, Fall 1990.

25.3   Dynamics of Organizational Change

The magnitude of technological change desired in an organization dictates the level of learning required of its personnel [5] (Fig. 25–5). Furthermore, the magnitude also determines the time required to adjust to the change. For example, a small change such as an engineer deciding to create his or her own library of reusable assets for personal use requires less time than a large change such as the adoption of a reuse program. Because the latter involves relearning at the corporate culture and strategy levels, such an undertaking requires more time and effort on the part of the organization.

25.4   Change Management

A stranger came upon a farmer and his dog. The dog was lying at his master's feet and was audibly moaning.

"Why is the dog moaning?" inquired the stranger.

"Because he's lying on a nail," replied the farmer.

"Why doesn't he get up from the nail?" asked the stranger.

The farmer paused and then said "Because it doesn't hurt enough."

—Author unknown

Because human beings are creatures of habit, we find it easier to pursue the path of least resistance and are reluctant, and sometimes resistant, to change. Przybylinski et al. [2] identify two means of change. The first is the "hammer" approach which mandates that change will occur (e.g., "You will use the new technology beginning next week"). The assumption behind this approach is that there is little or no gap (in terms of skills, desire, etc.) between the current state and the target state. The second involves "unfreezing" from the present state into a state of transition and then "refreezing" into the desired state. In unfreezing, people must perceive a need to change their current ways of doing things. The intermediate transition state is characterized by uncertainty, discomfort, and resistance. The refreezing to the desired state is characterized by progressing into a work habit, increasing comfort, and exhibiting a new set of behaviors.

25.5 Technology Transfer Group of the Workshop on Software Reuse

The Technology Transfer subgroup of the Management and Technology working group at the Workshop for Institutionalizing Reuse (WISR 93) [6] developed a framework that consists of three stages: introducing, institutionalizing, and sustaining software reuse. At the introduction stage, the group identified a cycle that consists of:

1. contact;
2. initial study;
3. further analysis.

Within this cycle, the reuse advocate is likely to encounter and should be prepared for resistance. Specific activities are associated with each phase in the cycle. For example, in the initial study phase, the reuse advocate would identify the bounds of the domain, determine a business model, and recommend a process for domain analysis.

Some of the activities associated with the institutionalizing stage include: facilitate plans; provide/find education, tools, technology, etc.; tailor and install support; record lessons learned and history; maintain momentum through personal contact; disseminate reuse opportunities and resources; and report and assess progress.

At the sustaining stage, activities include: reducing the technology transfer role; collecting information and providing feedback; providing consulting; optimizing the reuse process and the technology transfer techniques if necessary; and assessing the effort [6].

Buxton and Malcolm [7] suggest that for late adopters, the transfer ought to be performed by parties who have already adopted the new technology rather than the inventor(s) of the technology. With their unique perspective, such parties can ease the adoption process for the late adopters.

25.6   Approaches for Implementation

By Scope.   After an organization has been identified as a suitable candidate for reuse, an appropriate approach must be selected for implementing reuse. In this section, we describe four implementation approaches for reuse in the organization [8].

    Parallel Conversion.   Parallel conversion in an organization involves operating both the current and the new method simultaneously. When the organization is confident that the new method will perform satisfactorily, the current method is discontinued (Fig. 25–6).

    Parallel conversion hedges the risk involved in switching over to a new method and provides a means of comparing results between the new and current approach for the same development project(s). However, because of this duplicity and demand on resources, this method is unrealistic for most organizations.

    Direct Conversion.   Direct conversion consists of discontinuing the current method and starting up the new method in a very short period of time (Fig. 25–7). While this approach entails risks, organizations have utilized it because of the resources that are freed. These resources, when focused on making the new method work, can serve to make it successful. Another advantage to direct conversion is that the entire organization is transformed to a reuse development system, i.e., the organizational design, tools, and techniques interact together in such a way that reuse is optimized for the organization.

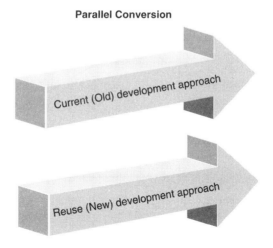

Parallel Conversion

Current (Old) development approach

Reuse (New) development approach

FIGURE 25–6   Parallel conversion.

Direct Conversion

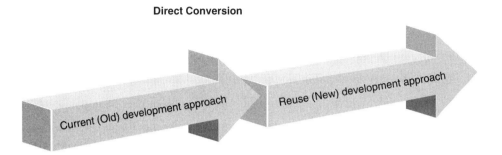

FIGURE 25–7   Direct conversion.

Phased Conversion.   Phased conversion occurs when the current method is gradually phased out as the new method is phased in (Fig. 25–8). This can be accomplished in a number of ways. For example, projects can begin by designing for reuse and reusing in a portion of the total product/system (e.g., test cases and test suites), and then gradually progress to implement reuse in the other portions of the systems (e.g., code, designs, and specifications) in subsequent releases and/or other product/systems. The difficulties inherent in this approach can arise when concurrent use of two methods causes conflicts. For example, under the old method, engineers are rewarded on the basis of the quantity of code developed. However, with the new method, reuse success is achieved when fewer lines of code are developed.

Phased Conversion

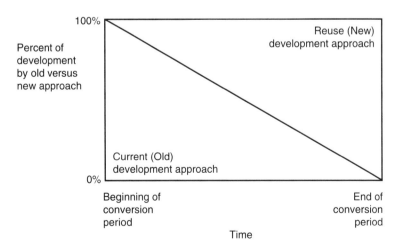

FIGURE 25–8   Phased conversion.

Pilot Conversion. A pilot conversion involves implementing the new method in a select portion of the ultimate implementation area (Fig. 25–9). For example, if the ultimate implementation area is a division which consists of multiple projects, one or more of these projects is chosen as a pilot. If the project operates satisfactorily under the new approach, the approach is fully implemented across the division. While the pilot method avoids some of the disadvantages of the other approaches, it still must be demonstrated that the new approach works under industrial use. It may also be difficult to isolate a project that is independent yet has the same conditions to which the rest of the projects would be subjected. The advantage of using this method is that the new approach can be tried on a single project from start to finish without risking all the organization's projects.

Note that these approaches are not mutually exclusive. For example, an organization may choose to select a pilot project which undergoes a phased approach.

By Speed. The speed at which an organization begins utilizing and producing reuse can be a critical factor to its success. If an organization attempts to implement reuse too quickly, several factors may jeopardize its success, including the inability of its personnel to rapidly absorb/learn the reuse techniques and tools. On the other hand, if an organization establishes reuse too slowly, then it may not realize the benefits of reuse in a timely fashion, lose managerial and other support, and be outperformed by competitors.

Incremental/Evolutionary. Incrementalism is "a policy or advocacy of . . . change by degrees" [9]. Reinertsen [10] asserts that the advantages of incremental implementation with smaller steps and smaller teams are as follows:

Pilot Conversion

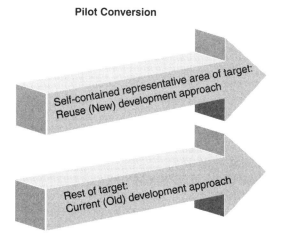

FIGURE 25–9   Pilot conversion.

- clearer targets;
- less communication required;
- less communication delay;
- lower risk;
- team autonomy;
- less decision making;
- less front-end analysis;
- less project approval delay;
- faster development cycles.

Among software reuse practitioners, Prieto-Diaz [11] describes some of the advantages of implementing reuse incrementally as follows:

- provides immediate return on investment;
- builds confidence within the organization;
- is easier to manage;
- allows for tuning and refining the reuse process;
- facilitates monitoring and evaluating reuse.

Griss [12] has also detailed some of the advantages of starting a reuse program incrementally. He emphasizes that by introducing process changes incrementally, people adapt more readily to as their reuse experience increases.

But among the disadvantages of an incremental approach is whether results can be achieved within the required time frame. Another disadvantage is that an incremental change to one aspect or portion of the system may not allow us to achieve reuse. For example, establishing the process for engineers to use reusable software will not succeed if they still are evaluated under an incompatible performance system, e.g., the number of new lines of code produced.

Revolutionary.   More dramatic, or revolutionary, changes are for organizations that have concluded that an evolutionary approach will not be acceptable.

Business process reengineering (BPR) is such an approach. BPR "does not lead to incremental improvements of the type usually associated with traditional quality improvement programs. The changes are radical: 'It is discarding conventional ways of working and replacing them with totally new ones.'" [13]

Among the factors to be considered when deciding whether to pursue an evolutionary or revolutionary implementation approach are as follows:

- Can the organization absorb the new paradigm?
- Is the organization open to reuse?
- How quickly can the organization learn the new paradigm?

- How urgently does the organization need to transition?
- Does the organization need to deliver its product to market before the competition?
- Is there currently or will there be a backlog of development projects?

Erickson [14] of the United Technologies Research Center (UTC) discusses the issue of whether to introduce reuse into the software development process in increments or in a single step. He cites the use of the incremental approach advocated by Prieto-Diaz within UTC but also contrasts it with the revolutionary approach used at NASA where a group "leaped" from a "FORTRAN-based environment to an Ada-based one, using generic architectures and object-oriented design."

By Driver.   By driver, we mean where the reuse program should begin implementation and by whom. This includes targeting parties to ensure that they are aware, informed, educated and are offered support. We examine some of the alternatives below.

Top Down.   A top down approach consists of obtaining support from management to pursue reuse. Upper management has the strategic view and, in many cases, can perceive the commonality from a product/system level. Although there are examples of reuse being mandated from the top, an edict from upper level management generally is undesirable because it may change the behavior but not necessarily the belief in the value of reuse. A conclusion of the working group on Management and Technology at the Workshop for Institutionalizing Reuse (WISR 93) [6] was that "edicts alone don't work; persuasion was necessary." Consequently, it is not desirable to have upper management conduct all the reuse planning and merely inform the subordinates of the way the reuse program will be implemented. Management, however, are the only ones who can provide legitimacy and resources.

Bottom Up.   A bottom up or "grass roots" approach seeks support from the engineers. Personnel at this level are usually aware of the need for new technology and are adept at making technological decisions. While sanctioning at this level is necessary, efforts at implementing reuse without management support are ill-fated because, among other factors, the reward system may not be aligned for reuse.

Combination.   Some organizations have pursued a combination approach, where legitimacy from upper management and support at the grass roots level has provided a strong alignment of interests for successful reuse.

Summary

A formal and systematic approach to reuse implementation increases the likelihood of success. Change agents may be a useful intermediary between producers and consumers of reuse technology. Among the factors to consider in the adoption of reuse are scope (the portion of the organization that is converted); speed (an evolutionary or revolutionary rate of conversion); and driver (whether reuse is driven from the top, bottom, or both directions).

References

1. J. G. Glynn, "Technology transition model," Ferranti International, 1990.
2. S. M. Przybylinski, P. J. Fowler, and J. H. Maher, "Software technology transition tutorial," *13th International Conference on Software Engineering,* May 12, 1991.
3. E. M. Rogers, *Diffusion of Innovations.* New York, NY: Free Press, 1995.
4. D. R. Conner and R. W. Patterson, "Building commitment to organizational change," *Training & Development Journal,* vol. 36, no. 4, pp. 18–30, Apr. 1982.
5. P. S. Adler and A. Shenhar, "Adapting your technological base: The organizational challenge," *Sloan Management Review,* vol. 32, no. 1, pp. 25–37, Fall 1990.
6. J. Tirso, "Report of the working group on management and technology transfer," in *5th Annual Workshop on Software Reuse,* Oct. 26–29, 1992.
7. J. N. Buxton and R. Malcolm, "Software technology transfer," *Software Engineering Journal,* vol. 6, no. 1, pp. 17–23, Jan. 1991.
8. J. O. Hicks, *Management Information Systems: A User Perspective.* Saint Paul, MN: West, 1984.
9. *Merriam Webster's Collegiate Dictionary.* 10th ed., Springfield, MA: Merriam, 1997.
10. D. Reinertsen, "Outrunning the pack in faster product development," *Electronic Design,* vol. 39, no. 1, pp. 89–96, Jan. 10, 1991.
11. R. Prieto-Diaz, "Making software reuse work: an implementation model," *SIGSOFT Software Engineering Notes,* vol. 16, no. 3, pp. 61–68, July 1991.
12. M. L. Griss, "Software reuse: From library to factory," *IBM Systems Journal,* vol. 32, no. 4, pp. 548–566, 1993.
13. M. Hammer and J. Champy, "What is reengineering?," *InformationWEEK,* no. 372, pp. 10–24, May 5, 1992.
14. R. E. Erickson, "Software reuse adoption: Some practical issues," *5th Annual Workshop on Institutionalizing Software Reuse,* Oct. 26–29, 1992.

Monitoring and Continuously Improving the Reuse Program

A reuse program should be monitored in order to determine whether its goals and objectives are being met. This monitoring can be achieved through the collection and analysis of quantitative and qualitative data and by interviewing participants in the reuse process.

Continuous improvement is a process by which an organization constantly strives for and progresses toward a specified goal(s). In our context, the goal is to develop a system for continuous learning, improvement, and innovation in the reuse infrastructure that enables the organization to continue producing and consuming software. By learning, we mean that the internal experience and knowledge gained in reusing needs to be captured and evaluated and an appropriate course of action taken to improve the reuse infrastructure. By improvement we refer to the process by which change is introduced into the reuse infrastructure. Guided by learning, improvement enables the infrastructure to achieve its goals. Finally, innovation is the introduction of new concepts, methods, and processes into the reuse infrastructure.

26.1 Monitoring

As we discussed in chapter 19, monitoring the reuse program is essential because managing without information is difficult. The manager can only make informed decisions and keep the reuse program on course if sound information is available. Reasons for monitoring the reuse program include ascertaining whether the reuse program is progressing according to plan and determining whether the reuse program is fulfilling its intended goals.

Qualitative and quantitative information should be collected to monitor the progress of the reuse program. The following information is used to "take a snapshot in time" to track the progress of the reuse program:

1. *Relative to the past.* This activity monitors, e.g., the level of reuse occurring and savings from reuse.
2. *Relative to the present.* Is the program meeting milestones? Is it addressing the needs of current consumers and customers?
3. *Relative to other reuse programs in industry.* Benchmarking is performed.
4. *As it evolves itself to meet the challenges of the future.* Will it meet future customer needs? Will it have adequate time and resources?

26.2   Continuous Improvement

Continuous improvement is essential for a variety of reasons, including:

1. New and improved methods, processes, and tools are constantly being developed by personnel as they become more experienced and from external sources that may be appropriate for the reuse program.
2. The competition continues to improve upon its practices enabling them to bring products of higher quality to market in a shorter time.
3. The technical environment (e.g., standards, operating systems) continues to change, rendering the existing reuse infrastructure ineffective.
4. Consumer and end-users needs and preferences change.
5. If unattended, the reuse infrastructure tends to degrade over time.

For continuous process improvement to succeed, we must consider multiple aspects of the organization, e.g., people, technology, and process. The needs for continuous process improvement are as follows:

1. Document, examine, and distill lessons from the experience and data; this information will be instrumental in identifying further opportunities for improvement.
2. Modify the current direction of the reuse program as necessary.
3. When appropriate, identify when to begin the cycle for changing the reuse infrastructure as business and technical conditions change. Factors to monitor and examine when beginning a cycle include:
   • business conditions change, for example:
     - new products/systems need to be developed;
     - more unique systems to be developed; hence fewer opportunities for reuse;

- more common systems to be developed; perhaps should consider generators for development.
- technical conditions change, for example:
  - internal or external standards change;
  - major development environment change.

In considering when it is appropriate to embark on a new cycle for implementing change in the reuse program, take into account the magnitude and accumulation of necesssary changes.

26.3 Learning and Innovation

A learning organization evolves by capitalizing upon its experience. Senge [1] highlights this aspect and Bailin, Simos, and Levine [2] reiterate its importance in the context of software reuse. Among the reasons for learning are as follows:

1. The costs accrued from the learning process are less than the costs of not doing so. Harrington points out that "training is not costly . . . it is ignorance that is costly." [3]

2. Focusing on merely operating the reuse infrastructure does not provide the opportunity to reflect, examine, and suggest improvements or innovations to the infrastructure.

3. Growth in knowledge and understanding is an essential aspect of personnel development.

Innovations are the significant leaps over the status quo. An innovation differs from improvement in that it is a benefit of greater magnitude.

Although an established reuse infrastructure may be operating properly, little or no innovation may occur if it is not explicitly encouraged and integrated into the process. Periodic meetings should be held to explore innovations generated from both internal and external sources.

Summary

By monitoring the reuse program, we can determine whether it is progressing according to plan and whether its goals are being met. Continuous improvement is essential because new and improved methods are being developed, the competition continues to improve, and consumer and end-user needs and preferences change. Both learning and innovation should be explicitly encouraged and integrated into the process.

References

1. P. Senge, *The Fifth Discipline: The Art and Practice of the Learning Organization.* New York, NY: Doubleday, 1990.

2. S. Bailin, M. Simos, and L. Levine, Informal Technical Report for Software Technology for Adaptable Reliable Systems (STARS) Learning and Inquiry Based Reuse Adoption (LIBRA): A Field Guide to Reuse Adoption through Organizational Learning, Loral Defense Systems-East, Manassas, VA, STARS-PA33-AG01/001/02, Feb. 6, 1996.

3. H. J. Harrington, *Business Process Improvement.* New York, NY: McGraw-Hill, 1993.

FUTURE TRENDS

27.1   Introduction

Software reuse is an inevitable outcome of software development maturity. Reuse will never replace tailored programming in every development situation, nor should it. If there is one message the reader should take from this book, it is to embrace the philosophy of, rather than the methods of reuse. Because reuse affords us a spectrum of development alternatives other than tailored programming, we challenge the software industry to rethink the way software should be developed.

This chapter explores the immediate future of reuse by examining present trends. Specifically, we will compare the history of reuse adoption with other methods and technologies that have been introduced to society in general and the software industry in particular. We will then examine what will be necessary to achieve reuse at the company, national, and international levels of reuse.

27.2   Where We Are Now

Currently, the majority of reuse is being practiced at the personal and intraproject levels (Fig. 27–1). However, more corporate and interenterprise reuse programs are being established. Examples of enterprise reuse include corporate programs such as those of Hewlett-Packard, IBM, and Nortel (formerly Bell Northern Research). Interenterprise reuse is being conducted by organizations such as Trans World Airlines, Inc., and IBM. At the national level, ASSET (http://source.asset.com) is establishing itself as a provider of "a marketplace for the collection, certification, categorization, and dissemination of software related assets and services and to help other organi-

Scope of Reuse:

1. *Personal reuse* is practiced by the individual software engineer. Over time, the engineer typically accumulates a personal library of routines primarily for his or her own use.

2. *Intraproject reuse* usually involves designating one or more engineers to create the reusable assets within a project (typically a function library) for the other project members to reuse.

3. *Interproject reuse* is the practice of reuse across multiple projects. Reuse at this level highlights the issues of coordination and organization among several groups and often requires steering committees and new job classifications. In addition, issues related to funding and having projects in different geographical locations may arise.

4. *Enterprise-wide reuse* characterizes reuse throughout an enterprise, and may require support and coordination of multiple levels of management in multiple organizations.

5. *Interenterprise reuse* describes reuse across enterprises. An example of this is the practice of reuse across several different companies. Issues that are raised at this level include copyright, pricing, and enterprise-proprietary issues.

6. *National reuse* is the reuse of assets on a national basis. At this scope, management issues are of utmost importance.

7. *International reuse* describes the reuse of assets across countries. Prominent issues raised at this level include issues of language, international copyright laws, and even greater management issues.

FIGURE 27–1   Scope of reuse.

zations establish their reuse programs based on suitable standards." [1] The Reusable Component Marketplace (http://components.software.net) is positioning itself as an Internet-based broker of third-party reusable components. While there are organized reuse or reuse-related efforts in Europe and Japan, and the International Workshops in Software Reuse have brought researchers and practitioners together to examine and discuss reuse issues, at the international level, there are still very few coordinated efforts in reuse.

27.3   Where We Are Headed

Time Lines.   Software reuse is not a new concept. More than a quarter of a century has elapsed since McIlroy [2] introduced the notion at a 1968 NATO conference of a software components industry. Since we currently do not have a widespread components industry, we may legitimately ask the question "How mature is software reuse?".

The timelines of other methods that have been advanced before society and then applied may aid us in answering this question. Research into this area [3] indicates significant differences between the date when the innovation is conceived and when it enters the marketplace (Fig. 27–2).

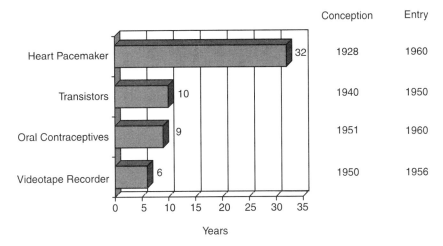

FIGURE 27–2 Adoption lag times for specific advances. *Source:* K. J. Dakin and J. Lindsey, *Technology Transfer,* Chicago, IL: Probus, 1991, p. 47.

Likewise, in the field of software engineering technology, we can see differences in technology maturation. In 1984, Redwine et al. [4] were commissioned by the Software Technology for Adaptable Reliable Systems (STARS) program to conduct in-depth case studies of various technologies. They constructed a timeline which depicted the major stages of the technology's maturity [4]. The stages of maturity are shown in Fig. 27–3.

The maturation timelines for four of the 14 technologies are shown in Fig. 27–4. Each technology possesses its own unique timeline signature for maturation.

Redwine [4] identifies the factors which affect the maturation of a technology. These include:

- conceptual integrity;
- clear need;
- contracting incentives;
- prior positive knowledge;
- management commitment;
- knowledgeable managers;
- incremental change;
- slow internal transfer;

Software Technology Maturation Phases
- **Basic Research**
  - investigation of ideas and concepts that later prove fundamental to the technology
  - general recognition that a problem exists and discussion of its scope and nature
- **Concept Formulation**
  - informal convergence of ideas
  - convergence on a compatible set of ideas
  - general publication of solutions to part of the problem
- **Development and Extension**
  - trial, preliminary use of the technology
  - clarification of the underlying ideas
  - extension of the general approach to the broader solution
- **Internal Enhancement**
  - major extension of the general approach to alternative problem domains
  - use of the technology to solve real problems
  - stabilization and porting of the technology
  - development of training materials
  - derivations of results indicating value
- **External Enhancement**
  - same activities as for Internal Enhancement but they are carried out by a broader group including people who have not been involved in the technology maturation up to this point.
- **Popularization**
  - appearance of production-quality, supported versions
  - commercialization and marketing of the technology
  - propagation of the technology throughout a receptive community of users

FIGURE 27–3   Software technology maturation phases. *Source:* S. T. Redwine et al., U.S. Department of Defense related software technology requirements, practices, and prospects for the future," Institute for Defense Analysis, Alexandria, VA, Technical Report IDA Paper P-1788, June, 1984, p. 85.

- high cost;
- malleability;
- psychological hurdles;
- latent demand;
- incentives;
- training.

We now map software reuse onto a similar timeline according to its maturation phases (Fig. 27–5).

Basic Research.   Although reuse had been practiced informally, appearance of the key idea behind formal reuse was articulated in McIlroy's [2] seminal paper at the 1968 NATO Conference where he proposed an industry of software components.

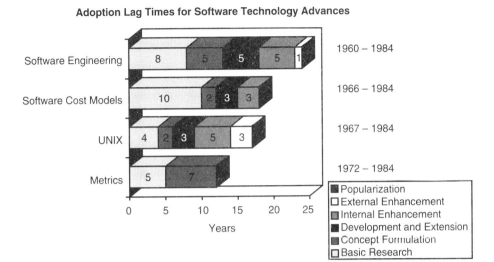

FIGURE 27–4 Adoption lag times for software technology advances. *Source:* S. T. Redwine et al., U.S. Department of Defense related software technology requirements, practices, and prospects for the future," Institute for Defense Analysis, Alexandria, VA, Technical Report IDA Paper P-1788, June, 1984, pp. 87–89.

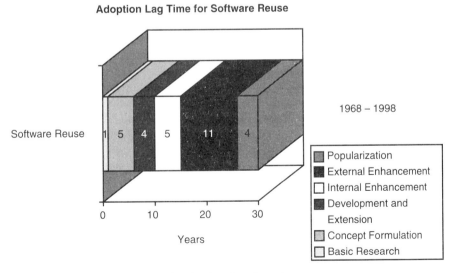

FIGURE 27–5 Adoption lag time for software reuse.

Concept Formulation.   Hitachi built its software factory in 1969. Although reusability at Hitachi was truly established in the 1980s when specific tools and techniques were integrated, its early work in this area aided development of the reuse concept.

Development and Extension.   While the Systems Development Corporation (SDC) coined the term "software factory" in 1974 [5], it was the Japanese who carried the concept further by establishing and furthering the concept of reuse. In the same year, the NEC Fuchu Works was the focus of innovation in software process and was informally referred to as a "software factory [5]". The company began pushing software development toward a level of discipline and productivity comparable to modern engineering and factory operations by utilizing process standardization, quality control, reusability, and automated tools [5]. NEC formed a distributed software factory network to meet the varying demands of customers. (Not all customers needed state-of-art products.) Products were developed using standardized methods and tools. By 1977, Toshiba had established a software factory for creating real-time control software for industrial applications which emphasized the reuse of components.

Freeman [6] had established reuse research at the University of California at Irvine. In this research program, Neighbors [7] wrote a thesis on software reuse.

Internal Enhancement.   In the mid- to late-1970s, Lanergan and Poynton [8] had successfully implemented reuse within a COBOL environment at Raytheon. They observed that up to 60% of the code they had created for their business applications were redundant and thereby offered the potential for reuse. By 1982, Ford Aerospace had begun a reuse program and created reuse coding and library guidelines [9], [10]. IBM conducted research on reusable software methods [11].

External Enhancement.   The ITT Workshop on Reusability [12] in 1983 was a landmark conference. The practitioners and researchers of the early 1980s presented their efforts and convened to discuss reuse issues. Furthermore, in the same year, Raytheon had spun off a company called MasterSoftware [13] (which billed itself as "The world's first fully reusable software company") and offered their reuse software system externally.

Popularization.   Portions of a reuse solution, such as reuse repositories and standards, are now being offered. One survey on the proliferation of reuse suggests that, as of 1994, reuse had reached at least a 40% penetration level among a sample of corporations in both North America and Europe [14]. Another survey by Frakes in 1992 indicates that "a quarter of the respondents (25%) work for companies with a reuse organization, though some more (17%) report planning one." [15] Further details of these surveys are discussed in Chapter 5.

Scope.   What is required for reuse at the interenterprise, national, and international levels?

Interenterprise.   The majority of software reuse efforts have been intracompany endeavors. Systems and products developed internally may be comprised of three types of assets (Fig. 27–6). The first type, external assets, are purchased on the market external to the company. Purchase of such assets is made because they are less expensive than what could be developed in-house or the expertise for creating such assets are not available to the company. The second type, internal assets, are assets developed in-house for internal use only. They are usually proprietary because they serve as a source of competitive advantage for the company. The third type, marketed assets, are internally developed assets which are used internally, as well as sold by the company on the external market. This type of asset serves as an additional source of revenue for the company. In some cases, they may also influence the external development of other assets, e.g., third parties may want to ensure their product is compatible with these marketed assets.

A number of these intracompany efforts have resulted in the offering of reuse products and services externally, spurring the development of a national reuse market. An example is the early successes of Raytheon's reuse efforts, which resulted in the creation of a company called MasterSoftware which marketed the reusable COBOL development environment. (The company has since been acquired and no longer markets the reuse products.) As a byproduct of its internal reuse program, IBM is currently marketing its reuse educational course offerings to industry. Westinghouse developed a reuse repository for internal use, and for a period of time, marketed the system externally. Trans World Airlines, Inc., provided an internally developed reusable application template so that Canadian Airlines International Ltd. could develop its frequent flier application in half the time normally required [16].

For more interenterprise reuse to occur, corporations must recognize the value of creating "marketed assets." This involves developing assets that are not only reusable within their own corporations, but in others as well. As with any other commercial product, such assets need to be fully supported. Legal matters such as reproduction and modifications should be clarified between the corporations.

1. External Assets (purchased).
2. Internal Assets (proprietary).   FIGURE 27–6   Systems may be de-
3. Marketed Assets (internal assets sold externally).   veloped from three types of assets.

National

What is needed: For reuse to thrive at the national level, we will need an appropriate national infrastructure to support reuse. Areas to be addressed include:

Standards.   Standards enable a common language among libraries, assets, and taxonomy for communication. Efforts by groups such as the Reuse Interoperability Group (RIG), the IEEE, and the Object Management Group serve that end. For example, the RIG has published standards that will aid in the effort to "enable users to easily link disparate libraries and access them with just one user interface, query method, and downloading procedure [17]".

Producer/Broker/Consumer Network.   This network is the creation of a producer, broker, consumer chain for the development and utilization of value provided by reuse. As companies bring their expertise, tools, and assets from their in-house experiences, we will need to encourage the roles of producer, broker, and consumer at a national level. We will also need to enable them to communicate and collaborate with each other. As mentioned earlier, we are beginning to see vendors enter the reuse market as producers of assets (e.g., Rogue Wave Software, EVB Software Engineering, Inc., Rational, Inc.); libraries (e.g., EVB Software Engineering, Software Productivity Solutions, Inc.); and expertise (e.g., Lombard Hill Group, Software Engineering Guild, Software Productivity Solutions). The broker role is being fulfilled by both the producers (in marketing their products and services), by the consumers ("gatekeepers" who search for and maintain tabs on new developments), and even by the emergence of "pure" brokers whose emphasis is on the distribution of assets (e.g., ASSET, the Reusable Component Market).

Distribution channels may increasingly utilize the Internet for purchase and retrieval. A means of regulating and tracking the payments for such assets needs to be identified.

Education.   Education on reuse should start earlier at the university level when students are taught the principles of reuse. Reuse should not necessarily be a separate course, but rather incorporated into existing curriculum. Several workshops sponsored by ASSET have examined reuse courses taught at the university level.

4. Economic Incentives.   Commercial producer organizations would like to see a return on their investment that is commensurate with the risk they bear. Products/concepts brought to market fall into at least two categories: those which are self-evident in their purpose and benefits (e.g., a better mousetrap) and those which require education on the part of the consumer (e.g., a novel or complex product). While reuse is simple in concept, its "buy-in" requires educational/cultural change. Consequently, commercial organizations that are pioneers in the field of reuse (e.g., the MasterSoftware spin-off from Raytheon) face hurdles in educating the potential consumers as well as the risks that accompany a new venture. This risk can be shared through consortium-type efforts, some of which are underway. Reduction of such risks can help assure a reasonable economic return for companies that enter the reuse market.

For government contractor organizations, the issue is more complex. Under certain contract arrangements (e.g., cost-plus), there may be little or no economic incentive to reuse. Some have suggested that the economic benefits from reuse be shared between the government and the contractor, thereby providing incentives for the contractor to reuse and allowing the government to enjoy some of the savings. Others have suggested that reuse be explicitly entered into a contract agreement between the contractor and the government, with the latter experiencing all the benefits. Again, risk from pioneering the reuse of software may play a factor in contractors reusing software. However, with increasing competition, we may see reuse becoming a necessity, not an option, as contractors utilize it to offer lower bids to the government.

Legal.   Legal matters pertain to the intellectual property issues of the production and consumption of reusable assets. Issues that must be addressed include end-user protection from damages arising from use of software created from defective assets. The deficiencies of the current legal framework to address software reuse concerns stem more from deficiencies of the framework to address software issues in general, i.e., what subject matter may be copyrighted and patented is still unclear.

Government Stimulus.   In the area of industrial policy, the role of the government in stimulating a reuse industry has been hotly debated. Efforts of the Japanese government through its agencies (e.g., Ministry of International Trade and Industry) in supporting technologies have been well publicized. However, as an end-user of software, the government can at the very least stimulate the production of reusable software as a customer. Several examples may be cited where government demand has accelerated a technology field. Cox [18] notes how the government, through its decision to purchase interchangeable-parts small arms, accelerated the manufacturing process and industry of such arms. The U.S. Navy's war needs also accelerated the development of the field of operations research [19]. Redwine et al. [4] comment on how the maturation of software cost modeling accelerated in the mid-1970s because the U.S. Army, Navy, and Air Force acquired an early version of the model and began using it in its procurements.

There are at least three levels where the government can encourage software reuse. At the first level, it can stimulate the reuse industry as a customer, e.g., as in the operations research and software cost modeling examples. At the second level, it can encourage commercialization of government reuse know-how to the private sector. At the third level, it can fund reuse research that has promise of having a positive impact on the U.S. economy.

International.   At the international level, in addition to the points in the previous section, areas that should be addressed include the following.

Standards.   Standards which are accepted at the international level would facilitate an international market in reuse. If each country has its own set of standards, we will encounter a situation similar to the dilemma every international traveler has faced: varying electrical outlet interfaces and power levels. The degree of international standards would affect the next category.

Localization.   Assets need to be tailored to the needs of the particular country or community. Such localization is a combination of reuse-specific standards as well as community standards (e.g., unit of measure, currency, and language).

Legal.   International intellectual property laws and regulations need to encourage the reuse of software. For example, issues in the area of international copyright and patent laws, policies, and methods of recourse need to support reuse.

Government Cooperation.   There must be greater cooperation on the part of various governments to encourage software reuse. Significant reuse efforts in Europe, Japan, and North America, for example, have much to learn from each other that would aid the effort in creating an international reuse market.

27.4   The Future of Reuse

If the obstacle of cultural change is overcome, we will see more organizations implement formal reuse programs, greater demand in the marketplace for skill sets in the area of reuse, and more offerings of reuse tools and components in the marketplace.

Near Term.   In the near term, as reuse and other technologies continue to mature, we will see the following.

1. Reusable software will assume a greater role in the way decisions are made to purchase development systems.

   Vendor offerings in the marketplace may be grouped into three stages. In the first stage, system suppliers provide both the hardware and proprietary systems software necessary for development. In the second stage, independent systems software developers (e.g., Microsoft, Novell, and others) offer products which in some cases drive the developers' hardware purchase decision. For example, applications which are critical for a company and operated only on PC-based platforms would drive the company's decision of which type of hardware to purchase. We have also begun to see companies that specialize in hardware only (e.g., Compaq, Dell). For the third stage, we will see suppliers of system software which have been optimized to run reusable components as well as the development of an industry for software components. These software components (e.g., kits, objectware) will become a greater driver in the developers' decisions regarding the type of systems software and hardware to purchase for their development needs.

2. Greater use of networks and the Internet as a distribution channel for reusable software assets.

   Companies such as MITRE and DEC are utilizing the capabilities of the Internet and related services to internally distribute and obtain reusable assets. Organizations such as ASSET and the Reusable Component Marketplace utilize the World Wide Web to serve as brokers in distributing reusable software.

3. Greater skill specialization in the production and consumption of reusable assets.

   Specialists who develop expertise in creating reusable assets will be in greater demand. Assembling assets will become a greater portion of the consumer engineer's responsibilities or even constitute an entirely new type of engineering position. Similar to the division between systems and applications programming, some envision a division between the activities of producing and consuming software. Postings for specialists in the creation of class libraries may be found in the employment marketplace even now.

4. Reengineering of organizations to fit the new development paradigm.

   There will be formal recognition of the need for domain-specific, systematic reuse. This will involve redefining job roles, responsibilities, and a change in mind-set.

Long Term. In the long term, greater emergence of the long-awaited "reuse industry" will occur. More organizations which have developed in-house expertise in reuse, reusable assets, and tools will offer such products or services in the external marketplace. These companies will create their systems by purchasing commercially available assets, creating the unique and proprietary portions of their systems, and licensing the use of their nonproprietary assets in the reuse marketplace. Vendors will offer domain-specific kits of reusable components, reuse libraries, tools, and expertise. Brokers will emerge to offer catalogs of components to prospective consumers.

Companies will increasingly differentiate themselves by providing their value-added through the addition of unique portions to core reusable assets which are available industry-wide. To ensure that the core reusable assets are not steering an industry in a sub-optimal direction, the core reusable assets and the standards associated with them will need to be revisited and reengineered in a time frame matching the rate of business and technological change specific to the domain

If we can achieve the cultural change necessary, this will be reflected in the behavior, attitude, and belief systems of the producers and consumers of reusable software. At that time, reuse activities may become more implicit than explicit.

Utilizing our framework for the scope of reuse, we will see the following.

1. The establishment of a greater number of enterprise-wide reuse programs.
2. Interenterprise reuse will initially occur as informal sharing of assets between organizations. This will be followed by more formal, packaged licensing of reuse products and delivery of services. Most of the software components sold will be in sets (e.g., kits, classes) or as a stand-alone asset of large granularity (e.g., template). More effective and efficient means of distributing reusable assets will be needed before reusable assets can be sold at a lower level of granularity (e.g., per component).
3. National reuse will have more specialized repositories that broker reusable assets for *particular domains.* These repositories may eventually be interconnected to other specialized repositories. We will then see the emergence of suprarepositories, which will cater to a breadth of domains.
4. International reuse will occur first through subsidiaries of international corporations. If disparate standards exist between producer and consumer, only the projects which reflect high value-added (because of the additional effort required to accommodate use of nonstandard components) from reuse will conduct international reuse.
5. The trend toward end-user programming will continue. After the telephone was introduced and its usage escalated, many predicted a shortage of telephone operators. At that time, operators were needed to connect telephone users. This potential problem was solved through the invention of the telephone rotary dial, effectively "making every telephone user an operator." [18] This analogy may be extended by noting the increasing popularity of automated attendants and call routing menus. With automated attendants, callers route themselves to their parties by dialing an extension or the name of the desired party with their telephone keypads. A call routing menu enables callers to select menu options, routing them to company departments or mailboxes.

    This analogy may be applied to software development and the impending shortage of software engineers. *End-user programming* enables users to perform their own programming with even limited software engineering skill and knowledge. An increasing number of end-users (e.g., accountants, bankers, lawyers) are developing applications using tools such as macrolanguages which allow them to incorporate the specifics of their business without having to know the technical aspects of software development. End-users customize software without writing code by utilizing code libraries and prepackaged debuggers [20]. Software reuse is an important technique in furthering this trend in end-user programming [21].

Reuse is an aspect that is implicit in many mature engineering disciplines. Prieto-Diaz states that the ultimate success of reuse will be marked by its disappearance when it is integrated into good software engineering practice [22]. Until then, we challenge the software industry to rethink the way software should be developed.

Summary

The majority of software reuse is currently being practiced at the personal and intraproject levels. Mapping the software reuse timeline against Redwine's maturation phases suggests that reuse is at the beginning of the popularization phase, where there is commercialization and marketing of the technology. In the near term, we will see: 1) reusable software playing a greater role in the way decisions are made to purchase development systems; 2) greater use of networks and the Internet as a distribution channel for reusable software assets; 3) greater skill specialization in the production and consumption of reusable assets; and 4) reengineering of organizations to fit the new development paradigm. In the long term, we will see: 1) the establishment of a greater number of enterprise-wide reuse programs; 2) interenterprise reuse initially occurring as informal sharing of assets between organizations; 3) emergence of more specialized repositories that broker reusable assets for particular domains; 4) international reuse occurring first through subsidiaries of international corporations; and 5) a continued trend towards end-user programming.

References

1. J. Moore and C. Lillie, "Asset source for software engineering technology (ASSET)," presented at the *National Symposium: Improving the Software Process and Competitive Position Via Software Reuse and Reengineering,* 1991.
2. M. D. McIlroy, "Mass produced software components," in *Software Engineering Concepts and Techniques,* J. M. Buxton, P. Naur, and B. Randall, Eds. New York, NY: Petrocelli/Charter, 1976, pp. 88–98.
3. K. J. Dakin and J. Lindsey, *Technology Transfer.* Chicago, IL: Probus, 1991.
4. S. T. Redwine, L. G. Becker, A. B. Marmor-Squires, R. J. Martin, S. H. Nash, and W. E. Riddle, "DoD related software technology requirements, practices, and prospects for the future," Institute for Defense Analysis, Alexandria, VA, tech. rep. IDA paper P-1788, June 1984.
5. M. Cusumano, *Japan's Software Factories.* New York, NY: Oxford University Press, 1991.
6. P. Freeman, "Reusable software engineering: A statement of long-range research objectives," Department of Information and Computer Science, University of California, Irvine, tech. rep. 159, Nov. 10, 1980.

7. J. Neighbors, "Software construction using components," Department of Information and Computer Science, University of California, Irvine, tech. rep. 160, 1980.

8. R. Lanergan and B. Poynton, "Software engineering with standard assemblies," *Association of Computing Machinery Proceedings,* Dec. 1978.

9. W. C. Lim and S. Rubin, "Guidelines for cataloging reusable software," *Hewlett-Packard Software Engineering Productivity Conference,* Aug. 1987.

10. S. Rubin and W. C. Lim, "Guidelines for modularization and reusability," *Hewlett-Packard Software Engineering Productivity Conference,* Aug. 1987.

11. S. J. Schappelle, "A methodology for reusable software," IBM internal rep., 1982.

12. A. Perlis, T. Biggerstaff, and T. Cheatham, *ITT Workshop on Reusability in Programming.* Newport, RI: ITT, 1983.

13. "MasterSoftware literature," MasterSoftware, Inc., Wellesley, MA, 1983.

14. N. Vitalari and W. Matorelli, "1994 index summit: Survey of systems development directors," *CSC Index,* Cambridge, MA, 1994.

15. W. B. Frakes and C. J. Fox, "Software reuse survey report," *Software Engineering Guild,* Sterling, VA, 1993.

16. G. H. Anthes, "Software reuse plans bring paybacks," *Computerworld,* vol. 27, no. 49, pp. 73–76, Dec. 6, 1993.

17. G. H. Anthes, "Users look for standards on reuse libraries," *Computerworld,* vol. 28, no. 21, p. 97, 1994.

18. B. J. Cox, "There is a silver bullet (reusable software components)," *Byte,* vol. 15, no. 10, pp. 209–218, 1990.

19. F. Hillier and G. Lieberman, *Introduction to Operations Research.* New York, NY: McGraw-Hill, 1990.

20. J. McMullen, "End users create PC applications," *Datamation,* vol. 35, no. 23, pp. 41–43, Dec. 1, 1989.

21. D. Marques, G. Dallemagne, G. Klinker, J. McDermott, and D. Tung, "Easy programming: empowering people to build their own applications," *IEEE Expert,* vol. 7, no. 3, pp. 16–29, June 1992.

22. R. Prieto-Diaz, "The disappearance of software reuse," in *Proceedings 3rd International Conference on Software Reuse: Advances in Software Reusability,* (cat. no. 94TH06940), 1994, p. 225.

For Further Reading

1. V. R. Basili and J. D. Musa, "The future generation of software: A management perspective," *Computer,* vol. 24, no. 9, pp. 90–96, Sept. 1991.

2. R. Prieto-Diaz, "Historical overview," in *Software Reusability,* W. Schafer, R. Prieto-Diaz, and M. Matsumoto, Eds. London, England: Ellis Horwood, 1993.

3. W. Tracz, "Software reuse: Principles and practice," University of California, Irvine, Feb. 26–28, 1990.

4. P. Freeman, "Reusability: Progress or repetition," presented at *1st International Conference on Software Reuse,* Dortmund, Germany, 1991.

A REUSE INFRASTRUCTURE AND IMPLEMENTATION PLAN OUTLINE

A software reuse infrastructure and implementation plan serves two primary purposes [1]. First, it serves as a proposal to garner support from management and constituents. Second, it serves as your guide to reuse in the organization. For example, it enables you to crystallize your understanding of the organization, why you are pursuing reuse, who your end-users, consumers, and producers are, and what roadblocks you can expect to encounter. While not all organizations that practice reuse have a reuse infrastructure and implementation plan, those who do are in a better position to succeed. The following outline may be used in part or in its entirety to help you construct a successful reuse infrastructure and implementation plan.

A.1   Software Reuse Infrastructure and Implementation Plan

I.   Executive Summary

1. Describe the industry, company, organizational, and product context.
2. Describe the goals and critical success factors that must be addressed.
3. Describe alternative development strategies.
4. Describe the rationale for a reuse-based development strategy.
5. Outline the key organizational and technical aspects of the reuse infrastructure and implementation strategy.

II. Industry

1. Competitors
   a. Describe existing and potential competitors and their strategies.
   b. Describe how the competitors differentiate themselves in the marketplace.
2. Collaborators
   a. Describe existing alliances which provide a competitive advantage.
   b. Examine potential alliances which can provide a competitive advantage.
   c. Describe the existing and potential collaborators of competitors.
3. Customers
   a. Describe the customer (end-user) market segment the company is targeting.
   b. Identify the needs and desires of those customers.
4. Suppliers
   a. Describe the supplies and resources required to create the company's products and/or services.
   b. Identify whether the availability of resources affects the choice of a product/service offering and the software development strategy.
5. Society
   a. Describe any legal, regulatory, institutional, social, or political factors and trends that impact the business or product.
   b. Identify existing or new products that will be affected by societal changes.
6. Industry Critical Success Factors
   Describe the critical factors for achieving success in this industry.

III. Organization

1. Type of Business
   State the nature of the business (e.g., telecommunications, banking, utilities).
2. Products and/or Services offered
   a. Describe the product (e.g., manufacturing resource applications, electronic instrument firmware) or service offered (e.g., accounting, application development).
   b. Describe the delivery channels for the product or service.
3. History
   Describe the history, image, and reputation of the company and events that may have affected the organization's development.
4. Vision and Mission
   Describe the vision and mission of the organization relative to the constituents that it interacts with and serves.
5. Strengths/Limitations
   a. Describe the organization's strengths and how they can be used to gain competitive advantage.

    b. Describe which strengths would be difficult for a competitor to emulate or supplant.

    c. Describe the organization's limitations and weaknesses.

6. Organization Critical Success Factors
Describe the critical factors of achieving success for the organization.

IV. Business/Product Strategy

1. Goals
Describe the organization's achievable goals in the context of its strengths, weaknesses, and industry position.

2. Business/Product Strategy
Describe the organization's business/product strategy for achieving success in the marketplace.

3. Business/Product Critical Success Factors
Describe the critical factors of achieving success for the organization.

V. Software Engineering Strategy

1. Relevant Reuse Assessment Results
Describe applicable reuse assessment results, e.g., baseline metrics, reuse improvement opportunities, software quality factor importance, and feasibility of reuse.

2. Alternative Software Development Strategies
Describe alternative software development strategies available to fulfill critical success factors.

3. Rationale for a Reuse-based Software Development Strategy Choice
Describe the rationale for choosing a reuse-based software development strategy over the alternatives.

VI. Reuse Infrastructure Plan

1. Role of the Corporate/Enterprise Reuse Program Organization
Describe the role of the corporate reuse program. Define the level of involvement, types of products and/or services offered, and mechanisms for interacting with constituents. For example, describe how the corporate reuse program will interact with other reuse programs in industry, academia, and any relevant consortia.

2. Rationale for Selection of the Target Organization/Domain
Describe the rationale for choosing the target organization/domain as a candidate for reuse.

3. Reuse Vision and Mission

Describe the reuse vision and mission for the organization. A reuse vision describes the state which the organization strives to attain. A reuse mission statement articulates the operational reuse goals of the organization.

4. Staffing
   a. Define the roles and responsibilities of the reuse staff. These include roles such as reuse champion, domain analyst, domain expert, domain asset manager, reuse producer engineer, reuse consumer engineer, reuse analyst, reuse economist/metrician, librarian, and reuse manager.
   b. Define the motivation and incentive structure for reuse in the organization. Examples of such mechanisms include recognition and performance reviews.
   c. Describe education and training for reuse. Courses should be geared toward the appropriate audiences in areas such as planning and organizing for reuse, development and use of reuse metrics, design for reuse, design with reuse, library management, and domain analysis. Time and resources should be allotted for training on the job.
   d. Define career progression in a reuse context. Career paths with increasing responsibility should be defined within the reuse organization.

5. Organizational Structure
   Design an appropriate organizational structure and identify appropriate integration mechanisms according to the organization's reuse strategy, current environment, unique characteristics, and culture. Integration mechanisms are rules and procedures that facilitate coordination among parties, e.g., a reuse steering committee.

6. Finance and Accounting
   a. Identify the cost/benefit of the reuse program for the organization. Determine the time horizon, cash in/and outflows, and appropriate discount rate for the return-on-investment calculation. Cost estimation models may be used to project the cost and savings.
   b. Describe the amount required to finance the organization's reuse program via a pro forma cash flow statement.
   c. Identify sources of initial and ongoing funding for the reuse program. Initial funding, for example, may come from grants, loans, or some other form of funding. Ongoing financing may come from taxation or payments.
   d. Determine whether the organization will attempt to recover its costs for its reuse products and/or services from consumers. If yes, describe the mechanism used for recovering the expenses. For example, a transfer price (the charges that one suborganization levies on another for the use of a product or service) may consist of royalties or taxes.
   e. Design the reuse management control system (RMCS). The RMCS assures that resources are obtained and utilized efficiently and effectively from reuse strategy development to implementation. Part of the RMCS is the de-

termination of whether the reuse producer will be designed as a revenue center or profit center. Describe the audits and reviews which will be implemented and the entity which will perform them.

   f. Describe how the cost/benefit of potential reusable assets will be determined. This ensures that only economically feasible assets are created.

7. Metrics
   a. Describe the set of metrics which are currently being collected or have been collected.
   b. Identify a core set of reuse metrics for corporate reuse program use. These metrics are used to obtain a picture of reuse across the corporation. They should be consistent, comparable, and aggregable.
   c. Describe the process to be used in identifying and collecting reuse metrics.
   d. Describe the reuse metrics if they have been identified. These may include quality, productivity and time-to-market metrics, reuse economic metrics, reuse library metrics, reuse process metrics, reuse product metrics, and reuse asset metrics.

8. Marketing
   a. Describe the product and service mix the reuse organization will offer.
   b. If the reuse organization will charge for its reuse products and/or services, describe how the price will be set. Alternative methods include, for example, cost-plus pricing, variable-cost pricing, and consumer-benefit pricing.
   c. Describe the channels of distribution of reuse products and services to the consumers. These include assets, training, and support services. Forms of electronic distribution include local area network, file transfer protocol (FTP), and Intranets.
   d. Describe the forms of promotion planned to increase awareness of reuse concepts, products, and services. These include, for example, brochures, newsletters, presentations, seminars, and technology conferences.

9. Legal and Contractual
   a. Identify applicable legal and contractual issues in reuse.
   b. Determine the appropriate form of intellectual property protection for the producer, if necessary. These include, for example, copyrights, trade secrets, and patents.
   c. Identify the legal implications of reusing assets from internal, external, and third party sources for the consumer.
   d. Understand the contractual implications of creating and reusing assets by producers and consumers. These include, for example, licensing and warranty issues.
   e. Describe contractual incentives for contractors to develop and reuse assets if applicable.

10. Reuse Processes
    Describe the processes necessary for supporting software reuse.

    a. Producing Reusable Assets
       Describe the life cycle for producing reusable assets (domain engineering).

       1. Analyzing Domain
          Describe the method to be used for domain analysis (e.g., FODA, Prieto–Diaz Sandwich method, etc.)

       2. Producing Assets
          Describe the approach(es) to be used for producing assets (e.g., prefabricate, retrofit). Assets include architectures, designs, code, etc. This includes testing of reusable assets.

       3. Maintaining and Enhancing Assets
          Describe the approach to be used for maintaining and enhancing reusable assets, e.g., regression tests.

    b. Brokering Reusable Assets
       Describe the process for brokering reusable assets.

       1. Scouting Assets
          Describe how potential internal and external assets will be identified.

       2. Assessing Assets for Brokering
          Describe the criteria by which the potential assets are evaluated (e.g., fulfills domain requirements, cost, quality, documentation, supportability).

       3. Procuring Assets
          Describe the process of procuring the required asset. For example, can the broker determine whether to buy the asset, buy and reengineer it, create it in-house, or reengineer an existing in-house asset for reusability?

       4. Certifying Assets
          Describe the method to be used to certify the reusable assets. For example, this can include verification that the assets meet certain quality levels and are accompanied by necessary documentation.

       5. Adding Assets
          Describe the method used to add assets. Adding assets includes the process of formally cataloging, classifying, and describing the asset. This also includes the actual placement/storage of the asset into a repository.

       6. Deleting Assets
          Describe the method used to delete assets, including exit criteria.

    c. Consuming Reusable Assets
       Describe the process for utilizing the reusable assets by consumers.

       1. Identifying System and Asset Requirements
          Describe the method to be used for translating end-user needs into system and asset requirements.

2. Locating Assets
   Describe the method used to locate assets through the reuse library, directory, or other means to identify assets which meet or closely meet the requirements.

3. Assessing Assets for Consumption
   Describe how the assets will be evaluated for their suitability for consumption. For example, possible factors are: Would the asset require modification? Would modification eliminate asset support from the producer group?

4. Adapting/Modifying Assets
   Describe the method for adapting the assets to meet requirements and environment. If modification is necessary, ensure that the changes are well-documented.

5. Integrating/Incorporating Assets
   Describe how the reusable assets will be integrated with new assets created for the application.

   d. Operating Reuse Library

1. Describe the process for operating the reuse library.

2. Describe the organizational scope from which the library will be accessible.

3. Describe who will control access to and have access to the library.

   e. Quality Assurance
   Describe quality assurance processes to be used to ensure that, for example, the assets are high-quality and processes are improving. Describe defect tracking for reuse.

11. Reuse Tools
    Describe the tools necessary to support reuse.

    a. Reuse Library
    Describe the requirements and features of the asset repository. This includes, for example, the representation method (e.g., keyword, classification scheme), information elements/display scheme, configuration management, and entry and exit criteria. Describe how security issues will be addressed.

    b. Reusability Guidelines
    Describe design, coding, or general guidelines which will be used to create reusable assets. Also indicate the standards (e.g., interface and documentation standards) to which producers will adhere.

    c. Reuse Tools
    Describe reuse tools which will be used to support reuse. These include, for example, objected-oriented languages and tools, application templates, generators, computer-aided software engineering (CASE) tools, transforma-

tional systems, module interconnection languages, architectural frameworks, very high level languages, subroutine libraries, parameterized systems, and problem-oriented languages.

VII. Reuse Implementation Strategy

1. Technology Transfer
Describe how reuse technology will be diffused within the organization via a transfer life cycle.

2. Change Management
Describe the change management approach that will be used to implement reuse.

3. Conversion Strategy
Describe the strategy for converting the organization to a reuse-based development strategy, e.g., the parallel, direct, phased, and pilot conversion approaches.

4. Evolutionary–Revolutionary Approaches
Describe the rate of change intended for the organization for converting to reuse. This includes, for example, the incremental/evolutionary and revolutionary approaches.

5. Top-Down and Bottom-Up Approaches
Discuss the implications of utilizing a top-down (management-to-engineer), bottom-up (engineer-to-management), or combination approach. Describe the approach selected and the rationale for choosing it.

6. Resources and Schedules
Outline the resources and schedules for the proposed reuse implementation over an appropriate time frame. Identify key milestones. Gantt or some other appropriate charts may be used. Describe resources required (e.g., person engineers, equipment, time, and funding).

VIII. Issues

1. Risk Analysis
Describe any risks or impediments to implementing reuse in the organization and describe how these risks will be addressed or minimized.

2. Substitutes for Reuse
Describe any substitutes or competition for reuse foreseeable in the organization where reuse will be implemented.

A.2 APPENDIX

1. Reuse Assessment Results
2. Working Group Results

Reference

1. "Reuse infrastructure and implementation plan," Lombard Hill Group. For more information, visit http://www.lombardhill.com or e-mail reuse@hotmail.com.

SOFTWARE REUSE LEXICON

Version 1.1
Mike Ogush
Software Initiative on Reuse
Corporate Engineering
Hewlett-Packard
e-mail: ogush@hpcea.ce.hp.com

Version History
Version 1.0, initial external version, Oct. 1992.
Distributed at 5th Annual Workshop in Institutionalizing Software Reuse (WISR) for comments from the reuse community.
Version 1.1, Nov. 1992, integrated comments received at WISR.

Note: To ensure consistency with terminology used in the book, portions of this lexicon have been adapted.

Acceptance Criteria
The criteria a software product must meet to successfully complete a test phase or meet delivery requirements.

Acceptance Testing
Formal testing conducted to determine whether or not a system satisfies its acceptance criteria and to enable the customer to determine whether or not to accept the system. See also qualification testing, system testing [11].

Adaptive Maintenance
Maintenance performed to make a software product usable in a changed environment [12].

Adaptive Reuse
A restricted form of leverage in which the functionality of the system remains unchanged and the system is adapted to a different hardware or operating system environment.
Synonyms: *port, porting*

Application Architecture
The gross architecture of the entire distributed application, such as a software bus.
Synonyms: *macro-architecture, framework architecture*

Application Program Interface (API)
The set of procedure calls/method invocations in some language that the implementor of a (framework conforming) component must use to access the infrastructure services of the framework, and to provide information, registration about this component.
Synonyms: *framework-API, application-program-interface*

Architecture
The organizational structure of a system or component [7].

Assets
Formal and informal records or documents pertaining to software products (e.g., software components, domain characterization, reusability requirements, etc.). Each asset includes a documented description of the rationale behind any decisions made during the production of the asset and all historical information concerning modifications to the asset.
Synonyms: *artifacts, workproducts*

Asset Classification
A set of terms that can be used in storing, searching for, and retrieving an asset. The classification relies heavily on the domain lexicon and configuration scheme. Classification of assets is especially important when there are large numbers of assets or when the assets are complex [15].

Audit
1. An independent review for the purpose of assessing compliance with software requirements, specifications, baselines, standards, procedures, instructions, codes, and contractual and licensing requirements. See also *code audit.*
2. An activity to determine through investigation the adequacy of, and adherence to, established procedures, instructions, specifications, codes and stan-

dards, or other applicable contractual and licensing requirements and the effectiveness of implementation [2], [11].

Baseline

1. A specification or product that has been formally reviewed and agreed upon, that thereafter serves as the basis for further development, and that can be changed only through formal change control procedures.

2. A configuration identification document or set of such documents formally designated and fixed at a specific time during a configuration item's life cycle. Baselines, plus approved changes from those baselines, constitute the current configuration identification. For configuration management, there are three baselines as follows:
   a) Functional baseline: the initial approved functional configuration.
   b) Allocated baseline: the initial approved allocated configuration.
   c) Product baseline: the initial approved or conditionally approved product configuration identification [11].

Binding Time

The last time when the interpretation of some name used in a system is resolved for all subsequent phases/times of that system. Typical binding times are: compile time, link time, system initialization time, and run-time. A name can be resolved multiple times with a given time phase, say compile time.

Black Box Reuse

To employ existing assets (as is) in the software product development process, preserving asset integrity. See also *Leverage* and *Controlled Evolution*.
Synonyms: *direct reuse, reuse without modification*

Broker Reusable Assets

A process the objective of which is to qualify or certify, configure, and maintain reusable assets. This process also includes classification and retrieval for assets in the reuse library.
Synonym: *support reusable workproducts*

Builder

Tools to help users assemble components into complete programs, install into framework, ensure correct usage of API and completeness of component set, etc. The user "manually" selects components, and tools provide support to interconnect them, and to write an interconnection (or programming) language. May provide assistance in setting parameters of the selected components and may be driven by a builder template.

Carry-Over Reuse

Software reuse that occurs when one version of a software component is taken to be used as is in a subsequent version of the same system. This kind of "reuse" is distinguished from black box reuse because it does not represent a distinct or novel usage of the same components. See also *Controlled-Evolution Reuse, Leverage, Black Box Reuse.*

Certification
1. A written guarantee that a system or computer program complies with its specified requirement.
2. The formal demonstration of system acceptability to obtain authorization for its operational use.
3. The process of confirming that a system, software subsystem, or computer program is capable of satisfying its specified requirements in an operational environment. Certification usually takes place in the field under actual conditions, and is utilized to evaluate not only the software itself, but also the specifications to which the software was constructed. Certification extends the process of verification and validation to an actual or simulated operational environment.
4. The procedure and action by a duly authorized body of determining, verifying, and attesting in writing to the qualifications of personnel, processes, procedures, or items in accordance with applicable requirements [1], [11].

Code Review
The specified process for ensuring that developed source code meets the module specifications.

Compositional Reuse
The construction of new software products by assembling existing reusable assets.

Configuration Scheme
A well-defined plan for the organization of assets to be managed as configurations.

Consume Reusable Assets
A process the objective of which is to produce systems using reusable assets.
Synonyms: *use reusable workproducts; design with reuse (DWR)*

Consumer
A person or agent using reusable assets or components to produce end-user products or further reusable assets.
Synonyms: *user*

Corrective Maintenance
Maintenance performed specifically to overcome existing faults [12].

Definitional Model
One form of domain model. It includes an intentional statement specifying what is and is not in the domain. It may include a lexicon and domain language (e.g., grammar).

Deposition Ratio

A set goal that a product development project deliver some percentage of reusable assets for future products. These could be packaged and reprocessed by a components group, or mined by the components group from the project, without project members' assistance.

Derived Reuse

Software reuse that is accomplished via the object-oriented principle of subclassing.

Domain-Specific Reuse

Software reuse that is targeted for a specific domain as opposed to reuse of general purpose assets. Typically, domain-specific reuse involves reuse of larger assets (subsystems, architectures, etc.) than general purpose reuse.
Synonyms: *high-level reuse, vertical reuse*

Domain

A coherent set of systems that exhibits common features and functionality across existing and proposed instances. A domain may be defined as a vertical or horizontal component within a larger context. For example, window systems are a horizontal domain; microwave instrument firmware is a vertical domain.

Domain Analysis

1. The process of identifying, collecting, organizing, analyzing, and representing a domain model and software architecture from the study of existing systems, underlying theory, emerging technology, and development theories within the domain of interest.
2. The result of the process of 1.
3. The process by which information used in developing software systems is identified, captured, and organized with the purpose of making it reusable when creating new systems [7].

Domain Analysis Objectives

A clear statement of goals for the information to be produced and activities to be undertaken in the domain analysis. The objectives may be as simple as capturing the knowledge of a departing project, or as far-reaching as exploring potential new lines of business. In typical situations, domain analysis will have the objective of producing complete domain models for use in producing reusable assets in a familiar domain.

Domain Analyst

A person who has expertise in extracting and analyzing information about a domain from existing components, domain exemplars, product plans, domain experts, and from other sources of domain knowledge in order to produce domain models. (Our point of view about the domain analysis process is that it deals only with the analysis and modeling phase of development. The software architecture is part of the design phase, which is also referred to as *domain engineering*.)

Domain Boundary Model
A description of what domains are related or nearby a particular domain and the relationships between the related domains and the focus domain. A domain context diagram is one example of how one might illustrate the domain boundary. See *Domain Model.*

Domain Definition
A formal definition of the domain that can be used to determine whether a arbitrary system is a part of that domain or not. This statement must be intentional, that is, a person should be able to determine whether a given system belongs in the domain by determining whether the system fits criteria of the domain definition statement. An example of an intentional definition is "A mammal is a warm-blooded animal, vertebrate, having hair, and secreting milk for nourishing its young" [8].

Domain Engineering
The construction of components, methods, tools, and their supporting documentation to solve the problems of system/subsystem development by the application of the knowledge in the domain model and software architectures [7].

Domain Exemplar
A system, subsystem, or component selected for detailed analysis as part of domain modeling. The exemplar is represented as a collection of assets, artifacts, and development history documents, as opposed to being merely the source code for the system in question.

Domain Expert
A person who is very knowledgeable about a particular domain. This person will generally be aware of existing and planned products in the domain.

Domain Feature Model
A type of conceptual model that enumerates features and their variants as they appear in existing and projected domain exemplars and accounting for desirable novel combinations of those feature variants.

Domain Functional Model
A type of domain model that emphasizes the standard generation and variants of functions as they appear in the domain exemplars. Process models or data flow diagrams are kinds of functional models. (Current modeling tools often provide only weak support for modeling functional variants.)

Domain Knowledge
Knowledge about systems in a specific domain that may be obtained by interviewing domain practitioners (e.g., product developers, technical marketing staff, sys-

tems analysts), or analyzing technical literature in the domain, where the knowledge may pertain to existing systems, technology projections, the relationship of this domain to others, experience in reusability, etc.

Domain Knowledge Sources
Any resources that can provide information about the domain. Examples:
- the assets of existing systems;
- published research in the domain;
- unofficial (i.e., non-asset) documentation: on-line directories, prior project notebooks;
- folklore or "techlore" in the domain: personal, oral history sources.

Domain Lexicon
The vocabulary or terminology of the domain. It includes clustered synonyms and antonyms. The reuse lexicon document itself can be considered a domain lexicon for the domain of "software reuse process."

Domain Modeling Language
A machine-processable language the terms of which are derived from the domain model and is used for the definition of components.

Domain Requirements Model
A model that links features with the environment (e.g., where systems operate, with what they must connect).

Domain Scope
This is an aggregate of the domain definition (statement), the domain boundary, the domain exemplar portfolio, and the domain requirements model. These assets are grouped together to form the scope because they each define a different view of the scope. Thus a change in any one of them will generally require changes to the other two. See *Domain Model.*

Domain Structural Model
A level of notational abstraction that describes functional units, connections, and interfaces in a system. This aspect of a domain model is developed during the domain engineering activity in the process of producing reusable assets.
Synonyms: *domain architecture specification*

Entity–Relationship–Attribute (ERA) Diagram
A diagrammatic notation for describing and documenting data items and the relationships between data items using an ERA model. Entities are shown as boxes in the ERA diagram and have an entity name; usually names are required to be unique. Attributes are generally shown as annotations of entity boxes. Relationships are shown as lines between entity boxes. Markings on the lines indicate the nature of the relationship (one to one, one to many, or many to many) [9].

Entity–Relationship–Attribute (ERA) Model

A model of a set of data relationships in terms of the entities, relationships, and attributes involved. Entities have attributes and have relationships with other entities. They have an entity name; usually names are required to be unique. Entities are often implemented as a record comprising a number of fields. Attributes are usually represented as a data dictionary and describe the characteristic features of the entity. Each attribute is named; usually the names of attributes are required to be unique. Attributes are often implemented as fields with values. Each relationship is named; usually relationship names are required to be unique. There can be more than one relationship between a pair of entities [9].

Engineer Reusable Assets

A process with the objective of constructing components, methods, and tools and their supporting documentation to solve the problems of system/subsystem development by the application of the knowledge in the domain model and software architectures.
Synonyms: *domain engineering*

Error Analysis

1. The process of investigating an observed software fault with the purpose of tracing the fault to its source.
2. The process of investigating an observed software fault to identify such information as the cause of the fault, the phase of development process during which the fault was introduced, methods by which the fault could have been prevented or detected earlier, and the method by which the fault was detected.
3. The process of investigating software errors, failures, and faults to determine quantitative rates and trends [11].

External Reference Specification (ERS)

The specification of a system suitable for clients (users) of that system. Only the interface to the system is specified; all internal details of implementation are omitted from this document.

External Reuse

Reuse of assets produced in one project and consumed by another. Measure external reuse level by comparing units written against units taken from an explicit external library at that abstraction level [13].

Feature

A user-detectable characteristic of at least one of the systems within the domain. Fundamentally, a feature is a basis for distinguishing between different variants within the domain. Features can therefore be specified at varying degrees of abstraction and granularity, and may take a number of variant forms.
Synonyms: *attribute* [6]

Framework

A set of assets (or infrastructure) that behave as a skeletal system or application and implement the common functionality in an architecture. A framework provides a shell for the systematic development and interconnection of assets, ensuring common appearance and behavior via use of common services.

Generation-Based Reuse

Software reuse accomplished via the use of application generators to build new applications from high-level descriptions. Examples include 4GLs and user interface generators.

Generator

A higher-level automatic builder that hides the manual interconnection of components using a problem-oriented language, template or option filler, or a visual programming environment. The generator enables concise specification of the desired (piece of) the application, and then generates appropriate code and/or procedure calls in some other language.

Generic Application

A customizable/extendible application that captures most of the interesting, common parts of an application domain. A complete application is built by adding missing parts, adjusting parameters, or selecting alternative components. It is often built upon an application framework. It can also be a prototypical or skeletal application, consisting of the infrastructure, some components, and some preset interconnection language scripts to simplify the task of creating complete, conforming applications for some domain. This may be just a shell into which additional components should be plugged to produce an executable application. Or it may be a trivial but complete application that needs to be evolved into the final/desired/customized application via the addition or replacements of components and changes in interconnection language.

Impact Analysis

An assessment of the potential repercussions of making a proposed change. In reuse, the dimensions of impact include not only what other assets would have to change or would behave differently, but also any impact on the reusability of the workproduct and its configuration.

Infrastructure

The software that implements the services of the framework, and presents it through the API. Some of the software may consist of distinguished conforming components or (in a layered framework) of a set of components from a lower level.

Inspection

1. A formal evaluation technique in which software requirements, design, and code are examined in detail by a person or group other than the author to de-

tect faults, violations of development standards, and other problems. Contrast with walkthrough. See also *Code Audit.*

2. A phase of quality control that wherein examination, observation, or measurement determines the conformance of materials, supplies, components, parts, appurtenances, systems, processes, or structures to predetermined quality requirements [2], [11].

Institutionalized Reuse
Systematic reuse that is a significant practice throughout an organization.

Interconnection Language
A language, usually interpreted, used to simplify the task of interconnecting components to form applications.
Synonyms: *framework language, process language, user-extension language, agents language, scripting language, glue language*

Internal Reuse
Avoiding redundant implementation of functionality within a single project by careful design and inspection at early stages so that selected components are identified for distinct uses within the project (system or subsystem).

Internal Reuse Level
A metric comparing the unit count of components used repeatedly in distinct contexts with unit count of components used only once. This is of interest in development projects with teams of programmers, and when writing object-oriented systems by developing common class libraries. (The "unit count" is normally non-commented source statements (NCSS), lines of code (LOC), or function points).

Kit
A coherent set of tools, methods, and reusable assets for producing software with systematic reuse in a particular domain.
Synonyms: *domain-specific, reuse-based software construction kit* [16]

Layered Architecture
An architecture designed as a series of abstract machines, or service layers, where each layer is ideally described only in terms of services provided by the layer immediately below. It is believed that portability, reuse, and evolution are enhanced, though many layered implementations seem to suffer in performance (a good example being OSI "protocol-stack" for network services).

Layered Framework
An application framework built as a series of layers, each layer factoring out additional, more domain-specific common services to further restrict the application domain that this framework naturally supports.

Leverage
To start with existing assets in the software development process, modifying as needed to meet specific system requirements. Leverage results in distinct

"branches" of versions of the modified components requiring separate maintenance.
Synonyms: *leveraging reuse, code scavenging, white box reuse*

Librarian

1. A person who accepts, classifies, maintains, searches, configures, and re-
   trieves assets from a reusable software library.
2. A person responsible for establishing, controlling, and maintaining a software
   library [11].

Maintenance

Modification of a software product to correct faults, to improve performance or
other attributes, or to adapt the program to a changed environment. See also *Adaptive Maintenance, Corrective Maintenance, Perfective Maintenance.*
Synonyms: *software maintenance* [12]

Mega-Component

A large-grained component, often a complete application or application fragment that
can be an encapsulated pre-existing application, reengineered so that it can be combined with other components within a framework, conforming to the framework API.
Synonyms: *application-component*

Operational Environment Characteristics Model

A description of the external environmental conditions that a system in the domain
must operate under (i.e. hardware constraints, embedded system versus not, con-
nected to LAN versus not, etc.)

Opportunistic Reuse

Reuse through identification of previously unplanned-for opportunities to reuse assets.
Antonyms: *systematic reuse*

Perfective Maintenance

Maintenance performed to improve performance, maintainability, or other software
attributes. See also *Adaptive Maintenance, Corrective Maintenance* [12].

Performance Requirement

A requirement that specifies a performance characteristic that a system or system
component must possess; for example, speed, accuracy, frequency [11].

Performance Specification

A specification that sets forth the performance requirements for a system or system
component [11].

Produce Reusable Assets

A process the objective of which is to develop, generate, or reengineer assets with
the specific goal of reusability. The process includes domain analysis and domain
engineering activities.
Synonym: *produce reusable workproducts*

Producer

A party who creates reusable assets with the specific goal of reusability.

Proof of Correctness

1. A formal technique used to prove mathematically that a program satisfies its specifications. See also *Partial Correctness, Total Correctness.*

2. A program proof that results from applying this technique [11].

Qualification Testing

Formal testing, usually conducted by the developer for the customer, to demonstrate that the software meets its specified requirements. See also *Acceptance Testing, System Testing* [11].

Reengineering

Changing a asset to meet new conditions or needs [3]–[5], [13].

Regression Testing

Selective retesting to detect faults introduced during modification of a system or system component, to verify that modifications have not caused unintended adverse effects, or to verify that a modified system or system component still meets its specified requirements [11].

Return-On-Investment (ROI) Metrics

ROI metrics are collected for cost/benefit models that provide a measure of the output relative to the size of the input. Some of these models account for risk and cost of capital. The value that these models provide may itself be considered an ROI metric. Examples of cost/benefit models include: net present value, internal rate of return, and payback methods.

Reusability

An attribute of software assets that measures the degree to which they can be used in more than one computer program or software system [10], [14].

Reusability Analyst

A person who has expertise in extracting and analyzing information about a asset users' work style in order to produce a set of relevant reusability requirements.

Reusability Knowledge

Lessons learned, metrics and data analysis, recommendations acquired in using reusable assets that identify factors affecting reusability of assets.

Reusability Metrics

Measures by which an individual may evaluate the reusability of assets.

Reusability Requirements

A set of requirements for each class of domain asset that reflects decisions about how users reusability criteria will be handled in the reusable domain assets. The requirements cover those related to business objectives, user work style, and user computing environment constraints.

Reuse

1. To employ existing assets in some form in the software product development process, preserving asset integrity.
2. The application of existing solutions to the problems of systems development.

Reuse Level

A consistent set of metrics to measure the amount of product external and internal reuse for improvement and comparison. Done by comparing ratios of software elements (non-commented lines of code (NLOC) or other program units) at an appropriate level of abstraction.

Software Component

A set of software artifacts that comprise a coherent module. A complete software component would include at least source code; header files; documents (product requirements, external requirements specification, internal requirements specification, system architectural specification); test data and scripts; and build instructions.

Software Library

A controlled collection of software resources and related documentation designed to aid in software development, use (reuse), and maintenance [7].

Software Metrics

A collection of algorithms and measures designed to assess features of software.

Software Repository

A collection of software assets providing permanent, archival storage for software assets and related documentation (note distinction from *Software Library*) [7].

System Design

The definition of the software architecture, components, modules, interfaces, test approach, and data for a software system to satisfy specified system requirements.

System Requirements

The customer, user, and market requirements for a specific, planned software system.

Systematic Reuse

The planned reuse of assets with a well-defined process and life cycles, with commitments for funding, staffing, and incentives for production and use of reusable assets. Synonyms: *planned reuse, managed reuse, formal reuse*

Validation

The process of evaluating software at the end of the software development process to ensure compliance with software requirements. See also *Verification* [11].

Verification

1. The process of determining whether or not the products of a given phase of the software development cycle fulfill the requirements established during the previous phase. See also *Validation*.

   2. Formal proof of program correctness. See also *Proof of Correctness.*

   3. The act of reviewing, inspecting, testing, checking, auditing, or otherwise establishing and documenting whether or not items, processes, services, or documents conform to specified requirements [1], [11].

Walkthrough

A review process in which a designer or programmer leads one or more other members of the development team through a segment of design or code that he or she has written, while the other members ask questions and make comments about technique, style, possible errors, violation of development standards, and other problems. Contrast with *Inspection* [11].

References

   1. ANSI/ASQC A3-1978.
   2. ANSI N452.10-1973.
   3. R. S. Arnold and W. B. Frakes, "Software reuse and reengineering," *CASE Trends*, vol. 4, no. 1, pp. 44–48, Feb. 1992.
   4. R. S. Arnold, "Software reengineering at SPC," in *Software Productivity Consortium*, Herndon, VA, Aug. 1991.
   5. E. K. Chikofsky and J. H. Cross II, "Reverse engineering and design recovery: A taxonomy," *IEEE Software*, pp. 13–17, Jan. 1990.
   6. "Feature oriented domain analysis (FODA) feasibility study," Unisys RLF Design Report, Simos90 CMU/SEI-90-TR-2 1.
   7. A. S. Peterson, "Coming to terms with software reuse terminology: A model based approach," *ACM SIGSOFT Software Engineering Notes*, vol. 16, no. 2, Apr. 1991, pp. 45–51.
   8. J. F. Sowa, *Conceptual Structures Information Processing in Mind and Machine.* Reading, MA: Addison-Wesley, Jan. 1984.
   9. *Dictionary of Computing.* Oxford, England: Oxford University Press, 1990.
   10. IEEE90-6 10. 12, via 14, below.
   11. IEEE Standard 729-1983, Standard Glossary of Software Engineering Terminology.
   12. Technical committee 97 (Information Systems), Subcommittee 1, (Vocabulary) of The International Standards Organization, via 11, above.
   13. W. B. Frakes, "An empirical framework for software reuse research," in *3rd Annual Workshop: Methods & Tools for Reuse, CASE Center*, Syracuse University, Syracuse, NY, June 1990.
   14. P. Oman, J. Hagemeister, and D. Ash, "A Definition and Taxonomy for Software Maintainability," tech. rep. 91-08 TR, U.I. Software Engineering Test Lab, Jan. 1992.

15. R. Prieto-Diaz and G. Arango, "Domain analysis: Acquisition of reusable information for software construction," in *IEEE Computer Society Press Tutorial*, New York, NY, 1991.

16. Software Reuse Department, Hewlett-Packard Laboratories.

Other Reuse Lexicon Sources

1. S. Katz, C. Dabrowski, K. Miles, M. Law, "Glossary of software reuse terms," NIST Special Publication 500-222, Computer Systems Laboratory, National Institute of Standards and Technology (NIST), U.S. Department of Commerce, Gaithersburg, MD, Dec. 1994.

INDEX

IF YOU WOULD LIKE TO RECEIVE MORE INFORMATION ABOUT REUSE, PLEASE COMPLETE AND RETURN THE POSTCARD BELOW.

Name: _____ Title: _____

Company: _____

Address: _____

City: _____ State: _____ Zip: _____

Country: _____ E-mail Address: _____

Phone: _____

❏ Please contact me.
    We expect to require reuse consulting services in the areas of:
       ❏ Reuse Training   ❏ Assessment   ❏ Metrics   ❏ Processes
       ❏ Tools   ❏ Domain Analyses   ❏ Other (please specify)
    Timeframe:
       ❏ Immediately   ❏ In 3 Months   ❏ In 6 Months   ❏ In 1 Year
       ❏ Other (please specify)

❏ We don't require reuse consulting services. However, please add me to your mailing list for information updates on software reuse.

The Lombard Hill Group
c/o 1621 Blackhawk Drive
Sunnyvale, CA 94087-4656